ANCIENT TOLLAN

MESOAMERICAN WORLDS
FROM THE OLMECS TO THE DANZANTES

GENERAL EDITORS: Davíd Carrasco and Eduardo Matos Moctezuma

Ancient Tollan: Tula and the Toltec Heartland, Alba Guadalupe Mastache, Robert H. Cobean, and Dan M. Healan
After Monte Albán, Jeffrey P. Blomster, editor
The Apotheosis of Janaab' Pakal, Gerardo Aldana
Carrying the Word, Susanna Rostas
Commoner Ritual and Ideology in Ancient Mesoamerica, Nancy Gonlin and Jon C. Lohse, editors
Conquered Conquistadors, Florine Asselbergs
Empires of Time, Anthony Aveni
Encounter with the Plumed Serpent, Maarten Jansen and Gabina Aurora Pérez Jiménez
Fanning the Sacred Flame, Matthew A. Boxt and Brian Dervin Dillon, editors
In the Realm of Nachan Kan, Marilyn A. Masson
Invasion and Transformation, Rebecca P. Brienen and Margaret A. Jackson, editors
The Kowoj, Prudence M. Rice and Don S. Rice, editors
Life and Death in the Templo Mayor, Eduardo Matos Moctezuma
The Lords of Lambityeco, Michael Lind and Javier Urcid
The Madrid Codex, Gabrielle Vail and Anthony Aveni, editors
Maya Creation Myths, Timothy W. Knowlton
Maya Daykeeping, John M. Weeks, Frauke Sachse, and Christian M. Prager
Maya Worldviews at Conquest, Leslie G. Cecil and Timothy W. Pugh, editors
Mesoamerican Ritual Economy, E. Christian Wells and Karla L. Davis-Salazar, editors
Mesoamerica's Classic Heritage, Davíd Carrasco, Lindsay Jones, and Scott Sessions, editors
Mexico's Indigenous Communities, Ethelia Ruiz Medrano, translated by Russ Davidson
Mockeries and Metamorphoses of an Aztec God, Guilhem Olivier, translated by Michel Besson
Negotiation within Domination, Ethelia Ruiz Medrano and Susan Kellogg, editors; translated by Russ Davidson
Networks of Power, Edward Schortman and Patricia Urban
Rabinal Achi, Alain Breton, editor; translated by Teresa Lavender Fagan and Robert Schneider
Representing Aztec Ritual, Eloise Quiñones Keber, editor
Ruins of the Past, Travis W. Stanton and Aline Magnoni, editors
Skywatching in the Ancient World, Clive Ruggles and Gary Urton, editors
Social Change and the Evolution of Ceramic Production and Distribution in a Maya Community, Dean E. Arnold
The Social Experience of Childhood in Mesoamerica, Traci Ardren and Scott R. Hutson, editors
Stone Houses and Earth Lords, Keith M. Prufer and James E. Brady, editors
The Sun God and the Savior, Guy Stresser-Péan
Sweeping the Way, Catherine DiCesare
Tamoanchan, Tlalocan, Alfredo López Austin
Thunder Doesn't Live Here Anymore, Anath Ariel de Vidas; translated by Teresa Lavender Fagan
Topiltzin Quetzalcoatl, H. B. Nicholson
The World Below, Jacques Galinier

ANCIENT TOLLAN

TULA AND THE TOLTEC HEARTLAND

ALBA GUADALUPE MASTACHE,
ROBERT COBEAN, AND DAN HEALAN

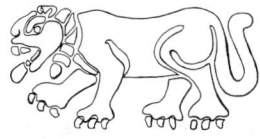 

UNIVERSITY PRESS OF COLORADO
Boulder

We thank the Instituto Nacional de Antropología e Historia for allowing us to reproduce the following illustrations: Figs. 4.3, 5.8A, 5.12, 5.13, 5.15, 5.17, 5.19, 5.22, 5.23, 5.25, 5.26, 5.28, 5.33, 5.34, 5.35, 5.36, 5.37, 5.38, 5.40, 5.41, 5.43, 5.44, 6.12, and 6.14.
Reproducción Autorizada por el Instituto Nacional de Antropología e Historia—Conaculta-INAH-México.
Reproduction Authorized by the Instituto Nacional de Antropología e Historia—Conaculta-INAH-México.

© 2002 by the University Press of Colorado

Published by the University Press of Colorado
5589 Arapahoe Avenue, Suite 206C
Boulder, Colorado 80303

All rights reserved
First paperback edition 2015
Printed in the United States of America

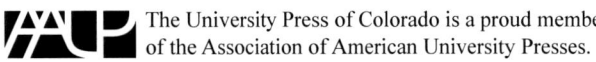 The University Press of Colorado is a proud member of the Association of American University Presses.

The University Press of Colorado is a cooperative publishing enterprise supported, in part, by Adams State University, Colorado State University, Fort Lewis College, Metropolitan State University of Denver, Regis University, University of Colorado, University of Northern Colorado, Utah State University, and Western State Colorado University.

The paper used in this publication meets the minimum requirements of the American National Standard for Information Sciences—Permanence of Paper for Printed Library Materials. ANSI Z39.48-1992

Library of Congress Cataloging-in-Publication Data

Mastache, Alba Guadalupe.
  Ancient Tollan : Tula and the Toltec heartland / Alba Guadalupe Mastache, Robert H. Cobean, and Dan M. Healan.
    p. cm. — (Mesoamerican worlds)
Includes bibliographical references and index.
  ISBN 0-87081-616-0 (alk. paper) — ISBN 978-1-60732-361-7 (pbk. : alk. paper)
  1. Tula Site (Tula de Allende, Mexico) 2. Toltecs. I. Cobean, Robert H. II. Healan, Dan M. III. Title. IV. Series.
F1219.1.T8 M368 2002
972'.46—dc21

2002003123

For my mother, Esther Flores de Mastache, with love.

To the memory of my grandmothers, Benigna Ramirez and Dolores Salgado.

—A.G.M.

Contents

	List of Illustrations	ix
	Foreword by Davíd Carrasco and Eduardo Matos Moctezuma	xiii
	Acknowledgments	xv
	Introduction	xvii
1	Tula and the Tula Region Project	1
2	The Tula Region: Physical Environment and Land Use	17
3	Chronology and Periodification	41
4	Classic, Epiclassic Occupations and the Early City	51
5	The Early Postclassic: The Tollan Phase City	77
6	Habitation in the City	151
7	The Hinterland	179
8	The Tollan Complex in the Tula Area	217
9	Subsistence Activities	237
10	Hinterland Settlement	275
11	Conclusions	301
	Appendix: Site Descriptions and Clusters	309
	Bibliography	379
	Index	403

Illustrations

FIGURES

1.1.	Locations of excavations and structures in Tula's ancient city	5
1.2.	Survey area	6
1.3.	Tula area	7
1.4.	The study area and surrounding valleys	8
1.5.	Tollan Complex: Selective and Systematic Collections	14
1.6.	Tollan Complex: Tepetitlan and Obsidian Workshop; Surface and Excavation Collections	15
2.1.	Tula area	18
2.2.	Tula area geology	21
2.3.	Tula area soils	25
2.4.	Tula area soil classes	27
2.5.	An eroded limestone zone in the southeast Tula area	29
2.6.	Present-day land use	31
2.7.	The Tula area alluvial valley from the east	32
2.8.	Nineteenth-century land use in the Tula area	34
2.9.	Present-day irrigation systems	36
2.10.	Traditional irrigation systems in the Tula area	37
2.11.	Dike on the Tula River	38
2.12.	Flow gates of the colonial Las Cadenas Dam built by the Tlahuelilpan hacienda	39
3.1.	Principal types of the Tollan Complex	47
4.1.	Classic occupation	53
4.2.	Irrigation canals and associated sites of the Zanja Romera and Zanja Nueva systems	54
4.3.	Plan of Chingú	56
4.4.	Classic period remains in Tula's Urban Zone	58
4.5.	Transitional occupation	61
4.6.	Coyotlatelco occupation	63
4.7.	Map of La Mesa	64
4.8.	La Mesa: Platform 12, Unit 33, a structure with a columned portico	65
4.9.	La Mesa: Platform 1	66

4.10.	La Mesa: Circular Structure 1 associated with Platform 1, containing over thirty burials		67
4.11.	Tula: The early city. Probable urban grid alignment for the Corral Phase		73
4.12.	Tula Chico		75
5.1.	Tula: East view		80
5.2.	The Tula area seen from the north		81
5.3.	Topographic restitution of part of Tula's urban zone		83
5.4.	Tula: "Tolteca A." Urban alignment grid		84
5.5.	Tula: "Tolteca B." Urban alignment grid		86
5.6.	Tula: Topographic restitution of the monumental zone		88
5.7.	Tula: The sacred precinct		90
5.8A.	Topographic map of Tula's sacred precinct before it was excavated		91
5.8B.	Location of the principal buildings on Tula's sacred precinct		92
5.9.	View of the sacred precinct: Pyramid B		93
5.10.	The Pyramid of the Sun and the Pyramid of the Moon at Teotihuacan		94
5.11.	Tula: A view of the east side of the plaza with Pyramid C		95
5.12.	Relief panel from the south balustrade of Pyramid C at Tula		96
5.13.	Pyramid B at Tula: A relief panel of a composite being		97
5.14.	View of the summit of Pyramid B		98
5.15.	Reliefs on the four faces of Pillar 4		99
5.16.	The personage on Side B, Pillar 4		100
5.17.	The recently identified upper section of Pillar 3		101
5.18.	The personages with attributes of Tlaloc and Tezcatlipoca on the upper section of Pillar 3		101
5.19.	The lower section of Pillar 3, Side B of which represents a bearded figure		102
5.20.	Detail of the elements that join together the upper section of Pillar 3		102
5.21.	Pillar 3, Side B: The bearded personage who probably represents Topiltzin Quetzalcoatl		103
5.22.	Some personages on the pillars of Pyramid B		106
5.23.	Stela 1, found in the pre-Hispanic trench in Pyramid B		107
5.24.	Pyramid B and the South Vestibule		108
5.25.	The South Vestibule and the "Palace to the East"		109
5.26.	The Friso de los Caciques		110
5.27.	Perspective of the Vestibule and the "Palace to the East of the Vestibule"		112
5.28.	The relief on the altar at the "Palace to the East"		113
5.29.	Plan of the "Casa de las Aguilas" at the Templo Mayor of Tenochtitlan		115
5.30.	Plan of the Palacio Quemado		118
5.31.	Perspective of the Palacio Quemado		119
5.32.	The north side of the Palacio Quemado		120
5.33.	The bench frieze of Cuarto 4 in the Palacio Quemado		120
5.34.	Sculptural elements that form the upper friezes in the central patios of the Palacio Quemado		121
5.35.	Reclining figures from the patio friezes of Sala 1 in the Palacio Quemado		122
5.36.	Relief panel in the north corner of Sala 2 showing two warriors, one of them elderly		123
5.37.	Bench frieze on the east side of Sala 2 in the Palacio Quemado		124
5.38.	Palacio Quemado. Bench frieze on the north side of Sala 2		125
5.39.	Offering found in the center of Sala 2		126
5.40.	Relief panels from Building J depicting Tlaloc with a long hooked nose		130
5.41.	Relief panel from Building J of a composite being		130
5.42.	Plan of Building K		131

5.43.	The Tlaloc Warrior statue from Ballcourt 1	135
5.44.	Reconstructive drawing of Pyramid B at Tula	137
5.45.	The Templo Mayor of Tezcoco with the chapels of Huitzilopochtli and Tlaloc on the summit	139
5.46.	The Templo Mayor of Tenochtitlan as represented in the *Codex Aubin*	140
5.47.	Tula relief panel depicting a warrior having a circular shield decorated with a human-skull profile	141
5.48A.	Plan of the so-called Palacio Charnay	146
5.48B.	Plan of the Tecpan excavated by Susan Evans in Cihuatecpan	147
6.1.	The House Groups of the El Canal excavations	153
6.2.	The El Canal excavations	154
6.3.	Hypothetical reconstruction of the House Groups of the El Canal locality	155
6.4.	U27-28: Another example of a House Group in Tula's urban zone	156
6.5.	U98: Sectors of what appear to have been two different House Groups in the same complex	157
6.6.	The structure of the El Corral excavation	158
6.7.	Plan of the House Group excavated at Tepetitlán	160
6.8.	The Tepetitlán excavations	161
6.9.	Location of probable spatial units in the Late Tollan Phase city	164
6.10.	Habitational and ceremonial structures of ZU17 in Tula's northeast urban zone	166
6.11.	Location of probable *barrios* of potters and obsidian workers	168
6.12.	Mounds mapped in the pre-Hispanic city by Yadeun	172
6.13.	Topographic map of the El Canal locality showing two ceremonial mounds	174–175
6.14.	El Corral Pyramid facing a plaza	176
7.1.	Early Postclassic: Collection Units in the Tula area	180
7.2.	Types of sites and present-day land use	181
7.3.	Types of sites and topography	182
7.4.	Different categories of Collection Units in the northeast quadrant of the Tula area (Tollan Phase)	184
7.5.	Groups of habitational and ceremonial structures	187
7.6.	Early Postclassic site types	189
7.7A.	Site type frequencies	190
7.7B.	Sites with previous occupations	191
7.8.	Early Postclassic zones	196
7.9.	Early Postclassic: Zone 1	197
7.10A.	Sierra Tasguada, looking north	198
7.10B.	Potential pre-Hispanic land use	199
7.11.	Early Postclassic: Zone 2	200
7.12.	Zone 3, alluvial valley, looking northeast	201
7.13.	Early Postclassic: Zone 3	202
7.14.	Early Postclassic, Zone 3: Site types	203
7.15.	Early Postclassic: Zone 4	204
7.16.	Early Postclassic: Zone 5	205
7.17.	Early Postclassic: Zone 6	206
7.18.	Early Postclassic: Zone 7	207
7.19.	Spatial distribution of rural site ranks	208
7.20.	Early Postclassic: Clusters	213
7.21.	Potential irrigation zones for the Tollan Phase	214

8.1.	Tollan Complex General Surface Collection, city and hinterland	219
8.2A.	Tollan Complex General Surface Collection, habitational structures, city and hinterland	220
8.2B.	Tollan Complex General Surface Collection	220
8.2C.	Tollan Complex General Surface Collection, hinterland site types	221
8.3.	Tollan Complex Intensive Surface Collection, hinterland	222
8.4.	Tollan Complex Intensive Surface Collection and excavations	223
8.5.	Biplot of Factor 1 (ordinate) and Factor 2 (abscissa) from the correspondence analysis of the data in Table 8.4	226
9.1.	Tepetitlán U56 distribution of *Phaseolus* and *Zea Mays*	251
9.2.	The Early Postclassic settlement in the Basin of Mexico	254
9.3.	Tepetitlán U56: Locations of diverse archaeological elements	259
9.4.	Pollen diagram for Tula	260
9.5.	Early Postclassic: Distribution of basalt scrapers	267
9.6.	Tepetitlán U56: Distribution of faunal remains	273
10.1.	Early Postclassic: Sites with ceremonial architecture	284
10.2.	Early Postclassic: Settlement Groups	286
10.3.	Early Postclassic: Clusters and sites with ceremonial architecture	287
10.4A.	Early Postclassic: Zone 6	292
10.4B.	Early Postclassic: Zone 6, site types.	293
10.5.	Early Postclassic: Zone 4	295
10.6.	Early Postclassic: Zone 3 (alluvial valley)	296
10.7.	Early Postclassic: Lithic and ceramic workshops	298

TABLES

3.1.	Chronology for Tula	42
3.2.	Selected Central Mexican Chronologies	44
3.3.	Chronology for the Tula Urban Zone	49
7.1.	Correspondences between Hierarchical Site Ranks and Site Types	192
7.2.	Distribution of Rural Sites by Zone and Rank	192
7.3.	Distribution of All Rural Sites by Zone	193
7.4.	Nearest Neighbor Coefficients for Site Ranks	209
7.5.	Estimated Population for the Tula Area	211
8.1.	Comparative Distribution by Zone of Full Tollan versus Late Tollan Rural Sites	233
8.2.	Comparative Distribution by Rank Size of Full Tollan versus Late Tollan Rural Sites	233
8.3.	Relative Occurrence of Classic Period Occupation at Full Tollan versus Late Tollan Rural Sites	233
8.4.	Matrix of Factor Loadings from the Correspondence Analysis	234
9.1.	Contexts of the Archaeological Maize Specimens from the Tula Area	239
9.2.	Nutrients of Various Food Sources	247
9.3.	Area of Municipalities in Tula Region	248
9.3A.	Classification of Agricultural Lands	249

Foreword

by David Carrasco and Eduardo Matos Moctezuma

An ancient Mesoamerican myth tells that Quetzalcoatl went inside of Sustenance Mountain to retrieve the sacred corn so that the newly created human beings could live and thrive in the new age, the Fifth Sun. Quetzalcoatl had to work hard and use magical techniques to overcome adversaries and create the conditions for new life. In this significant book, *Ancient Tollan: Tula and the Toltec Heartland,* Alba Guadalupe Mastache, Robert H. Cobean, and Dan M. Healan have done something, in archaeological and interpretive terms, almost as remarkable. They have dug into the physical environment and archaeological ruins of Quetzalcoatl's ancient kingdom and come out with a new appreciation and understanding of the dynamic social, agricultural, and architectural relations between the Toltec capital of Tula and its hinterlands. The book is outstanding for many reasons, but especially because of the combination of respect and creative use of previous scholarship as well as a new vision of the "Tollan Complex" in central Mesoamerican geography, settlement patterns, and urban form.

Ancient Tollan is especially welcome in Mesoamerican studies because it brings the science about Tula back into powerful focus at a time when Teotihuacan, Oaxaca, and a number of sites in the Maya regions have been the subject of innovative studies and interpretive works. These authors insist on seeing Tula and the Toltec state as "long events" by working out clearer chronological patterns, urban zone sequences, and more detailed views of the rich subsistence activities of the remarkable people who carried the Feathered Serpent traditions to what was later remembered as an ideal-type achievement. We are particularly pleased to have this book in our series because, along with H. B. Nicholson's recent close reading of the Topiltzin Quetzalcoatl tradition, it provides readers with a well-rounded vision of what one ancient source called "The Great Tollan."

Acknowledgments

Throughout the various stages of this investigation, the authors have received the generous help and support of many people, to all of whom we express our sincere thanks. The specific contributions of some of them are mentioned in the text. Nevertheless, here we would like to mention the special support of some colleagues and friends.

We thank the kind invitation of Eduardo Matos Moctezuma to Mastache to participate in the Tula Project, which he directed, along with his help in many ways over the years. The initial general surveys of the Tula area were done in collaboration with Ana Maria Crespo, and that period was very stimulating personally and professionally.

It has been a great privilege having from the beginning the guidance and advice of Professor William T. Sanders, who with great generosity oriented and enriched the key stages of this investigation by pointing out major lines of study. He was the director of Mastache's doctoral dissertation, which was the principal antecedent for this book. We greatly appreciate his invaluable comments and suggestions on a preliminary version of this text.

Richard A. Diehl introduced Cobean and Healan to the archaeology of Tula, and our field seasons with Dick's project were the foundation for our careers as Mesoamerican archaeologists. We also thank Dick for his kindness in supplying us with the cover illustration for this book.

Jeffrey Parsons, colleague and friend, helped us greatly in many ways, especially in sharing his profound experience in Mesoamerican archaeology.

We also express special thanks to Evelyn C. Rattray, who with kindness and expert knowledge helped define many of the Tula area ceramic complexes, and to Angel García Cook who provided very useful suggestions, especially during the first field seasons. He and Leonor Merino have supported our project in many ways. We appreciate the valuable comments and suggestions of Davíd Carrasco on an earlier version of this book.

The Foundation for the Advancement of Mesoamerican Studies generously provided a grant to help prepare this volume, especially regarding the costs of translation and preparation of illustrations, for which we are very grateful.

It is a pleasure to thankfully acknowledge the collaboration and advice we have received from numerous specialists, especially Lauro González Quintero, Oscar Polaco, Rafael Márquez, Efraín Hernández Xolocotzi, Bruce Benz, Lawrence Kaplan, and Emily McClung de Tapia. The help and guidance of Dr. Rafael Ortega, Ing. Jorge Duch, and Dr. Moisés Mendoza of the Universidad Autonoma de Chapingo were of key importance for our research, above all concerning the study of agriculture and soils. We also want to thank Gianfranco Cassiano of the ENAH for his generous advice and help, particularly regarding Chapter 2.

ACKNOWLEDGMENTS

Colleagues from the original INAH and University of Missouri Tula projects who have helped or advised us in more recent research include Juan Yadeun, Carlos Hernández, Clara Díaz, James Stoutamire, Agustin Peña, Carmen Rodriguez, Alicia Blanco, Lawrence Feldman, Alejandro Pastrana, Terrance Stocker, Robert and Alice Benfer, and Margaret Mandeville.

The theses and other investigations of our students were important for this book, and we sincerely thank Fernando Getino Granados, Elizabeth Jiménez García, Javier Figueroa Silva, Rosa Elena Moncayo Ochoa, María Elena Suárez Cortés, George Bey, María Guadalupe Sánchez, José Clemente Salazar, Héctor Patiño, Lourdes Camargo, Donald Jackson, Charles Rees, Aarón Arboleyda, Raúl Aranda, and Guizella Romero.

Edward Calnek made key observations on sections of this book and generously shared with us information from his landmark study of Tenochtitlan. Luis Reyes García likewise enlightened us with his analyses of the Toltec chronicles. With his insights, Karl Taube enriched our perspective concerning religion and ideology at Tula. Thomas and Cynthia Charlton, with their profound knowledge of Central Mexico, have helped us in many ways over the years. Susan Toby Evans graciously sent us comments and information on Mesoamerican elite residences.

Throughout the course of our work, we were inspired by the pioneering investigations of Jorge R. Acosta and Hugo Moedano. The analysis of Tula's sacred precinct presented here only was possible because Acosta and his staff excavated and reported their findings with such care. Wigberto Jiménez Moreno's, Barbro Dahlgren's, and Paul Kirchhoff's writings and classes also were an inspiration.

In recent years we have benefited from field visits and discussions with many colleagues and friends, including Beatriz Braniff, Mari Areti Hers, Michael Coe, Ruben Cabrera, Barbara Stark, Robert D. Drennan, Mari Carmen Serra, Christopher Pool, Fernando López Aguilar, Kenneth Hirth, William and Barbara Fash, Nigel Davies, Cynthia Kristan-Graham, William R. Fowler, Ana Alvárez Palma, María Elena Morales, and Rebeca Sandoval, some of whom made specific comments on an earlier version of this book.

We are extremely grateful to Arq. Jesús Acevedo, Mario Pérez, and Oscar Moran de Anda, who used their excellent computer skills to help us produce many maps and architectural plans. Preliminary maps were drawn by Arq. Leticia Rivas. Graphs and some other illustrations were drawn by Fernando Getino.

Jorge Mastache Flores and Sofía Ruíz provided very important help during the initial coding of the project's regional data for computer analyses. We also appreciate the valuable help of Lilia Mastache Flores.

Most of this book was originally written in Spanish, and the English version is due to the efforts of Graham McSkimmings and Robert H. Cobean. We thank Graham for his very fine professionalism.

We thank Joaquín García Bárcena and Enrique Nalda, who during different periods as Secretario Técnico of the INAH authorized special permissions for several months to Mastache, which provided valuable time to write and analyze data for this text. We also thank Alejandro Martínez and Norberto González for help in this.

Jose Vergara as Director of the Centro-INAH Hidalgo kindly aided us in many ways during recent periods of fieldwork and analysis of materials.

We also must mention our great debt to Tula residents Florentino Jiménez, Bernabé Jiménez, Zenón Jiménez, and Guadalupe Alcántara. Using their immense experience and talent, they were crew chiefs and specialists in several excavations and surveys of our project. Constantina Martínez López supervised many activities in the preparation and organization of our field collections for laboratory analyses. We are very grateful as always to Sr. José Ramírez and Sra. Enriqueta Guadarrama, Sra. Juana Gama, and Sra. Minerva Olmos of the Coordinación de Arqueología and the Dirección de Estudios Arqueológicos for their very valuable help in the preparation of this book.

Darrin Pratt, Laura Furney, and the staff of the University Press of Colorado have shown us much kindness and patience during the making of this book. We thank them for their thorough professionalism.

Mastache desires to express special thanks to Gloria Benedito for her support and understanding over the years.

Introduction

Among the cities of varying magnitude that emerged in the Central Highlands of Mexico during two millennia, Tula, together with Teotihuacan and Tenochtitlan, was one of the most important urban centers in Mesoamerica during the pre-Hispanic era. Tula had a long life of around four centuries, and by A.D. 1000 it probably was the largest contemporary city in ancient Mexico. Its area of influence extended over much of Central Mexico along with other regions of Mesoamerica including areas of the Bajío, the Huasteca, the Gulf Coast, the Yucatan peninsula, and such distant places as the Soconusco, on the Pacific Coast of Chiapas and Guatemala, and El Salvador.

In contrast with Teotihuacan, the monumental and archetypical city, which has been the focus of extensive investigations and excavations for more than a century, and with Tenochtitlan, which was a living city when the Spaniards arrived and for which almost ethnographic reconstructions of many aspects can be made, ancient Tula has been surrounded by much speculation and confusion. For generations this site has been the object of controversies and debates concerning its nature and its identity, perhaps not only because history and myth in this place have been fused but also because of its association with Topiltzin Quetzalcoatl, the culture hero par excellence of ancient Mexico, and surely in great measure because systematic investigations at Tula only began in 1940.

With this book, we intend to give an up-to-date synthesis of available knowledge about the nature of this city, its chronology, urban structure, and developmental processes, along with the settlement systems in its hinterland, although for some of these topics there are more questions than answers. This work basically contains the results of a long-term interdisciplinary project concerning the ancient city and especially its heartland. We also integrate findings from other archaeological projects conducted at Tula during recent decades by different institutions. The central themes deal with the formation processes and, above all, the period of apogee of Tula's urban center. Because an organic relationship existed between this city and the surrounding rural populations, the study of the core of its sustaining area permits a wider vision of some aspects of its political and economic structure.

The regional investigations cover an area of nearly 1,000 square kilometers surrounding Tula, and include settlement pattern studies involving both general surveys and several sampling strategies, intensive surveys and excavations in sites of various periods, studies concerning present-day land use and modern and traditional irrigation systems, palynological and geological studies, and historical research in archives and published sources concerning the Tula region during the Colonial period and the nineteenth century.

INTRODUCTION

In the chapter regarding the physical environment and land use in the Tula region, we treat the definition, limits, and characteristics of the study area. This chapter also includes a section on the paleoenvironments and the traditional irrigation systems, the study of which makes possible estimates of the region's irrigation potential.

A key element for the study of cultural processes is the periodification and the chronological placement of the different phases of occupation of the city and its hinterland. There now exist more exact definitions for the development periods of Tula supported by a series of radiocarbon dates that extend from the initial urban settlement to the apogee and abandonment of the city. In order to investigate the formation processes for this center, some chapters treat the occupations of the area in previous periods, especially the Classic and Epiclassic, that constitute a fundamental antecedent without which the emergence of Tula cannot be understood.

The study of the urban center is divided into three parts: the sacred precinct, other zones of the monumental area, and habitation in the city. An extensive chapter is dedicated to Tula's sacred precinct and its principal buildings, the architectural and iconographic analyses of which permitted an understanding of fundamental aspects of the Toltec state and of significant ideological continuities between Teotihuacan, Tula, and Tenochtitlan. A general panorama about the residential zones of the city is the subject of another section that treats the distinct stages of Tula's growth, which involve modifications in the orientations of the urban grid along with other changes in architecture and ceramic traditions. The available information concerning urban planning and spatial organization is analyzed, and some hypotheses are proposed about the city's territorial divisions and the existence of neighborhoods, some of which probably were defined in relation to the specialized activities of their inhabitants.

An extensive section is dedicated to settlement systems in Tula's hinterland in conjunction with the study of pre-Hispanic irrigation systems, specific crops and other types of natural-resource exploitation. The regional studies identified approximately five hundred archaeological sites of differing extension and complexity corresponding to distinct periods. The sites coeval with Tula's apogee are defined in terms of a series of aspects such as kinds of remains, ecological setting, extension, and complexity, and are tentatively classified into other categories such as Clusters and Settlement Groups. In Chapter 10, comparative ethnohistorical information is analyzed from fifteenth- and sixteenth-century settlement and political administrative systems, especially in the Basin of Mexico, Morelos, and Tlaxcala.

The study of the hinterland of this city began as part of the Instituto Nacional de Antropología e Historia (INAH) Proyecto Tula directed by Eduardo Matos, who proposed a settlement pattern investigation in the city's sustaining area. As cited in Chapter 1, the initial surveys of the area were done in collaboration with Ana María Crespo, producing several publications and a survey data bank at the disposition of both Mastache and Crespo. A new project coordinated by Mastache and Cobean began in the 1980s, which has done additional surveys and studies of specific sites in different parts of the area including Tula. These investigations involve intensive surface surveys, the production of site maps, and excavations in settlements of different periods. The specific characteristics and objectives of these investigations are treated in Chapter 1. The principal antecedent for this book was the doctoral dissertation of Mastache, who also wrote the lion's share of the present text.

ANCIENT TOLLAN

1

Tula and the Tula Region Project

This chapter consists of two sections: the first concerns investigations in Tula's ancient city, and the second deals with the Tula region project, which was a central aspect of our research.

TULA

Although it is true that all urban centers share a series of features and elements that define and characterize urban life, in order to understand the phenomenon of urbanism in Mesoamerica and its complexity, detailed studies of these centers are required, because the cities that developed in this area over at least two millenia are entities of different range and magnitude. Each one possesses its own characteristics and specific development pattern, which expresses its particular way of life and conception of the world, as well as its historical circumstances.

Most Mesoamerican cities, like others in the ancient world, were political, economic, religious, and administrative centers that constituted the axes of a complex system of relationships of a diverse nature. To speak of urbanism is in general to refer to societies divided by classes, with complex systems of production and labor organization—human groups with differential access to production, social wealth, and consumption—with some sectors of the population detached from agricultural activities and the production of goods, who instead governed and organized the society. These societies usually possessed complex institutions and a developed religion, which in the early states permeates all other spheres of society, constituting an important element of ideological control by which it gives moral legitimacy to the system.

Significant methodological progress for the study of urban centers has been developed by geographers, sociologists, economists, architects, and others who investigate living cities from different approaches and points of view. It is evident that the levels of analysis that can be used for an archaeological city are different from those for a living city, but some proposals of these disciplines can be viable in the study of archaeological cities. It also is important to evaluate which strategies and methodologies are relevant for archaeology and permit the application of techniques that may be useful for the urban analysis of these cities. The investigation of archaeological cities involves various problems related to the nature of these centers and the characteristics of the preserved information, which require the development of an adequate methodology.

Some urban centers of the Central Mexican Highlands, including Tula, are very extensive settlements with areas exceeding 10 square kilometers: for example, Teotihuacan's area is approximately 20 square kilometers, Tula's 16, Cholula's more than 10, Cantona's 12, and Tenochtitlan's around 12. The very size of these cities makes their study a complex problem because it is not possible to investigate on the same level of detail the totality of sites having such dimensions, even if they have been well preserved.

Another important aspect is the relative contemporaneity and chronology of the preserved remains. In general, these sites developed over several centuries and each city is not conserved at a specific moment in its life, but is the product of a complex sequence of occupation wherein it is difficult to detect which structures were contemporaneous with a given period. In Tula, there are sectors of the city, especially in the monumental center, with stratigraphic sequences several meters deep, covering almost a thousand years of occupation, including the Colonial period.

During the process of the growth of a city, the buildings of the first stages are covered, altered totally, or partially destroyed by transformations of various kinds. Later, diverse processes, such as erosion, reoccupations of distinct magnitudes, and different soil uses, that take place over the course of centuries in these sites destroy important areas of any archaeological city. Like other urban centers, Tula has been severely damaged, especially in recent decades. It has undergone rapid destruction for various reasons, which include recent urban expansion and the development of new towns, the construction of extensive cultivation and irrigation terrace systems, the extended use of mechanized agriculture, and the industrialization of the area that has involved the building of various complementary infrastructure works, all of which have destroyed large sectors of the ancient city and numerous outlying rural sites.

On one hand, the problem of erosion in Tula is more serious than in other urban settlements of the Central Highlands, because most of the habitation units were made of adobe, with stone only being used for making foundations. Thus, the structures are generally quite damaged and are difficult to detect using only surface surveys. In contrast, at Teotihuacan the buildings were constructed with quarried stone, and they are clearly delimited by walls that may still be observed on the surface. The Cantona, Puebla, site is another example of good conservation due to the construction techniques, including the use of stone.

It also must be emphasized that urban analysis is more difficult for Tula than for Teotihuacan, which possesses architectural characteristics (and a very detailed map for the entire city) permitting precise urban studies, or for Tenochtitlan—a city for which it was possible to make an almost ethnographic reconstruction thanks to the conquistadors' descriptions and numerous other historical sources. Given Tula's architectural characteristics and its conservation problems, in addition to the fact that the investigation projects concerning the city were not focused on defining its planning and specific urban features, we know little about its urban plan and structure and its specific forms for organizing urban space. Thus there are few data available for making a rigorous urban analysis of this site.

Our current knowledge about the city of Tula is fundamentally derived first from the pioneer studies made by Jorge R. Acosta over almost twenty years in the monumental zone beginning in 1940, to which we have referred in detail in other publications (Cobean and Mastache 1988, 1999), and subsequently from a series of projects undertaken by various institutions that started between 1968 and 1970 with approaches and objectives that generally reflect the technical and theoretical orientations of archaeology in that period, which emphasized investigation of this site beyond the limits of the monumental zone. These research programs included the definition of the extension and general characteristics of the pre-Hispanic city, excavation of residences, typological studies of ceramic complexes and redefinition of the sequence of occupations of the site, research in some zones of craft production, and regional studies of settlement patterns.

As part of the University of Missouri Project, directed by Richard Diehl and Robert Benfer, the investigations of Stoutamire (1974, 1975; Healan and Stoutamire 1989) defined for the first time the limits of the urban zone and conducted a statistical-sampling program of the surface materials within the city, which encompassed 844 collection units. Based on his studies, Stoutamire calculated that Tula covered an area of 13 square kilometers. His urban survey essentially used as criteria the presence and density of ceramics and other materials, as well as the evidence for architecture on the surface. In addition, Yadeun (1975), a member of the Instituto Nacional de Antropología e Historia (INAH) project directed by Eduardo Matos, redefined the limits of the city; this study principally took into account the distribution and density of mounds within the urban zone based on aerial photographs and a photo-grametric restitution that covered part of the city. Yadeun also sampled surface materials in various locations of the urban zone, collecting units of 1 meter by 1 meter, every 100 meters. His investigation centered on the presence of mounds, which were divided into two groups: those that were more than 2.5 meters in height and those at least 1 meter but less than 2.5 meters high, without considering those of less than 1 meter high, which excluded a large part of the habitation mounds of Tula. Yadeun took as a starting point the limits established by Stoutamire to define his area of study, later reducing them based on the density of mounds in some zones and proposing that the city of Tula covered an area of 11.38 square kilometers according to this criterion.

With respect to the planning of Tula, Mastache and Crespo (1982) made a study based principally on aerial photographs, which enabled them to define three different alignment grids for the city, corresponding to different phases. The alignments of the city were defined on the basis of the analysis of the aerial photographs of various dates, considering all the alignments visible in the photographs, although in many cases they were no longer visible on the surface. There was also a survey and sampling program of surface materials, starting from the outlying area and going toward the city, in order to verify the limits of the city previously defined by other projects. Based on the distribution of the alignments and their survey, it is estimated that the city had a maximum extension of 16 square kilometers. The principal difference between this figure and the area calculated by Stoutamire lies in the fact that he did not include the zones on the lower foothills of Cerro Magoni, situated to the west of the Tula River, which evidently formed part of the urban zone, and an area in the north of the city with platforms and structures having alignments visible in aerial photographs, but which have few surface ceramics.

Thus, in order to define the extension of this center, different criteria and approaches were used that are partly complementary, although unfortunately a detailed topographic map and a survey of the urban zone were not made for recording the various types of extant architectural structures and units, complemented with systematic surface collections by structure, with a total coverage of the city, that is, a study similar to the one that Millon ([ed.] 1973, 1981) and his collaborators did in Teotihuacan. The absence of research with these characteristics constitutes a severe limitation for investigations focused on defining the urban plans and the internal structure of the city in its growth process.

Tula unfortunately has been subjected to intensive destruction, especially during the last fifteen years, mainly due to the rapid urban expansion of this area and the diverse public works carried out by several institutions, such as PEMEX, S.R.H., the Federal Electricity Commission, and the construction of the "bullet train," as well as the mechanization of agriculture with its extensive use of tractors that disturb the subsoil to a depth of more than 1 meter. These developments now make it almost impossible to produce a map that covers the entire settlement and a study of the characteristics mentioned, although there are still small parts of the ancient city that can be mapped.

The study of pre-Hispanic habitation units has been the center of various research projects. However, to date in the city of Tula only about a dozen habitation structures have been excavated, including those investigated by Charnay in the last century: the Casa Tolteca and Palacio Tolteca (Charnay 1885), Dainí (Peña and Rodríguez 1976), the Colonia Pemex habitational structure (Matos 1974), El Corral (Mandeville and Healan 1989), El Canal (Healan 1989a), Cerro La Malinche (Abascal 1982; Paredes 1990), El Vivero (Fernández 1994), El Salitre (Healan 1986; Healan, Kerley, and Bey 1983), Units U27 and U28 (Getino and Fuentes 1986; Salazar 1991), and U98 (Hernández et al. 1999).

Some of these domestic structures, located in various parts of the city (see Fig. 1.1) were only partially excavated, and the methodology and techniques of excavation have differed with varying levels of accuracy in the recording of information and control of materials. Nor in all cases were the materials obtained analyzed or were detailed records kept of finds, descriptions of the stratigraphy, and their contexts. Some studies were often also lacking maps and basic plans that would make it possible to determine the internal plan and construction sequences of the phases of occupation of the buildings, and that would permit identification and detection of specific activity areas.

The reports derived from these excavations are equally variable in content, and only some have been published. The above deficiencies mean that the information available for the excavated domestic units is very incomplete and the data for the different excavations are not always comparable with each other. Therefore, we can only make generalizations based on a small sample regarding the domestic architecture that constituted most of the settlement of the city.

The most complete study of this subject is that published by Healan (1989a and b) concerning the El Canal and El Corral structures, the first of which includes totally excavated residences. Based on these excavations, Healan made a detailed reconstruction of the constructive and stratigraphic sequence of the habitation complexes, the number of rooms and units that made up these complexes, the identification of numerous activity areas—such as kitchens, other food preparation zones, storage areas, weaving and other craft areas, dormitories, among others—as well as demographic calculations.

Other aspects that have been studied by various scholars include the city's production areas, especially those concerning obsidian working (Healan 1986; Pastrana 1990) and ceramics. Probable production zones have been detected for the manufacture of shell, bone, jade, serpentine, and tecalli objects and figurines and ceramics (Healan and Stoutamire 1989; Diehl and Stroh 1978). Excavations have been done of three workshops: one obsidian (Healan, Kerley, and, Bey 1983) and one for ceramic tubes (Healan 1989a) and another pottery workshop (Hernández et al. 1999). The studies of ceramics conducted by Cobean (1978, 1990), based on excavation and surface materials, permitted him to elaborate a typology and investigate the functions of the specific ceramic types, and to propose a more precise chronology and periodification for the city, which is analyzed in greater detail in the following chapters.

Figure 1.1. Locations of excavations and structures in Tula's ancient city:
1. Monumental Precinct, **2.** Plaza Charnay, **3.** Tula Chico, **4.** El Corral Pyramid, **5.** El Corral Excavation (University of Missouri, 1970), **6.** El Canal Excavation (University of Missouri, 1970–1972), **7.** Unit 17 (ZU-17), **8.** Boulevard Norte (Centro INAH, 1998), **9.** Obsidian Workshop (Tulane University, 1980), **10.** El Cielito, **11.** Boulevard (Centro INAH, 1996), **12.** Main Plaza, Tula de Allende, **13.** Colonia PEMEX, **14.** Mormon Church (Centro INAH, 1986), **15.** Unit 27–28, (Dirección de Monumentos Prehispánicos, 1986), **16.** La Nopalera (Centro INAH, 1982), **17.** El Vivero (Centro INAH, 1982), **18.** El Museo (Centro INAH, 1982), **19.** Toltec House (Charnay, 1887), **20.** Toltec Palace (Charnay, 1887), **21.** Zapata 2 (Centro INAH, 1982), **22.** La Malinche M.1 (Centro INAH, 1982), **23.** La Malinche P.18-19 (Centro INAH, 1982), **24.** Viaducto (Centro INAH, 1982), **25.** La Mora (Dirección de Salvamento Arqueológico, 1996), **26.** Daini (Dirección de Monumentos Prehispánicos, 1976).

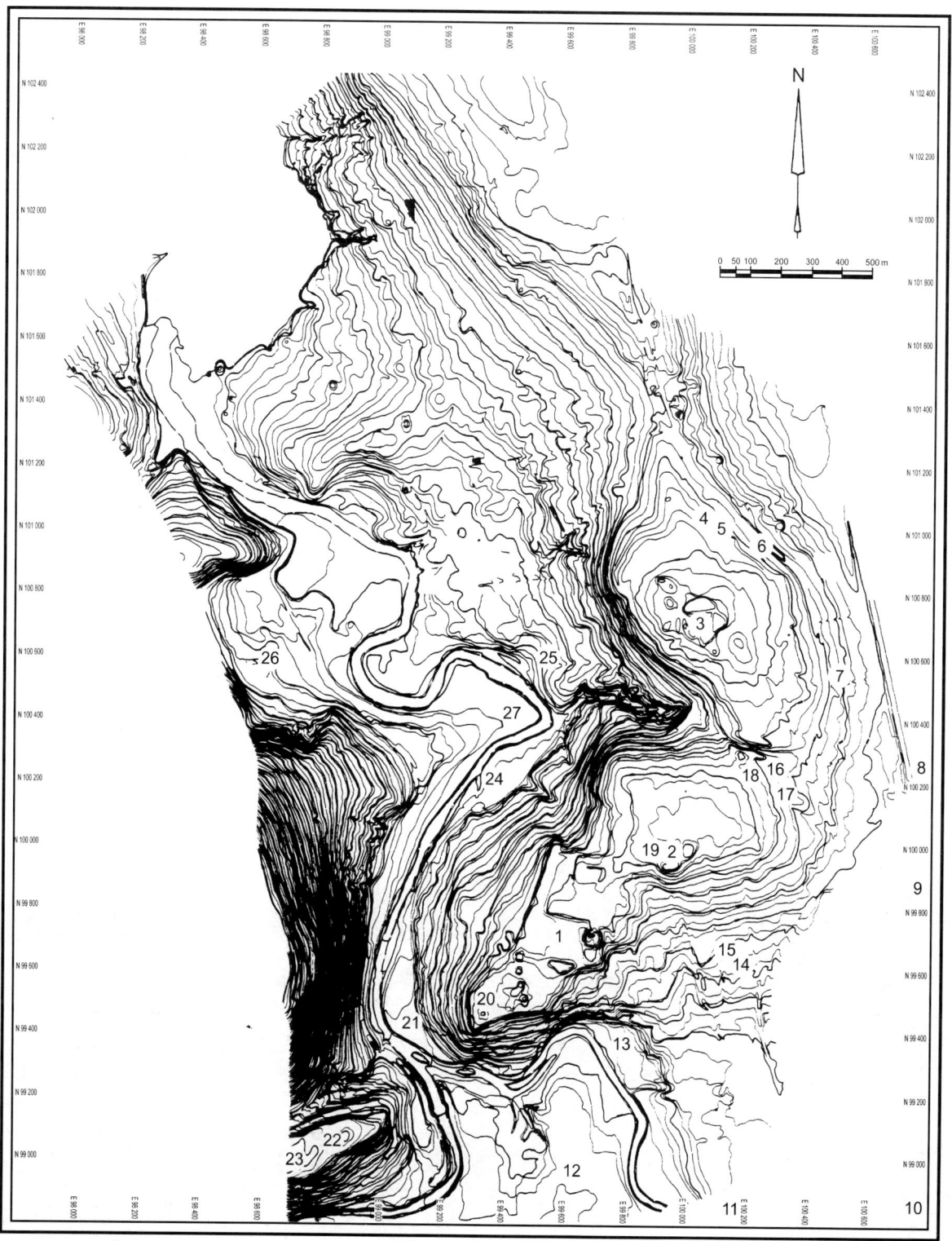

CONTOUR INTERVAL 50 METERS

Kilometers 10 0 10

Miles 10 0 10

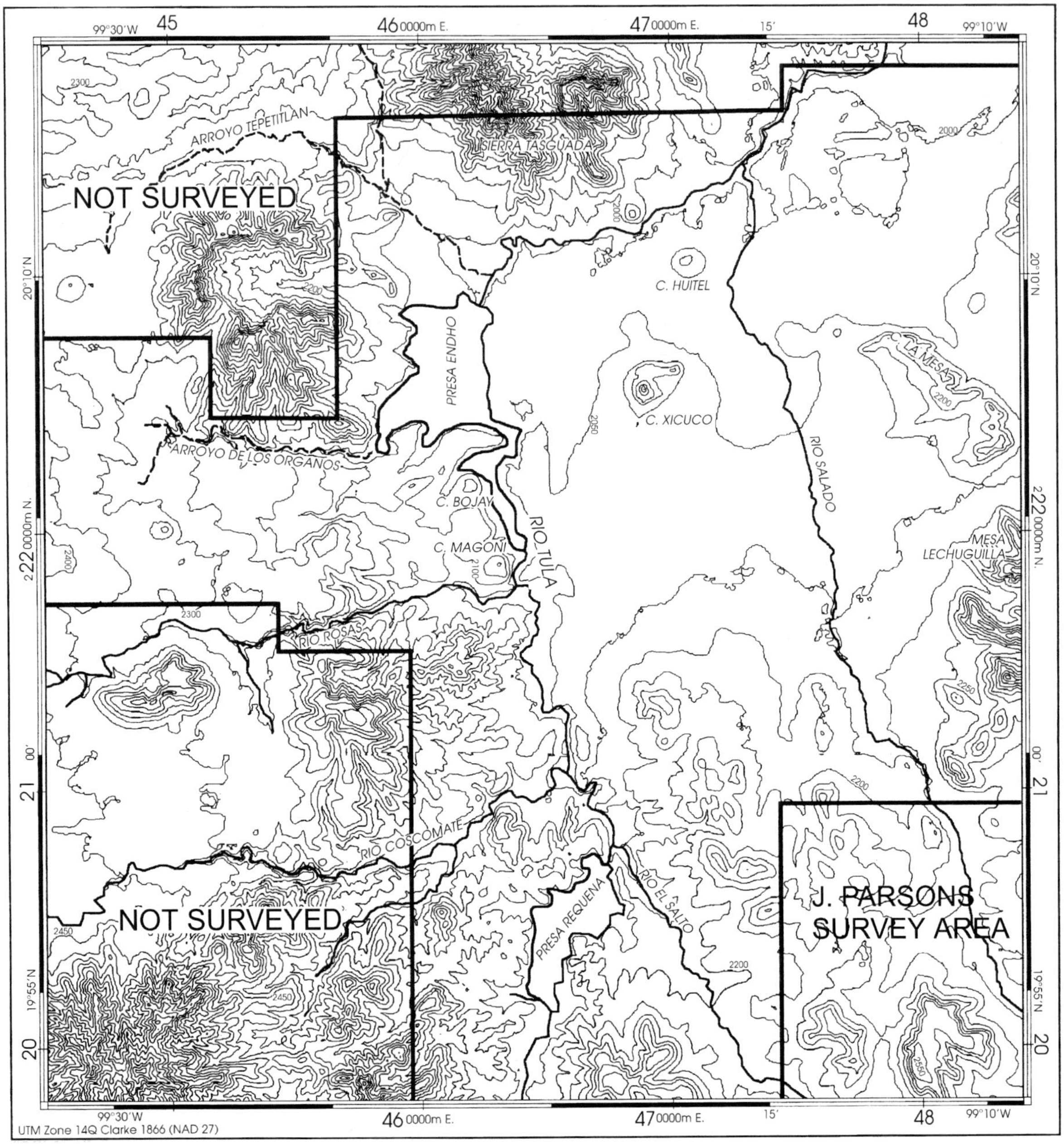

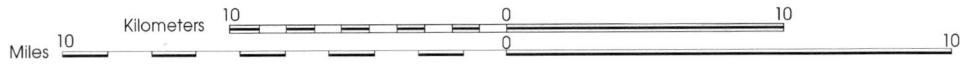

Figure 1.2. Survey area.

Figure 1.3. Tula area. The white lines indicate rivers and the limits of the Tollan phase city, and the black squares indicate rural sites of this period.

THE TULA REGION PROJECT

The central objective of the project concerning the Tula region was to obtain a regional perspective about the formation process of this city and the Toltec state, as well as to study the city's rural environment at its apogee. Consequently, we conducted a regional study of the city's hinterland, this being the territory that constituted the nucleus of this city's direct sustaining area and its immediate interaction area (Fig. 1.2).

The initial step was the definition of the study area, that is, to establish the extension of the city's immediate rural environment. Because there was no clearly defined physiographic unit, as in the case of the Valley of Teotihuacan, various criteria were followed to define the area to be studied. Initially, using the geographic criterion of the central place, a radius of 17 kilometers around Tula was drawn, which is the approximate distance to the north and south between the present city of Tula and the closest important towns of the area. Thus defined, this zone was the basis of the preliminary surveys. However, the intensive archaeological surveys conducted later did not cover the same area, because the preliminary studies showed that very probably the principal zone of interaction of the ancient city did not coincide with the entire area previously established, especially taking into account that much of the western area (which possesses very uneven topography) apparently had been uninhabited during most of the pre-Hispanic period. Thus Tula was located close to the western end of its rural environment, and not

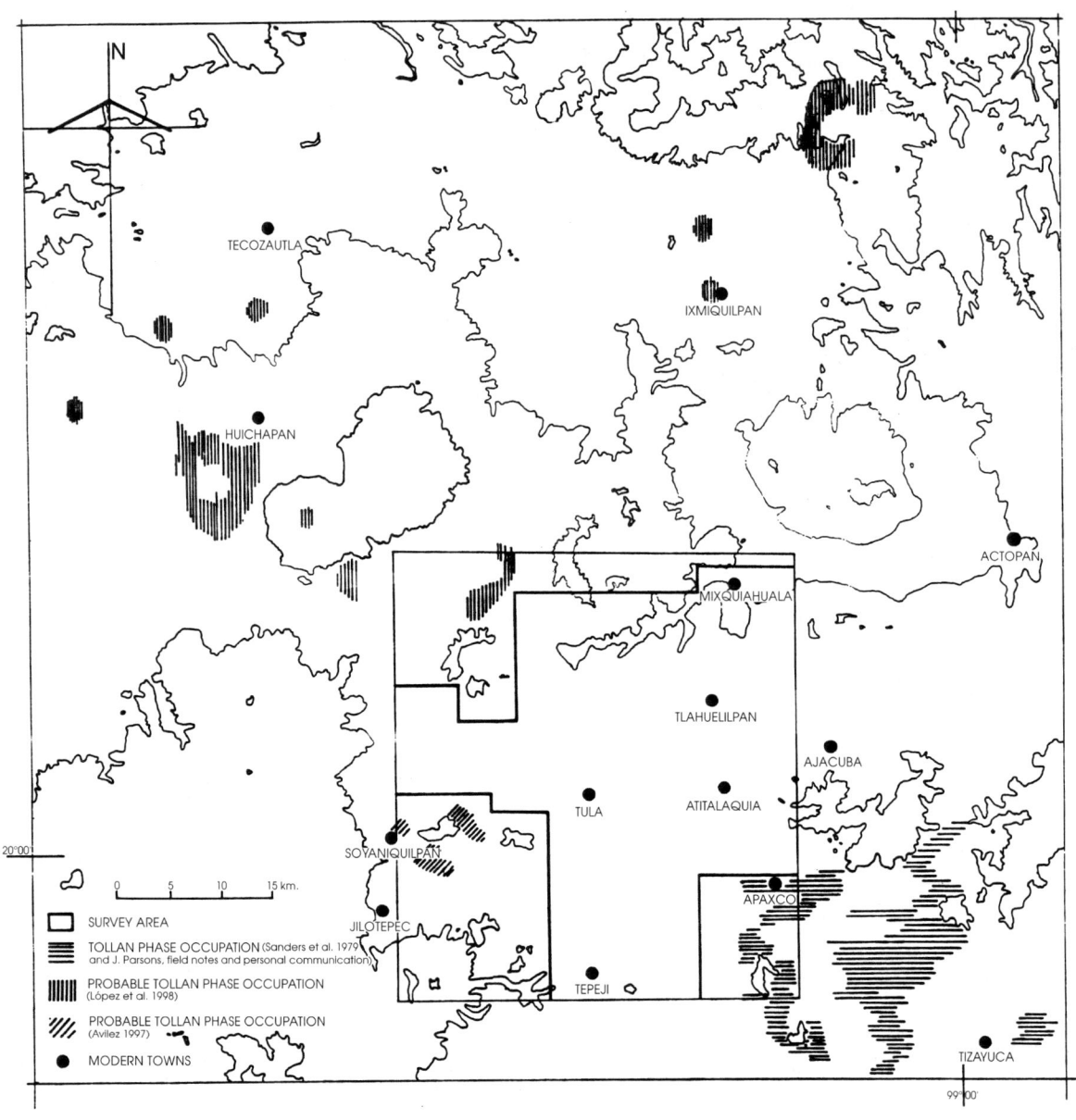

Figure 1.4. The study area and surrounding valleys.

in the center as had been supposed initially. Consequently, the proposed limits were modified and the intensive archaeological survey mainly covered the eastern part of the area. The survey area, however, was expanded to the north to include the end of the alluvial valley up to the town of Mizquiahuala, and to the southeast to border on the area surveyed by Parsons (1990) (see Figs. 1.3 and 1.4).

The area thus defined has an extension of approximately 1,000 square kilometers and forms part of the Tula River Basin, limited to the south by the Basin of Mexico and the north by the Valle del Mezquital. The most important present towns include Mixquiahuala and Tepetitlan to the north, Heroes de Carranza and Jilotepec to the west, Tepeji del Rio to the south, and Tlahuelilpan, Atitalaquia, and Atotonilco Tula to the east (Figs. 1.2 and 2.1).

It is important to emphasize that we consider the study area to constitute only the core of the heartland for the city, because without doubt the sustaining area for Tula was a larger geographic unit including some of the surrounding valleys and part of the Basin of Mexico, which would have been integral components. These zones probably were tied economically and politically to Tula, forming a kind of second ring of interaction for the city (Fig. 1.4).

Settlement Patterns

A regional settlement pattern study is an investigation that deals with regional settlement systems and the dynamic interaction existing between the population and the environment, rather than the analysis of specific sites. It is in reality a geographic study because it uses methods and techniques of geography and many of the basic fundaments and general principles are the same, although the nature of the archaeological data require special methodological techniques and include a series of limitations in terms of the scope of these studies that are not encountered by geographers when they study present-day settlements. The analysis of the settlement in a given region implies the study of multiple natural, historical, economic, and social factors that determine the way in which the population was distributed, and which are constantly interrelated. The specific systems and patterns of population distribution and the organization of space of human groups are closely associated with their level of technological development, on the one hand, and their social, economic, and political structure on the other.

Consequently, the study of population systems must be quantitative and qualitative, that is, it must include the description of the forms of distribution and groupings of the population, as well as search for the relationships between the specific location and the factors that determine the permanence of the population in this place (George 1974a and b). Thus, it is necessary to examine the particular conditions of the region and its specific historical circumstances, which implies the analysis of elements of a distinct nature, from which it is then necessary to select those that may easily be identified in the archaeological records, and to establish hierarchies according to their nature and the explicative level that they permit.

A fundamental aspect of these studies is the analysis of environmental conditions, above all to determine what has been called the carrying capacity of the area. In this respect, is important to take into account the fact that the physical environment and natural resources constitute a series of potential elements that on their own do not determine the sustenance capacity of area, because they may be modified, developed, or annulled according to the level of development of the productive forces—that is, in terms of the existing productive potential and technology, as well as the forms of organization of production and the nature of the material and ideological needs of that society, including specific consumption patterns.

As correctly shown by George (1976:15–16), the climate, water resources, and the quality and fertility of soils do not automatically generate high-yield agriculture and, on the other hand, unfavorable climatic conditions may be modified by the use of appropriate techniques. Forests, other plant and animal species, as well as diverse mineral resources may or may not be exploited, depending on the technology and the complexity of the extant institutions, the cultural traditions, and the needs of that society. On the other hand, the population that constitutes both the work force and the consumption base is not a determining factor in itself, because the efficiency and productive capacity of the population, as well as its consumption characteristics, do not depend solely on the extant number of inhabitants and demographic density, but are subordinate to multiple factors, especially economic and political ones.

Thus, natural conditions, technical capacity, forms of production organization, distinct types of needs, and cultural consumption patterns constitute an inseparable whole in constant interaction, which determines the production and therefore the sustaining capacity of the area. In general terms, most of the settlement pattern studies of Mesoamerica have contemplated these aspects, although it is evident that there are specific variations and significant differences between the projects in terms of the particular theoretical orientation of the investigators and the concrete objectives of each investigation, which has determined, among other things, the emphasis in the study of given aspects and the specific forms of analysis as well as the introduction of a framework and the level of conclusions reached. In this respect, the exhaustive study by Nichols (1996) concerning settlement pattern studies done in Mesoamerica from 1960 to 1995 should be consulted. Nichols's essay is a general overview of this type of investigation and a description of the principal characteristics, approaches, and accomplishments.

Through the course of history and in anthropological literature, there is a plethora of examples concerning the different ways in which the same region has been occupied and exploited over time in terms of particular historical circumstances and the existing economic and political systems. The case of Tula is a clear example of this fact because the forms of settlement and population distribution in the area and the use and exploitation of its resources gave rise to very different patterns during the diverse periods of occupation, basically due to the general economic and political system of which the area formed part. The changes in the forms of grouping and distribution of the population over time express different social relationships and distinct levels of political organization, diverse forms of labor organization, and different degrees of development of the productive forces, of which the resources of the area constituted a fundamental part. Thus, the analysis of the settlement of this region permits a greater understanding of its general historical process and the development of the Toltec state in particular.

The study of the settlement patterns in the Tula area generally followed the guidelines proposed for the previous work of Sanders and his collaborators for the Valley of Teotihuacan (1965) because the general objectives of this study were similar to that of Tula, and the conditions of these areas are similar in terms of the environment. A study essentially based on archaeological surveys was an initial indispensable stage that served as a basis for later specific investigations with concrete hypotheses and questions.

The investigation had various stages. First, some preliminary surveys were made with the purpose of obtaining a general panorama of the pre-Hispanic population in the area, principally the occupation density, site distribution patterns, size, conditions of conservation, and general chronology. Maps furnished by the Ministries of Defense and Water Resources and aerial photographs at a scale of 1:25,000 were used in the initial surveys (Crespo and Mastache 1973; Mastache and Crespo 1974).

Aerial photographs were used as a guide to the area in terms of access routes, topography, hydrography, present population distribution, and above all for the location of points with favorable conditions for human settlement, rather than for the location of archaeological sites. The principal criteria for the location of archaeological sites during this first stage of the research were principally local informants and the survey of zones that were accessible by roads. The corresponding information was recorded in forms that included sketch maps of the sites. The sites were located on the aerial photographs and other topographic maps and a general sample of surface materials, especially ceramics, was taken at each site. The collections obtained during the initial surveys were designated the "Selective Collection," which is composed of a selective sample of surface artifacts, mainly ceramics obtained by unsystematic pickup, a method comparable to "grab" sampling commonly used in archaeological surveys and environmental surveys conducted by the United States Environmental Protection Agency. As noted, the Selective Collection was intended only to provide a preliminary overview of the pre-Hispanic cultural sequence prior to the implementation of the "Systematic Collection" described below.

A survey was then made of the present population patterns and land use in the area, together with a study of the traditional and modern irrigation systems, while simultaneously obtaining information about various aspects such as hydrography, vegetation, agriculture, crop types, soil conservation techniques, water control and distribution systems, and the exploitation of various kinds of mineral resources. The initial step of the investigation concerning irrigation was the location of existing systems in the area by means of field studies and aerial photography. Afterward, investigations were conducted on published historical sources referring to the sixteenth and seventeenth centuries as well as in the General Archives of Mexico (Archivo General de la Nación), especially in documents of the Ramo de Tierras, which provided valuable information regarding the eighteenth and nineteenth centuries (Crespo 1976; Mastache 1976; Feldman and Mastache 1990).

During the associated field surveys, and while registering the irrigation systems, some archaeological sites were also located that were not sampled, and only subject to an on-site revision of surface materials and given a general chronology based on the diagnostic material. These sites are designated as sites without material (see Appendix). Pollen studies were also made (González Quintero and Montufar 1980) that essentially consisted of the analysis of two drilled cores of various meters in depth obtained at different points of the area, as well as a geological study (Márquez 1986) fundamentally focused on the location of potential areas for the exploitation of limestone, basalt, rhyolite, and chert.

Finally, a full-coverage survey was made beginning in 1975 and ending in 1977. The survey covered the eastern part of the area that was the principal zone of occupation during the pre-Hispanic period. In general terms, this is the region between the Tula and El Salado Rivers, extending up to the foothills of the mountains that limit the area to the west (Fig. 1.2). The sampling procedure corresponding to the full-coverage survey is designated here as the "Systematic Collection." This survey had as its basis a concept similar to that of a "siteless survey" (Dunnell and Dacey 1983). This approach to sampling assumes an archaeological record comprising a "more or less continuous distribution of artifacts over the land surface with highly variable density characteristics" (p. 272), which is certainly an appropriate characterization of the region surrounding Tula and comparable pre-Hispanic cities and their hinterlands. Siteless survey is a flexible approach that allows for the recovery of artifacts without making assumptions regarding subsurface realities, while at the same time providing the opportunity to identify surface features that normally do constitute surface manifestations of subsurface remains commonly considered as "sites." Once identified, such features, which include mounds, artifact concentrations, and other surface anomalies, may themselves be units for collection, which was the procedure used in this case.

For the survey, aerial photographs of different flights and scales were used because there was no flight that covered the entire study area, and there was no budget to make enlargements or to prepare a general mosaic at the same scale, as would have been desirable. However, one 1:7,500 flight that covered a large part of the study area, especially the northwestern quadrant that goes from the Tula River up to the mountains that limit the area to the east, was especially useful. Although it would have been preferable to have photographs at the scale of 1:5,000, like those used by Sanders and his collaborators in the study of the Valley of Teotihuacan, the scale of this flight was still adequate for the survey, and the fact that it covered the entire alluvial valley was especially important because as mentioned before, the preliminary survey studies (1973–1974) show that this sector had been the principal area of occupation during the pre-Hispanic period.

The photographs were used in the field as maps; they were organized into grids of 1 square kilometer, each of which was subdivided into twenty-five units. The survey and sampling were done on the basis of these units, which were fully surveyed and indiscriminate samples of materials present were taken throughout the unit. In cases where there were mounds, structures, or special concentrations of materials, specific collections were made that were independent of the general sample of the unit, taking the latter only as a reference.

Although the object of study for this investigation was the sustaining area of the pre-Hispanic city and not the city itself, the investigation of which was covered by other projects (Tula Project of the INAH directed by Eduardo Matos Moctezuma and the Tula Project of the University of Missouri directed by Richard Diehl), it was decided to include in the intensive full-coverage survey sampling program a small part of the periphery of the urban center so that the study area would overlap with that of the city, determining more precisely the spatial limits between the urban and rural zones. This involved the delineation of the same square-grid system used in the eastern periphery of the urban zone, which was then sampled using the method outlined for the Systematic Collection in the area. As mentioned before, this would also make it possible to verify the limits of the city established previously by other projects (Stoutamire 1974 and Yadeun 1975), except that this time we started from the periphery and moved toward the urban center. It was also necessary to have a sample of the surface materials of the city that had been obtained with the same criteria as the sampling of the rural area, so that they would be comparable with each other. As mentioned before, in order to try to define the planning and general layout of the city, as well as its urban grid system (aspects that had not been clarified by the other projects), a study was carried out between 1977 and 1978, a central part of which was the analysis of the aerial photographs from flights corresponding to different dates, as well as a very general surface survey of the pre-Hispanic city (Mastache and Crespo 1982).

In 1982, the Tula and Its Direct Interaction Area Project was started under the direction of Cobean and Mastache, the investigations of which include surface studies and excavations corresponding to distinct periods in different locations of the city's hinterland, including Tula. Some of the investigations of this project already have been published; some are still in progress and will be the subject of specific monographs.

The materials obtained in the general surveys (the preliminary survey and the full-coverage surveys) and those obtained from intensive sampling were fully analyzed. The chronology of the sites was established on the basis of the diagnostic ceramics collected, which were correlated with already defined ceramic chronologies, especially those for the Basin of Mexico and Tula itself. The sites were thus grouped together according to the principal periods established for Mesoamerica, following the general chronological framework used by Millon ([ed.] 1973) for the Basin, although it cannot be stated with certainty that the specific phases established for that region have an exact correspondence to the Tula area, especially in reference to the Classic period. Consequently, the maps for the periods presented cover large chronological blocks, which places some sites as contemporary even when this may not have been so. In this respect, the excavations made later on the various sites of the area are important because they have made it possible to obtain more detailed knowledge of the sequences of occupation for some settlements and to obtain absolute dates, as well as to verify the phases established for Tula. This has made it possible to subdivide some general periods that can also be applied to the rural area.

The typology and ceramic sequences established by Evelyn Rattray for Teotihuacan (Rattray 1973, 2001) were taken as a base for the ceramics of the Classic period, and we used the sequence and types defined by Cobean (1978, 1990) for the Epiclassic and the Early Postclassic, which will be referred to in greater depth in the following chapters because they constitute the principal point of reference for settlement of this period. Studies by Griffin and Espejo (1947, 1950), Parsons (1966), and Vega Sosa (1975) were used for the Aztec ceramics. The chronological placement of the settlements and the characteristics of the ceramic sequences used are aspects that will be analyzed in greater depth throughout this book.

Once the study of materials was finalized, as a starting point in the settlement analysis, the surface samples and their contexts were considered as units in themselves, irrespective of their category, in order to be able to interpret the information referring to each one independently with the same detail. This permitted a level of analysis that would not have been possible if the different elements of each site had been grouped together a priori from the beginning, especially in the case of the occupations corresponding to the Early and Late Postclassic periods, which are almost uninterrupted in some zones, without the limits between one site and another being clear.

These units were designated "Collection Units" (URs) and they were classified in the following categories according to the characteristics of occupation and the density of surface materials: dispersed artifactual material, concentrated artifactual material, habitation structures, inferred habitation structures, and ceremonial structures. The characteristics of these different categories of Collection Units are described in Chapter 7.

The information referring to each one of these units was coded in a uniform way that permitted computer analysis. The form corresponding to each collection unit thus contains data referring to its location, coordinates, aerial photographs, subdivision square unit, and a progressive number known as the "collection number," as well as data concerning the kind of occupation—dispersed artifactual material, concentrated artifactual material, habitation structures, etc.—the association with other cultural periods and density of the materials corresponding to the different periods of occupation, topography, distance from water, present land use, potential archaeological land use, level of erosion, and finally counts of the ceramic and lithic materials. In the case of the habitation structures and ceremonial mounds, the distance to the closest archaeological mound was recorded and defined based on aerial photographs.

The analysis of these variables by computer made it possible to have a series of lists and maps for the distribution and correlation of the elements and aspects referring to the settlement. On a second level of analysis, large distinct entities that we call sites were then defined, which consist of a variable number of URs. The criteria for the definition of sites are also dealt with in Chapter 7.

The topographic base map used to locate and show the settlement distribution in the area during different periods was prepared by using four Dirección General de Estudios del Territorio Nacional (DETENAL) 1:50,000 scale maps (Maps F14C–88 [Tula de Allende], F14C–89 [Mixquiahuala], E14A–19 [Zumpango de Ocampo], and E14A–18 [Tepeji del Río]).

An effort was made to place the symbols that represented different types of occupation on the map as accurately as possible. However, there is an obvious problem of scale because the symbols occupy a disproportionate area on the map so as to be visible, especially in reductions. Their size is thus overly large in relation to the real size of the structures and the scale of the map.

The general surveys of the area correspond to the Selective Collection and Systematic Collection, the criteria for which we have referred to earlier. We also conducted more intensive site surveys of two types, called "Intensive Sample" and "Intensive Sample A." The first was used in two habitational structures in the urban zone, one on El Cielito and the other in the unit designated ZU17 (Mastache and Cobean n.d.), and also in the rural habitation unit in the site of Tepetitlan that was excavated afterward. This sampling procedure covered the total surface of the structures, using a grid system divided in squares measuring 3 meters by 3 meters. One hundred percent of the materials in each square were collected and analyzed. The results of these sample analyses are discussed in Chapter 7. This same technique was used by Healan (1986) in his investigation of an obsidian workshop in the city, the data from the surface sample and excavation of which also are included in Chapter 7.

Intensive Sample A refers to additional sampling studies of nine sites of the area: Teltipan, Arroyo Tepetitlan, San Francisco Bojay, Hacienda Bojay, Xicuco, El Venado, Chingú, Mixquiahuala, and Tlahuelilpan, which were chosen on the basis of two criteria concerning the representivity of different zones in the study area and the presence at some of these sites of early Tollan Phase ceramic types that had been detected in the general surveys and sampled previously. This sample was obtained and analyzed by George Bey (1986). The criteria and sampling units used by Bey varied, but most often employed collection squares measuring 10 meters by 10 meters placed generally in plowed fields with high densities of materials, mounds, and looted sectors.

Our analyses of the Tollan Complex in the rural area and the city (using data from our own research and other projects) include the study of paired surface and subsurface samples obtained from both controlled intensive surface collection and subsequent excavation at three localities within Tula's urban zone—El

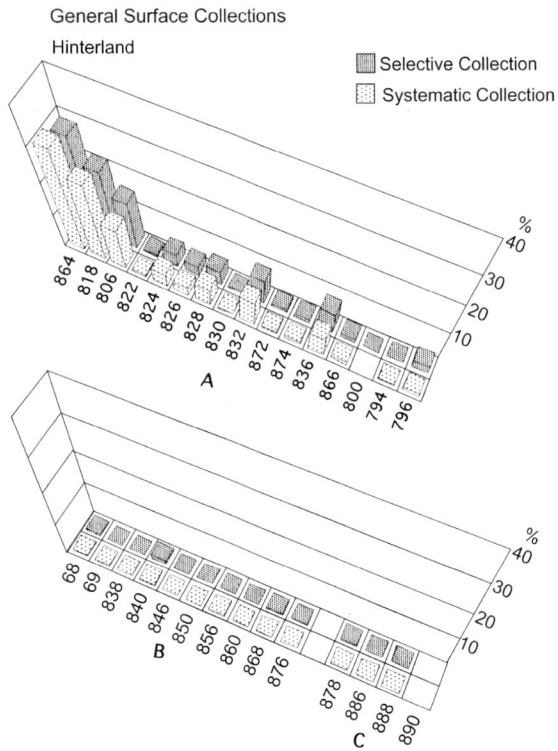

Figure 1.5. Tollan Complex: Selective and Systematic Collections: A. Principal Types; B. Less Frequent Types; C. Foreign Types.
68. Mazapan Figurines, **69.** Drain Tubes, **794.** Joroba Orange on Cream, **796.** Mazapa Red on Brow, **800.** Tolteca Red on Buff, **806.** Macana Red on Brown, **818.** Jara Polished Orange, **822.** Ira Stamped Orange, **824.** Proa Polished Cream, **826.** Sillón Incised, **828.** Rebato Polished Red, **830.** Manuelito Plain Brown, **832.** Toza Smoothed, Brown, **836.** Blanco Levantado (Watermarked), **838.** Abra Coarse Brown: Cylinder Variety, **840.** Abra Coarse Brown: Abra Variety, **846.** Abra Coarse Brown: Plain Hourglass Variety, **850.** Abra Coarse Brown: General, **856.** Alicia Openworked, **860.** Tarea Polished Red, **864.** Soltura Smoothed Red, **866.** Bordo Red on Brown, **868.** Mendrugo Semi-Smoothed, **872.** Acta Polished Red: Acta Variety, **874.** Acta Polished Red: Bowl Variety, **876.** Unnamed Black on Orange *olla*, **878.** Tohil Plumbate, **886.** Huastec ceramics, **888.** Gulf Coast Ceramics, **890.** North and West ceramics.

Canal, El Cielito, and the obsidian workshop—and one locality at Tepetitlan, a rural site north of Tula. These data provided a unique opportunity to compare surface and subsurface materials from the same locality at no less than four independent locations. Indeed, in every case comparative analysis showed a strong correspondence between surface and subsurface artifact assemblages that is similar to the correspondences between surface and excavation materials shown for some other sites in North America (Binford et al. 1970; Roper 1976).

It is important to emphasize some of the implications and results of the different kinds of sampling done as part of the general surveys in the area, the intensive surface studies done in specific sites, and the analyses of materials from excavations. The totals for ceramics (sherds), which appear in the graphs corresponding to the different samples mentioned, refer only to the total of Tollan Complex materials according to Cobean's (1978, 1990) typology. The identifying numbers correspond to the three-digit computer code for each type.

It is notable that in the Selective Collection, consisting of 203 Collection Units and a total of 5,171 sherds, and the Systematic Collection, with 1,394 Collection Units and 27,106 sherds, there is a great similarity in the graphs for the ceramic types and their percentages despite the differences in the numbers of collection units included in each kind of survey and the differences in the total numbers of sherds. Both kinds of collections detected all the basic types of the Tollan Complex, although there is a tendency for the minor types to be present in lower percentages in the Selective Collection (see Fig. 1.5).

With regard to intensive surface samples, there is a surprising similarity in the graphs for surface and excavation materials of the Tepetitlan structure, even though in one case the collection is little more than 5,000 sherds and in the other almost 30,000 sherds. The fundamental difference in both graphs concerns the presence of minor types in excavated materials that are not represented in the surface sample, even though there are cases such as those of types 836 (Blanco Levantado) or 866 (Bordo Red on Brown)

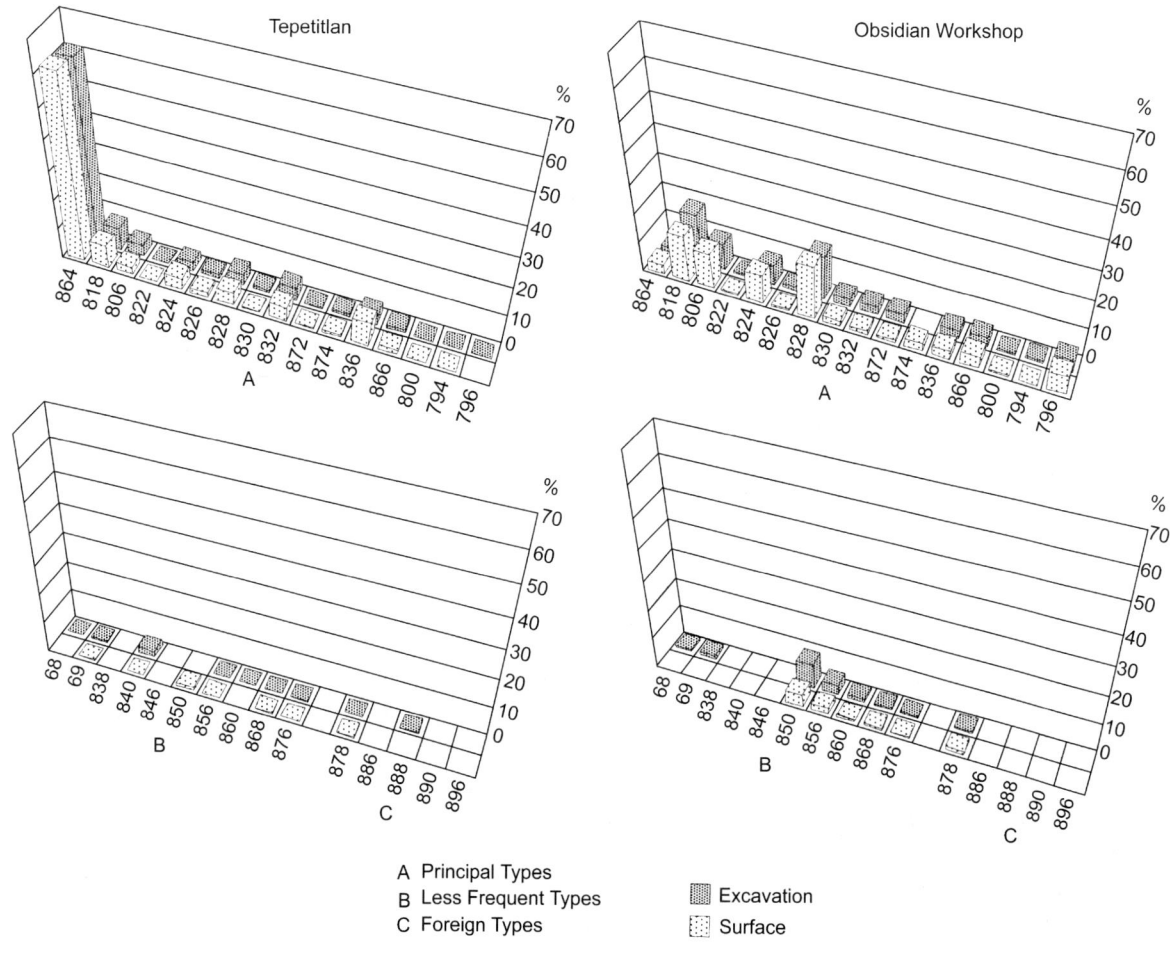

Figure 1.6. Tollan Complex: Tepetitlan and Obsidian Workshop; Surface and Excavation Collections.

with slightly higher percentages in surface materials than in the excavated assemblage (Fig. 1.6).

The same situation occurs in general terms in the sample for the obsidian workshop in the urban zone excavated by Healan (1986). In this investigation, there are some minor types found on the surface that were not recovered in the excavated materials, along with a higher percentage on the surface than in the excavation of some of the principal Tollan Complex types such as 806 (Macana Red on Brown) and 828 (Rebato Polished Red).

In our opinion, it is of considerable importance in terms of methodology that there are such similarities in both cases for the types represented and their percentages on the surface and in excavations, thus showing that a relation clearly exists between the surface materials of a site and the stratigraphic deposits of its various occupations, indicating the validity and representiveness of intensive surface samples, especially when they can cover 100 percent of a particular unit.

It is important to note that in the cases studied here the occupational sequence and stratigraphic contexts are different. In the rural structure of Tepetitlan, there is little stratigraphic complexity with essentially only one occupation; in contrast, the obsidian workshop located within the pre-Hispanic city has a longer and much more complex human habitation, and thus a more complicated stratigraphy.

2

The Tula Region: Physical Environment and Land Use

GENERAL DESCRIPTION

The study area is bounded by 19°53'10" and 20°15'00" north latitude and 99°08'18" and 99°28'14" west longitude. To the south it borders on the Basin of Mexico and to the north on the Mezquital Valley. It covers an area of approximately 1,000 square kilometers and includes the following municipalities: Atitalaquia, Atotonilco Tula, Tepeji del Río, Tepetitlán, Tezontepec de Aldama, Tlahuelilpan, Tlaxcoapan, and Tula de Allende. The modern city of Tula is located in the center (Fig. 2.1).

There are two prevailing climate types: dry steppe with average temperatures of 18°C and average annual precipitation of 450 to 600 millimeters, and dry temperate lands with a mean temperature of 12°–17.5°C and average annual rainfall of 700 millimeters, most between June and September (BS_1 kw[i']gw"). E. García (1966, table 13), recorded the data from fourteen stations located in the study area, with precipitation ranging from 400 to 700 millimeters annually. The highest levels correspond to this last zone.[1]

Physiographically, the area belongs to the Tula River hydrographic sub-basin, which forms part of the Pánuco River drainage system. It is situated in the physiographic region of the Central Plateau, between the Sierra Madre Oriental and the Neo-Volcanic Axis. The main river has four tributaries: the Coscomate, Rosas, Salado, and El Salto Rivers. The Tula and Salado Rivers drain from south to north and join near the northern limit, while the Coscomate and Rosas Rivers run from west to east. The ancient city developed on the confluence of the Rosas and Tula Rivers.

Most of the area is covered by mountain ranges that generally run from southwest to northeast, with altitudes of up to 3,050 meters. In the southeast portion, the slopes correspond to the channels of the Tula River and two of its tributaries. The alluvial plain seems to have buried part of the foothills, while

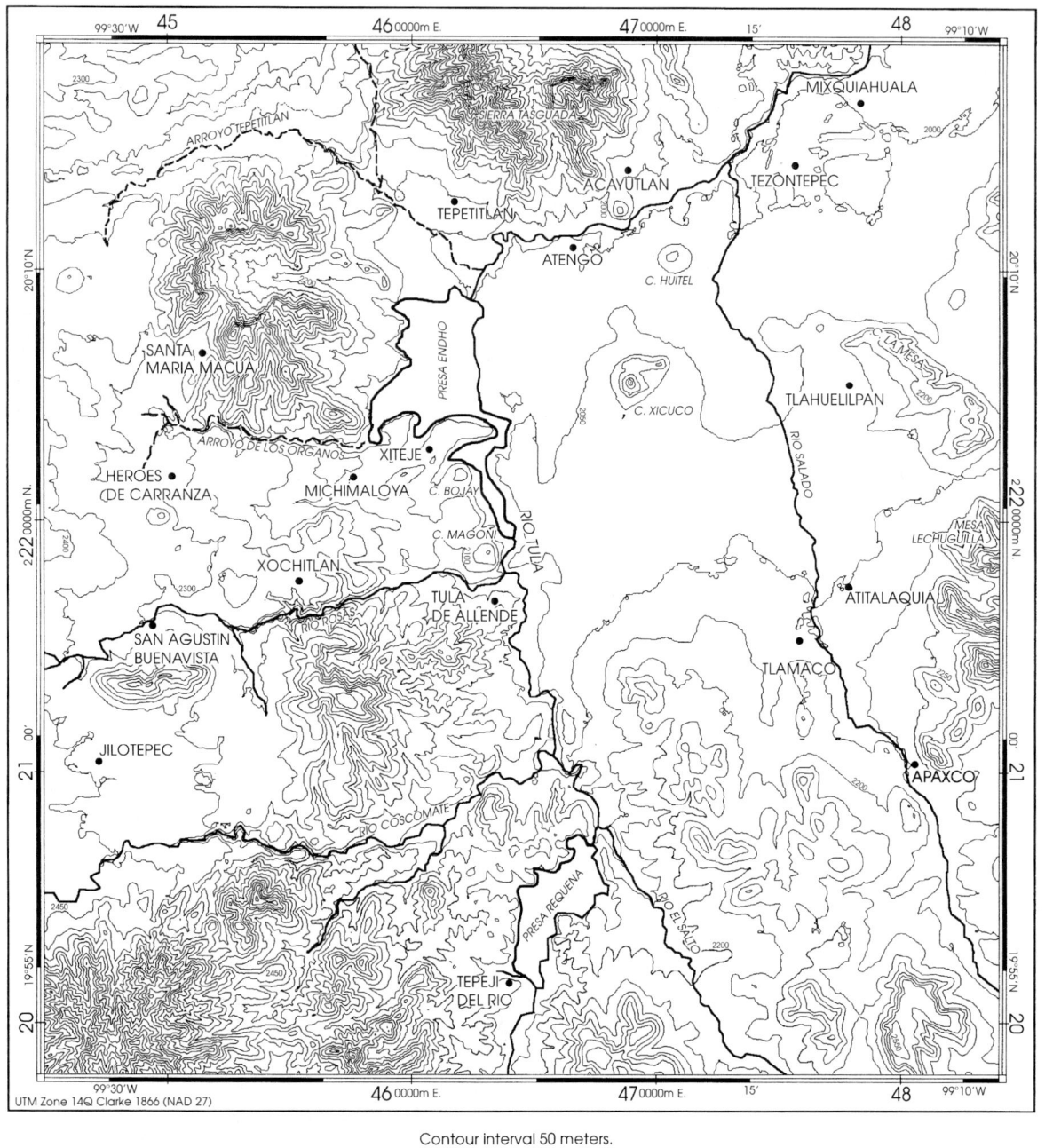

Figure 2.1. Tula area.

in the southern part there are sedimentary elevations with extensive, gently sloping foothills. The western part of the region has very uneven topography, with altitudes ranging from 2,050 to 2,650 meters; however, there are also intermountain valleys in this area that include the alluvial plain between the Rosas and Coscomate Rivers.

The northern limit is formed by the Sierra Tasguada, which reaches heights of 2,700 meters. It is a system of mountains that are mostly volcanic in origin, with small marine limestone sediment outcrops to the north. There are numerous intermittent streams, some fed by springs, and to the northwest there is a small valley that connects with the Chapantongo region.

The northeast quadrant is a wide alluvial plain between the Tula and Salado Rivers. This plain is interspersed with isolated volcanic outcrops such as Cerro Xicuco. To the east, the area is bounded by a mountain range that reaches altitudes of up to 2,800 meters in some parts.

The area is predominately one of steep volcanic formations without many foothills. At the bases of these formations there are canyons with streams.

GEOLOGY

The synthesis given below of the geology of the study area is based on studies made by Márquez (1986) as part of our project. As this author mentions, his work was based on previous studies of the region's geology and was largely focused on potential areas for the exploitation of various rocks as the source of raw materials for the manufacture of artifacts and as construction materials.

The Tula region is highly complex in geological terms because it lies between two physiographic provinces: the northern foothills of the Neo-Volcanic Axis and the western flank of the Sierra Madre Oriental. The appearance of the region today is a result of a sequence of geological events ranging from the Mesozoic to the Late Cenozoic. This can be seen in the complexity of the interdigitation of clastic, lacustrine, and pyroclastic sediments and lava in a changing climate (Márquez 1986).

The region consists of thick Tertiary and Quaternary continental deposits that partially fill a tectonic gap or hole. Volcanic activity during the Cenozoic period favored the formation of basins or sub-basins. These radically modified the landscape with the development of a large number of small lakes in areas that were not covered or partially covered by igneous material, while interrupting the drainage system and affecting the climate. The Late Cenozoic is marked by the extinction of magmatic activity and by pyroclastic and continental deposits in small basins.

Geomorphology: Relief-Forming Events

In our area, the Sierra Madre Occidental, which consists of marine sediments, is interrupted by the Neo-Volcanic Axis that lies in a negative tectonic area. This is evidenced by "islands" in various locations formed by Upper Cretaceous rocks. Furthermore, to the south and southeast of Tula there are limestone outcrops of the Lower Cretaceous, which implies the presence of underlying Mesozoic sediments (Fig. 2.2).

The construction events of the landscape took place in the Tertiary and Quaternary periods and were restricted to igneous activity and consequent erosion deposits. The processes that culminated in the current landscape are given below because of their importance and close relationship with human settlements (Márquez 1986).

Mesozoic. There is a deposit of carbonated and clastic marine rocks with outcrops of the remains of Middle-Upper Cretaceous limestone. At the end of the Mesozoic and the beginning of the Cenozoic periods, these rocks were folded to produce syncline, anticline, and blanketed structures that gave rise to the Sierra Madre Oriental. After the folding, the marine sedimentary rocks collapsed to produce a negative structural area or tectonic pit that favored the formation of lakes. This last point has been hard to prove since later volcanic activity has erased all direct evidence, although it can be inferred from the abnormal abundance of caliche derived from the dissolution of limestone.

Cenozoic. After the formation of the tectonic pit, a volcanic cycle started that ended in the Pleistocene and that constitutes the primordial forms of the current relief. Even supposing the nonexistence of prevolcanic basins, the emission of igneous material led to endorreic drainage, with the consequent formation of a lake zone. Finally, during the Late Cenozoic (Pliocene-Pleistocene) there was a final extrusive magmatic phase of basalt and basic and intermediate porous volcanic ash, as well as the drainage of the lake basin. This was probably the last significant geological event.

1. *Tertiary igneous activity.* This is represented by effusive events of volcanic ash and rhyolitic, andesitic, and dacitic lava (Fries 1962, quoted in Márquez 1986), which may be found under more recent volcanic material and as small isolated mountains or promontories on the plain. In the first case, the mountainsides show slope changes due to differential erosion.

   Associated with these, there is intrusive magmatic activity with an acid and intermediate composition that cuts the Mesozoic formations and gives rise to the two most important mining districts in the country, Pachuca and Zimapán, which border on Tula.

2. *Quaternary volcanic activity.* This is evidenced by lava and pyroclasts with an intermediate and basic composition and is responsible for the formation of higher elevations. These correspond to three forms:

a. Semi-destroyed craters with steep sides and occasionally with escarpments that correspond to high mountains with prominent peaks, such as the basalt complex to the east of the Endhó Dam, which reaches a height of 2,700 meters.

b. Basalt spills that cover rhyolites and form small, low and elongated mountain ranges, which are sometimes isolated on the plain, rounded and without large prominences, and the development of *mesetas* (small mesas) on the summits. They have gentle slopes that break in contact with the lithological zone.

c. Lava spills at the foot of volcanic apparatuses that form foothill *mesetas*.

3. *Continental detritus deposits.* This is the predominant formation process during the Cenozoic; there is constant eluviation and alluviation that is only interrupted by pyroclastic emissions interspersed with materials moved and deposited on the slopes, plains, and inundated areas. The deposits originated

GEOLOGIC FORMATIONS

Recent Pleistocene:
- **Qal** Alluvium and clastic material with local lenses of volcanic ash, Travertine, freshwater limestone, and gypsum.
- **Qb** Lava flows and associated pyroclastic rocks, principally of basaltic or andesitic composition, locally interdigitated with alluvium.

Tertiary:
- **Tpt** The Tarango Formation: predominantly clastic material with local lenses of freshwater limestone and volcanic ash locally interdigitated with mafic lava flows.
- **Ttpt** Lenses of freshwater limestone within the Tarango Formation (Fries, C., Jr.)
- **Tpb** Lava flows and associated pyroclastic rocks (basalts or andesites) locally interdigitated with the Tarango Formation.
- **Tomv** Includes volcanic rocks of the Pachuca Group and undifferentiated rocks constituted by rhyolites, andesites, and dacites that are locally interdigitated with silts and freshwater limestone.

Late Cretaceous:
- **Ksm** The Mezcala Formation: Interdigitated layers of lutite, siltstone, sandstones, and limestones of marine origin.
- **Ksc** The Cuautla Formation: thick layers of limestone and marine reef facies, has lateral contacts with the Soyatal Formation.
- **Kss** The Soyatal Formation: thin to medium layers of limestone, with interdigitated sandstone layers and lenses of flint.

Early Cretaceous:
- **Kid** The El Doctor Formation: marine limestones in layers of varying thickness with flint nodules and dolomite layers.

GEOLOGIC CONTACT: Inferred or uncertain contacts represented by a broken line.

GEOLOGIC FAULT SHOWING SUNKEN SECTOR

RAVINE-ARROYO

SOURCES OF RAW MATERIAL

- Ⓑ BASALT
- Ⓡ RHYOLITE
- Ⓒ KAOLIN
- Ⓣⓡ RED OR PINK VOLCANIC ASH (RHYOLITIC OR DACITIC)
- Ⓣ VOLCANIC ASH
- Ⓚ LIMESTONE, FLINT, AND CALCITE
- Ⓢ CHERT

Sources of information:
1. Fries, C. Jr. 1982
2. INEGI (México): Maps E14-C88, E14-C89, E14-A18, E14-A19

by this process may be grouped into the following types:

a. Alluvial fans. These are zones of river and stream discharge at slope changes. The loss of capacity and load power of the water current leads to a chaotic accumulation of materials ranging in size from

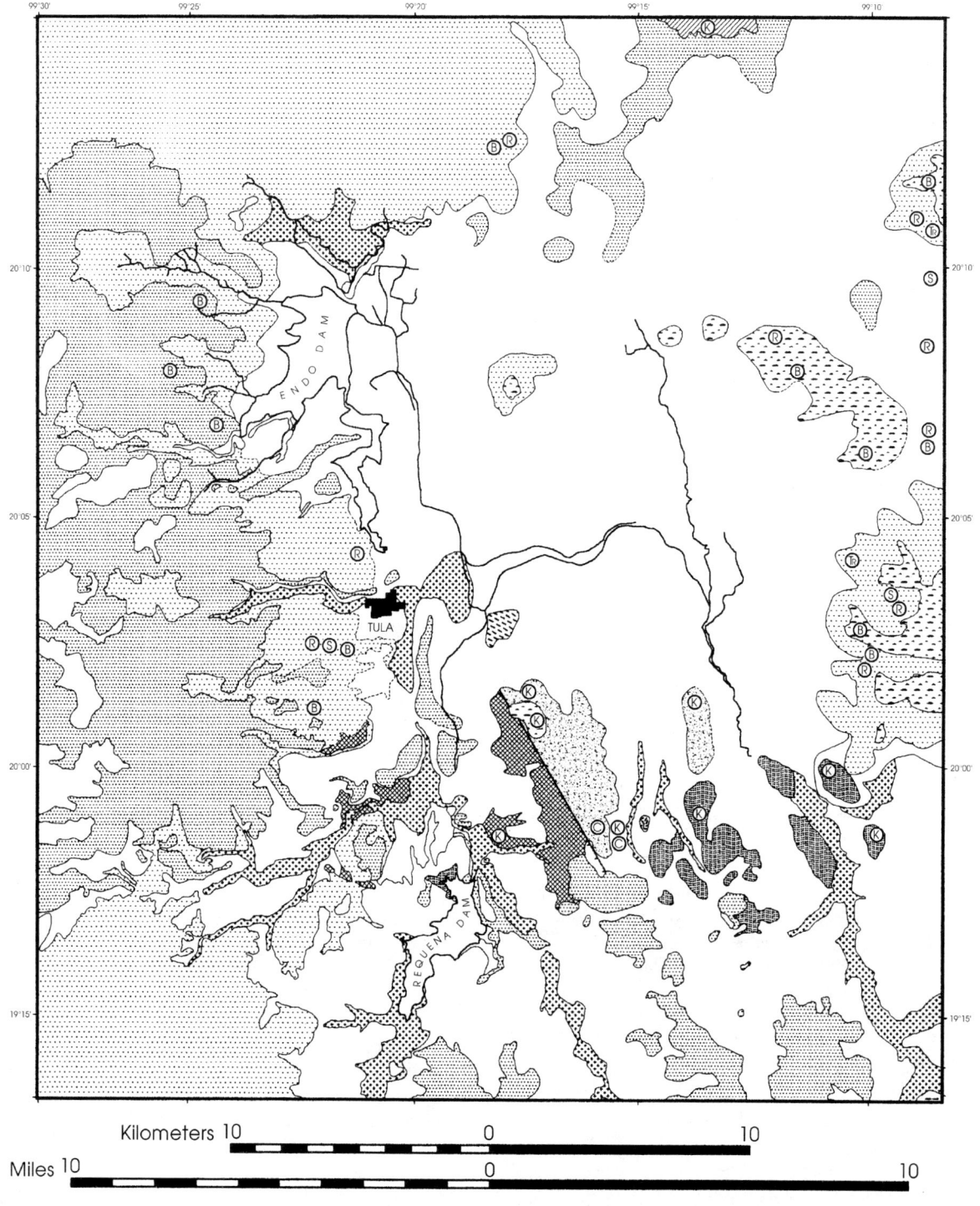

Figure 2.2. Tula area geology.

blocks, boulders, and pebbles to sand, silts, and clay. The formation is complete when an erosion cycle is complete, in which case the current dissects the alluvial fan or slightly changes course because the material that is being transported accumulates and becomes an obstacle. The interruptions of cycles stand out, hence the formation of alluvial fans caused by the appearance of new volcanic apparatuses, by large fluctuations in the lake zone, and by human activity.

b. Soil formation. This is a process of little importance since it occurs in very small areas, such as small platforms on top of horizontal lava spills. These areas are currently used for agriculture, with the well-known drawback of removing blocks of parent material, but with the advantage of low salinity.

4. *Lake region deposits.* The accumulation of sediments on inundated surfaces is the most important geomorphological construction feature in the area. Judging by the maximum inundation levels at the 2,150-meter contour that is 100 meters above the current level, and the caliche horizons, it may be inferred that there were severe water-level fluctuations and at least three desiccation periods due to climatic or drainage changes. On the other hand, these sediments are interspersed with pyroclastic materials in various locations. The change from a lake basin to a valley implied significant climatic changes and the interruption of the erosion cycle to give rise to a new one that is evidenced by a deepening of the rivers and the dissection for the recently formed lake region deposits and the foothill fans. Some of the runoff filtered into the alluvial deposits and lake zones.

It should be mentioned that these "reworked" sediments, based on continental deposits of lake-region origin and partially cemented by caliches of the same origin, are currently used for agriculture, with generally negative results due to the high salt content.

The current location of the lake-region sediments has the following variations:

a. Hills or small hillocks inside the basin with gentle slopes where there is evidence of attempts to cultivate, with negative results. There is abundant pyroclastic material in the profiles mixed with lake sediments and many caliche horizons, with a thickness varying from a few millimeters to 15 centimeters. When these horizons are thick, they are mixed with sand and clay materials.

b. Foothills that are formed by clay, silt, and even blocks due to the action of the lake element together with the ejecta of materials due to erosion. These have well-rounded shapes with gentle slopes and occasionally keep the appearance of alluvial fans upon which the elluviation can be clearly seen. The low salt content and abundance of pyroclasts create conditions that are favorable for agriculture.

c. Flat areas are the most common geoform and extend beyond the Tula area. These correspond to deep-water lake deposits. These areas are currently cultivated despite the high salinity of the soil, which is modified by using organic materials (irrigated with sewage) and fertilizers.

Relief Altering Phenomena

1. *Weathering.* This is determined by climate: the region has been subject to two radically different kinds of weathering. The oldest took place under conditions of high humidity, which is inferred from the lake area; mechanical weathering caused the fracturing of rocks with the chemical leaching of their minerals. These two actions were predominant while the lake conditions persisted. The other kind of weathering, which has lasted until the present, took place under conditions of low humidity. Here the chemical and mechanical activity is reduced to a minimum and the latter has only been increased by the recent intervention of man.

The main products of weathering in the region are caliches (sulfates and calcium carbonates) and chalk (calcium sulfate), which abound in the Cenozoic formations, and clay and soils formed by pyroclastic material deposited in water or by consolidated rocks.

2. *Erosion cycles.* We can associate two kinds of erosion with each of the two major climatic conditions inferred—humid in flooded areas and dry in drained flooding areas. Thus, along with the alterations caused by human activity, two major erosion cycles can be seen in the endorreic basins starting in the Middle Cenozoic.

a. Humid climate with flooded areas. Severe weathering: the detached and leached material is transported to the lake where the large particles are deposited at the bottom and fine and colloidal particles are transported in suspension and deposited in shallower parts. The predominant transportation mechanism was the drainage that dissected the constructional elements. It is estimated that erosion was severe, as can be seen in the mountains and lava flows and on pyroclastic deposits. All of this gave rise to a high volume of lake sediment.

b. Moderately humid to dry climate in drained area. It is possible to assign a final extrusive magmata phase to the Late Cenozoic (Pliocene-Pleistocene), which is represented by intermediate and basic basalt *tobas* (volcanic ashes) and the lake basin drainage event that constitutes the final important geological event for the zone. The change from a basin of lakes to a valley implies significant climatic changes and the start of a new erosion cycle marked by the drainage of the region and characterized by the deepening of the drainage paths, the dissection of the recently formed lake deposits, as well as foothill fans. This kind of erosion cycle is mainly caused by wind and water in the rainy season; consequently, the latter factor is now unimportant due to the short rainy season. Finally, man's intervention is accelerating the erosion cycle and the desertification process becomes increasingly irreversible with activities such as extracting underground water, tree felling, the establishment of industries, and the saturation of permanent runoff with industrial contaminants, which has led to saline oversaturation (Márquez 1986:25).

The intensity of the current impact of erosion depends on the kind of rock, the incline, altitude, precipitation, and human action during the last two millenia, with activities that have affected the natural drainage, such as agriculture, deforestation, construction, grazing, hydraulic works, and the extraction of raw materials.

3. *Fluvial dissection*. The drainage is not integrated because of the interruption of the first erosion cycle, climatic variations, and human intervention. There are two kinds of currents: intermittent and permanent.

Intermittent currents produce:

a. Poorly defined riverbeds in hillside rocks that disappear when they reach lake region sediments or foothills. When there is runoff, the water infiltrates such deposits.

b. Streams that have managed to dissect the alluvial fans and lake sediments and form ponds in flat areas or filter into the subsoil.

Permanent currents produce:

a. Well-defined riverbeds that generally flow into larger rivers and form a system. The Tula River belongs to this category—its course and bed have been drastically modified by man, as is the case of the geothermal springs that are characteristic of the state of Hidalgo, and which are used for irrigation, infiltrate the subsoil, or are tributaries of the Tula River.

On the other hand, the factors that form the drainage structure are the tectonic features that are determined by altitude, slopes, rock type, physical barriers, and karsting that cause underground water capture both under the volcanic material and on the surface. Here, the Tula River was captured by the Moctezuma River and became part of the Pánuco hydrographic system, which empties into the Gulf of Mexico at Tampico.

SOILS

Soil characteristics depend on the topography, the parental material, precipitation, and vegetation coverage. In the high parts of the mountains where there is more erosion than deposition, the soils are thin or nonexistent. The zones with the steepest slopes and that have limestone formations have soils with the poorest nutrients, less developed and less deep than those on the alluvial plains, which are formed by sediments of volcanic origin, with a predominance of silt and clay. These are richer in nutrients and have better horizon development. In the northern part of the area, there is soil in natural and artificial terraces on the hillsides.

The soils formed on the lake beds are very saline and must be modified for agricultural purposes with fertilizers and the introduction of organic materials. In contrast, the soils in the foothills are more favorable for agriculture because of the lower salt content and the abundance of pyroclasts. Some zones with permanent irrigation, especially floodwater irrigation, may also be negatively affected because in the long term this technique causes salinization and the loss of nutrients and fertility (Márquez 1986:21–22).

According to Instituto Nacional de Estadística, Geografía, y Informática (INEGI) maps, there are four soil types in the area: Rendzinas (E), Vertisoles (V), Feozem (H), and Litosoles (I)[2] (see Fig. 2.3) (DETENAL, 1974 Soil Classification System, FAO-UNESCO, Modified. Maps: Tula de Allende,

Mizquiahuala, Tepeji del Río, and Zumpango de Ocampo). Only some of the most general characteristics are mentioned below, for more technical details please refer to Ortíz and Ortíz (1990).

Rendzina is mostly found in the eastern part of the area on mountain slopes and lowlands. It is dark clay that is less than 50 centimeters deep and has more than 1 percent organic material that releases nutrients and gives consistency and porosity to the soil, and therefore fertility. It may be in the petrocalcic stage, i.e., over a consolidated horizon that is rich in calcium carbonate, or, more rarely, in the lithic stage when there is underlying rock (other than limestone) at less than 50 centimeters deep.

Feozem is the most frequent soil type, and it belongs to the intermediate group of soils, without distinctive characteristics, with medium texture and light brown color. These are generally moderately developed soils with a medium to high natural fertility. The depth varies in the area from shallow (between 10 and 50 centimeters in the petrocalcic stage), moderately deep (50 centimeters), and, infrequently, very deep at more than 1 meter. It occurs in three variants: Feozem haplico, which contains chalk; Feozem calcarious, which has calcium-carbonate residues; and Feozem in the duric surface stage, when it is over volcanic ash or tepetate at less than 50 centimeters, and deep when the *tepetate* (caliche) is between 50 centimeters and 1 meter.

Vertisol is generally dark clay soil with a massive and compact structure when moist, and with cracks more than 1 centimeter wide during the dry season. It is more than 50 centimeters deep and very fertile. It is found in small proportions on the margins of some rivers, in flat zones, and at the bottoms of valleys.

Litosol is a very shallow soil, less than 10 centimeters deep, interspersed with abundant rock outcrops; it is variable in color and organic-material content. It predominates in the high parts of mountains, such as on summits and in canyons in the steep slopes.

Soil Classes

One of the ways of quantifying and distributing soil use is by dividing it into classes according to suitability for cultivation, grazing, and other purposes (see Ortíz and Ortíz 1990:315–325) and by using attributes such as type, topography, depth, and use limitations, while considering the needs and limitations of the soils, the risk of damaging them, and management responses. This proposal, employing an eight-category classification system, has been applied to current soil use based on modern cultivation technologies, but it is considered useful when formulating hypotheses on the productive potential of various areas in the pre-Hispanic period, taking into account that traditional soil preparation and tillage techniques could modify and use areas that currently have low agricultural potential.

Figure 2.4 contains a map showing soil-type distribution drawn up on the basis of the information contained in the INEGI edaphological maps and prepared by Professor Jorge Duch, a researcher at the Autonomous University of Chapingo (personal communication 1995, Chapingo).

Class I. Class I lands are suitable for cultivation, with few use restrictions, that are almost flat and without danger of erosion, deep, generally well-drained with good moisture retention, adequate nutrient

SOIL TYPES

	RENDZINA
Ⓗ	FEOZEM
Ⓘ	LITOSOL
	LITOSOL + RENDZINA
	VERTISOL PELICO
I	LITOSOL
V	VERTISOL
L	LUVISOL
B	CAMBISOL
R	REGOSOL

Source:
México, Secretaria de Programación y Presupuesto
Edafologia: Cartas E14-C88
E14-C89
E14-A18
E14-A19
1982, Primera Edición

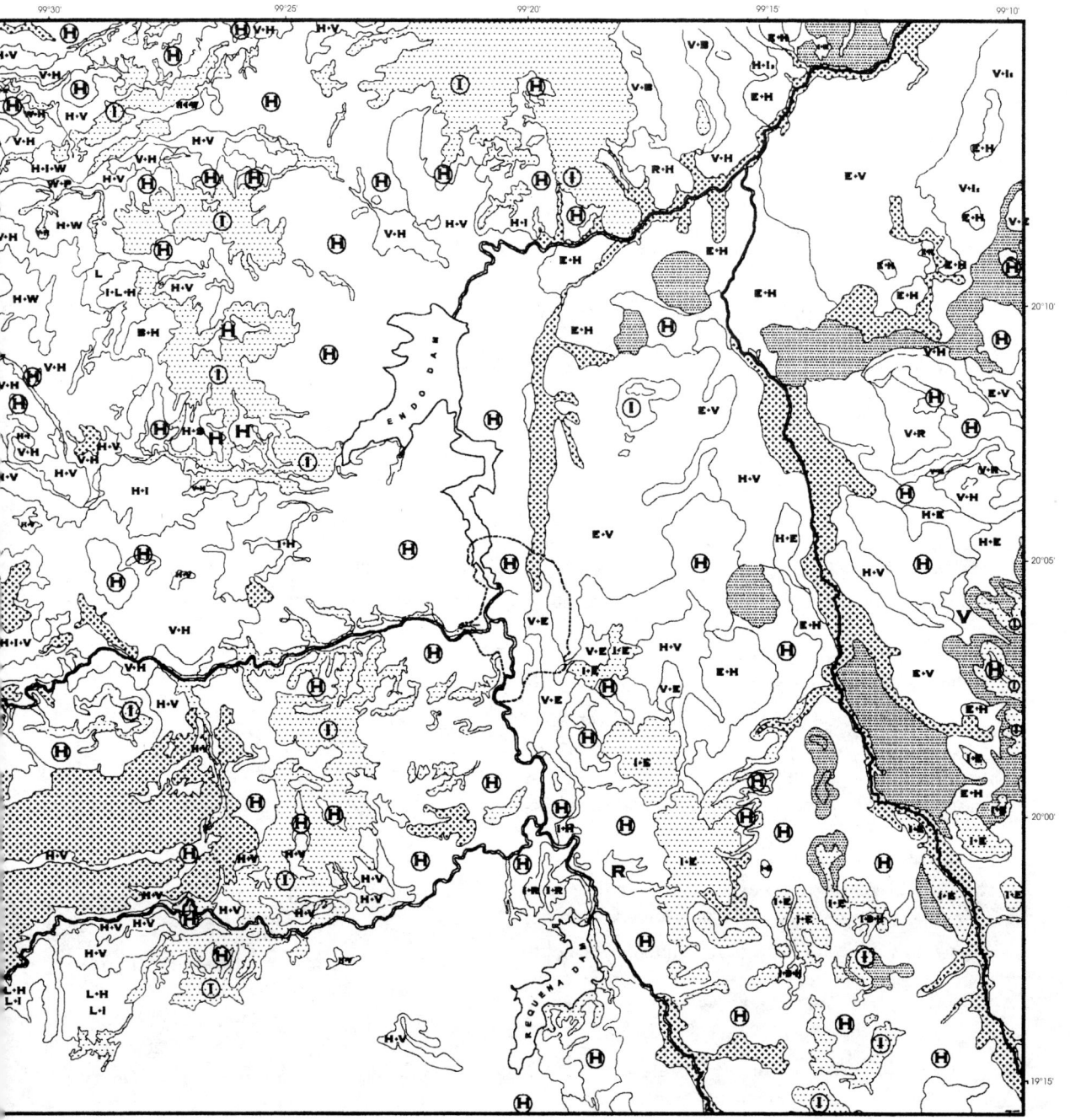

Figure 2.3. Tula area soils.

flow, and high response to fertilizers. They are not subject to damage by flooding, and are productive and suitable for intensive cultivation, with deep rooting zones. In irrigated areas, they are maintained by relatively permanent irrigation works. There are no salinity problems due to flooding, erosion, or capillary rising.

Class II. Class II soils are those with limitations in terms of variety of crops and require moderate conservation practices. They have the following simple or combined limiting features: moderate slope, medium vulnerability to wind and water erosion, shallow, slightly unfavorable structure, salinity or low or moderate alkalinity, occasional harmful flooding, waterlogging that can be corrected with drainage, and slight climatic limitations.

Class III. Class III soils have limiting factors that reduce the selection of plants and/or special conservation practices. These factors in isolation or combined are as follows: steep slopes with high vulnerability to erosion, heavy flooding that damages crops, poor permeability, persistence of humidity even after drainage, shallow depth, low fertility and humidity-retention capacity, salinity or moderate alkalinity, and moderate climatic limitations.

Class IV. Class IV includes soils with severe limitations on the choice of crops and require very careful handling. The simple or combined limitations are as follows: steep slopes that are highly vulnerable to erosion, severe effects of erosion in the past, shallow and low-humidity retention, frequent flooding with severe damage to crops, excessive humidity, high salinity or alkalinity, and moderately adverse climate.

Class V. Class V land is not suitable for cultivation. Some examples of this type are frequently flooded lowlands, rocky soils, and areas where water stagnates and there is no drainage.

Class VI. Class VI includes soils with severe limitations, such as steep slopes, danger of intense erosion, effects of past erosion, rocks, very thin rooting area, excessive humidity and flooding, salinity or alkalinity, and inadequate climate.

Class VII and Class VIII. Class VII and VIII soils have limitations that prevent use for cultivation that are more severe than the above type regarding slope, erosion, soil thinness, humidity, rockiness, salinity, alkalinity, and climate.

Thus, Class I has no limitations while Class VIII has very severe limitations and basically has very low use potential. In general, the first four classes are suitable for cultivation (Ortíz and Ortíz 1990). Classes V to VIII are currently more common and account for approximately 50 percent of the Tula area. They are principally located in the mountains and steep slopes. Classes III and IV prevail in the lower parts and account for 30 and 40 percent of the total area, respectively; the main restrictions are shallow depth and steep slopes. There are also Class I and II soils, albeit in a smaller proportion, and they account for 15 and 20 percent of the area, respectively. They are located in the river meadows and have deep soil proportions associated with very old traditional irrigation systems.

PRESENT-DAY VEGETATION

The prevailing dry steppe climate defines a large part of the area as semi-arid. The dryness depends on factors such as precipitation, parental material, altitude and slopes' edaphological characteristics, erosion levels, plant communities, microclimate, and human activity.

The climatic regimen and biotic and abiotic components determine the composition, structure, and distribution of the vegetation. The characteristics of the climate are reflected in the predominantly xerophytic landscape that has been disturbed by centuries of human occupation (González Quintero and Montufar 1980:185). On the alluvial plain, which is currently used for agriculture, it is still possible to reconstruct the natural vegetation that was surely dominated by mesquite (*Prosopis laevigata*). With regard to the other substrata, it is only possible to conjecture that the limestone area had desertic brush or desertic plains with *huizache* (*Acacia farnesiana*), while the tertiary volcanic substrata maintained *crasicaule* brush with an abundance of *garambullo* cactus (*Myrtillocactus geometrizans*), thorn bush (caduceus), and *nopal* (*Opuntia* spp.).

The upper slopes of the valley have the following kinds of vegetation (González Quintero 1967): between 1,700 and 2,000 meters there is alluvial desert

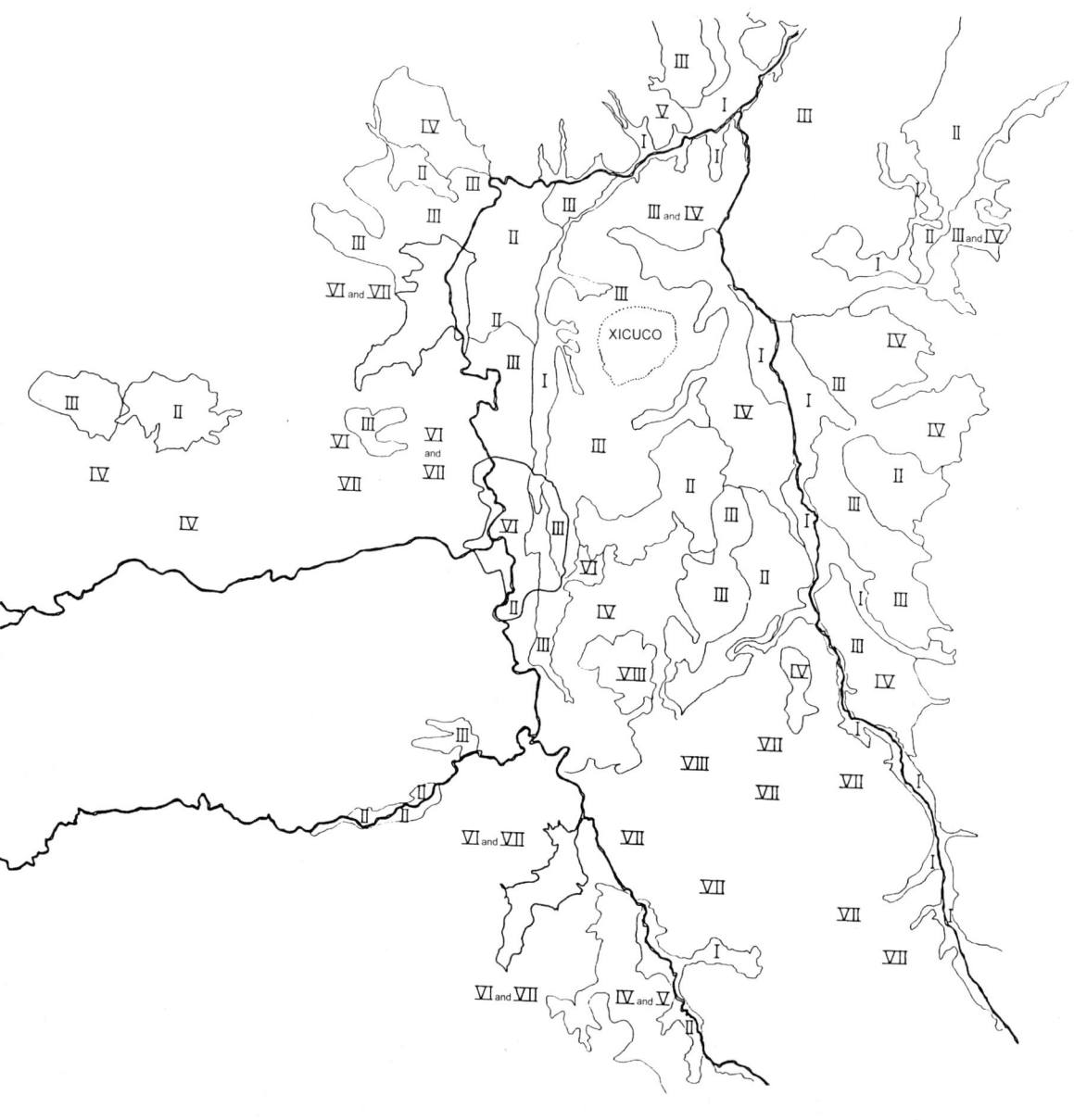

Figure 2.4. Tula area soil classes.

brush dominated by mesquite, with *huizache* (*Acacia tortuosa*) and a significant amount of *crasicaule* and various species of *Opuntia* and *garambullo* cactus. The herbaceous plants include grasses and labiates, which are potentially useful. *Flourencia cemua* dominates the poorest substrata.

Desert calcicole brush is to be found on the desert limestone (see Fig. 2.5). This community is very important and rich in species, especially in the herbaceous and scrub strata, while the bush stratum is relatively poor. The lechuguilla (*Agave lechuguilla*), palmita (*Hechtia glomerata*), and *Agave striata* are characteristic. Cactuses, labiades, and grasses also abound.

There is *crasicaule* brush on the igneous slopes between 1,800 and 2,700 meters that are physionomically defined by their association with *garambullo* cactus, thorn bush (*Opuntia streptacantha*), the *candelabro* (*Stenocereus dumortieri*) and mesquite, together with *huizache* and *Bursera fagaroides*. The bush and herbaceous strata are very diverse and contain many useful species. This was obviously a very important community in the past.

Oak and oak shrub (*Quercus spp.*) with *madroño* (*Arbutus spp.*) and juniper (*Juniperus flaccida*) are found above 2,300 meters with other species and a brush stratum. This association indicates higher humidity and in the upper limits it is enriched with pine, with mixed forest in the southwestern mountains. Human exploitation is currently intense in the region and the forest is in danger of disappearing.

The grasslands are less important; they include both natural and planted lands. The former are to be found on old saline lake beds or as grass coverage in forest and bush communities (González Quintero 1967; González Quintero and Montufar 1980:185; Crespo 1976:39). The gallery forests along the banks of the Tula River are dominated by *ahuehuetes* (*Taxodium mucronatum*), accompanied by poplars (*Populus sp*) and willows (*Salix bomplandiana*) in the forested part and by organisms typical of flooded areas such as grass and rushes (Crespo 1976). The thorny desert brush, which includes the *crasicaule* and calcicole brush of González Quintero (1967), covered 29 percent of the area in the 1970s, while scrub land accounted for only 4 percent and mixed forest was a mere 2 percent (Crespo 1976).

Deforestation is the major factor in vegetation changes. The felling of trees in the mixed forest and in other wooded lands to obtain lumber and fuel is severe since only secondary vegetation and grass develop afterward, while land clearing for agricultural purposes especially affects the thorn brush and mesquite.

PALEOENVIRONMENT

A pollen study done by González Quintero and Montufar (1980:85–92) provides interesting information about the alternating occurrence in the region of various climatic and biotic regimens. Based on a core obtained in the ancient city of Tula from the El Salitre swamp, the authors propose four climatic periods, in a regressive order of antiquity according to depth: Warm-Dry Stage (0–115 centimeters), Temperate-Humid Stage (115–260 centimeters), Warm-Dry Stage (260–370 centimeters), and Cold-Dry Stage (370–470 centimeters).

Based on the pollen diagram, these researchers try to reconstruct the vegetation existing during different stages. It should be mentioned that there was little palynological material between 490 and 610 cm, which indicates the existence of a cold climate.

The Cold-Dry Stage, the oldest, is thus named because of the high representation of grasses and ambrosia, elements that are typical of an alluvial plain and indicate a desert steppe with few trees. The increase of pine and oak pollen during this stage could indicate an increase in precipitation and an expansion of the mixed temperate forest at the expense of the herbaceous and bush communities (González Quintero and Montufar 1980:190).

The following stage has been named Warm-Dry because the temperature increased gradually until it reached a level similar to current conditions; however, the most important elements of the alluvial plain indicate lower precipitation. The dominance of arboreal elements in the middle levels could imply an increase in precipitation and the pine and oak forests probably started to appear as separate entities. In the rest of the area, there are traces of thorn bush, which indicates a very arid climate. In summary, the following communities can be indicated: oak forests, *Juniperus* forests and steppe that partially gave way throughout the stage to *subinerme* xerophile bush indicated by *Yucca, Celtis,* and Euphorbiaceae that finally regain their previous coverage.

The Temperate-Humid Stage is perhaps the largest extension of communities recorded. Because there was higher rainfall, there was a greater representation of arboreal elements. This is the period with the greatest pollen diversity and there are records of aquatic plants such as Nenuphar, Ranunculus, Urticaceae, Umbelliferae, and Typha. All the above-mentioned

Figure 2.5. An eroded limestone zone in the southeast Tula area.

communities are present and the pine forest dominates the initial part while the oak forests become more important toward the end and extending to the lower latitudes. As well as *rosetophile* bush (agave and yucca scrub), fir (*Abies religiosa*) trees were also present.

In the final Warm-Dry Stage, the temperature curve once again exceeded precipitation, that is, there is a water deficit, although it is different in proportion to the second stage with the same name and the *rosetophile* scrubland is better represented. The arboreal elements have decreased noticeably, although the numbers on the alluvial plains have increased. Finally, the transition from the previous stage is marked by a sudden increase in *Yucca*. The previous communities declined in number, such as the *nanophile* desert (small leaf) bush and *crasicaule*, which actually disappeared. Only the desertic brushland tends to increase (González Quintero and Montufar 1980).

The sequence of climatic changes in the area is very interesting, but unfortunately there is a lack of absolute dates for various parts of the core. Consequently, we do not know how long these stages lasted or their probable correlation with different periods of occupation of the area in the pre-Hispanic period, and thus we can only make conjectures about this last point. Other pollen cores taken in adjacent areas such as Ixmiquilpan and Texcoco present the same problem, but information about areas further to the north and northwest in Mexico also point to a general trend to aridization, with a high point around A.D. 1000 (Brown 1992; Martín 1963).

In the Tula area, as mentioned before, the last Warm-Dry Stage is characterized by an increase in elements that represent the steppe, such as grasses, with a progressive decline in the pine and oak coverage. There are moments of greater precipitation that do not significantly alter the trend toward desertification. Some of these features could be the product of man-made disturbance. In the latter case, it could coincide with some phase of the occupation of the ancient city of Tula since, according to the pollen graph (see Fig. 9.4), it also corresponds to an increase in the pollen of cultivated plants, especially maize and amaranth and other amaranths and chenopods, which are associated with other crops such as weed plants. It is therefore possible that the decline in the oak and pine population could be related to the fact that they are species used widely by man, especially as fuel.

This reasoning clearly could be applied to earlier cultural phases, but the evidence of the Formative and Classic stages in the area indicate a more limited occupation; therefore the dating to the Early Postclassic seems logical. Nevertheless, the above correlation is totally speculative, because first it would be necessary to answer other questions. For example, how would the later stages such as the colonial period and the current era be represented, or is it feasible to correlate climatic events defined by pollen studies having different methodological bases?

PRESENT-DAY LAND USE

The area studied is now severely deforested and altered, but there is a degree of diversity of plant communities and a complex soil-use problem. Together with traditional practices of wild resource gathering and grazing, there is intensive and extensive exploitation of deposits of various materials and rainfall-based and irrigated farmlands, which alternate with ever-expanding inhabited land, as well as the continued construction of numerous highways, bridges, reservoirs, and cement factories such as Cruz Azul or thermoelectric facilities such as the Federal Electricity Commission plant or the enormous Pemex refinery. All of this, together with mechanized agriculture, has drastically transformed the landscape of the region, especially since the 1960s (Figs. 2.6 and 2.7).

For further information about soil use and the current population pattern in the study area, the study

	Irrigated land
T	Rainfall agriculture land
	Floodwater irrigation
	Matorral
	Pasture
	Evergreen oak forest
	Evergreen oak forest with secondary growth
E	Erosion

Source: INEGI

Maps: F14-11
F14-2

Ana María Crespo made in the mid-1970s (1976) is a useful source. According to this study, 51 percent of the land is used for agriculture, of which 26 percent is irrigated land, 6 percent is half irrigated, and 19 percent is used for seasonal farming. Another study made by Ramón Figueroa (n.d.), apparently in the same decade, is based on the 1970 census and also contains estimates on the extension of the area's agricultural lands. This study indicates that cultivated land accounts for 43 percent (418 square kilometers) of the total area, of which some 250 square kilometers, or approximately 60 percent, is used for rainfall farming and 165 square kilometers (39 percent) is irrigated farming, while only approximately 2.5 square kilometers are wet or humid farmlands. Thus, according to Figueroa, there is more rainfall farmland than irrigated farmland, while the study by Crespo indicates the opposite. The fundamental difference between the authors' conclusions seems to lie in the fact that Crespo based her work largely on the analysis of aerial photographs and covered a slightly larger area.

Land Use in the Nineteenth Century

Figure 2.8 is a schematic map of land use during the nineteenth century that is principally based on the National Archive's (AGN) Ramo de Tierras data and information obtained from eighteenth- and

Figure 2.6. Present-day land use.

THE TULA REGION: PHYSICAL ENVIRONMENT AND LAND USE

Figure 2.7. The Tula area alluvial valley from the east.

nineteenth-century maps of some of the haciendas in the region, on which the zones set aside for grazing, irrigated farming, and rainfall agriculture are indicated (Mastache 1976). Some calculations for the extension of land use must be taken with a degree of reserve, which is mostly due to problems of scale derived from the schematic characteristics of the old maps that were used as a basis to draw up this general map. Consequently, it is better to consider it as a sketch rather than a map.

According to our study, the following haciendas, which varied in size and importance, existed in the area: Atotonilco, Denguí, El Salto del Agua, Jasso, La Cañada, La Goleta, San Antonio Tula, San Francisco Bojay, San Isidro Bojay, San José Bojay, San Lorenzo Endó, San Miguel Chingú, San Pedro Nextlalpan, and those in Tepetitlán and Tlahuelilpan (Mastache 1976) (Fig. 2.8). That is a total of fifteen haciendas, some of which occupied vast tracts of land during the eighteenth and nineteenth centuries, often to the detriment of various towns and villages, which led to frequent conflicts that dragged on for centuries. Many of these conflicts between the towns and the haciendas were due to land dispossession and disputes over water rights or the distribution of water among various localities that benefited from irrigation systems, and are documented in numerous files of the AGN by Ramo de Tierras and other Ramos documents. They constitute important sources of information about the area during this period.

The total of the irrigated area marked in Fig. 2.8 is approximately 101 square kilometers, that is, 10,191 hectares. This figure is based on the maximum capacity of the traditional irrigation systems (of the villages and haciendas) recorded in the study area. Further information about the nature of the data and the methodology used, as well as the characteristics of the irrigation system, is provided in Mastache (1976).

The rainfall farming land covers 151.44 square kilometers, that is, a little more than 15,144 hectares, of which about 47, or slightly less than 5,000 hectares, were used exclusively for the cultivation of the maguey plant. The areas left blank on the map are areas about which there is a lack of information, and these could be grazing zones or rainfall farmland, which means the total area dedicated to rainfall farming may have been greater than the figure mentioned.

The cultivation of the maguey plant, as in other regions of the Central Highlands, was done in two ways. On one hand, there was the exclusive cultivation of maguey, which is marked with number "III" on the map, and, on the other, mixed cultivation of maguey and maize, which is still practiced in some parts of the area where magueys are planted as hedges between maize fields. The maguey plantation zones were especially in the southeast and northeast of the area, whereas the mixed cultivation was almost entirely in the zones marked as rainfall farmland. Apparently the cultivation of maguey reached its peak in the last decade of the colonial period and the nineteenth century. This period saw the expansion of the *pulque* haciendas, when large areas were planted with maguey basically for the production of *pulque* (a fermented beverage) to supply a growing export market that included Mexico City.

During that period, other important crops in the area included maize and wheat, the latter on irrigated land. Fruit trees were also cultivated, especially along the Salado River in Tepeji del Río and in towns with springs such as Xochitlán and Santa María Magdalena in the western part of the region.

Irrigation Systems

In this kind of habitat, where water has been a limiting factor for agriculture, irrigation was undoubtedly of vital importance for the people who occupied the area in various periods. Consequently, it was essential to carry out studies on the traditional irrigation systems in the area in order to determine its agricultural potential. This is especially so because the geomorphological characteristics of the region and its hydrographic features largely dictate the location of dikes and canals, for it is very likely that the pre-Hispanic works of this kind were located on the same points as the later systems. Thus, the pre-Hispanic irrigation systems must have been similar in terms of location and characteristics to the traditional systems in the area, some of which were still being used in the 1970s.

Our study was mainly based on the analysis of aerial photographs and field reconnaissance, as well as research on seventeeth- and eighteenth-century documents in the AGN, especially those in the Ramo de Tierras (Mastache 1976). As mentioned before, this and other Ramos documents sometimes offer valuable data about the age and characteristics of the traditional irrigation systems associated with various towns and haciendas in the area.

There are two types of irrigation systems, the modern and the traditional, each with its own characteristics. The modern irrigation system forms part of the 03 Irrigation District of the Ministry of Water Resources (Secretaría de Recursos Hidráulicos) and it is fed basically by two large storage dams: Requena and Endó. The Requena Dam was built in 1919 on the Tepeji River, to the north of Tepeji del Río. The canals fed by this dam are essential for the irrigated agriculture of the area. They run from south to north and are used to irrigate most of the lowlands of the eastern part of the study area, especially the alluvial valley (Fig. 2.9).

The Endó Dam on the Tula River was built between 1947 and 1951 in order to use the river's waters for irrigation purposes. At this point, the Coscomate and Rosas Rivers feed into the Tula River. The canals fed by this dam especially benefit the northern zone between Mixquiahuala and Ixmiquilpan in the main part of the Mezquital Valley; consequently, this system is not of much interest for the study area.

The Tlamaco feeder dam is on the Salado River and it was also built in the twentieth century. The dam was not built essentially for irrigation purposes, however, although some land is irrigated along the run to the Juandó hydroelectric station, especially that near San Pedro Tlaxcoapan.

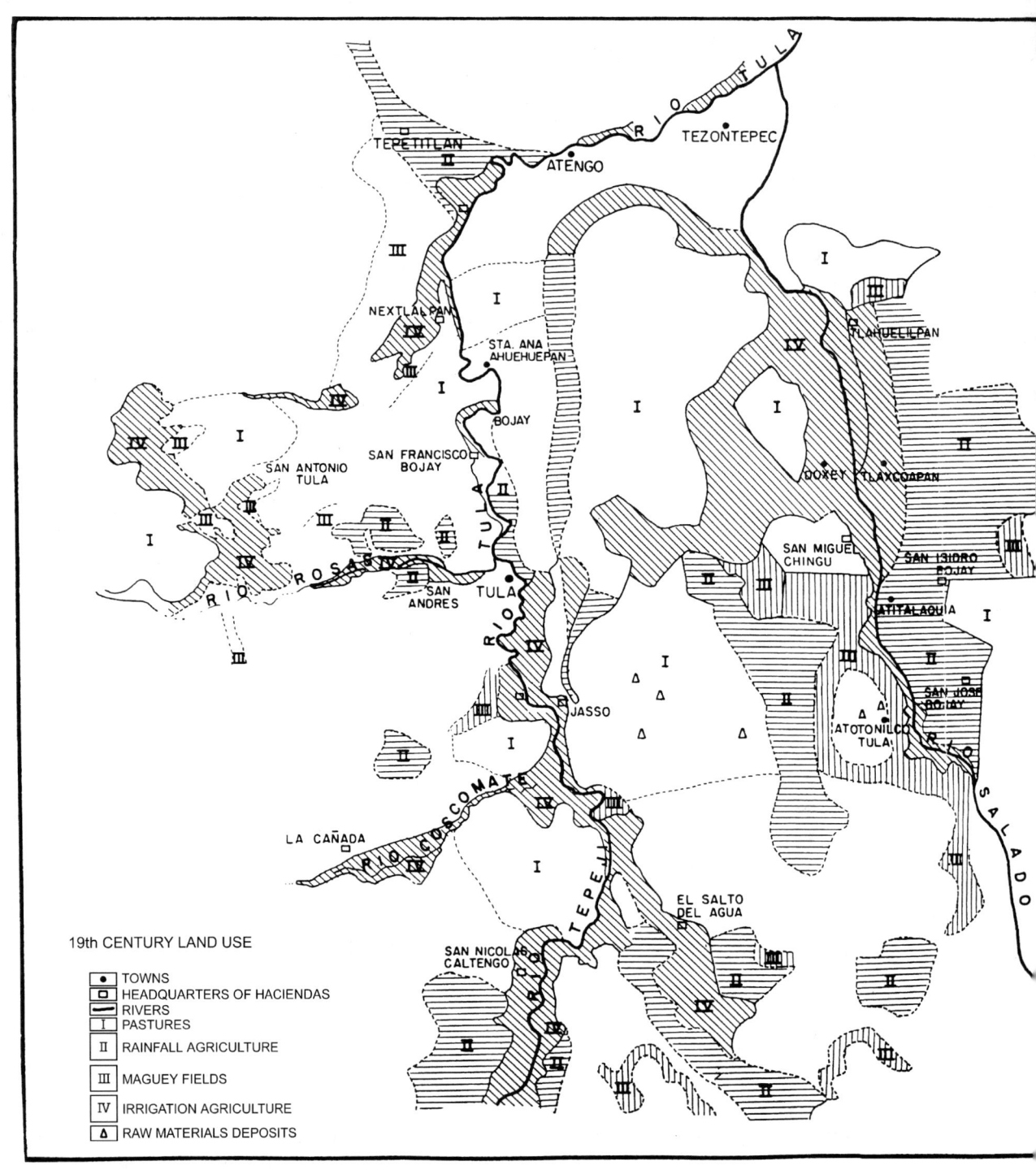

Figure 2.8. Nineteenth-century land use in the Tula area.

Some traditional irrigation systems associated with towns and haciendas still function alongside modern irrigation canals. These systems were fed by the main permanent streams in the area and they vary greatly in complexity from small dikes or weirs that channel water to canals of varying lengths, and also to more complex and sophisticated hydraulic works with concrete feeder dams and canals of several kilometers in length that, in some cases, have aqueducts and underground sections. In general, the systems associated with the towns are simpler constructions. They have small dikes or weirs made of boulders that divert river water into one or two canals. The first section of these canals is frequently made of concrete, but most of the channels consist of simple earthen ditches that generally irrigate narrow strips of land along the length of the feeder canal (Figs. 2.10 and 2.11).

The irrigation works for the haciendas were generally based on more complex hydraulic works than those for the towns. Some were abandoned after the Mexican Revolution, but others continued to be used, with modifications in some cases, despite the change in land tenure. These systems were fed by permanent rivers and streams, although some of them were directly fed by springs, as in the case of the El Sabino spring in the far northwest of the area. Another less common irrigation system was based on ponds, such as the small system located in the extreme west of the area that irrigated some of the La Goleta hacienda's lands. Rainfall farming was occasionally helped by ponds and water from mountain runoffs, which in some examples constitute real irrigation systems, as in the case of the system built on the San Isidro Bojay hacienda on the mountains bordering the area to the east.

Some of the works consist of concrete feeder and storage dams with several sluice gates to regulate the flow of water to canals, which are sometimes several kilometers long and occasionally have underground sections and aqueducts. Due to their characteristics, these systems make it possible to irrigate zones that are farther from the rivers. It could be argued, however, that all the traditional systems irrigated narrow strips of land. It is possible to irrigate large continuous tracts of land with modern systems because they have large reservoirs.

All the traditional eighteenth- and nineteeth-century irrigation systems identified in the area in both fieldwork and maps are recorded on the map showing traditional irrigation (Fig. 2.10). The most important systems include those that fed the alluvial valley lands. In those times, as now, it was necessary to channel the water from the extreme southern part of the area by means of long canals.

During the colonial period, the Zanja Romera, also known as the Zanja del Correo Mayor, was one of the most important traditional irrigation systems, and it was controlled by the Chingú hacienda. The Zanja Romera started in a stone dam on the Tepeji River to the south of Tepeji del Río. The dam channeled the water into a canal more than 30 kilometers long that irrigated the lands of various haciendas along the run, especially in the alluvial valley. This system is now abandoned, except for small stretches near Tepeji del Río. There are numerous references to La Romera in eighteenth-century maps and documents.

Another irrigation system that fed the valley was known as the Zanja Nueva. We do not know how old it is, but the name suggests that it was constructed after La Romera. As can be seen in Figure 2.10, its route was similar to that of the La Romera, but shorter. The system started at the Tepeji River with a dike that was later covered by the Requena Dam. It has some underground sections and aqueducts and ends to the west of Tlahuelilpan. The Zanja Romera and Zanja Nueva systems are of great interest for our study because the distribution of Classic and Tollan Phase sites in the area suggests that there could have been a system with a similar route since those periods.

The Salado River fed various irrigation systems—the Cadenas, Presa Vieja, and Yocua Dams with which the lands of the Tlahuelilpan hacienda were irrigated (Fig. 2.12). In the nineteenth century, this hacienda was the most important in the area and owned most of the land in the alluvial valley. To the south, the hacienda bordered on the town of Tula and the Jasso hacienda and to the north it bordered on Atengo and Tezontepec and the Ulapa hacien-

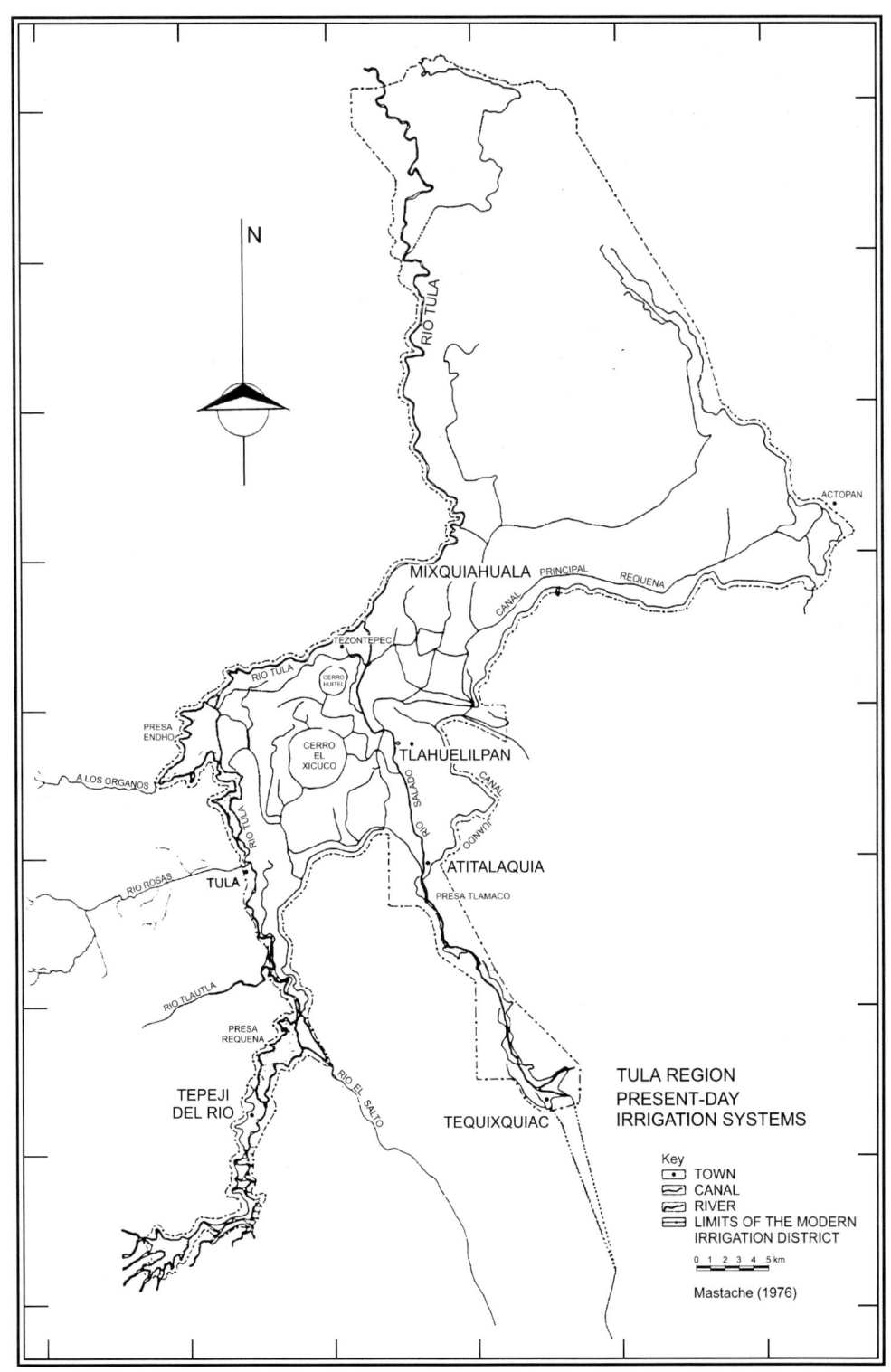

Figure 2.9. Present-day irrigation systems.

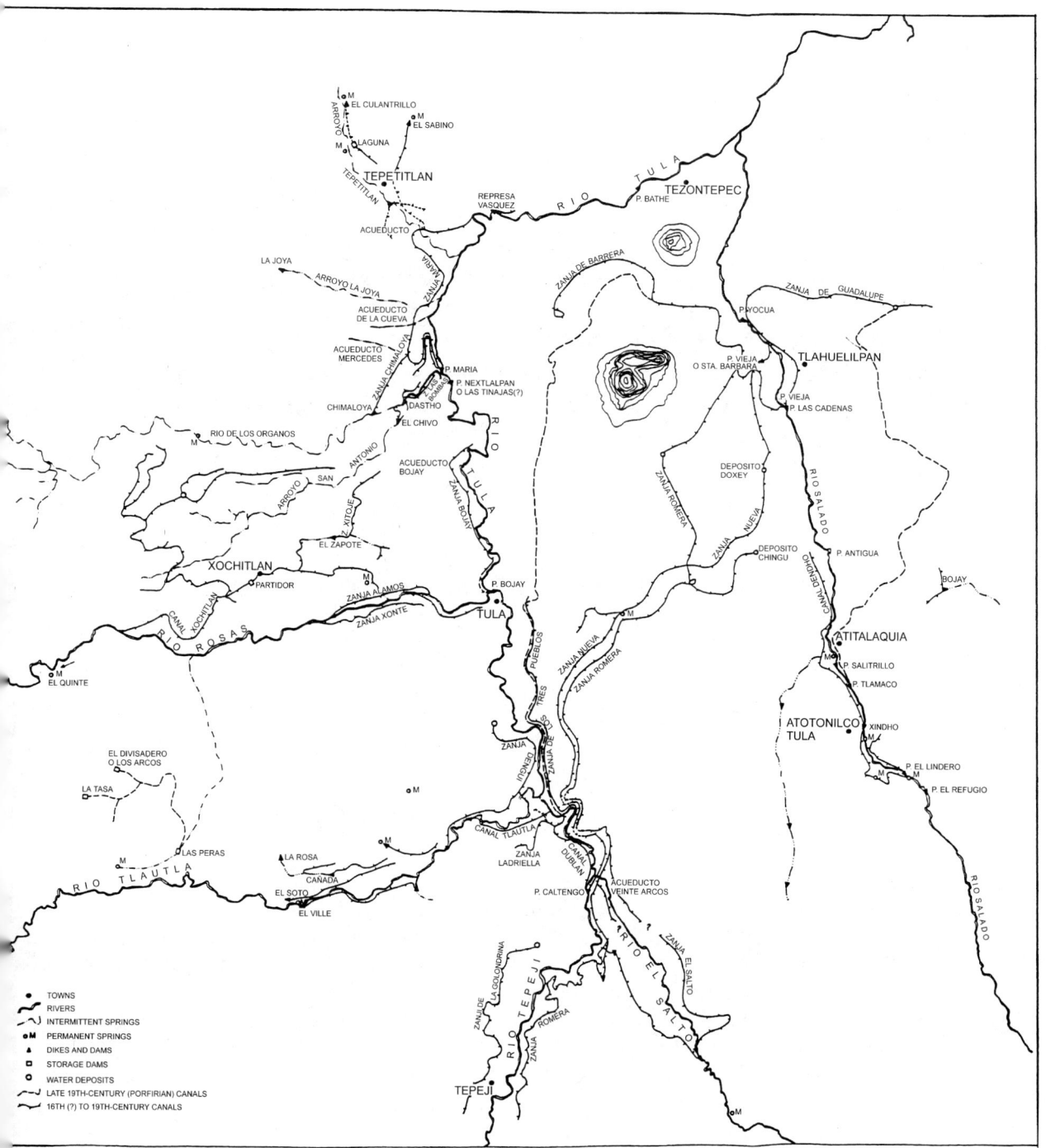

Figure 2.10. Traditional irrigation systems in the Tula area.

THE TULA REGION: PHYSICAL ENVIRONMENT AND LAND USE

Figure 2.11. Dike on the Tula River.

da. Another important system on the Salado River irrigated the lands of Atitalaquia, Tlaxcopan, and Tlahuelilpan. Since Atitalaquia is closer to the dam and upstream of the other towns, it was in charge of controlling the irrigation system, which we suppose was pre-Hispanic in origin.

The Tula River was the origin of various irrigation canals. One of the most important was the Zanja de los Tres Pueblos, which was still partially used up to the 1970s. It started with a small dike, located approximately 2 kilometers north of the Requena Dam, by which water was fed into a canal that ran along the right bank of the river. It was a simple ditch almost 10 kilometers long that irrigated land in San Miguel Vindhó, San Marcos, and San Lorenzo Xipacoya, which are towns to the south of the pre-Hispanic city (Fig. 2.11).

There was another small irrigation system within the limits of the ancient city that started with a dike under the suspension bridge located between the modern city of Tula and the archaeological zone. This system belonged, at least in the nineteenth century, to the San Francisco Bojay hacienda. The dike water drained to a canal that ran along the left bank of the river to the hacienda and irrigated lands that are now under the Endó Dam. It irrigated a narrow strip of land covering almost 100 hectares. Downstream, there was a series of small systems having characteristics much the same as those described above.

The Xochitlán irrigation system requires special mention. This is a semidispersed town some 8 kilometers to the west of Tula. Xochitlán still controls an irrigation system of vital importance for various

Figure 2.12. Flow gates of the colonial Las Cadenas Dam built by the Tlahuelilpan hacienda.

towns in the area, including the city of Tula itself. The system is fed by a spring called El Quinte or San Francisco, which is located near the town of San Francisco Soyaniquilpan in the Jilotepec region of the state of Mexico. The water from this spring is channeled in the Rosas River down to San Agustín, where it joins water coming from other springs.

The volume of water in this system is now very low, especially because it has to be shared by several towns: Xochitlán, San Andrés Nantza, Michimaloya, Xitejé, and Tula. The system used to channel the water to these towns is rather complex because it combines stretches where water flows in rivers and streams with sections of canals and earth ditches several kilometers long. However, from a construction point of view, its technology is very simple since there are no aqueducts or underground sections.

Because Xochitlán is closest to the springs and is higher than most of the other towns supplied by the system, it controls water distribution. On the outskirts of the town there is a rectangular pond divided into two sections that is called a *partidor* (starting gate). Local sources indicated that half of the water is set aside for Xochitlán and the other half is divided among the other six places mentioned. Each town has its own water rights during certain hours of the day and on a fixed schedule. The places that benefit from the system must keep the canals and ditches that correspond to them clean and well maintained. In some places, the job is done on a rotational basis by the town's men, who are chosen by the community to be *canaleros* (canal men) for a set period of time.

The conflicts caused by the distribution of the water in the system between the haciendas and the villages benefiting from it date back a long time, including most of the colonial period and into the nineteenth century. The respective archive documents contain very important data about the age of the system, indicating that in the seventeenth and eighteenth centuries the system supplied the same towns as it does now, in addition to the San Antonio and San Agustin (also known as La Goleta) haciendas. The latter is located very close to the springs that feed the system.

The archive data also indicate that the same system was used to deliver water to the towns as in the 1970s, traversing along the Michimaloya and Nextlalpan canyons to Xitejé and Michimaloya and then by the Rosas River to Xochitlán, San Andrés, and Tula. Also, the irrigation ditch that fed water from the dam to the colonial mill in Tula was very probably the same, or at least a ditch that followed a very similar route to the one in use when we made our study. This ditch starts at the meadow in San Andrés, irrigates the river meadows, and ends in a reservoir that supplies the city of Tula. Some documentary sources state that this water was essential for the functioning of the mill in Tula, which was already working in 1539. On the other hand, in the records of the conflicts between the haciendas and the villages, Xochitlán claims its rights "since time immemorial" to use and possess these waters for its maintenance and the irrigation of its lands (Mastache 1976:62).

The research on the traditional irrigation systems in the study area made it possible to determine the potential of the ancient systems and propose some hypotheses about the operation of some of them in the pre-Hispanic period, especially in the case of towns that have been inhabited continuously from the Postclassic period until now. There is ethnohistorical information about some of these towns, suggesting that they had irrigation, at least in the period immediately before the Conquest. In Chapter 7 there are maps of pre-Hispanic potential irrigation in the area.

NOTES

1. E. Garcia (1966), using the Köppens system of climate classification, designates Tula's immediate climate as $BS_1 kw(i')gw"$, that is: dry steppe, with moderate to cold temperatures that do not oscillate much, with the warmest period occurring before June. Particular local precipitations (in millimeters) are: Atitalaquia, 947.3; Binola 585.7; Héroes de Carranza, 633.6; Jasso, 482.6; Juandó 419.2; Sur de Miz-quiahuala, 508.8; Requena, 432.7; Requena Presa, 600; El Salto, 659.2; Tepeji, 734.9; Tezontepec, 507.9; Tula, 699.4; Xochitlan, 469.5.
2. This type of determination is based on the classification proposed by the FAO and is mainly based on the soil profile morphology, expressed in "diagnosis horizons" through physical characteristics such as color, texture, and horizon thickness, and chemical and organic material content, pH, and salinity.

3

Chronology and Periodification

THE URBAN ZONE SEQUENCE

The periodification that currently exists for Tula, and which constitutes the chronological framework for the present investigation, was defined twenty years ago by Cobean (1978), who proposed seven phases of occupation for the pre-Hispanic city (see Tables 3.1 and 3.3).

The Prado and Corral Phases correspond to the first major occupation of Tula's urban zone. The ceramic types used to define the Prado Phase are associated with the city's earliest occupation and most are closely related to Coyotlatelco Sphere complexes in the Basin of Mexico.

The types defining the Corral Phase also are closely related to Coyotlatelco pottery assemblages and correspond to the first extensive occupation of the monumental center known as Tula Chico. The Terminal Corral Phase corresponds to the destruction and abandonment of the Tula Chico center (Cobean and Suárez 1989; Cobean 2000), and probably to the initial expansion of the city that reaches its apogee during the Tollan Phase.

The Tollan Phase, marking the maximum expansion of the city, is the best-defined period, with a great deal of information and an extensive diagnostic ceramic complex. The Fuego and Palacio Phases, associated with Aztec ceramic types, correspond to occupations after the apogee of the city and its role as capital of a state. The Tesoro Phase, associated with colonial ceramics, represents the sixteenth- and seventeenth-century occupation that existed in some parts of the urban zone (Cobean 1990, 1994).

The principal basis for the periodification consists of three groups of data: (1) Acosta's previous chronology based on his excavations of the monumental zone, (2) the available chronologies for the Basin of Mexico, which in many cases include ceramic complexes that are similar to those in Tula, and (3) Cobean's analyses of ceramic collections from

Table 3.1—Chronology for Tula

Phase	Approx. Dates (A.D.)	Period
Tesoro	1520–1650	Late Postclassic
Palacio	1350–1520	
Fuego	1150–1350	Middle Postclassic
Tollan	900–1150	Early Postclassic
Terminal Corral	850–900	
Corral	750–850	Epiclassic
Prado	650–750	

surface surveys and excavations of the University of Missouri Tula Project during the 1970s, which included extensive excavations of habitational structures and Cobean's test pits in several areas of the city (Stoutamire 1975; Healan and Stoutamire 1989; Healan 1973; Cobean 1978, 1982, 1990), along with stratigraphic excavations done by the INAH at Tula Chico (Matos 1974; Cobean 1982). In the definition of the diagnostic ceramic complexes, Cobean mainly uses the stratigraphic sequences of occupations in the city and other excavation materials, but he also found the urban zone surface materials to be important because these made it possible to detect some types that were not well represented in the excavations; especially for the Coyotlatelco and Aztec occupations.

The initial excavations in Tula Chico (Cobean 1982) were especially important for defining phases preceding the city's apogee because they permitted the identification of different complexes related to the Coyotlatelco culture at Tula and of the ceramics associated with the beginning of the Tollan Phase with more detail than the previous investigations of Acosta (1945, 1956–1957). The subsequent excavations in different sectors of Tula Chico (Cobean and Suárez 1989) and other studies in various sites in the area with Coyotlatelco occupations (Mastache and Cobean 1989, 1990) now provide a wider panorama concerning this period for the region being investigated. It is important to state that the diagnostic types that define the Prado Phase and correlated with the beginning of the city generally do not occur in the area's Coyotlatelco sites; in general terms, the ceramic complexes of these settlements are somewhat different from the Coyotlatelco assemblages in the urban zone.

Cobean (1978) originally expressed doubts concerning the chronological validity of the Prado Phase, and proposed that its ceramics only consisted of some kind of special complex that possibly was intrusive or belonged to a social elite having a limited distribution. Likewise, he originally was not sure of the validity of the Terminal Corral Phase in terms of whether or not its diagnostic types really defined a period that could be separated from the rest of the Corral Phase. The subsequent excavations at Tula Chico verified the existence of the Terminal Corral Phase and permitted a better definition of its ceramic complex, both in terms of the identification of new diagnostic types and obtaining radiocarbon dates (Cobean and Suárez 1989; Cobean n.d.).

More recently, the Fuego Phase, which is characterized by Aztec II ceramics represented fundamentally in contexts in the monumental precinct (Tula Grande), was better defined on the basis of excavations in Building K (Cobean 1994; Getino 2000), located on the southern side of the monumental plaza. Concerning this phase, which correlates with the destruction of Tula, we now possess more information. In Building K, the different contexts of the building's destruction by fire are principally associated with Aztec II ceramics. Along with this stratigraphic information, many new samples for radiocarbon dates were obtained from Building K. Also of importance are Wolfman's (1990) studies of archaeomagnetic dates for Central Mexico, which for Tula place the burning of the Palacio Quemado between A.D. 1150 and 1200 on the basis of several clay samples from this building; these dates coincide with the chronology proposed here for the transition between the Tollan and Fuego Phases.

The investigations in Building K and recent typological studies for Aztec ceramics in the Basin of Mexico (Hodge and Minc 1990) will permit a more precise definition of the Palacio and Tesoro Phases, associated with Aztec III and IV ceramics, which sometimes are problematic as chronological indicators. For example, Aztec IV ceramics appear in some areas together with Aztec III wares, and then disappear in the occupation sequence before Aztec III, which often continues until the early colonial period (Parsons 1966, 1976; Charlton 1972).

The cultural sequence proposed for different phases continues to be valid, even though later investigation at Tula and in some sites in the area have defined more precisely some aspects of the occupational sequence and of the ceramic complexes that characterize each phase (Cobean and Suárez 1989; Mastache and Cobean 1989; Bey 1986; Getino and Fuentes 1986; Salazar 1991; Getino n.d.; Cobean and Mastache 1995, 1999; Moncayo 1999; Hernández et al. 1999). With regard to the Tollan Phase, which spans approximately 200–250 years and corresponds to the apogee and maximum expansion of the city of Tula, it has been possible to define at least two subphases on the basis of the information obtained during the last fifteen years by several projects working in the city and at sites in the area that have provided radiocarbon dates, analyses of stratigraphic contexts, and studies of changes in the frequencies of various pottery types through time along with temporal changes in the attributes of specific types. For example, Macana Red on Brown (one of the most common and important types in the Tollan Complex) possesses variations in several attributes that Cobean used to define varieties that have chronological significance. Similar temporal variations in attributes exist for Soltura, Bordo, and some other types (Cobean 1990, 2000; Mastache 1996a).

Bey (1986) also has proposed a division of the Tollan Phase on the basis of his study of ceramics from Healan's (1986) excavations in an obsidian workshop in the urban zone. Moncayo (1999) recently published a large sample of late Tollan Phase ceramics from the site of Tepetitlán in the northern Tula region, and further information for the definition of an early subcomplex for the Tollan Phase was recovered in excavations of habitational structures of the ceramics workshop zone in Tula's ancient city (Hernández et al. 1999).

In addition, the changes in the planning and orientation of the Tollan Phase city detected by Mastache and Crespo (1982), along with similar changes in the orientation of habitational structures in the urban zone, all appear to have chronological implications that have not been analyzed sufficiently. The residential type of the El Canal excavations, which Healan calls a "House Group," may be the main type of habitation structure for the late Tollan Phase, while perhaps the Apartment Compounds, such as the El Corral unit excavated by Mandeville (Mandeville and Healan 1989), would be more characteristic of the early Tollan Phase (see Chapter 6).

According to Healan (1986:148–149), there were changes in frequencies and percentages of obsidian artifact types in the city, which in his opinion have a clear chronological significance. At the beginning of the Tollan Phase, approximately one-third of the obsidian artifacts are gray, made with material from Ucareo, Michoacán, while later on in this phase the gray obsidian becomes less common and about 90 percent of the city's obsidian is green material from Sierra de Pachuca, Hidalgo.

The analysis and correlation of these temporal changes in archaeological materials, which are only outlined here, will permit the division of the Tollan Phase into two or more subphases. As will be described in the next section, on the basis of recent investigations in both the Tula region and other areas of Central Mexico, and especially on the basis of recently obtained radiocarbon dates, we have been able to refine part of the Tula sequence for the Classic and Postclassic periods, placing the Prado, Corral, Terminal Corral, Tollan, and Fuego Phases fifty years earlier than was originally proposed (Table 3.1).

THE TULA REGION CULTURAL SEQUENCE OUTSIDE THE ANCIENT CITY

During the last decade, increasing numbers of new radiocarbon, obsidian hydration, and arqueomagnetism dates from ongoing investigations have inspired a series of reevaluations of major cultural chronologies in Central Mexico, most of which are still in process (for example: Rattray 2001; Parsons 2000; Parsons, Brumfiel, and Hodge 1996; Wolfman 1990; Hodge and Minc 1990; Hirth 2000; Evans and Freter 1996; Hernández 2000; Cobean 2000). On the basis of these investigations, along with a group of new radiocarbon dates from Tula's ancient city and some sites in the region provided by Professor Austin Long of the Department of Geosciences of the University of Arizona, we have modified the chronology for some phases in the Classic and Postclassic periods (Table 3.1). The new radiocarbon dates from the Tula region will be discussed in detail in a separate report.

Table 3.2—Selected Central Mexican Chronologies

Approx. Date		Rattray 2001: Teotihuacan/ Basin of Mexico	Teotihuacan Valley (Names)	Teotihuacan Valley (Numbers)	Tula Region
1500			—— Teacalco ——	—— Aztec IV ——	—— Tesoro ——
1400	Late Postclassic	Aztec	Chimalpa	Aztec III	Palacio
1300		Aztec	Zocango	Aztec II	
1200		Aztec	Atlatongo		Fuego
1100	Early Postclassic		Mazapan	Mazapan	
1000		Mazapan			Tollan
900			—— Xometla ——	—— Coyotlatelco ——	
	Epiclassic				Terminal Corral
800		Coyotlatelco	Oxtotipac	Proto-Coyotlatelco	Corral
700			—— Metepec ——	—— Teotihuacan IV ——	—— Prado ——
600	Classic	Metepec		Teotihuacan IIIa	La Mesa
500			Xolalpan	Teotihuacan III	Chingu
400		Xolalpan		Teotihuacan IIa–III	Classic
300			—— Tlamimilolpa ——	—— Teotihuacan IIa ——	
200		Tlamimilolpa			
		Miccaotli	Miccaotli	Teotihuacan II	
100 A.D.	Terminal Formative	Tzacualli	Tzacualli	Teotihuacan Ia	Terminal Formative
0				Teotihuacan I	
B.C.					
100		Patlachique	Patlachique		
		Tezoyuca			
200		Ticoman IV		Proto-Teotihuacan I	
300	Late Formative	Ticoman III	Late Cuanalan		Tepeji
400		Ticoman II	Middle Cuanalan		
500		—— Ticoman I ——	—— Early Cuanalan ——		
600					
	Middle Formative	Zacatenco			
700			Chiconautla		
800					

Adapted with modifications from Millon 1981: Fig. 7-7 and Rattray 2001: Fig. 1b.

There probably was a very sparse Middle Formative occupation (ca. 800–600 B.C.) in some parts of the Tula region. Two diagnostic Middle Formative sherds were identified by Mastache and Crespo (1982:13, photo 2) in materials from the excavation of a modern water pipe in the main plaza of Tula de Allende. A few sherds of Middle Formative Zacatenco-like materials have been identified in surface collections in Tula's urban zone and the region (Cobean n.d.).

The earliest occupation with well-defined settlements corresponds to the Late Formative period (ca. 400–200 B.C.) and contain nearly pure Ticomán III ceramics along with some Chupícuaro pottery and figurines (Vaillant 1931; Porter 1956; Hernández 2000; Cobean 1974). Only three such sites have been identified in the region (Mastache and Crespo 1974, 1976). Two of them are small hamlets approximately 0.5 to 1.0 hectares in area, but La Loma, the other site near Tepeji del Rio, covers over 15 hectares and contains a small ceremonial center (Cook de Leonard 1956–1957; Cobean 1974). The tentative phase name for these Late Formative occupations is Tepeji, corresponding to the largest site in the region for this period. The Terminal Formative (ca. 150 B.C.–A.D. 200) occupations in the region have not been well defined yet, and mainly appear to consist of early components in some of the area's Early Classic Teotihuacan-related sites, which contain some diagnostic Tzacualli ceramics (Chapter 4; Mastache and Crespo 1976; Cobean and Mastache 1989; Rattray 2001). No formal phase names have been proposed yet for the Terminal Formative in the Tula region.

Most Early Classic sites in the region possess substantial quantities of diagnostic Teotihuacan-tradition ceramics, and their internal chronologies probably can be subdivided according to major Teotihuacan ceramic complexes (especially Tzacualli, Tlamimilolpa, Xolalpan, and Metepec), as has been done for the large center of Chingú (Chapter 4; Díaz 1980). The tentative Classic Phase name for the regions Teotihuacan-related occupations is Chingú (ca. A.D. 200–650). As explained in Chapter 4, the Teotihuacan-related occupations in the Tula region reached their peak in Late Tlamimilolpa times (ca. 350 A.D.) and appear to have decreased in size afterward.

A crucial recent investigation for Central Mexican archaeology is Rattray's (2001) redefinition of the Teotihuacan ceramic sequence and cultural chronology. For the period under discussion here, it is important to take into consideration Rattray's redating of the Metepec Phase corresponding to the end of Teotihuacan's Classic city during A.D. 550–650. This is based on a rigorous analysis of many new radiocarbon dates, and places the Metepec Phase nearly one century earlier than most archaeologists have proposed (e.g., Millon 1981). As we will see, Rattray's new dates for the Metepec Phase constitute a key factor in our chronology for the transitional period between the last Teotihuacan occupations and the founding of the Classic Coyotlatelco settlements in the Tula region. In addition, the Classic sites with the proposed "Transitional" ceramics described in Chapter 4 may constitute occupations coeval with part of the Metepec Phase that are unrelated to the Teotihuacan tradition and can eventually, on the basis of more investigations, perhaps be used to define a local subphase that partially overlaps with Metepec.

Very probably there was a significant chronological overlap between the Metepec Phase (A.D. 550–650) occupations of the Teotihuacan tradition sites and the initial Coyotlatelco settlements in the Tula region. As is discussed later, the principal Coyotlatelco sites generally are located in different ecological zones from the Teotihuacan sites, and the great majority of the Teotihuacan sites do not possess Coyotlatelco occupations. The process of Coyotlatelco settlement in the region probably took place in at least two stages: first, the founding of most of the hilltop Coyotlatelco centers such as La Mesa, Magoni, Batha, Atitalaquia, and El Aguila by A.D. 550–600 during the first part of the regional La Mesa Phase, and then the founding of Tula Chico and some others sites on lower elevations by A.D. 650. The La Mesa Phase is named after the most thoroughly studied early Coyotlatelco site in the region (Mastache and Cobean 1989, 1990; Jackson 1990; Camargo n.d; Patiño 1994a; Bonfil 1998). This phase overlaps with the Metepec Phase (A.D. 550–650) occupations of the Teotihuacan-tradition sites, indicating as we have proposed previously (Mastache and Cobean 1989, 1990) that the Tula-region hilltop Coyotlatelco sites were founded before the lower-lying Teotihuacan sites were abandoned.

The ceramic complexes of La Mesa and the other hilltop Coyotlatelco centers are significantly different from that of the initial Coyotlatelco occupation (Prado Phase: A.D. 650–750) at Tula Chico in Tula's urban zone. Most of the diagnostic Prado Phase types (especially Guadalupe Red on Brown Incised, Ana María Red on Brown, and Clara Luz Black Incised; Cobean 1990) are rare or absent in Coyotlatelco sites in the region that we studied outside of Tula Chico. For this reason, the Prado Complex is defined as an early Coyotlatelco ceramic assemblage that occurs only in Tula's urban zone.

The types defining the Corral Phase (A.D. 750–850) are closely related to Coyotlatelco-sphere ceramic complexes in Central Mexico (Tozzer 1921; Rattray 1966; Blanton and Parsons 1971; Nichols and McCullough 1986). As discussed here and in Chapter 8, the Tollan Complex in the region is very similar to the ceramics assemblage for this phase in the city. The Aztec (Fuego and Palacio Phases) and early colonial (Tesoro Phase) occupations in the Tula region are still being analyzed and will be reported in a separate volume.

THE TOLLAN COMPLEX

The ceramic complex that is characteristic of Tula was first defined by Acosta (1945, 1956–1957), and afterward with more precision and completeness by Cobean (1978), as consisting of an assemblage of ceramic types that have been found together both in the monumental precinct and in the rest of the city. Although most of this complex is present during all of the Early Postclassic occupation sequence, changes in frequencies and attribute composition for some types have been detected that possess chronological significance (Fig. 3.1).

The ceramic assemblage corresponding to Tula's apogee was defined by Cobean as the Tollan Complex, which is composed of approximately twenty-five types that coexisted in the city during nearly 250 years (A.D. 900–1150). This complex is an integration of several cultural traditions and marks a major change from the characteristic complex of the Corral Phase. This plurality of cultural traditions manifested in the ceramics also is present in other aspects of Toltec culture, especially in the case of iconography.

Among the various ceramic traditions that make up the Tollan Complex, red-on-brown ceramics are especially important, being represented principally by Macana and Bordo and in lesser amounts by Mazapa Red on Brown and Manuelito. This tradition existed in Central Mexico since the Late Formative and is related to the Ticoman culture of the Basin of Mexico and to red-on-brown pottery traditions of the Formative and Classic periods in various areas of Queretaro, Guanajuato, and Michoacán.

Nevertheless, the tradition that is most characteristic and diagnostic of the Tollan Complex is composed of orange-and-cream ceramics that, as was stated previously, represent an innovative tradition that is foreign to the Tula area. The initial versions of these orange-and-cream ceramics appear just before the beginning of the Tollan Phase, and there is still considerable speculation concerning their place of origin.

On the basis of the forms and surface finish of the orange-and-cream types, Cobean (1978, 1990) proposes that they are related to ceramic traditions on the Gulf Coast, but until there are more detailed studies of Classic and Postclassic Gulf Coast ceramics, it is difficult to identify a specific area of origin. However, it is clear that culturally the orange-and-cream tradition is not related to previous ceramic complexes in Central Mexico, the Bajío, or the northern Mesoamerican periphery. In this respect, Jiménez Moreno's (1941) reconstruction is of interest, in which, on the basis of ethnohistorical studies, he proposed that the origins of Tula involved two ethnic groups: a group from the north (perhaps producing Coyotlatelco red-on-brown ceramics) and another group coming from the Gulf Coast, the Nonoalcas.

The change that takes place in the ceramic tradition and in other elements is a manifestation of an important transformation in the cultural tradition, the economic organization, and probably the ethnic composition of Tula's population. At the beginning of the Tollan Phase, Tula becomes a completely urban settlement, with a complex social and economic organization that is characteristic of a society that is divided into classes (Chapters 5 and 6). Ceramics production during this period was based on numerous workshops located both in the city and in sites in the area. The pottery types generally are very standardized and uniform with very well-defined attributes and little variation between vessels of the same type (Hernández et al. 1999).

Another important cultural influence in the Tollan Complex ceramics comes from the Huasteca, represented partially by pottery imported from this area and also by types such as Sillon Incised, "Ink Stamp" (Unnamed Black on Orange *olla*), and perhaps Acta Polished Red, all of which possess attributes related to Huastec ceramics but are of local manufacture. Even though the origins of these types are tied to the Huasteca, they became characteristic of Toltec culture (Cobean and Mastache 1985). A

Figure 3.1. Principal types of the Tollan Complex (drawing by Antonieta Castilla).
1. Soltura Smoothed Red *olla*, **2.** Blanco Levantado *olla* (Levantado Watermarked), **3.** Acta Polished Red: Bowl Variety, **4.** Abra Coarse Brown: Plain Hourglass Variety (*brasero*), **5.** Abra Coarse Brown: Abra Variety (*brasero*): cylinder form, **6.** Abra Coarse Brown: Abra Variety (*brasero*): hourglass form, **7.** Bordo Red on Brown (*olla*), **8.** Unnamed Red on Brown "Frying Pan" (censer), **9.** Tohil Plumbate, **10.** Macana Red on Brown: Macana Variety (bowl), **11.** Alicia Open-worked censer, **12.** Mendrugo Semi-smoothed *comal*, **13.** Sillón Incised (bowl), **14.** Manuelito Plain Brown (bowl), **15.** Proa Polished Cream (bowl), **16.** Jara Polished Orange (bowl), **17.** Joroba Orange or Cream (bowl), **18.** Rebato Polished Red (bowl), **19.** Ira Stamped Orange (bowl), **20.** Toza Smoothed Brown (*cazuela*).

tie with the Mixteca is represented by Alicia Openworked *incensarios,* which both Acosta (1944) and Cobean (1990) have linked with similar censer types that are common in Oaxaca during previous periods.

On the other hand, Abra Coarse Brown *braseros,* which occur in numerous varieties at Tula and constitute a key component of the Tollan Complex, have very diverse origins. *Braseros* having similar attributes are present in the Maya Lowlands as early as the Late Formative. *Braseros* decorated with appliqué clay spikes on the exterior surfaces are so common in various regions of Mesoamerica during several periods that it is difficult to identify them with a specific origin area; but it is clear that these *braseros* did not originate in the Toltec culture. Nevertheless, at Tula they were essentially re-created and diversified, becoming a diagnostic element for the Tollan Phase (Cobean and Mastache in press; Diehl 1993).

A pottery type that is a manifestation of the clear relationship between Tula, the Bajío, and northern Mesoamerica periphery is Blanco Levantado. Cobean (1990) and other investigators propose that this ceramic tradition in the Tula area probably correlates with the presence of Otomi groups.

During Tula's apogee, imported ceramics such as Tohil Plumbate constitute an integral part of the Tollan Complex even though they originated in a production area more than 1,000 kilometers distant. Plumbate ceramics are an example of the relations of domination or trade of the Toltec state with other regions. The constant flow of these and other foreign ceramics to the metropolis implies a permanent system of tribute or commerce between Tula and the production zones, in this case the Soconusco. In a sense, Tohil Plumbate was the "official" import and export ceramic of the Toltec state because, even though this pottery was not produced locally, Tula probably controlled its commerce, its internal distribution, and its redistribution to other regions.

The major part of the Tollan Complex is composed of what commonly is called "domestic pottery," that is, different types of vessels and recipients that Tula's inhabitants used during their daily life in order to satisfy a series of practical and ritual necessities—dishes, plates, jars, *molcajetes* (grater bowls), bowls, basins—and recipients for storage, transport, drinking liquids, and preserving grains, and *braseros* (braziers) for cooking, heating, and rituals in religious ceremonies. On the other hand, there also were imported ceramics, the access to which was limited to only some sectors of the population. Surely some locally made pottery also possessed status value and had a restricted access limited to only some groups of people. An especially important context for the definition of the Tollan Complex was a *bodega* of ceramics that Acosta (1945) excavated on the north side of the Palacio Quemado that contained large quantities of around fifteen central types for this complex.

It is important to consider the Tollan Complex on at least two different levels of distribution: at the first level are the central types that define this complex in the city of Tula, that is, the diagnostic types defined by Cobean (1990) for the Tollan Phase. This ceramic assemblage can be described in rather simplified form as the group of pottery types that would be found in almost any house in Tula during the Tollan Phase, although there would be variations in type frequencies depending on the specific chronology of the house along with the socioeconomic position of its neighborhood in the city. These central Tollan Phase types would include the following: Jara bowls and dishes, Soltura *ollas,* Macana grater bowls, Rebato dishes, abundant large Toza bowls, Bordo *ollas,* small quantities of Acta vessels (both bowls and *tecomates*), some Sillon Incised bowls, some forms of Abra *braseros* (especially those with appliqué spikes and the Plain Hourglass Variety with Tlaloc images), some Blanco Levantado *ollas,* a small number of Tohil Plumbate vessels (perhaps only two or three bowls or jars according to the status of the house) and one or more Alicia censers. Some additional scarcely represented types would include Manuelito bowls, Tarea small jars and Mendrugo *comals,* along with some Mazapan figurines and an architectural drainage system composed of lines of interlocking conical ceramic tubes.

In the case of an early habitation, Mazapa Red on Brown dishes and Proa bowls would be present, along with occasional Joroba dishes. But if the house was late Tollan Phase, these types would be absent or only present in very small quantities, and there would

CHRONOLOGY AND PERIODIFICATION

Table 3.3—Chronology for the Tula Urban Zone

A.D.	Phase	Comments
1520	TESORO	Aztec IV and other early colonial Aztec complexes.
1350	PALACIO	Pre-Hispanic Aztec III and possibly some pre-Hispanic Aztec IV.
1150	FUEGO	Aztec II–III transition.
	LATE TOLLAN	The Tollan Phase constitutes the only time when there was a large city at Tula. Its ceramics are related to the Mazapan and Atlatongo complexes of the Teotihuacan Valley.
900	EARLY TOLLAN	
850	TERMINAL CORRAL	A transitional complex containing some Corral and Proto-Tollan pottery types.
750	CORRAL	A local variant of the Coyotlatelco culture. Its ceramic complex has similarities with Coyotlatelco pottery in the Basin of Mexico and some distinctive elements.
650	PRADO	Has a hybrid ceramics complex that contains some Coyotlatelco types along with diagnostic types that may be related to Classic cultures in the northern periphery of Mesoamerica.

be fewer Macana grater bowls and more Jara and Ira dishes. Ira Stamped Orange is a late type that nearly always is scarce. The Mazapa, Proa, and Joroba types are restricted to specific times and zones, being an essential part of the Tollan Complex at its beginning but diminishing greatly afterward. In some cases, there would be other imported pottery from central Veracruz, west Mexico, the Maya Lowlands, or Central America that is scarce and possesses restricted distributions.

The other level of ceramic destribution is what Cobean (1990) calls the Tollan Sphere, i.e., the pottery of the Tollan Complex that is present outside Tula in contemporaneous sites in Central Mexico, including principally the Basin of Mexico, the Valley of Puebla-Tlaxcala, northern Morelos, and parts of the Valley of Toluca and the Bajío. The types that these sites generally share with the Tula area are Jara, Macana, Proa, Abra *braseros,* Manuelito, Blanco Levantado, Tohil Plumbate, and Mazapan figurines, even though frequently, in contrast to Tula, all of these types are not always found together in sites of this period. Mazapa Red on Brown also is quite common at some of these sites, but Cobean does not consider it diagnostic of the Tollan Sphere because, as mentioned previously, its place of origin seems to have been the Basin of Mexico and not Tula. In addition, Mazapa Red on Brown possesses different chronological durations in different areas of Central Mexico (Parsons, Brumfiel, and Hodge 1996).

In general terms, if Mazapa Red on Brown and Macana are common at a site, this settlement almost surely is coeval with the first stages of Tula's development, but not its apogee. The chronological implications of these types and their relation with Tula's beginnings will be treated in more detail in another chapter. Among the other Tollan Sphere types, Cobean considers Jara and Tohil Plumbate as the most useful diagnostics for identifying sites related to Tula and contemporaneous with the city's apogee.

In summary, the Tollan Complex is a group of pottery types that represent an integration of different cultural traditions. It is clear that the Toltec culture and the origins of Tula are linked to various cultural traditions that are very clearly manifested in the Tollan Complex, as in other cultural expressions such as architecture and sculpture. The majority of the Tollan types are found together in almost any kind of habitational context in the city of Tula, and they coexisted for approximately 250 years, disappearing with the destruction of the Toltec state. Even though it is clear that Tula was not totally depopulated at the end of the Tollan Phase, the ceramic tradition of the remaining people almost completely changed with the introduction of Aztec wares (Cobean 1990; Cobean and Mastache 1989).

4

Classic, Epiclassic Occupations and the Early City

In order to understand the emergence of the Toltec state, it is necessary to take into account processes that were initiated some centuries earlier, during the Teotihuacan and Coyotlatelco occupations of the area, because these cultures constitute fundamental antecedents without which it is not possible to explain the process of formation for Tula. For this reason, in this chapter we will refer to the most relevant aspects of the Classic and Epiclassic settlements in the area, although very briefly, in order to have a global panorama on the dynamics of populating the area, and of this period, prior to the emergence of the Tollan Phase city.

This chapter is divided into three parts: the first section treats sites having Teotihuacan affiliation, which principally represent the Classic occupation. The second part deals with the settlements that represent a different cultural tradition, apparently originating in the northern periphery of Mesoamerica, the inhabitants of which were bearers of the Coyotlatelco ceramics, among other elements. This ceramic complex is considered in Central Mexico as a diagnostic of the period designated the Epiclassic. However, some carbon 14 (hereafter, C^{14}) dates indicated that these sites were probably in part contemporary with the Teotihuacan settlements in the area. That is, there was apparently a chronological overlap of the Coyotlatelco sites in the area with the last phase of the Teotihuacan occupations, but it is difficult to define, using the data currently available and without excavations, the density and extension of Metepec Phase occupations, and therefore determine which Teotihuacan sites did indeed coexist with the Coyotlatelco population of the area. The third part of the chapter refers to the early city of Tula, which corresponds to the second phase of the Coyotlatelco occupation and constitutes the initial nucleus upon which the Tollan Phase city developed.

CLASSIC, EPICLASSIC OCCUPATIONS AND THE EARLY CITY

TEOTIHUACAN TRADITION OCCUPATIONS

The periodification and chronology of Central Mexico are subjects that are still widely debated, but in general terms and in accordance with the chronological framework presented by Rattray (2001: fig. 1b), the central part of the designated Classic era, covers about four hundred years, A.D. 200–600 (see Table 3.2) although the life of Teotihuacan was much longer because its beginnings date back to the beginning of the Christian era—the Tzacualli and Miccaotli Phases—and its collapse at the beginning of the seventh century A.D. (Rattray, personal communication).

During the Classic period, the area where Tula would later develop formed part of the direct sphere of influence of the Teotihuacan state, and this situation is clearly illustrated in the settlement characteristics of this period. The architecture and planning of most of the sites, as well as the ceramics, chipped and polished stone, and other elements permit the proposal that these sites represent the Teotihuacan colonization in the area, or at least settlements with close ties to the city.

There are three sites of this period having a placement and a ceramic complex that seem different, but further research is required to categorize them accurately and to be able to state whether they represent the local population of the area. They are located on small hills, with habitation zones covering the foothills and the ceremonial precincts on the summits, while the Teotihuacan sites are on hills or lowlands. As analyzed in detail in a study being prepared (Cobean n.d.), a local ceramic complex predominates in these sites that coexists with low percentages of diagnostic Teotihuacan ceramics, which permits their chronological placement, but more detailed studies and excavations are required for their proper definition.

As can be seen in Figure 4.1, the Classic occupation is basically located in the eastern part of the survey area. The settlement extends along the wide range of hills between the El Salto and Salado Rivers, and to the north on part of the alluvial valley and a strip that runs parallel to the Tula River. In the southern area, most of the occupation is located between altitudes of 2,100 and 2,200 meters, in a zone of low rolling hills that are principally the result of the fact that limestone is the dominant rock in the geological substratum. This is a very heavily eroded zone in which shallow Class V to Class VIII soils predominate that are not suitable for agriculture (see Fig. 2.4). On the other hand, the settlement in the northern part of the area mainly extends in the zone of foothills and the lowlands between the Tula River and the eastern side of Cerro Xicuco, which rises in the center of the alluvial valley, and it is interesting to note that in these zones all the sites of this period are located on good Class II and III soils and next to a strip of Class I soils that are potentially very productive.

The regional settlement system during the Classic period basically consisted of three different site hierarchies: larger sites, with an area of more than 80 hectares (which appear on the map in Fig. 4.1 as Level 1 sites); concentrated sites of between 10 and 15 hectares in area (which appear on the map as Level 2 sites); and zones of dispersed occupation, which in some cases probably correspond to small sites with a very few households or zones of dispersed material that represent both the immediate environment of other sites and zones of cultivation or other activities, which apparently did not imply permanent settlement.

Chingú

The Chingú site is located almost at the center of the territory occupied during this period. It is a settlement that covers slightly more than 2.5 square kilometers, which is undoubtedly the most important Classic period site of the area. Its location is strategic, not only because of its central position, but also because it is located on the boundary of two different zones: the limestone area to the south and the alluvial valley to the north, each of which possess different potential resources. The apparent association of this site with one of the most important traditional irrigation systems of the area, the Zanja la Romera (Fig. 4.2), and with the extensive zone of potentially irrigable land to the north is highly significant.

The Chingú site, at an altitude of 2,100 meters, was identified during the general survey of the

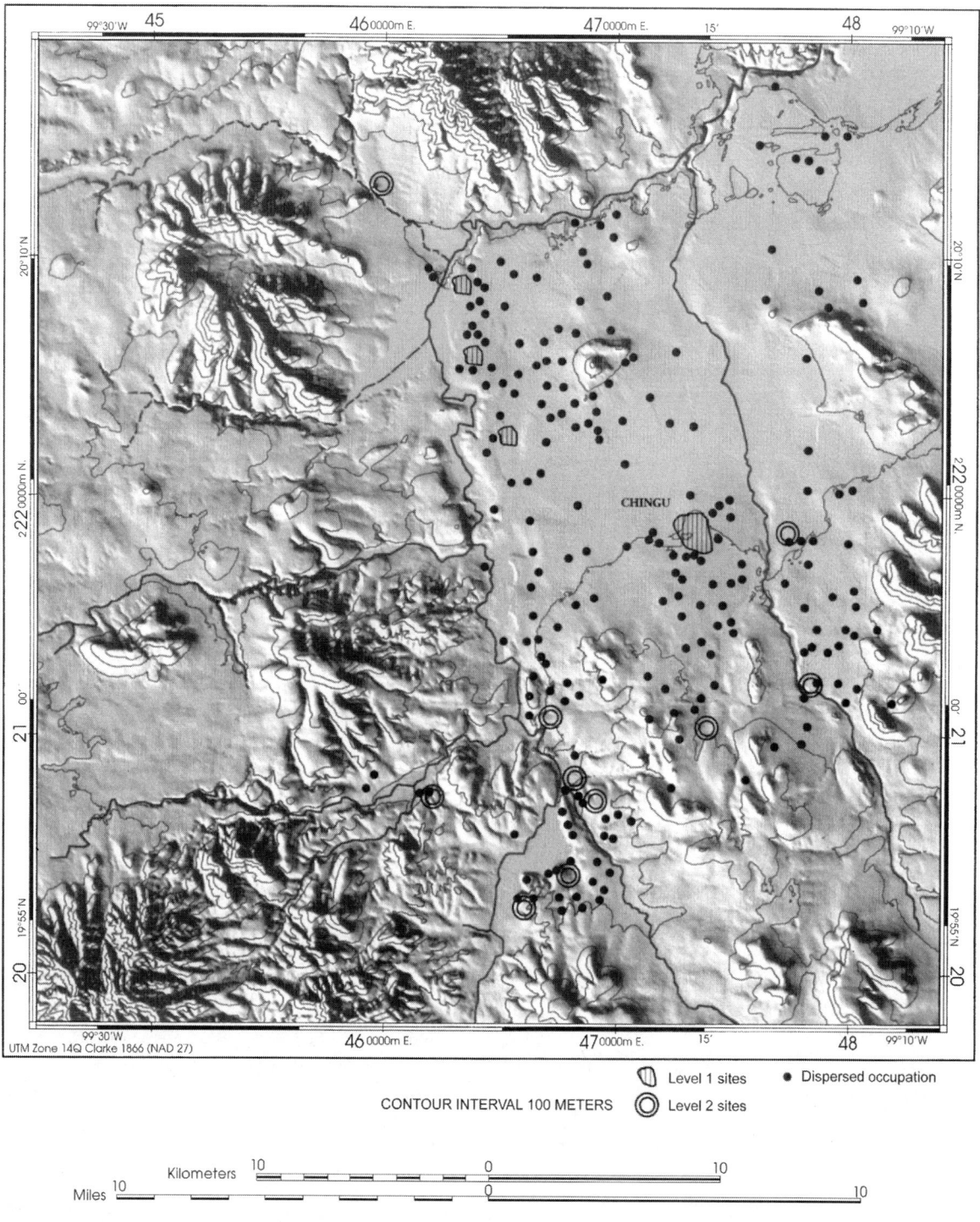

Figure 4.1. Classic occupation.

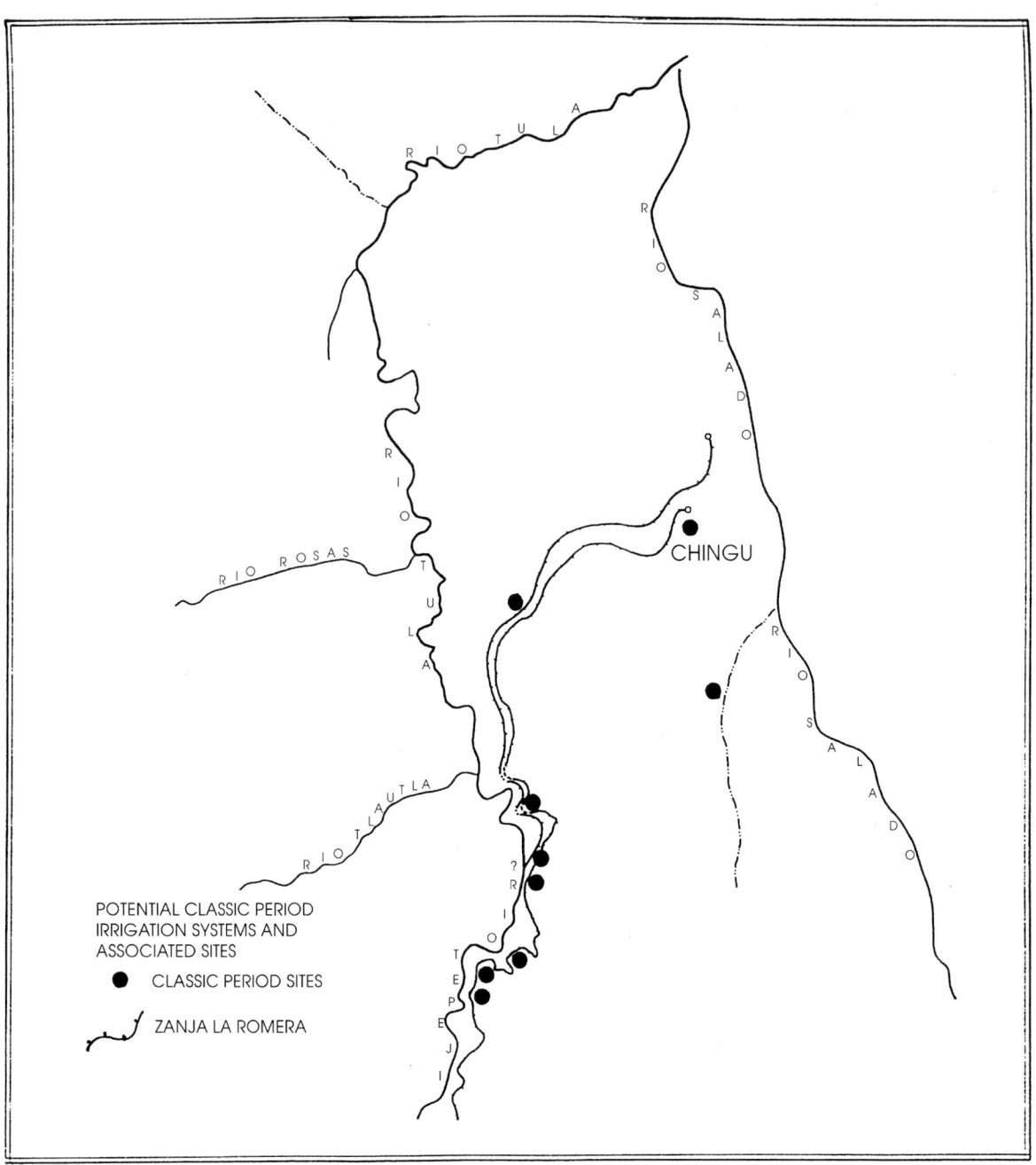

Figure 4.2. Irrigation canals and associated sites of the Zanja Romera and Zanja Nueva systems. The question mark indicates probable location of a dike.

area and, due to its importance, was the subject of a detailed surface study that included topographic maps and intensive sampling (Díaz 1980). This study indicates that the moment of maximum expansion for the site corresponds to the Tlamimilolpa Phase, with a considerable reduction in the area occupied during the Xolalpan and Metepec Phases. Much of the ceramics are identical to pottery from the same phases in Teotihuacan and probably were manufactured in that city, although there are also local versions of diagnostic Teotihuacan ceramics, and some types of local production (1980). The very high percentage of Thin Orange ceramics and pottery of a Oaxacan affiliation at Chingú is very noteworthy. In the area around the site, there is an extensive zone of dispersed occupation that apparently represents the immediate environs of this site and its areas of cultivation.

This small urban site was constructed along the lines of the city of Teotihuacan; there is the presence of *talud* and *tablero* facades and the general orientation of the settlement is the same as that of Teotihuacan. There are two extensive ceremonial precincts; the larger one possesses a plan and internal structure that are similar to the Ciudadela. The habitation complexes at Chingú appear to be small versions of the complexes characteristic of Teotihuacan (Díaz 1980) (Fig. 4.3). However, William Sanders (personal communication) observes that the residential compounds of Chingú, rather than being like small versions of Teotihuacan apartment compounds, are very similar to habitation compounds in some rural Classic sites in the Teotihuacan Valley.

Chingú was undoubtedly the regional center of the area during this period, that is, the paramount regional administrative and political center in the area and the link between the metropolis and this region, which seems to have been part of the direct sphere of influence of the Teotihuacan state.

Chingú is followed in importance by three sites that make up a strip of almost uninterrupted occupation parallel to the Tula River; these settlements of approximately 80 hectares in size also have many Teotihuacan elements. The settlement in the extreme south, which is located in part of the present town of Julián Villagrán, is a site that had already been severely looted in the 1970s; its architecture with *talud* and *tablero* was evident, together with the existence of plazas and also a Ciudadela-type precinct and the presence of diagnostic Teotihuacan ceramic types. Apparently an occupation corresponding to the Tlamimilolpa Phase also predominated in this site. Clara Díaz conducted a surface study here that included intensive sampling, but it has not yet been published. The other two settlements to the north are similar in size to the Julian Villagrán site, and they were also substantially destroyed. It is interesting to stress that a strip various kilometers long of almost uninterrupted occupation of this period is found in the zone of good agricultural soil that extends up to the western foothills of Xicuco, where there is also evidence of extensive dispersed Classic occupation.

Tula

The information available indicates that there probably were no relevant Classic period occupations in the zone where the Tollan Phase city of Tula would later develop. There are only some dispersed materials at several points and a concentration of sherds in the modern city of Tula de Allende's excavation for drainage done by the municipality in the center of the city in the Plaza de la Constitución (Mastache and Crespo 1982:13–20). The materials recovered from these excavations include what Rattray (personal communication) considers to be local versions of types corresponding to the Tlamimilolpa Phase, and some ceramics of Oaxacan affiliation. But given the context of this find, in the center of the modern city, it is not possible to define if there was a settlement for this period here or whether it was just dispersed materials.

The surface materials corresponding to the Classic period detected within the perimeter of the ancient city include those of the University of Missouri Project (Healan [ed.] 1989: fig. 13.5; Cobean 1978), which recorded some sherds of the Tlamimilolpa Complex at various points, and those of Mastache and Crespo (1982:18), who detected dispersed materials that correspond, according to Rattray (personal communication), to the Tlamimilolpa, Xolalpan, and principally Metepec Phases, including ceramics of

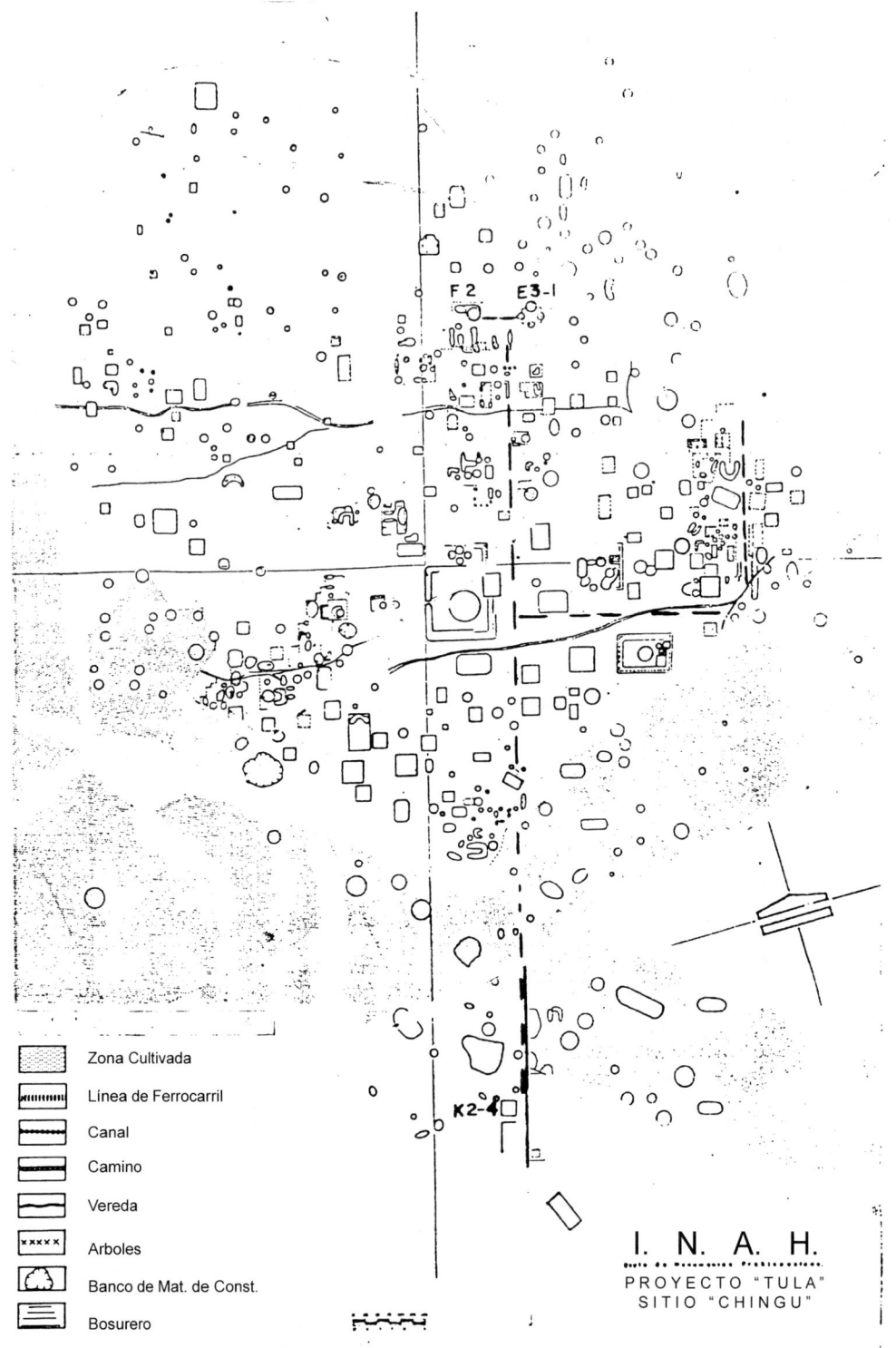

Figure 4.3. Plan of Chingú (Díaz 1980).

Oaxacan affiliation and fragments of figurines, in El Cielito, Plaza Charnay, around El Salitre, and in a strip around the present town of Tultengo (see Figs. 4.4 and 1.3). Cobean (1982), on the other hand, recorded a Xolalpan figurine in his excavations in Tula Chico, and Stocker (1974) two more figurines, one Miccaotli and another Metepec, in the excavation of the El Canal unit. Thus to date there are only isolated data that seem to indicate there was some type of dispersed Classic occupation in the zone that would later be the city of Tula (Fig. 4.4).

El Tesoro and Acoculco

In the southeastern zone of the study area, most of the Classic occupation is located at an altitude of between 2,100 and 2,200 meters, in the zone of low hills. The dispersed occupation alternates with some concentrated Level 2 sites. On the foothills on both sides of the Salado River, there are four small sites close to the present towns of Atotonilco, Progreso, and Ocampo, in the center of the intensive limestone exploitation zone; the site near the town of Atotonilco is on the right bank of the Salado River.

On the other hand, in the environs of the Requena Dam, on the summits of two small elevations, there are the sites designated El Tesoro and Acoculco, in addition to the dispersed material areas, that we will refer to in some detail. The site in the extreme south designated El Tesoro has been subject to previous investigations (Cook de Leonard 1956–1957).

As analyzed in a previous study (Crespo and Mastache 1981), these two sites are of great interest for our understanding of this period because they furnish important information about the Teotihuacan colonization in the Tula area. El Tesoro covers an area of approximately 10 hectares, and it possesses a ceremonial precinct formed by various platforms and mounds. In the 1950s, Cook de Leonard conducted excavations in the ceremonial precinct, concluding that the settlement corresponded to the Early Postclassic (1956–1957:117–120). However, the survey by Crespo and Mastache indicated that the principal occupation of the site corresponds to the Classic period, fundamentally to the Late Tlamimilolpa and perhaps Metepec Phases (Crespo and Mastache 1981). The Acoculco site is situated approximately 2 kilometers northeast of El Tesoro and is similar to this site in terms of placement, size, and chronology.

It is very important to note that in both these sites a ceramic complex of Oaxacan affiliation predominates, which is represented by diagnostic Monte Albán II and IIa phase types. As indicated in the above-mentioned study (Crespo and Mastache 1981:100–101), in both sites there are diagnostic Teotihuacan ceramics, principally of the Tlamimilolpa and Metepec Phases (Rattray 1973 and personal communication), that account for between 15 and 17 percent of the sample, while Oaxacan pottery constitutes 63 percent in El Tesoro and 54 percent in Acoculco.

According to the typology of Caso, Bernal, and Acosta (1967), the Monte Albán G12, G3, G21, and G1 types are present in order of importance, together with local variations of some of these types. In recent archaeological salvage excavations in the El Tesoro site, directed by Carlos Hernandez of the Hidalgo Regional Center (personal communication, 1994), a looted tomb of Oaxacan style was found with ceramics of that region, including two G12-type *sahumadores* and a G12 vessel. The fact that some types are only present at El Tesoro and that apparently there is a higher quantity of local Oaxacan ceramic variants at Acoculco suggest that the initial nucleus was probably in El Tesoro and later the population extended to the neighboring hill (Crespo and Mastache 1981:102).

There are also numerous signs, including burned sherds and in-process materials, that suggest that ceramics were manufactured in this area, especially local buff-and-orange variations of the G12 and G1 types (Crespo and Mastache 1981). It is interesting to note that the Oaxacan ceramics of the types mentioned and the local versions thereof are present in small amounts in all the settlements of this period in the area, including Chingú.

The existence of these two "Oaxacan" sites in an area colonized by Teotihuacan populations ought to be explained by taking into account the existence of the Oaxacan Barrio in Teotihuacan, rather than a possible direct or indirect tie between the Tula region

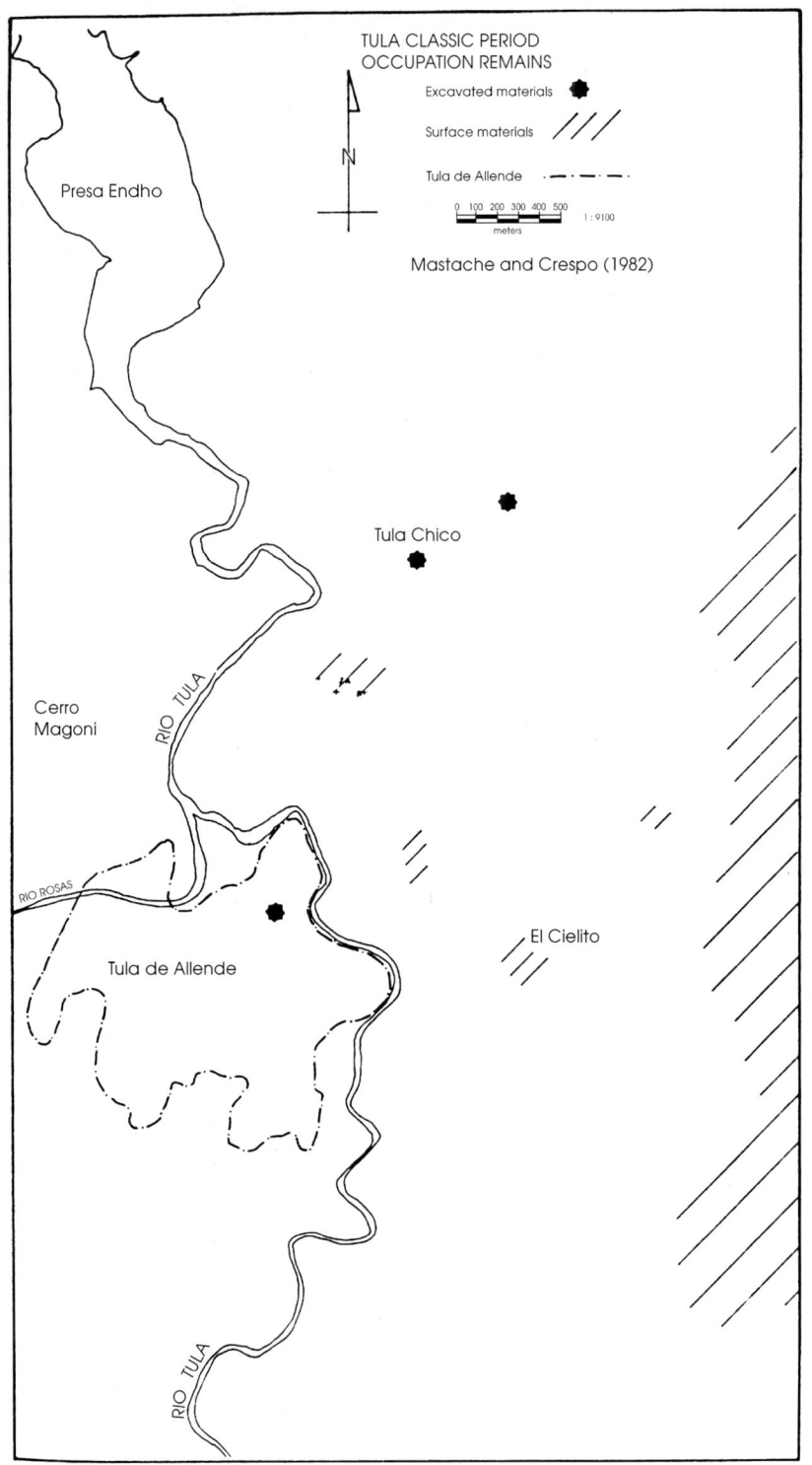

Figure 4.4. Classic period remains in Tula's Urban Zone.

and Monte Albán. The similarity between the El Tesoro and Acoculco ceramic complex and that of the Oaxacan Barrio in Teotihuacan seems to indicate that their inhabitants shared a common tradition, apparently based on the fact of their belonging to the same ethnic group, and they would reflect the ethnic composition of the Teotihuacan population upon their arrival in the Tula area. These people, which in Teotihuacan formed a *barrio* with its own characteristics, apparently continued to be differentiated and separated from the majority population when they migrated to another area where no city existed, settling in different localities than those occupied by the rest of the Teotihuacan population.

An important aspect of the settlement of this period is its apparent association with potentially irrigable lands, especially in the case of Chingú and the occupations close to the Salado River, located on the edge of the limestone zone and in front of the alluvial valley, with a wider zone to the north of quality soils that could have been irrigated by means of a system, similar to that of the colonial period, known as Zanja la Romera and La Zanja Nueva canals. As indicated in Chapter 2, this canal complex originated in the Tepeji River, to the south of the town of Tepeji del Río. It is a very extensive irrigation system that permitted taking water from the extreme south of the area to irrigate lands of the southern alluvial valley (see Fig. 2.10).

The Zanja la Romera canal is around 30 kilometers long, and along its course it irrigated lands of several colonial haciendas, principally those of the hacienda of San Miguel Chingú, via a side canal almost 5 kilometers long that went east, ending at the boundaries of the hacienda. Because there are Classic period sites at various points along the courses of the Zanja la Romera and La Zanja Nueva, and this canal system ends precisely next to the largest settlement for this period (Chingú), it has been proposed that there existed a similar irrigation system during the Classic period (Mastache 1976) (see Fig. 4.2).

In summary, various cultural elements, principally ceramic complexes, architecture, and settlement layout, suggest that the population of the Tula area during the Classic period consisted of three different groups: (1) people directly tied to Teotihuacan, who would constitute the majority population of the area and apparently represent the colonization of the metropolis toward this region; (2) people of Oaxacan affiliation, who were probably linked to the inhabitants of the Oaxacan Barrio in Teotihuacan; and (3) local inhabitants, who apparently constituted a minority in comparison with the Teotihuacan population.

The probable presence of groups of a Oaxacan affiliation strengthens the hypothesis that a population originating in the metropolis settled directly in the area. The colonization seems to have reached its apogee during the Tlamimilolpa Phase, but probably started by the Terminal Formative, due to the presence of the Tzacualli Complex ceramics in most of the Teotihuacan sites of the area. Considering the zones occupied and the distribution of the sites, it seems probable that the interest of Teotihuacan in this area was especially based on obtaining agricultural products through irrigated and rainfall cultivation, and especially in the exploitation of the large limestone zone, bearing in mind the importance that lime must have had for this city in the distinct stages of its development. In this regard, William Sanders (personal communication) has suggested that some of the Oaxaca-affiliated populations at Teotihuacan and the Tula region were masons or other specialists in the production of lime, and cites the existence of stucco floors and other lime architectural features in Monte Albán before lime appears at Teotihuacan.

The Decline of Teotihuacan

The decrease in the population in the area after the Tlamimilolpa Phase, which culminated in the apparent abandonment of the sites during the Metepec Phase, appears to be directly related to the process of the decadence of Teotihuacan as a center of political and economic power (Millon 1988; Rattray 1991), as part of a generalized phenomenon of radical changes in the distribution of population and in settlement systems, as well as the political and economic reorganization of most of the Central Highlands during the decline and collapse of the Teotihuacan state (Sanders, Parsons, and Santley 1979:183–219). Similar population movement processes have been detected in other regions of the Central Highlands during periods corresponding to the Xolalpan and Metepec Phases, especially in Morelos (Hirth 1981), Puebla-Tlaxcala (García Cook 1981), and in the Valley of Toluca (Sugiura 1993).

In the Tula area, a very vaguely defined ceramic complex that we have tentatively designated "Transitional" seems to correspond to this moment. These ceramics are reminiscent in shape to some Teotihuacan types, but also possessing attributes that are similar to Coyotlatelco ceramics, without corresponding to either specific types. There is, however, the possibility that these may be Coyotlatelco types that are not yet well defined and poorly represented on the surface because the designated Transitional occupation essentially consists of scarce and dispersed material, especially in the alluvial valley and the northeastern limit of the area (Fig. 4.5). In some points, higher concentrations suggest that they represent habitation structures corresponding to this moment, although it is clear that a certain degree of accuracy in this respect can only be obtained with excavations and more intensive sampling. Sanders (personal communication) proposes that the transitional ceramic assemblage in the Tula region may be similar to the Oxtotipac Complex in the Teotihuacan Valley.

The Transitional occupation seems to overlap spatially with the dispersed Teotihuacan and Coyotlatelco occupations in some points of the alluvial valley. There is dispersed material of both occupations that seems to coincide with Transitional dispersed materials. This correlation is dealt with in greater depth in Chapter 5, but it is interesting to observe that these Transitional materials probably represent the chronological overlap between the Teotihuacan and Coyotlatelco occupations of the area.

THE COYOTLATELCO OCCUPATION

Despite the fact that during the last fifty years researchers have indicated that the peoples of the Coyotlatelco tradition played a fundamental role in the decline of the Teotihuacan state and the emergence of Tula, Coyotlatelco is one of the most enigmatic and least known of the Central Highlands cultures (Armillas 1950; Sanders 1965; Rattray 1966; Mastache and Cobean 1989). There is no general agreement on its origins, and there are basically two approaches on the matter: some specialists propose that the Coyotlatelco people originated in the Central Highlands close to the Basin of Mexico and that the Coyotlatelco culture is just a transformation of the Teotihuacan culture (Sanders, Parsons, and Santley 1979; Dumond and Muller 1972); others propose that at least part of the Coyotlatelco population and many elements of this tradition have their origin in the northern periphery of Mesoamerica in regions such as the sierra between Jalisco and Zacatecas and perhaps the Bajío in Guanajuato and Querétaro (Rattray 1966; Braniff 1972; Hers 1989; Mastache and Cobean 1989, 1990).

For this period, there is a total change of settlement patterns in the area because, as was mentioned before, the alluvial valley and limestone sites that had important occupations during the previous period are essentially uninhabited now, while other zones, principally on the summits of hills and high hillsides, were occupied. There is also a change in the ceramic tradition, with various types of the Coyotlatelco Complex being characteristic of the period. The chronological placement of this complex in the Tula area is partly based on its correlation with sites in the Basin of Mexico and also on Cobean's excavations in Tula Chico (1978, 1982; Cobean and Suárez 1989), in addition to information derived from surface studies and excavations in other sites in the area (Mastache and Cobean 1989, 1990), as well as C^{14} dating.

As proposed previously (Mastache and Cobean 1989, 1990), the Coyotlatelco occupation in the area can be divided into two main stages:

1. The first one, placed between ca. A.D. 550 and 650, is represented by sites located on hilltops and high slopes, as is the case of the settlements of Magoni, La Mesa, Atitlalaquia, and Panoaya, which could be partially coeval with some Teotihuacan sites.

2. The second phase, between A.D. 650 and 750/800 (Prado Phase), would correspond to the development of Tula Chico as a small, quasi-urban nucleus upon which the Tollan Phase city would develop.

As can be seen in Fig. 4.6, the sites of this period are located, in some cases, in defensive positions atop hills, and in a sense surround the area instead of

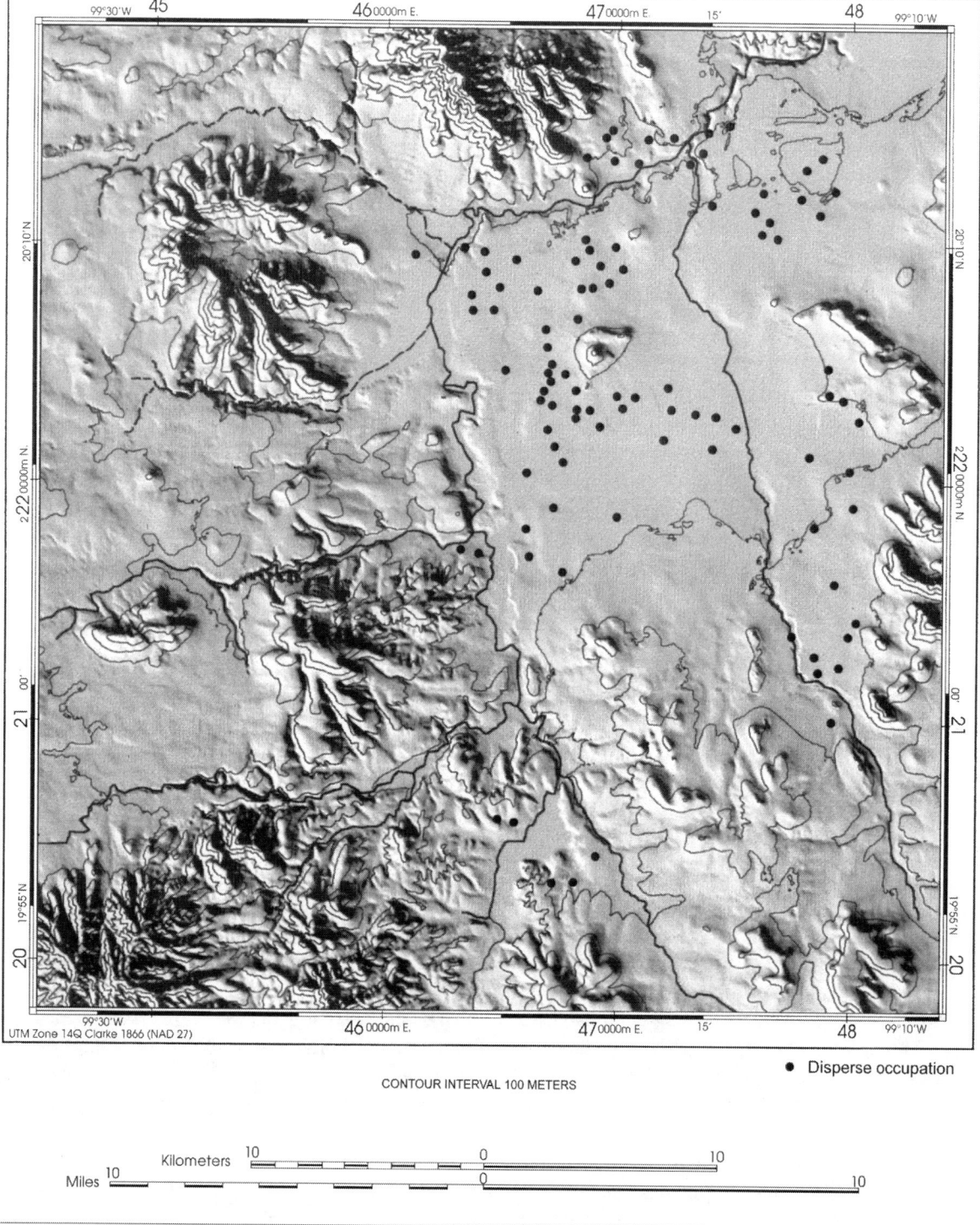

Figure 4.5. Transitional occupation.

occupying it. This could perhaps be because at that time the lower lands and the alluvial valley were still occupied by Teotihuacan populations, or because the situation of political instability did not permit settlement, since although these zones presented better potential living conditions and better access to water and other resources, they were very vulnerable from a defensive point of view.

Thus the Coyotlatelco settlement system and forms of population distribution are different from those of the Teotihuacan occupation. Indeed, there are fewer than ten Coyotlatelco sites that may be easily defined as units, with dispersed material surrounding them that apparently make up their immediate environment. The extensive zones of dispersed Coyotlatelco materials surrounding Xicuco stand out, especially those to the northeast and those that extend to the northwest of the limestone hills, which are probably not contemporaries of the settlements on the hills and in fact may represent the agricultural lands and rural environment of Tula Chico.

In addition to the ceramic complex, the Coyotlatelco sites present other elements that distinguish them from the Teotihuacan settlements. This is explained in another study (Mastache and Cobean 1990) and concerns the existence of a different cultural tradition, which is evident in the planning and internal structure, construction techniques, and architectural style, as well as a different lithic industry (Mastache and Cobean 1990; Patiño 1994a; Rees 1990; Jackson 1990). On the other hand, the settlement system and the forms of population distribution in the area are also different from those of the Teotihuacan occupation and indicate a distinct regional economic and political organization.

The early settlements of the Coyotlatelco culture constituted entities with their own cult zones composed of plazas having ceremonial architecture and religious precincts of similar dimensions, but each with its own peculiarities in terms of the shape, size, and distribution of the buildings. Some sites have more than one plaza with ceremonial architecture, as in the case of La Mesa, which has three.

Most of these sites also have systems of artificial habitational and agricultural terraces. In some cases, there is evidence for local ceramic production, and there are few products of commerce and importation, which indicates little long-distance exchange. There are variations in the size and extension of the settlements of this period. The size of the Magoni site is notable, but it is not evident that during the La Mesa Phase there was a center with greater hierarchy upon which the other sites of the area depended politically.

A brief description is given below of the general characteristics for two sites of this period where various intensive surface and excavation studies were carried out. Some of the results have been partially published, while others are in process.

La Mesa

The site designated La Mesa is, in our opinion, one of the earliest Coyotlatelco settlements in the Tula region. It is located on the top of a hill with the same name, to the southeast of the modern town of Tlahuelilpan, approximately 14 kilometers to the east of Tula. It is located at an altitude of approximately 2,100–2,260 meters.

This settlement covers an area of about 1 square kilometer, but it has some zones without structures. Apparently it is a site with a low population density. The site is structured in three sectors; each one is surrounded by extensive systems of terraces/platforms that, as in the case of other contemporary sites, were apparently habitation and cultivation zones (Figs. 4.7 and 4.10).

The placement of this site is very strategic: from its heights one can observe to the east the extensive valley of Ajacuba and Tepepango, and to the west Tula's alluvial valley. Even though La Mesa is very eroded, at the beginning of the 1980s this site had not been looted and was largely intact, with long terrace walls, remains of stairways, and numerous foundations of rectangular and circular structures having variable dimensions visible on the surface. This site possesses three different ceremonial precincts that differ from the closed plazas characteristic of Teotihuacan or Tula. In the case of La Mesa, the plazas are open with a rectangular form and built over a system of terrace platforms occupying the highest part of the settlement. Each plaza has a pyramidal building and a long rectangu-

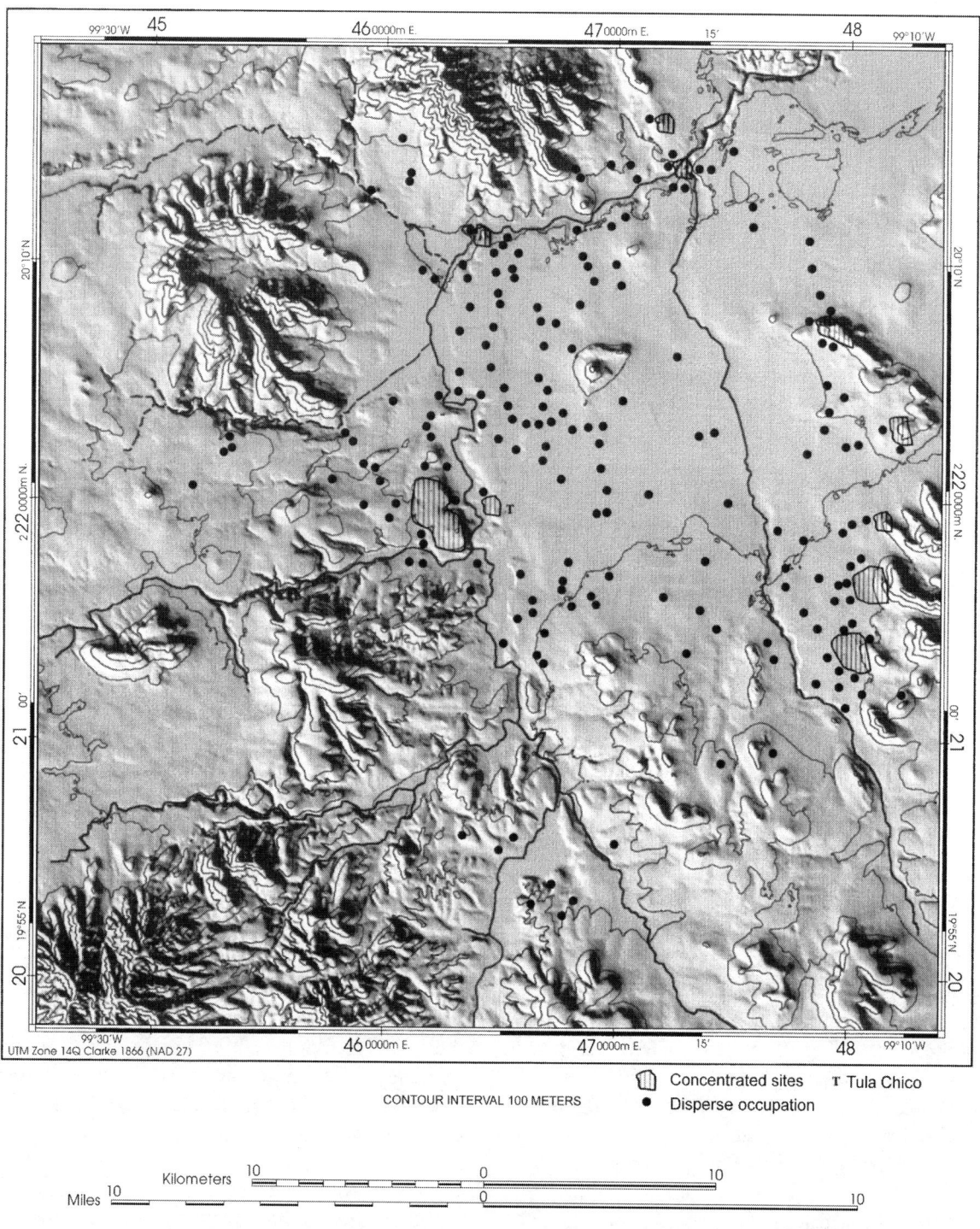

Figure 4.6. Coyotlatelco occupation.

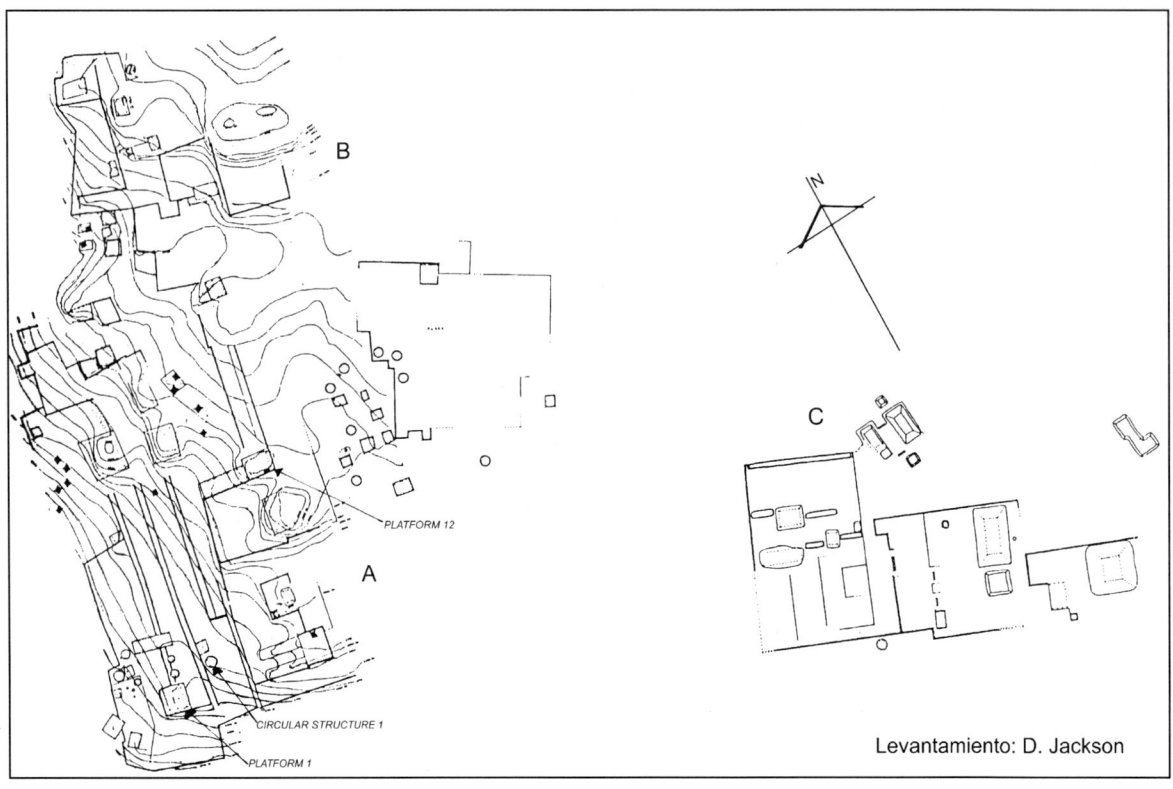

Figure 4.7. Map of La Mesa.

lar structure. What appears to have been the principal precinct (Fig. 4.7, A) is located in the central part of the most densely populated sector of the site. The spatial relationships of the buildings on this plaza are notable: the pyramidal structure is located on the east side of the plaza, with the principal facade facing west in the same position as that of Pyramid C on the Tollan Phase sacred precinct of Tula. On the north side there is a long rectangular building (Platform 12, Unit 33) with a placement similar to that of Pyramid B and the Palacio Quemado of Tula.

The excavations done in this rectangular structure indicate that it consisted of at least two different spaces: a columned vestibule placed in front of a rectangular hall having a very narrow entrance (Fig. 4.8). It was constructed on a platform approximately 1 meter high, having a preserved small stairway with balustrades on its western limit that permitted access to the upper level. Although initially we believed that this construction could have been a palace-like structure or an elite habitation, no characteristic contexts for domestic activities were detected, and it is very probable that this building possessed cult and ritual functions. The presence of a portico with columns here and in a domestic building excavated in the same site (Platform 1, Unit 99—Mastache and Cobean 1989: fig. 9) is very interesting because these porticos are the direct antecedent for the portico buildings and vestibules with columns that characterize Toltec monumental architecture, forming part of the architectural tradition of northern origin defined as "Salas-Claustros" by Hers and Braniff (1998).

It is worth noting that in sector C of the site (Fig. 4.7) there are two parallel structures that appear to correspond to a ballcourt, but without excavation it is difficult to be certain about the function of this architecture complex.

Figure 4.8. La Mesa: Platform 12, Unit 33, a structure with a columned portico.

Two types of residential architecture have been identified at La Mesa: rectangular structures approximately 10 meters on a side constructed on small platforms and circular structures having diameters varying between 1 and 10 meters and usually only surviving as foundations formed by double rows of thin basalt slabs. This means that the domestic architecture of La Mesa and other contemporary sites in the area is conceptually different from Teotihuacan and Toltec residential architecture because it consists of isolated individual houses and not groups of houses surrounding patios, as is the case of the habitational compounds of Teotihuacan and Tula (Healan 1989a; Millon 1981; Patiño 1994a). At La Mesa, the rectangular domestic structures possess a frontal portico supported by columns through which there is access to the principal part of the house, which consists of one or two rooms (Fig. 4.9). The construction method using small stone slabs (Toltec Small Stone) in La Mesa is a direct antecedent of the use of this technique in Tula that is so characteristic of the Tollan Phase (ca. A.D. 900–1150) (Healan 1989a).

It is very probable that the slab construction technique originated in the northern periphery of Mesoamerica, as there it is present in Classic era sites such as Cerro del Huistle, Jalisco (Hers 1989); La Quemada, Zacatecas (Jiménez 1989; Nelson 1997; Kelley 1971); San Bartolo, Guanajuato (Castañeda 1989); and Toluquilla and Las Ranas, Querétaro (Velasco 1989; Marquina 1964:239–242).

The La Mesa excavations indicate that the circular structures are associated with the rectangular buildings and that both had domestic functions. However, it is probable that some of the circular structures specifically functioned as kitchens and storage areas; the smaller ones could have been used as granaries. There are some differences in the construction techniques for different building types that deserve mention. In general, the rectangular structures are made with better materials: they have stucco floors and walls made of tabular stones and adobe, occasionally covered with sculpted stone panels. The circular structures, however, have earthen floors and the walls are apparently made of mud and wattle. There are burials under the floors of both types of buildings, but they are more numerous in the circular structures. In one of them, measuring approximately 9 meters in diameter, more that thirty burials were found, which were studied by Camargo (n.d.) (Fig. 4.10).

Some of the La Mesa buildings have relief sculptures with iconography that is similar to the monumental art of Tula during the Early Postclassic (Mastache and Cobean 1989:60, fig. 8). The most complex sculpture is a limestone panel with a relief that is vaguely similar to the images that Acosta identified as Tlahuizcalpantecuhtli on Pyramid B of Tula (Acosta 1945: fig. 19; Jiménez 1998). The La Mesa stone panel was found in the excavation of a rectangular residence (Platform 1, Unit 99), and perhaps represents the maize god, Centeotl (Mastache and Cobean 1989). A small sculpture in the shape of

Figure 4.9. La Mesa: Platform 1.

a human skull decorated the facade of the structure located north of the pyramid in sector A (Fig. 4.7) of the site (Platform 12, Unit 33).

The excavations at La Mesa recovered little evidence of social strata or internal status differences in the offerings with the human burials. Most of the offerings consist of one or two objects, generally tools and belongings pertaining to the individual's daily life: hoes, stone scrapers, and ceramic vessels. There are no formal tombs; most of the bodies were deposited in pits dug beneath the floors or in simple excavations in the *tepetate* (caliche). It is important to note that there are gray obsidian instruments placed as offerings in various burials. Long (up to 20 centimeters), complete prismatic blades without signs of having been used, large projectile points, and knives stand out, which shows that obsidian also had a ceremonial use with a special value, perhaps

due to its scarcity. Preliminary studies indicate that the gray obsidian used to produce instruments at La Mesa and other Coyotlatelco sites in the region probably came from mines in the Zinapécuaro-Ucareo region of Michoacán (Cobean 1991; Healan [ed.] 1989).

More than 80 percent of the stone for tools used in La Mesa is local basalt from the outcrops located on the same hill as the site, and they include scrapers, blades, and stone chips (Jackson 1990). Jackson's survey identified small areas for the production of basalt instruments, without evidence of specialized workshops. There are smaller quantities of instruments made of rhyolite, silex, and obsidian, and it is probable, as Jackson indicates, that many of the basalt instruments were used for the exploitation of maguey to work fibers and produce *aguamiel* or *pulque*. It seems feasible that most of the terraces

Figure 4.10. La Mesa: Circular Structure 1 associated with Platform 1, containing over thirty burials.

radiocarbon dates available, indicate that the occupation of La Mesa probably only lasted one century between approximately A.D. 550–650. Although the ceramic complex present in the site includes types that are similar to the Coyotlatelco complexes of the Basin of Mexico and the assemblage defined by Cobean (1990) in Tula Chico, there are also considerable differences in terms of the shapes, frequencies, and decorative elements. The red-on-brown decorated ceramics of La Mesa generally have more simple designs than the characteristic decoration of similar types in the Basin of Mexico and Tula Chico, and their frequencies are lower. There is also a series of brown-and-red monochrome types, including *ollas,* that have not been identified in the sites in the Basin of Mexico or in Tula Chico (Mastache and Cobean 1990).

surrounding the settlement were mainly planted with maguey. Numerous basalt scrapers associated with fragments of enormous Coyotlatelco *ollas,* 70–100 centimeters in diameter, which probably were used as recipients for water, *aguamiel,* or *pulque,* were found on the surfaces of these terraces.

Preliminary analyses of the ceramics of this site and its uncomplicated stratigraphy, along with the

Magoni

This site also apparently corresponds to the La Mesa Phase, and constitutes the most complex and extensive Coyotlatelco settlement in the Tula area. It is perhaps the direct antecedent of Tula Chico, which is located just 1 kilometer to the east. Magoni is situated on the hill with the same name near the ancient city of Tula and next to the two most important rivers in the area: the Tula and the Rosas. The settlement covers an area of approximately 4 square kilometers, and extends over the top and upper slopes of Cerro Magoni. The site has an extensive system of habitation and cultivation terraces several kilometers long that runs along the length of this elevation. An important production area for rhyolite instruments is located on the eastern foothills.

On the summit is the ceremonial zone, consisting of two different precincts surrounded by cult buildings and structures that probably were the residences of the ruling group. Despite its size, this site cannot be considered as an urban settlement because it appears to have had a low population density and little internal complexity.

The excavations made at various locations in the site show that the plaza and perhaps one of the main precinct structures have only one stage of construction, which together with the rather simple stratigraphy in the habitational zones indicates a relatively short occupation period, which, as in the case of La Mesa, appears to have been no more than one century. Apparently most of the Magoni habitation units are rectangular structures similar to the typical dwelling types of La Mesa, but without evidence of round structures.

The ceramic types correspond almost entirely to the Coyotlatelco Complex, and in general are more similar to the ceramic complex present in Tula Chico than to the La Mesa types. It is interesting to note that the figurines correspond stylistically to three different types, some of which are of the characteristic Coyotlatelco style of the Basin of Mexico (Rattray 1966), while others have attributes related to the Teotihuacan tradition and there are isolated examples of figurines similar to those of western Mexico.

There are three rhyolite instrument production zones on the foothills of Magoni. The principal zone covers an area of two hectares; the workshops produced a variety of instruments: scrapers, hoes, blades, and notched chipped stone. Many of these tools were probably used in the production of maguey fiber and *aguamiel,* and also perhaps to work wood. No other Coyotlatelco site of the area has lithic workshops that are as extensive and specialized as these zones of Magoni (Rees 1990).

El Aguila and Atitalaquia

Other coeval sites of the area share many of the characteristics (placement, architecture, ceramic complex, lithics) of the Magoni and La Mesa sites; however, unlike the Teotihuacan settlements or Tollan Phase sites that appear to be quite homogeneous, each one of the sites of this period had variations in terms of site planning, size, and internal structure. For example, the El Aguila site located in the extreme northeast of the region is very compact, with a dense settlement concentrated on a small *meseta* between two deep ravines at the confluence of the Tula and Salado Rivers—a privileged defensive position. In contrast, it is difficult to define the extension of the Atitalaquia site, because unlike other settlements of this period, it does not cover a well-defined topographic unit and some parts of the site have been severely damaged by current land use. The ceremonial precinct is located on an almost inaccessible hilltop with basalt cliffs occupying the highest point of the site. On the same hilltop, there is an extensive habitation nucleus, of which there are visible surface traces of numerous rectangular and circular structure foundations and parts of the long walls of the terraces. On the lower levels, on the foothills, there is an extensive, very altered and destroyed habitational zone.

The ceramics of Atitalaquia are very similar to those present in La Mesa, and thick, large *ollas* also abound, which were probably used to store liquids. The lithic industry shows some differences with that of other sites in terms of both the raw materials and the technology used (Jackson 1990).

There are few detailed studies of other sites of this period in the area. An important preliminary finding was published by Martínez (1994), who in a salvage study of the site located on top of Cerro El Elefante, in the north of the area, found a sculpture of a male figure that could possibly be of the Coyotlatelco era. On the southeastern limit of the area, as part of the survey of the Basin of Mexico, Parsons (1974) studied an extensive Coyotlatelco settlement on the top of Cerro La Mesa Ahumada, which has some similarities with Magoni in its planning and placement. Because of its size and location at the limits between the Basin of Mexico and the Tula area, this important site should be excavated and intensively studied.

As will be discussed later, it is important to emphasize that the Coyotlatelco sites in the area of Tula do not constitute a homogenous entity, and although most of the sites seem to share a common cultural tradition, there are notable differences in terms of particular aspects. It is clear, for example, that the La Mesa site is divided into three sectors, each with its corresponding ceremonial-administrative precinct, while Magoni, even though it is larger, has only one ceremonial center consisting of two adjacent sunken closed plazas surrounded by structures that are rather similar to the ceremonial precinct of Tula Chico. In contrast, the La Mesa plazas are open, having only one pyramidal structure with a smaller building. The precincts of other sites also present differences in terms of structuring, shape, and size. The orientation of the settlements and the residential architecture are also varied; the circular structures that are so frequent in La Mesa are rare in other settlements.

The rectangular habitation structures that are common in all the sites of this period also have differences in terms of size and construction techniques; those in La Mesa are generally larger. In Atitalaquia, the rectangular structures have thick stone walls and apparently lack columns. Further excavations of diverse sites of the area are required to define the diversity in the residential architecture of this period in the area.

The preliminary analysis of both the surface and excavation ceramics also indicates little uniformity in the types and in their distribution. Some of the principal varieties of Coyotlatelco Red on Brown ceramics are present in all sites, but there are important differences in the painted decoration styles and in the shapes. Much variation in terms of the frequency also exists for other characteristic types. There is, for example, a type of red monochrome vessel that is very common in La Mesa that is not frequent in other sites. There are also considerable fluctuations in the size, shape, and color of the *ollas,* and apparently in many cases these were made locally in each site, which constitutes a common pattern in settlement of different periods and regions. The transportation of these large vessels is not practical, because they often measure more than 1 meter in diameter and in some cases weigh about 40 kilograms.

Furthermore, the lithic industries differ from one site to another, basically in terms of the raw materials used (basalt, rhyolite, chert, obsidian) and sometimes in terms of the morphology of the instruments. Apparently, the lithic production in each site was almost exclusively for self-consumption. For example, despite the considerable extension of the rhyolite instruments workshops in Magoni, no significant amounts of the products of these workshops were found in the other coeval sites of the area (Rees 1990; Mastache and Cobean 1989).

The lack of homogeneity of the Coyotlatelco culture in the Tula area could be due to the fact that these groups had the same origin in general terms, but were different in particular terms, perhaps because they came from a region with a common cultural tradition, but with local variations, or they were the result of various migrations in different episodes or among different ethnic groups. Another important factor in explaining this phenomenon is the political fragmentation in the area, in that apparently at this time there was no dominant center in the region, and there was an absence of a state with the complex social, economic, and political institutions that characterized the Tollan Phase.

The Northern Periphery of Mesoamerica

It is not possible to understand the Coyotlatelco population in the Tula area without taking into account the probable northern origin of many aspects that are surely related to institutions and ideological concepts expressed in the planning and structure of the settlements, placement, architecture, construction techniques, and ceramic and lithic complexes, among others.

The placement of most of the sites on top of rather inaccessible hills is similar to the numerous centers of the culture designated Chalchihuites, such as La Quemada, Altavista, and Las Ventanas (Kelley 1971), or Cerro de Huistle and Cerro del Pueblo "Tenzompa" in Jalisco, studied by Hers (1976, 1989). Perhaps this is just a superficial similarity, because the location of a site could be largely determined by the topographic characteristics of a region or by particular political conditions, but it could also show cultural trends or the preference of some groups for this kind of location.

There are also important architectural similarities between the Chalchihuites culture tradition and the Coyotlatelco sites of the Tula region that include halls and porticos with sets of columns, types of plazas and the extensive use of tabular slabs in the construction of walls, and the frequent presence of circular structures.

Circular buildings and especially round habitation structures are not common in Central Mexico. Rattray (in press) recently excavated some Early Classic circular structures in the Merchants Barrio of Teotihuacan that appear to be associated with foreign non-Teotihuacan populations. Sanders (personal communication) proposes that these structures functioned as storage areas. Hers has found round structures of various sizes similar to those in La Mesa in the Classic era sites of the Sierra del Nayar in Jalisco and Zacatecas (1989 and personal communication). Additionally, Weigand (1979, 1985) describes circular residences and ceremonial buildings for the Teuchitlán culture in the highlands of Jalisco. In the same state, in the zone of Tomatlán, Mountjoy (1982) has excavated round houses that are very similar to those of the Tula area. According to Beatriz Braniff and L. F. Nieto (personal communication), in the Bajío there are circular Classic period buildings in sites of eastern Guanajuato. Margarita Velasco (1989 and personal communication) mentions that there are numerous circular structures in the Ranas site in the sierra of Querétaro.

The Huasteca is another region where circular buildings are common. There is a tradition of circular residences and ceremonial structures from the Middle Formative to the Late Postclassic at Tamuín, Loma Alta, San José del Tinto, and Tanleón, among others, that are representative sites (Merino and García Cook 1987 and personal communication; Stresser Pean 1971). However, the connection of the Coyotlatelco population in Tula with this region does not seem likely because other elements that are characteristic of the Huasteca during this period are absent in the area.

In pioneer studies over thirty years ago, Rattray (1966) and Braniff (1972) proposed that the Coyotlatelco ceramics are part of the red-on-brown pottery tradition that probably originated in the northern periphery of Mesoamerica. The Coyotlatelco red-on-brown pottery of the Tula area is more similar to the northern complexes than the examples of this type in the Basin of Mexico (Cobean 1990, 1982). The designs painted on the Coyotlatelco ceramics of Tula are generally coarser and simpler than the decorative elements of this type in the Basin (Rattray 1966; Nichols and McCullough 1986).

Although there are few detailed studies on the ceramics of the northern periphery of Mesoamerica, various northern types of the Classic era have been identified that are probably related to the Coyotlatelco complexes of the Central Highlands. Braniff (1972, 1975, 1999) published a series of red-on-brown types of the Bajío and San Luis Potosí that have very similar motifs to the Coyotlatelco designs of the Tula area, especially the San Juan Rojo/Bayo type of Villa de Reyes, San Luis Potosí, and a group of types present in San Juan del Río, Querétaro, and San Miguel de Allende, Guanajuato. Nalda (1975, 1991) describes a type for the Classic of southern Querétaro ("R/B El Mogote"), which has simple linear motifs that are almost identical to the Coyotlatelco red-on-browns of Tula (Cobean 1982, 1990). Some of the main types of red-on-brown and red-on-cream pottery of the Canutillo (A.D. 200–500) and Vesuvio (A.D. 500–950) Phases of the Chalchihuites culture in Zacatecas and Durango have simple linear and geometric designs that are very similar to the common decorations of Coyotlatelco ceramics in Tula (Kelley 1971; Kelley and Kelley 1971).

It is probable that many aspects of the Coyotlatelco lithic complexes also have their origin in northern cultures. During the Classic era of the Bajío and in San Luis Potosí, there are instruments made of basalt and other local raw materials that are rather similar to the Coyotlatelco lithics of the Tula area (Braniff 1961 and personal communication 1986; Crespo 1970). Many of the artifacts that Spence (1971) published for the Chalchihuites culture are almost identical to the Coyotlatelco instruments of the Tula area (Jackson 1990; Rees 1990).

Although there are few "absolute" detailed chronologies for the specific areas of the northern periphery of Mesoamerica (Kelley 1971; Braniff 1974; Hers 1989; Jiménez 1989; Trombold 1985; Nelson 1997), there are sufficient chronological data that make it possible to propose some hypotheses concerning the most probable region of origin for most of the northern elements present during this period in the Tula area. We have mentioned that these elements have specific similarities with two regions: the Bajío zone and the "macro-region" covering parts of the states of Zacatecas, Jalisco, and Durango, where the Chalchihuites culture expanded during the Classic era. Based on data of diverse nature, which are analyzed in detail in studies being prepared, we propose that most of the northern influence in the Coyotlatelco culture has its origin in the Chalchihuites culture or in other cultures that are closely related to these peoples. Almost all of the "northern elements" of the Coyotlatelco settlements are present in the Chalchihuites culture. However, the location, internal planning, and architecture of the known Bajío sites are somewhat different. The red-on-brown pottery of the Classic era in the Bajío is perhaps more similar to the Tula region Coyotlatelco ceramics than the red-on-brown types of the Chalchihuites culture.

It is important to stress that the red-on-brown ceramics of the Classic era in the Bajío always appear to be associated with high percentages of the ceramics known as "Blanco Levantado," a pottery tradition that is predominantly *ollas* (Braniff 1972; Kelly and Braniff 1966). However, Blanco Levantado is totally absent in the Coyotlatelco complexes of the Tula region, which, together with considering the other elements present in these sites that are similar to the Chalchihuites cultural tradition area, leads to the conclusion that this is the most likely region of origin of these groups. In Chalchihuites sites, there are similar red-on-brown complexes without the presence of Blanco Levantado.

THE EARLY CITY
Tula Chico

The city of Tula had a long life of more than four centuries, during which it underwent multiple changes and transformations. The initial stage of its urban development is a period full of questions, especially concerning the time of the settlement's beginning, its size, and its characteristics.

The early city corresponds to the Prado and Corral Phases, and its principal nucleus (A.D. 650–850) was around the plaza known as Tula Chico. The Prado Complex is undoubtedly the diagnostic ceramic assemblage for the initial stage of the settlement, but we do not know whether an urban occupation already existed at the time. Prado ceramics have been recorded in the deep levels of the excavations made in Tula Chico (Cobean 1982; Cobean and Suárez 1989) associated with the oldest structures of this monumental precinct, and on the surface they extend over a zone of approximately 2 square kilometers around Tula Chico.

It is worth mentioning that the Prado Complex shares some types with the earliest Coyotlatelco Sphere sites of the area, although in some cases there are significant differences in terms of shape and decoration style. On the other hand, the Prado assemblage includes some kinds of red-on-brown ceramics that are very similar to types common in Classic sites in the Bajío, Querétaro, and zones of the northern periphery of Mesoamerica (Cobean 1978, 1982, 1990; Braniff 1999; Martínez and Nieto 1987; Lopez Aguilar, Solar Valverde, and Vilanova de Allende 1998; Fernando Lopez, personal communication). But there is a substantial number of types that are not found in other Coyotlatelco sites of the area; the most characteristic ceramics of this complex includes cylindrical tripod vessels with incised relief or painted decoration (Cobean 1978, 1990), which have also been recorded in various, apparently contemporary sites of the neighboring zones of Chapantongo and Huichapan and in the south of Querétaro (Lopez Aguilar, Solar Valverde, and Vilanova de Allende 1998; Fernando Lopez, personal communication; Nalda 1975).

It is interesting that the Tula Chico lithic industry is clearly different from that of other Coyotlatelco sites in the area, since many of the instruments are made of obsidian, and in the opinion of Cobean and Healan, this material comes from three different sources: Ucareo, Michoacán, as the principal source, and probably Zacualtipan, Hidalgo, and Sierra de las Navajas. There are probable remains of a prismatic blade production zone near the monumental area of Tula Chico, and there is also evidence of long-distance ceramic trade, principally from central Veracruz and probably the Huasteca (Cobean 1982, 1990).

Undoubtedly, during the Corral Phase (ca. A.D. 750–850) Tula Chico was an urban or quasi-urban settlement, but there is no certainty about whether this early city of 5 to 6 square kilometers in size was already a fully developed urban center in terms of the socioeconomic complexity that characterizes a city, because we know little about its internal structure and its occupation density. Surface studies and research on the urban grid or layout of Tula (Stoutamire 1975; Yadeun 1975; Mastache and Crespo 1982; Healan and Stoutamire 1989) indicate that there was a habitational nucleus of approximately 3 square kilometers surrounding the monumental precinct of Tula Chico that constituted the political-religious center of this settlement. To the south, there are other zones of occupation for this period on the Cerro La Malinche and on the hill of El Cielito, and on the elevation where the monumental precinct of the Tollan Phase city would later be constructed (Fig. 4.11).

We do not know to what extent these zones of occupation were integrated with each other, and we have no knowledge of the continuity and density of settlement of this period, because with the exception of Tula Chico, all the area was covered by the Tollan Phase city. We do not know whether these zones were *barrios* or small satellite sites of the principal nucleus located at Tula Chico, or if all of them were part of an uninterrupted occupation of urban settlement with a continuous area of between 5 and 6 square kilometers. We believe that the latter possibility is the most probable, but it is evident that more stratigraphic excavations are required to be certain about the occupation density of this initial settlement and to determine its internal structure.

Tula Chico is located on top of an elevation formed by basalt outcrops and limestone, bounded to the west by cliffs. A large part of the surface of this hill was transformed by an extensive system of artificial terraces and platforms upon which the plaza and its constituent buildings were constructed. The principal precinct measures approximately 100 meters long and is surrounded by several kinds of structures that have not been excavated, which seem to correspond to pyramid bases, ballcourts, and large platforms that could have been buildings that are similar to the columned structures of the monumental precinct of the Tollan Phase. The few stratigraphic excavations made in this zone (Cobean 1982; Cobean and Suarez 1989) indicate that some structures have at least four construction stages.

The analyses of the urban layout of Tula done on the basis of aerial photography (Mastache and Crespo 1982) detected that this urban center apparently had three distinct grid systems with different orientations during the time of its development. The first of these grids seems to correspond to the Corral Phase settlement, and exhibits an urban layout and organization with a north-south orientation that includes the Tula Chico monumental precinct and the terrace systems that surround it (Fig. 4.11). There is also evidence of what seems to be an extensive complex of terraces and platforms with the same orientation on the hill where the monumental zone of the Tollan Phase would later be constructed. The corresponding plan (Fig. 4.11) also shows alignments that could correspond to the boundaries of habitation complexes, streets, avenues, or terraces, all with the same north-south orientation.

These and other data suggest that the early city of the Corral Phase included the hill on which the Tollan Phase monumental complex would later be constructed. The alignments detected by Mastache and Crespo in this zone seem to correspond to a complex system of terraces and platforms that, like Tula Chico, has a north-south orientation. On the other hand, the studies by Jorge Acosta in the 1940s detected a Coyotlatelco occupation in various points of the Tollan Phase monumental precinct, along with a structure under the Palacio Quemado that probably corresponds to this early occupation (Acosta 1945). Additionally, more recent excavations by Cobean (1994) identified architectural elements under Building K and the Vestibule south of the Palacio Quemado that may also correspond to platforms contemporary with Tula Chico.

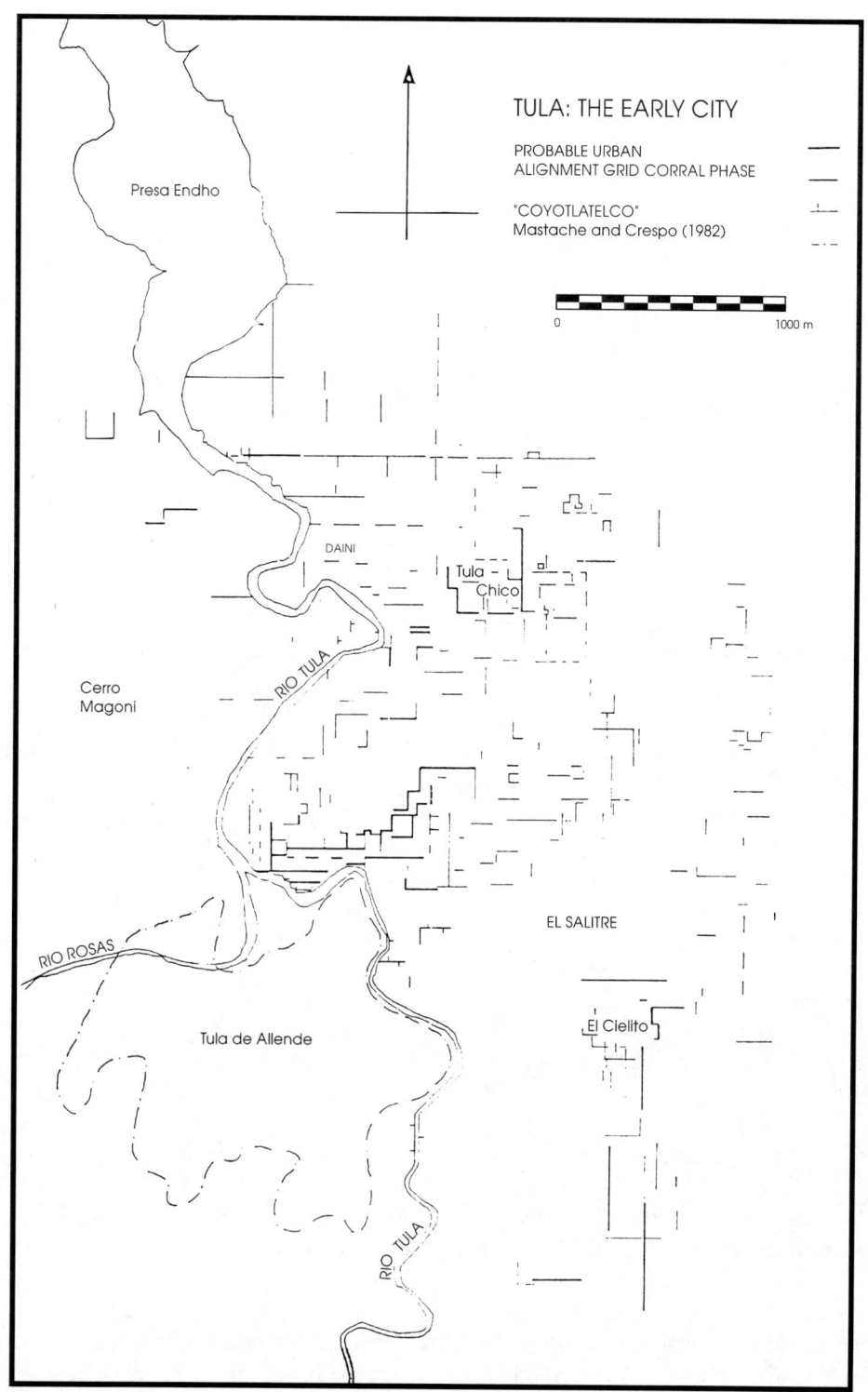

Figure 4.11. Tula: The early city. Probable urban grid alignment for the Corral Phase.

With the data now available, it is not possible to determine the nature of the Coyotlatelco structures existing under the Tollan Phase monumental center, but it is very likely, as has been proposed previously (Mastache and Crespo 1982:23–24; Diehl 1983) that the early city of the Corral Phase had two ceremonial precincts, one in this place and the other in Tula Chico. This proposal has important implications concerning the ethnic composition and political and social structure that the early city may have had, because the existence in this period of two monumental precincts would suggest the possibility of a less centralized government than that of the Tollan Phase, or the existence of distinct ethnic groups or factions that could correspond to the protagonists of the legendary conflict between Topiltzin Quetzalcoatl and the followers of Tezcatlicopa referred to in various chronicles.

Apparently, the moment of maximum expansion of this early city was during the first half of the eighth century, about A.D. 750. Tula Chico was abandoned approximately one century later and very probably burned and looted. The excavations made by Cobean and Suárez found evidence of burning in some of the Tula Chico buildings. The best documented example corresponds to what seems to be the last construction stage of a building located on the eastern edge of the main plaza (Platform 1) where there were numerous fragments of charcoal scattered on the burned floor along with the remains of what appears to be burned and collapsed roof beams. Here two Terminal Corral Phase *braseros* also were found, apparently crushed when the roof fell, and there are also other associated ceramic types of the same phase (Cobean and Suárez 1989; Cobean 2000).

Radiocarbon dates determined by Professor Austin Long of the Geosciences Laboratory of the University of Arizona aided the interpretation of these excavations. (The detailed interpretation of these and other dates from Tula will be presented in a separate publication with Professor Long.) He dated a total of five specimens from Tula Chico, four of which come from this excavation, and two (A-5852 and A-5853) are carbonized roof beams found in the center of Platform 1 that correspond to the final construction stage of this structure and its abandonment.

The other two specimens (A-5856 and A-5855) are fragments of carbonized wood associated with two prior construction stages of the same building. The dates obtained, calibrated to 2 SIGMA, have a wide approximate range of between A.D. 700 and 900, which does not allow for the precise establishment of the building's period of occupation and abandonment. However considering the stratigraphic data and the ranges of the dates obtained, it is viable to propose that the first construction stage of this platform could have been around A.D. 700, because there is at least one construction stage prior to the context dated (A-5855), and that the abandonment and probable burning of the building could be placed between A.D. 800 and 850.

The fifth specimen dated by Long is from another context. It is a carbonized maize cob (A-5039) from the deepest levels of the principal ballcourt of Tula Chico. Thus, the date of the sample is associated with the first construction stage of this structure at the beginning of the occupation of Tula Chico, and it could be as early as A.D. 600–650.

In addition to the abandonment during the ninth century A.D. of the political-religious center of the early city, there was a radical transformation. The changes include the construction of a new monumental center of much larger proportions than Tula Chico's, on the nearby elevation to the south, very probably covering a preceding Coyotlatelco precinct. There is also a change in the orientation of the grid of the city, which is now oriented like the new sacred precinct, with a deviation of approximately 17° to the east (which is the same as in Teotihuacan). Apparently streets, avenues, and buildings follow the new orientation, and during the following century (Early Tollan Phase), the initial urban nucleus becomes a more complex city that covers an area of almost 13 square kilometers (see Fig. 5.6). As mentioned in Chapter 3, these transformations also correspond to important changes in the ceramic traditions.

It is only possible to speculate about the causes behind such a drastic urban transformation, but it is evident that the abandonment of Tula Chico and the creation of a new monumental precinct are related to important political and religious changes. As pro-

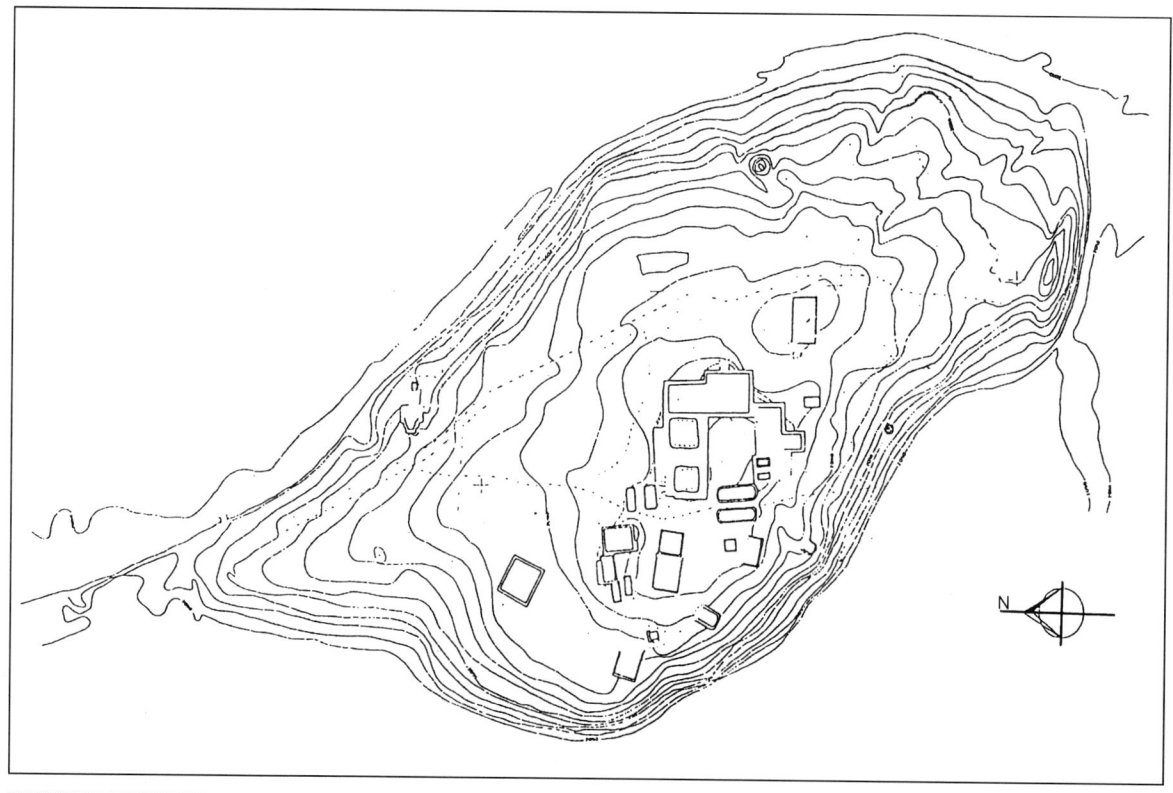

Figure 4.12. Tula Chico.

posed before (Mastache and Crespo 1982; Mastache and Cobean 1985), this transformation could have been linked to some of the central events referred to in diverse chronicles and historical sources regarding the conflict between the priest-king Topiltzin Quetzalcoatl and the followers of Tezcatlipoca, which ended with the expulsion of Quetzalcoatl and his group. There is no consensus in the various sources about the date of this event. Some historical records associate it with the foundation of Tula, while others relate it to the city's apogee or a period immediately prior to the end of the city. But irrespective of whether the Quetzalcoatl-Tezcatlipoca conflict is legendary or historical, the research that has been done to date on Tula Chico indicates that the main plaza and its buildings were abandoned without new buildings being erected, and that during the following centuries this center continued to be uninhabited although it was surrounded by the living city of the Tollan Phase. Perhaps, as observed by Stocker (1983), this abandonment was maintained as a monument and permanent testimony to the magnitude of the events that took place there.

It is evident that we have more questions than answers about the beginning of Tula and the early city. Intensive studies in this almost unknown zone of the city are required in order to understand the formation process of this urban center. The fundamental themes to be investigated concern the chronology of the beginning and end of the early city and the characterization of this settlement. Also needed is a study of the ethnic and cultural origins of Tula that apparently integrates populations associated with preceding Teotihuacan culture and groups having ties with the northern periphery of Mesoamerica (Jiménez Moreno 1941, 1959; Mastache and Cobean 1985, 1989, 2000; Hers 1989; Hers and Braniff 1998). Some of the founding population of Tula

Chico probably were direct descendents of the preceding Teotihuacan peoples in the region.

As analyzed in the following chapter, Tula's cultural ties with Teotihuacan, as well as its northern origins, are evident not only in the ceramics, but also in the planning, architecture, and the iconography of the Tollan Phase sacred precinct, but we do not know what the situation was in the case of Tula Chico. We are unsure of the kinds of buildings that formed this precinct, their architectural characteristics, function, and iconography, because to date we only have a schematic map of the plaza and its buildings (Fig. 4.12). It is significant that the plaza of Tula Chico does not seem to share the similarity that the Tollan Phase precinct has with Teotihuacan, in terms of the location of the two principal pyramids (see Chapter 5). In Tula Chico, the two mounds that appear to be pyramid bases do not seem to have the same spatial relationship as Pyramids C and B. In the location that corresponds to Pyramid C, there is a long rectangular platform (Platform 1), which in contrast seems to be similar to the Palacio Quemado. Only the ballcourt seems to have a similar location to Ballcourt No. 2 in the Tollan Phase precinct (Fig. 4.12). Thus, research concerning the ideological, religious, and political continuity and discontinuity between this initial urban nucleus and the Tollan Phase city is crucial for our understanding of the formation processes of Tula and its urban development, its institutions, and its ideology.

5

The Early Postclassic: The Tollan Phase City

A key aspect of the settlement system in the Tula area during the Early Postclassic is the existence of a great city, which indicates a fundamental difference with respect to the other occupation periods and determines the particular population distribution along with a different kind of exploitation of natural resources. For the first time, the area was the heartland of a large state, and the complexity of the existing institutions is manifested in the size and internal structure of the city together with the population distribution and the specific settlement patterns in the city's direct sustaining area.

During this period, Tula and the sites in the area formed a territorial, political, and economic unit that constituted the core state, and the regional settlement cannot be explained without considering the city and vice versa. The city itself never constitutes a complete entity: the metropolis and its surrounding region are inseparable; they are parts of the same system and form an organic unity. For these reasons, we will begin the analysis for this period with the ancient city.

THE CITY

No one knows better than thou, wise Kublai, that one should never confuse the city with the discourse which describes it.
—ITALO CALVINO, *Las Ciudades Invisibles,*
México: Ediciones Minotauro

Among Mesoamerican peoples, as in other cultures, essential principles exist for the organization of space that are closely linked to the world view of these societies and to the functions and specific nature of the settlements. In the structure and planning of Mesoamerican urban centers, there are symbolic, ideological, and functional aspects, along with other factors related to cosmogony, the organization of production, characteristics of consumption patterns, and the expression of a specific structure of social classes.

A city can be structured in very different ways, organizing the urban space in elements and units having variable character and dimensions. As Castells (1982) and others have shown, the study of specific forms of a city's organization is based on the premise that urban space is not organized randomly and that its structuring expresses ideological aspects along with specific social and economic processes. Thus the spatial units inside a city are the expressions of diverse kinds of key entities.

In the case of Tula, some elements that are necessary for a formal urban analysis are lacking, not only due to the limitations and the specific nature of the archaeological record, but because fundamental information, such as the fact that no detailed map of the ancient city was ever made, is now lost to us.

An urban analysis of a city involves the study of many aspects concerning its topographic-ecological setting, form, extension, planning, and structure. This includes investigating specific forms of the organization of space: density of buildings, continuity and discontinuity of urban spaces, proportions of open spaces and masses of constructions, the separations between building complexes, and the definition of different levels of spatial units, including their dimensions and the characteristics of their specific forms of articulation such as axes and circulation routes, among many other aspects. This type of investigation also involves the qualitative analysis of the units composing the city: the definition of the nature and function of the constructed spaces and of the open ones, of the public and private zones—plazas, cult areas, administration areas, storage areas, temples, markets, and habitation zones—which can be continuous or discontinuous, homogeneous or heterogenous.

Obviously, because no detailed map exists for most of ancient Tula, there are important limitations for analyzing its general urban plan and for defining its basic units, together with their characteristics and functions. In addition, we can say little concerning the city's internal communication network, including the routes that articulated and communicated between different urban units, such as streets, thoroughfares, and principal arteries or axes. We only possess some general ideas concerning the planning, the grid systems, and the internal structure of the city, along with other important aspects of its spatial ordering. In this chapter, we will present problems and working hypotheses that in some cases can still be investigated in the field more than we will deal with data and conclusions.

Location and Setting

The study of the specific location or setting of an archaeological site concerns the relation of this settlement with its surrounding physical environment, its placement with regard to local topography, and many other factors that might have been considered in the development of this place such as soils, geology, proximity to water sources, wind directions, relationships to cultivated lands and other settlements, the possibility of controlling specific resources, proximity to strategic routes or other communication systems, or perhaps the symbolic importance of the place in terms of sacred ideology or cosmogony. This means that the placement of a settlement depends not only on physical factors, but also on a multitude of aspects and circumstances that varied from one society to another and from one period to another (George 1976). The ideal settlement location for a specific human group could be quite inappropriate for a different group. If, for example, defensive needs are a high priority for a population, or a strategic placement with regard to a specific resource or to important commercial routes, the settlement perhaps will develop in a place that apparently does not possess easy access to important resources such as water or agricultural lands, but will possess attributes that provide for the essential needs of survival for this society in terms of its historical circumstances, or that correspond to fundamental cosmogonic concepts of the people involved.

Thus the location of a city or other site should be studied within a perspective that goes beyond the site itself and its surrounding area to consider a multitude of factors that could have determined the selection of this specific place based on the characteristics of the society and its particular historical conditions. A region can possess numerous settings, all of which are potentially adequate for a city, but urban centers do not develop in all these places because, in the process of urbanization, various aspects intervene besides the physical setting, such as ideological, historical, political, and economic factors.

In the case of Tula, if the city's setting is analyzed in a context larger than its specific region, it is evident that it has a priviledged location because no natural barrier exists between the Tula area and the Basin of Mexico. In this sense, the Tula region can be considered a northern prolongation of the Basin, with which it shares some advantages of a central location in terms of access to a great variety of important economic resources, trade networks, and natural passes connecting it with other regions of Mesoamerica, especially the Central Highlands, the northern Mesoamerican periphery, and western Mexico.

The region where the ancient city developed possesses direct access to north and west Mexico via southern Queretaro, which connects to the Bajío and the central highlands of Michoacan without encountering significant geographical barriers. The Michoacan highlands were especially important because, among other factors, it contains the Ucareo-Zinapecuaro obsidian source that was the principal supplier of obsidian for Tula during the beginning of its urban development. The strategic location of the Tula region is well illustrated by considering, as an example, its relationship to obsidian sources: Tula also has direct access to the Teotihuacan Valley and to the Sierra de Pachuca, both of which possess key obsidian quarries—especially the Sierra de Pachuca, which contains obsidian quarries such as the Sierra de las Navajas mines that were extensively exploited by the Toltec state (Healan [ed.] 1989; Cobean 1991).

Another series of geographic relationships concern the Tula River, which forms part of the great Río Pánuco drainage system crossing the Huasteca and emptying into the Gulf of Mexico. In this case, no direct passes exist (like those to north and west Mexico) because the river is not navigable until it reaches the coast, but it probably was an important route to the Huasteca, where several authors have proposed hypotheses concerning ties with Tula that are evident in its ceramic complexes, architecture, and other aspects (Stresser Pean 1971; Davies 1977; Cobean and Mastache 1985). It is worth noting that another obsidian source that supplied Tula is in the area of Zacualtipan, Hidalgo, located on the course of the Río Pánuco (Cobean 1991).

With regard to the specific setting of the city, it is obvious that Tula possessed a very strategic location from several points of view. Tula's city developed on an elevation at the confluence of two of the three most important rivers in the area, occupying a place that dominates the alluvial valley and adjacent irrigable lands (Figs. 5.1 and 5.2). The elevation where the principal nucleus of the city is located is surrounded by cliffs on the south and protected on the west by Cerro Magoni. The small Magoni-Bojay mountain range to the west not only protects the city against winds and possible enemy attacks; its summit provides an ideal lookout point for the vigilance of a very large area extending especially toward the north and the east.

Thus the city possessed a very favorable setting in a defensible area, adjacent to irrigatable land, and at the confluence of two permanently flowing rivers. In addition, the monumental precinct, which constituted the religious, political, and administrative center of the city, also possessed particularly strategic conditions in that it was surrounded by great terraces and platforms and by steep cliffs next to the river (see Figs. 1.1 and 2.1).

With regard to land exploitation, Tula had a key setting; the placement of most of this urban center on an elongated mesa is due without doubt not only to the defensive potential of this zone, but also to a need by the city's people to avoid occupying lower-lying lands that were better used for agriculture. Most of the city extended over zones with poor agricultural potential, much of which apparently was bare bedrock without soil. Healan's ([ed.] 1989) stratigraphic analysis of the University of Missouri excavations at the El Canal and El Corral habitation units shows that these houses located on the east side of the ancient city were constructed directly on the limestone conglomerate bedrock (Márquez 1986). Likewise, the habitational structure that Healan (1986) excavated in the obsidian workshop zone in the extreme south of the city was built directly on

THE EARLY POSTCLASSIC: THE TOLLAN PHASE CITY

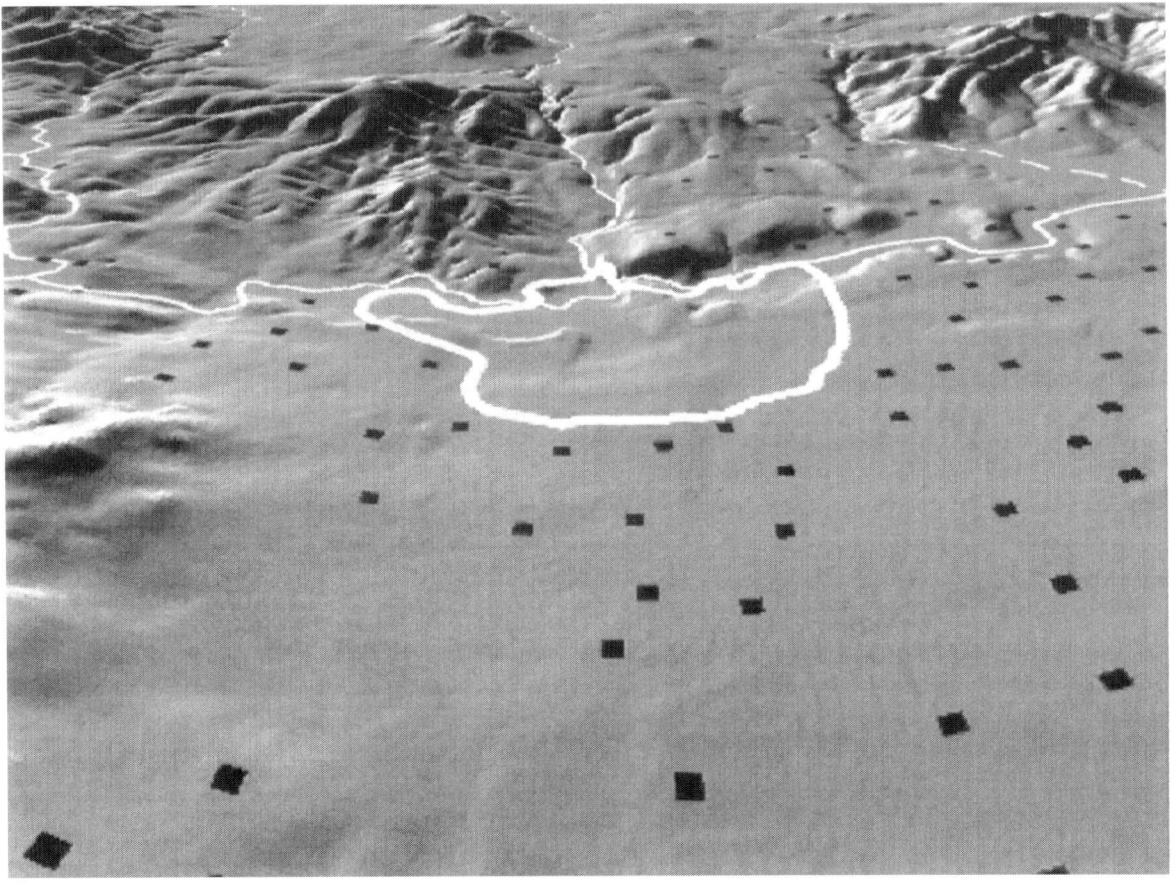

Figure 5.1. Tula: East view. (In this and other digital maps, the white lines indicate rivers and the limits of the Tollan Phase city, and the black squares indicate rural sites of this period.)

heavily eroded terrain, thus supporting this author's proposal that only a few sectors of the ancient city possessed soil of any kind.

The rocky substrata over which much of the city was built also constituted a basic construction material that the inhabitants used for making the foundations and walls of dwellings and other structures. Near one of the house groups in the El Canal excavation, Healan (1989a) found what appears to have been a small quarry for obtaining blocks of *tepetate* that were used in the construction of a nearby building.

When considering the possibility of other potential sites for the city within this region, it is noted that the western half of the area is unsuitable, especially because of the uneven terrain. However, if on the contrary the urban center was in the lower-lying lands of the alluvial valley, in the eastern part of the area, almost 16 square kilometers of cultivatable land would have been used, some of which is suitable for intensive agriculture, in addition to the city's losing its strategic location regarding the rivers and defensive possibilities.

The Teotihuacan site of Chingú is a direct antecedent of urbanism in the area. It is a small urban settlement of over 2 square kilometers that could be considered a feasible potential site for the development of the Toltec city, but Tula did not arise in this place and there is no direct continuity between this Classic center and the Early Postclassic city.

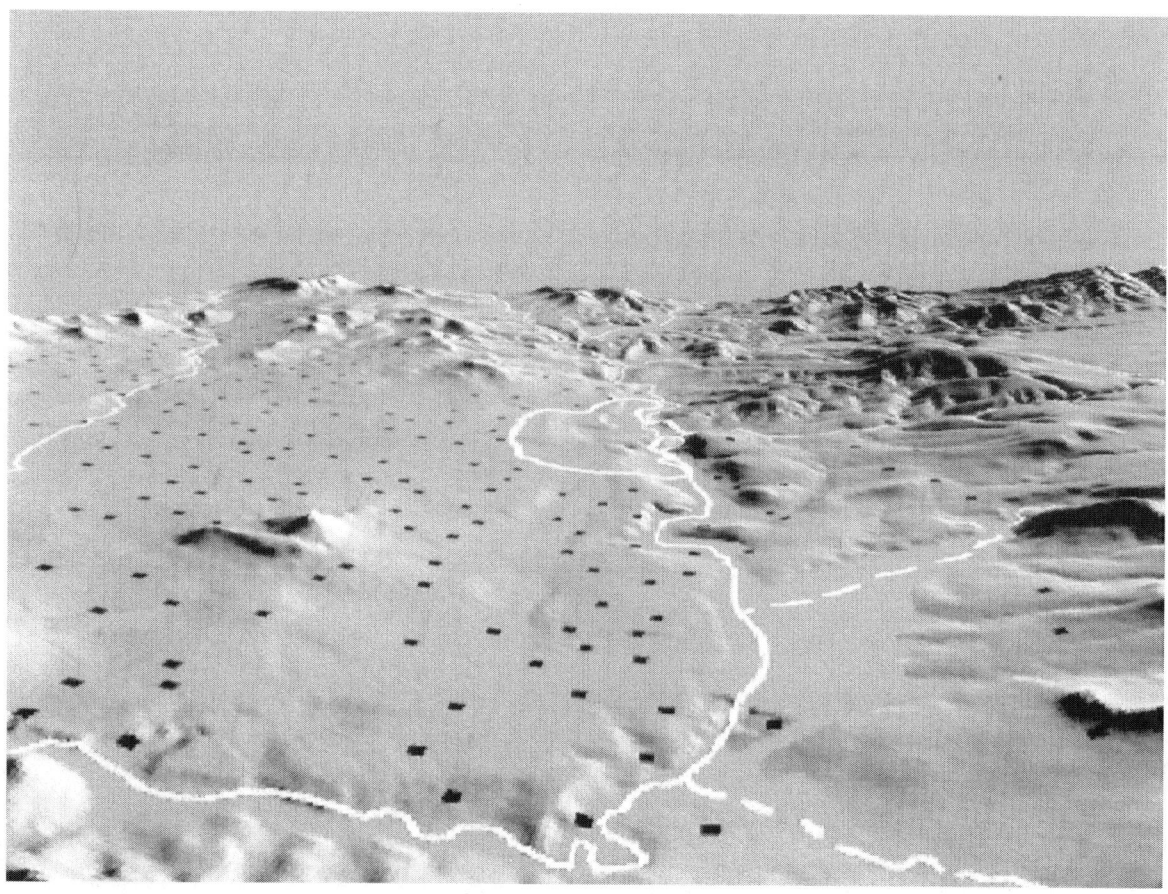

Figure 5.2. The Tula area seen from the north.

Shape, Size, and Limits

The shape and general plan of the site are closely linked aspects. The relief and topography influenced the distribution and planning of the settlement, but the shape and planning also seem related to the nature of the city and various kinds of necessities, practical needs, production, circulation and consumption needs, and what we would call ideological needs, that is, with a specific vision of the world and with diverse social and ideological factors.

The nature of the city, its institutions and peculiar forms of life, are expressed in the particular fashion of the organization of the territory, in the ordering of the urban space. As Lefebvre rightly expresses: "Each mode of production has produced a type of city as something fundamental, which is immediately reflected by giving form to the most abstract social, juridical, political and ideological relationships" (1983:30).

The detailed analysis of a site contributes to the knowledge of the way in which the settlement was organized and the definition of its principal units and forms of articulation. The layout is related to its physical characteristics, its topography, location, and setting, and expresses functional needs regarding the daily lives of its inhabitants and ideological aspects tied to their view of the world. Here, as Castells points out (1982), the life of a city can, to a certain extent, be read by analyzing its structure and the distribution of space and by approaching the essential aspects of the ideology and the institutions of that society, which are also expressed in the plan and structuring of the settlement.

Sites such as Teotihuacan, Tula, and Tenochtitlan, which share the fact that they are Mesoamerican cities and are located in the Central Highlands, as well as having strong cultural ties, do however present vast differences in terms of site layout and the structure of their urban territory. These differences undoubtedly express cultural and ideological specificities, characteristic institutions, and the particular forms of life of these cities.

The shape, size, and limits of Tula varied with time: everything seems to indicate that during the initial phases (Prado and Corral Phases), the fundamental core was, above all, around the precinct called Tula Chico and on the hill located to the south, where the Tollan Phase monumental precinct was later built (Fig. 5.3), and that the city of Tula, during its long life, apparently had two great urban transformations. The first of these included the abandonment of Tula Chico's monumental precinct and the construction of a new monumental center having much greater proportions than the previous one, along with a change in the orientation grid, which like the new sacred precinct now is oriented approximately 17° east of north (the configuration called "Toltec A" in Mastache and Crespo 1982: fig. 4). The city also increased in size, reaching an extension of about 13 square kilometers. The second urban transformation appears to correspond to the late Tollan Phase ("Toltec B," 1982: fig. 5), that is, the stage of apogee and maximun expansion of the site. The urban orientation grid again changes, this time to approximately 15° west of north. The magnitude of this change is impressive if one considers that it must have involved a massive program of construction activities, with streets, avenues, and buildings being constructed or reconstructed in accordance with the new grid orientation. Nevertheless, it can be said that this new urban transformation was not as drastic as the previous one because it did not include the construction of a new ceremonial precinct; and the same center, with its plaza and buildings, conserved the previous orientation although the majority of its structures were modified and enlarged. As will be analyzed in a subsequent section, this urban transformation also appears to correspond with a change in the architectonic conception of the domestic structures, along with changes in the ceramic complex involving as an important aspect the increase in various types of an orange-and-cream ware tradition. It is this stage of maximum expansion of the city that we will take as the basis for the following analysis (Figs. 5.4 and 5.5).

Shape refers to general layout, extension, and features, which are related to the site's urban conception and use of space. In Tula, the topographic relief and the course of the river must have been important factors in its planning and layout. In general terms, the ancient city was rectangular in shape with very irregular contours on the edges, which were undoubtedly determined by the elevations to the south of the modern city of Tula de Allende and the topography of the Magoni-Bojay hills, which form a natural barrier to growth toward this western zone, while to the east, where there are no topographical barriers, the town spread from the higher foothills to the lowlands and neighboring hills (see Figs. 1.3, 5.1, and 5.2). The uneven topography includes hillsides, hilltops, and lower lands, with heights ranging from 2,005 to 2,060 meters in the higher parts. It could be said that the Tula River constituted the north-south axis of the city, although it did not run exactly through the center of the settlement, but rather on its western flank. The city's limits thus included the confluence of the Rosas and Tula Rivers.

During its apogee (Tollan Phase), Tula covered an area of almost 16 square kilometers, with a maximum length (north-south) of 6 kilometers and a maximum width (east-west) of 4 kilometers, although in some points it was only 3.25 kilometers. As mentioned before, the size that we take here as a base is that of the time of maximum expansion; the data on this come from studies by diverse researchers: Stoutamire (1974, 1975), Healan and Stoutamire (1989), Yadeun (1975), and Mastache and Crespo (1982).

From this total we need to deduct the El Salitre area, a swamp zone of approximately 1 square kilometer, which was within the perimeter of the urban center but not populated. The neighboring Alpuyeca

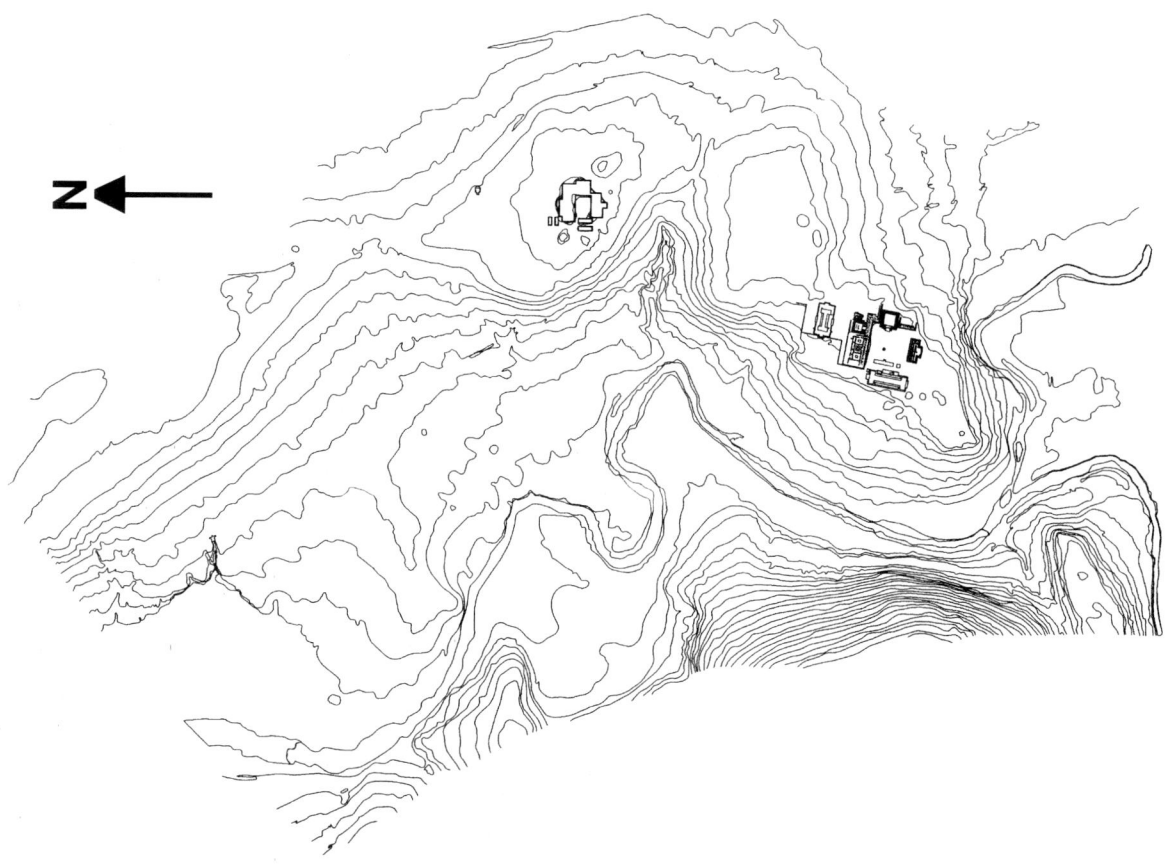

Figure 5.3. Topographic restitution of part of Tula's urban zone, showing Tula Chico to the left and the sacred precinct to the right.

saltwater spring feeds it and stagnates in this area. Undoubtedly for the inhabitants of Tula it was useful to have a saltwater swamp as well as a river within the city limits as a source of various resources, lake flora and fauna such as water plants and reeds and various species of fish and algae. The limits of the pre-Hispanic city included: to the east, the current towns of San Lorenzo, Tultengo, and El Llano and the hill known as El Cielito; to the southwest, a large part of the modern city of Tula and the La Malinche elevation; and to the south, a large zone of lowlands on both sides of the Tula River continuing to the current town of San Marcos.

The ancient urban limits are clear, although they are not bounded by walls or any other type of construction, nor do they coincide with any specific topographic unit. It is surrounded by an uninhabited area between 1 and 3 kilometers wide that marks the limits and constitutes a kind of well-established frontier between the town and the rural environment. Surely, as in the case of Tenochtitlan, and as was frequent in preindustrial cities, there would have been specific access points along this strip related to certain streets and avenues and perhaps check and control points for products entering and leaving the city.

This unoccupied strip would have been a kind of symbolic wall, an administrative and political limit that separated the urban community from the rural community, the city dweller from the inhabitants of

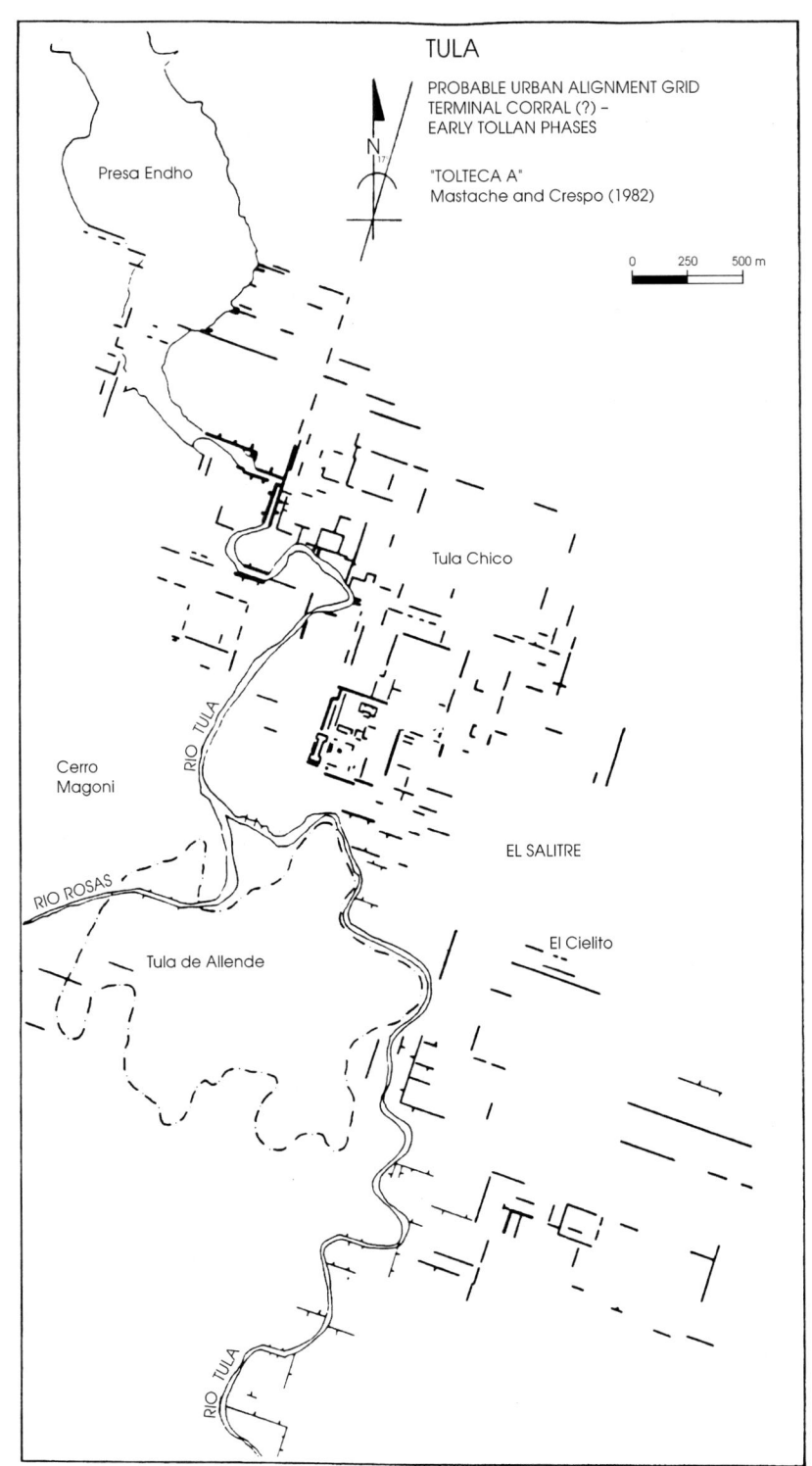

Figure 5.4. Tula: "Tolteca A." Urban alignment grid.

the area, although we do not know exactly what this meant in terms of status, rights, and privileges within the class structure of Toltec society. It is very likely that this zone was also an area of farmland immediately attached to the urban center and cultivated by its inhabitants.

Planning and Layout

It has already been mentioned that Tula had three different layouts during its history, each with different orientations that were surely related to fundamental political and ideological changes (Mastache and Crespo 1982); here we especially refer to the plan that corresponds to its apogee stage (Toltec B) (Fig. 5.5).

The Tula urban network is difficult to analyze, since there are no maps of the entire settlement, but also because of the architectural techniques and construction materials used. Tula was fundamentally an adobe city and was not articulated on long, straight axes, as in Teotihuacan, which would facilitate analysis. There is no evidence of avenues such as the Street of the Dead or the four avenues that started in the sacred precinct in Tenochtitlan. It is true that the urban zone has been severely altered and destroyed, especially in the last twenty-five years, and no research has been done to clarify this problem, but if avenues had existed with these characteristics, they would be obvious from aerial photography and within the site itself.

The topographic variation of the land that includes the El Tesoro, El Cielito, and La Malinche elevations, slopes, and lowlands and the Tula and Rosas Rivers, as well as the El Salitre zone, undoubtedly played a decisive role in the layout of the site, since the numerous natural barriers and uneven topography would make it difficult to have straight roads that crossed the city from one end to the other.

Some of the numerous alignments detected in the aerial photographs (Mastache and Crespo 1982) seem to correspond to different kinds of internal streets and communication thoroughfares. In the two layouts corresponding to the city of the Tollan Phase, there are signs of the existence of at least three avenues that cross a large part of the site from north to south. These axes seem to be separated from each other by a distance of about 400 meters (Figs. 5.5 and 6.9).

Some alignments suggest that the streets in Tula were interrupted at certain intervals to turn in a kind of L shape, which would mean that there would not be very long straight streets and that there would be 90° turns every now and then, with the street then continuing. However, the signs of L-shaped streets are more evident in aerial photographs than on the site itself. This is clearly seen in the stretch that communicates the two ballcourts of the monumental precinct and other alignments in various points in the city.

It is important to stress that the access to the habitational complexes was also in the characteristic L shape, as can be seen in the Toltec House excavated by Charnay, in the complexes studied by Healan (1977, 1982, 1989a and b), and in Building 1, located to the east of Pyramid B. These L-shaped entrances to the residential units imply that there was no direct visual access from the street and that in order to enter it was necessary to make a 90° turn. These accesses to the houses are so narrow that they only allow one person to pass at a time. The L shape is also present in the planning of the sacred precinct and in the shape and structuring of some of its buildings. The presence of this feature in the domestic and monumental architecture of Tula, and apparently in the layout of the streets and internal communication thoroughfares in various zones of the city, seems to indicate that this was a characteristic architectural and urban element in the site.

However, it should be clarified that streets interrupted with L-shaped turns do not appear to be a concept that is exclusive to Tula or to this period. Millon's plan of Teotihuacan (1973) shows numerous streets and secondary thoroughfares interrupted at certain intervals by small 90° turns, which then continue. That is, despite the axial symmetry of the city, many roads did not run straight for great lengths without L-shaped turns every now and then, like those detected in Tula. The presence of this element in Teotihuacan is somewhat surprising, since the principal axes of the city are straight avenues—the Street of the Dead and East and West Avenues—and this city

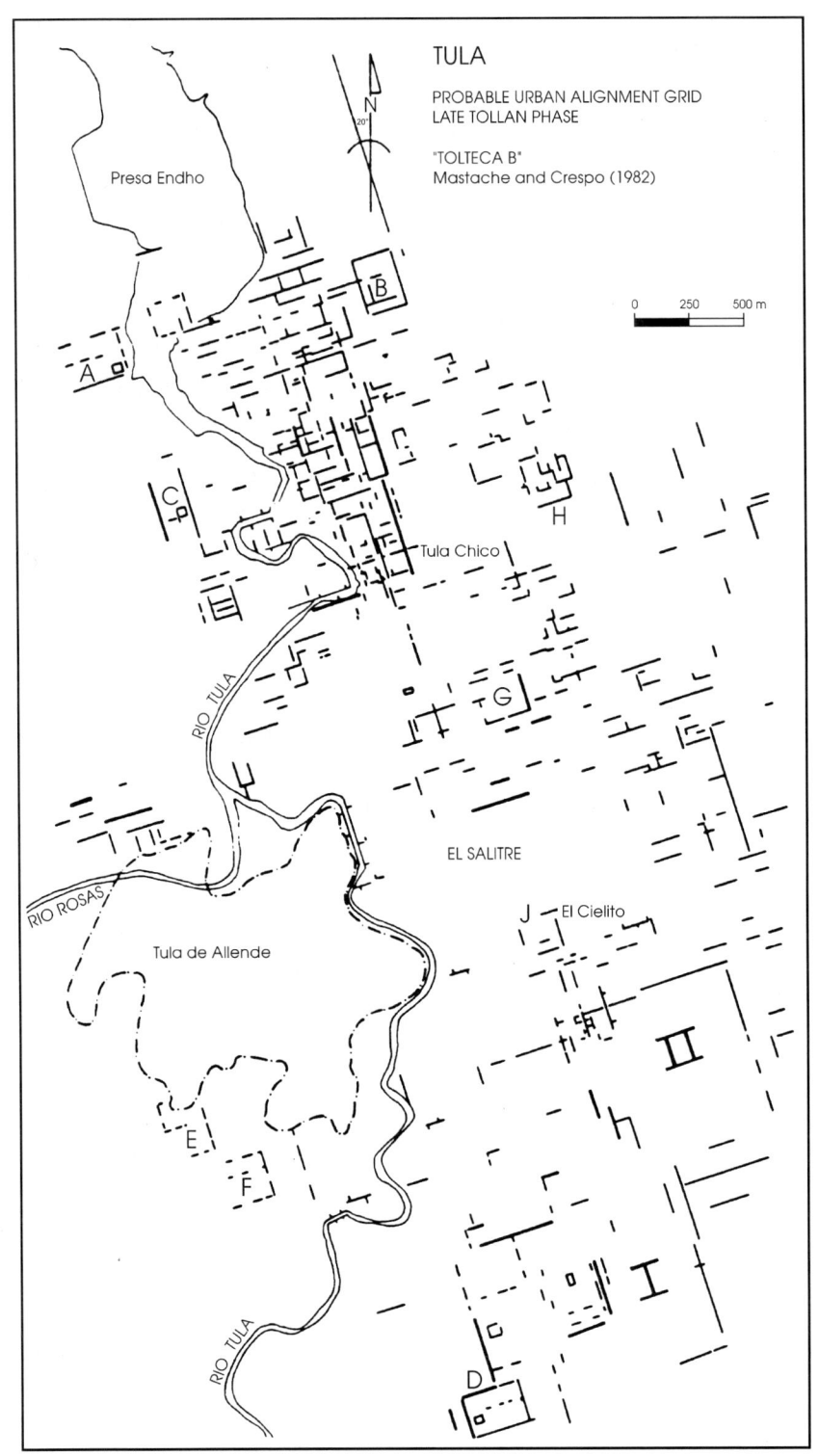

Figure 5.5. Tula: "Tolteca B." Urban alignment grid.

had a clear orthogonal plan based on axial symmetry. Additionally, unlike Tula, most of the Teotihuacan city had a rather regular and homogenous topography and was built at the same altitude, without being interrupted by abrupt elevations.

In the Cantona site in Puebla, with architectural characteristics and a good state of conservation that make it possible to very clearly appreciate the general plan of the settlement and the urban fabric, there are some roads with the characteristic L-shaped architectural turns. Recent excavations show a network of well conserved elevated avenues and streets, one of which is avenue No. 2 and some of its secondary streets, which are interrupted at various points by 90° turns, and which García Cook and Merino (1996 and personal communication) attribute principally to the topography of this part of the site, although these authors believe it could have implications on the control of the circulation in some streets.

It is interesting to add that in the Tula museum there is a clay model published by Acosta (1957) that represents the front of a temple in which the L shape of the access can clearly be seen in relation to the axis of the building. However, it must be clarified that the model was associated with the Aztec occupation of the monumental precinct.

Internal Structure

Speaking of the internal structure of a site implies the spatial analysis of the settlement (the constructed spaces and the open spaces), an analysis of the general plan (the diverse units that make it up and their nature), as well as of the specific forms or articulation (the principal axes and the ways of access); all of these aspects regarding the urban fabric are closely related and cannot be analyzed separately.

The first differentiation that can be made is between the public and private areas, between the monumental and what Lefebvre calls the "habitational." We agree with this author when he indicates that the monumental zone represents the global level of society, its essence, the areas of control; it is the center of power and divinity, and the concrete expression of the institutions that govern the society. The inhabited area, on the other hand, projects social life, everyday events, the economic processes of production and consumption, and family organization (Lefebvre 1983:94).

The monumental congregates, it is the center of political, ritual, festive, administrative, and religious life; the home separates, isolates, individualizes. The inhabited zone is made at a human scale, while the monumental is at a superhuman scale, exceeding, overflowing, and overwhelming the human being; its scale is the scale of divinity, of divine government, of abstract institutions that dominate society. The monumental zone is thus the axis or symbolic center of the city; it is a strategic enclave in terms of how the urban spaces are organized and articulated, which, however, cannot be defined in themselves but instead by their relationship with the rest of the social and spatial structure (Castells 1982:270). A city cannot be characterized by its monuments nor can the entire symbolic structure be reconstructed through them, but the monuments are a key point in the structure.

In the Mesoamerican cities, as in many others, the monumental center was the heart of the city, its religious, political, and administrative center, the seat of divinity and government, the place where spatial configuration and the order of the cosmos and the universe are reproduced and materialized.

The Monumental Center and the Sacred Precinct

In Tula, the importance of the monumental precinct as a symbolic axis and architectural center of the city is manifested on one hand in its central position, since the monumental plaza is indeed located in the center of the site, taking into account a hypothetical north-south longitudinal axis about 6 kilometers long. On the other hand, its hierarchy is stated by its height, since it is on the highest and most prominent point in the city, which physically dominates the urban space. The edification of this vast architectural complex on a natural elevation implies an enormous public work that includes the modification of the original hill through an extensive system of terracing, with artificial landfill zones of up to 7 and 8 meters in depth for the leveling of the plaza and the construction of the platforms that serve as a base for these edifices.

THE EARLY POSTCLASSIC: THE TOLLAN PHASE CITY

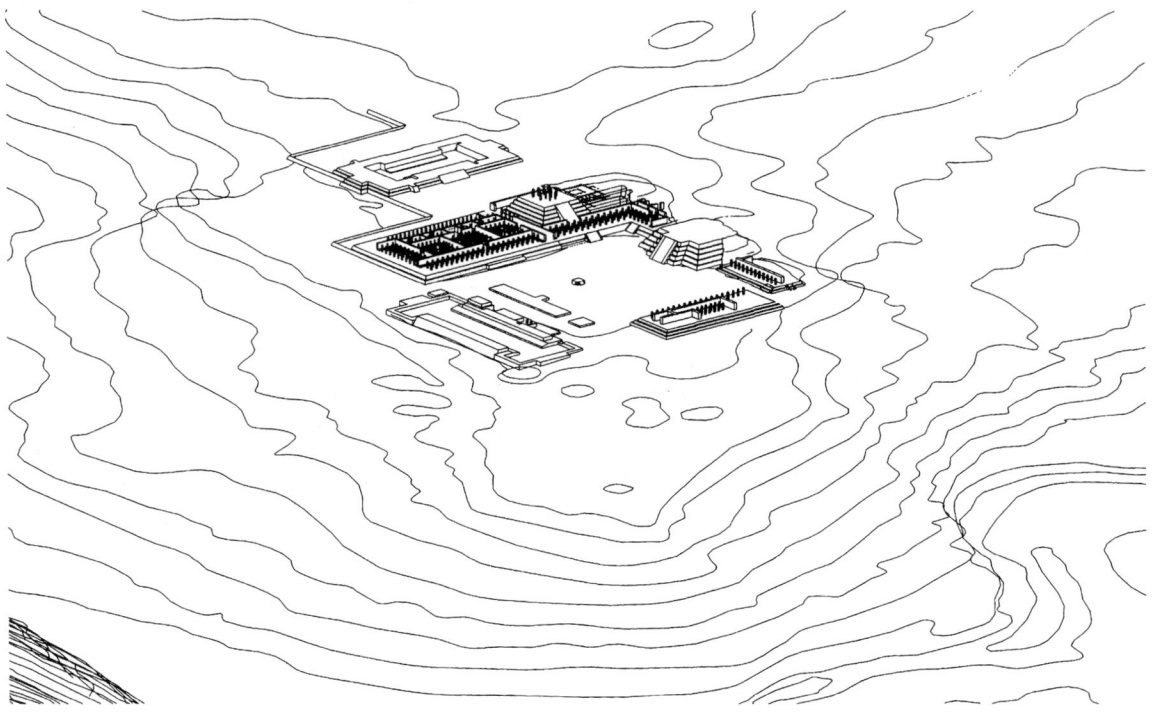

Figure 5.6. Tula: Topographic restitution of the monumental zone.

The volume of the pyramids as such is not very great if compared with the Pyramids of the Sun and Moon in Teotihuacan, for example, or the main pyramid of Cholula, but its location in the most prominent part of the city offsets this fact. Indeed, the monumental zone as a whole is an enormous pyramidal structure made up of an extensive system of terraces and platforms that raised the original height of the promontory upon which the principal plaza rises (Fig. 5.6).

The terraces and platforms that make up the great architectural complex upon which they were raised enhanced the size of the pyramids, and the entire complex resembled a huge pyramidal structure topped by two pyramids. This situation is different from Teotihuacan or Tenochtitlan, where the entire city, including the monumental zone, was on the same flat terrain. Teotihuacan and other Mesoamerican centers, especially those of the Classic period, have very large pyramidal structures whose height and volume were achieved by the mass of the buildings, that is, through the sheer volume of the pyramids themselves. In general, the Postclassic pyramid structures tend to be smaller than the Classic ones, a difference that seems to be tied to changes in the nature of the religious and political institutions that took place after the Classic period. Even at Tenochtitlan, capital of a large empire and a religious center, we do not find the same monumental scale of religious architecture that we find at Teotihuacan.

It is evident that the placement of the monumental center at Tula is strategic, not only because it occupies an easily defended place, but also because of its central setting at a dominant point having great visual impact to inhabitants in every part of the city and within view of many rural sites. Stated in Lefebvre's (1983:46) terms, the monumental zone has the spaciousness of an area that overflows its material limits and is not circumscribed to a specific place; indeed it occupies all of the city, like the institutions it represents. "The monumentality spreads, develops, condenses and concentrates everywhere. A monument goes beyond itself, its facade, its interior space; the essence of the monumentality is generally the height and depth."

The kind of placement that Tula's precinct has on the summit of an elevation is common in various areas of Mesoamerica and the north of Mexico. Without doubt, one of the most outstanding examples of this type of acropolis-like setting is La Quemada, Zacatecas, which also shares with Tula a number of architectonic elements including columned halls (Hers 1989; Nelson 1997). Hers observes that in the region that she studied (in the limits between the states of Jalisco and Zacatecas) and generally in sites of the Chalchihuites culture, settlements placed at high elevations are common. In some cases, only the ceremonial center and elite habitations were located in high points, while the majority of the population occupied lower areas. In the Central Mexican Highlands, sites having monumental centers placed on high elevations were common during the Late Classic and Epiclassic, and include Xochicalco, Teotenango, Cantona, and Cacaxtla-Xochitecatl, along with most Coyotlatelco sites in the Tula region.

As in other cities of ancient Mexico, Tula's urban plan must have been determined by the sacred precinct being the symbolic and physical axis around which the urban territory would have been structured and articulated. However, since there is an absence of the elements required to make an urban analysis, such as a detailed map of the settlement, we only can present a somewhat incomplete approximation of the city's architectural and urban concept, as well as the way in which the monumental complex, and the sacred precinct in particular, determined the general planning of the site, its axes, proportions, units, and forms of articulation.

THE SACRED PRECINCT

We know that Tula experienced several changes and transformations during its long life, but it is evident that the city's conception and urban structure were defined according to a master plan when the monumental precinct was built. At the place where the sacred precinct was constructed, there very probably was a Coyotlatelco center corresponding to the city's initial development stage, that is, an occupation coeval with Tula Chico, over which the Tollan Phase monumental center was built (Mastache and Crespo 1982; Diehl 1983; Cobean 1994).

As is common in Mesoamerican cities, the pyramidal structures and other buildings in Tula's monumental precinct contain various construction stages and enlargements. In his excavations, Acosta found several substructures and additions in the majority of the buildings. The monumental precinct and its buildings generally have between three and four construction stages corresponding to the Tollan Phase (A.D. 900–1150), which was Tula's apogee (Acosta 1944, 1945, 1956a; Cobean 1994; Getino and Figueroa n.d.).

There is evidence that the principal buildings on the ceremonial precinct were intentionally burned at the end of the Tollan Phase (ca. A.D. 1150), and that some structures were looted and partially reoccupied during the Late Postclassic (A.D. 1200–1520). The reoccupations during this period are evident principally in the so-called Palacio Quemado, Building K, the central altar, and Ballcourt 2, among other buildings (Acosta 1944, 1945, 1956a, 1956–1957, 1961a; Cobean 1994).

The limits of the monumental center are difficult to define with precision because no detailed topographic map has ever been made of the entire complex, and because various platforms and structures conforming it have not been excavated yet. Restoration and excavation programs have concentrated fundamentally on the buildings surrounding the main plaza.

The dimensions for structures and architectural features presented in the following discussion are based principally on the map of the monumental precinct published by Acosta (1956–1957) and the schematic maps of the different orientation systems of Tula's city (Mastache and Crespo 1982) where the approximate limits of the monumental center can be detected. Considering the extension determined from maps, the monumental precinct measures approximately 350 meters north-south and 300 meters east-west; with the northern edge being Ballcourt 1, the southern limit being Building K (recently excavated by Cobean [1994]), the east marked by the rear facade

THE EARLY POSTCLASSIC: THE TOLLAN PHASE CITY

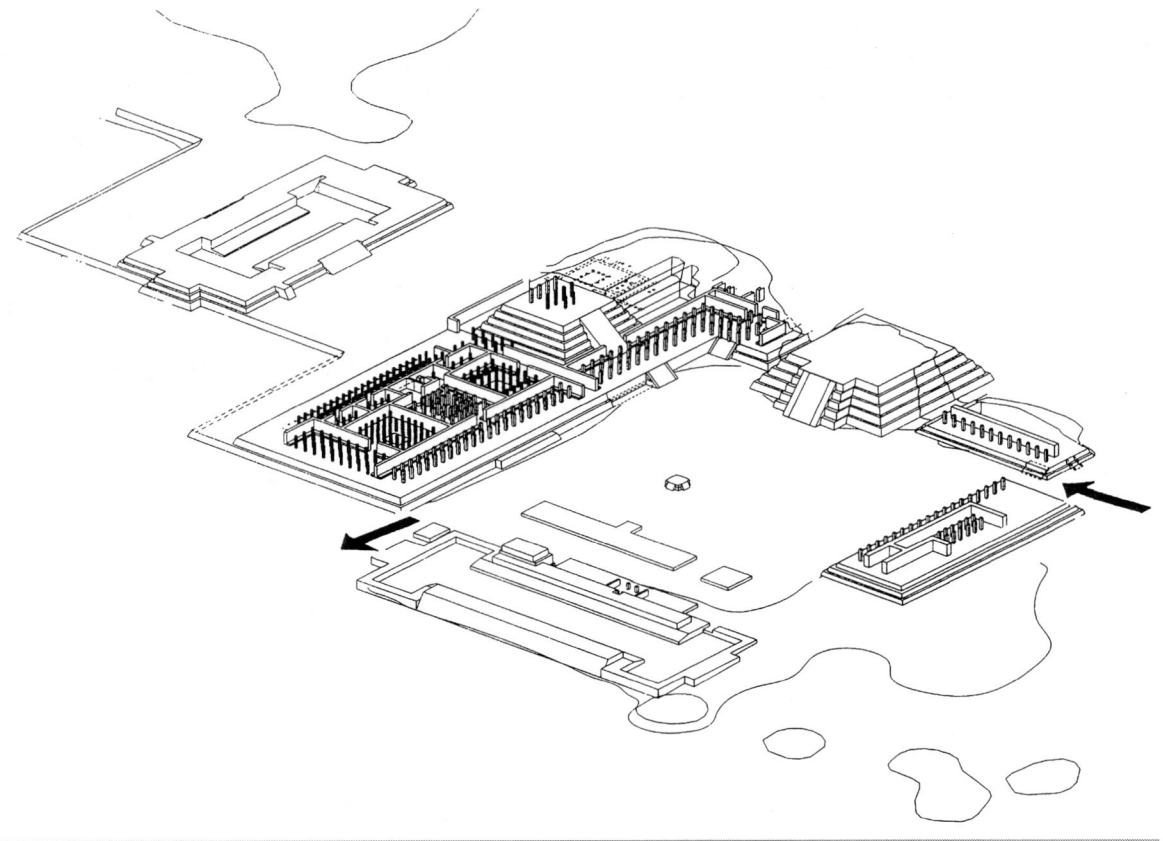

Figure 5.7. Tula: The sacred precinct.

of Pyramid C, and the west determined by the large mound on the southwest edge of Ballcourt 2. Alternatively, if only the exterior limits of the buildings surrounding the plaza are used, the precinct would measure approximately 260 by 230 meters, with the longest axis being east to west. The interior space of the plaza can be determined with more precision, constituting a nearly square form measuring around 120 by 135 meters, with the longest axis being north to south (see Figs. 5.7, 5.8A, and 5.8B).

The monumental precinct is a huge quadrangle that is open on its northwest and southeast corners. It is composed of two complexes that have the form of two opposing right angles or of two capital L's that are not completely joined, leaving the corners open in diagonals. These open corners were the principal entrances to the plaza. This is especially evident in the topographic map made by Acosta's (1940) project before his excavations (Fig. 5.8A). The largest right angle, measuring approximately 140 meters on a side, is formed by Pyramids C and B and by adjacent structures with columned halls. The lesser right angle (of about 120 meters on a side) is constituted by Building K and Ballcourt 2 (Figs. 5.7, 5.8A, and 5.8B). Thus Tula's plaza was surrounded by different types of buildings, the specific functions of which have not been defined in all cases.

In a sense, we can say that the sacred precinct is divided in two zones of distinct hierarchy and differing character. The northeast complex is the most important because of its greater dimensions and, above all else, because of the nature of the buildings that compose it, especially the two pyramids that, together with the adjacent buildings, are without

THE EARLY POSTCLASSIC: THE TOLLAN PHASE CITY

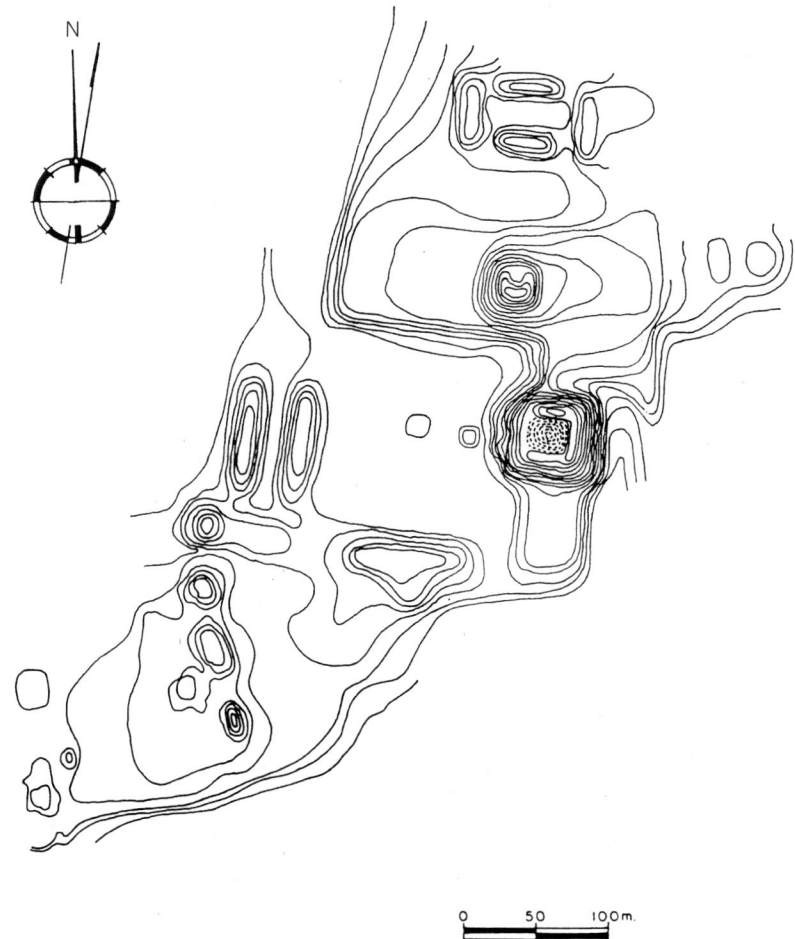

Figure 5.8A. Topographic map of Tula's sacred precinct before it was excavated (Acosta 1941). This well illustrates the two opposing L-shaped building complexes that form the precinct.

functions of the buildings, but also expresses spatially essential cosmogonic concepts and marks two different realms of distinct nature and hierarchy within the religious and political structure of the Toltec state.

A noteworthy aspect in the planning of the monumental center is the placement of both pyramids in relation to the structure of the total precinct. The pyramids appear to be displaced to one side instead of being in a central position, especially if they are observed from a point inside the plaza. Nevertheless, if the general plan of the precinct is analyzed, taking into account its external limits, it is clear that Pyramid C is the fundamental architectural element, not only because it is the largest structure in the city, but also because of its location and relationship with other buildings in the plaza. When the entire monumental compound is considered in its totality as an architectonic unit, the impression of asymmetry and displacement of the two pyramids in the precinct disappears, and it is evident that Pyramid C is clearly the principal structure, the very probable *axis mundi* and predominant element on the basis of which all the plaza was planned, possibly along with the rest of the city. Pyramid B, on the other hand, has a secondary position due to its smaller size and less prominent setting within the precinct.

Both pyramids are placed adjacent to each other, forming a 90° angle, with their main facades

doubt the most important architectural elements in the entire precinct (Figs. 5.8B and 5.9). Thus this section can be considered the most essentially sacred part of the monumental center. The lesser symbolic and architectonic hierarchy of the southwest section is expressed in its smaller volume and dimensions, and in a different level of internal articulation, because, while Pyramids B and C are articulated with other structures (vestibules and columned halls), Building K and Ballcourt 2 can be considered separate units that only are integrated in the sense that they were built on the same platform.

It is very probable that the structuring of the buildings on the monumental plaza in two separate units not only constitutes an architectonic solution to designate differences in the importance and the

THE EARLY POSTCLASSIC: THE TOLLAN PHASE CITY

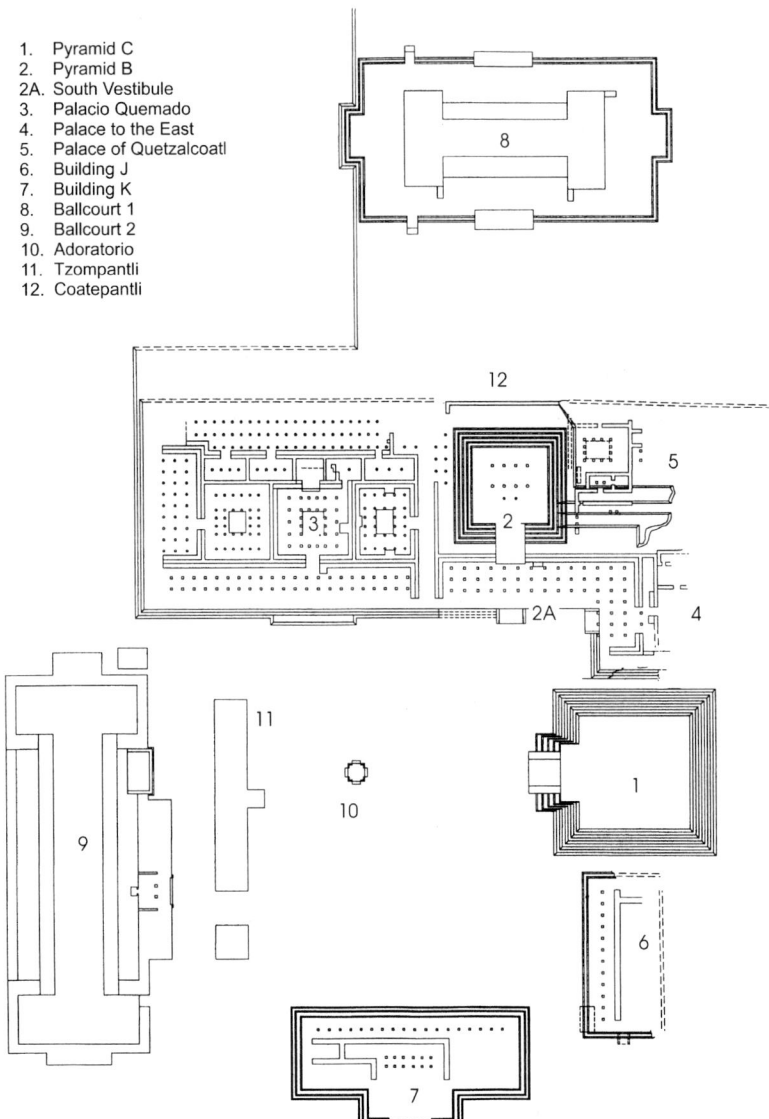

1. Pyramid C
2. Pyramid B
2A. South Vestibule
3. Palacio Quemado
4. Palace to the East
5. Palace of Quetzalcoatl
6. Building J
7. Building K
8. Ballcourt 1
9. Ballcourt 2
10. Adoratorio
11. Tzompantli
12. Coatepantli

Figure 5.8B. Location of the principal buildings on Tula's sacred precinct (based on Acosta 1956–1957, 1967; Matos 1976; Diehl 1983; and Cobean 1994).

In contrast to Tula, at Teotihuacan the two pyramids are not on the same plaza, but the pyramids at both sites are placed in similar positions in relation to each other. Another important aspect that coincides is the general orientation of the precincts in that, like Teotihuacan, Tula's monumental center is aligned approximately 17° east of astronomical north (Acosta 1944:147; Gali, 161–163, in Acosta 1944). It is obvious that these similarities are not casual and do not merely refer to a formal aspect of urban planning, but instead indicate a continuity of cosmovision and fundamental ideological concepts that were shared by both cultures, which also are evident in iconography and other elements to be discussed later.

On the other hand, many other aspects of planning and urbanism in the two cities are different. The planning of Teotihuacan's monumental center has fundamental differences with that of Tula, the most evident being that it is not structured around a central plaza, but instead along the great axis of the Street of the Dead, where the Pyramids of the Sun and the Moon are located. The Pyramid of the Moon, the smallest, is nevertheless hierarchically emphasized by its placement as the central point where the Street of the Dead begins. The Street of the Dead is the city's symbolic and architectonic axis, articulating the various plazas and

facing the plaza: Pyramid C toward the west and Pyramid B toward the south. There are notable similarities with the Pyramids of the Sun and Moon at Teotihuacan, not only because of the existence of two pyramids, with one larger than the other, but because in Teotihuacan, as in Tula, the largest pyramid faces west and the smallest faces south, and above all because they possess the same spatial setting with regard to each other as can be seen in Figure 5.10.

Figure 5.9. View of the sacred precinct: Pyramid B.

precincts having different sizes and importance that constitute the monumental zone.

Obviously, there also is a great difference in scale between the pyramids of Teotihuacan and those of Tula, but the difference in proportion between the two structures is similar at both sites, that is, the difference in volume between the larger and smaller pyramid. It is worth noting that in terms of scale and dimensions, Pyramid C and especially Pyramid B are more similar to the Temple of Quetzalcoatl at Teotihuacan than to the much larger Pyramids of the Sun and Moon,[1] as also is the case of the Templo Mayor in Tenochtitlan.

It is noteworthy that the plaza of Tula Chico (Fig. 4.12), which is earlier than the Tollan Phase precinct, lacks the similarities that the latter has with Teotihuacan with regard to the placement of pyramidal buildings, because in Tula Chico the two mounds that appear to be pyramidal platforms do not possess the same spatial relationship as Pyramids B and C. The two probable Tula Chico pyramids are placed together on the northern side of the plaza (in a position equivalent to that of Pyramid B) with the principal facades oriented south. Here, in the place corresponding to that of Pyramid C, there is a large rectangular platform that apparently is similar in plan to the Palacio Quemado (Cobean and Suárez 1989). The principal ballcourt at Tula Chico appears to be in an equivalent location to that of Ballcourt 2 in the Tollan Phase precinct.

It should be considered, however, that the monumental zone know as Tula Chico has been looted extensively, probably since pre-Hispanic times, and without excavations it is difficult to be certain (only on the basis of surface topography) that the largest mounds really constitute pyramidal platforms and to determine accurately their architectonic characteristics and the precise spatial

THE EARLY POSTCLASSIC: THE TOLLAN PHASE CITY

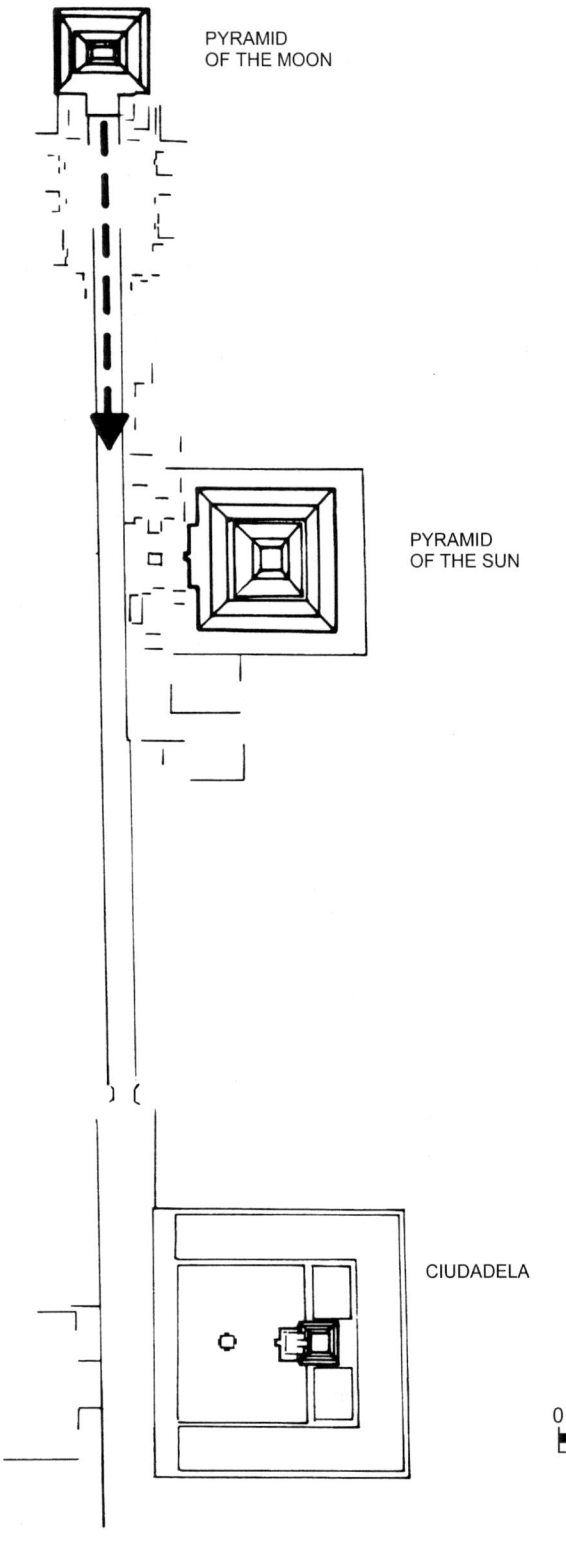

relations of the different structures that conform this monumental complex.

Pyramids C and B

Pyramid C is a building formed by five vertically superimposed *talud* platforms. On its principal (west) facade supporting the stairway is a lateral platform that Acosta (1956a:55) called "cuerpo adosado" in the central part of the facade. This element constitutes another important similarity between Tula and Teotihuacan, because as Acosta stated, the *cuerpo adosado* of Pyramid C is similar "with those of the two great pyramids of San Juan Teotihuacan (p. 55). Actually, if one studies maps of these buildings, the major similarity is between Pyramid C and the Pyramid of the Moon, because the general plans of both structures are very much alike. A feasible similarity between Pyramid C and the Pyramid of the Sun is that both probably are constructed with five *taluds*, although a debate still exists concerning whether the Pyramid of the Sun originally had five *taluds* before it was restored by Leopoldo Batres.

Pyramid C is one of the most badly damaged buildings in Tula's sacred precinct. Acosta's (1944, 1945, 1956a) investigations in the 1940s found great destruction apparently caused by pre-Hispanic looting. A large trench had destroyed much of the stairway and other sections of the west facade, and there also were looting pits at the summit and the east side of the pyramid. The north side was more intact than the south; Acosta (1945) identified four different construction phases for Pyramid C, including remains of three interior substructures (Fig. 5.11). This structure very probably was covered with relief panels and other sculptured elements like those of Pyramid B, but most of this sculptural

Figure 5.10. The Pyramid of the Sun and the Pyramid of the Moon at Teotihuacan. Based on Millon (1973). Drawing by Fernando Getino.

Scale: 1: 10,000

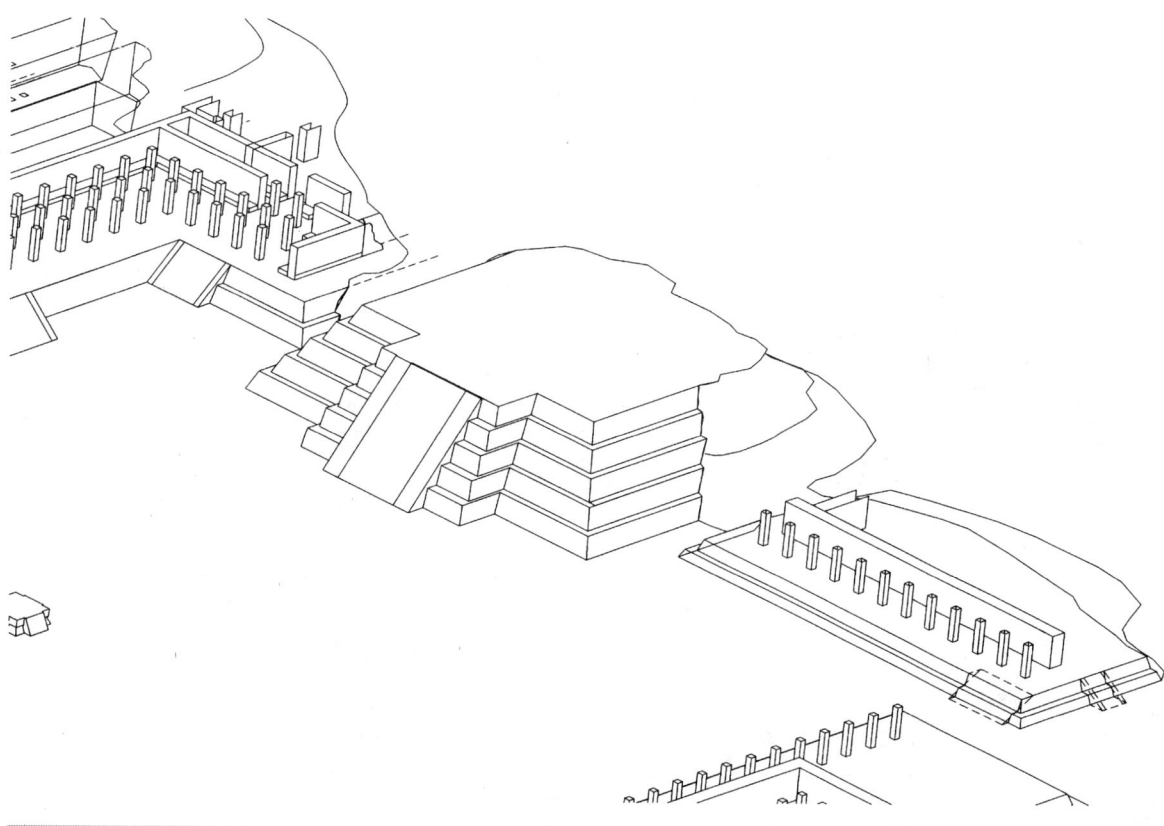

Figure 5.11. Tula: A view of the east side of the plaza with Pyramid C.

program was dismantled and looted in pre-Hispanic times; thus, what we know concerning this pyramid's appearance during its last construction stage is very incomplete. The only in situ relief panel was found on the west facade at the base of the south balustrade; the decoration of which Acosta (1956a: fig. 5) interpreted as a cross section of a conch shell, a symbol of Venus and the god Quetzalcoatl to whom Acosta proposed the pyramid was dedicated (Fig. 5.12).

In the hallway at the north edge of Pyramid C, Acosta (1956a: fig. 49) found a headless Chac Mool and a small incomplete Atlante sculpture. Another Chac Mool fragment was recovered nearby. Acosta proposed that these sculptures originally were on Pyramid C. Previously, he had stated that the various fragments (mainly feet and legs of giant Atlante sculptures at Tula and the National Museum of Anthropology) that were similar to the Atlantes of Pyramid B, but having greater dimensions, probably originally were looted from Pyramid C (Acosta 1944:146). Of course, it is also possible that these unprovenienced Atlante fragments correspond to an earlier construction phase of Pyramid B.

Pyramid B faces south, also having five *taluds* and a square ground plan. Acosta (1956a:89) emphasized the difficulty he had interpreting what appear to have been three principal construction stages for this building, because in some cases there are partial superimposed platforms that were built only on one or two sides of the pyramid during different periods. Acosta clearly identified two interior substructures, the first of which was covered by unsculptured stone panels painted white. The second and third (last?) stages of the pyramid were covered with relief panels having the same sculptural elements: processions of felines and canines, panels with eagles or vultures, and a composite creature having human, reptile,

THE EARLY POSTCLASSIC: THE TOLLAN PHASE CITY

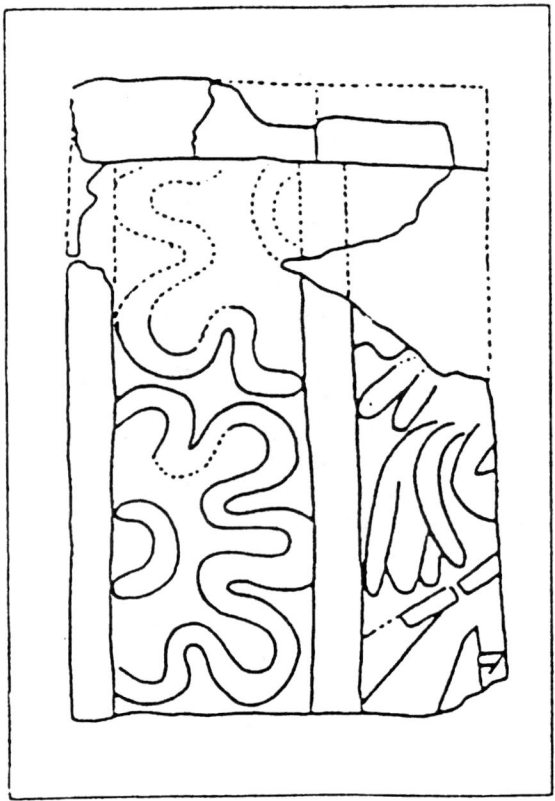

Figure 5.12. Relief panel from the south balustrade of Pyramid C at Tula. Acosta interpreted this motif as representing the cross section of a conch shell symbolizing the planet Venus (Acosta 1956a: fig. 5).

and avian attributes, which Acosta (1956a) and Moedano (1946a) consider to be a representation of Tlahuizcalpantecuhtli, the god Quetzalcoatl in his embodiment as the planet Venus, the evening star (Fig. 5.13).[2]

Pyramid B, as it now stands restored, corresponds to two different building stages because Acosta left exposed fragmentary facades from the last two construction periods: the relief panels on the east facade correspond to the penultimate building stage, and the relief panels on the north are from the last stage (Fig. 5.13). Acosta (1956a:59) proposed that the last construction stage in Pyramid B also corresponded with the final stages of the Palacio Quemado, the south Vestibule of Pyramid B, and the so-called Palace of Quetzalcoatl, which adjoins Pyramid B on the east partially covering its two lowest *taluds* or tiers.

The rich diversity of iconographic elements associated with Pyramid B has been described in detail and analyzed by Acosta and other scholars. Among the outstanding elements are the aforementioned relief panels that covered the facades, along with other associated sculptural and architectonic features such as the pillars, columns, and monumental sculptures that were integral parts of the pyramid and of the temple that very probably existed on its summit. The best-known sculptures at Tula are the so-called Atlantes or caryatids presently placed on top of Pyramid B, which consist of anthropomorphic columns 4.6 meters high that apparently supported the original temple roof. These represent high-ranking Toltec warriors whose elaborate ceremonial costumes have been analyzed in detail by Acosta (1941, 1943, 1961b) (Fig. 5.14). Important costume elements include the cylindrical headdress, the butterfly-shaped breast plate or pectoral, the disk (*tezcacuitlapilli*) divided in four sections and decorated with fire serpents (Xiuhcoatl) on the warrior's back, and weapons such as a dart thrower (*atlatl*), a fending stick, and a knife. Kristan-Graham (1989) also analyzes key elements of the Atlantes' dress.

The Pillars of Pyramid B[3]

We will discuss the pillars on the summit of Pyramid B in some detail because the reliefs on them are key elements for understanding fundamental aspects of the Toltec state.

These consist of four pillars covered with reliefs on all four sides, which apparently were originally painted. On each pillar there are four representations of human figures, with two personages on the lower section and two personages on the upper half of each pillar, totalling sixteen figures on the original four pillars, although only twelve personages have been preserved completely along with fragments of two other figures. All these personages possess the attributes of warriors, along with other shared aspects such as being depicted in profile in the act of walking, but they also have specific elements that differentiate each figure. Among these elements are the

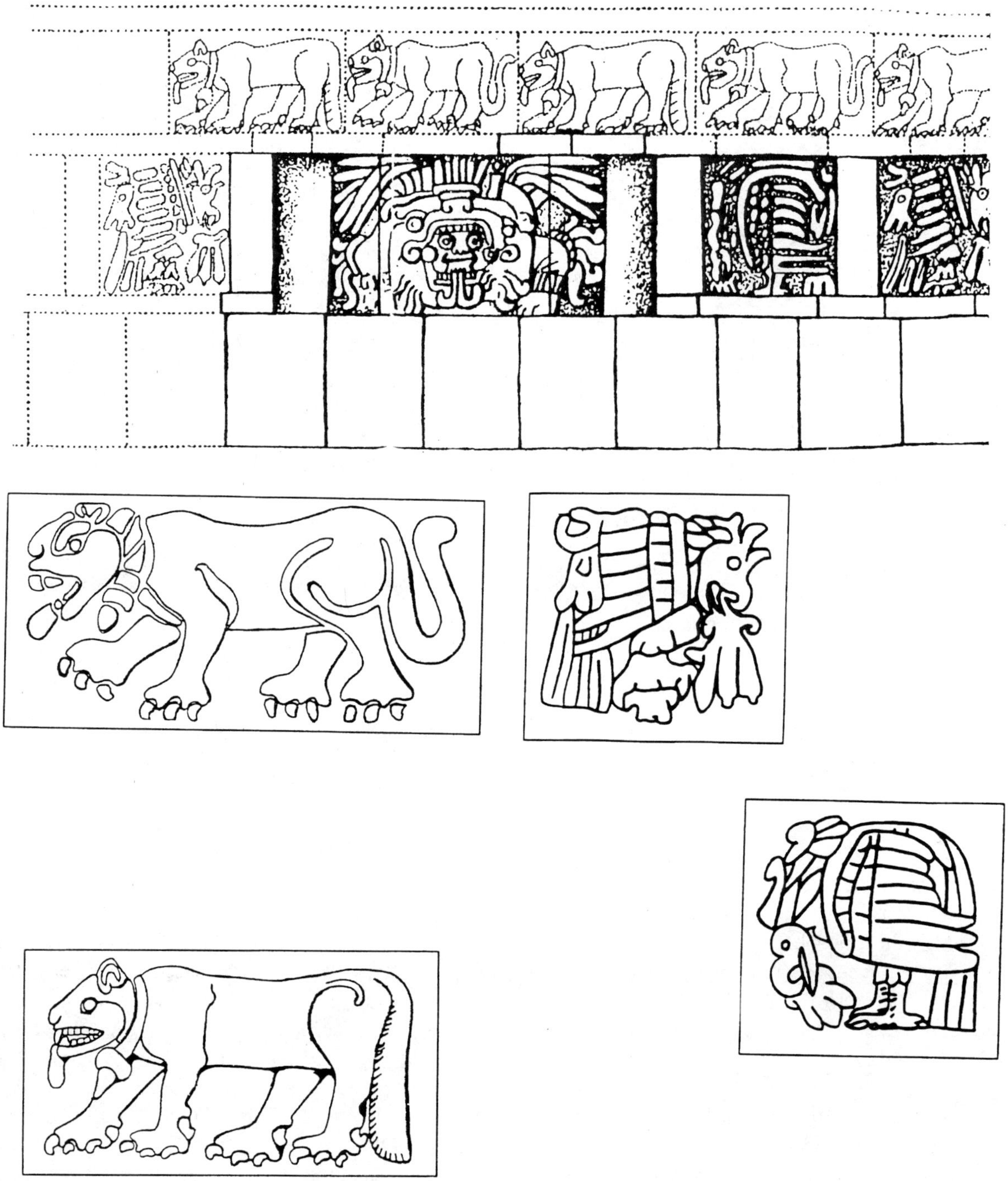

Figure 5.13. Pyramid B at Tula: A relief panel of a composite being that Acosta (1944) and Moedano (1946a) considered to represent Tlahuizcalpantecuhtli, along with reliefs of felines, canines, and raptorial birds (from Jiménez 1998).

THE EARLY POSTCLASSIC: THE TOLLAN PHASE CITY

Figure 5.14. View of the summit of Pyramid B with sculptured pillars and other elements.

glyphs or symbols that some personages have near the upper part of their heads, which appear to refer to their names, positions, or rank, and which some researchers have cited as evidence that the pillar figures depict historical personages who really existed, probably governors of Tula or high ranking nobles who were members of Toltec dynasties (Acosta 1968; Kristan-Graham 1989; Jiménez 1998; Mastache and Cobean 2000).

Alternating with the human figures are representations of spear or dart bundles on four sections of each pillar (Figs. 5.15 and 5.16). Another element is the Cipactli symbol, which is placed on the upper and lower edges of each personage, in a sense framing these figures. This symbol often is linked to royal lineages, and it no doubt is significant that the date 1 Cipactli constitutes the first day of the Mesoamerican 260-day calendar and also is the initial date of creation in myths of the origin of the universe (Taube 1993). 1 Cipactli was a favored date for the enthronement of Mexica kings (Kristan-Graham 1989:236; Nicholson 1961).

There are seven surviving figures on the Pyramid B pillars with glyphs near their heads. It is pertinent to cite here an illustration of the lords of Tenochtitlan in Book 8 of the *Florentine Codex* (reproduced by Carrasco 1971: fig. 2) in which, beside each lord, is a symbol that identifies him; these symbols are similar to the glyphs on the Tula pillars. Kristan-Graham, whose study of these pillars is the most rigorous to date, indicates the similarity between the symbols for various Mexica kings, especially Cuauhtemoc and Izcoatl, and the glyphs of some figures on the Pyramid B pillars (1989:241, 317, 334). She proposes that the Tula pillars could be commemorative monuments for the enthronement of rulers, some of whom could predate the Tollan Phase, and that members of the same dynasties, or even the same individuals, could be represented in the reliefs of Tula and Chichén Itzá because at both sites there are personages possessing similar elements, such as the descending bird motif on some of their helmets and headdresses (pp. 251, 317).

A New Pillar Fragment

During the 1980s, a conservation project directed by Roberto Gallegos in Tula's archaeological zone recovered part of a pillar on the north side of Pyramid B. No report was published on this find and the exact location where this sculpture was found has not been specified, but apparently it was excavated near the large trench where Acosta (1944, 1945) recovered the majority of the sculptures and pillars that now are on the summit of Pyramid B.[4]

Although incomplete, the newly found pillar is of great interest in terms of its iconography because a relief on one side represents a personage having physical and costume elements of the god Tezcatli-poca, and on the opposite side there is a figure with attributes of Tlaloc (Figs. 5.17 and 5.18). The other two sides of the pillar depict spear bundles similar to those represented on the known Pyramid B pillars. When the newly found pillar fragment was exhibited for the first time, we did not think that it formed part of the pillar group that Acosta had placed on the summit of Pyramid B, and we tentatively concluded that this fragment came from an earlier sculpture complex. This impression mainly was due to the apparent differences in sculptural style and quality of the new fragment compared to the other pillars, and also because in contrast to the original pillars, the new fragment represents two deities. However, on the basis of our recent analysis we concluded that this fragment is without doubt the upper section of the incomplete pillar on Pyramid B (Pillar 3 according to the system of Jiménez 1998:113–116). The supposed differences in sculptural technique apparently were due to the eroded state of the original pillars, which have been exposed on top of Pyramid B for nearly 50 years, while the newly recovered fragment has not been damaged (Mastache and Cobean 2000).

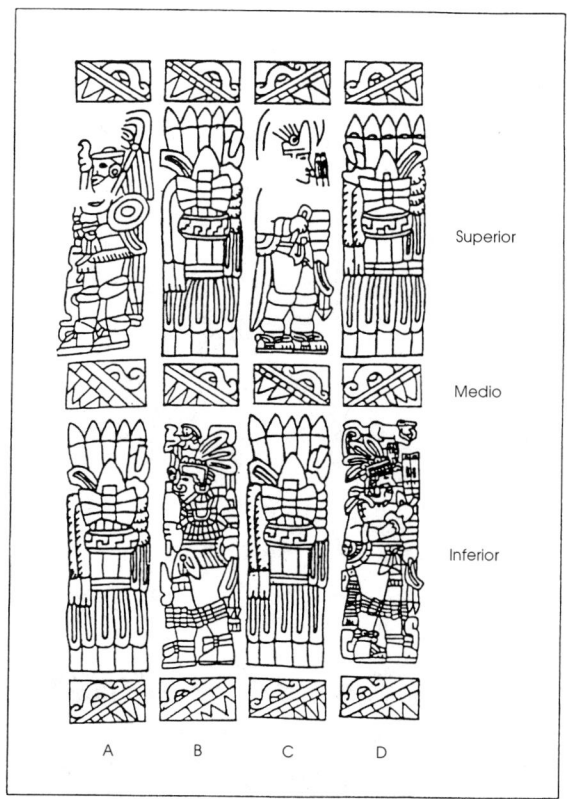

Figure 5.15. Reliefs on the four faces of Pillar 4 (from Jiménez 1998: fig. 20).

The measurements of the fragment coincide with those of Pillar 3, and the sculptured elements on the four sides of Pillar 3 and the fragment correlate perfectly. The side of the fragment that displays a personage with attributes of Tlaloc lacks the personage's feet, which appear on the upper edge of the west side of Pillar 3 (Fig. 5.20). In addition, the missing elements on the lower section of the fragment's representation of Tezcatlipoca appear on the upper part of the east side of Pillar 3, which in relief displays the single sandle of the god's only complete foot along with parts of the circular smoke rings coming out of the smoking mirror that has replaced his other lower leg. Also, the upper parts of the north and south faces of Pillar 3 contain reliefs of the missing end sections of the spear bundles depicted on two sides of the fragment. (See Figs. 5.19 and 5.20.)

Figure 5.16. The personage on Side B, Pillar 4. Photo, Humberto Illera.

the figures of the other pillars, is depicted in profile dressed as a warrior carrying a knife, a fending stick (*arma curva*), and a dart thrower (*atlatl*) and wearing a disk on his back (probably a *tezcacuitlapilli*). The headdress or helmet has the form of a bird's head (an eagle) topped by three large feathers;[5] other distinguishing costume elements include a noseplug and earplugs in the form of long cylinders, anklets similar to feline claws, and a semicircular pectoral made of rectangular plaques (perhaps shell or turquoise) with a T-shaped motif in its center.

Taube (1994:233, 239, fig. 29) identifies this type of pectoral, which also appears on personages in the reliefs of Chichén Itzá as an early version of a *xolocozcatl*—the Mexica turquoise pectoral—noting that on the Chichén figures with preserved surface paint, these pectorals always are turquoise blue.

Pillar 3 is precisely the sculpture with a bearded figure that Acosta thought very probably represents Topiltzin Quetzalcoatl (Fig. 5.21), surely because this personage is bearded and has a feathered serpent glyph above his head (Acosta 1967:38, fig. 14). Nicholson, on the other hand, proposes that this figure represents a priest of the cult of Quetzalcoatl (personal communication in Kristan-Graham 1989:326). This personage is shown walking toward the left and, like Besides the bearded figure on Pillar 3, two other personages on the Pyramid B pillars have this kind of pectoral.

The other personage on the lower section of Pillar 3 also is depicted in profile walking (but toward the right) (Fig. 5.19). He is costumed as a warrior, wearing a *tezcacuitlapilli* (back mirror) and carrying a knife, fending stick, and *atlatl,* but his helmet is different from that of the Quetzalcoatl figure and

Figure 5.17. The recently identified upper section of Pillar 3 with reliefs of two personages: one shown as Tezcatlipoca and the other with attributes of Tlaloc (from Jiménez 1998: fig. 51).

Figure 5.18. The personage with attributes of Tezcatlipoca on the upper section of Pillar 3. Photo, Humberto Illera.

his glyph has the form (apparently) of a fox with its tongue coming out of its mouth. Especially interesting are the large (probable) speech scroll in front of this figure's face and the angular steps near the temples of his helmet, which is decorated with two types of feathers along with a small bird in descending position on the helmet front. The personages represented on the lower sections of Pillars 2 and 4 also wear these stepped helmets decorated with descending birds.

In addition, the recently recovered fragment that constitutes the upper section of Pillar 3 (Fig. 5.18) shows two personages likewise represented in profile; the figure dressed as Tezcatlipoca faces and walks toward the left, and the other figure goes toward the right. This last figure having attributes of Tlaloc lacks the upper portion of this head, but clearly wears the gogglelike circles characteristic of this deity around his eyes. This personage is dressed as a warrior and carries two spears and a fending stick in his left hand and an *atlatl* in his right hand. On his chest is a disk with two small perforations, very similar in form to the plain pyrite mirrors found in the offerings of Sala 2

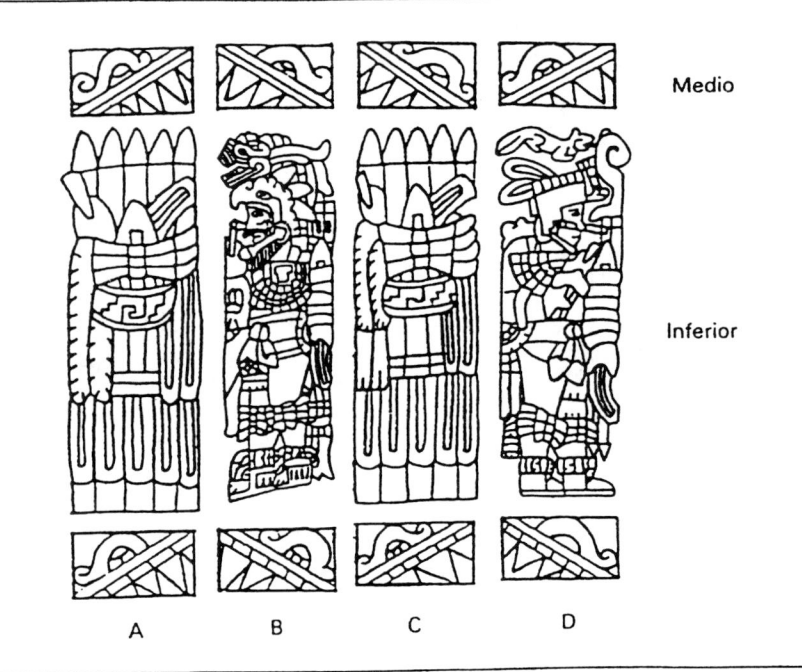

Figure 5.19. The lower section of Pillar 3, Side B of which represents a bearded figure (accompanied by a feathered serpent) who Acosta (1967) proposes was Topiltzin Quetzalcoatl (from Jiménez 1998: fig. 49).

Figure 5.20. Detail of the elements that join together the upper section of Pillar 3. The upper limits of this side show the feet of the Tlaloc figure.

Figure 5.21. Pillar 3, Side B: The bearded personage who probably represents Topiltzin Quetzalcoatl. Photograph by Robert H. Cobean.

in the Palacio Quemado (Acosta 1964; Cobean and Mastache n.d.). In these offerings, the sandstone bases of the mirrors possess the same perforations, apparently indicating that these mirrors were worn suspended as pectorals.

The personage with attributes of Tezcatlipoca on the opposite face of the pillar is dressed as a typical Toltec warrior with a butterfly pectoral, a *tezcacuitlapilli* on his back, a fending stick, an *atlatl,* and a knife sheathed in the cotton armor of his upper left arm. A double speech scroll comes out of his mouth, and he appears to be wearing a stepped helmet typical of Toltec warriors, although the upper section of the helmet is missing along with the upper section of the pillar where there might have been an identifying glyph for this personage. He has the characteristic motifs of this god, that is, the incomplete fleshless leg ending in a smoking mirror. In this figure the fleshless knee joint of the right femur is visible and the tibia and fibula of the lower right leg are missing, being replaced by the smoking mirror. It is worth emphasizing that this is the only clear-cut representation of Tezcatlipoca known for Tula, and constitutes the oldest image of this deity identified so far in the Central Highlands. It is striking that no other sculptures of this god have been recovered at Tula despite his presence in the epic cycles concerning the founding and subsequent history of Tollan, and specifically the legendary conflict between Quetzalcoatl and Tezcatlipoca that had this city as its setting.

In contrast, there are several representations of warriors with Tezcatlipoca attributes in Chichén Itzá (Thompson 1942). Tozzer (1957: figs. 239, 240, 241) presents three personages from reliefs on columns at this center that possess Tezcatlipoca motifs; especially the personage in figure 239 who has a fleshless leg and smoking mirror motif very similar to those of Tula's Pillar 3 representation and also has the same type of legging (*rodillera*) on his knee. The personages in figures 240 and 241 of Tozzer possess a *tezcacuitlapilli*, an *atlatl,* and a fending stick like the Tula Tezcatlipoca figure, but none of these Chichén figures wear a butterfly pectoral, and only one (fig. 241) of them has a stepped helmet. It is worth noting that the personage in figure 239 also is similar to the Tula Tezcatlipoca in that the right leg is fleshless, while in the Chichén figures 240 and 241 it is the left leg that is fleshless.

The Tezcatlipoca personage on Tula's Pillar 3 is similar in some aspects to the famous representations of Mexica kings depicted with Tezcatlipoca attributes in the Tizoc Stone, the commemorative stone for Axayacatl, and the recently recovered *cuauhxicalli* (vessels with sacrificed hearts) of Moctezuma I (Nicholson 1971; Wicke 1976; Pérez Castro et al. 1989). Many of the images of Mexica emperors on these monuments possess archaic Toltec-style warrior-costume elements (especially butterfly pectorals and stepped helmets) but a fundamental difference is that in contrast to the Tezcatlipoca representations in Tula and Chichén, these Mexica figures have their lower legs complete and only have one foot replaced by a smoke scroll without a mirror. Another difference with the representation of Tezcatlipoca in Tula is that in these Mexica sculptures the incomplete leg with the smoke scroll is the left one, like those in Tozzer's (1957) figures 240 and 241 from Chichén Itzá. In the Tizoc Stone, the smoking mirror appears in the figures' headdresses.

It is of great importance that the fragment originally missing from Pillar 3 of Pyramid B is precisely the segment with representations of Tezcatlipoca and Tlaloc. If we follow Acosta's (1967) assumption that the bearded figure on Pillar 3 represents Topiltzin Quetzalcoatl, a series of implications emerge regarding the fact that this key protagonist in the myths and histories of Tula is depicted on the same monument with Tezcatlipoca. The placement of images of Tezcatlipoca and Topiltzin Quetzalcoatl on the same column, and on one of the two most sacred monumental buildings at Tula, indicates that the narratives written in the indigenous chronicles concerning the Toltec and ancient Tollan definitely are represented in the iconography and writing of Tula, whether or not these accounts describe historical events or are purely legendary. The complete sculptural group of Pillar 3 suggests the probable coexistence of Topiltzin Quetzalcoatl with the cult of Tezcatlipoca, and supports the possibility that the conflict between this king and the followers of Tezcatlipoca described in the chronicles really could have occurred, ending with the expulsion of Quetzalcoatl and his faction from Tula.

It also is very significant that on the same pillar and exactly opposite the Tezcatlipoca figure, a warrior is represented with some attributes of Tlaloc. The presence of this figure on one of Pyramid B's columns very probably is related to the Tlaloc warrior cult of Teotihuacan tradition, which is the same cult to which Karl Taube (n.d.) proposed the offering with the shell garment and plain pyrite mirror in Sala 2 of the Palacio Quemado was dedicated. The presence of a Tlaloc warrior sculpture on Pyramid B and some other Tlaloc figures in the sacred precinct, which will be discussed in a subsequent section, supports Taube's conclusions concerning the relevance of this cult in Toltec ideology. In addition in the iconography of Chichén Itzá, there are various representations of warriors having goggle eyes and other attributes of Tlaloc similar to those of the figure on Tula's Pillar 3; for example: Tozzer (1957: figs. 217, 518, 528, 625) and Lothrop (1952: fig. 39e). Likewise, the images of Tlaloc and Tezcatlipoca appear together on Pillar 3 suggesting that these could have been the two principal deities or cults at Tula probably related to royalty with Tezcatlipoca being the new god.

Among Kristan-Graham's (1989:315–317) interpretations concerning the pillar reliefs on Pyramid B, she proposes that perhaps all of the personages represented are portraits of kings, and that the pairs of human figures on the upper and lower sections of each pillar may depict a recently enthroned king along with a portrait of the deceased preceding king. In our investigation of the pillar figures (Mastache and Cobean n.d.2), we propose an alternative interpretation that suggests that the personages depicted may belong to two different hierarchies, and that only those having glyphs above their heads represented kings or rulers, while the other figures may correspond to secondary but high-ranking elites, perhaps equivalent to the Cihuacóatl of the Mexica or the Toltec supreme pontiff referred to by Kirchhoff (1955) in his analyses of the chronicles. Thus the kings or sovereigns of Tula would be represented in the lower sections of the pillars, while the personages of the upper sections (with one exception) would correspond to a secondary rank. Because there always is a difference in the directions toward which the figures on each pillar walk, with two figures walking toward the left and two others walking toward the right, we suggest that the personage pairs walking in the same direction could be coeval—one figure representing a king and the other a secondary ruler.

Concerning the possibility that Tula had a dual government, a proposal by Luis Reyes (n.d.:5) in his analysis of the *Historia tolteca-chichimeca* is of great interest:

> [There are] the two principal military priests of the Toltec: Quetzalteueyac and Icxicouatl, who have many pictorial representations; in one occasion, Icxicouatl is depicted as a male with his mantle, but Quetzalteueyac appears dressed in a woman's huipil. From this we can understand that the Toltec had a type of dual government, the [personage dressed as a] man was in charge of masculine affairs, and the other figure [was responsible for] internal administrative affairs that were considered feminine. This refers to a situation similar to that which later is found among the Tenochca [Mexica] with their Tlacateuhctli and their Ciuacoatl.

Likewise for this subject, it is important to mention a frieze in the Temple of the Jaguar at Chichén Itzá analyzed by Linnea Wren (cited in Schele and Mathews 1998:223–224, fig. 6.19), in which a leader is depicted with a skirt of serpents and woman's breasts. Wren proposes that this personage is a prototype for the Cihuacóatl of the Mexica. In our opinion, it is also significant that this figure is shown with attributes of a Toltec warrior, as are the three personages facing him in the frieze.

Perhaps dual rulership was more common in Central Mexico than we suppose. According to Graulich (1998) a dual power existed in Cacaxtla and is illustrated in the portraits of two sovereigns in the murals of Edifico A on each side of a doorway. This author observes that the Olmeca-Xicalanca of Cholula described in the *Historia tolteca-chichimeca* possessed two kings, the *áquiach* and the *tláchiach* (Reyes n.d.).

Our interpretation concerning the differences in rank of the personages represented is based principally on the fact that all of the personages on the lower registers of the Pyramid B pillars have glyphs near their heads that identify them, along with distinctive costume attributes. Only one of the figures represented in the pillars' upper sections has some of these features. These attributes principally are: (1) a helmet with angular steps near the wearer's temples decorated by two types of feathers and a small bird (usually in descending position) in front; and (2) leggings (*rodilleras*) made of a series of tied knots on the front of the lower legs. An interesting exception is that the figure that probably represents Quetzalcoatl possesses a different kind of helmet (Fig. 5.22).

Tozzer (1930, 1957), in his investigation of Chichén Itzá iconography, cites the headdresses with descending birds as a key diagnostic element of Toltec warriors represented at Chichén. For almost a century scholars have related the descending bird motif with royal lineages of Chichén Itzá. According to Kristan-Graham (1989: 132–134) these descending birds (which at Chichén usually are painted blue) can be identified with a lineage that still existed in northern Yucatán during the Late Postclassic—the famous "Tutul Xiu," who had a partially Mexican origin. Because the term *xiututul* in Nahuatl means "turquoise bird," the descending blue bird motif has been identified with the Xiu royal lineage. In turn, if this motif at Chichén is associated with an elite of Mexican origin, it would not be surprising for the descending bird-on-helmet representations at Tula to be identifying attributes for kings.

Taube (1994:234–239, fig. 23) in his analysis of Chichén Itzá iconography directly associates the descending-bird motif with Xiuhtecuhtli because this element is a normal part of the costume for this principal god who during the Late Postclassic was a patron of the ruling class and an important war deity. As an example of the presence of this god among the Postclassic Maya, Taube cites a representation of Xiuhtecuhtli in the *Dresden Codex* that includes the descending-bird motif, and observes that Seler identified the descending birds in the headdresses of Toltec warriors at Chichén Itzá as the Xiuhtototl, or *cotinga* bird, which is on the headdress of Xiuhtecuhtli. In synthesis, Taube (1994) proposes that figures with the

THE EARLY POSTCLASSIC: THE TOLLAN PHASE CITY

Figure 5.22. Some personages on the pillars of Pyramid B who have glyphs near their heads identifying them (from Jiménez 1998: fig. 176).

descending-bird motif in their headdresses are associated with rulers and war forming part of a complex that he calls "the Toltec Turquoise warrior."

At Chichén, there are numerous personages represented in sculpture, painting, and metalwork who wear stepped helmets with a descending bird in front very similar to these costume motifs on the human figures depicted on the lower sections of the Pyramid B pillars. Many of these personages at Chichén clearly correspond to representations of rulers whether or not they are historical or mythical. More examples exist in the gold disks from the cenote (Lothrop 1952: figs. 30, 32, 34, 36) and in the mural in the Temple of the Jaguars (Tozzer 1957: fig. 396).

As indicated previously, the personages in the reliefs on the lower sections of the Pyramid B pillars wear special leggings on their lower legs having a series of tied knots or bows, which Kristan-Graham (1989:161, 258) observes are similar to important costume elements for Classic Maya kings who used them in rites of autosacrifice that were key obligations for Maya rulers. She proposes that the leggings on the Tula pillar figures are knotted cloths stained with the kings' blood after they performed rituals of autosacrifice. We agree that this type of legging was a distinctive part of the costume for Tula's kings. It is interesting to note that the only stela that was recovered from Pyramid B (Fig. 5.23), and which may represent Topiltzin Quetzalcoatl, includes this kind of leggings as a costume element, and likewise the central personage probably representing a Toltec king on the altar reliefs at the entrance of Tula's "Palace to the East of the Vestibule" (please see below) also wears these leggings (Acosta 1944, 1945, 1956–1957; Jiménez 1998: fig. 52).

The South Vestibule

Pyramid B is limited on the south by an L-shaped columned vestibule that is 54 meters long and 12 meters wide, with its longest section oriented east-west and its shortest section oriented north-south (Fig. 5.24). This vestibule was open only toward the principal plaza (Acosta 1945:38–40). Its north, east, and west sides were closed by adobe walls with benches and cornices that originally were covered with sculptured panels having polychrome reliefs. A total of fifty rectangular columns supported the roof that covered the entire vestibule (Fig. 5.25). Some antecedents for this type of portico with columns can be found in ceremonial and domestic structures at the Coyotlatelco site La Mesa (see Fig. 4.9) (Mastache and Cobean 1989, 1990; Patiño 1994a; Bonfil 1998) and at Classic period centers in the north like Alta Vista and La Quemada (Hers 1989; Nelson 1997).

According to Acosta (1945), the Vestibule was built during the same period as Pyramid B, and like that structure consists of several construction phases, the first of which did not have benches. During the last phase, the decorated benches were added along all three walls of the Vestibule, along with an altar near the eastern edge of Pyramid B's stairway. The southeast section of the Vestibule contains two stepped platforms that go down nearly to the level of the plaza, and on the southeast adjoin a passageway several meters wide that separates the Vestibule from Pyramid C. Two lower stairways, one on the south edge and another on the east edge, permit access from the plaza to the Vestibule. The southern stairway is aligned with the north-south axis of Pyramid B, and gives access to the pyramid, while the eastern stairway is an access to what Acosta (1956a) called "The Palace to the East of the Vestibule."

The benches that bordered the walls of the Vestibule nearly totally survived, but the friezes that covered them were preserved only in a section covering about 8 meters in the northwest corner. The cornice of this frieze is decorated with reliefs of undulating plumed serpents, which is a common motif on the existing sculptured bench cornices at Tula.[6] The polychrome frieze of Pyramid B's vestibule is known as the Friso de los Caciques (Acosta 1945; Moedano 1947) (Fig. 5.26), and has been analyzed in some detail by a number of scholars, including

Figure 5.23. Stela 1, found in the pre-Hispanic trench in Pyramid B (from Jiménez 1998: fig. 52). This figure probably represents a king of Tula.

THE EARLY POSTCLASSIC: THE TOLLAN PHASE CITY

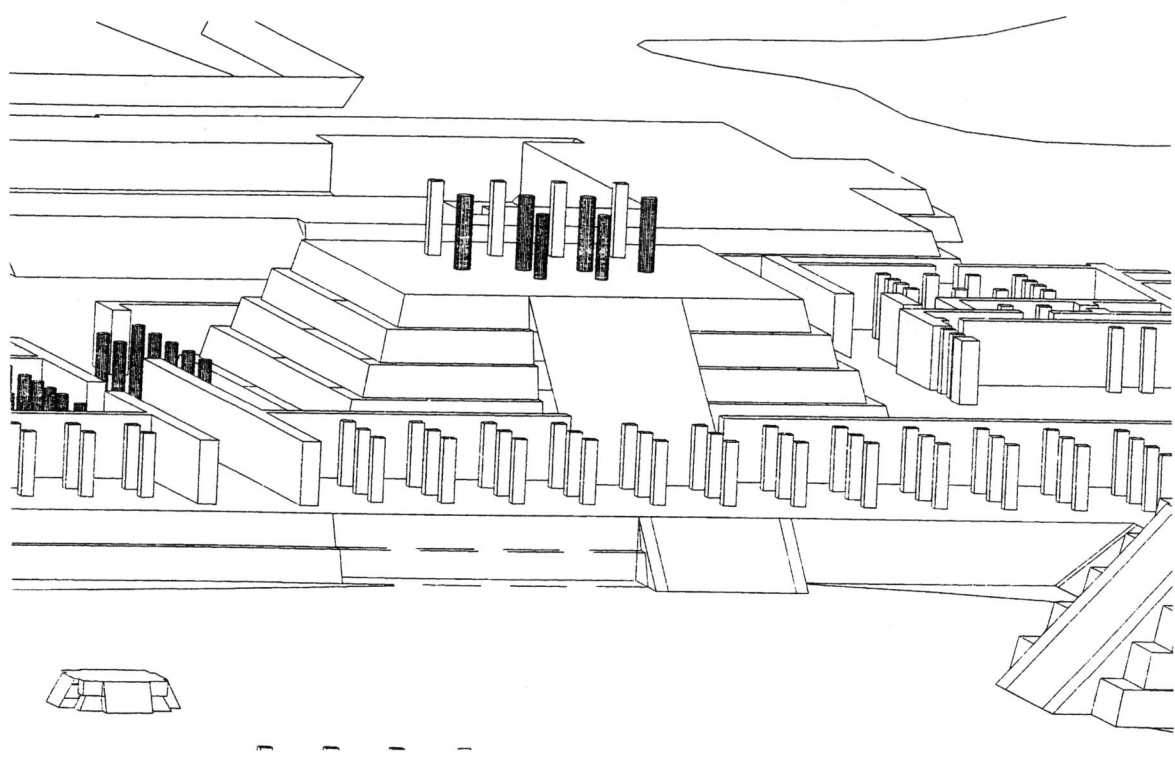

Figure 5.24. Pyramid B and the South Vestibule.

Kristan-Graham (1989), Umberger (1987), and Klein (1987), who have discussed the similarity of these reliefs with those of benches at Chichén Itzá and the sacred precinct of Tenochtitlan. Taube (in press a) recently has shown that prototypes for Tula's benches with feathered-serpent reliefs are to be found in Classic Teotihuacan where probable benches with feathered serpents are depicted in the murals of Techinantitla, and he identified another kind of bench-throne in Tetitla.

The Friso de los Caciques at Tula consists of nineteen richly costumed personages who walk from left to right, that is toward the east and the stairway of Pyramid B. In the opinion of Moedano (1947:133), who excavated this sculpture group, the preserved part of the frieze represents: "A procession of principal nobles (señores) . . . of the principal peoples subject to Toltec domination . . . because of this we find personages with headdresses and other attributes of diverse forms and richness, ranging from a noble with a simple headdress to one who wears a Xihuitzolli [crown] . . . [and others with] headdresses and attributes of warriors, because these chiefs possessed among their principal functions that of the military command, although just nominal, of their own armies."

Kristan-Graham (1989:274–275; 1993) proposes that the persons represented in this frieze could be *pochteca* (merchants) and not noble lords or warriors. To support this interpretation, she cites Sahagún's description (Book IX) of a ritual that the *pochteca* performed before leaving for a journey, in which they formed two rows facing each other, with old merchants on one side and young ones on the other; but she notes that this *pochteca* ritual differs from the scene in the Friso de los Caciques in that all the merchants were seated. She also observes that *pochteca* in some rituals carried a staff in one hand and a shield in the other, as do some of the personages in the Friso de los Caciques. Other evidence

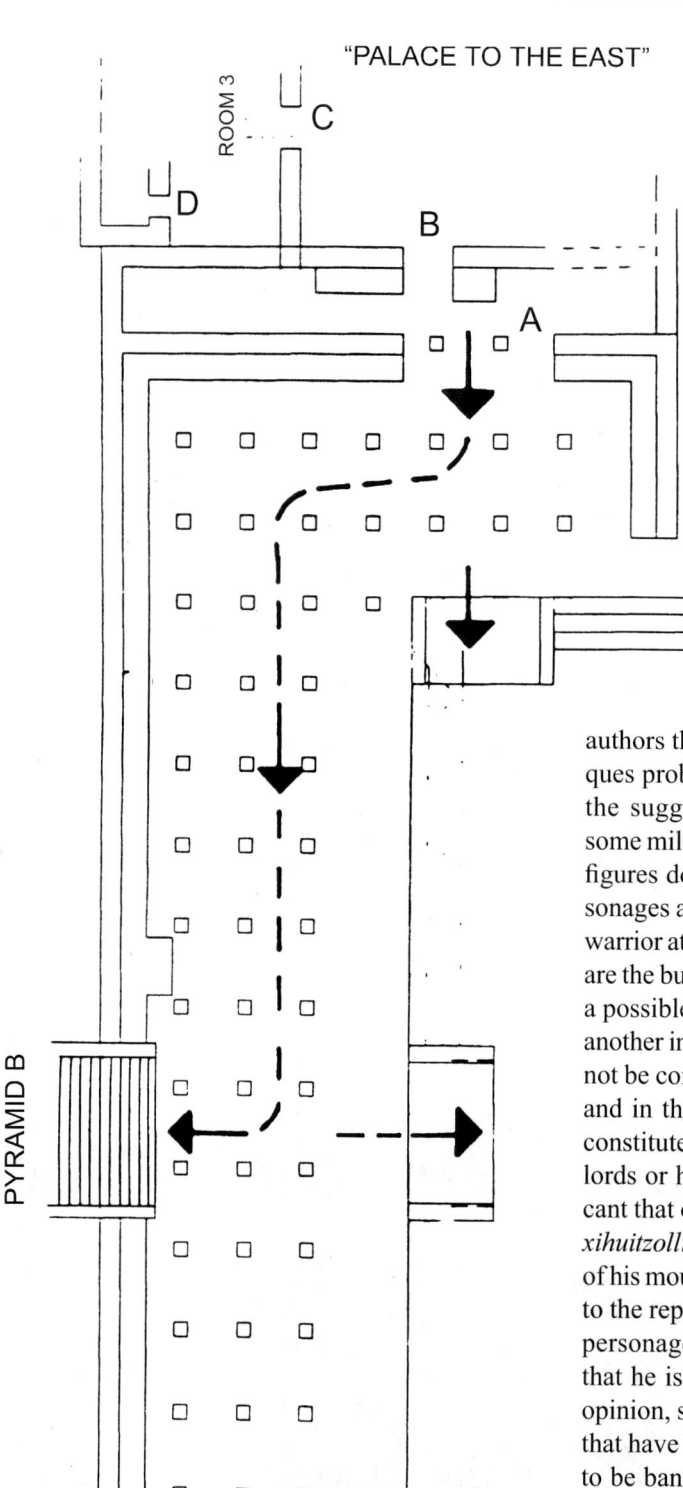

Figure 5.25. The South Vestibule and the "Palace to the East." Based on Acosta (1960).

for the representation of *pochteca* in this frieze that Kristan-Graham cites includes the notion that one of the figures appears to be carrying a bundle on his back, and the proposal of Moedano (1947:124) that another figure carries what could be a fan in his hand, this being a symbol associated with *pochteca* and traders in Mesoamerica.

We agree with these authors that the personages in the Friso de los Caciques probably are not warriors, and especially with the suggestion of Moedano that the presence of some military elements in the representation of some figures does not automatically mean that these personages are warriors. Otherwise, the only additional warrior attributes that we have identified in this frieze are the butterfly pectorals that three figures wear, and a possible fending stick or slashing weapon held by another individual, but in our opinion the shields cannot be considered an exclusive attribute of warriors, and in the context of this frieze could more likely constitute an important element in the costumes of lords or high ranking nobles. It is no doubt significant that one of the personages in this frieze wears a *xihuitzolli* (crown) and has a speech scroll coming out of his mouth—both these elements do not correspond to the representation of a *pochteca,* but because this personage does not carry weapons, it is unlikely that he is a warrior (Jiménez 1998: fig. 95). In our opinion, some elements in the Friso de los Caciques that have been identified as arms more likely appear to be banners, staffs, scepters, and elaborate rattles similar to the ones described by Sahagún and other chroniclers, which the Mexica used in processions, festivals, and other rituals.

THE EARLY POSTCLASSIC: THE TOLLAN PHASE CITY

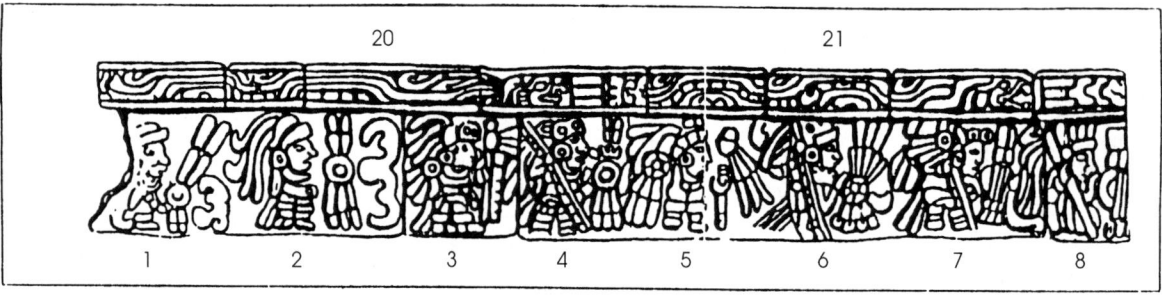

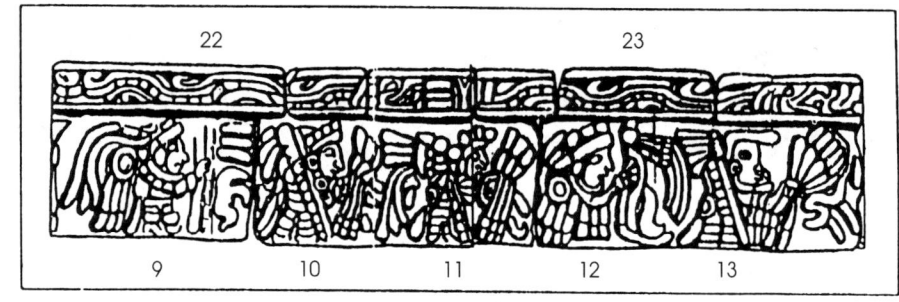

Figure 5.26. The Friso de los Caciques (from Acosta 1945 and Jiménez 1998: fig. 95).

In the eastern sector of the Vestibule, Acosta (1956a:74, fig. 2) found fragments of another bench frieze representing personages walking from right to left, and in the Vestibule's southeast limit, he found a panel in situ depicting two figures walking in this direction. On this basis, both Acosta and Moedano (1947) propose that the bench friezes in the Vestibule show two processions: one starting from the extreme west and another from the east, with the two processions meeting at the stairway of Pyramid B. Thus, it seems beyond doubt that the Vestibule's bench friezes do represent two processions, but it is not clear that these met at the pyramid stairway, and to us it is more probable that the meeting point of the processions was the altar directly east of the stairway. Not much can be said concerning the procession that, starting in the southeast of the Vestibule, eventually met the Friso de los Caciques procession at or near the altar. The few surviving fragments, with only one panel found in situ, merely depict a sequence of personages walking from right to left and the only complete figure appears to represented a warrior carrying a fending stick (*arma curva*) in his right hand (Acosta 1956a:74, fig. 27). Thus it is very likely that the two processions of the Vestibule were of different character: one was composed of warriors and the other of nobles or other high-ranking personages, with both groups converging on a central unknown motif that could have been a *cuauxicalli*.

On the basis of the similarity of these friezes at Tula with those studied by Beyer (1955) and those recently excavated in the Casa de las Aguilas (Matos 1988) near the Templo Mayor of Tenochtitlan, both cases of which have the processions of personages converge on a *zacatapayolli* (a symbol representing a ball of grass with maguey spines jutting out of it for autosacrifice), various authors (especially Klein 1987 and De la Fuente 1990) have proposed that it is probable that also in the Friso de los Caciques the central motif for the convergence of the processions was a *zacatapayolli*. De la Fuente, for example, mentions that Acosta (1957:141, fig. 21) found a relief panel with this symbol in the southwest corner of the Vestibule. However, this panel actually was in a secondary context and had been reused in the construction of the balustrade of a stairway. It was set in the balustrade with the relief facing inward, out of view. Thus there is no certainty that this panel originally formed part of the Friso de los Caciques. In addition, Acosta identified the symbol on this relief as a *cuauhxicalli* and not a *zacatapayolli*.

Thus we do not know what the central motif was for the two processions of personages on the bench reliefs of the Vestibule, but it is probable that the ritual being represented dealt with sacrifice ceremonies, and very probably the penitence and autosacrifice rites performed by Tula's king and his principal functionaries and priests in the Vestibule and associated with Pyramid B. These ceremonies perhaps were similar to the penitence rituals that Klein (1987) proposes could have taken place in Tenochtitlan's Casa de las Aguilas.

Building 4 or "The Palace to the East of the Vestibule"

On the east side of the Vestibule there is an entrance to a building complex that Acosta only partially excavated that he called "Building 4 or the Palace to the East of the Vestibule" (1956a:44–46, 77–80). He describes this structure as an "enormous palace" where he only was able to explore parts of four rooms, but his project reports do not explain why more sectors of this "complicated system of rooms" were not excavated. "The discovery of a wide entrance on the east side of the Vestibule led us to an enormous and complicated system of rooms constructed with adobe having [preserved] walls which sometimes reached four meters in height" (Acosta 1964:60).

It is worth emphasizing that the "wide entrance" to this room complex measured almost 9 meters in width and was subdivided by two pillars supporting the lintels. Thus, this was no ordinary entrance, but a very special access of great dimensions divided into three sections, similar to the entrance that Acosta (1967) proposed in the reconstruction for the temple on the summit of Pyramid B, and which is a common plan for the entrances of pyramid temples both in Central Mexico and in Maya centers.

The remains of Building 4, which are still visible on Tula's precinct and especially in the maps of Acosta, consists only of sections of four different rooms (Fig. 5.27). Acosta (1964) mentions that the adobe walls in the third room were preserved to a height of 4 meters, and that he found in situ the wooden beams for the entrances to this room. We only know that part of this building consisted of a long narrow room that extended for the entire length of the Vestibule's east side, and beyond this narrow room to the east there are sections of three other rooms, two of them located on the north, but we do not know the complete dimensions and the internal structure of the building, which without doubt constituted a very important structure on Tula's sacred precinct due to its proximity to the two pyramids and its direct access to Pyramid B.

Embellishing the base of the interior wall of the first room was a rectangular altar with a cornice that is aligned with the great entrance of the building. Both the main register and the cornice of the altar originally were covered with reliefs, the surviving panels of which cover part of its main (west) face and its south side. The reliefs of this altar depict a procession of richly costumed personages walking from east to west and from south to north toward a central motif, which in this case is a human figure with his torso sculpted frontally, and his head facing south toward the personages in the procession. An undulating blue plumed serpent forming an S is in the background of the central figure, whom Acosta

THE EARLY POSTCLASSIC: THE TOLLAN PHASE CITY

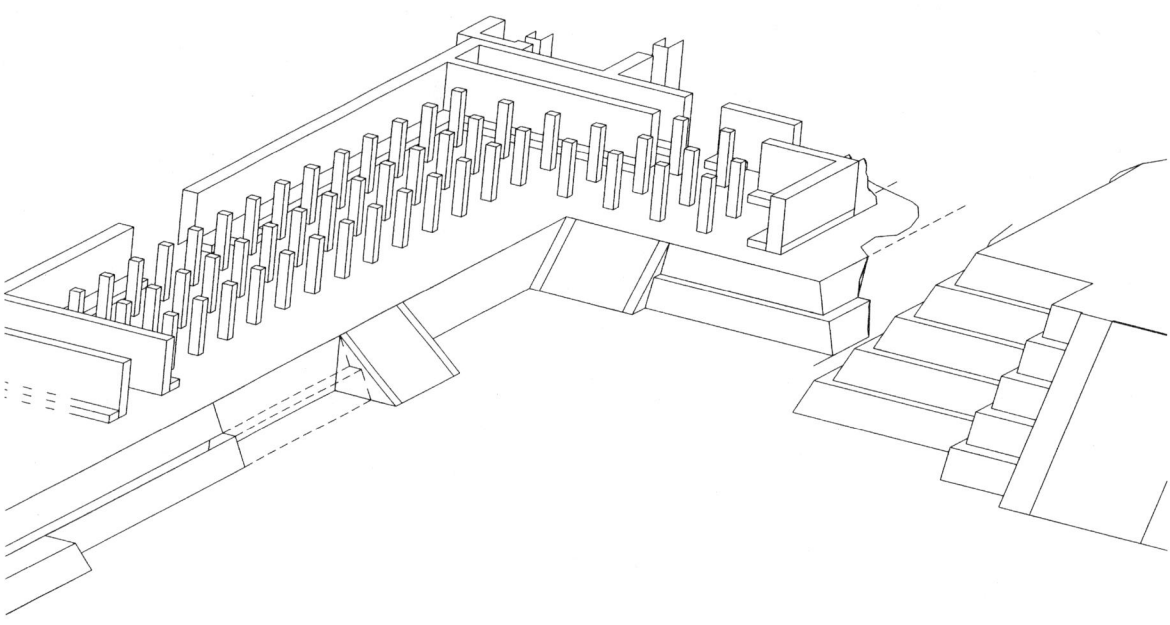

Figure 5.27. Perspective of the Vestibule and the "Palace to the East of the Vestibule." Based on Acosta (1960).

(1956a:74–80, figs. 28 and 29) calls the "Great Priest Quetzalcoatl" ("el Gran Sacerdote Quetzalcoatl"). Armillas (1947:178) proposed that the plumed serpent or Quetzal-coatl could have been at Tula a title of Ce Acatl Topiltzin as "sacerdote mayor del dios de las aguas." More generally, we think that in the art of Tula the serpents in form of an S are symbols of royalty, possibly signifying the title of ruler, and that personages with the serpent behind them represent Toltec kings (Mastache and Cobean n.d.2). The rest of the relief on the main face and the north side of the altar has been destroyed, but on the north edge of the central figure are depictions of feathers that very probably are part of a banner or headdress for another (missing) figure, which indicates that there was probably another procession of personages going in the opposite direction, with both processions converging on the plumed serpent figure (Fig. 5.28).

The costumes, placement, and other attributes of this central personage and the other members in the altar processions suggest that this relief may represent an important ceremony, wherein the protagonists consist of the king (perhaps recently enthroned) and lords from other regions who are greeting or paying homage to the newly invested sovereign. This scene suggests a situation similar to a ceremony described by Sahagún that was part of the festivities in the election of a new Mexica emperor who "sent his ambassadors to all surrounding Kingdoms, from Quautimalan to Michoacan, and from sea to sea, and then came the same lords or their dignitaries to attend . . . the festival of the election, all the invited participants were together some days before the festival" (Sahagún 1956: II, Book 8, p. 324).

There is a notable similarity between this altar frieze and the bench reliefs at the Mercado and the friezes in the Temple of the Jaguar at Chichén Itzá (Marquina 1964: photos 435, 436; fig. 272), both of which depict processions of richly dressed figures centered around a great personage with an undulating feathered serpent in the background. The reliefs in the Mercado are especially similar to the Building 4 reliefs because the Mercado benches have cornices with plumed serpents like those of most Tula bench cornices, including those of Building 4.

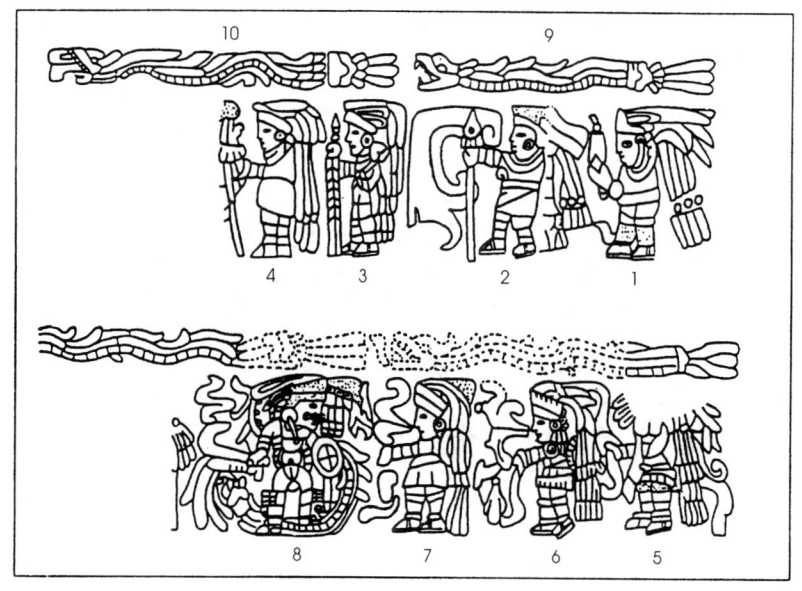

Figure 5.28. The relief on the altar at the "Palace to the East": A procession of richly costumed personages walking toward a central figure who probably is the king of Tula (from Acosta 1956 and Jiménez 1998: fig. 97).

It is important to emphasize that although the Palace to the East is adjoined on the north by the so-called Palace of Quetzalcoatl, there is little probability that these buildings had direct communication because platforms and other architectural barriers exist between them. Probably the greatest barrier was that the floor level of the Palace of Quetzalcoatl was several meters above that of the other palace.

Several investigators have discussed correlations between the sculptured benches in the Casa de las Aguilas (Building E) in Tenochtitlan and those of two structures at Tula: the Vestibule (the Friso de los Caciques bench) and the Palacio Quemado, emphasizing for both centers' bench reliefs the existence of processional figures with similar style, ritual themes and iconography, and the presence of cornices decorated with plumed serpents (Klein 1987; Umberger 1987; Kristan-Graham 1989; De la Fuente 1990; and López Luján 1993). Klein (p. 307) observes that the east room of the Casa de las Aguilas has a sunken patio with drains comparable to the halls in Tula's Palacio Quemado and the Mercado at Chichén Itzá; especially emphasizing the compositional and iconographic similarities between the bench friezes near the Templo Mayor and the Friso de los Caciques at Tula. López Luján (p. 82) also mentions that the spatial distribution of the Casa de las Aguilas (Building E) and the form, proportions, and decoration of its benches are reminiscent of the Palacio Quemado in Tula and the Mercado in Chichén Itzá.[7]

Even taking into account that the similarities proposed by the just-cited authors do exist, we are in agreement with Molina Montes (1987) and Francisco Hinojosa (cited by Molina Montes:102), who show that the spatial organization of the Casa de las Aguilas is similar to that of the building excavated by Acosta to the east of the Vestibule, stating that in "both cases the access is up a stairway, through a portico which is part of an L-shaped colonnade . . . this portico entrance is gained through a doorway located axially with the stairway into a long, narrow chamber. From here one proceeds into the patio through a doorway not located on the same axis but displaced to one side."

It is important to note that there are other elements shared by the Palace to the East of the Vestibule and the Casa de las Aguilas besides the similarities described by Molina Montes. In both complexes, the principal axes are oriented east-west with a secondary axis oriented north-south, and the vestibules possess square pillars and two stairways: one on the north side and the other on the east side. In addition, in both Tula and the Templo Mayor the group of rooms is located on the east side of the vestibule, and at the entrance of these rooms there is long narrow rectangular space with an altar placed against its inner wall. In both cases, the altar is aligned with the principal entrance, and the architectonic relationship between the building entrance and the altar with the east stairway of the vestibule (all are roughly aligned) is the same.

In the Casa de las Aguilas, adjoining the first room on the north is another room that on its south side has a sunken patio with columns. At Tula, we can observe in the same location part of a room that appears to have a similar form (e.g., Room 3, where Acosta found the doorway beams in situ). This room is adjoined to the north by a smaller room that has a second doorway in its northwest corner, apparently like the plan of the equivalent room in the Casa de las Aguilas (see Fig. 5.29). The letters A, B, C, and D in Figures 5.25 and 5.29 indicate the rooms and the doorways of the two structures that are similarly placed. Nevertheless, in Tula the sector to the south of Room 3, where the columned patio would be, was not excavated (and may have been destroyed in pre-Hispanic times). Because of this, we do not know if the rest of this building also was similar in plan to the Casa de las Aguilas, as is the part near the portico, but even so, the correlations in terms of general plan and location are notable.

But probably even more significant is the fact that the location and spatial relationship of both buildings with the nearby pyramids are the same. The setting and architectural relationship of the South Vestibule with Pyramid C are clearly the same as those that the Casa de las Aguilas has with the Templo Mayor. In both complexes, the vestibule and its rooms are placed on the northwest side of the pyramid, in a location next to the pyramid but separated from it by a hallway.

It is important to state that the total sizes and forms of these two buildings are unknown, and that different sections of each structure were conserved at Tula and Tenochtitlan. In the case of the Casa de las Aguilas, the rooms of its east wing are known almost in their totality except for the northern limit, which is covered by the modern street of Justo Sierra. Due to this, the length and width of the building's north wing are unknown, as is the total number of columns in this section. The existing excavation uncovered a row of six columns, but there may have been more. At Tula, in contrast, much of the "east wing" (consisting of Acosta's "Palace to the East of the Vestibule") of the complex has not been excavated, but we know the size and characteristics of the adjoining sector (the Vestibule), and we also know the nature of the building to the north with which this complex was integrated, this being Pyramid B, for which the Vestibule constituted its only direct access.

If, as we believe, the north wing of the Casa de las Aguilas really was part of a long narrow portico similar to the South Vestibule of Pyramid B, it is logical to ask if this portico was articulated toward the north with another structure, and that being the case, what were the characteristics and nature of this building.[8]

Another possibility is that directly to the north of the Casa de las Aguilas, there was a plaza or another kind of open area such as those found at Chichén Itzá north of the colonnade (which also has small stairways) to the southeast of the Temple of the Warriors, or to the north of the vestibule on the west side of Chichén's plaza. On the other hand, it may be possible that the Casa de las Aguilas constituted an independent architectural unit in itself, with the form of an L, and was not specifically integrated with another building to the north. Without knowing the total plan and dimensions of the Casa de las Aguilas, including especially its north wing, in our opinion it is highly speculative to attempt to make an architectural reconstruction of this building.

In the case of Tula, it is important to emphasize that only the occupants of the "Palace to the East of the Vestibule" had direct access to Pyramid B and the temple on its summit; from this structure, it was possible to walk directly to the stairway of the pyramid without going down to the plaza. No other building had such direct access to this pyramid. The great columned doorway of this palace probably was the starting point for ceremonial processions going to the summit of the pyramid. It is evident, therefore, that the Vestibule and the "Palace to the East" constituted an architectonic unit that was integrated with Pyramid B. It is worth adding that even though on first impression it might appear that the Palacio Quemado and the Palace of Quetzalcoatl also had direct access to Pyramid B, this was not so because despite the proximity of these buildings, different types of architectural barriers exist between them.

THE EARLY POSTCLASSIC: THE TOLLAN PHASE CITY

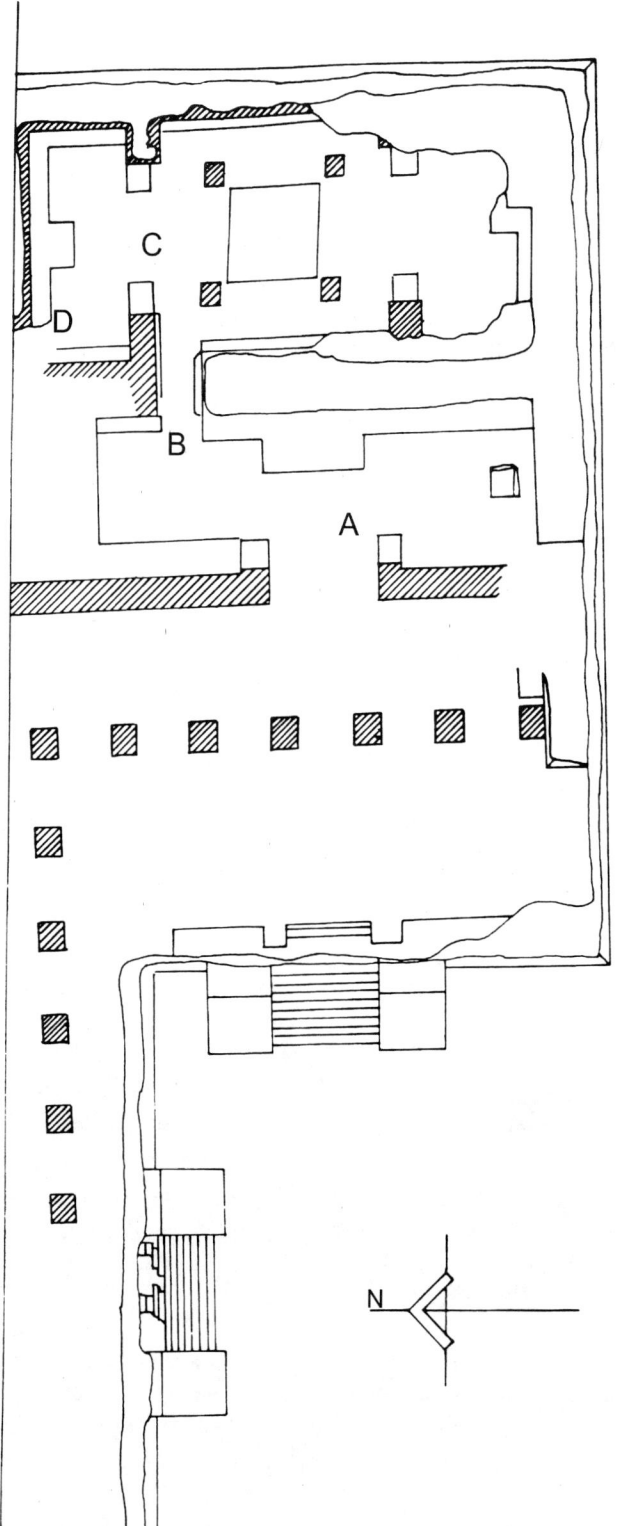

Figure 5.29. Plan of the "Casa de las Aguilas" at the Templo Mayor of Tenochtitlan. Courtesy, Eduardo Matos.

The Palace of Quetzalcoatl or Building 1

As can be seen clearly in the topographic map of Tula's monumental center before excavations (Fig. 5.8A), Pyramid B was constructed at the center of a great elongated platform and is flanked by two large architectonic compounds: the Palace of Quetzalcoatl to the east and the Palacio Quemado to the west, with these three structures together constituting a kind of great complex. This is another parallel between Pyramid B and Teotihuacan's Pyramid of the Moon, which also is flanked on the east and the west by great compounds forming a similar complex (Millon 1973: maps N5W1 and N5E1).

Adjacent to Pyramid B on the east, and in some sense overlapping with part of the pyramid, is the building that Acosta (1964) called the "Palace of Quetzalcoatl" or Building 1, in which he identified three principal construction phases, some of them covering part of the lower two *taluds* or tiers of Pyramid B on its east side. According to Acosta (pp. 58–61) this building measures approximately 60 meters east to west, and its east base ended in a stuccoed *talud* that in some sectors was at least 2 meters high, apparently with a cornice on its upper edge and the remains of connecting walls at its base. On the east face of this *talud* there was a mural painted on a clay surface, of which only the lower portion survived, representing the feet of two personages walking toward the south along with part of a circular motif placed between the two figures.

Even though Acosta's excavations only exposed one columned hall of the Palace of Quetzalcoatl, his topographic map provides an idea of the probable form and extension of this building (1956–1957: map 1) (see Fig. 5.8A),

115

which during its last construction stage appears to have constituted an architectonic complex similar to the Palacio Quemado, that is, a long platform composed of one or two tiers (*taluds*) on which were constructed several columned halls aligned along an east-west axis.

The floor level of the excavated hall is approximately 4.5 meters above the base of Pyramid B and the South Vestibule. This hall was slightly rectangular like Salas 1 and 3 of the Palacio Quemado, but smaller, having only one row of columns to support the roof. Toward the west, the hall is adjacent to Pyramid B but located several meters above its base; toward the east this hall probably was followed by a similar columned room of which only some remains of walls and pillars were found. The completely excavated hall has two entrances; one, probably the principal access, is located exactly in the center of the north wall, perhaps communicating with a vestibule or other room on this side. Another access, this one in form of an L, existed in the southwest corner of the hall and provided communication to another room that was bordered on the north by three smaller rooms.

Unfortunately, little more information is available concerning the plan and internal structuring of this building and its specific contexts, but nevertheless its placement next to Pyramid B and on the Plazoleta Norte indicates its importance. It is interesting that this building partially covers the lower tiers of Pyramid B's west facade, and that its floor level is raised up several meters above the South Vestibule and the Plazoleta Norte, which indicates that the Palace of Quetzalcoatl did not have direct access to these spaces, nor to the main plaza farther south. Perhaps the principal entrance to the Palace of Quetzalcoatl was on its east side on the extreme eastern limit of the platform on which this structure was built. The mounds of the so-called Ballcourt 3 are near the eastern limit of this building, although there exists a significant difference in elevation between these structural complexes, as can be seen in Acosta's (1956–1957) map (Fig. 5.8A).

During the excavations of the Palace of Quetzalcoatl (Edificio 1), Acosta (1956a:56–60) found a lateral platform overlapping the east base of Pyramid B. He defined six different construction stages for this platform, "of which three correspond to Stage 1 of the pyramid, two to Stage II and one to Stage III" (1956a: plan 1). The last enlargement of this platform reached a height of 4.5 meters and consisted of three tiers (*taluds*) covered by plain-surfaced limestone panels. Apparently these lateral platforms extended between 50 to 60 meters to the east of Pyramid B, forming a barrier between the Palace of Quetzalcoatl and the "Palace to the East of the Vestibule."

The Palacio Quemado or "Burned Palace"

Among the columned buildings on the sacred precinct, the largest and perhaps the most important is called the Palacio Quemado. This architectonic complex has a rectangular form measuring approximately 90 meters by 60 meters, and is located directly west of Pyramid B, from which it is separated by a narrow passageway. Acosta (1956a) found remains of a polychrome mural on the stucco surfaces of the adobe walls of this passageway.

The Palacio Quemado basically consists of three great quadrangular columned halls with central sunken patios (*impluvios*). These halls are independent and do not interconnect in common entrances or passageways. Each hall possesses its own entrance on different sides: Sala 1 on the east, Sala 3 on the west, and Sala 2 on the south, which means that only Sala 2 had direct access toward the main plaza (see Fig. 5.30). These halls are adjoined on the north by a row of six long narrow rooms. The three rooms (*cuartos* number 1, 5, and 6) on the western and eastern ends of the row only have doorways toward the north and do not connect with the main halls, whereas the central three rooms (2, 3, and 4) are closed on the north but have direct communication with Sala 2 on the south.

Acosta (1956a) emphasized that a significant aspect of this structure is the existence of columned vestibules (*columnatas*) that surround it on three sides: south, north, and west. These vestibules are independent or isolated, with transverse walls that block communication between them and separate them from one another. The existence of architectural barriers between the vestibules conditioned the possibilities of circulation for most spaces in the Palacio Quemado complex. Most of the Palacio Quemado apparently did not have direct access to Pyramid B, because the vestibules of both buildings were separated by a walled passageway (Figs. 5.31 and 5.32), which blocked circulation to the pyramid. Only Sala 2, through its southern entrance, would have had access to Pyramid B via the plaza.

Some differences exist in the columns and pillars supporting the roofs of the three halls and the vestibules. The halls (Fig. 5.30, *salas* 1 and 3) on the extremes of the Palacio Quemado have circular columns along with the north and west vestibules that communicate with them. In contrast, Sala 2 and the southern vestibule of the palace possess square columns. Probably the reason for placing columns with the same forms in specific halls and the vestibules with which they communicate was not merely to achieve greater architectural unity, or harmony in particular sectors of the structure, but also as a means of marking two different categories of space. Only the spaces with square columns had direct access to the plaza, that is, Sala 2 and the southern vestibule.

As can be seen in Figures 5.31 and 5.32, the three great portico halls that form the Palacio Quemado are very similar but not identical. The halls placed on the extreme east and west (1 and 3) are slightly rectangular in form, while the central hall is square (measuring 26 by 26 meters). The central location of Sala 2, its having three small annex rooms on the north, and its being the only hall with direct access to the plaza indicate, as Acosta (1961a:56–57) observed, that Sala 2 was without doubt the most important room in the Palacio Quemado. Also of special importance was Cuarto (Room) 4, located on a higher level than Sala 2 to the north, which had access to the *sala* via a small stairway aligned exactly on the palace's north-south axis; Acosta (pp. 34, 37) states that this small room surely constituted "a sanctuary where the most sacred rites were celebrated."

In the interior of this small room, there was a bench or altar from which some polychrome friezes survived that represent figures dressed as warriors. The two preserved personages are depicted frontally instead of in profile like most Tula friezes. They are shown with characteristic Toltec arms (*atlatl* and fending stick) along with butterfly pectorals and a *tezcacuitlapilli* back mirror. Behind one figure is an undulating plumed serpent forming an inverted S motif, while the other warrior lacks a serpent but is followed by a panel fragment with the relief of the tail of another feathered serpent. Thus, originally this frieze probably consisted of alternating figures with one personage having a plumed serpent and the next one lacking the serpent (Acosta 1961), which suggests that each figure had a different status. We agree with Acosta that this room was no ordinary place. It clearly constituted an important ritual setting having restricted access, perhaps only for the sovereign, and possessing significant roles in the ceremonial functions of Sala 2 (Fig. 5.33).

The three great columned halls (*salas*) of the Palacio Quemado can be reconstructed in some detail on the basis of Acosta's excavation reports. He found the roofs fallen on the floors and damage by burning. The roofs originally had a central open section (*impluvio*) that provided light to the interior of each hall. The upper parts of these open patios were decorated with polychrome relief panels that possessed three principal motifs: reclining human figures, great solar disks like the dorsal disks of the Atlantes, and representantions of *cuauhxicalli* or vessels with sacrificed hearts (Acosta 1956a). Fallen sculptures also were found of *chalchihuites* (precious stones or drops of water) and bundles of columns (*atados de columnillas*). The patio roofs, in addition, were decorated with merlons (*almenas*) in the form of a G, which Acosta interpreted as depicting the cut cross section of a conch shell, and thus being a Venus-Quetzalcoatl symbol (Fig. 5.34).

In Sala 1, Acosta (1956a, 1957) was able to reconstruct the greatest number of relief panels because they were less damaged than in the other two halls. In Sala 1 he recovered fragments corresponding to eight solar disks and four *cuauhxicalli*, but even more numerous were the panels with reclining personages that totalled at least twenty, of which only seven were reconstructed. These reclining figures are armed and have costume elements of

THE EARLY POSTCLASSIC: THE TOLLAN PHASE CITY

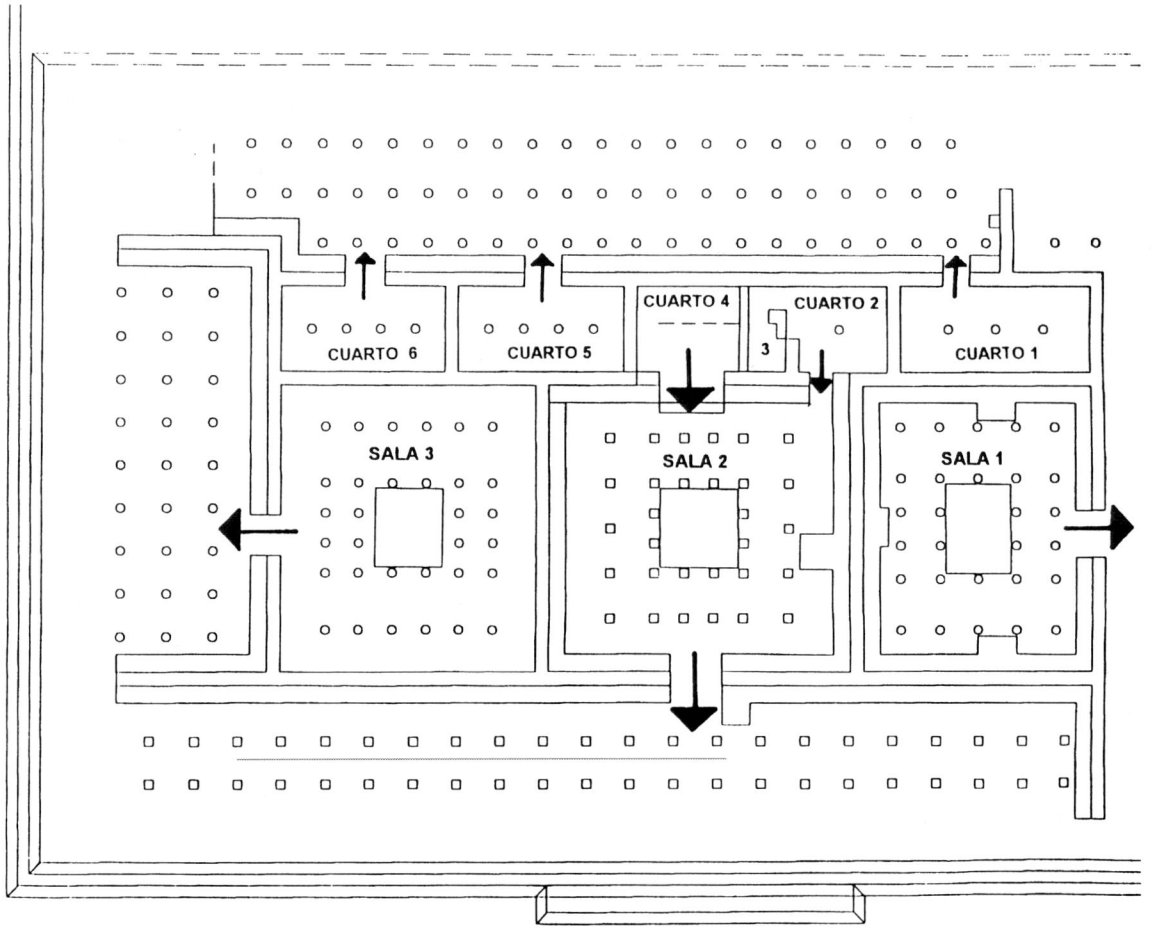

Figure 5.30. Plan of the Palacio Quemado.

Toltec warriors. Some have feathered serpents in the background, and others wear a large transversally cut conch shell as a pectoral. Although Acosta managed to reconstruct only a few of the panels with reclining figures, his illustrations indicate that these figures look in different directions: most of the figures looking toward the right have serpents, while the other figures look toward the left, which suggests that in the original sculpture group, the reclining personages (Fig. 5.35) were divided in rows of figures looking in the same direction, with groups of figures looking to the left and to the right arranged around one or more central motifs that could have been the *cuauhxicalli* or the *tezcacuitlapilli* (solar disks), or both (Fig. 5.34). It is significant that four of the reclining figures have leggings with tied bows, which may constitute symbols of royalty. The other personages have plain round leggings or knee protectors (*rodilleras*).

Anatomical and costume attributes of the reclining figures in the Palacio Quemado suggest that they may represent some of the same personages who are depicted on the pillars of Pyramid B. Like the figures of the Pyramid B pillars, the Palacio Quemado roof panels may represent personages of two different categories—kings or rulers and other personages having a lesser status or function—but only a detailed analysis of all the restored panels and the hundreds of

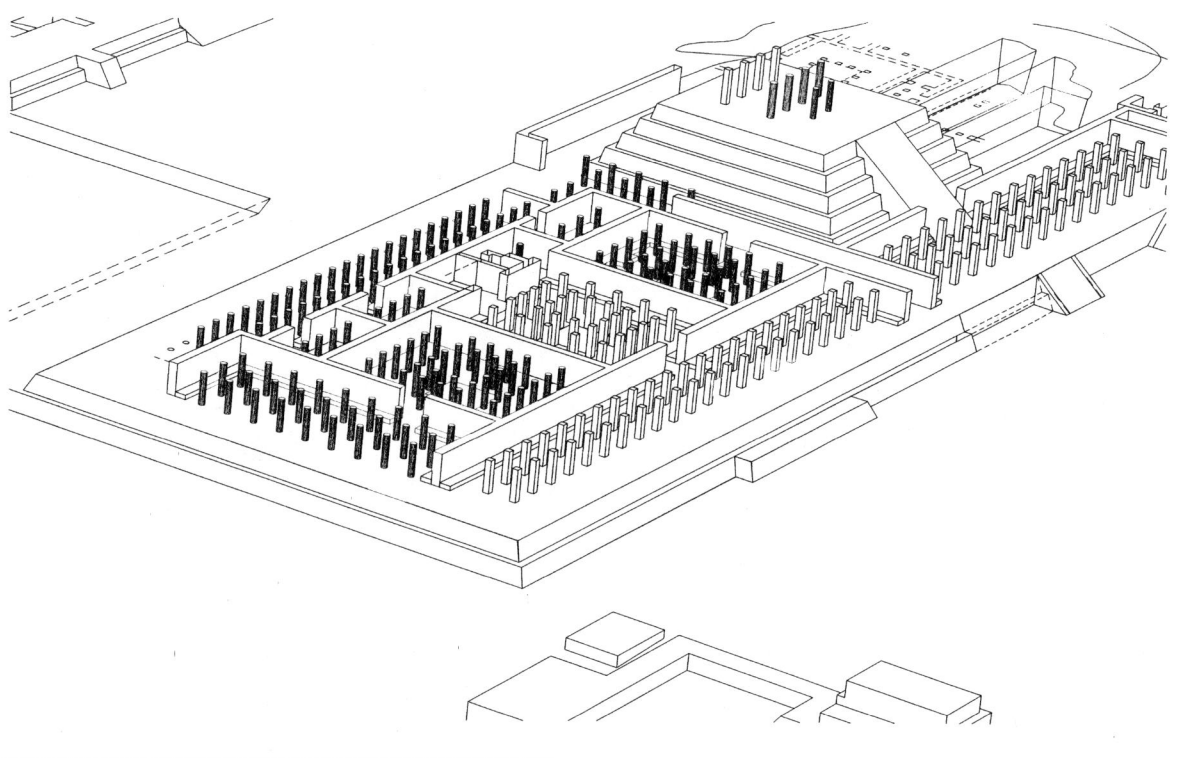

Figure 5.31. Perspective of the Palacio Quemado.

fragments found on the palace floors would determine if these proposals are viable.

The benches and altars originally located in the interior of Salas 1 and 2 were similar in size and architectural characteristics to those of the Pyramid B Vestibule. The Palacio Quemado benches and altars doubtlessly also were covered with friezes, but these reliefs only were preserved in three areas of Sala 2 and in Cuarto 4 to the north. In addition, the three vestibules surrounding the Palacio Quemado all probably possessed sculptured benches and altars, but only a few reliefs have survived in situ in the North Vestibule (Acosta 1957, 1961a).

The principal preserved friezes in Sala 2 include an important relief panel in the northeast corner at the east side of the entrance for Cuartos 2 and 3, which depicts two warriors walking from left to right, one of whom is bowed like an elderly person (Fig. 5.36). Surely this frieze continued for the bench's entire length until it connected with the surviving relief panels on the east side of the hall's principal entrance. Here Acosta found a section of bench friezes representing six personages in procession from left to right, with three figures on the north face of the bench and three figures on the east face at the main entrance. The procession on the north face turns the corner at the entrance and is shown leaving the building on the east bench face (Acosta 1957: 131, 153, 168, figs. 8 and 31).

The personage who leads this procession out of the building possesses the eye goggles characteristic of the god Tlaloc, and is without doubt the most important figure in the frieze (Fig. 5.37). His high status is expressed in his leading the procession, his being represented with greater stature than the other figures, and his having the most elaborate costume. This leader also has the most elaborate speech scroll in the procession, and it is noteworthy that one of the figures following him wears a *xihuitzolli*. All the surviving figures in this procession are armed (usually with fending sticks or spears), but do not have butterfly pectorals or other attributes of high status Toltec warriors.

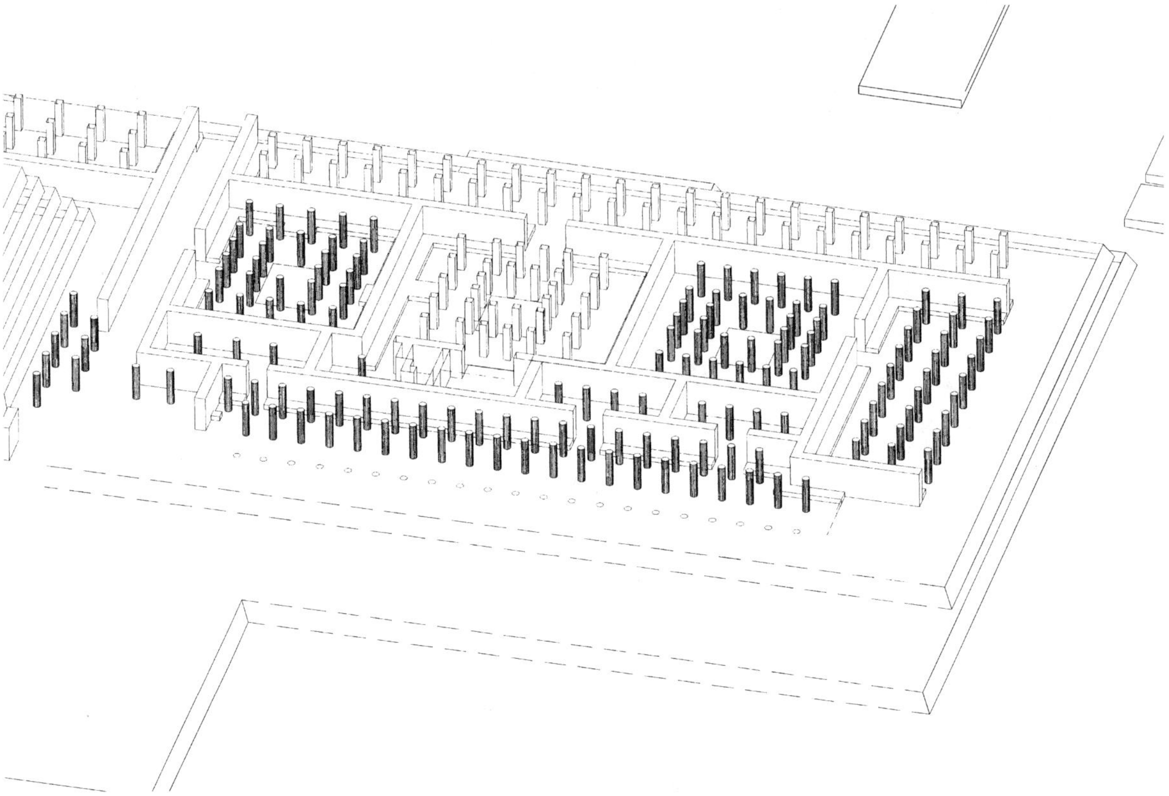

Figure 5.32. The north side of the Palacio Quemado.

Figure 5.33. The bench frieze of Cuarto 4 in the Palacio Quemado. Based on Acosta (1961a) (from Jiménez 1998: fig. 91).

Figure 5.34. Sculptural elements that form the upper friezes in the central patios of the Palacio Quemado. Drawing from Acosta (1956a). Photos, Humberto Illera.

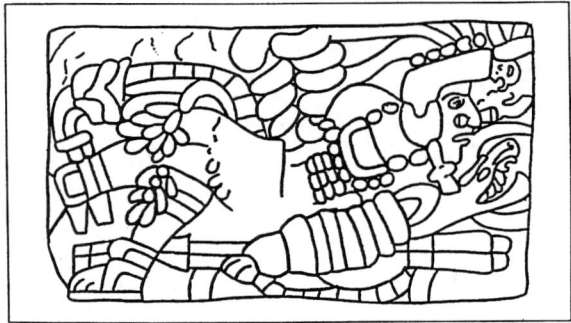

Figure 5.35. Reclining figures from the patio friezes of Sala 1 in the Palacio Quemado (from Jiménez 1998).

On the west side of the entrance to Cuartos 2 and 3 (Fig. 5.30), there is a bench with relief panels extending for more than 4 meters, representing thirteen personages walking from right to left along with six serpents in relief on the bench cornice, which also are depicted in motion from right to left (Fig. 5.38). The first three personages in the procession go toward the south, then turn west where the remaining ten figures are. The surviving frieze ends abruptly before connecting with what appears to have been an altar. The missing relief panels probably were removed in pre-Hispanic times and their broken basal stubs were found still on the floor when Acosta excavated them. The surviving cornice reliefs are interesting because the undulating serpents above the human figures have white scrolls on their bodies instead of feathers. Acosta (1957) suggests that these are cloud serpents and constitute a reference to the legendary lord or god Mixcoatl.

Acosta concludes that the two processions in the Sala 2 friezes (one going from left to right and the other from right to left) surrounded the entire hall going in opposite directions and then met at the main entrance in the south, probably finally leaving the hall to enter the South Vestibule: "Surely we are witnessing the representation of some important civic-religious ceremony that was celebrated in the precinct where the participants when entering in the rear (north of the hall) divide into two columns, and afterwards march in different directions, (eventually) joining again and leave via the principal entrance in order to direct themselves towards the Vestibule" (1957:168–169).

Acosta considers that the personages in the two processions are warriors, but only one figure (number 2 in Fig. 5.38) in the west procession is armed, and the others carry what we consider to be long banners or ceremonial staffs (scepters), decorated rattles, round banners (which may be shields), and at least one conch-shell trumpet (all of these objects are heavily ornamented with what appear to be feathers and scrolls), instead of weapons. It is significant that unlike the procession on the opposite side of the hall, no personage in the west procession has a speech scroll coming from his mouth, but there are speech scroll-like elements associated with the shell trumpet and the rattles, which we think probably represent the music or sounds produced by these instruments.

Figure 5.36. Relief panel in the north corner of Sala 2 showing two warriors, one of them elderly. These figures very probably formed the end of the procession that was led by the Tlaloc personage in Figure 5.37 (from Acosta 1957 and Jiménez 1998: fig. 93).

In contrast, the personages in the procession led by the Tlaloc figure on the east side of Sala 2 do carry weapons (and sometimes have cotton armor), and almost surely represent warriors, including the two personages on the extreme northeast of the hall (the apparent old man and young warrior) (Fig. 5.36). Of the eight surviving figures in this procession, five have speech scrolls coming from their mouths.

In our opinion, the two processions in Sala 2 possess different character or functions. The figures in the west procession appear to represent high ranking lords who are not warriors. These personages have the most sumptuous costumes depicted in any of Tula's friezes, and instead of weapons they carry what appear to be musical instruments or noisemakers. The east procession is composed of warrior figures, and the speech scrolls coming from their mouths, including that of the leading personage dressed as Tlaloc, could well be symbols of song or prayer. These friezes suggest a ritual similar to a ceremony for the sixth month, called Etzalqualiztli, described by the informants of Sahagún, in which priests formed processions led by the high priest of Tlaloc: "All of them richly costumed commenced their festival right away; they went in procession to the Temple (*cu*), at the lead of all of them went the priest of Tlaloc . . . following him all the other ministers and priests, they all went talking in the manner of one who prays while arriving at the Temple of Tlaloc." Afterward is a description that was part of the same festival: "They sang in the monasteries and played rattles that they usually bring in their arietos; with all these instruments they made very festive music" (Sahagún 1956: I, Book 2, p. 169). With this citation, we do not mean to suggest that the reliefs in Sala 2 represent the specific ceremony described by Sahagún, or that the friezes are related to these festivals, but only that the reliefs could depict a similar ritual, probably in honor of Tlaloc, which included processions with songs, music, and prayers. It also is very probable that in this case the Tlaloc figure who leads the procession was the king himself.

The greater architectonic and symbolic importance of Sala 2 in relation to the other halls in the Palacio Quemado also is manifested in the kinds of ritual contexts that have been identified there. It was precisely in the center of the patio of Sala 2 where a massive offering of marine materials was made, which included an elaborate ceremonial garment made of hundreds of finely carved shell plaques, and a subsequent offering at the same central point was also made (Cobean and Mastache [coord.] n.d.) that included a large pyrite mirror with turquoise mosaic fire serpents (i.e., a solar disk or *tezcacuitlapilli* like the disks sculptured on the fallen roof panels of Salas 1 and 2) (Fig. 5.39). In an analysis of these ritual deposits, Taube (n.d.) considers the offering with the cut-shell garment to be a manifestation at Tula

THE EARLY POSTCLASSIC: THE TOLLAN PHASE CITY

Figure 5.37. Bench frieze on the east side of Sala 2 in the Palacio Quemado represents a procession of warriors led by a personage with attributes of Tlaloc (from Jiménez 1998: fig. 94).

of the Teotihuacan tradition cult of Tlaloc as a war god, as was mentioned earlier. This interpretation is further supported by the existence in Sala 2 of the frieze procession showing warriors being led by a personage with Tlaloc attributes.

Besides the turquoise mosaic mirror in the latest Sala 2 offering, an undecorated pyrite mirror was deposited on top of the shell garment in the earlier offering (Cobean and Mastache [coord.] n.d.). These are not the only mirrors found in Sala 2. During the 1950s, Acosta (1957) recovered another turquoise mosaic mirror and several small pyrite mirrors among a group of offerings under the Chac Mool found in situ in front of the eastern altar in Sala 2. On the north side of Sala 2, Acosta (1957) encountered most of another Chac Mool that originally may have been placed in front of another altar in this hall. In Sala 1, he excavated a thorax fragment of a Chac Mool near the entrance (Acosta 1956a:70).

In our opinion, the iconography of the sculptures in Sala 2, together with its offerings and architectural features, suggest that its main functions were not related to rites of autosacrifice even though several authors (e.g., Klein 1987; De la Fuente 1990) have proposed this interpretation. The presence of two Chac Mools (with one placed in front of an altar) and the panels with *cuauhxicalli* (vessels with sacrificed hearts) in the patio roof friezes probably indicate

Figure 5.38. Palacio Quemado. Bench frieze on the north side of Sala 2 depicting a procession going in the opposite direction from the east-side relief figures. This procession represents sumptuously dressed personages carrying what appear to be long banners or ceremonial staffs, decorated rattles, round banners that may be shields, and probably a conch-shell trumpet (Acosta 1957 and 1967) (from Jiménez 1998: fig. 92).

human sacrifice rather than penitence and autosacrifice. It is pertinent for this conclusion that Miller and Samayoa (1998; Miller 1985) consider Chac Mools to be elements for cults of human sacrifice and especially the sacrifice of war prisoners. Peter Schmidt's recent recovery of a Chac Mool with its arms tied like a war prisoner in the Group of the Thousand Columns at Chichén Itzá supports this interpretation (cited in Schele and Mathews 1998:358).

In addition, both Miller[9] and Graulich (1984) propose a relation between Chac Mools and Tlaloc cults, and the find of Chac Mools in situ in front of the Tlaloc Temple on the summit of the Templo Mayor (Matos 1988) directly relates them to the cult of this god; as does of course the well-known Tlaloc Chac Mool recovered under the modern Mexico City streets of Venustiano Carranza and Pino Suarez, which has irrefutable attributes of this deity (Matos 1988; De la Fuente 1990: 49–52; Miller and Samayoa 1998:67–69). Thus, even though the Chac Mools of Tula are representations of warriors that lack specific attributes directly linking them to a particular deity, it is probable that the association between this type of sculpture and cults to Tlaloc, which is evident in the Templo Mayor, goes back to Tula, especially when considering that the only Chac Mool found in situ at Tula is next to the bench frieze procession led by a Tlaloc figure.[10]

Unfortunately, perhaps we never will know who the personage was leading the west procession going in the opposite direction. This would provide us with key insights into the nature of the ritual represented and the function of Sala 2. Thus we only can speculate that this was another Tlaloc figure like the personage at the head of the procession on the east, or possibly a figure with attributes of Tezcatlipoca, which would not be surprising because the association of both these gods already exists in this hall, as has been found in Taube's (n.d.) analysis of the two offerings that Cobean (1994) excavated there. The same association is found on Pillar 3, which has representations on its upper sections of precisely Tlaloc and Tezcatlipoca, with the warrior Tlaloc being linked with Teotihuacan and Tezcatlipoca a diety of Tula.

With regard to the importance that Tlaloc cults could have had in Tula, the widespread occurence of ceramic Tlaloc effigy *braseros* is significant. There are two diagnostic varieties of these *braseros* in the Tollan Complex (Acosta 1956–1957; Cobean 1990), which are decorated with great appliqué images of this god's face. Both varieties are widely distributed in domestic and ceremonial precinct contexts in Tula's ancient city, which is especially impressive because these *braseros* often are nearly 1 meter high and weigh over 20 kilograms.[11] Tlaloc *braseros* also

THE EARLY POSTCLASSIC: THE TOLLAN PHASE CITY

Figure 5.39. Offering found in the center of Sala 2, including an elaborate ceremonial garment made of hundreds of finely carved shell plaques. Photo, Humberto Illera.

are widely distributed in the Tula region, and very similar effigy vessels have been recovered in many other areas of Mesoamerica in Early Postclassic occupations, including regions as distant as Colima and Yucatán, constituting diagnostic markers of the "Toltec Horizon" (Cobean 1978, 1990:415, 425; Diehl 1993). There also is a continuity of these effigy *braseros* between Tula and Tenochtitlan, as is the case of the famous Tlaloc *braseros* found in the Templo Mayor that clearly are based on antecedents from Tula (Cobean 1990; Umberger 1987).

Returning to the iconography of the Palacio Quemado, Kristan-Graham (1989:288–289) proposes that the reclining figures in the Palacio Quemado reliefs could represent vanquished warriors and that the halls possessed a function related to the funeral rites of dead warriors, dead heroes, or fallen leaders.

With regard to this, it is worth noting (Mastache and Cobean n.d.2) that in the *Codice Borgia* (1963), the representations of deceased women (*cihuateteo*: p. 34), and especially of the ancestral sacrificed dead warriors (*huehueteteo*: p. 33), are shown in a horizontal position that is very similar to that of the reclining figures in the Palacio Quemado reliefs, even to the extent that in both cases the figures' legs and feet are in the same positions, with one limb bent above the figure's torso and the other resting in line with the torso. Kristan-Graham (1989) and Klein (1987) identified the functions of the Palacio Quemado as similar to those of the Mexica *tlacochcalco* ("Dart House"), based on Klein's studies of sixteenth-century accounts of the autosacrifice ceremonies of newly elected Aztec kings, and of the funeral rites for Aztec rulers and high-ranking warriors. Klein also notes that the *tlacochcalco* was the place where the Mexica emperor's cadaver was dressed and masked before it was cremated, and cites Mendieta and Duran as stating that the dead king and funerary images of dead warriors were put in this building. She concludes that according to various ethnohistorical sources, the *tlacochcalco* buildings were dedicated to the god Tezcatlipoca, and that according to Broda (1976) war captives were sacrificed in Tenochtitlan's Casa de las Aguilas (which Klein considers to have been a *tlacochcalco*) after Mexica military victories.

Klein's and Kristan-Graham's hypothesis that the Palacio Quemado had similar ritual functions to those of Tenochtitlan's *tlacochcalco* is highly suggestive, but difficult to confirm, because for Tula we do not have the vast ethnohistorical sources that exist for Tenochtitlan, nor the detailed descriptions of chroniclers concerning specific structures, rituals, festivals, and ceremonies that make possible nearly ethnographic reconstructions of the appearance and function of the buildings in the great precinct surrounding the Templo Mayor.

It is pertinent to discuss here another commonly cited context in the Palacio Quemado: Acosta's (1945) find of a pottery storage area (*bodega*) during the initial excavations in this structure. Here he recovered more than two hundred complete (but shattered) vessels of Tollan Phase types under a fallen burned roof. It is important to emphasize that this storage area was not within the main halls of the palace as some authors have reported, and even though Acosta in the published report does not give a clear description for the location of this find, a careful analysis of his unpublished reports and photographs in the INAH Archivo Técnico supports the conclusion that this group of vessels was found somewhere in the extreme northeast of the North Vestibule where Acosta also uncovered a series of fallen roofs. Even though this large group of ceramics has been interpreted as evidence for a domestic (living area) context in the Palacio Quemado, this conclusion is doubtful. This storage area for ceramics (which is not associated with kitchens or other food preparation areas) more likely was directly related to the ceremonial and ritual functions of the Palacio Quemado, because it is highly probable that some of the rituals there required the presence of priests and nobles during several days and involved ceremonial meals. It should be noted that in addition to dishes for serving food, ceremonial pottery was found in the storage area, including pipes, *braseros,* and incense burners.

Building J or "The Building to the South of Pyramid C"

South of Pyramid C (and separated from it by a passageway several meters wide) is a long rectangular platform designated "Building J," which Acosta (1961a:54) describes as "a big building of the 'Palace' type with an enormous colonnade on its front (west facade) which extends for the entire length of the platform." Like the cases of many structures in the precinct, Acosta detected several construction stages for this building, noting that he dug many test pits and trenches on the upper section of this platform without finding any offerings or burials. This is one of the structures at Tula with the least basic information concerning its architectonic characteristics, and the existing excavation reports lack key data about some contexts and finds. This structure probably had a narrow stairway on its southwest side, that is, toward the main plaza, but apparently its principal access was on the south side of the structure where there was a stairway with balustrades. In a reconstructive drawing made by Ponciano Salazar (Acosta 1968: fig. 17), this building is shown with a south stairway and two small open interior patios that are not mentioned in the published reports.

An important series of stone relief panels was recovered on the south section of this building that have key information concerning the iconography of this sector of the precinct. Acosta (1960:68–69) describes these reliefs and their probable original contexts as follows:

> Over all the explored surface [of the south part of the building] a series of sculptured stones appeared that without doubt belonged to relief panels which decorated the south face of the platform . . . A study of the reliefs, and of the locations where they they were found, shows that these sculptured panels ought

to have been similar to those which decorate Pyramid B . . . But now, what we do not know is specifically where the three different motifs were placed, that is, Quetzalcoatl, the god Tlaloc and the reclining personages; the first elements are easy to place because they only could be set in the [sunken] section of the panel group . . . hypothetically the [other] two motifs [Tlaloc and the reclining personages] were one in the upper frieze and the other in the intermediate panels . . . [I suppose] that the reclining personages were [directly displayed] in the middle part of the panel group, while the images of Tlaloc formed a procession in the upper frieze.

The image that Acosta refers to as Quetzalcoatl is identical to the representations in the friezes of Pyramid B, that is, the composite man-bird-reptile being that Acosta and Moedano identify as Tlahuizcalpantecuhtli. Whether or not this identification is correct, the presence of this motif on Building J is very significant because this indicates that the man-bird-reptile symbol was used in other structures on the sacred precinct that were not pyramids, which would mean that Pyramid B may not have been dedicated to this possible deity. The only illustration that Acosta (1960) published of this symbol found in Building J lacks the butterfly noseplug and is nearly identical to the being represented on the panels on the north facade of Pyramid B, which correspond to the last constructive stage of this building, whereas the man-bird-reptile motifs on the east facade of Pyramid B, which are chronologically earlier, do possess butterfly noseplugs, characteristic of high status Toltec warriors. Acosta states that he did not publish illustrations of all the relief panels of Building J with this motif because all of them were exactly the same. Thus we can assume that all the examples of this motif from Building J lacked the butterfly noseplug and were similar to the man-bird-reptile images of the final constructive stage of Pyramid B.

The presence of at least five relief panels with the man-bird-reptile motif on Building J also suggests the possibility that Pyramid C, which borders this building on the north, originally possessed panels with this image among the friezes that covered its facades. This motif probably was more common in Tula than has been thought. Another panel relief depicting it, also lacking the butterfly noseplug, was recovered at the El Corral residential compound in the northeast city (Mandeville and Healan 1989:184, fig. 12.11). Even though there is no doubt that this relief represents the same man-bird-reptile being, it possesses some stylistic differences compared to the sculptures of this motif on Pyramid B and Building J (Fig. 5.41). Another panel with this image in relief was found by Cobean on the urban zone surface approximately 80 meters east of the Tula Chico plaza.

It is important to observe that the representations of Tlaloc that formed part of the Building J friezes are different from nearly all the images of this god found in other structures of Tula's main precinct, in that the face of the god has what appears to be a large buccal mask with a long tubelike snout curling upward and ending in a hook (Acosta 1960: plates XVI, XVII, XIX). Acosta (p. 68, fig. 27) observes that the great curved noses of these figures are reminiscent of Maya Chac images in Yucatán (Fig. 5.40), but Karl Taube (personal communication) considers the Tlalocs of Building J to be more similar iconographically to images of the rain god at El Tajín than to Chac. In the recent excavation of Building K (to the southwest of Building J), a relief fragment was recovered with a Tlaloc image essentially identical to the version of this god found in Building J (Cobean 1994).

In the friezes of Building J, in addition to the images of Tlaloc and the man-bird-reptile being, there are panel reliefs representing reclining personages similar to the figures that originally were in the friezes placed in the upper sections of the patios in the halls of the Palacio Quemado, but in the case of Building J the reclining figures do not seem to carry weapons. One of these personages is accompanied by the glyph "9-Hand," which Acosta (1960) proposes is the calendrical name of this lord.

Building K

This is a long narrow rectangular structure marking the southern limit of the main plaza, which was excavated recently but found to be very damaged from pre-Hispanic (Aztec) and Colonial period looting and reoccupations (Cobean 1994). Like most buildings on the ceremonial precinct, it was burned at the end of the Tollan Phase (ca. A.D. 1150), and has partial reoccupations during Late Postclassic and early colonial times. The original structure has at least three construction stages: the first is associated with the Coyotlatelco culture (Corral Phase ca. A.D. 800), and the others with two constructions during the Tollan Phase (Getino 2000).

The final Tollan Phase version of Building K consists of three overlapping *taluds* (tiers), with the upper platform supporting a long columned hall and vestibule similar to those of Building J south of Pyramid C. The vestibule was closed on its southern limit by a long adobe wall with a bench that originally was covered by relief panels like the benches in other structures on the precinct. No friezes were recovered in situ, but several relief fragments were found fallen on floors, including the just mentioned Tlaloc image. A long row of square columns supported the roof of the vestibule's north side, which was open toward the plaza.

South of the vestibule, apparently there was a long, narrow columned hall (that was badly damaged subsequently) that had two rows of pillars placed together in two groups of six around a central space functioning as an entrance, or an open patio (*impluvio*). This columned hall was connected in the west with a long, narrow room that probably lacked other accesses. The walls of the columned hall form two Ls, the largest of which in terms of its placement and shape repeats the L formed by the vestibules on the north side of the plaza, especially that of the Vestibule of Pyramid B (Fig. 5.42).

Beginning with Ponciano Salazar's reconstruction drawing of the then unexcavated structure (Acosta 1968: fig. 17)), Building K has been consistently depicted as having its stairway on its south rather than north (patio) side, based on topographic evidence of a probable stairway along the south side and the absence of any such evidence along the north side of the building. This interpretation has changed drastically in light of recent excavations (Cobean, et al. 2012: 97; Gamboa and Cobean 2009) which, on the one hand, revealed that the south stairway was a later addition dating to the Aztec occupation of the structure. At the same time, excavations along the north facade encountered the foundation of a staircase at least 3.5 meters wide that that had been dismantled, perhaps by the builders of the South staircase. This revised interpretation makes Building K an integral part of the largely enclosed plaza and lays to rest the enigmatic question of why Building K would have been focused to the south with its back to the plaza of which it is an integral part. All of the illustrations in the present volume correctly show the Tollan phase version of Building K with a north rather than a south stairway.

No contexts were found indicating that Building K functioned as a residence (Cobean 1994; Getino 2000). From an architectonic perspective, it appears to synthesize two different concepts because it consists of a pyramidal platform composed of various superimposed tiers combined with a complex of columned halls. Its central location on the south side of the plaza, and its exact alignment with the transverse axis of the adoratorio located in the center of the plaza, emphasizes its importance in the overall plan of the precinct.

The Adoratorio

The importance of Pyramid C as the axis of Tula's sacred prencinct is manifested not only in its location and size, but also in its relationship with other architectonic elements of the precinct, such as the Adoratorio and Ballcourt 2. The Adoratorio is not placed exactly in the physical center of the plaza, but still possesses a central location if the exterior limits of the monumental complex are considered. In addition, it is clear that the Adoratorio is aligned with the central stairway of Pyramid C and with the center of Building K, which emphasizes the hierarchical position of the latter building within the general plan of the precinct.

The Adoratorio or central altar has been so badly damaged that we know little about it. This structure probably had stairs and a Chac Mool sculpture, but apparently it had been badly looted before Charnay's

Figure 5.40. Relief panels from Building J depicting Tlaloc with a long hooked nose (Acosta 1960) (from Jiménez 1998: figs. 78 and 79).

Figure 5.41. Relief panel from Building J of a composite being with human, reptile, and avian attributes (Acosta 1960: plate XVIII).

THE EARLY POSTCLASSIC: THE TOLLAN PHASE CITY

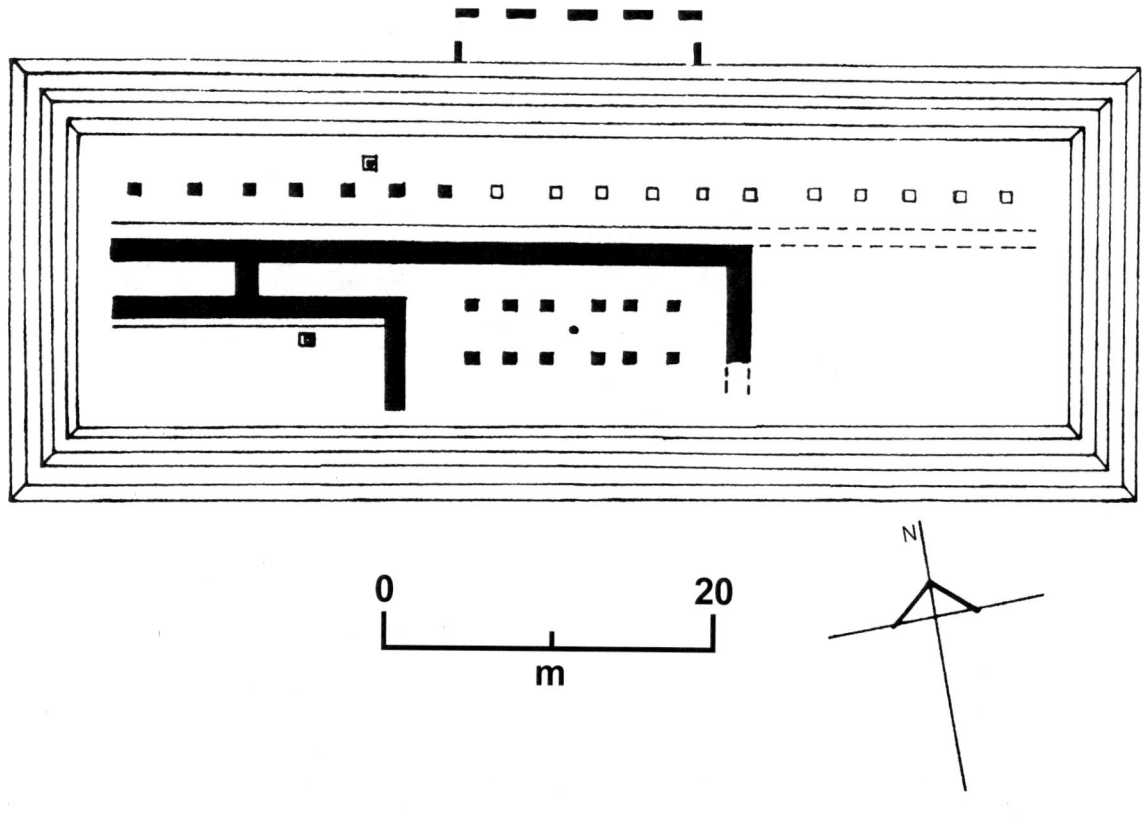

Figure 5.42. Plan of Building K (Cobean 1994; Getino 2000).

(1885) excavations. He found a burial (probably secondary and from the Aztec reoccupation) underneath the Adoratorio. There are clear architectural similarities between the Adoratorio and the much larger Plataforma de Venus at Chichén Itzá (Marquina 1964:886). The Chac Mool was found by Acosta (1944:148) in rubble on the east side of the Adoratorio. It is a large fragment lacking the head, like most Chac Mools from Tula. In various sectors of the altar, Acosta recovered shattered relief panels, one of which, representing a warrior with a feather cape in polychrome, is among the finest sculptures known for Tula: "[the figure] represents a richly dressed personage dressed with a feather cape which is realistically and delicately rendered . . . the personage, who is lacking the head and the upper part of the torso, carries a weapon which looks like a lance, but the point of which has teeth-like edges, and probably a bag of copal . . . The relief panel has traces of red, yellow and blue paint" (Acosta 1944:148, fig. 26).

In further excavations Acosta (1945:46–48) found a badly damaged earlier substructure within the Adoratorio. These explorations showed that most of the damage to the Adoratorio were pre-Hispanic, as is documented by the recovery of two different Aztec II offerings: one inside the structure containing more than thirty vessels (Acosta 1956a:50) and another in the rubble of the east side of the Adoratorio that was deposited after the destruction of this section (Acosta 1945:46–48).

The Ballcourts and the Tzompantli

Two ballcourts have been excavated and restored at Tula. The largest, Ballcourt 2 (excavated by Eduardo Matos [1976] at the end of the 1960s), occupies the western limits of the main plaza in front of Pyramid C; a smaller structure, Ballcourt 1 (excavated by Acosta [1940, 1941, 1945]), lies outside the plaza directly north of Pyramid B in an area called the Plazoleta Norte. Also outside the plaza to the northeast of Pyramid B is a small (almost miniature) unexcavated structure with two parallel mounds approximately 30 meters long, which may constitute a third ballcourt, but without a detailed topographic map and excavation of this zone we cannot be certain of the function for this complex.

The two excavated ballcourts have significant architectonic relationships with the two pyramids. Ballcourt 2 obviously was the most important structure because of its larger dimensions and location within the main plaza, being constructed directly opposite the largest pyramid (C). On the other hand, the smaller ballcourt is outside the plaza, and is related to the smaller pyramid (B). Even though Ballcourt 1 is behind Pyramid B and not in front, there is a clear spatial relationship between the two structures: The central axis of both buildings coincides and Pyramid B is aligned with the central part of Ballcourt 1. It is important to note that this relationship, pyramid-plaza-ballcourt, is found in various Mesoamerican centers, the most notable example of this being perhaps Cantona, Puebla, where García Cook and Merino (1996, 1998) have identified twenty-four Epiclassic ballcourts, twelve of which repeat the structure complex pyramid-plaza-ballcourt; but at Cantona, in contrast to Tula, there are no *tzompantlis* and the ballcourts always are longitudinally aligned with the pyramids, as is the case in the sacred precinct of Tenochtitlan.

Ballcourt 2. This structure is inside the sacred precinct in front of Pyramid C, and is the largest ballcourt in Tula. Its longitudinal axis is oriented north-south and measures 142 meters long and 60 meters wide. Two Tollan Phase and one Aztec construction stages have been identified in Ballcourt 2 (Patiño 1994b). The orientation of the Tollan Phase structures corresponds to what Mastache and Crespo (1982) define as Toltec A. Recent stratigraphic excavations in this ballcourt investigating its constructive sequence found no structures previous to the Tollan Phase (Patiño 1994b:33). Most of this ballcourt was excavated by Matos (1976), who found it even more damaged than Ballcourt 1. With the exception of a stone ballcourt ring fragment found out of context, no sculptural elements were recovered from this complex.

There are many similarities between Ballcourt 2 and the great ballcourt of Chichén Itzá. The proportions and architectural features of the two structures are closely analogous, including the specific locations of temples and other lateral buildings (Patiño 1994b; Marquina, 1964:855, fig. 264). The probable temple on the east facade has essentially the same location as the Temple of the Jaguars in Chichén, and the small platforms on the north and south sides of Ballcourt 2 possess the same proportions and forms as the north and south temples of the Chichén ballcourt, although at Tula the temples did not survive. In addition, the spatial relationship of Ballcourt 2 with Pyramid C is the same as that between the great ballcourt at Chichén Itzá and the Temple of the Warriors, and at both centers the *tzompantli* (skull rack) is in the same location in relation to the ballcourt.

The Tzompantli. Tzompantli or skull altars are structures for cults of human sacrifice and war that became frequent in ancient Mexico during the Late Postclassic (A.D. 1200–1520), and often are associated with ballcourts. At Tula, the *tzompantli* is located next to Ballcourt 2 to the west of the Adoratorio, and was excavated by Matos (1976) during the 1960s, who found a great number of human skull fragments associated with this structure. The major information concerning the specific contexts and the chronology of this platform has not been published, but its structural similarity and analogous location with the *tzompantli* of Chichén Itzá indicate that it surely is coeval with the other buildings on the monumental precinct.

In northern Mexico, the *tzompantli* appears to be earlier than in the Central Highlands. Hers (1989) identified an Early Classic skull rack at Cerro del

Huistle, Jalisco, and Spencer (1982) reports one for the Late Formative in the Cuicatlán Cañada, Oaxaca, although Hers and Braniff (1998:66) dispute the chronology of this find, saying that its contexts could correspond to the Late Postclassic Mexica conquest of the Cuicatec (Hopkins 1983), and that of the sixty-one human skulls recovered only two have possible evidence of perforations; thus, these skulls may not constitute a *tzompantli* (Spencer 1982:71, 75, 78, 236).

The apparent absence of a *tzompantli* associated with Ballcourt 1 may be specious, because various sectors directly north and west of this structure have never been systematically excavated. If real, this absence could be another indicator of a hierarchical difference between Ballcourts 1 and 2, and suggests that perhaps only Ballcourt 2, located within the plaza, was involved in human sacrifice rites such as those extensively documented in sixteenth-century chronicles and codices for Tenochtitlan and other centers. At present, with the exception of the skull rack at Cerro del Huistle, Jalisco (Hers 1989), which has different characteristics, the *tzompantli* of Tula is the oldest structure of its kind known for north-central Mexico, and is without doubt the prototype for Aztec *tzompantli*.

Ballcourt 1. This structure is located north of Pyramid B outside the main plaza. Ballcourt 1 was the first building extensively explored in Tula by Acosta (1941), who found it very damaged from what appear to have been systematic pre-Hispanic dismantling programs that had removed most of the panels on the facades, along with associated sculptures. This complex has a sunken I-shaped court nearly 70 meters long and 12 meters wide. On both sides of the interior lateral walls there are indentations, probably for mounting the ball rings and niches, and on the east and west interior walls there probably were diverse sculptures: "The position and placement of the niches in the interior extremes of the heads (cabezales) of the ballcourt (equidistant and in diagonal in relation to the longitudinal axis of the structure) architecturally relate this building with the ballcourts of Monte Albán and Atzompa" (Acosta 1945:57).

At the center of the exterior north and south facades of Ballcourt 1 were located the principal access stairways. Apparently Acosta (1945:26–27) identified three construction phases for this building, but this is not clear in his reports. He mainly restored the second phase structure, which was the best preserved. Acosta (p. 25) emphasizes that the construction of the west sector of this building constituted a much greater work than that of the east side because this involved leveling the original surface and building an extensive platform that forms the base of most of the ballcourt. Probably because this building was badly damaged in pre-Hispanic times, no evidence for temples or lateral structures like those identified in Ballcourt 2 was found.

The sculptural elements found associated with Ballcourt 1 include a relief panel representing a ball player (Acosta 1941: fig. 1) and another having the cut conch-shell motif along with a probable numeral (Acosta 1944: fig. 2A). The most impressive sculpture recovered from this ballcourt is a three dimensional representation of a Tlaloc warrior (Fig. 5.43) wearing a vest very similar to the shell mosaic garment found recently in Offering 2 of the Palacio Quemado (Acosta 1944: fig. 1; Cobean 1994; Taube n.d.). Even though it is not certain that the Tlaloc statue was found in situ, its association with Ballcourt 1 is significant. The fact that it has a costume that is nearly identical to the shell garment of Offering 2 further suggests the existence of important ritual ties between the Palacio Quemado (especially Sala 2) and its particular ceremonial functions with Ballcourt 1, and suggests a link between this ballcourt and the Tlaloc warrior cult. Koontz (2000) in a recent analysis of sculptural elements also links Ballcourt 1 with Tlaloc rituals. Beginning with his first report, Acosta (1940) made comparative studies of Ballcourt 1 with other ballcourts in Mesoamerican centers, including Xochicalco, the Maya regions, and other areas, concluding that this structure in terms of form, proportions, and specific architectural characteristics is very similar to a ballcourt at Yucuñunahui in the Mixteca (p. 188).

The Coatepantli

The Coatepantli or serpent wall constitutes an element of great symbolic relevance that marks the limit of sacred space, and is present in some highland centers during the Late Postclassic. The Coatepantli at Tula is the oldest structure of its kind known for Central Mexico and, as various authors have noted, surely was the prototype for this feature in some Aztec cities.

Acosta (1944, 1945) excavated and restored the Coatepantli, and Diehl (1989) presents an insightful analysis of this structure. Some scholars have assumed that the elements restored by Acosta are only fragments of a larger wall. Nevertheless, no other sections of this wall have been found in other parts of the precinct, and the probability that the existing structure constitutes the complete length of the original Coatepantli is suggested because its limits are aligned exactly with the width of Pyramid B and the length (east-west) of Ballcourt 1. Even though the Coatepantli symbolically delimits sacred space, it did not physically surround Tula's plaza.

The Coatepantli is a wall 40 meters long and about 2 meters high, not taking into account the merlons (*almenas*) that decorate the upper section, and is about 1 meter wide at the base with a construction core formed of large river cobbles and mud. The upper half of the wall is divided in three sections: the higher and lower sections are decorated with reliefs of stepped frets (*grecas escalonadas*), while the central panel depicts a series of serpents eating human skeletons that still have some flesh on the elbows, knees, and hands. The surviving central frieze elements are painted red, blue, yellow, and white and on each side of the wall form two opposing processions that coverge on a central motif or symbol, which has been destroyed. Acosta (1944:139–145) proposed that the serpents in the central friezes are devouring the god Tlahuizcalpantecuhtli, and on the basis of differences in sculptural technique and style, he detected evidence for the collaboration of at least five different artists in the production of these reliefs. Eleven merlons in the form of a G (representing the cut conch-shell motif) crown the upper limit of the restored Coatepantli, of which seven merlons are the original sculptural elements and the other four are modern copies (Acosta 1945:30). This author (1944:143–145) recovered two anthropomorphic standard-bearer sculptures at the two extremes of the Coatepantli that were not found in situ, but he proposes they were originally positioned at each end of the wall.

Symbolically, the Coatepantli does mark a sacred limit at Tula, indicating that the most sanctified area consists of the buildings surrounding the plaza, but does not include the Plazoleta Norte and Ballcourt 1. The placement of the Coatepantli indicates the separation of these two zones, showing that the Plazoleta Norte possessed a different status from the plaza in terms of function, sacredness, and surely also in terms of accessibility. Besides limiting sacred space, the Coatepantli emphasizes the architectonic relationship between Pyramid B and Ballcourt 1. The focus of Pyramid B is not completely on the plaza, where Pyramid C predominates as the central architectonic unit, but is directed toward the Plazoleta Norte, where it constitutes a fundamental architectural element.

The main precinct of Tula is thus limited both on the north and the south by two smaller plazas that complement it and constitute a kind of prolongation of the sacred zone, including the Plazoleta Norte and the other plaza to the south. Concerning the buildings on the Plazoleta Sur, their specific characteristics are unknown except for the so-called Toltec Palace excavated by Charnay (1885), which probably was one of the royal palaces. If this building was a royal residence, then Building K would constitute the connection between the south plaza and the sacred precinct, that is, between two different realms of the state. On the other side of the precinct, the Plazoleta Norte is articulated to the north with the compound called the Plaza Charnay (Matos 1974), concerning which we can say little of its characteristics and function because this zone suffered many alterations during the Aztec reoccupation, and because it has not been investigated in detail. But its monumental setting and its proximity to the main plaza suggest an important function, which may have been as the city's market. However, this hypothesis needs to be investigated with excavations.

Accesses

Tula's main plaza possesses two obvious entrances that are placed in diagonal corners of the

Figure 5.43. The Tlaloc Warrior statue from Ballcourt 1 (Acosta 1944) (from Jiménez 1998: fig. 34).

plaza. What doubtlessly was the main entrance is in the extreme southeast between Building K and Building J measuring approximately 20 meters wide and connecting with a great stairway that climbed Tula's acropolis from the lower terraces near the Tula River below. It appears to be significant that this access is directly in front of Pyramid B. The other access is in the plaza's northwest corner, between the north end of Ballcourt 2 and the Palacio Quemado; this is a narrow passage that connected the main plaza with the Plazoleta Norte. Another secondary entrance appears to have been located between the south end of Ballcourt 2 and Building K, which connected the precinct with the south plaza (Figs. 5.7 and 5.8B).

We do not know the manner in which the precinct entrances articulated this zone with the rest of the city, including immediately adjacent areas and more distant points in the urban zone. Also uncertain are the internal urban communication network and therefore the level of access that the city's nonelite inhabitants had to the sacred precinct. The great height of the acropolis, the limited number of entrances, and the sacred nature of the monumental plaza suggest that, although it dominated the urban space, its buildings may have been somewhat alien and inaccessible for the great majority of the population. Castells (1982) observes that the monumental center of a city is composed of great open spaces along with closed areas. There are public domains, but also inaccessible domains that are restricted to all but a few persons.

General Comments Concerning the Sacred Precinct

The previous analysis shows that Tula's sacred precinct was composed of different types of buildings, the specific functions of which have not been defined in all cases. The two pyramids, arranged adjacently forming a 90° angle, were without doubt the most important architectonic elements in all the compound, with Pyramid C being the largest and principal building and the predominant component on the basis of which all the monumental center was probably planned, possibly along with the rest of the city. Pyramid B, which faces south, has a secondary position or status that is manifested in its smaller size and its specific location within the precinct (see Getino and Cid [2000] for another interpretation of Pyramid B's role in the planning of the city).

It should be emphasized that the differences between the two pyramids do not only concern their volumes and placement within the plaza, but also that both these structures are conceptually distinct. Pyramid C, probably the *axis mundi* of the sacred precinct, in a sense constituted an entity in itself, that is, an autonomous architectural unit that was not articulated with other buildings. Even though

Pyramid C was flanked by two structures, in both cases these buildings are separated from the pyramid by passageways. The smaller scale of these side structures highlights the size and volume of Pyramid C.

As stated earlier, Pyramid C is architecturally similar to the Pyramids of the Sun and the Moon at Teotihuacan, because like these, it possesses a lateral stairway platform (*cuerpo adosado*) in the center of its principal facade, thus constituting the same architectonic conception, although of course on a smaller scale as the great Classic pyramids. In this sense, Pyramid C represents a continuity with Teotihuacan, constituting a conservative architectonic element that conceptually ties Tula with Classic Teotihuacan architectural traditions. Thus there is a clear Teotihuacan presence in the principal structure of Tula's sacred precinct.

Pyramid B, in contrast, is architecturally innovative, constituting a distinct entity that integrates in a single architectonic complex a pyramid-temple, a vestibule, and halls with benches and altars, thus uniting different kinds of spaces and functions in the same structural unit. From this perspective, Pyramid B represents essentially innovative aspects characteristic of Toltec culture. Just as Pyramid C links Tula with Teotihuacan, one can say that Pyramid B represents an essentially Toltec building, and emphasizes Tula's northern origins with its ties to northern architectural traditions. This new concept of a pyramid with a vestibule places a portico in front of a pyramidal structure, thus covering most of its principal facade and obstructing the visual impact of the pyramid toward the plaza, creating the effect of diminishing its volume and to some degree the magnificence characteristic of these structures.[12] Hers and Braniff (1998:65) have shown that this combination of a portico in front of a pyramid is surprising and apparently contradictory because it makes the pyramidal structure look like the second story of the portico (Figs. 5.24 and 5.44).

Nevertheless, we believe that this apparent contradiction is due to the two pyramids probably having different specific functions. As the principal building on the precinct, it was important for Pyramid C to be uncovered, thus being massive and powerful and dominating the sacred space. Pyramid B, with its frontal vestibule, would have been a more private and restricted space for performing different kinds of rites and ceremonies from those of the other pyramid. Pyramid B was probably, above all else, a monument related to royalty, government, and power; exalting the royal dynasties and the institution of war that was closely tied to the leadership and government of Tula. It should not be forgotten that the pillars in the temple on Pyramid B's summit apparently represent Tula's kings and other nobility, along with idealized versions of high-ranking Toltec warriors.

As we discussed before, the great Vestibule and the Palace to the East are part of the same complex integrated with Pyramid B. Thus these three buildings (the Pyramid, the Palace to the East, and the Vestibule) clearly conformed one basic architectonic unit. Even though the specific functions and many areas of the Palace to the East are unknown, the iconographic elements associated with this building, and the fact that it was the only structure having direct access to Pyramid B and the temple in its summit, strongly suggest that the three buildings constituted a kind of royal sanctuary, that is, a special temple for the king and his priests and dignitaries, where rituals and ceremonies were performed related to the functions of the sovereign. These ceremonies probably were centered around sacrifice, penitence, enthronement, war, and government, and perhaps were similar to rites that Klein (1987) proposes took place in Tenochtitlan's Casa de las Aguilas based on descriptions in sixteenth-century chronicles.

It is worth considering the possibility that the Palace to the East may not only have been a building possessing ritual functions tied to the king, but also could have constituted a type of royal palace or the royal palace itself: the residence place of the monarch and not just a religious space. With regard to this possibility, it is important to take into account this building's location, along with its dimensions (approximately 75 meters long by 30 meters wide), and to remember that Acosta only excavated a small section in the front of this structure. On the other hand, it also should be considered that the three large compounds associated with Pyramid B (the Palacio

Figure 5.44. Reconstructive drawing of Pyramid B at Tula (from Acosta 1968: fig. 15).

Quemado, the Palace of Quetzalcoatl, and the Palace to the East) form a great architectonic complex that as a whole could have been used as a royal palace, a kind of royal establishment, with each building having varied and complementary functions related to the administrative and political activities of a royal residence. Perhaps as William Sanders (personal communication) observes, this royal complex also could have included buildings on the lower terraces on the eastern limits of the monumental zone.

It is probable that the existence of two large pyramids at Teotihuacan and Tula, with the aforementioned correlations in placement and orientation, is related to the concept of duality, with the universe structured in pairs of opposing and complementary entities, which was a fundamental concept in the cosmovision of peoples in the Central Highlands and other areas of Mesoamerica.[13] We believe that the two pyramids in both centers express this duality and the existence of two principal cults; in the same way that in the Templo Mayor of Tenochtitlan and in other cities of the Late Postclassic, this binary conception is expressed in a single pyramid having two temples on its summit.

In Teotihuacan, the two pyramids are separated; centuries later at Tula, the pyramids are together on the same plaza. And at Tenochtitlan, apparently what was once two entities becomes one, that is, one pyramid with two temples on its summit. We think it is likely that because of this, in the Mexica Templo Mayor (and apparently in other Aztec centers) the north temple dedicated to Tlaloc was smaller than the south temple dedicated to Huitzilopochtli, probably as a remembrance that the north pyramid-temple should be the smallest and possess a different hierarchy (Figs. 5.45 and 5.46). This appears to have been a process that lasted several centuries, which manifests the continuities in the cosmovision and the fundamental ideological concepts shared by these three cultures. This continuity is also evident in iconography and some other aspects, although many central features, such as the urban conception and planning of the three cities, are different.[14]

We do not possess sufficient information to determine if the deities and cults of both pyramids at Teotihuacan and Tula were similar to the two gods of the Templo Mayor at Tenochtitlan, and this problem still is the object of speculation and controversy. It often has been assumed that the Pyramid of the Moon could have been dedicated to Tlaloc or to an aquatic goddess, fundamentally because of the great importance of Tlaloc in Teotihuacan iconography and the recovery of a monumental statue of a female water deity in the plaza near this pyramid (Bernal 1963; Seler 1915:407).

With regard to the Pyramid of the Sun, the general absence of representations of deities or other iconographic elements in mural paintings or sculptures associated with this building makes this subject even more speculative. Nevertheless, some indications exist that this monument could have been dedicated to a solar deity. Among this evidence are the descriptions of Boturini and Clavijero stating that in the eighteenth century there was still a monumental sculpture on the summit of the Pyramid of the Sun, which had a large golden disk on its chest—an observation that Seler (1915:407) considered a descriptive fantasy of these chroniclers.[15] But taking into account the recovery of several large pyrite mirrors mounted on slate disks in the offering in the cave under this pyramid (Heyden 1973: figs. 3 and 4), and the importance of mirrors and related solar cults that Taube (1992) has documented in Teotihuacan iconography, it is plausible that the principal cult of this pyramid involved a solar deity.

Heyden (1973) proposes that the slate-backed mirrors were intentionally broken when they were deposited in the offering. The reverse sides of some of the slate mirror backs are decorated with anthropomorphic figures, including one costumed as a jaguar and another as a bird. The personages represented on the mirror backs, especially the figure with the jaguar costume, are similar to some representations of warriors in Teotihuacan mural art that could constitute antecedents for the warrior orders of Tula and Tenochtitlan during the Postclassic period. It is important to observe, however, that the dedicatory offerings recently recovered inside Teotihuacan's Pyramid of the Moon also contain pyrite mirrors, including a slate-backed mirror in Entierro 3 measuring 30 centimeters in diameter (Sugiyama and Cabrera 2000:169).[16]

Another relevant find is the stone disk sculpture recovered by Robert Chadwick in 1963 in the plaza in front of the Pyramid of the Sun (Millon [ed.] 1973: fig. 216). This disk, measuring nearly 1 meter in diameter, is covered with traces of red paint and at its center has a frontal sculpture of a human skull with a tonguelike flat object coming out of its mouth. The skull is surrounded by a circle of radially sculpted lines. Millon emphasizes that human-skull representations are not common in Teotihuacan art (unlike the cases of Toltec and Aztec iconography). Chadwick (cited by Millon) mentions that this disk originally may have been put on a temple platform that is directly in front of the Pyramid of the Sun, and that there is a possible description of this sculpture as a "death god" in a *Relación* for the year 1580 for the Teotihuacan area (Castañeda 1905, cited in Millon [ed.] 1973: fig. 216).

The radial lines surrounding this skull-disk seem to suggest sun rays and a vague similarity with the Toltec-period disks called *tezcacuitlapilli,* which have a central motif surrounded by less clear radial lines that are only insinuated as small indentations on the disks' edges. Taube (personal communication), however, observes that the radial lines in the Teotihuacan disk appear to represent folded paper, which is associated with images of the death god in the Mexica culture. A Tula sculptured disk that is very similar to the Teotihuacan skull-disk is represented as the shield of a warrior (Jiménez García 1998:311–315, fig. 147). The Tula disk (Fig. 5.47) possesses radial lines surrounding a skull that are not as complete as the lines in the Teotihuacan sculpture, but the two images are very alike except that the skull in the Tula relief is shown in profile, which is a common trait in Toltec art.[17]

Taube (n.d.), in his analysis concerning mirrors in offerings and sculptures at Tula, illustrates

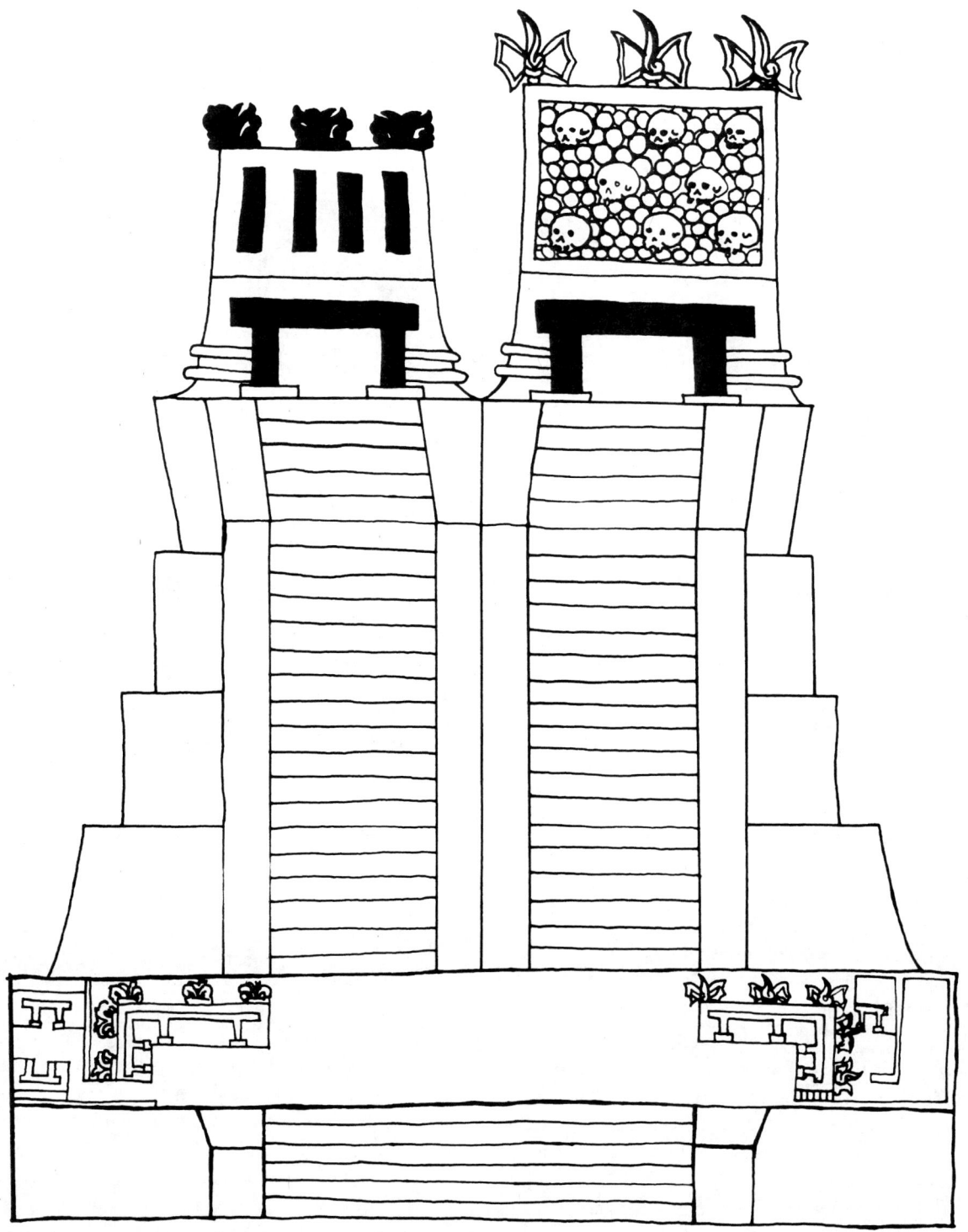

Figure 5.45. The Templo Mayor of Tezcoco with the chapels of Huitzilopochtli and Tlaloc on the summit (from *Codex Ixtlilxóchitl* 1976).

Figure 5.46. The Templo Mayor of Tenochtitlan as represented in the *Codex Aubin* (1963:81).

examples of *tezcacuitlapilli* with a skull representation in the center, one of which has a frontally depicted skull similar to that of the Teotihuacan sculptured disk. In another example, the skull is shown in profile and it is surrounded by clearly depicted radial lines, with a long object coming out of its mouth like the tonguelike object in the Teotihuacan disk, but in this case the motif in the mouth appears to be a flint knife. It also is pertinent to cite some early representations of the Templo Mayor of Tenochtitlan in which the characteristic decorations for the south temple dedicated to Huitzilopochtli are precisely images of human skulls. In a well-known illustration from the *Codex Ixtlilxóchitl* of the main temple of Tezcoco (in Boone 1987:85), the human skulls represented on the roof of the temple of Huitzilopochtli are shown frontally like the skull depicted on the Teotihuacan disk.

At Tula, Acosta (1956a: fig. 5) proposed that Pyramid C was dedicated to Quetzalcoatl in his embodiment as Venus the morning star on the basis that the only preserved sculpture in its original context for this pyramid was a balustrade relief with a symbol that he interpreted as a cut conch-shell motif characteristic of this deity. It is worth observing that a similar symbol called a five-pointed star (*estrella de cinco puntas*) is common in the Classic mural art of Teotihuacan (see De la Fuente [coord.] 1995: I[1]:63, fig. 8; 66, fig. 19; 77, fig. 6.13).

In addition, Acosta (1943) and Moedano (1946a) concluded that Pyramid B was dedicated to an embodiment of Quetzalcoatl as the evening-star version of Venus, which they identify as Tlahuizcalpantecuhtli. This identification is doubtful because Tlahuizcalpantecuhtli is principally associated with Venus as the morning star (Miller and Taube 1992:166–167), and the representations of a man-bird-reptile composite being on the reliefs of Pyramid B, which Acosta and Moedano identify as this deity, are not clearly associated with Tlahuizcalpantecuhtli iconographic traits (Kubler 1961; Taube n.d.). As noted before,

Figure 5.47. Tula relief panel depicting a warrior having a circular shield decorated with a human skull profile. Photo, Humberto Illera.

recent research has shown that a Tlaloc warrior cult of Teotihuacan origin could have been very important at Tula. The representations or attributes of this deity in Ballcourt 1, the offerings (Taube n.d.) and reliefs of the Palacio Quemado, and on the pillars of Pyramid B open the possibility that his cult was associated with this pyramid. It is worth noting that representations of armed Tlalocs have until now only been found on the north side of the precinct, given that the Tlalocs in Buildings J and K are stylistically different and do not carry weapons.

A probable continuity in the iconography of Pyramid B and the art of Teotihuacan, which has been cited for decades (Armillas 1950), is the similarity of the processions of seemingly domesticated canines and felines accompanied by eagles or vultures on this pyramid's facades with processions of animals in Teotihuacan murals, especially those at Atetelco. Even though no murals or reliefs with files of animals have been found at the Pyramid of the Moon, the recently recovered offerings in its interior precisely consist of skeletal canines, felines, and eagles, some of which Oscar Polaco identified as *Canis lupus, Puma concolor,* and *Aguila Chrysaetos* (Royal eagle) (Sugiyama and Cabrera 2000:167). As mentioned earlier, these are the same species that Polaco identified in the reliefs of Pyramid B. This similarity and continuity suggests that both pyramids could have been dedicated to similar cults. Further evidence concerning the deity to which the Pyramid of the Moon could have been dedicated is constituted by the eight Tlaloc effigy vessels that Sugiyama and Cabrera recovered in an offering associated with a ceremonial burial (Entierro 3) inside this pyramid.

We have mentioned previously that there are several elements that support the importance in Tula of a Tlaloc warrior cult of Teotihuacan origin, a cult that we believe is related to the office of kingship. Stela 1, which was associated with Pyramid B and very probably represents a king, wears an image of Tlaloc and the *glifo del año* (year glyph) as the principal elements of the headdress (Fig. 5.23). Two similar stelae in Mexico's Museo Nacional de Antropología, which supposedly come from Tula, also possess Tlaloc headdresses, one of which has a *glifo del año* (Jimenez 1998: figs. 53 and 54). Another representation is the Tlaloc personage who heads the sculptured relief figures in Sala 2, along with the Tlaloc on Pillar 3 of Pyramid B. All of this suggests that in Tula the reigning monarch possessed among his titles and functions the duty of being a priest of Tlaloc, or even more, that the king could be the incarnation of Tlaloc. In this sense, Taube's (2000:47) observation is significant that in Teotihuacan a metaphor for the sovereign was a Tlaloc figure accompanied by the glyph for cultivating the earth; thus the king would be the one who cultivates and feeds the people.

Tlaloc attributes in the representations of rulers exist at various Classic Maya centers.[18] William Fash (personal communication) observes that it is highly significant that the founding king K'inich Yax K'uk' Mo' of the Copán dynasty, who was a foreigner (either a Teotihuacano or someone with strong ties to Teotihuacan), is represented on Altar Q and on some other monuments with the eye-glass-like goggles of Tlaloc. Fash adds that there probably are traditions of Teotihuacan-derived royal rituals being expressed in the similarity between the sculptural groups of the eye-goggled K'inich Yax K'uk' Mo' heading the row of sixteen Copan kings depicted on Altar Q and the Tlaloc-costumed royal figure leading the procession in the reliefs of Sala 2 in the Palacio Quemado (personal communication; 1991:24–25, figs. 11–14).

It is important to note that various scholars have shown that the *glifo de año* is a common element in the headdresses of Maya kings and of rulers in some other cultures, probably constituting a symbol of royalty.[19]

Finally, we want to observe that in addition to the information in some historical sources concerning the existence of a dual government at Tula, there are elements in the iconography of the sacred precinct that suggests this, such as the pairs of personages represented in the pillars of Pyramid B and the series of paired reclining figures in the reliefs of the Palacio Quemado roof panels. We believe that this concept also is expressed in the recurrence of groups of two processions of personages converging on a central motif as the predominant theme in the reliefs of Tula's sculptured benches.

OTHER ZONES OF THE MONUMENTAL CENTER

The monumental center in Tula is not limited to the sacred precinct, although this is an essential part of it. There is a series of structures and platform terraces around and in the proximities of the principal plaza that are undoubtedly an integral part of the monumental zone. Their closeness to the main plaza and the shape and dimensions of some of these structures are clear indicators of the monumental nature of this area, which covered various kinds of open spaces, plazas, and buildings with different characteristics. The buildings in this zone of the city must have included palaces for the royalty and residences for the ruling elite, as well as buildings with diverse functions related to the governing of the city, but it is difficult to determine the limits and characterize an area that has not been excavated and for which there are no detailed plans or maps.

When analyzing an urban center with these characteristics, it is important to bear in mind that the state implied the existence of a series of institutions and a complex administrative and political apparatus. Each branch of government, religion, and economic life needed specialized personnel in the administrative, organizational, and justice apparatuses—various kinds of government officials, a corps of administrators, judges, high ranking military personnel, and a priestly class with various hierarchies—all of whom were necessary to develop the complex ritual, political, and economic life required by the functioning of the state. Complex institutions and social groups needed specific spaces in the settlement: residential areas; various kinds of council halls and meeting places for warriors, priests, judges, and various classes of officials; temples and other buildings for the preparation of ceremonies connected with the cults, schools, and areas for tribute storage and administration; and storage areas for food and other items, weapons, and clothing. There must also have been a court around the monarch in addition to his wives and children, as well as groups of nobles, relatives, servants, and dependents.

As Calnek (1976) states, it is important to establish the equivalents in the settlements of certain functions and institutions of the state, that is, the identifiable architectural markers that could link these institutions, activities, and social groups with a specific type of architectural complex and structure. It must be borne in mind that buildings with different functions are not always architecturally different; the differences may lie at less evident levels. That is, even if there is a degree of architectural uniformity, other elements such as the specific location of a building, its distance from or relation to other structures, orientation and height, or other attributes such as color, bas reliefs, or specific iconographic elements, may all be indicators of a building's specific functions.

Paradoxically, although for many years most of the archaeological research in Mesoamerica, especially institutional archaeological research, has focused on monumental zones and the excavation and restoration of plazas and monumental buildings, we know little (with the exception of some sites in the Maya area) about the internal structure and planning of many of these centers or about the function and characteristics of various kinds of buildings that make up the monumental zones. Few sites have topographic studies and detailed maps that cover the entire monumental center, with systematic investigations of their specific archaeological contexts, aimed at determining the nature and function of these monuments.

There is a tendency to divide monumental architecture into two large groups. On one hand, we have pyramids/temples and altars, the attributes of which make them easy to identify, and thus there is no problem in terms of defining their generic function. On the other hand, many of the buildings that are not pyramids are frequently called palaces. Structures with a wide variety of functions and diverse architectural characteristics are grouped together under this term.

It is important to review the validity of this concept and define it with more precision for different areas and periods, perhaps restricting it fundamentally to residential structures occupied by the king or the principal ruler of a center, and for the residences of the nobility. Marcus (1983) emphasizes that many of the buildings in the Maya area that are called palaces are not really residential structures and, in some cases, are a long line of rooms with separate entrances and no internal articulation.

Harrison's (1970) work in Tikal is of great interest in this respect. He excavated a series of different palaces and drew up a typology based on four classes of different functions for the buildings, and found that only some of them were residential, while the other structures were for various rites, storage, and other activities. Sanders (1989), likewise, has found in Copán important data about the existence of other palaces, in addition to the royal palace, with inscriptions that give specific information about the family ties of the inhabitants of those buildings to the king.

With regard to the royal palace, which is the residence of a king, buildings with specific characteristics should be designated under this term. First, it should be a place with habitable structures, with areas and dependencies to house the governor's extended family, relatives, and servants. Additionally, as stressed by Calnek (1976), the palace of the reigning monarch is also frequently the headquarters of secular government, where various kinds of officials meet and numerous activities are carried out regarding the administration and government, that is, a royal palace constitutes a political-administrative complex. Thus, in addition to extensive habitation zones, the palace would have suitable spaces to cover these needs, such as rooms of various sizes, halls, courtyards, and vestibules. The size and architectural attributes would naturally vary according to the kind of city in question and its degree of complexity.

Thanks to chroniclers and other written sources, we know that the royal palaces in Tenochtitlan and Texcoco were huge. According to the "Anonymous Conquistador," the palace of Moctezuma II, which was located near the sacred precinct but outside it, had a capacity to hold thousands of officials, and some of the halls were big enough to hold a thousand people. Netzahualcoyotl's palace, according to *Ixtlilxóchitl,* must have covered dozens of hectares (quoted by Bedoian 1973:87–88). There were storage rooms and kitchens open at all times in the royal palaces. Moctezuma II sometimes had six hundred visitors a day in the central patios of his palace, most of whom must have been nobles, because on entering they had the right to be treated as guests, according to court protocol (Evans 1998: 170). Although some of the descriptions of these buildings may be exaggerated, they give an idea of the complexity that a royal palace could attain in the Late Postclassic period, since it was not only the sovereign's place of residence, but also a site with multiple functions.

Sahagún describes the royal palace or Tecpancalli as "the house of the ruler or the government house, where the ruler is, where he lives or where the ruler or the townsmen, the householders, assemble. It is a good place, a fine place, a palace; a place of honor, a place of dignity ... There is glory ... There is bragging, there is boasting; there is haughtiness, presumption, pride, arrogance ... It is a place where one is intoxicated, flattered, perverted ... It is a center of knowledge, wisdom" (Sahagún 1956, Book 2:270, quoted in Evans 1991:65–66).

At the time of the Conquest, the Tecpan of Tenochtitlan was the Palace of Moctezuma II, while the Palace of Axayacatl was called the old Tecpan and functioned as a dormitory and residence for nobles who could not be housed in the principal palace and as a place for storing various products (Evans 1991). In Tenochtitlan, the royal palace also functioned during times of war as a refuge for nobles and allied sovereigns or to house the royal dynasties of places that had been defeated. It was common to incorporate noble widows, with their servants, in the royal palace. Sometimes these women married other members of the nobility; on other occasions, they became the concubines of kings or other nobles. Many of these princesses and noblewomen who inhabited the royal palaces became cooks and, especially, they were incorporated into the production of fine fabrics (p. 168). Various kinds of artisans inhabited the royal palace, especially feather, gold, silver, and lapidary craftsmen, who were frequently minor nobles. Evans observes that in the reign of Moctezuma II, a kind of crisis existed because there were too many hereditary nobles, and this king issued new rules stating that the inheritors of minor titles would not have the right to live in the palace, and therefore some of them became artisans in order to continue living in the royal palace.

A detailed ethnohistorical study of the Tecpan and minor palaces in the rural sites in Central Mexico done by Evans (1991) provides very interesting data about the characteristics of these buildings and their diverse types. She defines various levels and categories of buildings under this term. *Tecpan* means the place of the lord, the place where the king is, but it is also a community building, or structure for the community. It is the house of the leader, but it is also the house of government. It is where the leader is, where he lives, or where the leaders or townsmen and householders meet; it is the place where the objects for tribute are stored. The Tecpan was the red house and there was a hearth that was alight twenty-four hours a day in the central courtyard. The fire was not only symbolic, it was also there for the visitors to warm themselves, and thus one of the community's tribute obligations was to provide firewood for the fire (Evans in press: note 10).

This investigator discusses some of the archaeological indicators for the identification of these structures, especially in rural sites of the Aztec period, such as the Cihuatecpan site, which she excavated in the Teotihuacan Valley (Evans [ed.] 1988, 1991). She indicates that the Tecpan was not always a monumental construction, and it is sometimes only distinguished by specific iconographic elements and by its location within the settlement. Archaeologically, a nonurban *tecpan* is a building having a very large courtyard with an open part facing the exterior in the shape of a C. It is almost always the largest residence of the site, between three and five times bigger than normal houses. It is a structure with numerous rooms and several kitchens, which were necessary not only for the inhabitants but also for the numerous visitors who came to attend business with the Tlatoani and because it was a place of community gathering. There was a raised room in front of the open patio where the seated lord received people.

Returning to Tula, it is important to stress that there is no obvious structure with the characteristics of a royal residence in the monumental precinct and even though it is possible that the Palace to the East was a type of royal palace, as we mentioned before, and that this structure together with the complex of buildings that flank Pyramid B (the Palacio Quemado and the Palace of Quetzalcoatl) could have functioned together as a kind of royal establishment, nevertheless we do not possess clear evidence for this presently.

It also is very likely that in Tula, as in Tenochtitlan, the royal palace was outside the sacred precinct and that it was not just one building, but a complex of buildings. The structure called the Toltec Palace, which was excavated by Charnay (1887:107–110) more than a century ago, has the characteristics that suggest the possibility that it may have been the royal palace or part of the royal palaces. It is in a privileged and strategic location, being near the sacred precinct, but bordered by cliffs on two sides. This building is located on a corner to the southwest of the main plaza, at one end of the elevation on which the monumental zone rises. From here, there is a view of the entire valley, as indicated by Charnay (p. 108).

However, it is not clear whether this structure was totally excavated, and there is also scant information about its archaeological contexts, but it is evident that it was a residential building. Charnay identified, as mentioned by Healan (1989b), ten different apartments connected by staircases in this building, and he defined two different periods of occupation (Fig. 5.48A).

Charnay (1887:108) referred to the structure and its excavation in the following terms: "Here we attack a pyramid of considerable size . . . which, to my extreme delight, revealed an old palace, extending over an area of nearly 62 ft. on one side, with an inner courtyard, a garden and numerous apartments on different levels, ranged from the ground floor to 8 ft. high, exactly like the first house; the whole covering a surface of 2,500 square yards (2088 m^2). We will give description of it, together with the probable use of various apartments." He then describes the probable function of some of the rooms of the compound, which included various kinds of chambers of varying size; he also mentions benches, stairways, and passageways, noting that "the main body of the palace consists of ten apartments of different size with stuccoed walls and floors."

When studying Charnay's plan (1887:107) (Fig. 5.48A), one inevitably asks whether the building was really totally excavated or whether the plan corresponds to just part of the structure, because if the courtyard was in the center of the building, as was common in Toltec residential structures, then the wing corresponding to one of the sides is missing. This would mean that the building is more complex, and larger, than what is recorded in the plan published by Charnay.

However, this explorer writes that "the building we unearthed is entire, its outer wall is intact" (Charnay 1887:110) and there is an interesting similarity between the plan published by Charnay and Structure 6 of the Cihuatecpan site excavated by Evans (1991: figs. 3.10 and 3.11), especially in its having the general C shape and the location of the patio in relation to the chambers. There is also similarity between these two buildings regarding the shape and location of the rooms of their northern limits. The rooms are marked H, L, and A in the case of Cihuatecpan and No. 6 in the Charnay Palace of Tula. That explorer stated that "No. 6, No. 6 are a kind of yards, without any trace of roofs" (Charnay 1887:109), and it seems important that the areas marked H and A in Evans's reconstruction of the Cihuatecpan building also lack roofs (Fig. 5.48B). In these two spaces she recorded *temascales* (steam baths), while Charnay assumed they were orchards.

Despite the similarities indicated, it should be noted that the Charnay Palace is larger, with greater internal complexity, and it has more rooms than the probable *tecpan* of the Aztec period published

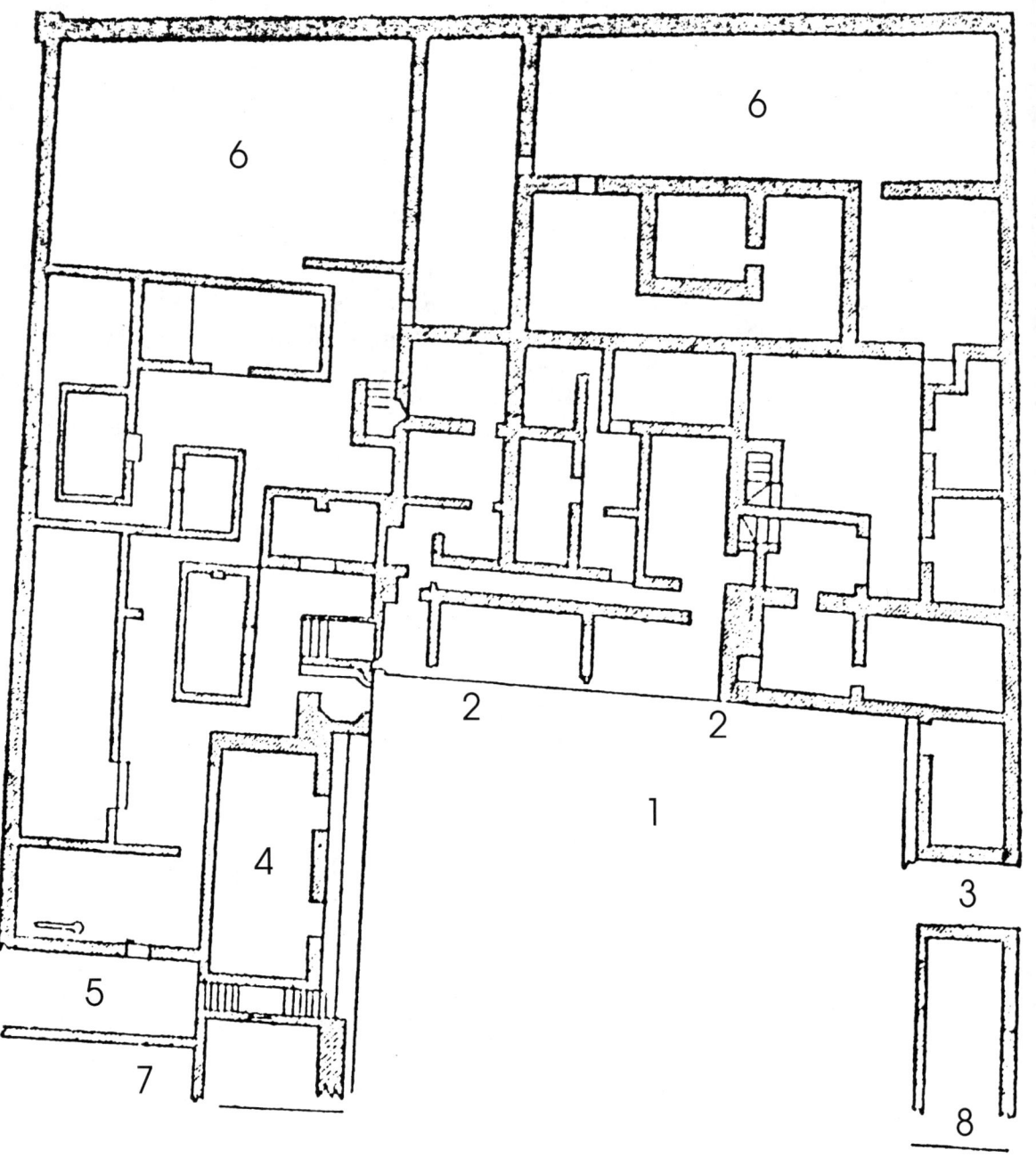

Figure 5.48A. Plan of the so-called Palacio Charnay (after Charnay 1887:107).

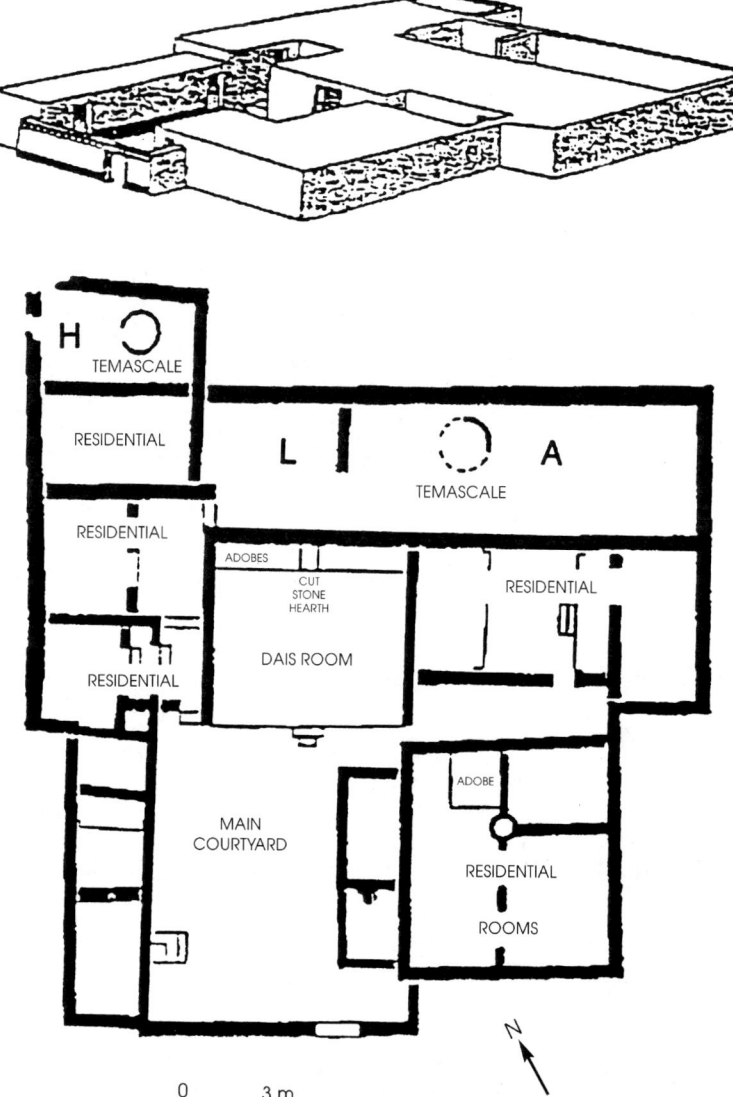

Figure 5.48B. Plan of the Tecpan excavated by Susan Evans in Cihuatecpan (Evans 1991, 1998). Courtesy, Susan Evans.

the primary contexts in Building 6 at Cihuatecpan. It is interesting to note that Elson, who analyzed the materials of the excavations made by Vaillant in the probable Aztec palace of Chiconautla, state of Mexico, also states in a recent article (1999:160, 164) that the numerous clay spindle whorls of various sizes found in the building undoubtedly indicate that the production of cloth was an important activity in the structure. Nevertheless, it should be mentioned that clay spindle whorls are frequent in many common nonpalace domestic contexts in Tula and other Postclassic sites in the Basin of Mexico.

The similarities we have referred to between the so-called Charnay Palace and the probable *tecpan* of the Late Postclassic period excavated by Evans pose the possibility that the prototype and antecedent of this kind of building is to be found in Tula. However, it is clear that

by Evans. It should also be emphasized that in the brief description made of the materials found in the building, Charnay clearly mentions the presence of clay spindle whorls of various sizes (1887:110), in this regard Evans (in press) proposes that a high frequency of spindle whorls in the Late Postclassic period could be an indicator of palatial buildings, because one of the important activities carried out in the palaces was the production of fine cloths, which was done by the women who lived there. However, Evans also notes that there were few spindle whorls in if we believe that the Charnay Palace is a building corresponding to Tula's zenith, further excavations will be required in order to determine accurately its chronology. On the other hand, the architectural technique and the fact that the Aztec occupation of the monumental center of Tula is limited only to partial reoccupations of some structures support our proposal that this building corresponds to the Early Postclassic period.

Undoubtedly, there are other possible locations in Tula for the royal palace, especially in the zone of large terraces and platforms that extends to the east of the main plaza, as we mentioned before, including the northeast and southeast limits. There has also been speculation about the likelihood of the sovereign's palace being in what Matos (1974) called the Charnay Plaza because that explorer also excavated a habitation structure there (Charnay 1887:105). This plaza is located to the north of the principal precinct of Tula. It is a large architectural complex that rises above an artificial platform and the structure excavated by Charnay is only a small part of this complex. In reality, this is an area that has not been studied extensively, and we have no knowledge of its plan or internal structure and its architectural characteristics. Considering that during the Late Postclassic period the *tecpan* was known as the Red House, it is interesting to note that Charnay observed the stucco floors of some of the building interiors that he excavated in this plaza were red in color. However, it is worth mentioning that remains of red floors were found in Building K and the Palacio Quemado, which suggests that this color was frequent for floors of buildings with ritual or religious functions.

It is very likely that over the almost three centuries of the Tollan Phase, several royal palaces were constructed or expanded in Tula by different sovereigns and, as in the case of the Mexica royal palaces, the old palaces were not always destroyed, but rather were kept as complementary buildings. However, given our current level of knowledge, trying to establish the correspondence between the royal palace or palaces or any other building with a given location in the monumental zone is quite speculative, because, as was noted before, with the exception of the buildings in the main plaza, this area is practically unknown. It is necessary to have detailed maps and extensive excavations in various parts of this zone in order to be able to propose concrete hypotheses about the nature and function of these spaces and buildings, and the probable correspondence between one kind of architecture and certain functions and activities. It is evident that an integral investigation of the monumental zone in Tula is essential for the understanding of various aspects of the organization and functioning of the Toltec state, its complexity, and the nature of its institutions, which were materialized very concretely in the monuments and in their relation with the entire spatial structure of the city.

NOTES

1. It should be noted that Getino and Cid (2000), in a recent archaeoastronomic analysis, propose that the placement and orientation of Pyramids B and C (as well as the Pyramids of the Sun and the Moon at Teotihuacan) may have been determined on the basis of the cycles and positions of the star Polaris and the planet Venus, and apparently that the *axis mundi* that determined the plan or urban grid of the city was Pyramid B and not Pyramid C. The orientation of the sacred precinct (Toltec A: Mastache and Crespo 1982) is the same as that of Teotihuacan (approximately 17° east of north). Getino and Cid conclude that this orientation is based on the declination cycle of Venus.

2. According to zoologist Oscar Polaco (personal communication 2000), the felines are pumas (*Puma concolor*) with the following diagnostic characteristics: short faces, round ears, typical claws on the feet, and naked tails. He states that the scale represented makes it more probable that the canines are *Canis lupus*. These animals are characterized by more or less round ears, claws, short faces, and bushy downturned tails. The birds consist of two kinds: royal eagles (*Aquila chrysaetos*) and a type of vulture that only can be identified on the level of family (Cathartidae). It is important to mention that Polaco states that royal eagles occur in the Central Highlands, but not in Yucatán, even though they also are depicted in Toltec iconography at Chichén Itzá.

3. For a detailed description of the reliefs on the pillars, see the thorough analysis of Kristan-Graham (1989) concerning these sculptures and Jiménez (1998), which is the source of the illustrations used here.

4. This fragment was on display for several years at the museum in Tula's archaeological zone and also was exhibited briefly in Mexico City at the National Museum of Anthropology. It is published in the catalogue of Castillo and Dumaine (1988:222, 244, fig. 2) as sculpture number 12, and Jiménez (1998:125–132, fig. 51) describes and illustrates it, calling it "Pilastra 5 (incompleta)."

5. According to Oscar Polaco (personal communication 2000) the bird represented in the helmet very probably

is a royal eagle (*Aguila chrysaetos*) characterized, among other attributes, by the upward-turned feathers on its head. This is the same species of eagle that is depicted on the facades of Pyramid B.

6. Oscar Polaco (personal communication 2000) observes that the serpents on the bench cornices along with those in the background of human figures on relief panels are rattlesnakes (*Crotalus sp.*), which in some cases are depicted with obvious ventral scales.

7. López Luján subsequently made a study of the Casa de las Aguilas for his doctoral dissertation, but we have not seen this text because the author was revising it for publication and could not give us more information when we consulted him.

8. According to Marquina's (1964) map, the Temple of Tezcatlipoca would be located nearby, and it is important to note that Klein (1987), on the basis of various ethnohistorical sources, identifies the Casa de las Aguilas with the *tlacochcalco* where recently enthroned Mexica kings performed rites of autosacrifice and the funerary rituals for kings and high ranking warriors took place. Klein also notes that the buildings called *tlacochcalco* were dedicated to Tezcatlipoca.

9. Concerning the relation between human sacrifice and Chac Mools, see the analyses of Mary Ellen Miller (1985; Miller and Samayoa 1998).

10. Coggins (1987:444, 466) also associates Chac Mools with Tlaloc, but emphasizes even more their roles in New Fire ceremonies at Chichén Itzá and Tula. She postulates that Chac Mools were used at these centers as the drilling base for making the New Fire, and that in this ceremony these sculptures are accompanied by *tezcacuitlapilli* mirrors, as is the case in the Palacio Quemado and the Castillo at Chichén Itzá. Getino and Figueroa (n.d.) and Taube (n.d.) provide further analyses of New Fire ceremony symbolism in the iconography of the Palacio Quemado. Broda (1982:47) published an observation by Seler proposing that the vessels on the Chac Mools' abdomens were used to store pulque in rites to the Tlaloque as gods of mountains and pulque (Angulo 1996:128). Cuéllar (1981), in a series of iconographic and ethnohistorical interpretations, also relates Chac Mools with gods and rites concerning pulque.

11. A description of this *brasero* type and its distribution is in Cobean (1990).

12. This combination of a pyramid with a frontal portico also occurs in the Temple of the Warriors at Chichén Itzá, although at this site apparently no adjacent building equivalent to the Palace to the East of the Vestibule existed. At Tula, as we have emphasized, Pyramid B, the Vestibule, and the Palace to the East constituted an architectural unit.

13. Regarding the concepts of duality in the universe among the peoples of ancient Mexico, see Lopez Austin (1973, 1980), who analyzes this topic thoroughly along with discussions of the most common types of opposition in Nahua cosmovisions.

14. See López Luján (1993:95–101) on the dual pattern of the Templo Mayor, including a summary and analysis of different proposals from diverse investigations and the controversy concerning the significance of the temples or "double chapels" on this pyramid's summit. This author also discusses the notable preeminence of the cult to Huitzilopochtli at the Templo Mayor, showing that indications of this superior status can be observed in the frequent generic reference to the Templo Mayor as the "Cu of Huitzilopochtli" in the early sources, and in the greater size of the "chapel" of Huitzilopochtli evident in the remains of the Templo Mayor at Tenochtitlan and Tlatelolco, and in sixteenth-century illustrations of these structures (p. 98).

15. The "phantasy" that Seler attributes to Clavijero and Boturini is an account of a great representation of a Sun God that was standing on the summit of the Pyramid of the Sun and that had a large golden plaque (a mirror?) on its chest that reflected the rays of the sun at dawn. We thank Karl Taube for informing us of Seler's commentary, and for his observations on the probable mirror and other attributes of this sculpture. We also thank Irmgard W. Johnson for translating Seler's text on this subject.

16. Pasztory (1997:73–95) proposes, mainly on the basis of the iconography of Teotihuacan's mural art, a debateable hypothesis that this pyramid was dedicated to a storm goddess, and the Pyramid of the Sun to a cave goddess.

17. At Tula, the representations of skulls in profile include, for example, the skeletal figures in the Coatepantli (Acosta 1944, 1945) and in the reliefs of the altar on the northeast edge of the El Corral temple (Acosta 1974).

18. In Stela 6 of Copán, the King Smoke Imix God K is shown with a headdress very similar to that of the personage in Tula's Stela 1, having Tlalocs and *glifos de año* (trapeze-triangle glyphs) as principal elements (Fash and Fash 2000: fig. 14.1; Fash 1991:80).

19. See Stone (1989:165) and Urcid (1993). Other examples are on Stela 2 of Aguateca and on Stela 16 of Dos

Pilas, where Ruler 3 of Dos Pilas is represented with Tlalocs on his lower garment and shield and trapeze-triangle glyphs in his headdress (Stuart 1998:13). Also, the king Nun Yax Ayin is depicted in the well-known Stela 31 of Tikal carrying a Tlaloc shield (Stuart 2000:472). In Stela 3 of Los Horcones, Chiapas (Navarrete 1986), the great Tlaloc figure in Teotihuacan style with a glifo de año headdress is considered by Taube (personal communication) to represent a king. A very similar Tlaloc image, probably related to warfare and rulership, is the principal element of Stela 2 at Xochicalco, Morelos (Smith 2000:91).

6

Habitation in the City

Numerous questions exist concerning the residential areas, which made up most of the urban zone and where most of the population lived, especially their planning and spatial organization, their territorial divisions, and the definition of the essential component units. However, there are few answers to these questions due to the fragmented and limited information available concerning residential areas. Consequently, here we only give a general panorama as to those aspects of the settlement about which we have information, and rather than concrete data, hypotheses are proposed that can still be corroborated in some cases.

Only a dozen residential structures have been excavated to date in the city, excluding those studied by Charnay and Acosta in the monumental area. This is obviously a very small sample, considering the long sequence of occupation and the size of the city (almost 16 square kilometers), which must have had thousands of houses. Healan (1973), based on his studies of habitation structures and Stoutamire's (1975) investigation of the urban zone, calculates that Tula probably had about two thousand housing complexes during the Tollan Phase. Although this figure is tentative and the criteria on which it is based are essentially surface surveys, it can be used to get an idea of what the city's habitational density must have been.

Other problems arise, on one hand, because the excavations of most urban habitation units done to date have been partial and seldom cover the entire residential structure, and on the other hand, because the methodology and techniques of different projects have very different levels of accuracy in recording; therefore, the data are not always comparable with each other. There is a serious problem in the lack of control over archaeological contexts within various excavations conducted on habitation structures in the city because there is little basic information as to their chronology and the functions of different areas and spaces that made up the structures. Walls, floors, and other elements corresponding to different phases of construction are sometimes depicted together on the same plan, without records of specific contexts or analyses of the associated materials, and without discriminating the archaeological elements corresponding to a given stage of occupation of the building. Only two of the studies published include detailed descriptions of the contexts excavated, their stratigraphy, the construction sequence of the buildings, and their chronology (see Healan 1989a; Mandeville and Healan 1989).

TYPES OF HABITATIONS

Healan proposes that in Tula there were at least three types of habitation units: Palaces, House Groups, and Apartment Compounds. The above-mentioned Charnay Palace represents the first category, about which we know very little. Probably most of the buildings of this kind were inhabited by nobles and members of the ruling elite and correspond to a series of structures and platforms located on the extensive terraces, especially to the south and east of the monumental precinct.

The second type, called the House Groups, is the most carefully studied and the one defined in more detail. It is fundamentally represented by the units in the excavation called El Canal, located in the east of the city and studied by Healan (1973, 1989a, 1989b). It is a residential complex, approximately 75 percent of which has been excavated, with a total length of 90 meters and a width of 36 meters. This housing complex consisted of three different residential units: the East Group, the Central Group, and the West Group, each one made up of three or more habitational houses placed around a courtyard that represented the focal point of each complex. We wish to emphasize here that the patio, and more precisely the central altar, was the physical and symbolic axis, the basis on which the space of all of the domestic compound was structured. In both the Central Group of the El Canal excavation and the rural domestic unit excavated in Tepetitlán, the central altar is aligned with the principal stairway, thus emphasizing the symbolic importance of the house located on the east side.

Apparently, this type of domestic compound reproduced a similar conception of space as that of the sacred precinct: with the plaza, central altar, and the principal structure being on the east side, in the same position as Pyramid C, and also perhaps the entrances were at the same points (Mastache and Cobean 1999b:61).

A total of eleven houses were defined in the entire complex, three in the West Group, six in the Central Group, and one temple and two houses in the East Group. However, this does not mean that this is the total number of houses in the complex, since the East Group was not totally excavated and some of the zones of the West Group had been heavily eroded. Indeed, the Central Group is the most thoroughly studied because it was fully excavated and also possessed a better state of conservation. Each House Group had one narrow entrance to the street in an L shape, which prevented observation into the interior from the outside and allowed only one person to enter at a time, as can be seen in the excavation plan (Fig. 6.1).

A distinctive feature of these complexes is that the houses making up each of the three House Groups have multiple rooms. Each house has a variable number of rooms and none has just one. Most of the houses have four or five rooms, but there are some with just two and others with as many as eight. A total of fifty-three rooms were defined in the entire El Canal complex. With the exception of one house, all of the complexes have the same orientation, with a deviation of between approximately 15° and 17° to the west of the astronomic north. This orientation was defined by Mastache and Crespo (1982) as Toltec B, and appears to be characteristic of the phase of apogee for the city.

The houses were built on a platform approximately 1 meter high; each house had its own entrance and there were no accesses communicating between the houses; that is, they were independent units that only communicated through the courtyard. They had stone foundations and mud (adobe) walls; most of the floors were made of tamped earth, although there were stucco floors in some of the houses. Healan considers them to be an indicator of status differences inside the complexes.

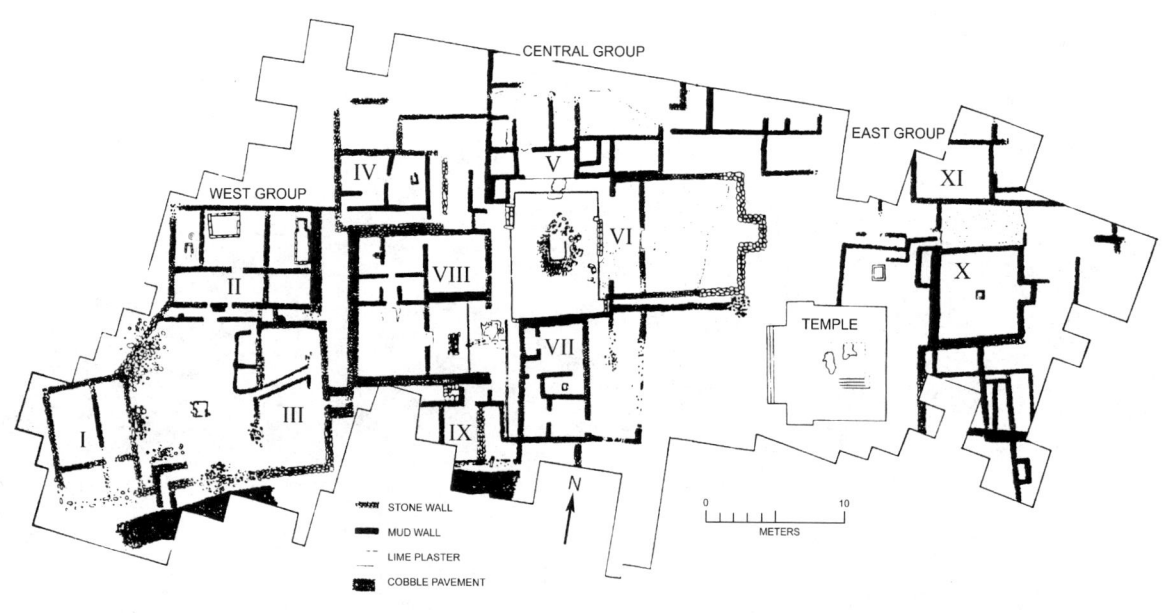

Figure 6.1. The House Groups of the El Canal excavations (Healan 1989c: fig. 7.7).

Different kinds of activity areas were defined in each house, the two most important being the kitchens, which were located inside the houses, and the food preparation areas, which were in open spaces such as the central courtyard and the house vestibules. On some occasions, two kitchens were found inside the same house, which in Healan's opinion seems to indicate that these habitations were occupied by more than one nuclear family. Healan proposes that each of the House Groups was occupied by an extended family, while each individual house was generally occupied by a single nuclear family, with the courtyard as a common area to share and carry out domestic chores and other activities in the company of other family groups.

The structuring of the El Canal complex indicates that there was constant interaction among the occupants of the three House Groups that made up the compound, with the patios as extensions of the houses. The patio provided additional space for domestic, craft, and religious activities, as is indicated by the presence of a central altar in the patio of each complex. It is very likely that the inhabitants of the three complexes had kinship ties and perhaps made up a lineage.

It is generally assumed that multifamily complexes of this kind, which were frequent in various parts of Mesoamerica, were inhabited by extended families, that is, by domestic groups made up of several, directly related nuclear families and corresponding to more than one generation. However, it is important to consider that the occupants probably were not always directly related nuclear families, and that the inhabitants of these complexes in some cases also could have included: widows, nephews and nieces, cousins and single distant relatives, servants (even slaves), dependents, various classes of workers, and, perhaps in the case of high ranking individuals, the different wives of the head of the household with their respective children. As mentioned elsewhere (Cobean and Mastache 1999b:300), in this respect, Carrasco's studies of documents in Nahuatl referring to the Marquesado of Morelos during the beginning of the colonial period (Carrasco 1964, 1972; Smith 1992), which indicate diverse possibilities and patterns of variability in the social and demographic structure of the domestic complexes, are highly suggestive.

Figure 6.2. The El Canal excavations. House VII appears in the foreground with the Central Group Courtyard in the background. (Note altar in the center of the courtyard.)

The number of houses and complexes at Tula changed with time, which was probably related to the growth of family units. In the Central Group there are two later houses, and the West Group was the last to be built, although obviously the space available must have imposed limits on the growth within each unit.

There was an associated temple in the East Group (Figs. 6.1 and 6.3), which was undoubtedly used for religious activities involving the occupants of the entire complex, that is, the families who lived in the three complexes, and it is interesting to note that there was also a ceremonial mound 3 meters high near the excavated unit to the south. Its closeness leads to the assumption that it was related to the habitation complex, although it is not possible to define the exact relationship between this structure and the residential buildings because the mound has not been excavated. As can be seen in Healan's topographic plan of the complex excavated (1989a:56, 57, fig. 7.2), there is another much larger ceremonial mound to the northwest of the same residential complex that is similar in size to the El Corral Pyramid excavated by Acosta. The plan for the El Canal complex also shows the remains of a cobbled street found on the limits of the excavated unit, and there is information that seems to indicate the presence of similar habitation groups adjacent to the El Canal structures (p. 148) (Fig. 6.2).

Another example of the House Group is from an obsidian workshop located in the southeast urban zone and also excavated by Healan (1986). Appar-

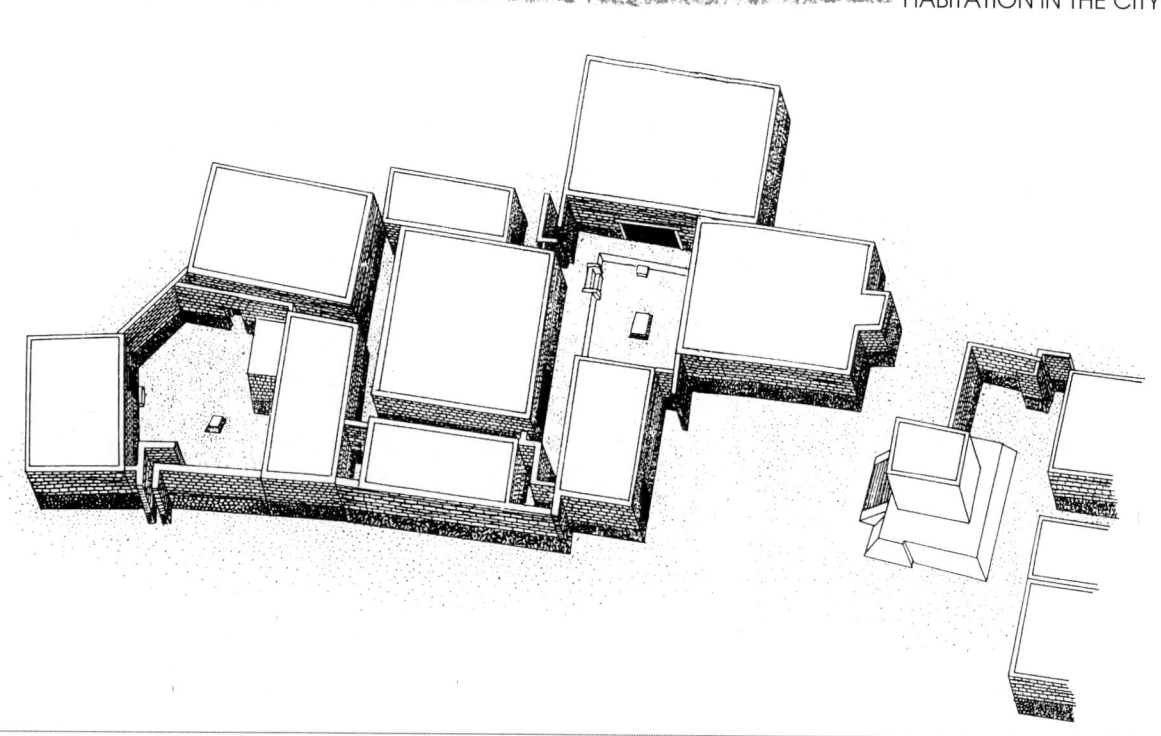

Figure 6.3. Hypothetical reconstruction of the House Groups of the El Canal locality (Healan 1989a: fig. 9.28).

ently, this habitation complex was similar in shape and size to the El Canal complex (90 meters long and 40 meters wide), although the exact dimensions are not known because it was only partially excavated, and the structure was severely altered by agricultural machinery just before the Tulane University project started. Healan indicates (1986: fig. 2) that there were two other structures next to this unit of similar dimensions, one of which was narrower.

We have two more examples of House Groups, both of which were unearthed by salvage excavations. One structure is located less than 1 kilometer east of the monumental precinct denominated U27 and U28 (Mastache and Cobean 1985; Getino n.d.) (see Fig. 6.4). This complex is apparently similar to the Central Group of El Canal, of which the northern end of the patio and part of the north and west houses have been excavated.

Another example was found in the rescue excavation conducted by Carlos Hernández and María Elena Suárez in 1998 as part of the Tula-Tlahuelilpan highway expansion program (Hernández et al. 1999). The excavations were made within the urban perimeter, in a zone that was probably a neighborhood of potters in the ancient city (Fig. 6.5), and exposed sections that seem to have been two different House Groups of the same complex. In the extreme north, part of two rooms and a courtyard were discovered. The courtyard is apparently similar to the one in the Central Group at El Canal. To the south, part of the complex was exposed with smaller dimensions, of which only a small courtyard and some rooms have been excavated. It seems likely that both habitation structures, which were apparently occupied by potters, formed part of the same complex and are similar to the House Groups at El Canal studied by Healan (1989a). However, since only a limited area was excavated, there is no certainty as to whether this was so.

The so-called Apartment Compounds are, according to Healan (1989b, [ed.] 1989), buildings consisting of groups of rooms that were also structured around courtyards, but that are similar in general layout and internal planning to the Teotihuacan Apartment Compounds, albeit smaller and simpler. However, there is no detailed knowledge of architectural characteristics because none of the Apartment Compounds in Tula have been fully excavated. These are apparently larger structures than the House Groups, with numerous rooms and various courtyards. There are interior systems with interconnected passages that connect various rooms, which do not exist in the House Groups, where there is a single passageway going around the courtyard. Another difference lies in the fact that there are two kinds of open spaces in these complexes: courtyards and roofed corridors with columns surrounding an *impluvium* (cistern). Unlike the House Groups, in these complexes it is difficult to delimit the group of rooms that provided housing units for each family.

Healan proposes that because the Apartment Compounds have larger interior spaces than those in the House Groups, central courtyards, and better-quality construction in which more stone and stucco are used, even including sculptured relief panels, it is probable that these structures were higher in status, while the House Groups were more common housing and characteristic of most of the city's population.

In Healan's opinion, the most characteristic example of this kind of residence is the so-called Toltec House excavated by Charnay. He also mentions, as another example of the Apartment Compounds, the unit called El Corral (Mandeville and Healan 1989) (Fig.

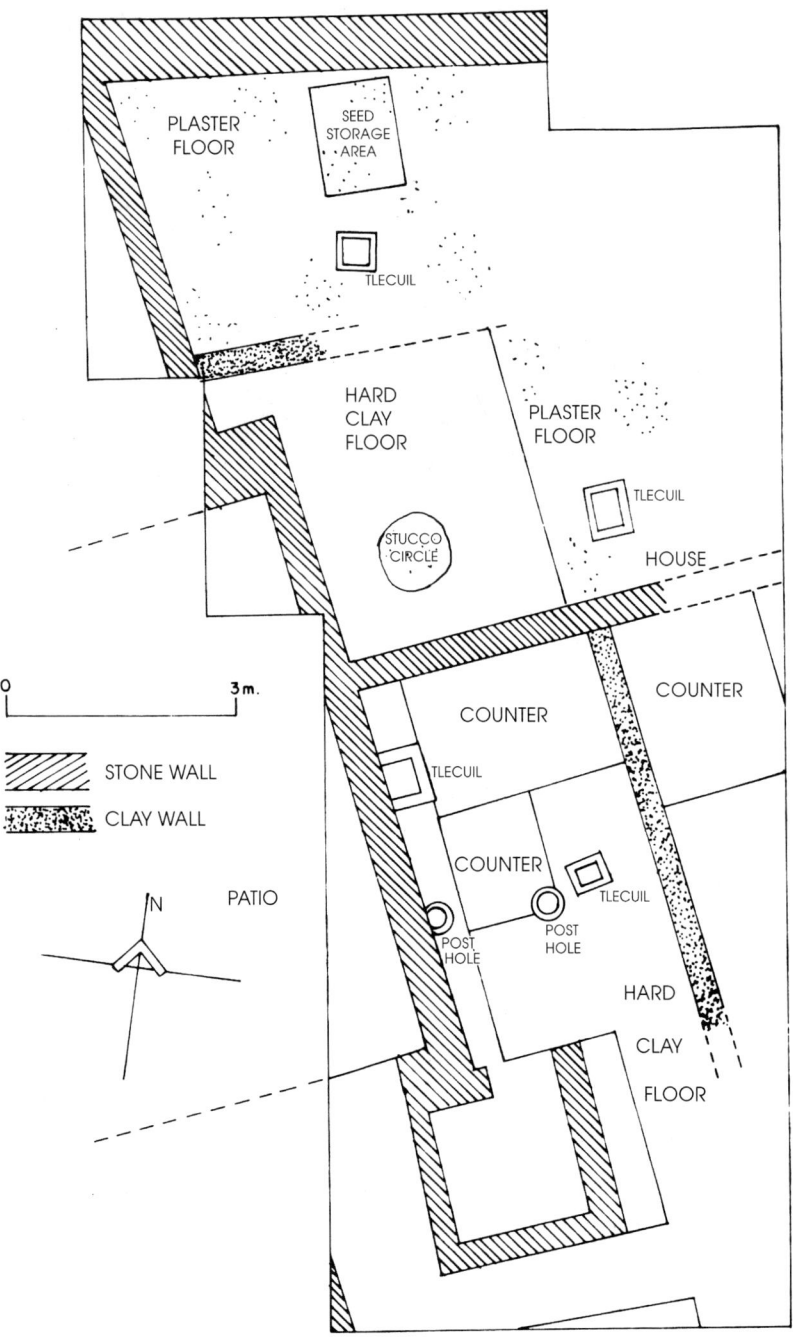

Figure 6.4. U27-28: Another example of a House Group in Tula's urban zone, of which the east sector and part of the patio were excavated (Getino n.d.).

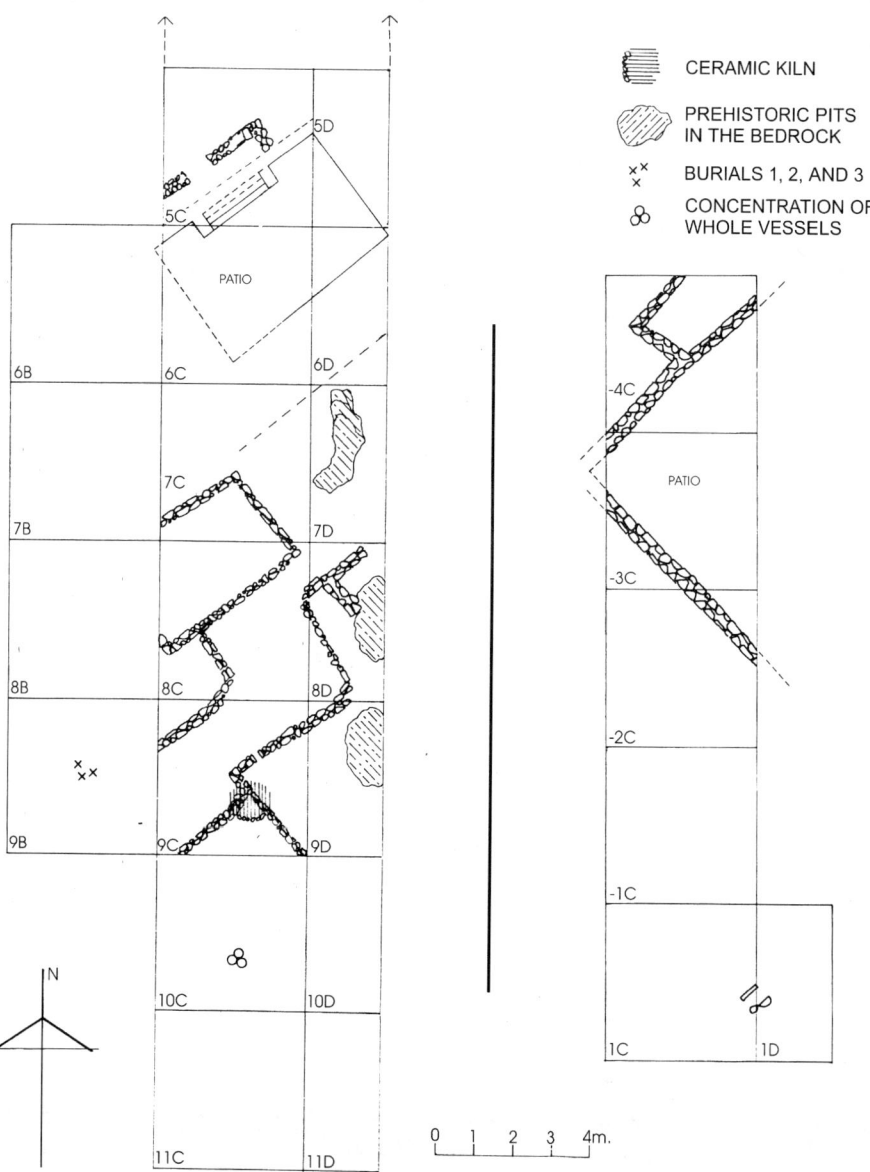

Figure 6.5. U98: Sectors of what appear to have been two different House Groups in the same complex located in the ancient city's ceramics-production *barrio* (Hernandez et al. 1999).

6.6), located in the northeast sector of the city close to the pyramid with a circular base having the same name, which was excavated by Acosta in 1950. Probably, other structures of this kind were some of the units excavated by the Hidalgo Regional Center at the beginning of the 1980s for the construction of the "Bullet Train," such as the structures located on the Cerro de La Malinche (Paredes 1990) and in the El Vivero area, close to the current site of the museum (Fernández 1986). Healan also proposes that the unit called Daini, partially excavated by Peña and Rodríguez (1976), could correspond to

HABITATION IN THE CITY

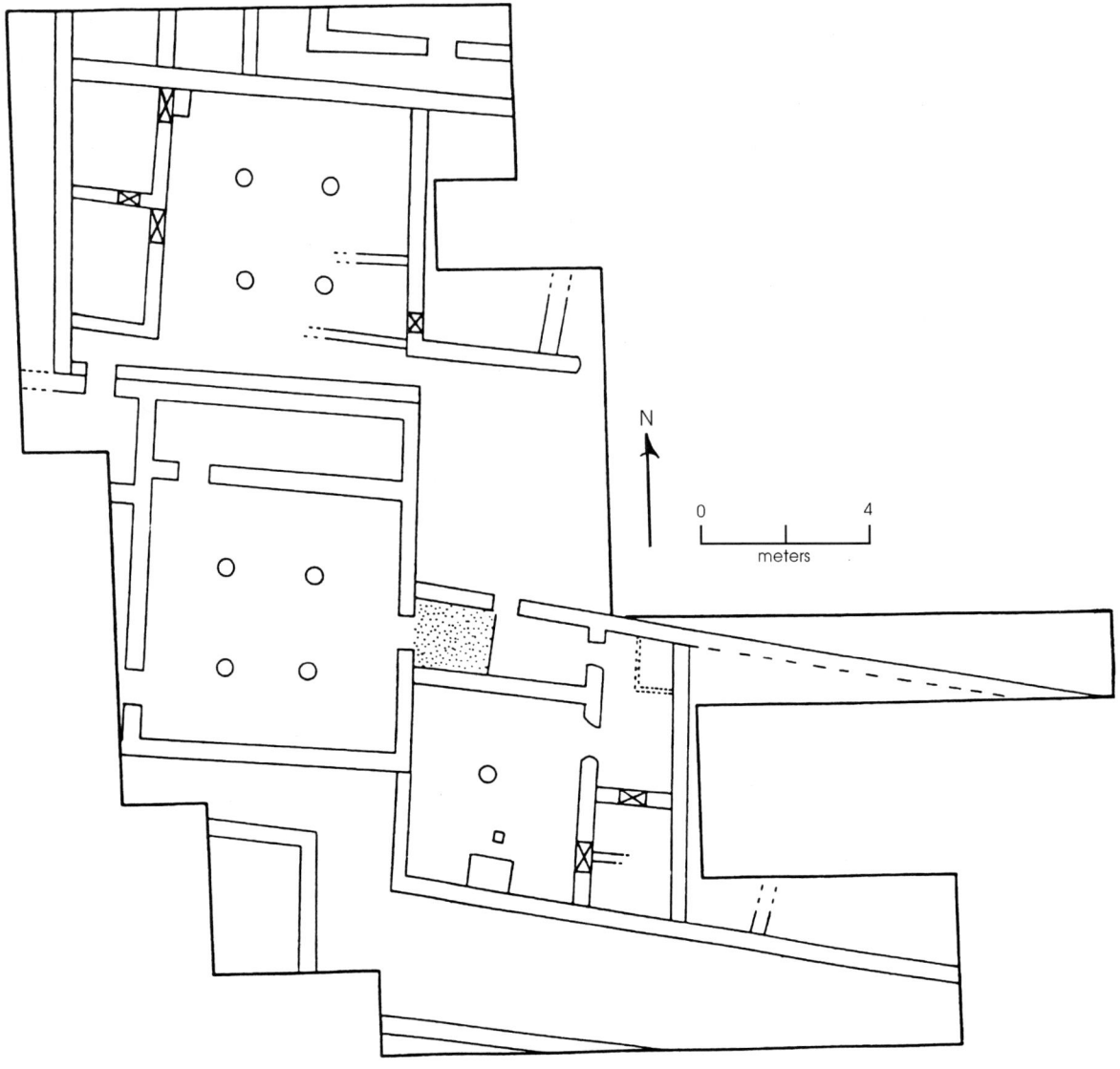

Figure 6.6. The structure of the El Corral excavation, which constitutes a typical apartment compound at Tula (Mandeville and Healan 1989).

this kind of habitation; however, given the limited area excavated, it is difficult to assure this (Healan 1989b: 419, table 1).

Regarding Healan's proposal that the complexes called House Groups were the most common kind of housing in the city, it is important to note that the surface studies and excavations done in the Tula area indicate that this kind of complex could also have been the most common kind of Tollan Phase rural housing in the area that sustained the city, especially in zones where dispersed and semidispersed settlements predominated (Cobean and Mastache 1999).

Cobean and Mastache (1999) excavated a rural domestic unit contemporary with the apogee of Tula at the Tepetitlán site located some 20 kilometers to the north of the ancient city. The excavated structure turned out to be a House Group and very similar to the El Canal Central Group studied by Healan. Unfortunately, it is the only Tollan Phase habitation structure excavated in the rural area to date.

There are striking similarities between the Tepetitlán rural habitation structure and the El Canal urban compound (see Figs. 6.7 and 6.8). They include the general planning and structuring of the unit, the shape and dimensions of the courtyard, the size, location, and characteristics of the central altar and the three stairways, and the presence of drainpipes and small stone facades at various points. Also, the general plan and internal structure of each one of the houses surrounding the courtyard are similar in Tepetitlán and El Canal. There are also some differences, such as the absence of stucco floors in the houses of the rural complex and the absence of sculptures on the central altar. The shared elements at both sites make it clear that the rural and the urban housing units followed the same basic model—a plan that expressed essential principles of space distribution in which there are undoubtedly present symbolic and practical aspects of the social structure.

Obviously, a single residential compound does not constitute a valid sample for proposing that this kind of complex is representative of the rural Toltec dwelling place, but the fact that a large number of the Tollan Phase habitation mounds located in the survey appear on the surface to be very similar (in terms of form and dimensions) to the mound excavated in Tepetitlán suggests that this kind of habitation complex could have been a common rural dwelling in the area that sustained the city during its apogee (Mastache 1996a).

Although, as has been stated before, the sample of domestic units studied in the city is small, it is clear that there were two basic types of dwellings in Tula: House Groups and Apartment Compounds, each one with its own distinct architectural characteristics. It is very likely, as Healan (1989b) states, that the existence of two kinds of habitation units is related to the differences in status in the population, and that those who lived in the Apartment Compounds enjoyed a higher status, while those who lived in the House Groups would be the common population and probably included a large part of the rural population.

However, even though this is just a hypothesis, we would like to indicate that the existence in the city of two different kinds of habitation compounds, each with a different architectural conception and use of space, could be related, not only to a specific division of classes, but also, as Edward Calnek has suggested (personal communication 1999), to the ethnic composition of the city. Historical sources clearly refer to the multiethnic origin of the population of Tula, with two main groups: the Nonoalcas, probably related to Teotihuacan, and the so-called Tolteca-Chichimeca peoples, who included various groups of mostly northern origin (Jiménez Moreno 1941, 1954–1955). Likewise, the archaeological studies in the city and the area show that Tula was largely a cultural synthesis of the preceding Teotihuacan people and of groups of northern origin linked to the northwest periphery of Mesoamerica.

The cultural ties between Tula and Teotihuacan are evident, as was analyzed in the previous chapter, in the planning, architecture, and iconography of the sacred precinct. Therefore, it is not strange that this relationship also would be manifested in the domestic architecture and that the Teotihuacan-affiliated population would perhaps be a minority consisting of higher status people who occupied the Apartment Compounds (which have planning and internal structure reminiscent of the Teotihuacan residential complexes and an orientation seemingly the same as that of Teotihuacan).

Apparently there are chronological differences between both kinds of dwellings: the Apartment Compounds correspond fundamentally to the Early Tollan Phase, while the House Groups were more common especially during the last stages of the city's apogee (Late Tollan Phase) (Cobean 1978). Likewise, it is significant that the orientation of the El Corral habitation structure apparently corresponds to the early orientation of the city (Mandeville and Healan 1989:172, fig. 12.1), which Mastache and Crespo (1982) called Toltec A, while the House Groups excavated so far have the later orientation, called Toltec B (Getino n.d.; Healan 1986; Hernández et al. 1999).

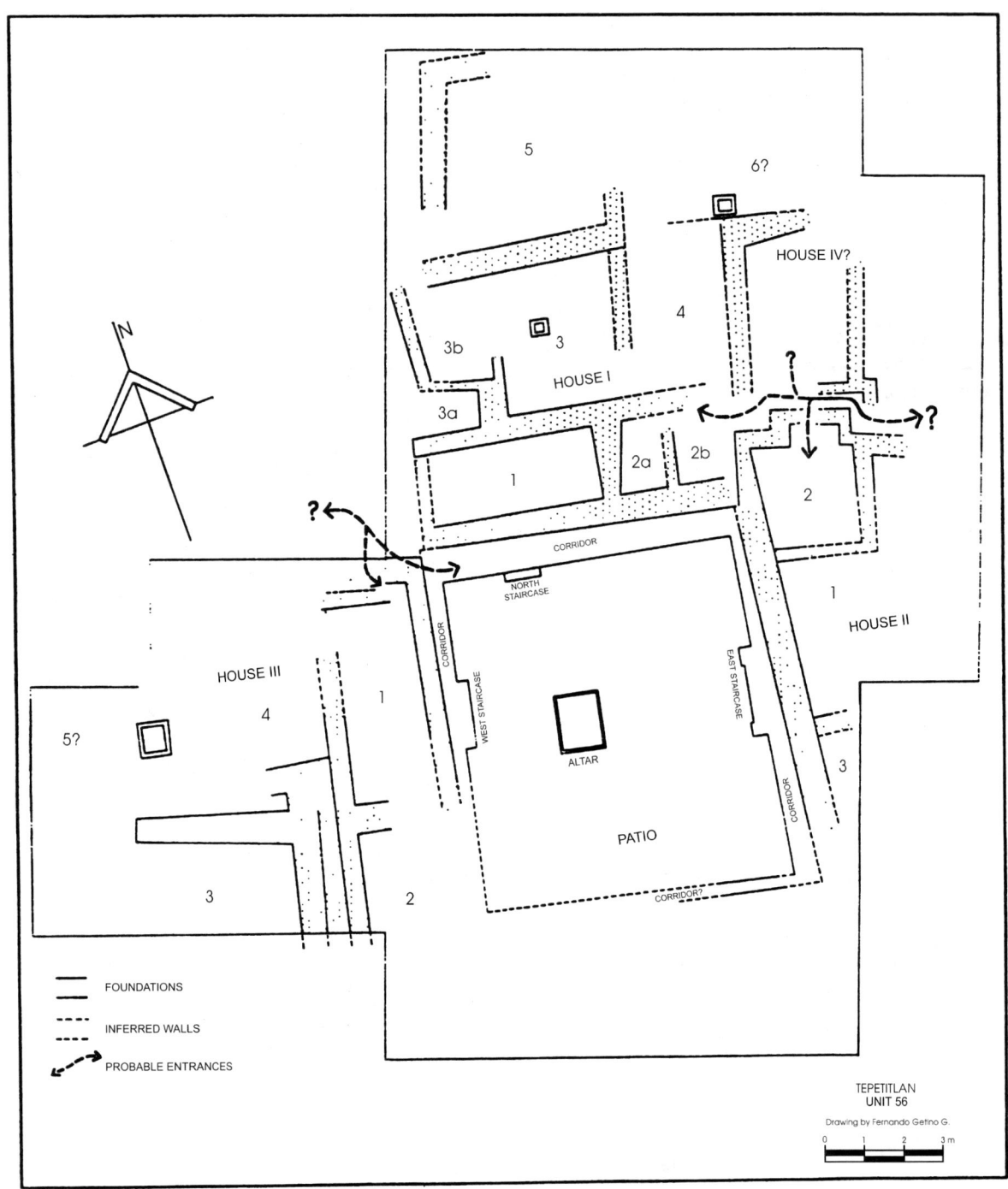

Figure 6.7. Plan of the House Group excavated at Tepetitlán (Cobean and Mastache 1999: fig. 1.25).

Figure 6.8. The Tepetitlán excavations.

All of the above make it possible to propose that the city of the Early Tollan Phase had an urban layout, including the monumental precinct, with an orientation of 17° to the east of the astronomical north (the orientation called Toltec A), and that the so-called Apartment Compounds apparently were most characteristic of this phase. During the Late Tollan Phase, which corresponded to the city's apogee and maximum expansion, the urban fabric would correspond to the layout and orientation called Toltec B, deviating toward the west, and the majority of the population lived in House Group–type dwellings. Nevertheless the Apartment Compounds were not abandoned in all cases, since there is evidence of continued occupation in at least two examples (Mandeville and Healan 1989; Fernández 1986) until the Late Tollan Phase. However, as we have emphasized, the sample known to date is too small to make definite conclusions on this matter. It is notable that Apartment Compounds and House Groups do not seem to be limited to any given zone of the city and that they were not mutually exclusive in distribution, which would indicate that they did coexist during some periods having both kinds of population spatially mixed in the same zones of the city.

If it is true that the Apartment Compounds essentially correspond to the Early Tollan Phase and the Toltec A orientation, and the House Groups to the Late Tollan Phase and the layout of the city with a Toltec B orientation, then there was a very significant urban transformation between one phase and the other that not only included the change of orientation in the plan of the city, but also an important innovation in domestic architecture with a different concept of dwelling and the use of space, changes that surely correspond to important ideological transformations and modifications in the socioeconomic structure of the city. The House Groups would thus correspond to that time of maximum population expansion, perhaps because their architectural concept and flexibility were more suited to the population boom that apparently took place in the tenth century, when the city reached its greatest extension, and these structures were better adapted to the socioeconomic changes.

The House Groups constitute a residential unit that offers various advantages because it gives the occupants privacy in using the individual houses, and it has the architectural flexibility of being able to expand, up to a certain point, thus allowing for differences in the sizes of individual families and the differences in status among the families (Healan, Cobean, and Diehl 1989:245). It must be remembered that in the El Canal complex there were some differences in terms of the use of space, construction quality, and specific contexts between different houses in the same complex, which Healan (1989a) considered could be indicators of internal hierarchical differences among the families that occupied these complexes.

The existence of multifamily complexes of this kind in Tula and the absence of isolated single-family dwellings clearly illustrates that during the apogee of the city, the basic socioeconomic unit within the urban (and perhaps rural) social structure was the extended family, and groups of extended families shared the same architectural unit. This kind of urban residential complex, especially the House Groups, represents three different levels of social integration: the nuclear family, the extended family, and groups of extended families. Healan, Cobean, and Diehl (1989) have already observed that the residential complexes, which house various nuclear families, are a common form of habitation in pre-Hispanic cities, and they reflect a successful form of adaptation to urban life. Their advantage lies in organizing, with different purposes, superfamily groups in semiautonomous fashion with their own social cohesion.

However, the differences present in this kind of architectural complex in distinct periods seem to be important. If the plans corresponding to the Teotihuacan, Tula, and Tenochtitlan habitation complexes are examined, it is evident that there was a gradual simplification in plan and a reduction in size through time.

Irrespective of the variation in the size and complexity of the various classes of residential complexes in Teotihuacan (Millon [ed.] 1973), they seem to be more uniform compounds and more complex and formalized units than the House Groups in Tula. In general, they are larger and seem to have housed a greater population than the dwelling complexes of Tula. The latter, in turn, despite their variations and flexibility, are clearly more uniform and complex in terms of layout, internal structure, and size than the Tenochtitlan habitation complexes. The courtyard is an important point of continuity between the Teotihuacan and Tula dwelling complexes because, as Susan Evans points out in both cases, it is the "focus of household life, central to all the living rooms, and having an altar in the middle, whereas the pattern changes in the later Postclassic (Aztec). At that time the patio becomes an entrance courtyard, a smaller version of the plaza it faces upon" (personal communication January 2000).

Calnek's studies (1974, 1976, n.d.) show that the residential units in Tenochtitlan and Tlatelolco seem to have varied greatly in terms of size and shape, and it is not possible to talk about a standard residential complex. These architectural units are widely variable and housed from two to six nuclear families. The space occupied by the individual dwellings varied from 10 to 30 or 40 square meters. The plans of urban dwellings in Tenochtitlan published by Calnek clearly show a greater heterogeneity among the domestic structures in contrast to the more standard residential units of Teotihuacan and Tula.

The differences in the architectural conception and the dimensions of the residential complexes in these cities are undoubtedly related to the particular socioeconomic structure of the centers, and show a tendency to live in ever smaller domestic complexes through time. The Teotihuacan residential complexes perhaps housed members of complete lineages who lived together, which Sanders (personal communication 1999) states is very probably tied to the fact that the economic function of these large domestic units was complex and the organization of labor was based, to a greater extent than in Tenochtitlan, on the cooperation of larger extended families, because the economic activity of these urban family units also included agricultural work. In contrast, Tenochtitlan would be an example of a more open and diversified urban economy, where commercial and market activities were more important than agricultural work. Being more open in terms of individual occupation (livelihood) opportunities, the existence of large extended-family corporative groups would be less important and there would less need to maintain large domestic units.

NEIGHBORHOODS, DISTRICTS, AND SECTORS

Neighborhoods (*barrios*) are collective, territorial, and often administrative entities that constitute a basic unit of urban life. The neighborhood has a fundamental meaning in the organization of a city. The structure of public, economic, religious, and festive life is based on the neighborhood, which frequently has a name that confers its own personality within the city (George 1974c:94–95; Castells 1982:125). In preindustrial cities, the neighborhoods are frequently of an ethnic, kinship, or lineage character, as well as having functional and economic links. They often have their own traditions and protecting god (*patrón*), as well as specific festivities, and there is a feeling of identity and belonging among the inhabitants.

According to Chombart de Lauwe, neighborhoods are elemental units in social life; they result from a specific combination of work life and the relations of production and consumption that are integrated within a given space (quoted by Castells 1982:127, 128). In the study of these urban entities, it is important to be able to determine what social ties define a neighborhood and the ideological, economic, or social processes that result in its structure, dynamics, and growth, as well as its permanence, together with the correlations of these processes with the organization of the urban space.

As in other large preindustrial cities, in Tula, between the monumental zone—which represented the central power and the institutions of the state—and the residential complexes that represented minimum social units (nuclear family, extended family, and groups of extended families), there must have existed one or more types of intermediate entities of different hierarchies that could have been neighborhoods, districts, or sectors. However, it is difficult, given the scant information available, to define what these units were, their number, dimensions, shape, location and spatial delimitation, and hierarchy. We agree with Castells (1982:126) when he proposes that it is possible to divide an urban space in as many units as desired, following diverse criteria for objectives of study or as a methodological technique, but above all it is important that these units correspond to real elements possessing significance within the social and economic structure, and that they define what was the social specificity of these urban entities.

In the layout of the city designated Toltec B (Mastache and Crespo 1982), there are alignments that suggest the existence of three different kinds of spatial units. However, since this study was essentially based on aerial photography, it cannot be stated with precision what architectural elements are represented by the alignments marked on the plan: streets, avenues, terraces, platform limits, walls, plazas, or canals, etc. Thus, these units are tentative and their specific meaning and nature are difficult to define without further field studies, which would have to include detailed topographic maps and excavations in the zones where this is still possible. In some cases, it was confirmed in the field that the alignments corresponded to the limits of specific architectural units, as in the case of the points marked A and B in Figure 6.9 and some of the alignments that appear in the northwest sector of the city.

The most frequent units are approximately between 90 and 100 meters wide with variable lengths. They are most commonly located in the northwest of the city, between the Tula River and Tula Chico, but there is also a broad distribution throughout the urban zone. There are other rectangular divisions that measure between 250 and 300 meters long and approximately 200 and 220 meters wide; the best defined are marked with A, B, and C in Figure 6.9.

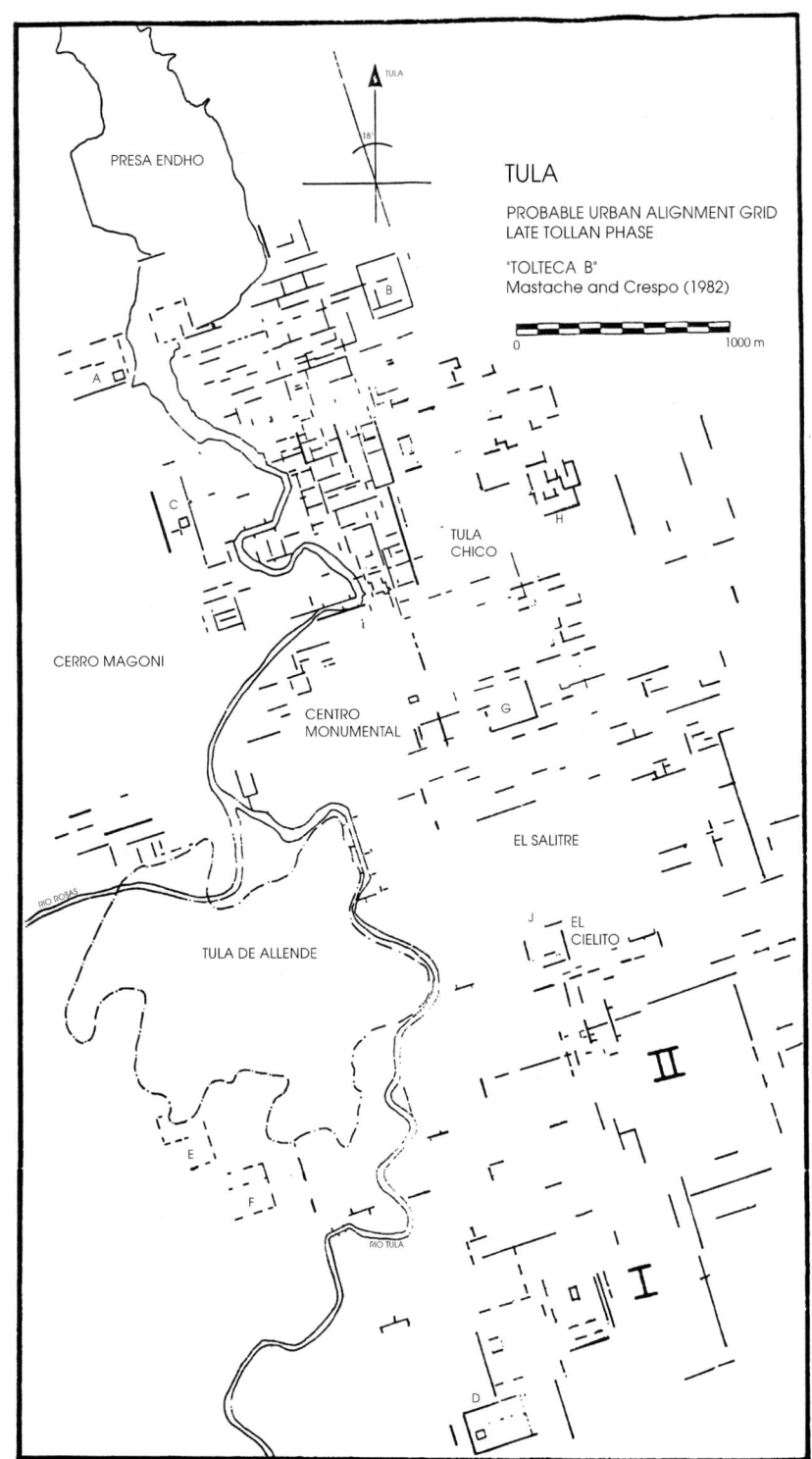

Figure 6.9. Location of probable spatial units in the Late Tollan Phase city.

Finally, in the southeast city there are signs of larger spatial units (marked with I and II) of approximately 1 kilometer long by 800 meters wide; other alignments can be seen within these units, which seem to be smaller subdivisions, but we do not know if these larger units correspond to territorial entities within the city.

In reference to the alignments between 90 and 100 meters wide mentioned in the above paragraph, it is interesting to note that the El Canal unit excavated by Healan measures approximately 90 meters long by almost 40 meters wide, the same dimensions as the habitation platforms studied by Healan in the obsidian workshop zone in the southeast of the city. In addition, the surface study of a group of habitational structures to the southeast of Tula Chico, called Urban Zone 17 (ZU17), directed by Cobean (Moncayo and López 1985) detected that the units sampled have different dimensions, albeit with similar ranges (Fig. 6.10).

We know that the habitation units were bounded by streets that permitted access to these units, which are evident in the excavations made by Healan in El Canal and in the above-mentioned study (ZU17). Frequently, there seem to be two different distances between streets, the shorter one being about 50 meters and the other between 90 and 100 meters, both of which seem to represent two minimum units for secondary roads within the city's internal urban communication network. The plan of ZU17 shows that the average width of the secondary streets or roads that interconnected various habitation complexes is between 8 and 10 meters. If this represents the average width of the streets in the city, they were certainly wide thoroughfares.

The above analysis makes it possible to propose that most of the alignments between 90 and 100 meters that appear on the plan very probably constitute the length of the habitation complexes and correspond to the streets that bounded them. The occurrence of most of these alignments in the northwest of the city, to the south of the Endó Dam, could be due to the fact that until a few years ago, this part was one of the least-damaged areas of the urban zone, and this is precisely where Healan and Stoutamire (1989) detected a high density of habitational structures (Healan, Cobean, and Diehl 1989:245, fig. 13.9).

Regarding the rectangular elements measuring approximately 300 by 200 meters that appear on the same grid plan for Toltec B, it was verified in the field that at least two of them were large platforms on which were constructed various habitation units. The platform marked with a B at the northern limit of the city (Fig. 6.9) was in a good state of conservation at the end of the 1970s, but unfortunately it was not possible to make a study of the characteristics and the internal distribution of the habitation units built on the platform. Some alignments could be seen in the interior that marked internal subdivisions of about 50 and 100 meters that seem to correspond to the above-mentioned complexes and access roads. Those marked with A and C also show smaller alignments and elements that seem to correspond to mounds or pyramid structures, which could be confirmed on the surface in the field in the case of unit A.

There are alignments in various sectors of the urban zone that suggest there probably were similar units of variable dimensions. Some examples are marked with the letters E, F, G, H, and J. In the ZU17 surface study, habitation mounds of various sizes were also found built on a large platform measuring approximately 300 by 200 meters and about 70 centimeters high.

These units probably corresponded to major territorial divisions within the city, with areas that varied between 40,000 and 60,000 square meters, which included various habitation complexes. It is very likely that these spatial units were territorial units with social and economic significance—administrative, political, religious, and constituted entities that may have been defined by kinship, economic activity, ethnic group, or other criteria—specific districts, sections, sectors, or neighborhoods, but we can only make conjectures on the matter with the scant information available.

Cowgill, Altschul, and Sload (1984:174) emphasize that units of this kind were frequently used by the state for the administration and control of the population, the organization of production, and sundry activities with religious connotations,

Figure 6.10. Habitational and ceremonial structures of ZU17 in Tula's northeast urban zone.

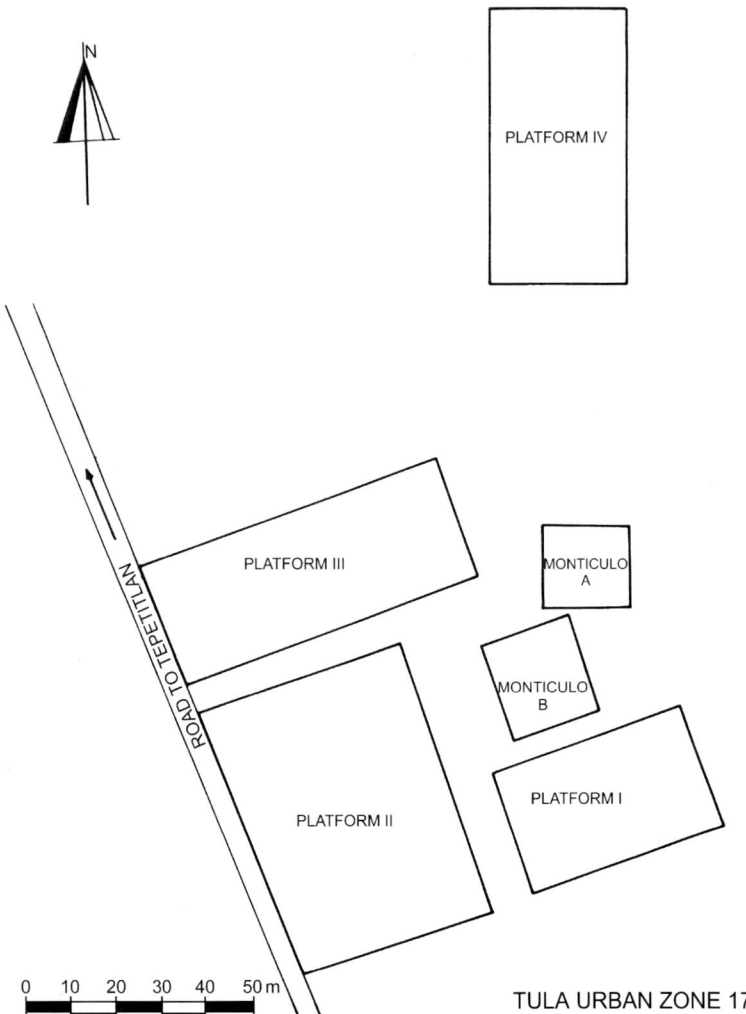

along with kinship and ethnic aspects, constituting, as Millon ([ed.] 1973:40, 41) proposes, urban entities with a corporate identity. That is, they are social groups with common interests, like being involved in the same economic activity, as we know happened in Tenochtitlan and apparently in Teotihuacan. In Tula, we only have signs of these units, but within an experimental framework it is possible to make some calculations and estimates. If it is accepted, as proposed by Healan, that the House Group was the most common residential structure in the urban zone and that the dimensions of the El Canal complex were typical of this kind of housing, and that the larger units of between 40,000 and 60,000 square meters, detected on the Toltec B map and in the field, were large platforms that house various habitation complexes, then we have the following figures:

El Canal Unit (100 x 50 m) = 5,000 m²
Larger Unit (300 x 200 m) = 60,000 m²

Assuming that the El Canal housing complex was a typical structure for the city in terms of size and characteristics, there would be twelve similar units (each one with three House Groups) in each unit of 60,000 square meters, if the size and distribution of dwellings were homogenous. On the other hand, the maximum size defined for the city is about 16 square kilometers, from which the El Salitre and the monumental zone could be subtracted to obtain a figure of approximately 13.5 square kilometers. If this area were divided uniformly into units of 60,000 square meters, there would be a total of 225 units of this size in the city and approximately 2,250 to 2,700 habitation units like El Canal.

However, it must be borne in mind that the proposal is hypothetical and is based on a homogeneity that undoubtedly did not exist. We know, on one hand, that there are small plazas in some parts of the city and ceremonial mounds near the habitation structures. Some of the mounds are 15 meters in diameter and 3 to 4 meters high, while others are much larger in size, 30 to 40 meters in diameter and higher than 4 meters (Healan 1989a:56–57, fig. 2.3; Healan, Kerley, and Bey 1983; Yadeun 1975; Moguel, Getino, and Martínez 1999), and the spaces corresponding to streets and avenues would also have to be subtracted. On the other hand, we know that both the House Groups and their individual houses were not homogenous in size and their total dimensions varied. It is evident that there were also variations in the dimensions of multiple House Group–type complexes and that there were other kinds of housing such as the Apartment Compounds, the frequency, dimensions, and internal structure of which have not been defined in detail.

Despite the above, when comparing the figures obtained through these calculations with the studies made by Millon (1981) and his collaborators at Teotihuacan (Cowgill, Altschul, and Sload 1984:174), as well as with the information available on Tenochtitlan, we find similar ranges in the number of possible residential compounds. The estimates made by García Cook and Merino (1996) concerning the number of "patios" recorded in Cantona, an urban site in eastern Puebla covering between 12 and 13 square kilometers, are also of great interest. These researchers have been able to determine that in the site's apogee (A.D. 600–800), there were about 7,500 patios, or habitational structures, many of which corresponded to single-family dwellings, although others seemed to have housed extended families. García Cook and Merino consider that their estimate is very accurate because of the state of conservation of the site and the construction techniques of the habitational structures, with the widespread use of stone, and because they made a detailed photogrametric map of the entire settlement that enabled them to accurately define the limits of the habitation structures.

It has been estimated that there were about 2,000 residential complexes in Teotihuacan and between 150 and 200 neighborhoods of very variable sizes, with a wide range of inhabitants per neighborhood (between 200 and 3,000 people). It has been proposed that this city was probably subdivided into thirty districts or larger units, each of which included various neighborhoods. It also has been stated that the inhabitants of the same complex tended to have the same economic specialization and there are examples of compounds occupied by foreigners of the same ethnic group, such as the Oaxaca Barrio and the Merchant's Barrio where there are concentrations of foreign ceramics from various parts of Mesoamerica, principally Veracruz and the Maya area (Millon [ed.] 1973:40, 41; Rattray 1993 and in press; Spence 1989).

The economic activity of the inhabitants is an important aspect in the definition of *barrios* in various preindustrial cities. This seems to have been the fundamental criteria in the structuring of the neighborhoods in Teotihuacan and Tenochtitlan, with the tendency for the occupants of a *barrio* to share the same trade, and in some cases to belong to the same ethnic group.

In Tula, there is evidence of craft production; however, in most of the cases there are only indications or indirect information. To date, probable production areas of *tecalli* bowls, shell objects, figurines, drainpipes, obsidian tools, and ceramics have been identified. There are two zones that without doubt were *barrios* inhabited by specialized craftsmen: (1) an area of obsidian workshops that is located in the extreme southeast of the city, the total area of which has not yet been exactly defined (Healan 1986; Pastrana 1990); the principal product seems to have been prismatic blades and other artifacts elaborated on the basis of blades (Healan, Kerley, and Bey 1983; Pastrana 1990); and (2) a ceramics workshop zone also located in the east of the city, which at some points overlaps with the obsidian instruments production zone (Hernández et al. 1999) (see Fig. 6.11).

Based on surface reconnaissance, Mastache and Crespo (1976, 1982) previously identified the approximate limits of what seems to have been a ceramics-production *barrio* within the pre-Hispanic city, where certain kinds of ceramics were manufactured that are diagnostic of the Tollan Phase. The surface samples detected irregular concentrations of burned and twisted sherds together with formless baked clay wasters that extended over an area of about 1.5 square kilometers, which, as mentioned before, partly overlaps the specialized obsidian instruments production area.

Recent excavations in the extreme north of this probable ceramics-production *barrio* (Hernández et al. 1999) verify the proposal made by Mastache and Crespo in that this was an area with Tollan

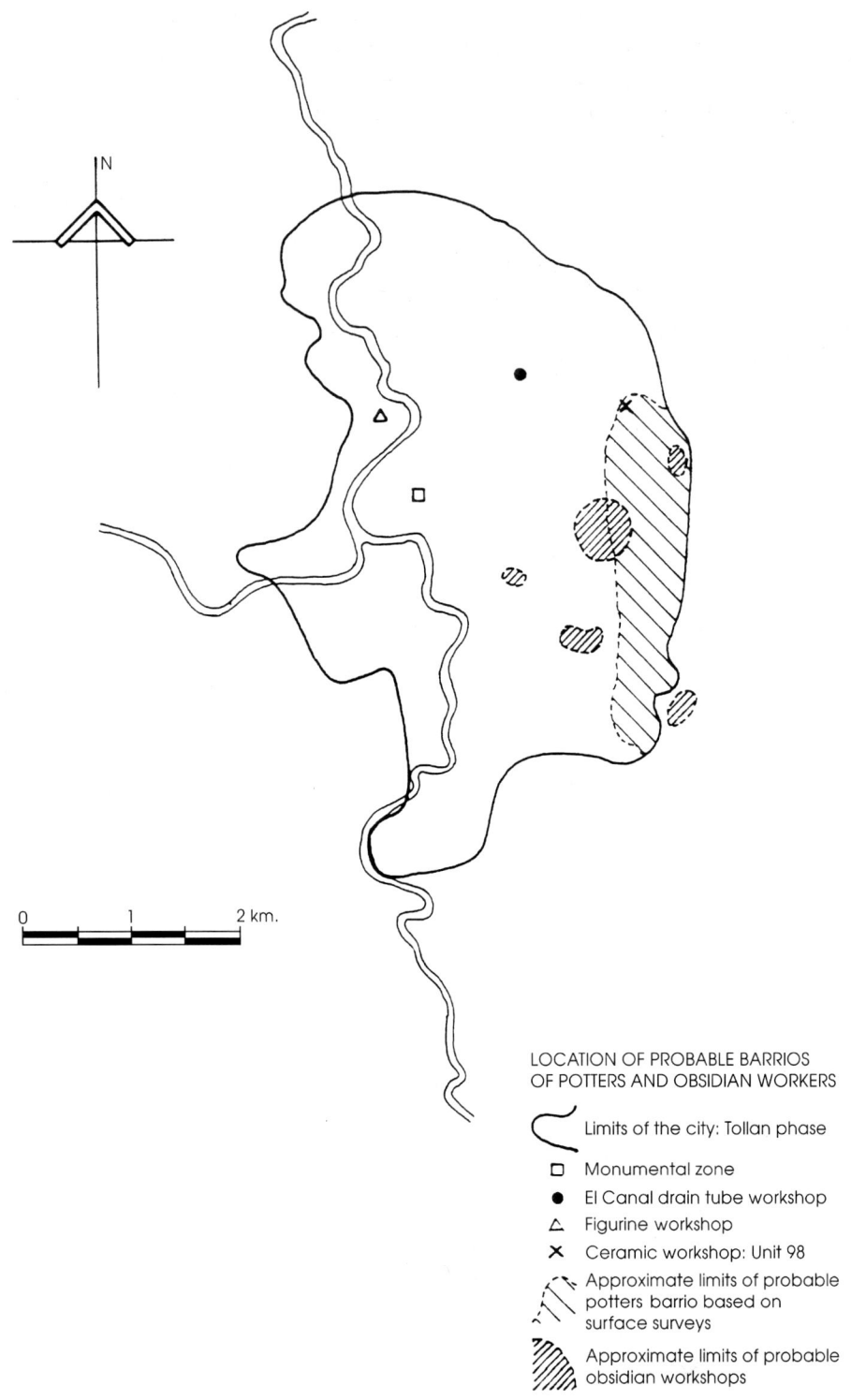

Figure 6.11. Location of probable *barrios* of potters and obsidian workers.

Phase ceramic workshops. One production unit for various kinds of ceramics associated with habitation structures of this period has been explored here. Nevertheless, more research is required to ratify whether this strip of about 150 hectares, located on the periphery of the city and defined on the basis of surface sampling, was completely occupied by potters and whether this was really a specific *barrio*. It is important to determine the occupation density and the characteristics of this zone and the relations that existed between these craftsmen and the obsidian-instrument producers. The fact that both of these groups seem to have occupied a peripheral sector of the city is probably related to the organization of production and to the status that this kind of craftsmen possessed within the class structure of Toltec society. On the other hand, considering that an important portion of the ceramic production in this neighborhood was devoted to copying types from the Gulf Coast and the Huasteca, it is probable that some of the potters belonged to ethnic groups originating from these regions, which would not be surprising because various historical sources describe Tula as a multiethnic society, and the presence of diverse ethnic groups having specialized activities was frequent in diverse cities of ancient Mexico (Jiménez Moreno 1941, 1959; Mastache and Cobean 1985).

It is important to note that just outside the western and southern limits of the city, there is evidence for basalt sculpture workshops near the Rio Tula and Rio Rosas where unfinished *atlante*-like and circular monumental columns have been found. A third zone for the production of basalt sculptures was identified to the north of the Presa Requena (Hernández 1995) (see Fig. 10.7). However, none of these sculpture workshop zones appear to be associated with residential structures.

Surely, a surface study with intensive sampling based on architectural units, as done by Millon ([ed.] 1973) in Teotihuacan, would have made it possible to detect other production zones in the city. This would have provided more elements to define the relationships that existed between the economic activity of the inhabitants and their being structured in *barrios* or other territorial, political, and administrative units. It is also important to consider that the topography might influence the definition of territorial organization within the city, because there are well-defined topographic units within the urban perimeter, such as: (1) the elevation upon which the monumental precinct rises, (2) the La Malinche and El Cielito hills, (3) the hill upon which Tula Chico rises, (4) the lower slopes of Cerro Magoni on the northwest side of the city, to the west of the Tula River, (6) the lowland zone in the south of the city, to the east of the Tula River, (7) the confluence areas of the Tula and Rosas Rivers, which include the zone of the current city of Tula, and (8) the northeast zone of the city, to the east of the Requena Canal. All of these zones could have constituted some kind of territorial and administrative entities of the pre-Hispanic city (see Fig. 1.3).

The studies conducted by Cowgill (Cowgill et al. 1984) and Altschul (1981) in some of the units previously defined by Millon ([ed.] 1973, 1976) concerning the nature and definition of *barrios* in Teotihuacan (based on the statistical analysis of architectural correlations with various kinds of ceramics and other artifacts) show very interesting results regarding the definition of specific *barrios* and the social-status differences between them. It was found that there was a mosaic of different kinds of neighborhoods spatially mixed in nonuniform distribution. Although the high-status *barrios* were principally located in the central district, close to the Street of the Dead, there were also neighborhoods of this kind on the outskirts of the city, mixed with others of a lower hierarchy, and there are also low-status *barrios* near the center of the city. On the other hand, it should be noted that Spence's research (1974), based on physical anthropology studies, indicates that the male inhabitants of the same apartment complex had genetic ties, which suggests a kind of patrilineal descent group and patrilocal residence.

In the case of Tenochtitlan, we know that the city was divided into four large territorial units: Cuepopan, Atzacualpa, Moyotlan, and Teopan, marked by the four main avenues that originated in the great ceremonial precinct, and oriented in accordance with the four cardinal directions. Based on various sources, Calnek notes that one great temple or complex of temples was located in each of these great districts, although there are no data on their size or architectural characteristics (1976: 296).

These four larger territorial units were subdivided into *barrios* of various sizes. Caso's (1956) research identifies a total of 108 barrios of different dimensions, each with its own name, in an area of approximately 13.6 square kilometers, which also includes Tlatelolco. Calnek states that these territorial units, *barrios* or *tlaxilacallis,* could correspond to a *calpulli,* a disputed concept with various meanings. Apparently, each neighborhood had its own patron god and most had their own plazas or market and a house for youths or *telpocchcalli.* According to Sahagún's illustrations of the *calpulli* temples, they do not seem to have been pyramids, but buildings similar to houses, built on a low stepped platform within a small plaza limited by a wall where there were other structures (Calnek 1976: 297). Sahagún (quoted by Calnek) states that the *barrio* temple was also the place of reunion of the elders and the focal point of important ceremonies organized by groups that carried out specialized economic activities.

Calnek's analyses conclude that Tenochtitlan, with an area excluding Tlatelolco of about 9 square kilometers (1976, n.d.), had between eighty and a hundred neighborhoods (*barrios*) of various sizes. The size of the *barrios* varied greatly, ranging from 2.5 hectares, as in the case of the Yopico *barrio,* to 19 hectares, like the Amanalco neighborhood; there was also a trend for the larger *barrios* to be located toward the outskirts of the city. Calnek notes (n.d.), in reference to the four large districts or divisions, that the Teopan district, divided into two, was the largest in area, followed by Moyotlan and then Cuepopan; the smallest was Atzacualpa, slightly larger than 100 hectares in size.

This author shows that the territorial organization of Tlatelolco was different from that of Tenochtitlan because the urban territory was not structured into four large districts divided into *barrios,* as in Tenochtitlan, but in "Large Neighborhoods" (Barrios Grandes) and "Small Neighborhoods" (Barrios Menores). Tlatelolco, which covered an area of 3 to 4 square kilometers, had between twenty-five and thirty *barrios* in the sixteenth century, including the nineteen Barrios Grandes identified in Alzate's map for Tlatelolco (Calnek n.d., 1976, and personal communication 1999). This author observes that some of the early colonial sources indicate that these Barrios Grandes were subdivided into a variable number of Barrios Menores. For example, the Xolalpan neighborhood consisted of only two or three smaller units, whereas Atezcapan and Atenantitech had between twelve and sixteen smaller *barrios.* The size of the smaller *barrios* also varied, while some only consisted of the houses of one street or even those on just one side of a street, others such as the Amaxac neighborhood, located to the extreme northeast, were much larger. This scholar also notes that most or perhaps all of the colonial churches were very probably built on pre-Hispanic temples that corresponded to the Barrios Grandes, temples that would be used by the entire population of the Barrios Menores that made up the bigger *barrios* (Calnek n.d., personal communication 1999).

In Tula there are numerous cases of association of habitational units with ceremonial mounds. In the El Canal excavation, there are two mounds of this type to the northwest and southeast of the residential complex at a distance of between 30 and 40 meters. These mounds are of different size; one is approximately 15 meters in diameter by 3 meters high, while the other one is between 30 and 40 meters in diameter by 4 meters high (Healan 1989a: fig. 7.2). Healan also mentions a ceremonial mound close to the domestic structures of the excavated obsidian workshop, approximately 20 meters to the west (1986, fig. 3). The same situation occurred in Daini, where a "temple base mound 30 meters to the southwest of the excavated structure" was found (Peña and Rodríguez 1976:86). There was a mound about 3 meters high approximately 20 meters to the south of the El Corral habitation unit in addition to the El Corral pyramid (Mandeville and Healan 1989), located 40 meters to the northwest of the excavated unit. In unit ZU17, there was also a small plaza and two ceremonial mounds near the residential platforms (Mastache and Cobean n.d.).

It is very likely that these structures were *barrio* temples similar to the *tlaxilacalli* temples in Tenochtitlan, or those mentioned by Millon in Teotihuacan:

"Many barrios have one or more temples in them, larger and distinct from those within compounds, suggesting the existence of barrio temples in at least some parts of the city. Barrio temples and a tendency to grouping by occupation or place of origin suggest that barrios, as well as apartment compounds, had some degree of corporateness" ([ed.] 1973: 40–41).

Various models may be derived from the information available on the probable structure of the city of Tula. On one hand, the fact that there are two mounds near some of the just mentioned residential compounds suggests that perhaps some *barrios* had more than one temple, as in Teotihuacan; however, since the specific relations between these buildings and the rest of the habitational units surrounding them have not been investigated, we do not know the real ratio between the habitational units and the ceremonial mounds.

Yadeun (1975) divides the mounds in the urban zone into two categories: mounds more than 2.5 meters high, that is, mounds that could be considered as pyramid structures, and mounds higher than 1 meter and less than 2.5 meters, which would mostly be habitational structures. He identifies 85 in the first group and 916 in the second, which would give a ratio of one pyramid per ten or eleven habitational mounds (Fig. 6.12). However, we know that most of the habitational mounds in Tula are between 30 and 70 centimeters high, and consequently it is obvious that many of them were not included in this researcher's map, because he only recorded those measuring more than 1 meter in height. On the other hand, we also know that the nonhabitational mounds that Yadeun classified as higher than 2.5 meters are not homogenous and can be subdivided into at least two categories: (1) mounds approximately 15 meters in diameter and 2.5 to 3 meters high, and (2) mounds between 30 and 40 meters in diameter and between 3 and 4 meters high. The latter are numerous, and it is clear from aerial photography and field studies that they are structured or placed in relation to small plazas and seem to be more frequent in the northern half of the city.

It is also necessary to consider the destruction of mounds in the urban zone before Yadeun's studies, due to the use of land for cultivation in an important sector of the pre-Hispanic city where the ceremonial mounds were a bigger obstacle to cultivation than the habitational mounds. According to information provided by local farmers, it is known that the mounds located to the east of the Requena Canal were destroyed with the construction of this large canal, which crosses part of the city.

Nevertheless, if it were considered that each *barrio* of the city had a pyramid structure, bearing in mind the number of mounds recorded by Yadeun, there would be a total of eighty-five *barrios*. If on the other hand, for the probable number of neighborhoods, the 225 units measuring 60,000 square meters proposed before is taken as a base, together with the eighty-five pyramid mounds recorded by Yadeun, then only about a third of the units would have a pyramid structure, which suggests the existence of *barrios* with different hierarchical levels. Although these figures are not exact and they only give a general idea of the ratio between habitational structures and pyramid mounds, it reasonably plausible that, as in Teotihuacan, not all the *barrios* in Tula had their own temples and some had more than one, as is suggested by the very irregular distribution of mounds on Yadeun's map (1975:45) and the data of ZU17 and the El Canal and El Corral excavations.

However, we would like to point out that the existence of two different categories of ceremonial mounds in the habitational zone of Tula—(1) mounds of 15 meters in diameter and between 2.5 and 3 meters high and (2) mounds between 30 and 40 meters in diameter and 3 to 4 meters high—suggests the possibility that each one of these categories might correspond to different classes of territorial units, with a different hierarchy within the internal structure of the city. Calnek's observation (personal communication 1999) is important, regarding the survey data analyzed here. He suggests that the internal organization of Tula might have been more like the system of Barrios Grandes and Barrios Menores of Tlatelolco, than the territorial organization of Tenochtitlan, which was divided into four large districts and subdivided into barrios. Thus, we think it plausible that Tula's larger ceremonial

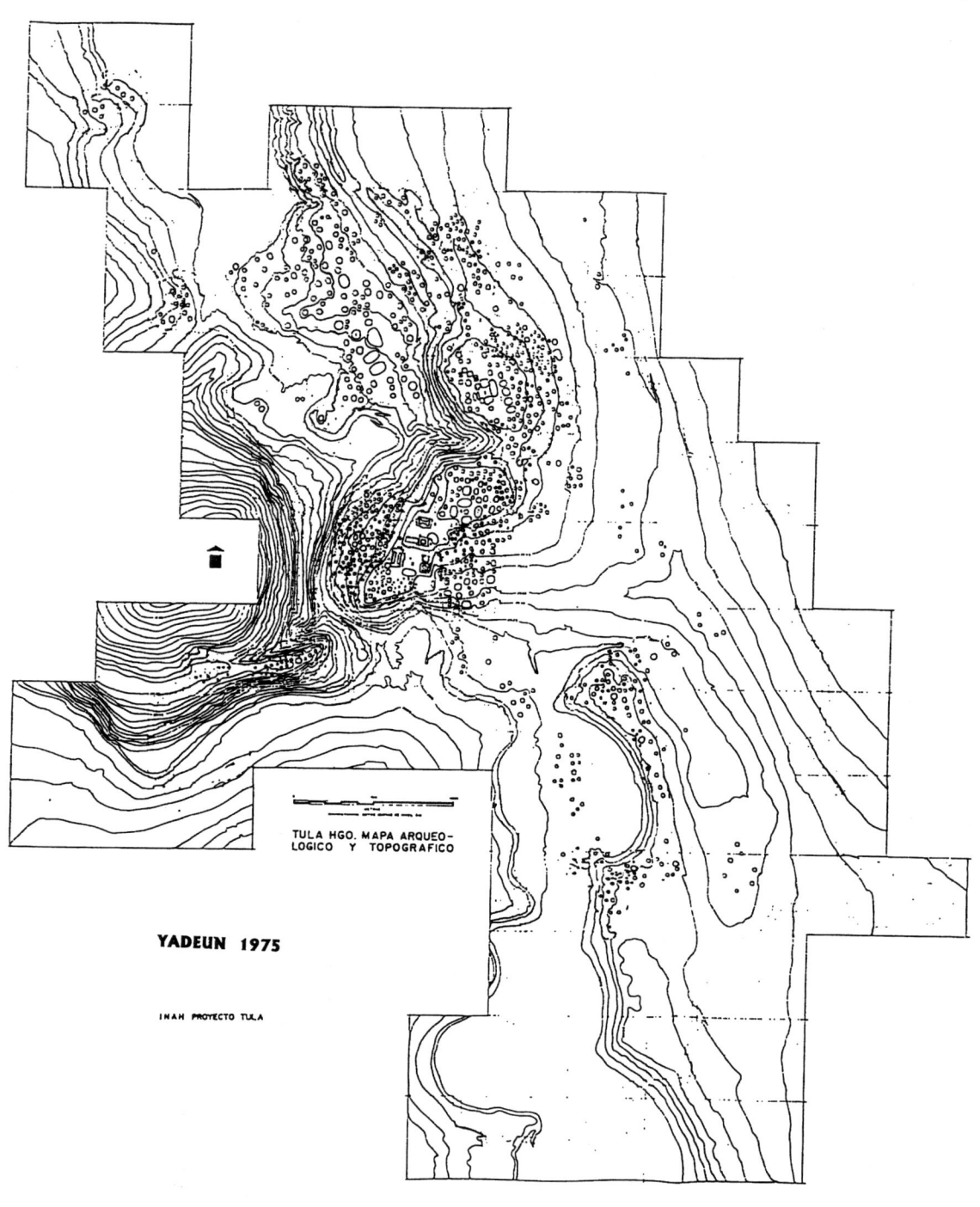

Figure 6.12. Mounds mapped in the pre-Hispanic city by Yadeun (1975).

mounds could correspond to the temples of larger territorial units of Barrios Grandes, and the smaller ones to the internal subdivisions. But since there are at least two cases (El Canal and ZU17) (Figs. 6.10 and 6.13) where the large and small mounds are close together and near habitational structures, it is also likely that in these hypothetical larger units or Barrios Grandes, there were both kinds of structures: a larger temple and another, smaller pyramid structure, perhaps dedicated to the lesser deity or the patron god of the *barrio*.

As mentioned before, several larger ceremonial mounds are situated in relation to the small plazas measuring about 50 by 50 meters. The recent excavation of two of these mounds, both in the north part of the urban zone—one in the foothills of the Magoni, to the west of the Tula River (Moguel, Getino, and Martínez 1999), and the other in the northeastern part of the ancient city excavated by Sterpone and Equihua—indicate, at least in the case of the latter, that this type of complex consists of a simple platform base with a portico at the front and a temple on the upper part. Remains of columns of various sizes were detected in both cases, and the association of the building with a plaza is clear. Thus, these are edifices that are similar to the *barrio* temples described by Sahagún (quoted in Calnek 1976), which suggests that perhaps, as occurred in Tenochtitlan, each *barrio* in Tula also had its own patron god and marketplace, as well as meeting places for several kinds of communal activities and ceremonies in which the inhabitants of the *barrio* participated, that is, urban spaces with religious, economic, and administrative functions.

The pyramid having two platforms and a composite base excavated by Ponciano Salazar and Acosta at the beginning of the 1950s, also in the northeastern part of the city known as El Corral (Acosta 1974), would be another building of this type, albeit *sui generis,* because of the mixed plan that is partly rectangular and partly circular, which gives the impression that it is a temple dedicated to the god Ehecatl (Diehl and Feldman 1974; Figueroa Silva 1994), although the associated stone panels and sculptured relieves do not seem to be related to this god (Fig. 6.14). It is interesting that the famous plumbate bowl covered with shell plaques, representing a bearded man looking through the jaws of a coyote, was found in the center of the altar located in front of this building. The El Corral pyramid, like the other large mounds mentioned, seems also to be associated with a wide open space, and various habitational structures are located nearby, although some researchers (Acosta and T. Stocker, personal communication) have considered the possibility that rather than being a *barrio* temple, the El Corral pyramid was a temple associated with a complex similar to the Mexica Tepochcalli or Calmecac.

All of the above shows that Tula possessed various classes of public and private ceremonial structures—a hierarchy of buildings topped by the sacred precinct of the city, followed by buildings of different ranks distributed throughout the urban territory and apparently linked with territorial units and socioeconomic entities of different levels and complexity. The larger mounds or architectural complexes, fundamentally consisting of a temple and a plaza, would represent a second level within this hierarchy of buildings constituting the link between the central power of the state and the urban population, an intermediate level that would correspond to the larger territorial units such as Barrios Grandes into which the city may have been divided. A third level would correspond to the pyramid structures of lesser dimensions that are more numerous than the just-mentioned complexes, many of which very probably functioned as temples associated with *barrios* of a lower hierarchy. The second and third types of temple platforms occur to the north and southeast of the El Canal habitation unit, as can be seen in Healan's (1989a: fig. 7.2) topographic map (see Fig. 6.13).

A fourth level would be represented by small pyramid structures such as the "temple" located next to the East Group of the El Canal habitational complex (Stocker 1974; Healan 1989a: fig. 7.7), with a location and characteristics suggesting that it was a place of cult activities that involved the occupants of the entire complex, that is, the extended families that occupied the three house groups (see Fig. 6.1). However, at this point, there is no certainty that there was a temple with these characteristics in all

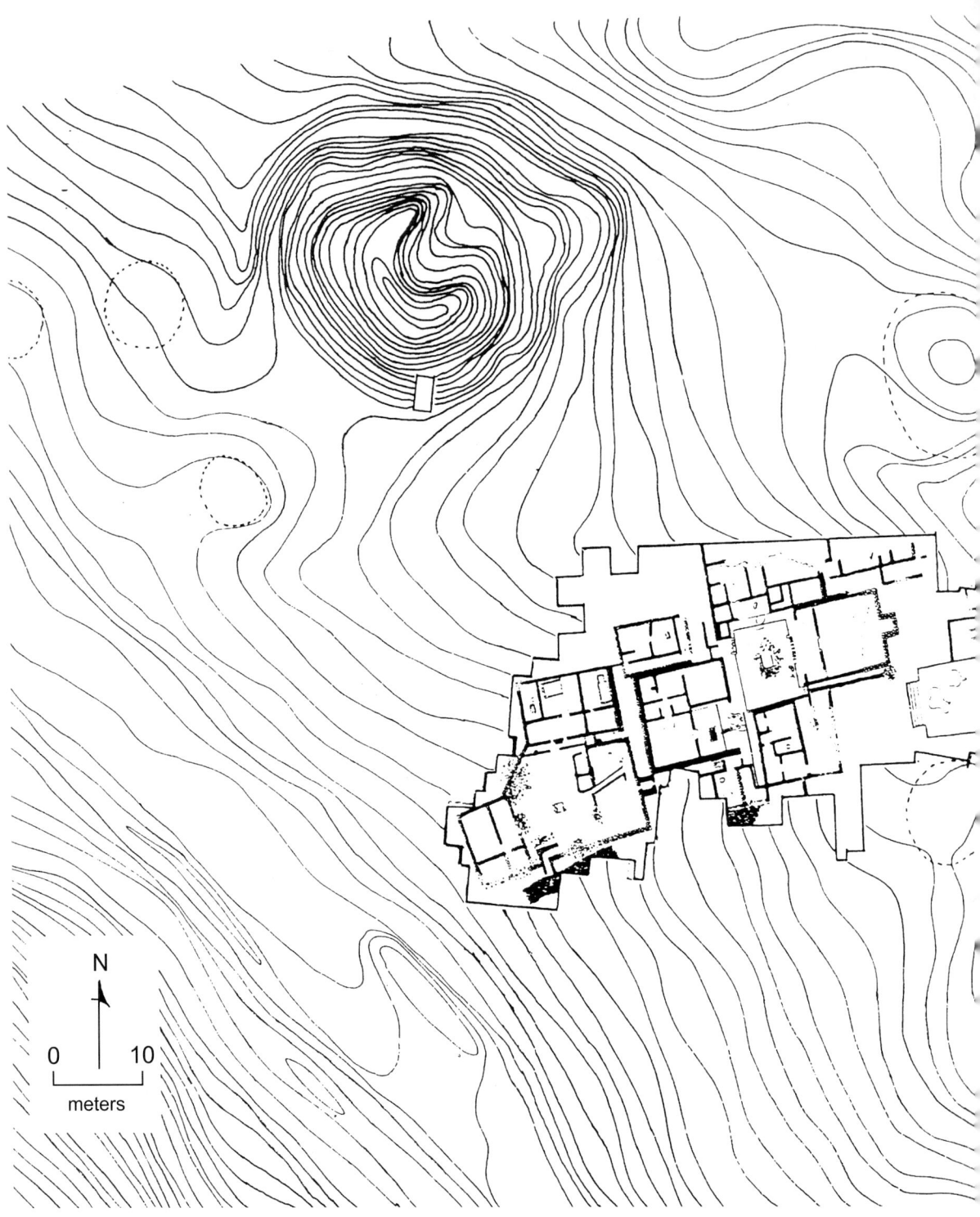

Figure 6.13. Topographic map of the El Canal locality showing two ceremonial mounds of different dimensions in its proximity (Healan 1989a: fig. 7.2).

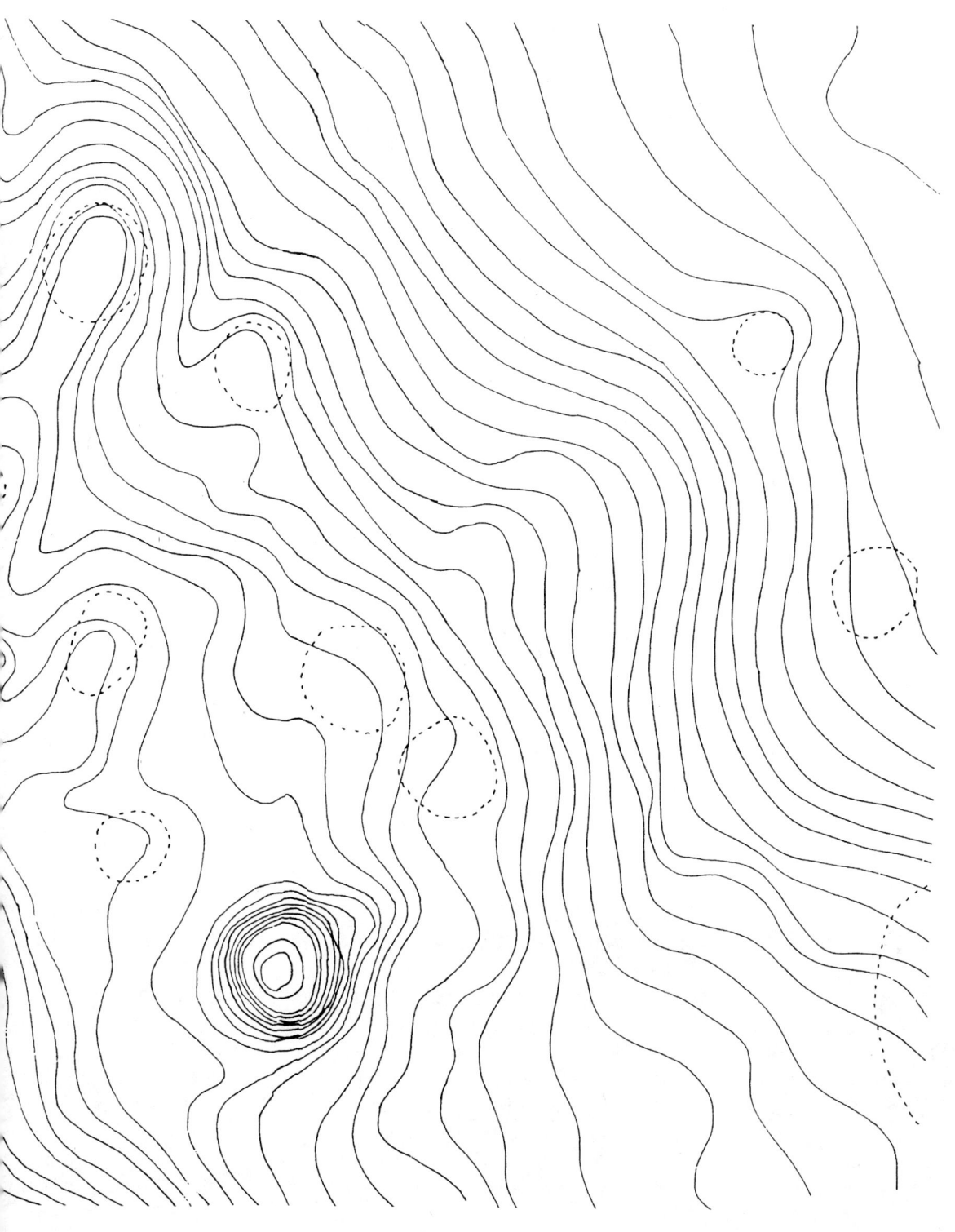

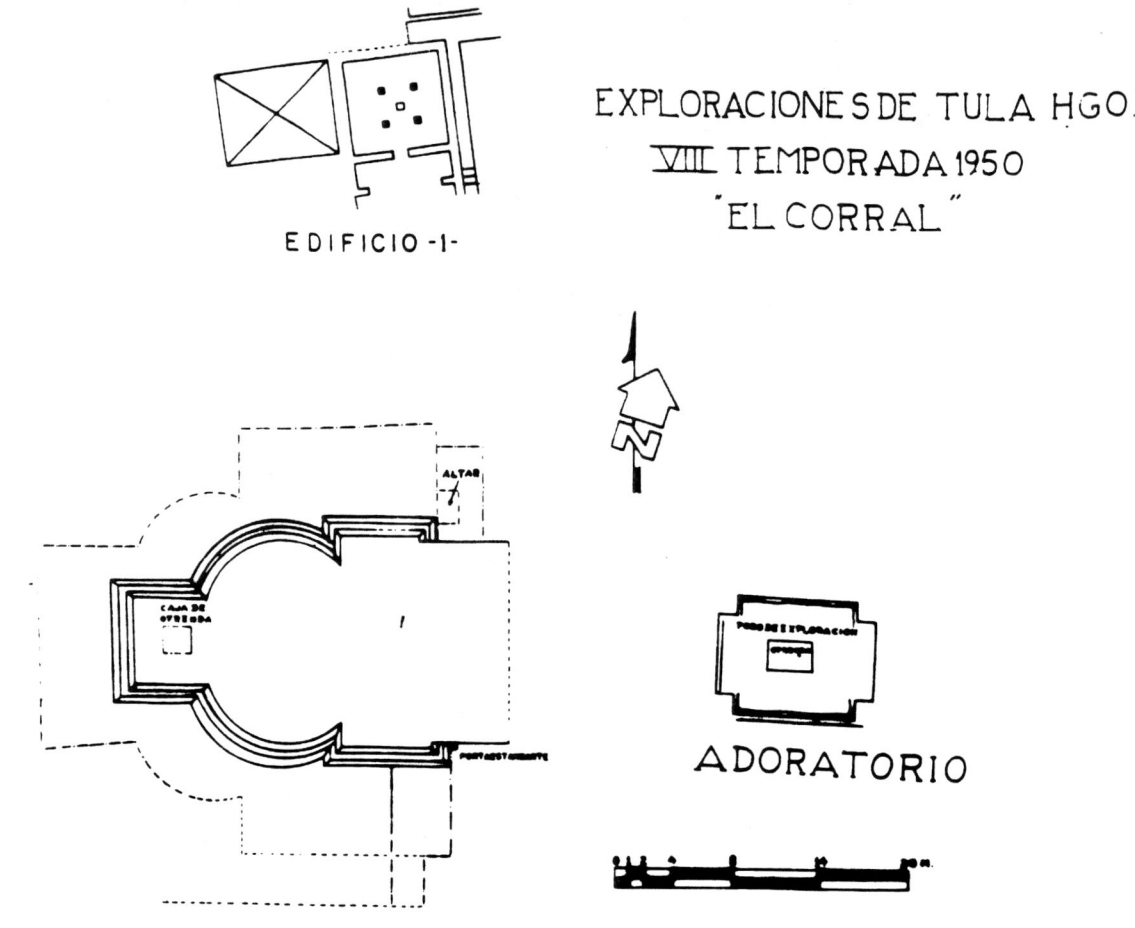

Figure 6.14. El Corral Pyramid facing a plaza (Acosta 1974: map 1).

the urban habitation complexes of the House Group type, because no other complexes of this kind have been fully excavated to date, other than El Canal.

The last level within this chain of ceremonial buildings related to the structure of the city and the ritual and religious life of its inhabitants is represented by the altars in the center of the courtyards inside the residential compounds. These altars are the physical and symbolic centers of the groups of houses that make up the residential complexes and were, undoubtedly, the focal point of daily religious rituals and domestic ceremonies that took place in the inner courtyard of each unit, and which involved only the members of the extended family who lived in the dwellings surrounding each patio.

It is evident that in order to answer the questions about the internal structuring and territorial organization of Tula as they concern the religious, economic, social, and political significance of the distinct levels of spatial units into which the urban territory was organized, further studies are required, centered on the analysis of the specific forms of the organization of this territory and the social relationships and processes that justify and give meaning to these spatial units.

In order to complete this section, we would like to mention that the studies by Luis Reyes on the *Historia tolteca-chichimeca*—a source written in the mid-sixteenth century in Cuauhtinchan, Puebla, that furnishes information of great topical interest—may be used, as this author indicates, to reconstruct some of the elements of the social and political organization of the Toltecs of Tula Xicocotitlan, because it presents the situation of Toltec migrants on their arrival at Cholula (Reyes n.d.:3). If indeed, as indicated in the Tolteca-Chichimeca history, these groups were a part of the population of the city of Tula that emigrated soon after the collapse of that center, the data on their political and social organization contained in this document, and analyzed by Reyes, constitutes a unique opportunity to approach some aspects of the structuring and nature of the ancient city that would be difficult using just archaeological data.

Reyes observes (pp. 4–7) that the migrant Toltec population was organized in two levels: *calmecac tlaca* (people of the *calmecac*) and *calpolleque* (people of the *calpulli*). He adds that the *calmecac tlaca* are *tepeuani* (conquerors or warriors), and that from their pictographic representation it can be seen that they are also priests because they have long hair tied with a strip of red leather. These conquerors are presented in a list of twenty-five persons grouped in five units. The five personages of the first group whose names are recorded, and which includes the two principal priests of the Toltec (Quetzalteueyac and Icxicouatl), were each represented in a rectangle. Only one person of each group appears in a rectangle of the second, third, and fourth groups, while there is no pictographic representation of the fifth group, which may indicate its secondary position. There is a wavy line inside the rectangles that probably refers to the uterus, indicating the "primordial fathers and mothers," founders of the lordly households (pp. 4–7). Reyes concludes that the conquerors were organized in seven military units, one priestly unit, and a ninth on which there is no information, and it could be said that there was a ruling priestly and military-type class in Tula.

This author notes that the *Historia tolteca-chichimeca* indicates that people of the *calpulli* moved more slowly, because the *calmecatlaca* first reached Cholula, followed by the *calpolleque,* who were said to constitute the "hands and feet" of the *altepetl* or ethnic *señorio*. The *Historia tolteca-chichimeca* also records a list of the *calpolleque* and their corresponding pictorial record. The list enumerates fifty-two persons grouped into eight units. Each unit with its respective name—the *quetzaluaque* (the owners of quetzal feathers), the *xiuhcalca* (those of the turquoise house), the *tecameca,* the *mizquiteca* (people of the mesquite), the *texploca,* the *quanhteca* (people of the eagle), the *xalteca* (people of the sand place), and the *calmecauaque* (people of the *calmeca*)—had a variable number of between three and twenty people. Only sixteen people are recorded in the pictograph, one on each side of the eight buildings. That is, each *calpulli* is represented in a rectangle within which there are two people with long hair, which indicates their priestly activity. Each one of the *calpolleque* represented has hair tied with a strip of leather that denotes his ties with religious activities.

Reyes observes that the given or generic names of the first, the *quetzaluaque* and the *xiuhcalca,* could be feather and stone artisans, and that a pictographic representation of the *calpolleque* indicates that they were devoted to irrigation cultivation and commerce. Based on these data and his analysis of some of the symbols of pictographic representation of their buildings, this author concludes that the *calpolleque,* originating from Tula Xicocotitlán, were specialists in irrigation cultivation, craftsmen, and merchants who were associated with particular temples and gods, and who also had a dual government.

7

The Hinterland

The specific forms of rural settlement and population distribution during the Tollan Phase, when the area was the heartland of a large state, will be analyzed in this chapter. This special status constitutes a fundamental difference compared to the other periods of occupation of this area, and determines the specific settlement pattern and a different exploitation system of resources. During the Early Postclassic, Tula and the sites of its hinterland made up a territorial, political, and economic unit; the urban and rural populations were parts of a whole, constituting an organic entity in which one cannot be explained without the other.

When the map of the occupation for this period is examined, it is interesting to note the higher density of the settlement in comparison with other periods, and the fact that there is an unoccupied strip around the ancient city of between 1 and 3 kilometers wide that clearly marks its limits and forms a kind of well-defined border between the city and its rural environs (Fig. 7.1). It is evident that there is now a larger population in the area, not only because of the presence of a great urban center but also because the rural population has spread to zones that had only been partially occupied previously, and to areas and ecological niches that were occupied for the first time. It is important to emphasize that slightly more than half of the collection units corresponding to this period do not have materials that indicate previous occupation, and they represent what could be called the Toltec colonization of the area.

These processes of occupying and populating the area are obviously related to the development and expansion of the city, which we know underwent at least two fundamental changes during the Tollan Phase. Thus it is very likely that the occupation and colonization of the city's direct interaction area corresponds to these two general stages of the city's growth—one that began about A.D. 900, and the other, which could correspond to the city's maximum

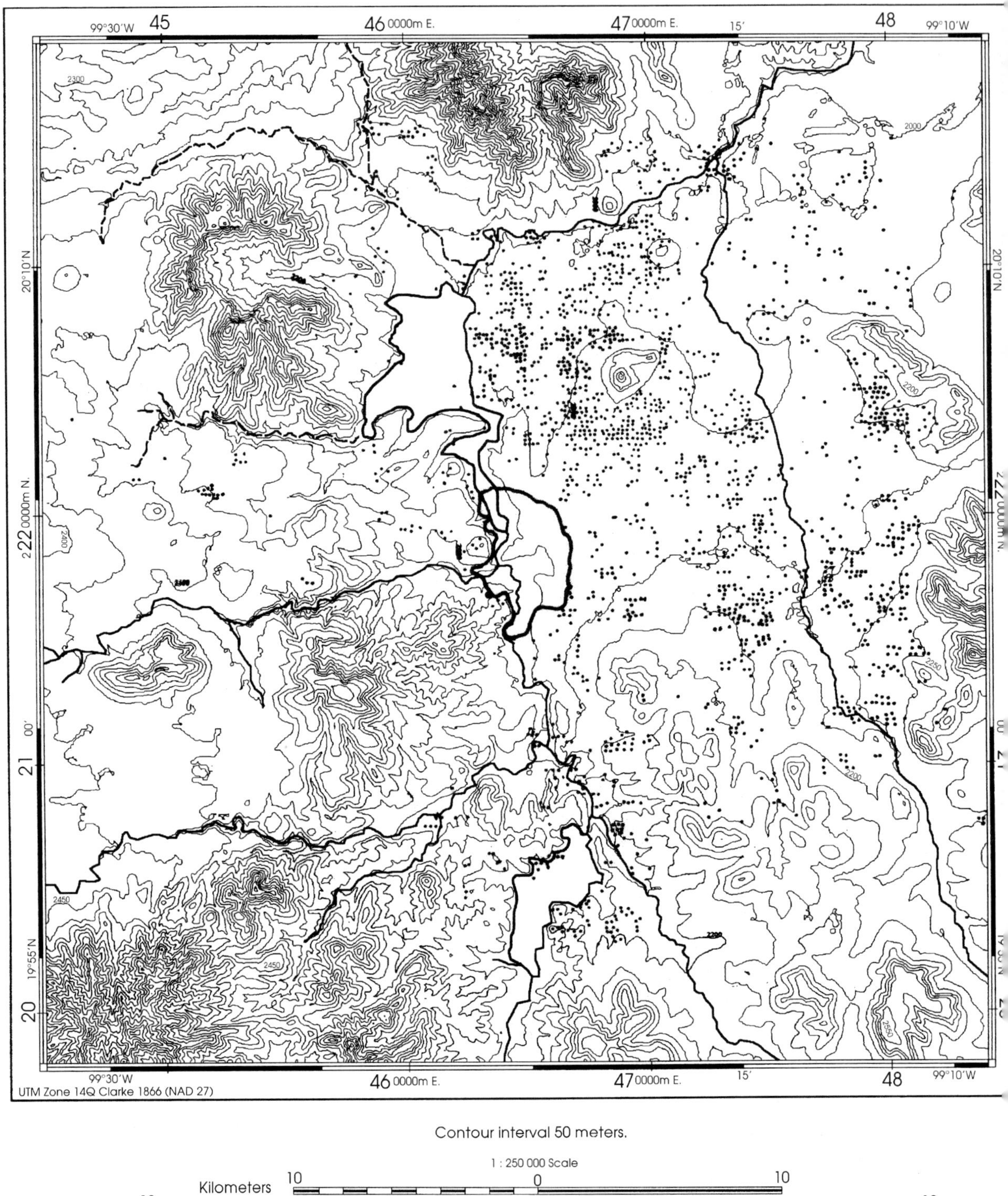

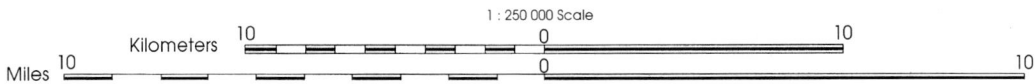

Figure 7.1. Early Postclassic: Collection Units in the Tula area.

THE HINTERLAND

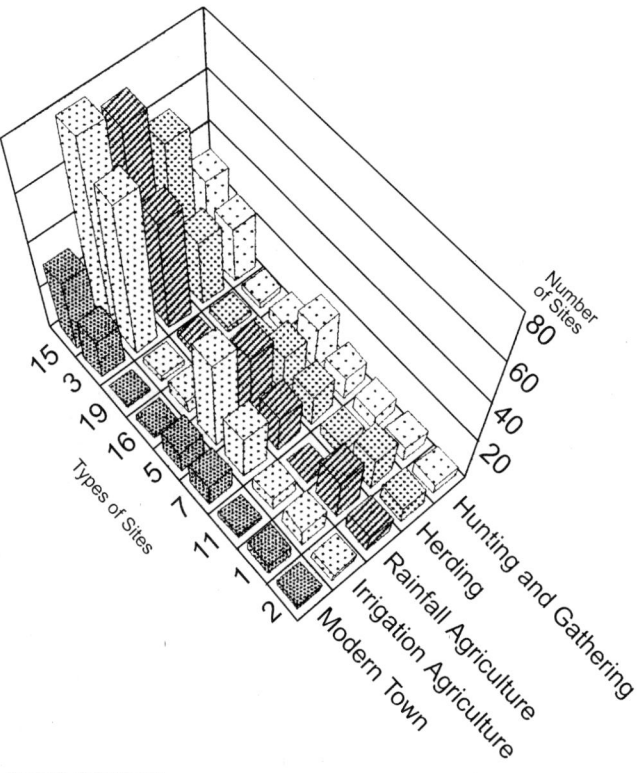

Figure 7.2. Types of sites and present-day land use.

TYPES OF SITES:

1 Sites with an indeterminate number of structures
2 Sites with an indeterminate number of structures and ceremonial architecture
11 Complex of 6–7 structures
7 Complex of 3–5 structures
5 Complex of two habitational structures
16 Complex of two structures: isolated habitational structures
19 Complex of two structures: one habitational, one ceremonial
3 Isolated habitational structure
15 Zones of dispersed occupation

expansion and apogee, between A.D. 1000 and 1050, as is analyzed in detail in Chapter 3.

The fact that most of the settlement is located principally in the eastern part of the region is noteworthy, because the western part, with very uneven topography, was almost uninhabited during the Tollan Phase, with the exception of some occupation points in small intermountain valleys. Thus, the pre-Hispanic city was located in the western part of the sustaining area, in a very strategic position in terms of topography and water sources, at the confluence of the Tula and Rosas Rivers, both of which are permanent hydraulic sources with a high volume of water, and facing the alluvial valley that extends to the east.

The present-day land use in the zones of the area that were occupied during this period is highly varied, including zones of irrigation and rainfall cultivation, wild plant and gathering lands, etc. Some figures of this chapter and the data in the Appendix treat aspects of the specific distribution of the settlements in relation to the topography, current land use, and relationship with water resources. Most of the occupation of the Tollan Phase is on land that is now used for irrigated and rainfall farming, while the zones that are currently used for herding, gathering, hunting, and forestry only occupy 25 percent of the total collection units corresponding to this phase. The current settlements in the area, especially the most important highly populated towns, undoubtedly cover part of the pre-Hispanic occupation, and only a low percentage (11.81) of the collection units of this period are located in currently populated areas, which is perhaps because the sampling opportunities are more limited here than in other contexts (Fig. 7.2).

The majority of the settlements of this period are located on the lower slopes of small hills and lowlands, principally between altitudes of 2,000 and 2,100 meters, and hillside and lowland occupation predominates, especially in the alluvial valley and other zones of the area, while settlements on high hill summits or high slopes are very scarce (Fig. 7.3). It is interesting to note that most of the occupation is not directly limited to the vicinity of the area's permanently flowing rivers, or close to intermittent water sources such as arroyos and *barrancas*. The fact that most of the occupation of the alluvial valley, especially around the Xicuco hill, is distant from water sources (permanent or

THE HINTERLAND

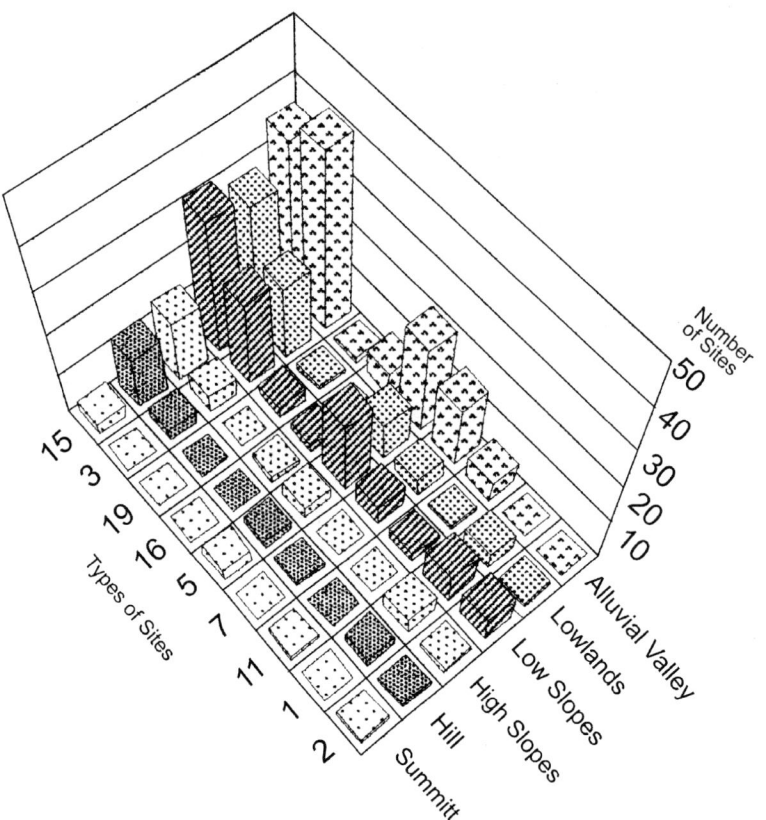

Figure 7.3. Types of sites and topography.

intermittent) stands out. This leads to the supposition that perhaps during the Tollan Phase there were springs and intermittent currents in the Xicuco zone that have since disappeared.

SITES

The definition of sites is one of the basic objectives and problems in settlement-pattern studies, since the identification and analysis of these entities and the determination of their characteristics make it possible to understand the nature of the settlement of a given area during a particular period, especially the structure, functioning, and complexity of the settlement system. As in other regional studies, here we confront the problem regarding the definition of sites, which is difficult not only because of the arbitrary and ambiguous nature of the concept, but also because of specific aspects of settlement for this period in the study area, as can be seen in Fig. 7.1. In some zones there is almost uninterrupted occupation, without clear limits between one site and another.

We agree with Adams (1981) when he observes that sites are not always a coherent and obvious category, and that the process of demarcating and identifying specific concentrations of archaeological remains implies the interaction of many variables, in which subjectivity intervenes. The density of materials is an important indicator, but in any region with a long history of human occupation, there are variable amounts of sherds and other materials in almost any place; the problem is to establish where the density of materials is sufficient to define a settlement.

Determining the limits and dimensions of a site also implies facing other problems regarding the uniformity of the data and the definition of the site itself. At one extreme there could be the remains of what corresponds to only one event, such as the breakage of a vessel or the accumulated refuse left by the transitory occupation of a family of cultivators; at the other, there would be the complex contexts of cities inhabited for long periods of time (Adams 1981). Obviously there is a wide range of occupations between these two examples, with limits and characteristics that are difficult to establish, which means that the criteria for defining a site are variable and they depend on the objectives of each investigation, as well as the specific attributes of the occupations of an area or of a given period.

The study by Kolb and Snead (1997:609–625) is very interesting because they discuss the correlations of the concepts of site and community, and they analyze the problem of the definition of the community based on archaeological data in detail. Their criticism of regional studies in archaeology is important because they stress that most studies of this type do not analyze the levels corresponding to communities in detail, nor do they make comparative and historical studies of such communities. These scholars suggest that there are three fundamental factors that must be considered in the concept of community: social reproduction, agricultural production, and the community members' sense of identity and belonging. They propose that the community is a minimum territory that includes individuals of both sexes who can reproduce and maintain themselves economically from one generation to another, and have ties with or form part of a larger society beyond the local community. They also point out that the community generally includes individuals of at least three generations.

Undoubtedly, the concept of community is an underlying factor in regional studies of settlement patterns and in the problem of the definition of sites as identifiable entities with archaeological indicators, and it is true that in many cases the community could be a category that is equivalent to the concept of the site. However, as mentioned by various authors and widely discussed by Willey and Sabloff (1993), a "site" in archaeological terms does not necessarily have to be a habitational settlement, but any *locus* altered by human activity.

Indeed, as indicated by Parsons, the concept of site is used implicitly in many of the settlement-pattern studies. Studies by Sanders and Parsons in the Basin of Mexico use Sanders's definition of "site," which states:

> An archeological site is . . . any localized area that shows signs of alteration by man as observable by archaeological method. This would include anything from an isolated home . . . or ceremonial structure, dams, canals, terrace systems, to a city of 100,000 inhabitants. The important point is that a site is "a spatially isolated unit" . . . [with] some cultural significance to the prehistoric population and not . . . simply an archaeological abstraction if such units are to be used conveniently in settlement pattern analysis. (1965:12–13; quoted in Parsons 1971:21)

Parsons stresses that in general there was no difficulty in distinguishing these "spatially isolated units," which can be interpreted as various kinds of residential settlements, temporary campsites, isolated ceremonial structures, and ceremonial precincts.

In the case of Tula, adopting two extreme positions, the city and the entire rural settlement of the area could, on the one hand, be considered as a single entity or site, because all constituted an economic, political, and social unit, and the city cannot be understood without its rural environs. On the other hand, each habitation structure could be considered as a site, because it is the minimum basic settlement unit.

Although both these positions are feasible, and the latter very useful as an initial means of analysis, we know that in terms of the social structure and economic and political life, in addition to considering the state as a general entity that encompassed the city and its hinterland, and the nuclear and extended families that made up the basic socioeconomic units, there were other intermediate levels of integration and basic territorial units within the general structure and the functioning of society: towns or villages, administrative centers (*cabeceras*), *barrios,* or *calpullis,* just to mention some of the possible entities that, in some manner, would be similar to the concept of a site in the way in which this concept is most frequently used in archaeology.

SETTLEMENT ANALYSIS

As mentioned in Chapter 1, two different levels of analysis were carried out in order to make a detailed study of the settlement system and its components: (1) an investigation prior to the definition of the sites based on different *Collection Units* that permitted a more detailed analysis of the settlement and its components, which would not have been possible if these units had been grouped a priori into sites from the beginning; and (2) a later analysis based on *sites* (different categories of discrete units that were originally or later grouped as sites), which were defined by considering different criteria such as the distance between structures and the density and distribution of surface materials, as explained below.

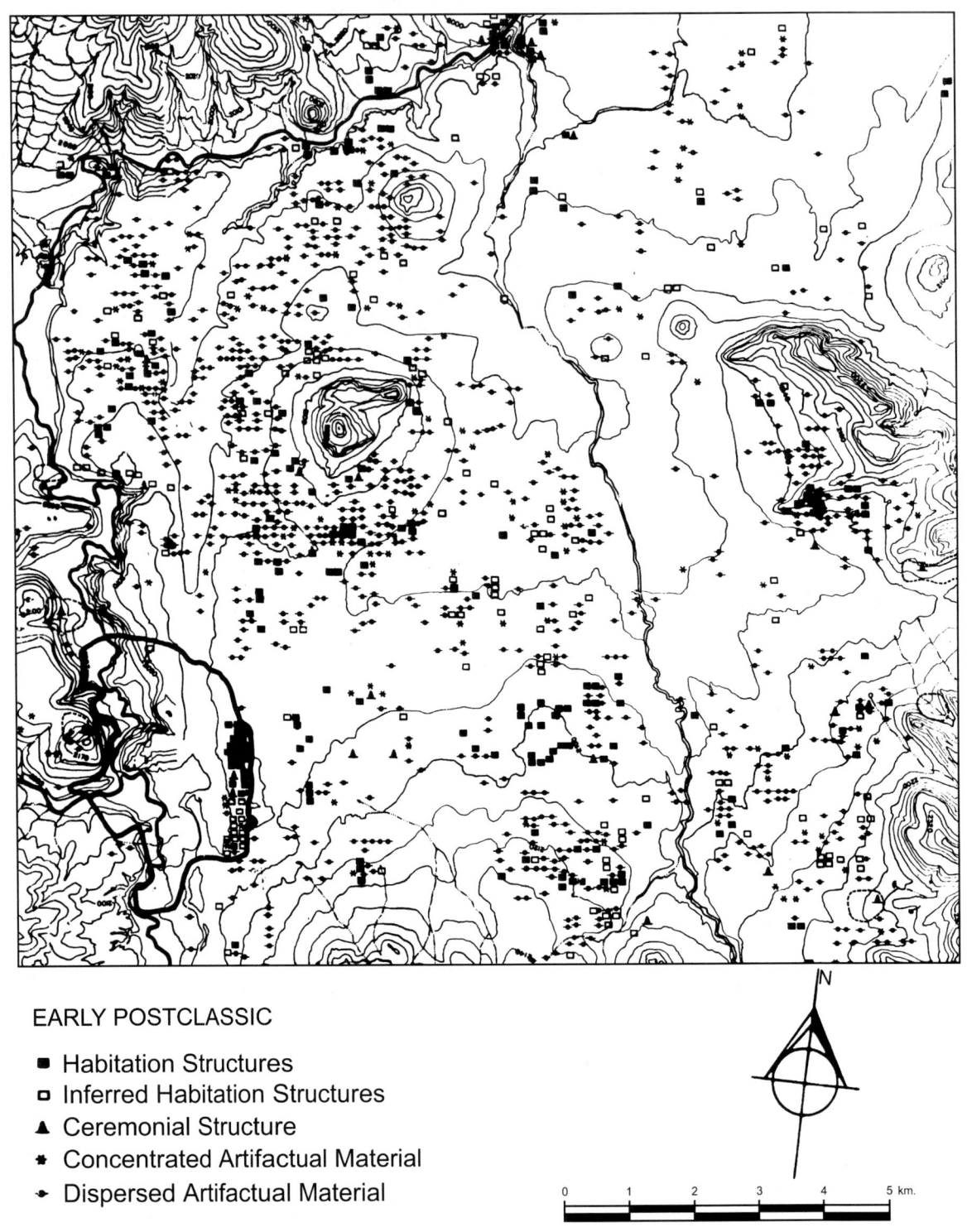

Figure 7.4. The map shows the different categories of Collection Units in the northeast quadrant of the Tula area (Tollan Phase), which is the sector with the densest occupation at this time.

Collection Units (URs)

Different categories (Fig. 7.4) were defined on the basis of the density of surface materials and the occupation characteristics, which were considered as units per se in order to analyze them independently with a similar level of detail, with the same information referring to each of them. These categories—Habitation Structures (Real and Inferred), Ceremonial Structures, Concentrated Artifactual Material, Dispersed Artifactual Material—were defined by considering the density of the materials on the surface and specific settlement characteristics.

Real Habitation Structures. In the URs assigned to this category, field studies showed clear-cut remains of habitation structures, and in some cases it was even possible to define their approximate dimensions. There is abundant ceramic material, polished stone, chipped stone, and the remains of construction material on the surface. Worked stone is common in the case of structures of this period, especially small, slablike, irregular-shaped limestone pieces that formed part of the structures and the walls, which were build with a technique that is very characteristic of this period, known as "Toltec small stone" (Healan 1989a). Thus, the habitation structures of the Early Postclassic frequently appear as white limestone-colored surface stains in the fields.

Inferred Habitation Structures. These are units in which there is no direct evidence of structures, but there are elements that make it possible to infer such: a significant concentration of ceramic material, dispersed construction material, and in some cases data from local informants about the existence of recently destroyed structures at these points. However, the principal criterion for defining these structures was the amount and concentration of sherds of this period at given locations, which include the presence of six to eight different diagnostic types for the Tollan Complex.

Ceremonial Structures. These basically consist of two types:

1. Mounds between 3 and 5 meters high, almost always with scant surface material; consequently, in some cases without excavation it is difficult to assign them to a specific chronological period. This is especially so in the case of isolated structures, or when the adjacent habitational structures have materials from various periods. The mounds that appear on the maps can be fairly accurately tied to this period due to their proximity to habitation structures or their association with diagnostic Tollan Phase material.

    Another problem regarding the identification of these mounds is the fact that they are a serious obstacle to cultivation because of their characteristics (height and the amount of stone forming their core), and consequently they are frequently razed and the stones are generally used in the walls separating fields. On numerous occasions, local informants assured us that there was a high and large mound or *mogote* in a certain field that had been razed, of which there were no remains at the time of our reconnaissance.

2. Plazas or platforms with a central altar, in some cases surrounded by habitations and/or ceremonial type structures. This type of complex almost always forms part of concentrated settlements.

Concentrated Artifactual Material. These are units with more abundant and concentrated (dense) material than those classified in the category of dispersed material. The surface material is generally concentrated in specific points. These may correspond to zones of temporary occupation or, in some cases, may be indicative of severely destroyed habitation structures in zones that have been altered by current land use. Some of these points were very difficult to classify, because based on the density of materials and the variety of ceramics present, the locations fell between the limits of this category and that of the inferred habitational structures.

Dispersed Artifactual Material. These are zones with very little material that is dispersed over the survey unit. They probably represent the environs or periphery of a site or a habitation structure or zones of temporary occupation associated with cultivation or other activities.

Zones with an Undetermined Number of Structures. This additional category contains zones that are concentrated settlement areas that require detailed surface studies because of their characteristics, and for which in a general survey it was difficult to determine accurately their size and limits, along with the internal structuring and number of constituent structures.

As indicated in Chapter 1, the information about each survey Collection Unit included its coordinates, topographic location, distance from water resources, current land use, potential land use, degree of erosion, association with other periods, and the analysis results of the ceramic and lithic materials samples from each unit. In the case of habitational and ceremonial mounds, records were also taken of the distance to the nearest structure, defined on the basis of aerial photographs. The coding and organization of the data bank with these variables permitted the analysis and correlation of different diagnostic elements and information concerning the settlements of the Tollan Phase. Some results of this analysis, prior to the definition of the sites, are included in this chapter and the Appendix.

Sites

On a second level of analysis, larger, different entities that we call "sites" were defined, which consist of a variable number of Collection Units (URs). The principal criterion followed in the definition of sites was the distance between architectural structures and the dispersed and concentrated materials zones surrounding them. The entities thus defined have different hierarchies and characteristics; some are undoubtedly permanent habitation settlements of varied size and complexity that correspond to the concept of community proposed by Kolb and Snead (1997), but some are probably just components of larger units, and others correspond to areas of specific activities.

Figure 7.5 shows the distribution of habitational and ceremonial structures in the area classified on the basis of the distance to the nearest structure. Both real and inferred habitation were taken into account by using the distance between them as the principal criterion. They were classified into four categories on the basis of the distance to the nearest structure:

A = Structures 0–50 meters to the nearest structure

B = Structures 60–250 meters to the nearest structure

C = Structures 260–490 meters to the nearest structure

D = Structures with a distance to the nearest structure of more than 500 meters. These are considered as isolated structures. This category was later subdivided into two variants: structures at a distance of 500 to 600 meters, marked with a <u>D</u> (underlined), and those at a distance of more than 600 meters, marked with a plain D.

Fig.7.5 shows these structures grouped under proposed "sites" that were defined on the basis of distance between structures. Those more than 500 meters apart were not included in the same "site" or complex, except in five cases in which various D or isolated structures were experimentally grouped together because they were about equidistant, and even though they were far apart, they seemed to form the same entity, which is clearer if the Dispersed Artifactual Materials zones surrounding them are taken into account.

The Concentrated and Dispersed Artifactual Material zones surrounding the structures were used as a complementary criterion for the definition of sites, in addition to the distance between them, because apparently in many cases, the Dispersed Artifactual Material zones represent the immediate environs of a site, the satellite area around it, and the space or social distance between one site and another, which together form the direct environs or sphere of influence of a site's inhabitants—its complementary space, areas of cultivation, waste disposal zones, etc. The attribution of Dispersed Artifactual Material zones to one site or another was arbitrary in many cases, and generally defined in terms of the distance from habitational structures.

In addition, the Dispersed Artifactual Material zones that are not associated with mounds were identified and given a site number because in some cases they constitute discrete complexes, even though apparently they often are just temporary occupation zones associated with cultivation or other activities, site satellite areas, and not settlements in themselves, or at least not permanent settlements. The localities classified under the category of Concentrated Arti-

THE HINTERLAND

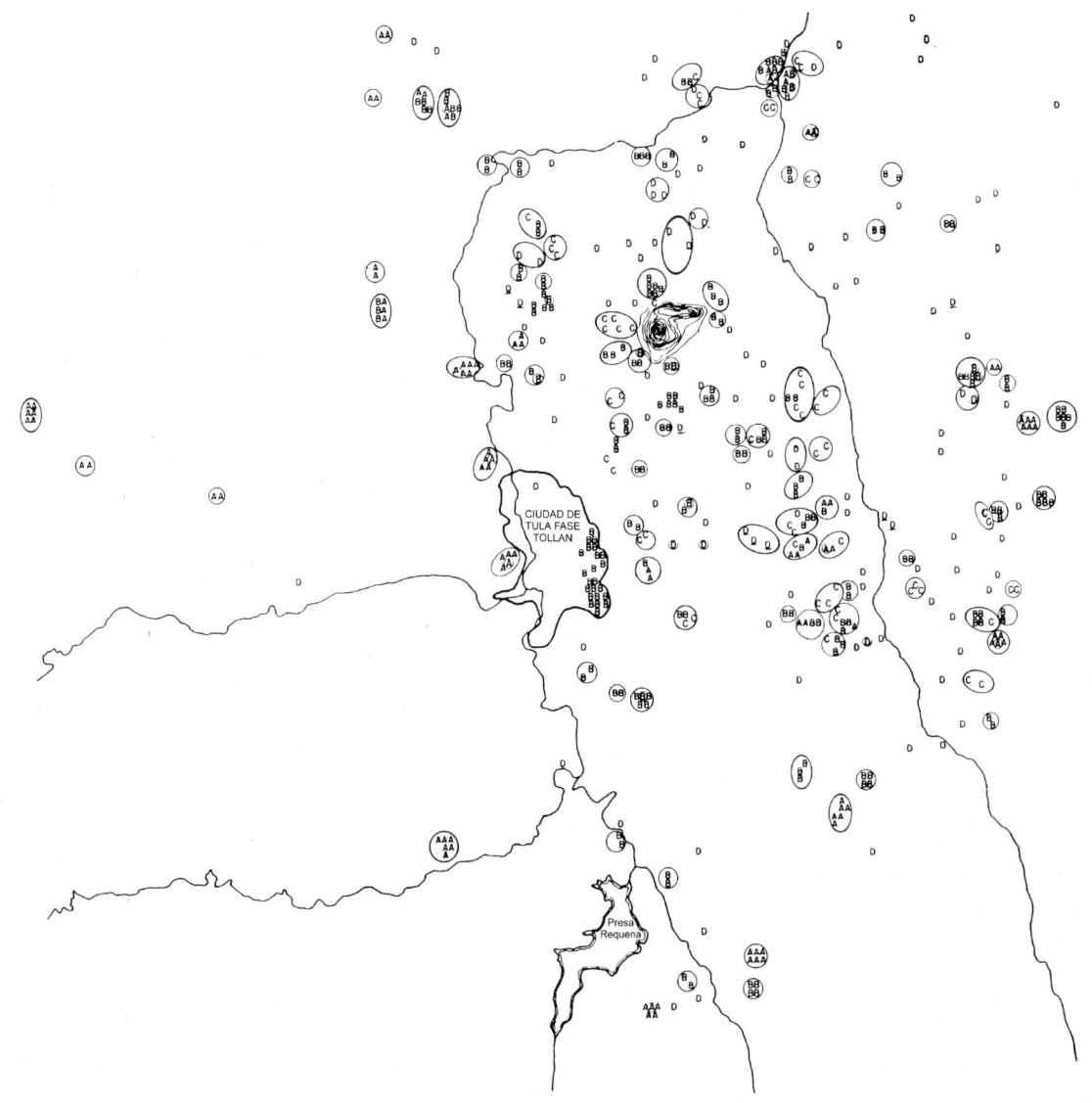

Figure 7.5. Groups of habitational and ceremonial structures.

factual Material could also correspond to areas of temporary occupation, although in some cases these were difficult to classify because they were on the borderline between this category and the Inferred Habitation Structures, based on the density of material and the variety of ceramic types present.

The settlements classified as Zones with an Undetermined Number of Structures require, as mentioned before, intensive special reconnaissance that was not done. Our general survey could not in all cases establish the exact limits or the exact number of habitation structures that make up a site. Thus, four or six structures were marked as conventions on Fig. 7.5, depending on the size of the site.

The maps (Figs. 7.5 and 7.6) show some trends and patterns in the kind of grouping for habitation structures. There is a noticeably high frequency of the following:

187

THE HINTERLAND

- Isolated structures that sometimes seem to form part of larger complexes
- Complexes formed by two nearby structures
- Complexes formed by two nearby structures and a third, more distant one
- Complexes of six or seven structures
- Sites with an indeterminate number of structures
- Dispersed artifactual material zones (or zones of disperse occupation)

The types of sites listed below, which appear in Figures 7.6 and 7.7A and B, were defined based on these patterns. It must be clarified that unlike the sites defined by Parsons (1971) and Sanders, Parsons, and Santley (1979:38–39) in their survey of the Basin of Mexico, the categories in the present case are more descriptive than interpretative. Consequently, there are not always clear equivalences between the Tula-region site types and categories that these authors define for the Basin. This is perhaps not so much due to the fact that the sites in both regions were very different during this period, but because the definition and analysis criteria are not the same in the two projects.

Type 1: Sites with Indeterminate Number of Structures (NIDE). This category is very general; it includes concentrated and semidispersed sites, the limits and number of structures of which are not evident on the surface. Consequently, it is probable that sites with different levels of complexity, size, and occupation density are grouped under this category. More detailed excavations, sampling, and surface studies are required for a better definition and a more precise typology of this kind of site.

Type 2: NIDE Sites with Ceremonial Architecture. These sites differ from those in Type 1 in that they have ceremonial architecture (generally mounds between 3 and 5 meters high and/or small mound complexes with a plaza), which seems to be an indicator that these sites would have a different hierarchy than those classified as Type 1. Evidently, as in the case of the Type 1 sites, more detailed surface studies, sampling, and extensive excavations are required for a better definition of the characteristics of this site type.

As can be seen in Figure 7.6, Type 1 and 2 sites are mainly located on the foothills and lower slopes of the mountains and sierras, and their distribution gives the impression of surrounding the rest of the occupation, as though outlining it. Type 1 and 2 sites are present in all the zones except the alluvial valley (Zone 3), which can be called the heart of the rural settlement during this period.

Some Type 1 and 2 sites are very close to each other and it is probable that in some cases these in fact would constitute just one site, or these sites' proximity was due to their constituting *barrios* or subjects of a site, or subjects of a larger entity, which is a frequent arrangement in the Late Postclassic. The distribution of the Type 2 sites in different zones of the area suggests that they could have functioned as the administrative centers (*cabeceras*) of a specific territory, as is analyzed more thoroughly in Chapter 10.

The Type 1 and 2 sites, most of which cover between 10 and 20 hectares, must have housed a larger population in less space than the sites consisting of isolated habitation structures. Type 1 and 2 settlements may correspond to the "Large and Small Nucleated Villages" categories of Sanders, Parsons, and Santley (1979).

Type 3: Isolated Habitational Structures. This is the most frequent settlement type in the area during this period. The type consists of domestic structures, with the exception of five ceremonial structures, that were included under this category because they are also isolated, and because it was not considered necessary to create a new type with such a low frequency.

TYPE		SITE TYPES
1	○	SITES WITH AN INDETERMINATE NUMBER OF STRUCTURES
2	▲	SITES WITH AN INDETERMINATE NUMBER OF STRUCTURES AND CEREMONIAL ARCHITECTURE
3	■	ISOLATED HABITATIONAL STRUCTURE
5	□	COMPLEX OF TWO HABITATIONAL STRUCTURES
19	▲	COMPLEX OF TWO STRUCTURES: ONE HABITATIONAL, ONE CEREMONIAL
16	⊡	COMPLEX OF TWO ISOLATED HABITATIONAL STRUCTURES
7	○	COMPLEX OF 3–5 STRUCTURES
11	⊙	COMPLEX OF 6–7 STRUCTURES
15	∴··	ZONES OF DISPERSED OCCUPATION

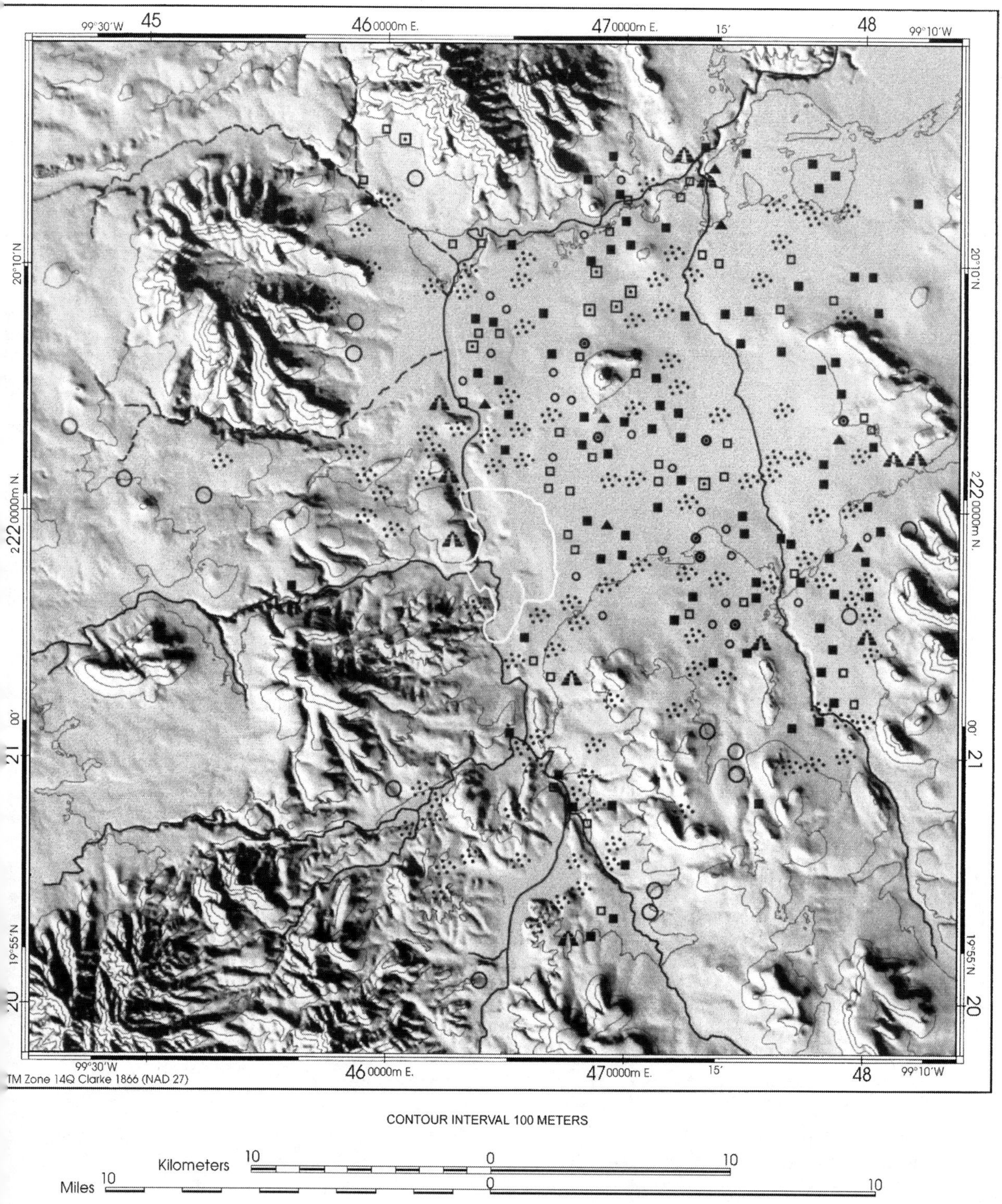

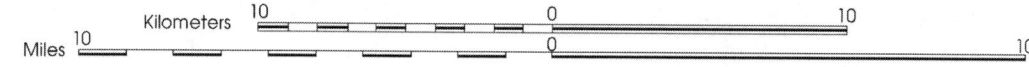

Figure 7.6. Early Postclassic site types.

THE HINTERLAND

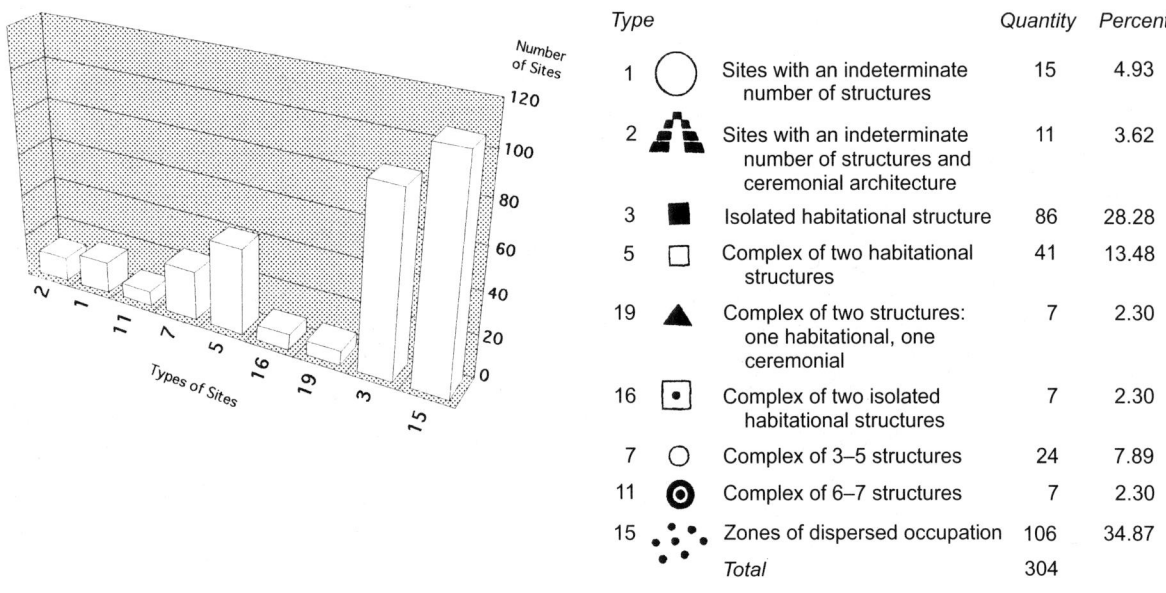

Figure 7.7A. Site type frequencies.

Most of these sites are at a distance more than 600 meters from the closest structure and only about 11 percent are less than 600 meters from the closest structure; the latter are marked on the map (Fig. 7.5) with a D. This type of settlement is not restricted to a specific zone and although it is frequent in the alluvial valley, it is also located on the foothills or mountain spurs of various zones of the area.

This is probably the most rural form of settlement, and pertains to the lowest hierarchy among the sites of the area. In some cases it is likely that they form part of very dispersed communities, similar perhaps to what Sanders, Parsons, and Santley call "Small and Large Dispersed Villages" (1979). Although these settlements have distances of less than 600 meters between structures, Type 3 settlements could well be part of the environs of more nucleated sites.

Because these structures are similar when observed on the surface in terms of size and other characteristics with a domestic structure excavated in the site of Tepetitlán (Site 290: Cobean and Mastache 1999), it can be proposed with a certain degree of accuracy that most of the isolated domestic structures that were detected in the area survey would be similar in terms of internal structure and architectural characteristics to the domestic complex excavated in Tepetitlán. That is, these domestic structures do not correspond to single-family houses, but to architectural complexes consisting of three or four individual houses surrounding a central patio that would house several related nuclear families, constituting an extended family.

Type 5: Complex of Two Habitational Structures. These are the most frequent sites after Type 3, and they also represent a kind of dispersed occupation, except that in this case the site consists of two structures instead of one. As in the case of the isolated structures, these sites are distributed over the entire area, except in Zone 2, with a higher frequency in the alluvial valley. Like the isolated platforms, at some points Type 5 sites seem to form part of larger groups, which could be the "Dispersed Villages" categories described by Sanders, Parsons, and Santley (1979).

It is likely that these sites originally were isolated structures and that the occupation expanded to two structures with the growth of the family. However, in the urban zone, where space was more limited, the alternative, given the growth of the family, would

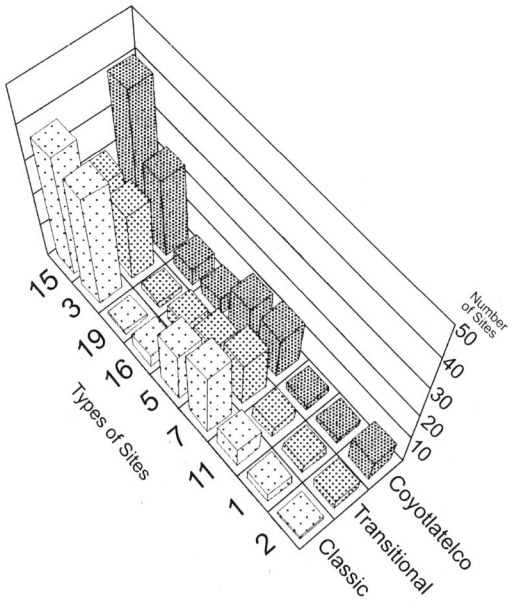

Figure 7.7B. Sites with previous occupations.

not be to build a new structure but to annex a new group of houses to the original complex, thus forming extended and complex House Groups like those studied by Healan in Tula (1989a).

Type 16: Complex of Two Isolated Habitational Structures. This type of site, as mentioned before, is really a variation of Type 3, because it also consists of isolated structures, but in this case it is not one but two. Most of these complexes are located in the alluvial valley, especially in the sectors north of Cerro Xicuco, although no specific distribution was identified.

Type 19: Complex of Two Structures: One Habitational and One Ceremonial. To a certain extent, this type of site also is a variation of Type 3 because it concerns an isolated structure, but in this case there is a ceremonial mound adjacent to the domestic structure, which seems to indicate that these complexes would have a different hierarchy than the rest of the isolated habitational structures. This is a very rare type that mainly occurs in the alluvial valley and to the west of the Salado River. Some sites of this type are near isolated habitational structures or two-structure complexes lacking ceremonial mounds, but there are cases in which they are near Type 2 sites, which also have ceremonial architecture.

Type 7: Complex of 3–5 Structures. This is a rare site type that follows Type 16 in frequency. It is a complex with three to five structures. Four Type 7 sites have ceremonial structures. Most of them are in Zone 2, especially in the alluvial valley and in an area between the ancient city and the Salado River. This kind of site could be considered as a first level of nucleation in the settlement system of the area, that is, an intermediate level between the diverse types of dispersed occupation mentioned above (Types 3, 5, 16, and 19) and the Type 1 and 2 sites.

Type 11: Complex of 6–7 Structures. Once again this type is scarce. Only one of these complexes, in Zone 6, has ceremonial architecture. It can be proposed that these sites correspond to a second level of the area's settlement nucleation and, in general terms, could be the equivalent of the "Small Nucleated Village" described by Sanders, Parsons, and Santley (1979) and an example of what Pierre George (1974a:126–129) calls the "Elementary Habitat Group."

Type 15: Zones of Dispersed Occupation. These undoubtedly represent a very common type of occupation in the area, although they probably do not constitute permanently occupied settlements, but rather, as mentioned before, the environs or periphery of diverse types of sites, constituting evidence of agricultural use of the land and other forms of exploitation, or activities such as hunting, plant collection, and obtaining firewood, but they are not residential sites. These areas may correspond to different levels of agricultural space according to George's (1974b:224, 225) model, which subdivides agricultural land into different types of occupation that he calls three different "aureoles": the first is closest to the settlement, with feces humus, cooking wastes, and, we would add, frequently vegetable garden cultivation; the second consists of a complex of fields cultivated in accordance with the rules of crop rotation, which provide the basic crops; and a third level is conformed by an area with land that is only occasionally cultivated.

This model is rather similar to the concepts of infield and outfield cultivation that various researchers (Palerm 1955; Wolf 1959; Sanders and Killion 1992) have used for Mesoamerica. The infield is the space cultivated adjacent to the dwellings, which could include the surrounding orchards and vegetable plots. The outfield, however, is the agricultural space consisting of the fields that provide the basic crops, which may be up to 2 or 3 kilometers from the house.

It is important to mention that some of these nine defined site types could also be classified as variations of the same type. This applies to Types 1 and 2; 5; 3, 16, and 19; and 7 and 11. Thus our site typology could be modified and reduced to four or five types (depending on whether the dispersed occupation zones are considered as sites or not) in the following manner:

- 1 and 2—Sites with an indeterminate number of structures (with and without ceremonial structures)
  Total: 26
- 3, 16, and 19—Isolated habitational structures (7 with ceremonial mounds and 7 grouped together in complexes of two)
  Total: 100
- 5—Complex of two habitational structures
  Total: 41
- 7 and 11—Complex of 3 to 7 structures
  Total: 31
- 15—Zones of Dispersed Occupation
  Total: 106

In addition, following a different criterion, Types 5 and 16 could be grouped together because both types consist of two habitation structures, except that in one case, the distance between structures is greater. It is also feasible to subdivide Types 7 and 11 by separating those complexes that have one

Table 7.1—Correspondences between Hierarchical Site Ranks and Site Types

	Site Type	*Hierarchical Site Type*
1	Sites with an indeterminate number of structures, NIDE	Rank 2
2	Sites with an indeterminate number of structures and ceremonial architecture	
7	Complex of 3–5 structures	Rank 3
11	Complex of 6–7 structures	
19	Complex of two structures: one habitational, one cermonial	Rank 4
5	Complex of two habitational structures	
16	Complex of two isolated habitational structures	
3	Isolated habitational structure	
15	Zones of dispersed occupation	Rank 5

Table 7.2—Distribution of Rural Sites by Zone and Rank

	Rank 2 sites			Rank 3 sites			Rank 4 sites			Rank 5 sites		
Zone	f_o	f_e	partial chisq.	f_o	f_e	partial chisq.	f_o	f_e	partial chisq.	f_o	f_e	partial chisq.
1	2	1.2	0.53	1	1.4	0.11	9	6.5	0.96	2	4.9	1.71
2	8	2.1	16.57	0	2.6	2.60	1	11.5	9.58	16	8.8	5.89
3	0	7.4	7.40	16	9.2	5.02	50	41.1	1.92	23	31.3	2.20
4	5	4.9	0.00	11	6.1	3.93	23	27.2	0.64	20	20.8	0.03
5	1	2.4	0.81	0	3.0	3.00	20	13.4	3.25	8	10.2	0.47
6	4	4.1	0.00	3	5.0	0.80	26	22.6	0.51	16	17.3	0.09
7	5	3.0	1.33	0	3.7	3.70	10	16.6	2.62	21	12.7	5.42
		total	26.64		total	19.18		total	19.51		total	15.84
			$p < .001$			$p < .01$			$p < .01$			$p < .02$

Table 7.3—Distribution of All Rural Sites by Zone

Zone	f_o	f_e^1	Partial chisq.
1	14	19.7	1.64
2	25	68.5	27.62
3	89	49.8	30.85
4	59	65.7	0.68
5	29	35.9	1.32
6	49	35.6	5.04
7	36	25.9	3.93
			71.12 (p <.001)

^{1}Based on relative size

ceremonial mound, or possibly subdivide the entire sample into two large groups, which would be those sites with ceremonial structures and those without.

The problem is not in the diverse classification criteria that could be applied to group different levels of units, but in knowing whether the complexes defined really represent some entity or territorial unit with significance within the economic and social structure of the Toltec state—that is, if these types of "sites" are really the spatial expression of basic socioeconomic units.

In the statistical analyses concerning these sites done by Healan, a different four-part hierarchy of sites was used (consisting of site Ranks 2, 3, 4, and 5). Rank 2 sites, encompassing Types 1 and 2, would include all concentrated sites, whether or not they had ceremonial architecture. Rank 3 sites include all sites with 3–7 structures, and Rank 4 sites those with only 1–2 structures. Finally, surface scatters or other dispersed material comprise a single category, designated Rank 5 sites (Rank 1 is reserved for Tula, the only urban site in the region). (Tables 7.1 to 7.3.)

TOLLAN PHASE SETTLEMENT AND PREVIOUS OCCUPATIONS

Before beginning the descriptions of Tollan Phase settlements in the survey area, we would like to make some observations concerning the sites of this period that show evidence of previous occupations on the basis of data from the General Survey Collections. This information is of great interest, especially for defining the zones in the area that were occupied for the first time during the Tollan Phase and investigating the continuity or discontinuity between settlements of the Early Postclassic in the area and the previous Teotihuacan and Coyotlatelco occupations.

These aspects are crucial with regard to our proposal that Tula was the result of a cultural and ethnic synthesis that integrated elements of both the Teotihuacan culture and the northern tradition represented by the inhabitants of the area's Coyotlatelco sites. Therefore, it is important to analyze what kinds of continuity and discontinuity are present in the rural settlements and how these processes are manifested.

In a separate investigation (Mastache 1996a), an analysis was made of Tollan Phase settlements having evidence of previous occupations (Teo-tihuacan, Transitional, Coyotlatelco), based on the Collection Units (URs) categories (Habitation Structure, Ceremonial Structures, Concentrated Artifactual Material, Dispersed Artifactual Material, and Zones with an Undetermined Number of Structures). In contrast, here our comments will be based fundamentally on the nine different site types defined for the Tollan Phase, although some of the results from the Collection Unit study will be mentioned.

Classic Teotihuacan

Some Teotihuacan materials are present in slightly more than 41 percent of the Tollan Phase rural sites. Figure 7.7B shows the number of sites for each type possessing Classic Teotihuacan materials. This graph clearly indicates that in absolute numbers, the highest frequency of sites with Teotihuacan material corresponds to Type 15 and Type 3 sites, that is, zones of dispersed occupation and isolated habitation structures, followed by site Types 7 and 5, and then by the site types with lower frequencies.

Nevertheless, it is worth stating that in terms of percentages, the sites of Types 15 and 3 represented in Fig. 7.7B constituted only 35 percent of the total Type 15 sites and 39.5 percent of the total Type 3 sites, whereas for Type 7 sites the percentage is 90 percent of total sites, and for Type 11 the percentage is 100 percent, or the total number of this site type. It is of interest that only one site of Type 2 has Teotihuacan material, which appears to indicate that rural sites of the highest hierarchy did not overlap with Early Classic period occupations.

When seen in terms of occupation density, the majority of the possible previous Teotihuacan presences in the Tollan sites consist of small points of disperse, very scarce material. The analysis based on URs also showed that the Teotihuacan occupations that overlap with Tollan sites are very light and dispersed, coinciding mainly with dispersed Tollan Phase occupations and isolated Tollan habitational structures. Only 3.31 percent of the total Tollan Phase URs have more dense Teotihuacan occupations, few of which overlap with dense Tollan remains. The cases of clearer correlations between these two periods consist of twenty-seven URs classified as Classic habitational structures, which also correspond to Tollan Phase habitational structures. Most of these are located in the alluvial valley on land having adequate soils for rainfall and irrigation agriculture, or in zones of limestone exploitation. However, without excavation it is difficult to determine if those structures represent continuity in occupations between the Classic and the Tollan Phase. In many cases it is not clear if there also was an intervening Coyotlatelco occupation, and it is very probable that some of these units represent the reoccupation of this zone during the Tollan Phase, when populations expanded to different zones of the area, especially to where there were good agricultural lands, some of which had been occupied previously by the Teotihuacanos.

It is interesting that in five of these structures, there occur some ceramic types that we have considered as Transitional (see Chapter 4), because they suggest a probable continuity in occupation, although in only two of these structures are there significant quantities of these materials. An interesting correlation is that 60 percent of the twenty-seven Teotihuacan-Tollan Phase habitational structures show some evidence of Coyotlatelco material, although in the majority of these cases this occupation appears to have been light.

Only one site on the southern foothills of Cerro Xicuco has clear continuity of occupation from the Classic to the Early Postclassic. This identification was surely possible, in part, because the site had been looted, indicating that only through excavation would it be possible to define continuity of occupation where only slight traces of Transitional and Coyotlatelco ceramics were detected.

Transitional

27.23 percent of the Tollan Phase sites possess ceramics that provisionally have been classified as Transitional. Although, as was indicated in Chapter 4, this ceramic category is very tentative and only can be defined adequately with excavations, because these types could be part of Teotihuacan or Coyotlatelco complexes as local variants, and they are poorly represented in surface collections.

As can be seen in Fig. 7.7B, Transitional materials are present in considerably fewer sites than those that have Classic (Teotihuacan) presence. Transitional ceramics were found in 20 percent of the Type 15 sites and in a little more than 24 percent of the Type 3 sites. The low frequency of those ceramics in site Types 1 and 2 also is notable. In the Tollan sites with previous occupations, the Transitional materials (like the Teotihuacan occupations) are predominated by scarce, dispersed remains that in many cases are associated with zones of Coyotlatelco and Classic materials, along with zones of dispersed Tollan remains. The analysis based on the URs showed that eleven units with a higher density of Transitional materials coincide with Collection Units classified as Tollan Phase habitational structures.

Coyotlatelco

Thirty-seven percent of the Tollan Phase sites have some Coyotlatelco ceramic types. As can be seen in Fig.7.7B, the highest frequencies occur also in site Types 15 and 3, that is, dispersed occupations and isolated habitational structures, only now the frequency for sites of Type 15 is higher, 41.38 percent of all the sites of this type. Also the frequency is high for Type 2 sites with Coyotlatelco materials, and is especially high for Type 1 sites, with a presence in 50 percent of these sites.

With regard to occupation densities for Coyotlatelco, once again very scarce, dispersed materials predominate, usually associated with zones of dispersed Tollan occupations. The analysis based on URs indicated that only 35 percent of the Collection Units with Coyotlatelco and Tollan occupations also have Teotihuacan materials. A third of these units correspond to Classic habitational structures, but with the exception of one structure, the Coyotlatelco presence in these cases consists of very scarce dispersed material.

On the other hand, ten Coyotlatelco habitational structures appear to have been reoccupied during the Tollan Phase, representing 0.62 percent of the total Collection Units. These structures correspond to different sites and are located in diverse zones of the area. It is probable that together with a great part of the Coyotlatelco dispersed presence located in the alluvial valley that overlaps Tollan occupations, these remains may represent the rural population of Tula Chico; that is, the direct sustaining area of the early city. This last proposal is speculative because of the limited data we have concerning these settlements and their chronology.

As we have seen, the Tollan Phase settlement in the area overlaps at some points with occupations of previous periods. A chi-square analysis of the area settlement data used to establish correlation levels between Tollan sites and previous occupations indicated that there is no direct correlation between Tollan sites and Teotihuacan or Coyotlatelco occupations. This analysis only detected a slight correlation between Early Tollan occupations and the Transitional ceramic assemblage (Early Tollan sites are those that have diagnostic early ceramic types, principally Mazapa Red on Brown, Joroba Orange on Cream, and Manuelito Plain Brown, that are described in more detail in Chapter 8). On the other hand, it is interesting that the Correspondence Analysis (see Chapter 8) suggests a kind of correlation between some Tollan and Teotihuacan occupations.

ZONES

In order to facilitate the description of the settlement system during the Early Postclassic, the area was subdivided into seven large zones that are listed below. The definition of these zones is arbitrary to a certain extent, although the hydrography and topography of the area, as well as the occupation characteristics during this period, were taken into account for their delimitation (see Fig. 7.8).

Zone 1

Zone 1 basically covers the foothills of the Sierra Tasguada that bounds the study area to the north. It is limited to the south and west by the Tepetitlán arroyo and to the east by the Tula River until its point of confluence with the Salado River (Figs. 7.9 and 7.10A). As can be seen in Figure 2.3, the soils include extensive zones of lithosols in the upper part of the sierra and an association with haplic feozem and dark vertisol soils in the foothills and spurs, with some inclusions of regosoles, which are shallow incipient sandy soils associated with rocky outcrops. On the banks of the Tula River, there are small areas of moderately deep vertisoles, with a stratum of rhyolite toba at a depth of less than 1 meter.

This zone was not subject to a total reconnaissance. Our survey was mainly centered on the west in the southeastern foothills of the Sierra Tasguada, up to the old Culantrillo Dam and on both banks of the Tepetitlán arroyo, and to the east to the town of Acayutlan up to the outskirts of Santa Maria Batha (see Fig. 1.2).

To the north of Tepetitlán, at an altitude of 2,000 to 2,200 meters, there is an extensive zone of occupation that is interspersed with concentrated and dispersed material points with isolated habitation structures (site Types 5, 15, and 16).

Apparently, the occupation extended almost without interruption along the foothills of the sierra from the dam and Culantrillo arroyo to the Las Animas arroyo in the east. The sector with the densest occupation is associated with an arroyo fed by the El Sabino spring and a traditional irrigation system that originated in the same spring to the northeast of the town of Tepetitlán; this is a site (Number 290, Type 1) that extends over a series of artificial terraces. A habitation mound contemporary with the apogee of Tula was excavated at this site in the 1980s. This is the only rural Tollan Phase residential structure excavated to date in the Tula area (Cobean and Mastache 1999).

There are other areas of occupation directly along the banks of the Tepetitlán arroyo, which feeds another traditional irrigation system. There are Class III soils surrounding the densest occupation of the zone, which are suitable for rainfall agriculture (see

Contour interval 50 meters.

1 : 250 000 Scale

Kilometers 10 0 10

Miles 10 0 10

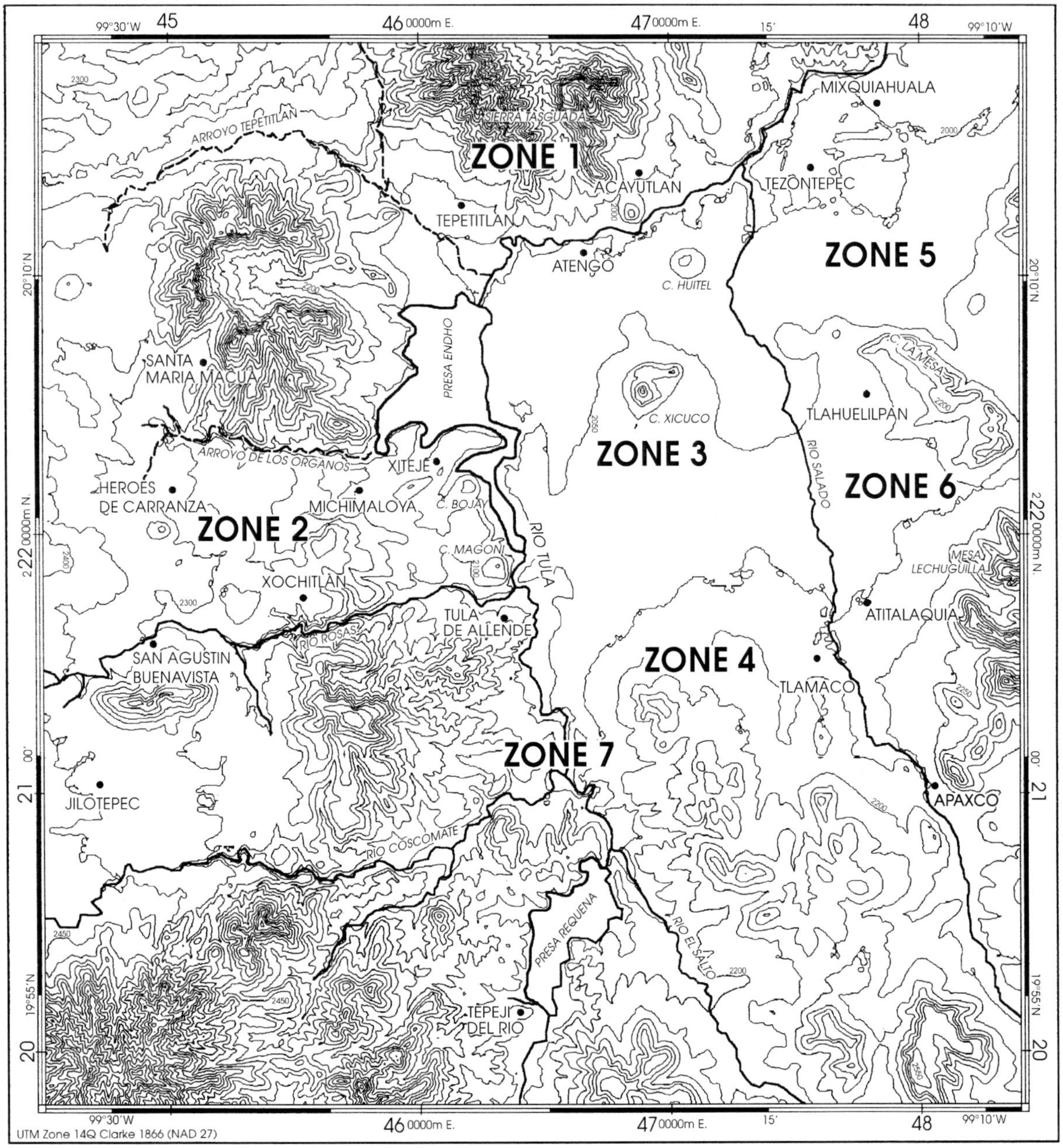

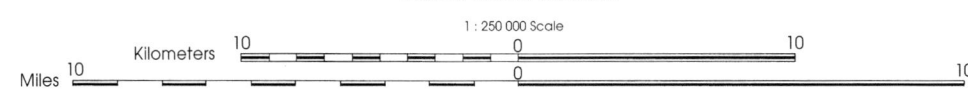

Figure 7.8. Early Postclassic zones.

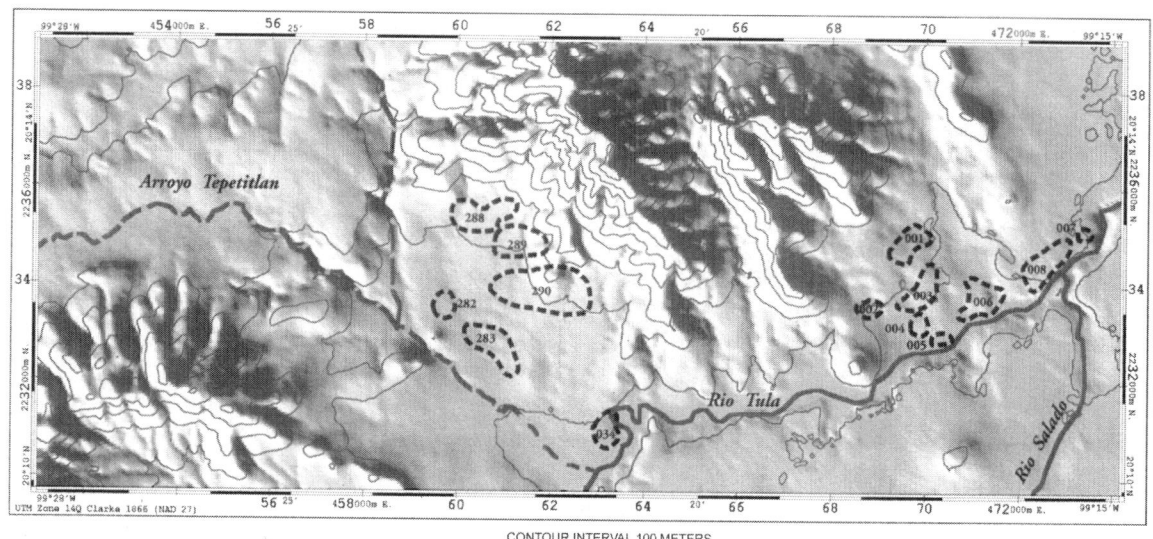

Figure 7.9. Early Postclassic: Zone 1.

Fig. 2.4), although there also is a small zone of potential irrigation of vertisols associated with feozem in the small valley to the south of the present town of Tepetitlán. However, rainfall agriculture now predominates in this zone, with maize and maguey being the crops. Climate is a limiting factor in this area because there are frequent frosts. There are small dispersed occupations below 2,000 meters on the Tula River banks next to a narrow strip of fertile vertisol-type, Class I soils (Figure 7.10A).

In the eastern limit of the area, at the confluence of the Tula and Salado Rivers, there is another nucleus of dispersed occupation associated with deep vertisols, and to the west of the foothills of the sierra, east of the present town of Acayutlán, there are zones with alternating dispersed occupation and habitation structures (site Types 3, 7, and 15) on sandy Class IV and V soils that are very poor for agriculture. Site 008 (Type 2), of almost 20 hectares, with ceremonial architecture, stands out impressively on the northern bank of the Tula River in this sector (Fig. 7.9).

Zone 2

Zone 2 is located to the west of the Tula River and the pre-Hispanic city. The northern part of this zone has very uneven topography; it includes the mountains to the northeast of Santa Maria Macua, with altitudes between 2,300 and 2,650 meters. Thin, basically haplic feozem soils predominate on the slopes, with lithosols on the upper parts of the sierra. These are generally soils with a medium texture in the lithic phase, that is, the underlying volcanic rock, mainly basalt and rhyolites, is at a depth of less than 50 centimeters. The mountains form a limit on the south with the Organos arroyo and there are hills and a small intermountain valley between it and the Rosas River, which is permanent, where there are deeper soils—vertisols and association with feozem soils. Most of the length of the Rosas River is between steep banks having lithosols and haplic feozem (Figs. 7.11 and 7.6).

There is scant settlement in Zone 2, and this is fundamentally located in three areas.

1. There are dispersed material zones (Type 15 sites) and two small concentrated sites (276 and 277; Type 1) close to intermittent arroyos in the eastern foothills of the above-mentioned mountains. This is a heavily eroded area with very shallow soils (haplic feozem in the lithic phase), over a substratum of volcanic rock mainly consisting of basalt, rhyolites, and andesites. These are Class VI and VIII soils that are not suitable for agriculture. It is interesting to

THE HINTERLAND

Figure 7.10A. Sierra Tasguada, looking north.

note that these settlements were production zones for stone grinding tools: *metates, manos,* and pestles. The survey found that the raw-material extraction zone was in the higher parts of the same mountains.

2. The Magoni-Bojay mountains to the west and north of the ancient city harbor three concentrated sites with ceremonial structures (sites 278, 279, and 280) on the spurs and foothills, as well as concentrated and disperse material zones (Type 15 sites). Haplic feozem and luvic soils also predominate here, the latter with a clay horizon in the middle. These are Class VI soils that are not suitable for agriculture.

As can be seen in Figure 4.6, there was an important Coyotlatelco settlement here with an extensive system of terraces, where the main activity was the cultivation of maguey, and it is very likely that this zone was used for the same purpose during the Tollan Phase. The Tollan Phase site is located on top of Cerro Magoni, where it must have been a good outlook post given its strategic position, in addition to its symbolic importance.

3. Additional occupation was on the hills and the lowlands between Arroyo de los Organos and the Rosas River. It is important to stress that the settlements and dispersed occupation points (sites 296 to 303) located in this zone between the Arroyo de los Organos and the Rosas River are directly associated with different collection points along the course of the traditional irrigation water canals, specifically Zanja San Miguel and Zanja Xitejé, which form part of the ancient and extensive irrigation system that originated in the Soyaniquilpan springs under the control of Xochitlan, which irrigated lands of seven different communities, including Tula. This is evidence, albeit limited, that

THE HINTERLAND

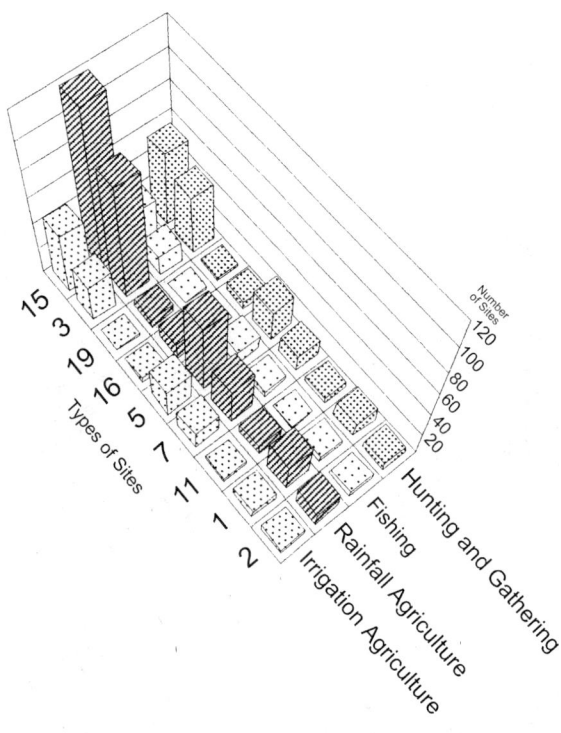

Figure 7.10B. Potential pre-Hispanic land use.

are numerous settlements surrounding the Cerro Xicuco and almost uninterrupted occupation areas to the north and west up to the Tula River. Most of the settlement of this zone is located between altitudes of 2,000 and 2,080 meters (the valley floor is at an altitude of 1,980 to 2,020 meters) and relatively far from permanent or intermittent arroyos. There are deep and shallow feozem and rendzina soils associated with vertisols, and it is one of the sectors where rendzinas predominate in the areas studied. These are Class III soils that are suitable for rainfall agriculture, with limitations only in terms of soil depth and topography (Figs. 7.13 and 7.14).

As can be seen in Figure 2.4, there are two strips of deep vertisol-type Class I and II soils that are very suitable for rainfall and irrigation agriculture; one is on the banks of the Salado River and the other crosses the pre-Hispanic city and runs to the north up to the Tula River. Thus, the almost continuous strip of occupation that runs from the north of the city up to the Tula River lies on a belt of deep vertisol and luvic feozem associated with Class I and II vertisol soils that include the east side of the pre-Hispanic city, although most of the urban zone is on Class VI soils.

There is also a wide strip of Class II soils (deep haplic feozem) more than 1 meter deep near the ancient city to the northeast. This land was largely irrigated by the ancient La Romera irrigation system and then more recently by the principal Requena and Endó Canals. Consequently, it is difficult to determine whether the soil quality and characteristics were the same during the Tollan Phase, due to the fact that this land has been irrigated for a very long time (Fig. 7.15).

As can be seen in Figs. 7.13 and 7.14, this zone was extensively occupied. As mentioned before, Zone 3 can be considered as the heart of the rural settlement of this period. Dispersed occupation predominates, with only a few points of nucleated occupation. All the site types are present, with the exception of Types 1 and 2, but the most frequent are the isolated habitational structures (Type 3) and complexes with two structures (Type 5), as well as the dispersed occupation zones classified as Type 15 (Fig. 7.6). There is evidence that some types of ceramics

the Tollan Phase occupation in this zone was of key significance, and it supports our proposal that chronologically this ancient and important irrigation system that terminated in Tula (Mastache 1976) dates back to the Early Postclassic.

Some sites in this zone are associated with Class II and III soils with good agricultural potential (deep duric-phase vertisols and feozems). This is the case of site 304, located next to the modern Macua Dam on the western edge of the area, on a small hill having Class VI soils but surrounded by Class II.

Zone 3

Zone 3 corresponds to a broad alluvial valley that lies between the Tula and Salado Rivers to the north and east of the pre-Hispanic city, with the Xicuco and Huitel elevations in the center and northeast as outstanding features (Fig. 7.12).

Zone 3 is important because a large part of the settlement for the Tollan Phase is located in this alluvial valley, which was extensively occupied. There

THE HINTERLAND

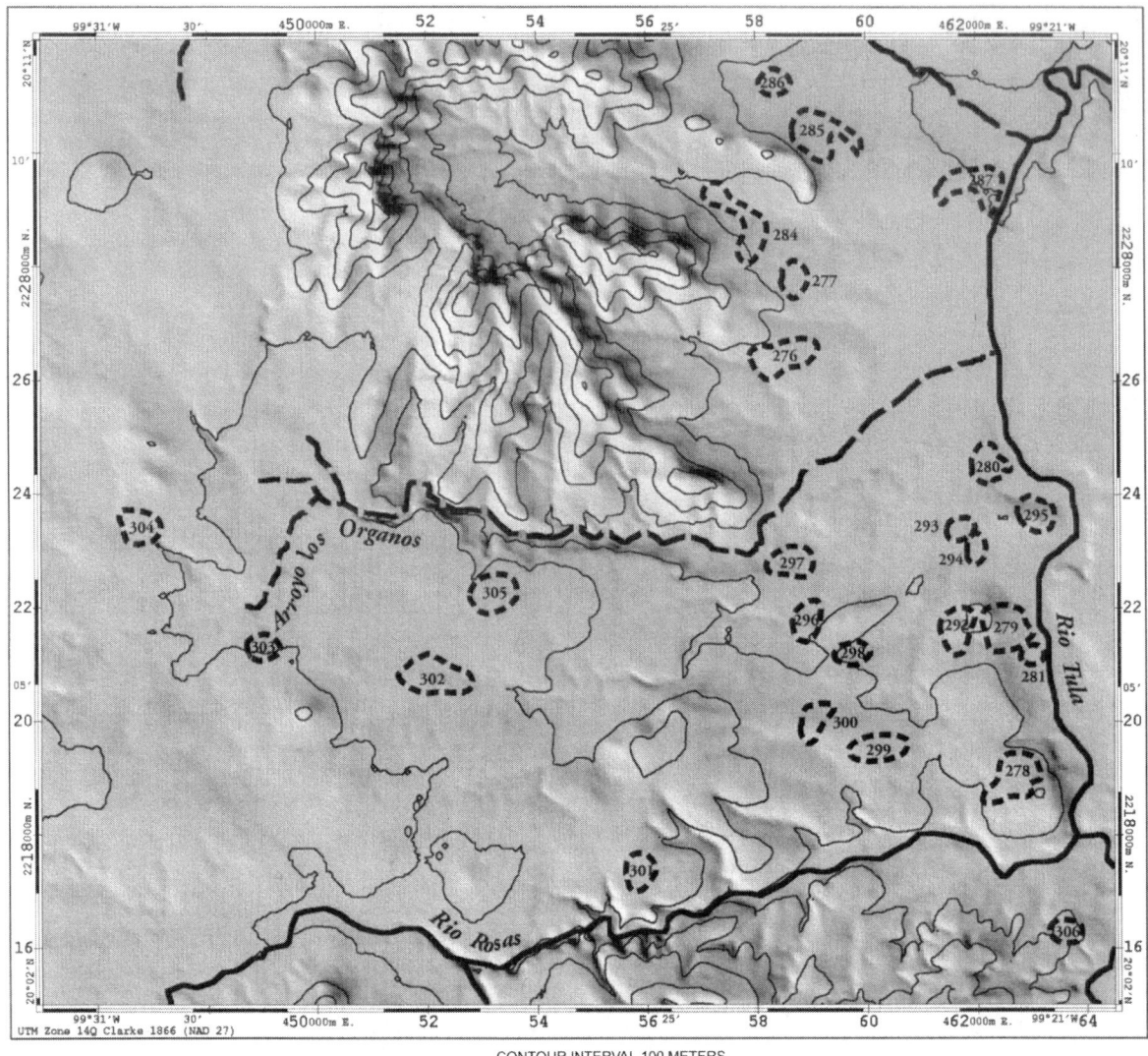

Figure 7.11. Early Postclassic: Zone 2.

characteristic of the Tollan Phase were produced in some sites to the south of Xicuco.

Zone 4

This covers the extensive mountain range between the El Salto and the Salado Rivers to the southeast of the pre-Hispanic city. This range, with altitudes of between 2,200 and 2,500 meters, includes low hills, and the elevations are less uneven than in other zones of the area; it has smooth and rounded contours, which is largely due to the fact that limestone rock predominates. This is a zone with severe erosion and shallow Class V–VIII soils that are not suitable for agriculture, consisting principally of haplic and calcareous feozem (with some points in the duric and deep lithic phase), as well as litosols, especially at the top of higher elevations. There are also small areas of rendzinas in the petrocalcious phase and pelic vertisols, the latter being Class I and II soils.

Figure 7.12. Zone 3, alluvial valley, looking northeast.

The settlements are located on the mountain foothills at an altitude of 2,100 to 2,200 meters, on slopes and hilltops in front of the ancient city and on the western spurs bounded by the Tula and El Salto Rivers. Small nucleated settlements with different characteristics predominate (Types 1 and 2) that alternate with large areas of dispersed occupation (Fig. 7.15). The settlement that extends to the east of ancient Tula to the Salado River largely occupies rendzina and pelic vertisol areas, the latter being high-quality Class I and II soils.

Zone 4 is the setting of the sites located to the south and east of the city (sites 232, 233, 235, 421, 107–111, and 113–116), near land that could be irrigated by the ancient La Romera and Zanja Nueva systems, and of the settlements on the left bank of the Salado River, which are on Class II and IV soils, but close to the Class I and II vertisol zones on the banks of the river and some of its tributaries.

Zone 5

This zone includes the lowlands of the northeastern end of the area. It is bordered to the south by the La Mesa sierra and the west by the Tula and Salado Rivers, where the Mezquital Valley begins (Fig. 7.16). There are large areas of vertisols associated with feozem, which are moderately deep soils in the duric phase due to the presence of a stratum of rhyolite rock at a depth of less than 1 meter, as well as shallow, petrocalceous rendzinas, with a limestone stratum at a depth of less than 50 centimeters. The occupation is essentially dispersed, and isolated habitation structures and complexes with two structures predominate (Types 3 and 5). There are extensive areas of Class I soils on the banks of the Salado River and in Zone 6, which are highly suitable for agriculture and can be irrigated by the traditional irrigation systems that originate in this river. These are largely river meadowlands, with a very high potential for irrigated or natural humidity

THE HINTERLAND

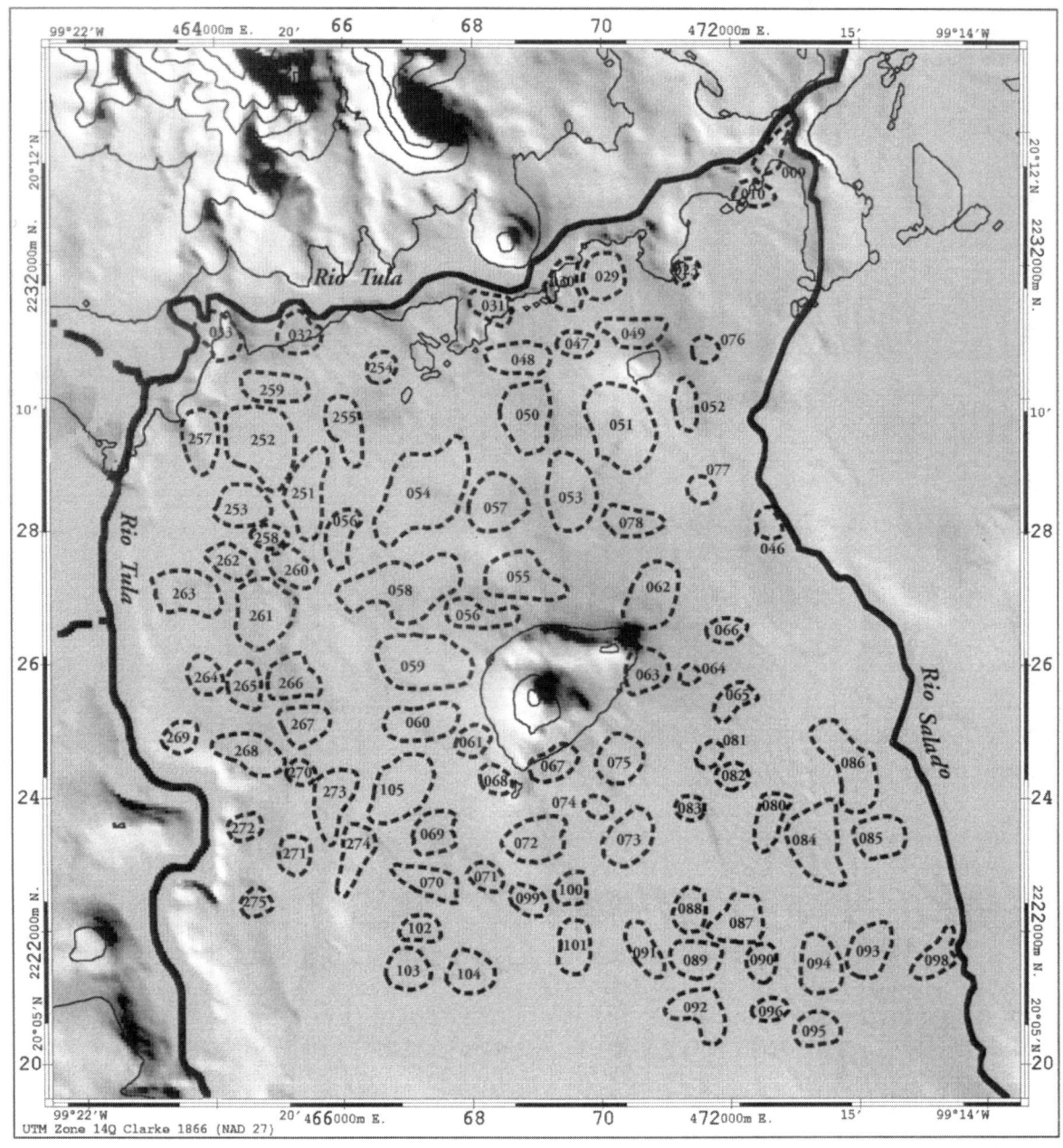

Figure 7.13. Early Postclassic: Zone 3.

agriculture, but because they have been irrigated since colonial times, it is difficult to determine accurately whether the soil conditions were the same during the pre-Hispanic period.

Zone 6

Zone 6 is to the east of the Salado River and is bounded to the north by the Mesa Lechuguilla range, with altitudes of up to 2,800 meters, but it

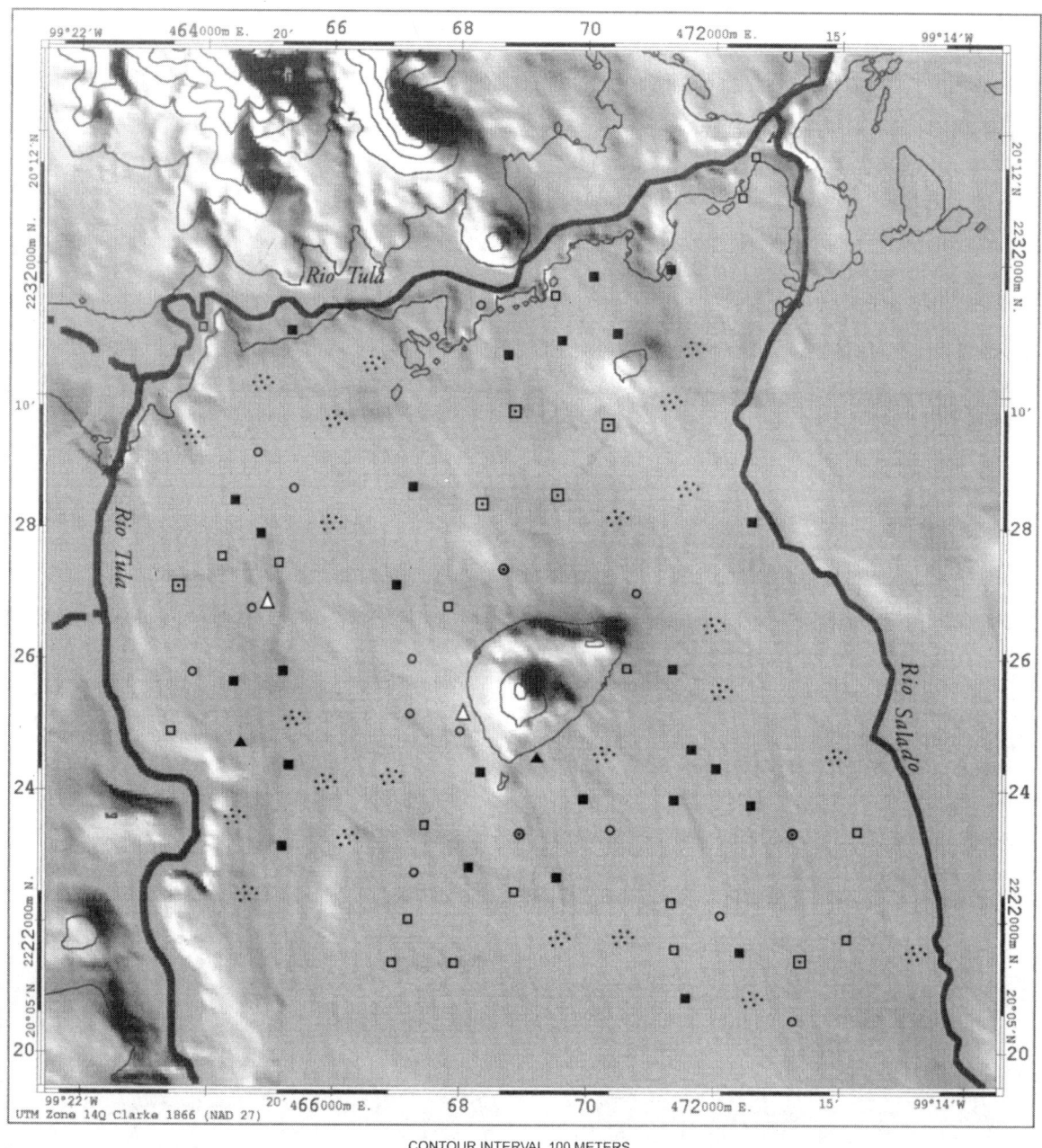

Figure 7.14. Early Postclassic, Zone 3: Site types.

also includes a broad strip of lowland between Tlahuelilpan, Atitalaquia, and Tlaxcoapan (Fig. 7.17). In the high part of the sierra the soils are lithosols and rendzinas, while vertisols and regosols predominate in the lowlands. There is an area of concentrated population (site Types 2 and 11) that extends over the lower foothills of Cerro La Mesa, to the southeast of Tlahuelilpan, and a large zone of dispersed

THE HINTERLAND

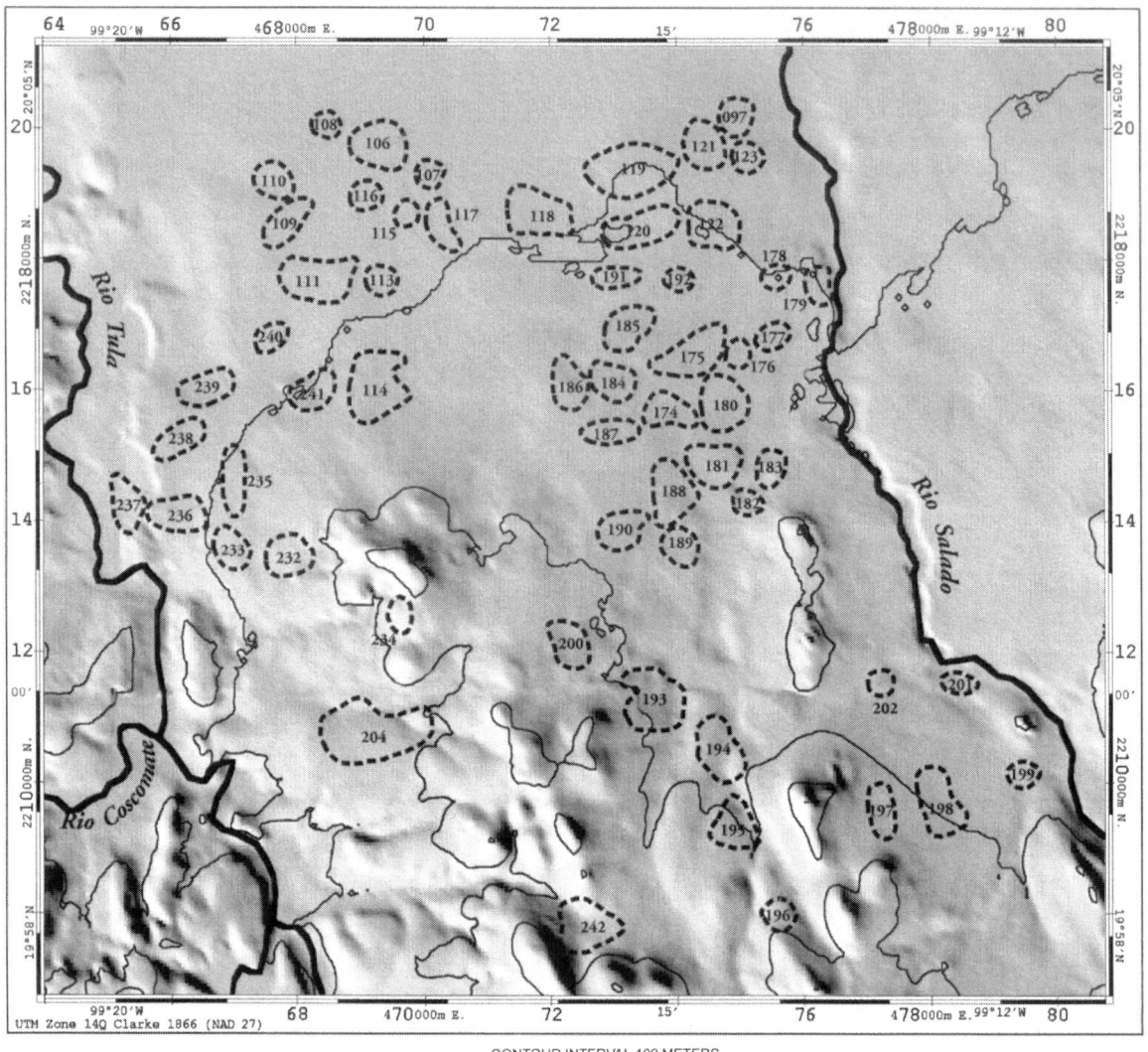

Figure 7.15. Early Postclassic: Zone 4.

occupation in the southern part of the area, on the foothills and spurs of the Mesa Lechuguilla that extends to the banks of the Salado River and is also associated with intermittent arroyos that flow from the sierra. Site Types 1 and 2 alternate with dispersed occupation in this zone; one site (160) was a zone that specialized in the production of chert bifaces, especially projectile points.

It should be noted that most of the settlements are on Class III and IV soils, which are suitable for rainfall cultivation, especially of agaves, but like Zone 5 this area also has soils that are highly suitable for irrigated or naturally humid land (*humedad*) crops in the river meadowlands.

Zone 7

Zone 7 includes the lands lying between the Coscomate and El Salto Rivers, from the point where the Tula River joins the Coscomate (Fig. 7.18). Most of the western part of this zone has very uneven topography, and is occupied by a mountain range with altitudes as high as 2,650 meters. Thin, mostly

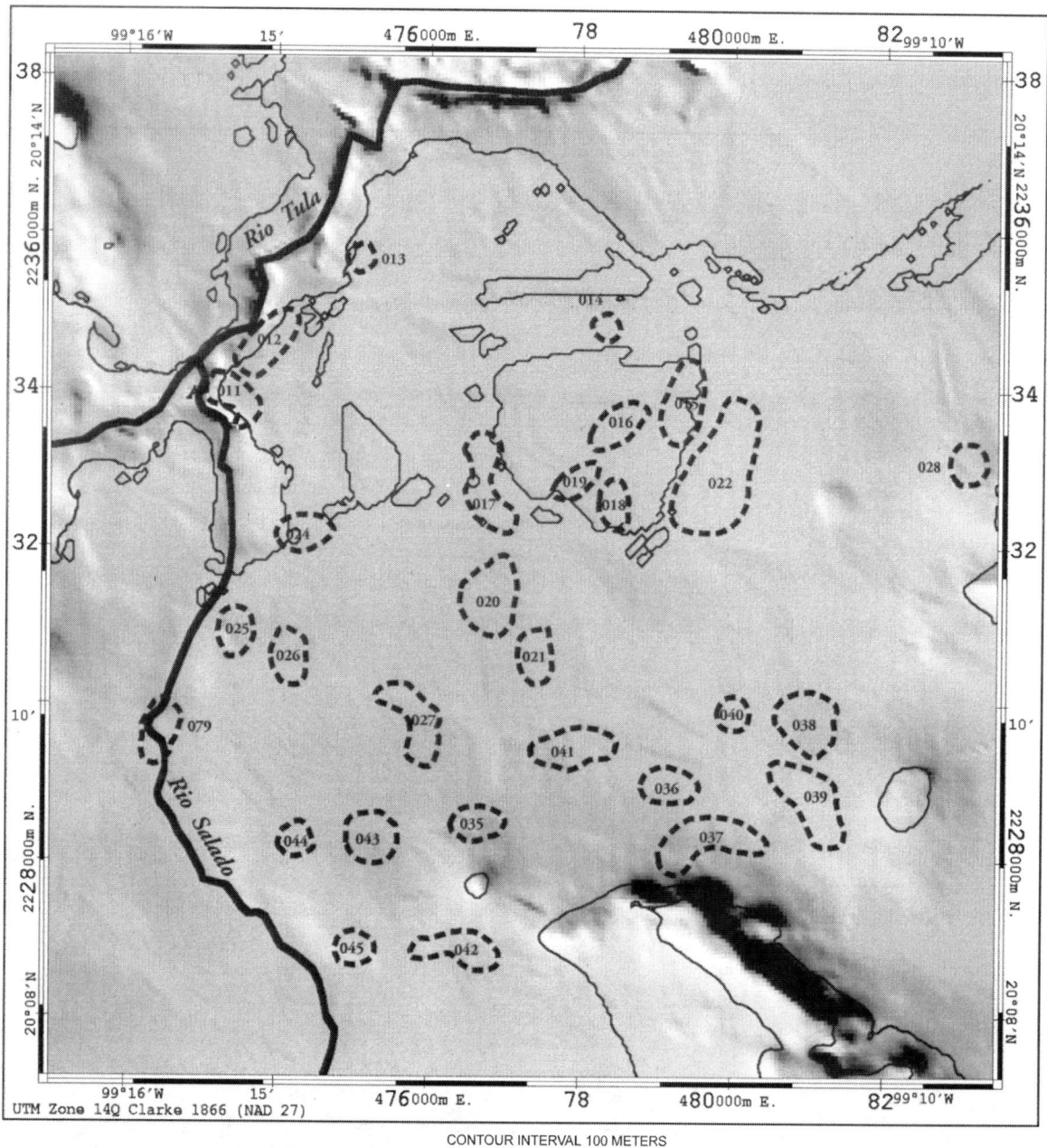

Figure 7.16. Early Postclassic: Zone 5.

haplic feozem soils predominate over the slopes, with lithosols in the higher part of the sierra. The soils are generally medium-texture lithic phase, that is, the underlying volcanic rock, mostly basalts and rhyolite, is at a depth of less than 50 centimeters.

The Tollan Phase occupation zones are located on the less uneven terrain areas with better soils, on land close to the Coscomate River, and on the foothills and spurs to the north and west of the Requena Dam, which has a geological substratum with

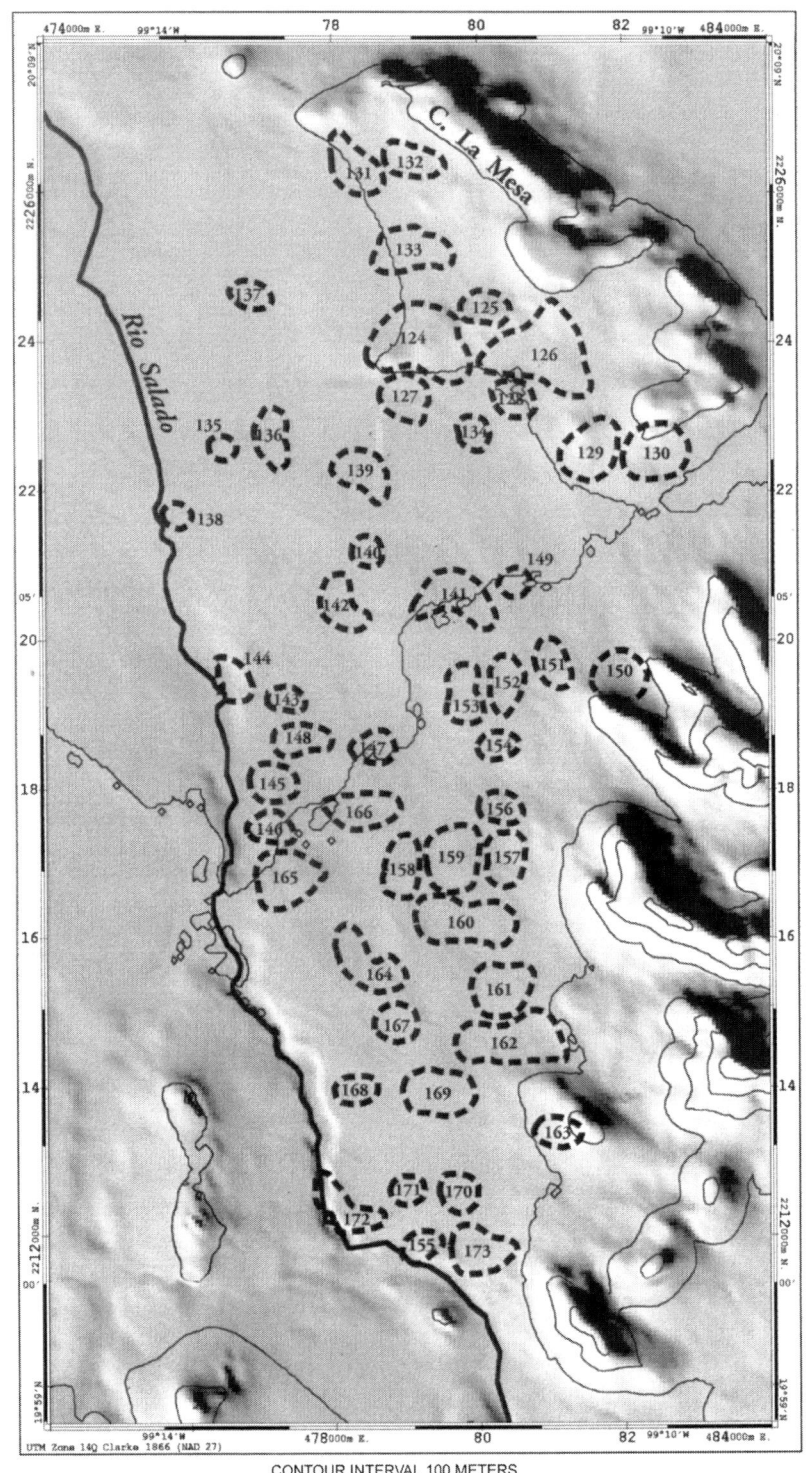

Figure 7.17. Early Postclassic: Zone 6.

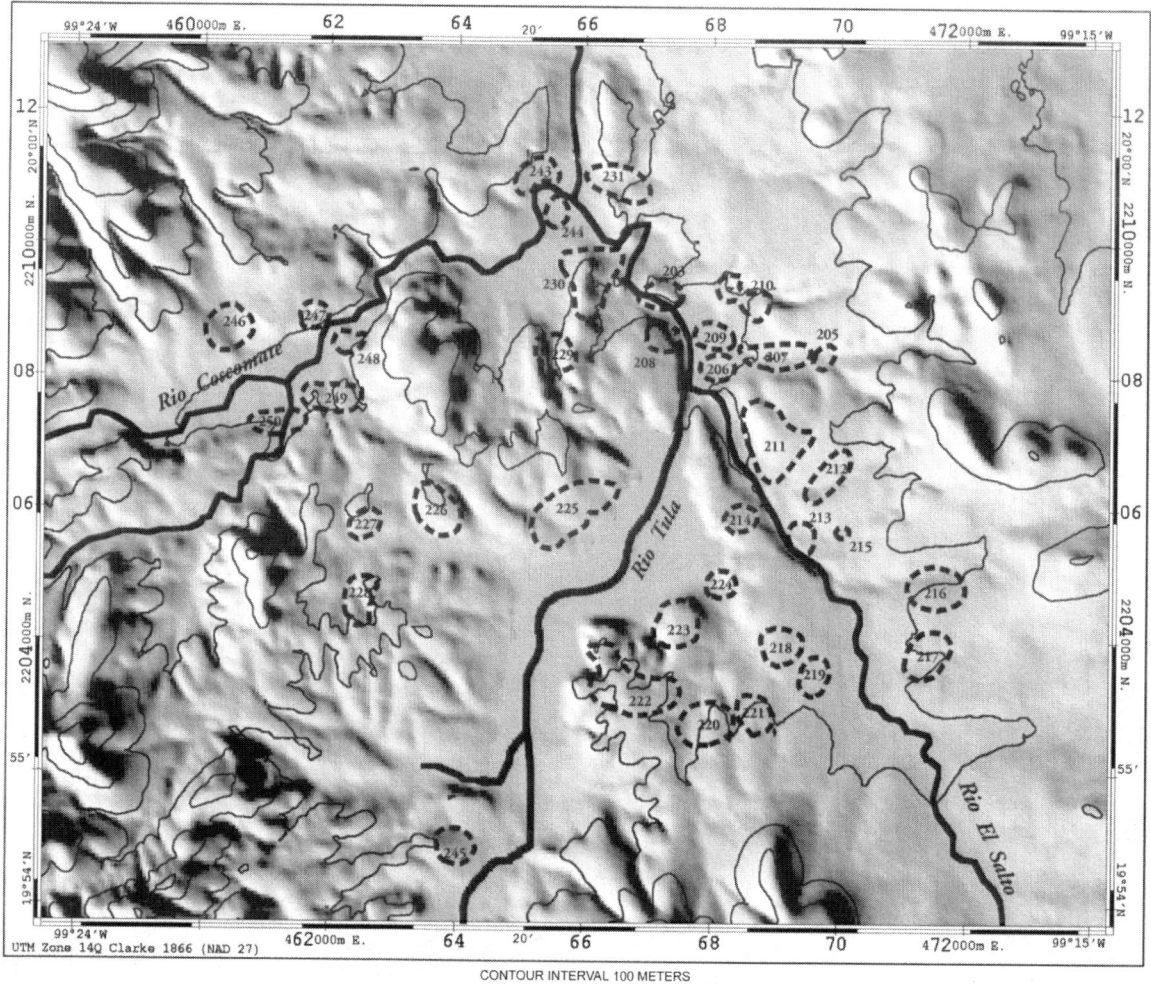

Figure 7.18. Early Postclassic: Zone 7.

feozem-type Class V and VI soils that are unsuitable for agriculture. Dispersed occupation also predominates in this zone, alternating with Types 1 and 2 sites near the El Salto and the Coscomate Rivers and close to the vertisol zones, which are potentially irrigable by the Zanja de El Salto. There are also narrow strips of deep vertisol and feozem, Class I and II soils, in the Coscomate riverbank meadowland.

Correlations Between Sites and Zones

The statistical analyses of the distribution by zone for each of the four ranks of rural sites (Fig. 7.19; Tables 7.1 to 7.3) used by Healan indicate that each category enjoys a unique pattern of distribution. Rank 2 sites have a disproportionately heavy occurrence in Zone 2, a discontinuous and sparsely settled zone to the west of Tula. In general, Rank 2 sites tend to occur in peripheral areas (Fig. 7.19), with disproportionately large numbers in Zones 2 and 7, while totally absent from Zone 3, seemingly the most densely settled zone situated in the heart of Tula's hinterland, which instead has a disproportionately heavy representation of Rank 3 sites. Rank 4 sites are virtually absent in Zone 2, but occur in disproportionately large numbers in Zones 5 and 3, relative to other zones. Curiously,

THE HINTERLAND

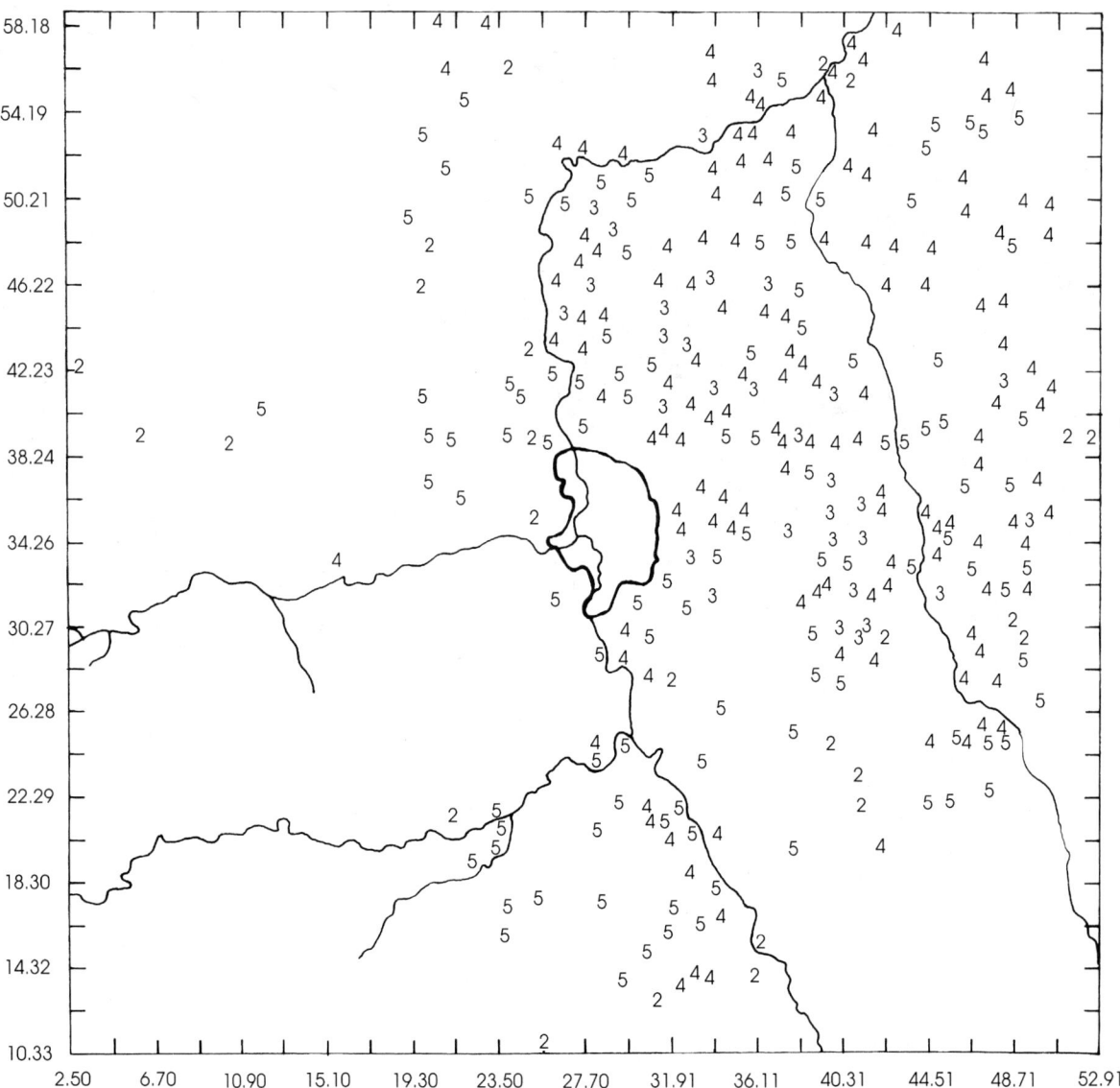

Figure 7.19. Spatial distribution of rural site ranks. The four rural site ranks are: Rank 2: site types 1 and 2; Rank 3: site types 7 and 11; Rank 4: site types 3, 5, 19, and 16; and Rank 5: site type 15.

Rank 5 sites exhibit a distribution similar to that of Rank 2 sites.

Table 7.4, "Nearest Neighbor Coefficients for Site Ranks," computed between the four categories of sites, suggests that the distributions seen in Figure 7.19 actually comprise three general patterns. The first of these, represented by the extremely high values for all intertype relationships involving Rank 2 sites, reflects the peripheral location of most of the largest rural sites. Conversely, the configuration of relatively low coefficients indicative of mutual clustering that is shared by Ranks 3 and 4 is a reflection of their centrally located, interspersed distribution, which can be seen in Figure 7.19. Finally, the intermediate nearest neighbor coefficients for relationships involving Rank 5 sites reflect a more intermediate (i.e., neither peripheral nor centralized), relatively more uniform, distribution, although the relatively low values with Rank 2 sites probably reflects their mutual concentration in Zones 2 and 7.

The above information may shed some light upon the nature of Rank 5 sites, or what was designated as sherd scatters or dispersed material, certainly a problematic category because it is not certain that these scatters consistently represent distinct, temporary, very small occupations. On the one hand, their co-occurrence in disproportionately large numbers with Rank 2 sites, especially in Zones 2 and 7, suggests that these scatters may simply be ill-defined extensions of these large, concentrated sites, whose limits were probably difficult to define with any certainty. On the other hand, Rank 5 sites in other zones, such as those in Zone 3, may indeed represent temporary or very small occupations perhaps associated with agricultural activity.

Dispersed and Nucleated Occupation

In summary, most of the site types of the area represent different forms of dispersed settlement, which is evident if it is borne in mind that Types 3, 19, 5, 16, and 15 add up to 247 sites, or 81.25 percent of the total sites defined in the area for this period. However, if the number of sites classified as Zones of Dispersed Occupation (106, which account for almost 35 percent of the total sites) is subtracted because, as mentioned before, they are not really sites in the sense of permanent settlements, then there is a total of 198 sites, of which Types 3, 19, 5, and 16, which represent dispersed sites, account for 71.21 percent (see Fig. 7.7A and B).

Type 7, formed by the complexes with 3–5 structures—which we have considered as an intermediate category between the dispersed and nucleated sites, and which in our opinion would correspond to what George (1974a:127) calls "elementary villages"— make up 12.1 percent of the sites, if a total of 198 sites is considered. Thus, only 16.6 percent of the sites (Types 1, 2, and 11) represent the concentrated occupation of the area.

It is not surprising that dispersed settlements make up the majority of the sites in the area, since dispersed occupation is a very common form of rural settlement, and it corresponds to what Pierre George calls Dispersed Habitat (1974a) in geographic terms, which consists of the isolated establishment of families or small family nuclei in the agricultural space. The maximum form of dispersion is the isolated family or isolated-family complexes, generally located in the center of the space exploited by the family unit.

Table 7.4—Nearest Neighbor Coefficients for Site Ranks

	Intratype (Principal Diagonal) and Intertype (Off-Diagonal) Nearest Neighbor Coefficients			
	Rank 2	Rank 3	Rank 4	Rank 5
Rank 2	0.84	2.43	2.25	1.13
Rank 3	1.42	0.57	0.78	0.90
Rank 4	1.41	1.14	0.88	1.03
Rank 5	0.98	1.72	1.41	0.87

The Dispersed Habitat has been considered the optimum relationship between the agricultural family settlement unit and its farmlands, and it is related to different types of agriculture, generally with extensive cultivation regimens. The Dispersed Habitat tends to be abandoned when man's direct relationship with the agricultural areas is no longer necessary, and the exploitation of the area can be done without the need to reside in the same place (George 1974a).

This type of occupation was very common in Mesoamerica, and as Sanders and Killion have indicated, the pre-Hispanic settlement pattern in the Basin of Mexico in general consisted of dispersed villages on sloping terrain situated on the more productive lands (1992:21–23, 29–30). The farmers try to live very close to the fields they work and thus minimize daily energy expenditure, which fosters dispersed population. Mesoamerican farmers were obliged to let a significant part of the agricultural land lie fallow for the soil to recover before being cultivated again, and they alternated fallow land with cultivated land, which led to the dispersion of the settlement. Thus, dispersed population is an obvious adaptation to maintain soil fertility through a land-rotation system, and to more efficiently exploit the productive land and minimize the farmers' use of energy.

George's (1974a) affirmation is interesting regarding the fact that, in some cases, the dispersed occupation is associated with new occupation of the area, that is, new settlements, and in the case of Dispersed Habitat countries, the formation of small villages is due to the growth of the family group of a dwelling that was originally isolated. In the Tula area, this could be the case of site Types 7, 11, and 5, but not Types 1 and 2, and especially not the concentrated sites with ceremonial structures, which must have represented instances of intermediate control between the central power of the state and the rural population, and which chronologically appear to be contemporary with or even earlier than part of the dispersed occupation of the area, and it is very likely that Types 1 and 2 represent the commencement of the colonization process of the city's sustaining area.

The fact that most of the sites correspond to various forms of dispersed population does not mean that the dispersed settlement constituted most of the population of the area. However, it is obvious, given the general nature of the data available, that it is not possible to make reliable estimates of the rural population of the area. But if the Sanders, Parsons, and Santley (1979) criteria for demographic calculation for the Basin of Mexico sites and Healan's (1989a) criteria for the urban zone of Tula are considered for indicative and comparison purposes, then we have some very general estimates of the population of the area during this period.

Sanders, Parsons, and Santley (1979:37–39) propose, based on ethnohistorical research and studies of the current settlement of the Teotihuacan Valley, a methodology that correlates settlement type and the density of surface archeological material in a given area with approximate estimates of the number of inhabitants. The "Moderate Occupation" and "Moderate-to-Heavy or Heavy" categories proposed by these authors (p. 39) that estimate an occupation of 25 to 50 persons per hectare and 50 to 100 persons per hectare, respectively, were considered for the approximate estimates of the Type 1 and 2 sites. Although in the Tula region the size of the majority of these sites varies between 10 and 20 hectares, and there are some sites covering 25 hectares, an average of 15 hectares for both site types was considered, but it should be considered, as mentioned before, that the sites are not precisely demarcated and there have been no detailed surface studies.

In reference to the sites with a specifically determined number of habitation structures (Types 3, 19, 5, 16, 7, and 11), Healan's (1989a:143) estimates for the El Canal excavation House Groups were considered, which were mainly based on ethnohistorical studies of the sixteenth century, ethnographic studies on the use of space in family units in different cultures, and the distribution of space and of defined activity areas in the units excavated.

Healan's proposals for the West Group and the Central Group were considered in the estimates for this kind of site. In the first case, he proposes that the complex formed by three single-family houses was inhabited by twenty-one or twenty-two people, according to his highest estimation, while the Central Group, which is much larger and more complex, would be occupied by a minimum of thirty-three to forty-one persons.

Although the unit excavated in Tepetitlán was very similar to the Central Group studied by Healan, because of its size and internal structure, and the fact that, as mentioned before, the structures located in the area are rather similar in terms of dimensions and surface characteristics to the Tepetitlán House Group, a figure of only twenty persons as a general average was considered for the habitation structures of the area. However, since this figure is really rather conservative, a second column with the results obtained by using the estimate of thirty-three persons per House Group was used for comparative purposes. The latter figure is Healan's lower estimate for a more complex habitation group (the Central Group) (Table 7.5).

Although the estimates given in the tables are very general and speculative, they provide approximate figures that between 65 percent and 80 percent of the population of the area lived in concentrated sites, between 7 percent and 12 percent in what we have called the Intermediate Sites (dispersed-nucleated), and only 12 percent to 23 percent of the inhabitants would make up the dispersed population (Table 7.5). This population distribution is surely

Table 7.5—Estimated Population for the Tula Area (Part 1)

	Site Type	No.	%	Moderate population 25–50/h	Dense population 50–100/h
1	Concentrated sites (15h)	15	4.93	5,625–11,250	11,250–22,500
2	Concentrated sites with a ceremonial structure (15h)	11	3.62	4,125–8,250	8,250–16,500
3	Habitational structure	86	28.28	1,720*	2,838†
5	Complex of two habitational structures	41	13.48	1,640	2,706
19	Complex of two structures: one habitational, one ceremonial	7	2.30	140	231
16	Complex of two isolated habitational structures	7	2.30	280	462
7	Complex of 3–5 habitational structures (average: 4)	24	7.89	1,920	3,168
11	Complex of 6–7 habitational structures (average: 6.5)	7	2.30	910	1,502
15	Zones of dispersed occupation	106	34.87	—	—
	Total	304		16,360–26,110	30,407–49,907

* 20 persons/structure; † 33 persons/structure. (Calculations based on Healan 1989.)

Table 7.5—Estimated Population for the Tula Area (Part 2)

	Moderate population 25–50/h	Dense population 50–100/h
CONCENTRATED SITES		
Type 1 (15 h)	5,625–11,250	11,250–22,500
Type 2 (15h)	4,125–8,250	8,250–16,500
Type 11	910	1,502
Total	10,660–20,410*	21,002–40,502†
INTERMEDIATE SITES		
Type 7	1,920	3,168
Total	1,920	3,168
DISPERSED SITES		
Type 3	1,720	2,838
Type 19	140	231
Type 5	1,640	2,706
Type 16	280	462
Total	3,780	6,237
Total Estimated Population	16,360–26,110	30,407–49,907

* 20 persons/structure; † 33 persons/structure. (Calculations based on Healan 1989.)

related to the forms of land use, cultivation and crop types, land tenure, the class structure, and the different hierarchies of the sites.

Clusters

Lastly, a series of larger units called clusters were defined that encompass various sites (Fig. 7.20). These constitute categories that are superior to sites, that apparently have an ecological significance, and perhaps are units employing the same types of land use. Nevertheless, the criteria for the definition of clusters are not so clear nor so uniform as those used in the definition of sites. Taking into account that in various cases clusters include at least one site with ceremonial structures, it is probable that some of them represent major political-administrative units, forming part of some kind of hierarchy in the settlement system of the area that perhaps reflects some institutions in the general sociopolitical and economic structure of Tula, as will be analyzed in Chapter 10. A list of clusters is included in the Appendix.

POTENTIAL IRRIGATION: EARLY POSTCLASSIC

As was observed in Chapter 2, the investigation of the traditional irrigation systems in the study area was fundamental for knowing the regional potential for this factor, and it is very probable that the majority of the irrigation systems shown in Fig. 2.10 were functioning since pre-Hispanic times. However, here we have considered as potential irrigation during the Early Postclassic only those systems associated with sites having occupations of this period. Figure 7.21 basically includes the traditional irrigation systems associated with those towns that have been continuously occupied from that period to date. Since the topography of the area largely conditions the possibility of locating dikes and channels, it is very likely that the pre-Hispanic hydraulic works were similar in terms of location and characteristics to the traditional systems recorded on this map, some of which still operate.

From a technological point of view, these hydraulic works are very simple and different from those systems associated with haciendas with aqueducts, arches, and other architectural elements characteristic of the colonial period. Most of the irrigation systems included in this map (Fig. 7.21) correspond to the towns mentioned in sixteenth-century records as sites with irrigation agriculture. Such is the case of Atengo, Atitalaquia, Atotonilco, Tezontepec, Tepeji de Río, Tepetitlán (?), Tlamaco, Tula, San Lorenzo, Xipacoya, San Pedro Nextlalpan, Santa Maria Illucan, and Xochitlán, quoted in the *Relaciones* published by Del Paso y Troncoso (1905–1948:1, 2, 21, 22, 209, 223, 226, 289, 301, 166 and 194) and in the *Libro de Tasaciones* (González de Cosío 1952:88, 89, 535). These references are very important, if it is accepted that the data contained in these sources generally reflect the situation of the area in the period immediately before the Conquest.

An example is San Lorenzo Xipacoya, whose lands were until recently irrigated by the Zanja de los Tres Pueblos, along the length of which there is occupation corresponding to the Early and Late Postclassic. On one hand, the topographic conditions of the Tula River limit the possibilities of dikes further downstream, and on the other hand, in order for these lands to be irrigated it is necessary to have a channel with a similar course to this ditch. Thus, it is very likely that the pre-Hispanic channel would follow a similar contour level to that of the current ditch. Similar situations arise in the other towns mentioned.

In the pre-Hispanic city's intermediate environs there are various points of potential irrigation. This is the case of the earthen ditch located to the east of the city, which if it had been irrigated it would have been by means of an extension of the Zanja de los Tres Pueblos, shown on the map with a dotted line. On the other hand, with dikes located at points similar to those of the Tres Pueblos, Puente Colgante, and San Andrés it would be possible to irrigate lands on the right bank of the Tula River from San Miguel Vindhó to San Lorenzo, and on the left bank from the Puente Colgante to San Francisco Bojay, as well as the end part of the meadowland of the Rosas River where this river joins the Tula. This last stretch is still irrigated, as in colonial times, by means of the system controlled by Xochititlán, which, as indicated in Chapter 2, is various kilometers long and covers seven different towns, including Tula.

The map also includes the traditional irrigation systems, called La Romera or Zanja del Correo Mayor, controlled by the Chingú hacienda, by which the alluvial valley was irrigated during the colonial period. The characteristics of this system and its association with various Classic and Tollan Phase sites suggests an irrigation system with a similar course to what existed in those periods.

The areas that could have been irrigated by means of the irrigation systems included in Figure 7.21 are generally just narrow strips of lands along the length of rivers. According to our calculations, the total potentially irrigable land in the area during this period is approximately 3,000 hectares. This estimate does not include those Colonial irrigation systems associated with haciendas, whose course and construction techniques make it unlikely that they date back to the pre-Hispanic period. Nor does the map include those systems that, even though

Figure 7.20. Early Postclassic: Clusters.

Figure 7.21. Potential irrigation zones for the Tollan Phase.

they constitute simple constructions from a technological point of view, are not associated with Early Postclassic settlement. Finally, our calculations on the amount of potentially irrigable land during the apogee the pre-Hispanic city is somewhat conservative.

Sanders, Parsons, and Santley (1979:396–400), based on our earlier study, proposed that a substantial amount of the Tula region could be permanently irrigated. These researchers calculate that approximately 10,000 hectares of land could have been irrigated by means of various systems that tapped the permanent water sources of the area. They also propose that at least half of the population that occupied the area and the city during the apogee of Tula, which they estimate at 120,000 inhabitants (pp. 41–143), could have been sustained with the production of these irrigable lands. More recently, Nichols and Frederick (1993:135), in a study on pre-Hispanic canals and *chinampas* in the north of the Basin of Mexico, restate this figure, indicating that this land area could have been irrigated in the Tula area during the Early Postclassic.

The fundamental differences between our estimates and those of Sanders and his collaborators lies in the fact they consider most of the zones irrigated during the nineteenth century as potentially irrigable land during the Tollan Phase, without taking into account the technological limitations implied in some of these systems in pre-Hispanic times and the specific distribution of settlement during the Early Postclassic. We need to take into account the capacity of the people to build smaller and less monumental dams upstream on the rivers to distribute the water in that area. They probably did not achieve the maximum figure of 10,000 hectares with pre-Hispanic techniques. In summary, what we can say is that the total amount of irrigatable land in the survey area probably varied from a minimum of 3,000 hectares to an absolute maximum of 10,000 hectares, and that the actual figure under irrigation was somewhere between these two estimates.

8

The Tollan Complex in the Tula Area

The presence of diagnostic pottery types of the Tollan Complex in Tula's rural environment permitted, in the first place, the definition of the sites that formed the hinterland of the ancient city, that is, those sites with Tollan Phase occupation, which therefore were contemporaneous with the city's apogee. In additon, we attempted to determine if the Tollan Complex as defined with its numerous types in the Tula urban zone (Cobean 1990) was also present in the rural sites of the area, and what were these types' specific forms of distribution, statistical tendencies, and variations. These investigations attempted to detect patterns of differential consumption between the city and its rural population, that is, different ceramic consumption, based on tendencies or types found exclusively in urban contexts, or other types used only by the rural population, along with studying variations in ceramic consumption between different kinds of rural sites.

In this sense, it is important to take into account that the existence of a large urban center implies, on the one hand, the massive, very uniform production of ceramics that we know is the case for diverse types of the Tollan Complex, as well as an established market and supply system for consumers in the city and the hinterland. A state structure also implies the existence of social classes with differential access to production, wealth, and the consumption of goods by the different groups of the population who formed Toltec society. The inhabitants in the city and the rural sites of the sustaining area constituted integral parts of this society, and ceramics, along with other goods for daily use or sumptuary functions, can be important indicators of this class structure.

It is evident that analyses based almost exclusively on surface survey samples will indicate only general tendencies, and that various kinds of excavations are required to corroborate these tendencies and their significance. However, it is worth emphasizing, as was observed in Chapter 1, that some types of surface sampling showed tendencies similar to those of excavated materials with regard to the ceramic types represented, and their proportions and percentages. This is especially evident for the obsidian workshop excavated in the city by Healan (1986) and the rural habitation unit excavated in Tepetitlán (Cobean and Mastache 1999; Moncayo 1999) (see Figs. 1.5 and 1.6). In addition to the samples derived from the General Surface Collections in the area, we consider the materials derived from intensive surface survey in various rural sites and in the city, along with excavated materials from urban habitational structures and the Tepetitlán domestic unit.

The information concerning the frequencies of each of the Tollan Complex types identified in the surface and excavation samples is presented here in general graphs, and the specific frequencies along with type distribution maps are presented in Mastache 1996a.

DIAGNOSTIC EARLY TOLLAN PHASE CERAMIC TYPES

Surveys and excavations, both in the region and in Tula's urban zone, have provided the basis for identifying at least three ceramic types that are useful in detecting early Tollan Phase occupations (ca. A.D. 900–950): Mazapa Red on Brown, Joroba Orange on Cream, and Manuelito Plain Brown. The first two types are principally diagnostic for the preceding Terminal Corral Phase when they are associated with Coyotlatelco sphere pottery, but they also occur in small percentages in early Tollan Phase assemblages (Cobean and Mastache 1989).

The INAH and Missouri Project investigations at Tula and in the region have produced some disconcerting facts concerning the famous "Wavy-Line Mazapan Red on Brown" (our Mazapa Red on Brown) pottery, which is commonly used as a key diagnostic type or horizon marker for the Mazapan Phase, sometimes referred to as "Late Toltec" in the Basin of Mexico and assumed to be contemporaneous with Tula's Early Postclassic city (Linné 1934; Vaillant 1938; McCullough 1966; Evans 1975; Sanders, Parsons, and Santley 1979:463–464;

Koehler 1986). In Tula's urban zone, Mazapa Red on Brown is partially coeval and overlaps with Coyotlatelco pottery, but generally is so rare there and elsewhere in our region that it is not very useful as a horizon marker by itself. Our data from Tula's urban zone and the regional survey suggest that the period of highest frequency for Mazapa Red on Brown mainly predates the major expansion of the Early Postclassic city during the Tollan Phase, although it is present in small quantities in pure Tollan Phase occupations (Figs. 8.1, 8.2A, B, and C). In addition, Toltec Red on Brown, also called "Sloppy" Red on Brown (Koehler 1986) or Toltec Red on Buff (Sanders, Parsons, and Santley 1979:464), is very rare in the Tula region and in Tula itself, although it is an important component of the Mazapan Complex in the Basin of Mexico.

As Diehl (1971) and Healan, Kerley, and Bey (1983:142–145) have suggested, the scarcity of Mazapa Red on Brown at Tula could be due to geographical as well as chronological factors in that this type may have been extensively traded only in the Basin of Mexico, perhaps with the Teotihuacan Valley as its major production area. Given our evidence for its relative unimportance in the Tula region, however, Mazapa Red on Brown should be used with considerable caution in Central Mexico as an indicator of occupations coeval with Tula's Tollan Phase city. If this type largely predates the period of the Tollan Phase elsewhere in the Central Highlands, as it appears to at Tula, then serious misinterpretations would result from using it as a horizon marker for Tula's apogee. As described below, Jara Polished Orange—called "Naranja a Brochazos" by Acosta (1956–1957)—is one of the key Tollan Phase pottery types and a much better diagnostic for marking Tula's Early Postclassic apogee than Mazapa Red on Brown. It is significant that the late Tollan Phase habitation unit excavated at Tepetitlán in the northern region recovered only a tiny percentage of Mazapa (Moncayo 1999) (Fig. 8.4).

Joroba Orange on Cream is present in small quantities in sites in many different sectors of the rural area, and its importance as a diagnostic for identifying rural sites that correspond to the early

THE TOLLAN COMPLEX IN THE TULA AREA

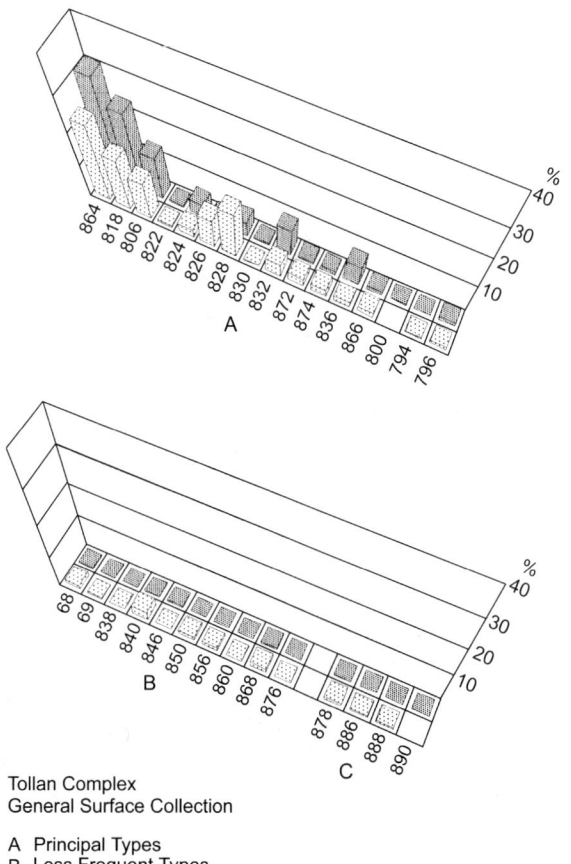

Figure 8.1. Tollan Complex General Surface Collection, city and hinterland.
68. Mazapan Figurines, **69.** Drain Tubes, **794.** Joroba Orange on Cream, **796.** Mazapa Red on Brow, **800.** Tolteca Red on Buff, **806.** Macana Red on Brown, **818.** Jara Polished Orange, **822.** Ira Stamped Orange, **824.** Proa Polished Cream, **826.** Sillón Incised, **828.** Rebato Polished Red, **830.** Manuelito Plain Brown, **832.** Toza Smoothed, Brown, **836.** Blanco Levantado (Watermarked), **840.** Abra Coarse Brown: Abra Variety, **850.** Abra Coarse Brown: General, **856.** Alicia Openworked, **860.** Tarea Polished Red, **864.** Soltura Smoothed Red, **866.** Bordo Red on Brown, **868.** Mendrugo Semi-Smoothed, **872.** Acta Polished Red: Acta Variety, **874.** Acta Polished Red: Bowl Variety, **876.** Unnamed Black on Orange *olla*, **878.** Tohil Plumbate, **886.** Huastec ceramics, **888.** Gulf Coast ceramics, **890.** North and West ceramics, **896.** Maya ceramics, **902.** Imported unidentified ceramic, **698.** Local exotic ceramics, **696.** Incised Oranges, **702.** Sapo Brown, **674.** Unidentified Bordo Red on Brown, **666.** Unnamed Incised Brown *olla*, **846.** Abra Coarse Brown: Plain Hourglass Variety, **838.** Abra Coarse Brown: Cylinder Variety.

Tollan Complex
General Surface Collection

A Principal Types
B Less Frequent Types
C Foreign Types
▓ Hinterland
░ City

Tollan Phase is especially supported by the results from sites surveyed with the Intensive Sample A methodolgy, which verified the existence of a series of early occupations (Fig. 8.3). Joroba is relatively common in the early Tollan Phase contexts of the obsidian workshop excavations, and it is rare at the late Tollan House Group at Tepetitlán (Fig. 8.4). A recent excavation of a kiln and houses at a workshop in what probably was a potters *barrio* in the eastern urban zone found direct evidence for the production of Joroba during the early Tollan Phase (Hernández et al. 1999) and confirmed Cobean's (1978, 1990) original proposal that Joroba was the prototype for the principal orange-and-cream types of the Tollan Phase, including Proa Polished Cream, Jara Polished Orange, and Ira Stamped Orange, which are present in the workshop in transitional forms. The ceramic workshop excavation materials also contain evidence that Joroba may be a copy of imported Gulf Coast orange-and-cream wares (Hernández et al. 1999).

Manuelito Plain Brown is useful in identifying early Tollan Phase occupations, especially when it occurs together with Joroba or Mazapa or some early varieties of Proa Polished Cream. Manuelito first occurs in small quantities during the Terminal Corral Phase. It is most common during the early part of the Tollan Phase, as is indicated by its high frequency in the obsidian workshop excavation and its relatively low frequency in the Late Tollan Tepetitlán excavated assemblage (Fig. 8.4). Manuelito possesses sufficient variations in attributes through time so that it should soon be possible to define early and late varieties of this type, making it more useful in subdividing the Tollan Phase.

The combined distributions of Mazapa, Joroba, and Manuelito in the region indicate that during the early Tollan Phase expansion of Tula's city, the same

THE TOLLAN COMPLEX IN THE TULA AREA

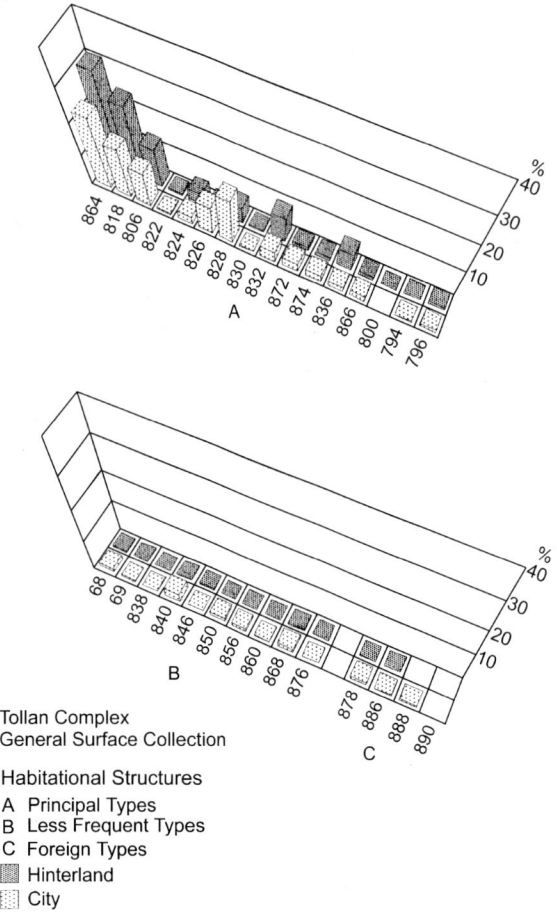

Figure 8.2A. Tollan Complex General Surface Collection, habitational structures, city and hinterland.

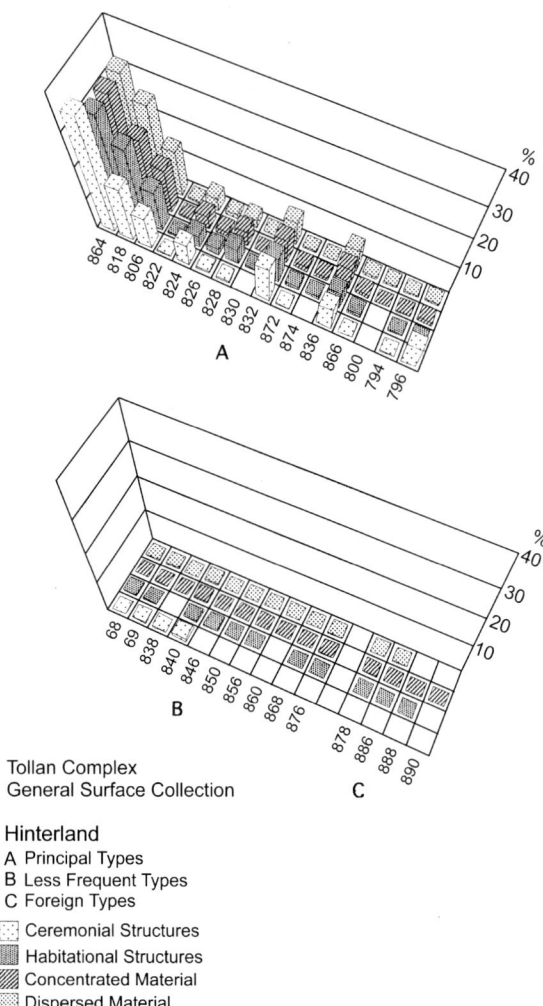

Figure 8.2B. Tollan Complex General Surface Collection.

rural zones were occupied that afterward would become the core of the hinterland during Tula's apogee, but these early occupations were less intensive than those of the later Tollan Phase populations. The fact that the same ecological zones were occupied in the initial Tollan Phase as those of Tula's later zenith suggests that the Toltec state employed the same system for exploiting the region's resources from the beginning of the Tollan Phase.

We believe that the ocupation and the colonization of the outlying region correspond to the two stages of growth and renovation that the city experienced during this period, that is, the Early Tollan Phase "Toltec A" urban orientation grid followed by the Late Tollan Phase expansion associated with the "Toltec B" urban orientation system (see Chapter 5, and Mastache and Crespo 1982). This colonization process is not fully investigated, and should be better understood when the regional cultural chronology is defined. Recent investigations in the city, especially at Tula Chico, suggest that direct antecedents for a number of key early Tollan Complex ceramic types exist in the preceding Terminal Corral Complex (Cobean and Suárez 1989; Cobean 2000). The better

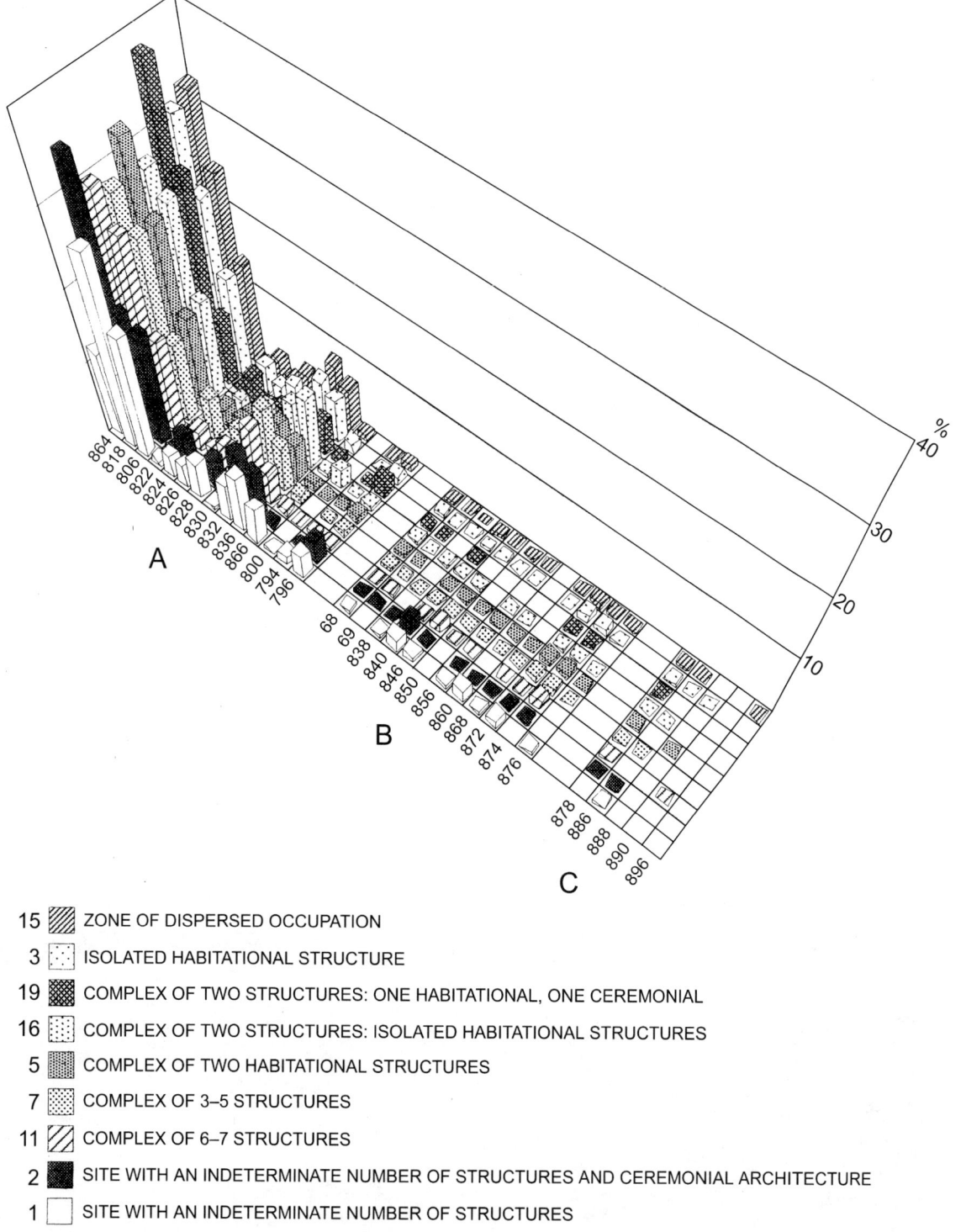

Figure 8.2C. Tollan Complex General Surface Collection, hinterland site types.

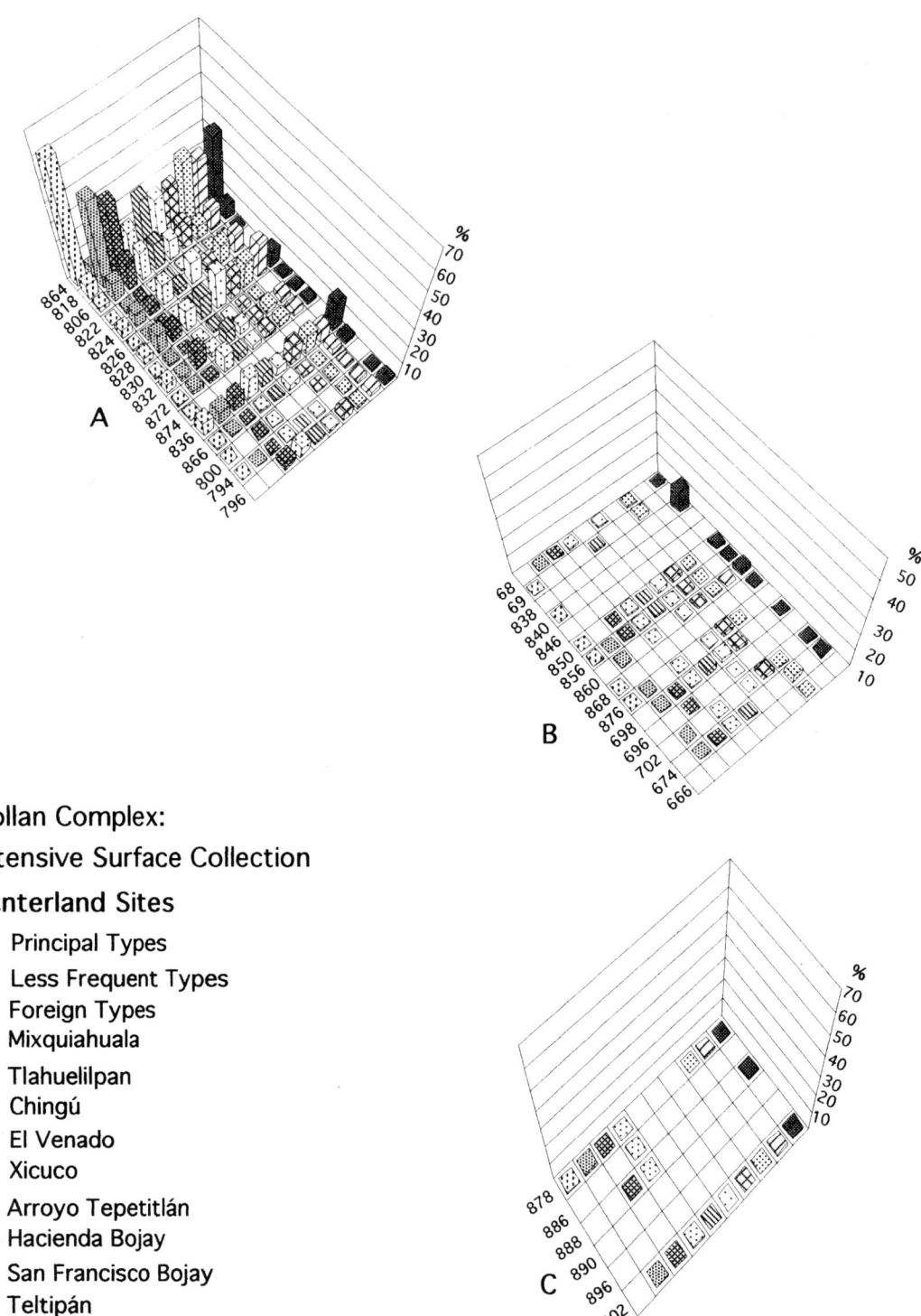

Figure 8.3. Tollan Complex Intensive Surface Collection.

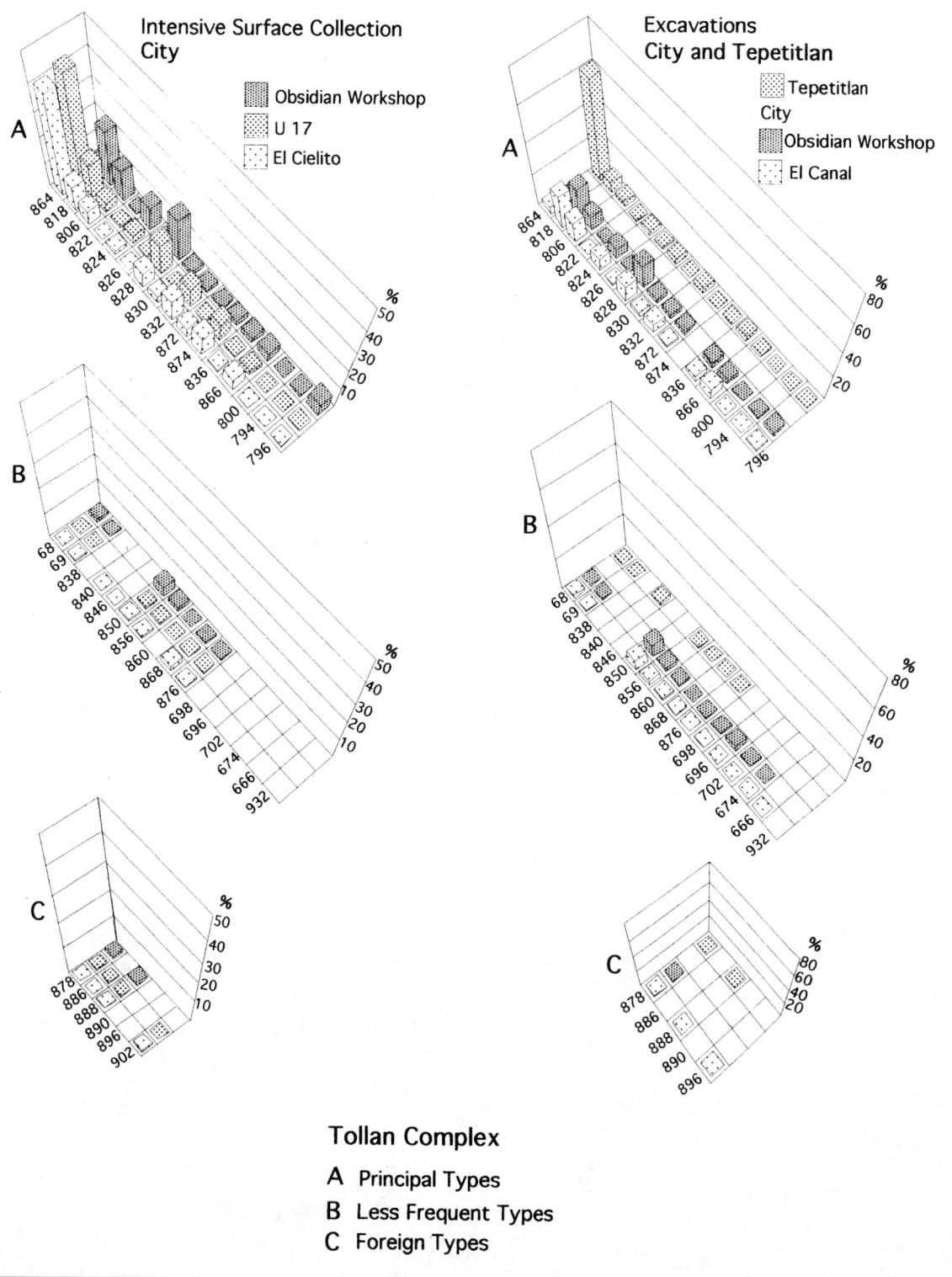

Figure 8.4. Tollan Complex Intensive Surface Collection and excavations.

definition of these early types, which are diagnostic of the Early Tollan Phase, together with Macana Red on Brown, which is more frequent in the initial contexts for this phase, should help identify the first stages of the expansion of the Toltec state in the area.

DIAGNOSTIC TYPES FOR THE TOLLAN PHASE IN THE AREA

The analysis of the materials from urban contexts and from the sites that made up the rural hinterland of the Tollan Phase city showed that basically the Tollan ceramic complex is present in the area in the same form as it was defined by Cobean (1978, 1990) for the city. These investigations permitted us to determine the approximate limits of this core rural hinterland and distinguish it from a second level of regional interaction that was composed of the Basin of Mexico and other surrounding zones, which without doubt constituted integral components of the sustaining area for the Toltec state, and were tied economically and politically with Tula. In these regions, diagnostic types of the Tollan Complex have been identified, but in different assemblages with other frequencies and characteristics. This second ring of outlying interaction zones is, in general terms, equivalent to what Cobean calls "spheres" of the Tollan Complex, which we will refer to later on.

The Tollan Complex (Fig. 3.1), as it was defined for the city, is composed of approximately twenty types, of which nine types constitute the central diagnostics for this complex: these are Jara Polished Orange, Macana Red on Brown, Rebato Polished Red, Proa Polished Cream, Sillon Incised, Toza Smoothed Brown, Abra Coarse Brown, Blanco Levantado, and Soltura Smoothed Red. These key types are present in almost any rural or urban domestic context in the area in more or less similar proportions. Many of the other types are equally diagnostic but less frequent, and some are more characteristic of urban contexts than rural ones and vice versa. Here, initially, we will refer to the first group of diagnostic types.

Macana Red on Brown is a crucial diagnostic for the Tollan Phase, both in the city and in the area. It has been divided into several varieties that have chronological significance, especially in the case of the proposed early varieties (Cobean 1990). Macana is present in 65 percent of the Tula-area Collection Units and in 81 percent of the urban Collection Units. It is less common in Late Tollan Phase occupations than at the beginning of the Tollan Phase, as can be seen in the differences in the percentages for this type in the excavation at Tepetitlán (Late Tollan) and the urban obsidian workshop that is mainly Early Tollan (see Figs. 1.5 and 1.6).

Macana is most common in the Type 2 rural sites (sites with ceremonial architecture), which often appear to have long occupation sequences that would correlate well with a high frequency for this type because they have Early Tollan Phase occupations. It is the third most common Tollan type in the General Surface Collection, but it has more variability in the Intensive Surface Collection's percentages. Macana also is an important marker for Tollan sphere occupations in Central Mexico beyond the Tula region, being widely reported for Early Postclassic sites in the Basin of Mexico (Vaillant 1938; Tolstoy 1958:42; Blanton and Parsons 1971; Sanders, Parsons, and Santley 1979:462–463), and existing in areas as distant as Guanajuato (Braniff 1972:323) and the Valley of Puebla (Müller 1970).

Macana, Jara, and Soltura are the most frequent types in all kinds of occupations in the Tula region for this period. The distribution of Jara Polished Orange in the area is nearly identical to the total distribution of Tollan Phase occupations. This type is present in 73 percent of the 1,604 Tula-area URs. In Healan's use of correspondence analysis to determine the patterns of interaction among the region's ceramic assemblages, presented at the end of this chapter, Jara was determined to be a key diagnostic type for Tollan Phase occupations. Like Macana, Jara is most common in the Type 2 sites, which are among the largest rural settlements. It constitutes 26.76 percent of the ceramic assemblage of the Type 2 sites and over 20 percent of the sherds from Types 3, 5, 7, 11, 15, and 19.

Even though Jara is present in the Tollan Complex for approximately two centuries, this type apparently did not change much through time in terms of its major attributes, and so far cannot be subdivided into "early" and "late" varieties. However, as mentioned, Jara is much more common in the region during the Late Tollan Phase than at the beginning of the Tollan Phase. Moncayo (1999) reports some differences in paste and other attributes between Jara varieties in Tepetitlán and the urban zone, which suggests that most of the Jara at Tepetitlán was produced at different workshops from those in the city, where there are both surface and excavated materials indicating the production of this type in the ceramic workshop *barrio* (Hernández et al. 1999).

In excavations of Late Tollan Phase urban deposits, Jara often constitutes nearly 50 percent of the decorated pottery. Years ago, Acosta (1945:56; 1956–1957:91) recognized the importance of "Naranja a Brochazos" (his name for the Jara type) as the best chronological marker for Tula's apogee, but his findings were not sufficiently appreciated by other archaeologists.

Jara Polished Orange is a key diagnostic for the Tollan sphere in the Basin of Mexico (Tolstoy 1958:51; Sanders, Parsons, and Santley 1979:465; Whalen and Parsons 1982:432), northern Morelos (Kenneth Hirth, personal communication), and northeast Guanajuato (Braniff 1972:323). This type has been especially well documented in the Teotihuacan Valley as diagnostic of the Atlatongo Complex, which William Sanders (personal communication) correlates with the incorporation of the northern Basin of Mexico into the Toltec state.

Ira Stamped Orange is basically a stamped version of Jara. It is never very common in any excavation or survey context in the area, but when it is present constitutes a clear diagnostic for the Tollan Phase. The recently excavated urban-zone ceramics workshop produced Ira, among other Tollan types, and numerous molds for making the characteristic Ira stamped designs were recovered in this excavation (Hernández et al. 1999: fig. 18).

The distribution map for Proa Polished Cream probably in part identifies Early Tollan Phase rural occupations because this type is more common at the beginning of the Tollan Phase than afterward, although one or more varieties of this type are present until the end of the Tollan Phase. Proa probably was the prototype for Jara Polished Orange (Cobean 1990). The Early Tollan Phase ceramic workshop producing Proa and Jara, recently excavated in the city's ceramic workshop *barrio* (Hernández et al. 1999), recovered materials that indicate that Proa, like Joroba, may have originated in Tula as an imitation of Gulf Coast cream ceramics, as mentioned above. The much greater occurrence of Proa in the Early Tollan contexts of the obsidian workshop excavation as compared to the Late Tollan Tepetitlán excavation supports the chronology for this type proposed here (Fig. 8.4).

Proa is most common in rural sites of Type 7 (complex of 3–5 structures) and also is fairly common in the Type 1 sites (Fig. 8.2C), but it never is as common as Jara Polished Orange in any site. Proa is an excellent marker for the Central Mexican Tollan sphere, occuring throughout the Basin of Mexico (Vaillant cited by Tolstoy 1958:51; Hicks and Nicholson 1962:502; Evans 1975; Sanders, Parsons, and Santley 1979:465) and occuring as far away as Guanajuato (Braniff 1972:323) and San Luis Potosí (Crespo 1976:43; Braniff 1975).

Sillon Incised is one of the most interesting pottery types found in the Tula region. It is mainly of local manufacture, but is of much better quality (fine decoration, fine paste, excellent surface finish, few firing defects) than most locally made Tollan Phase ceramics. Sillon almost surely is a copy of Gulf Coast or Maya Fine Orange tradition ceramics. Mastache and Crespo (1976, 1982), in their survey of the urban potters *barrio,* located a group of workshops producing Sillon. The recently excavated workshop in the north of this pottery production zone made large amounts of Sillon, among other wares (Hernández et al. 1999). The materials from Tula's pottery workshops are still being analyzed, but in the preliminary studies significant amounts of Huastec (Period V: Early Postclassic) incised fine-paste ceramics have been identified, very similar to a type described by Ekholm (1944: fig.21 R-4) from Las Flores, Tamaulipas. These Huastec ceramics probably were used by Tula's potters as models in the production of some varieties of Sillon Incised, and elsewhere we have proposed that some of these artisans may have been ethnic Huastecs (Cobean and Mastache 1985).

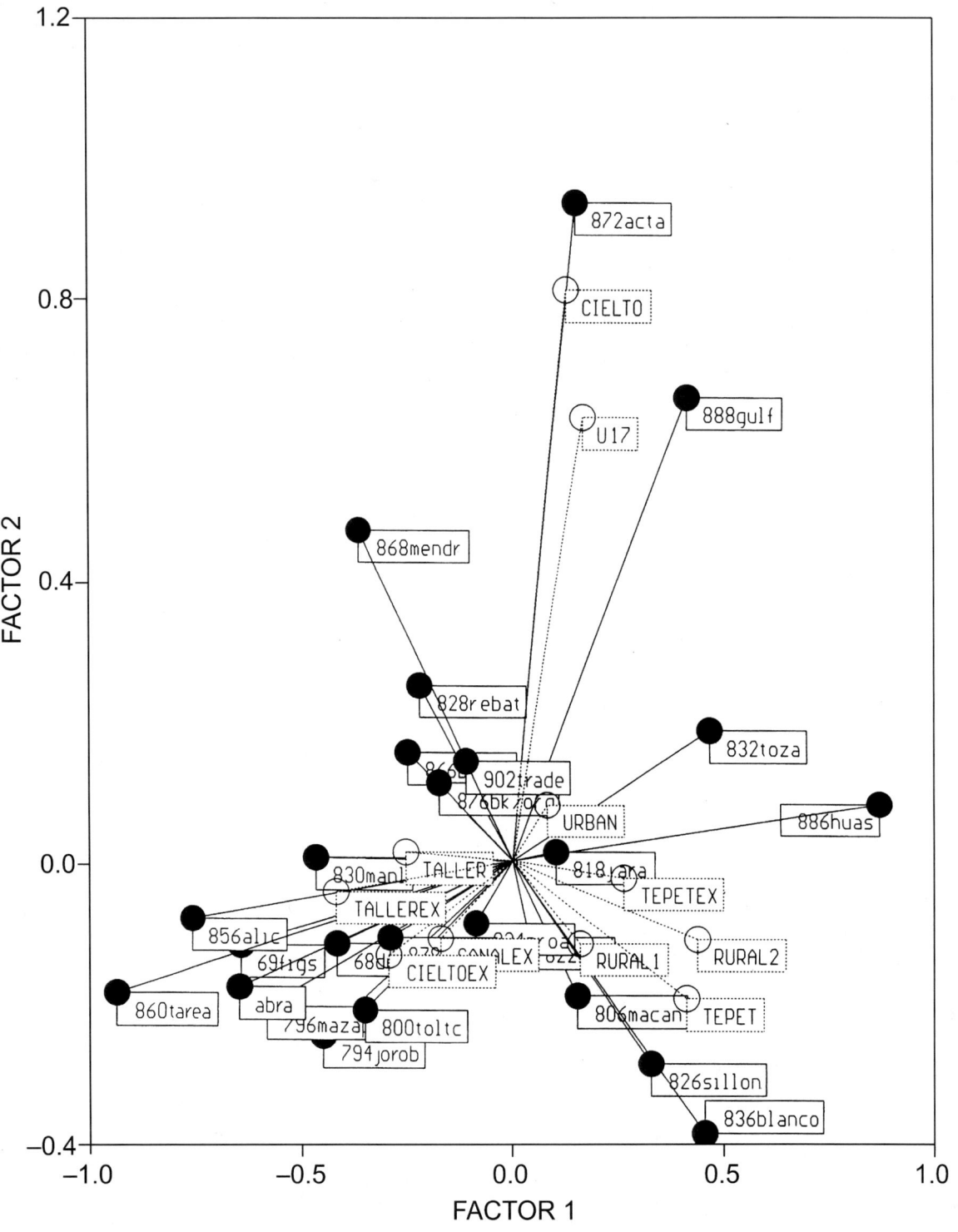

Figure 8.5. Biplot of Factor 1 (ordinate) and Factor 2 (abscissa) from the correspondence analysis of the data in Table 8.4. Solid circles denote ceramic types; hollow circles denote sites.

Cobean (1990) originally proposed that Sillon Incised probably constituted a "luxury" ceramic in Tula often associated with high-status social groups, and he predicted that it would be more common in the city than in the rural sites. This is not always the case, as can be seen in Figure 8.4. In addition, Healan's study using correspondence analysis showed Sillon to be apparently an important diagnostic for rural Tollan Phase ceramic assemblages, and less significant for defining the urban Tollan Complex (Fig. 8.5). It may be that precisely because Sillon Incised was locally made, it served as a status item for the region's rural elites who did not have the economic resources to acquire exotic imported wares, such as Plumbate, as the urban elite groups did.

Sillon is most common in Type 2 rural sites (Fig. 8.2C), where it constitutes 3.29 percent of the total sampled ceramics. Type 2 sites constitute those of highest hierarchy in the area. We propose that they probably functioned as *cabeceras* or administrative centers, being likely residence zones for rural elites who were probably consumers of Sillon as a "luxury" ware. Sillon shows a wide distribution in rural sites, but appears to be rare in Early Postclassic occupations outside the Tula region (Cobean 1990:382), although it exists in some nearby Tollan sphere sites in the northern Basin of Mexico (Jeffrey Parsons, personal communication). More aspects concerning Sillon Incised are referred to in the following section on Rebato bowls.

Rebato Polished Red is a common diagnostic type for the Tollan Complex in the region. It appears only to occur in areas very near Tula, such as the neighboring Ajacuba Valley to the east (Hortensia de Vega, personal communication), and does not seem to be present in Early Postclassic occupations in nearby sectors of the Basin of Mexico to the south (Jeffrey Parsons, personal communication). In the city's ceramics-production *barrio* workshops making Rebato, bowls were found in the surveys of Mastache and Crespo (1976, 1982) and in recent excavations (Hernández et al. 1999). Moncayo (1999) identified a large variety of Rebato at Tepetitlán that possibly was produced in rural workshops.

As we mentioned in Hernández et al. (1999), it is surprising that on the basis of excavations in Tula's pottery workshop zone, it is clear that the same craftsmen who made the probable "luxury" ware Sillon Incised also produced Rebato. In the excavated workshop, large quantities of waster sherds and broken vessels of both types were found in the same contexts, along with some "transitional" vessels that share attributes of both types on the same bowl (pp. 80–81). Thus the same urban workshop produced the finest locally made pottery along with a rather coarse utility ware and several other common domestic types. This was a surprise because we originally expected the workshops making Sillon to be specialized only for this type, especially because its fine paste is so different from that of other Tula types, including Rebato.

The chief function for Rebato probably was as a common dish for serving and eating food. It also is a fairly frequent offering in Tollan Phase human burials, where these bowls probably were buried holding food for the dead individual. It is interesting that Rebato bowls were not part of the great group of Tollan Phase vessels that Acosta (1945:35–37) recovered in a storage area on the north edge of the Palacio Quemado, even though numerous examples of "domestic" ceramics such as Macana, Jara, Ira, and Toza were present among these vessels. Perhaps Rebato, which is undecorated and often badly fired, was too unrefined for the ritual meals and other activities of the elite groups using the Palacio Quemado. Rebato is one of the few important pottery types at Tula that Acosta did not describe in his reports, although it may correspond to a ceramic he calls "Pintura Roja" (1945). Acosta's omitting Rebato may be the result of his investigations being concentrated in the main precinct, excavating elite and ceremonial contexts that would not have large amounts of coarse domestic pottery like Rebato.

Rebato is present in approximately 75 percent of the rural habitational structures surveyed. It is most common (5.40 percent of the ceramics) in the Type 2 rural sites. In the Intensive Samples of some sites, Rebato occurs in very high frequencies, especially in Xicuco (19.76 percent) and Tlahuelilpan (18.21 percent). Its 15.52 percent occurence in the urban obsidian workshop excavation also is unusually high (Fig. 8.4). The General Sample surface collections suggest that Rebato is significantly more common in the city (almost 15 percent of the total sherds) than in the rural occupations (about 5 percent of the sherds) (Fig. 8.2A).

Apparently its major attributes did not change much during the Tollan Phase, and no attempt has been made to subdivide this type into early and late varieties. There exists a rare early prototype for Rebato in some urban Terminal Corral Phase contexts. These early vessels often are more brown than red, and are not as well polished as Tollan Phase examples of this type.

Toza Smoothed Brown *cazuelas* were the most common cooking vessels for both the urban and the rural people during the Tollan Phase. Sherds of this type are often found in excavations with soot on their surfaces and occasionally with remains of burned food, especially *pozole*-like maize kernels. Toza is one of the most frequent types in rural sites, occuring in about 80 percent of the region's habitation structures. These vessels are most common in rural site Types 7 and 11 (complexes of between 3–7 structures) where they constitute 10–11 percent of the total ceramics (Fig. 8.2C). In both the city and the region, Toza is much more common than Tollan Phase *comals* (Mendrugo Semi-Smoothed), which may mean that maize cooked in Toza *cazuelas* (as a *pozole* broth or as tamales?) was more common in the Tula region than the cooking of maize in the form of tortillas.

Several workshops producing Toza *cazuelas* were identified in the area to the south of Cerro Xicuco (Chapter 10), and no doubt there were urban workshops for this type, although none have been identified yet. Toza is very diagnostic for Tollan Complex occupations within the Tula area, but does not seem to occur in significant amounts in the Basin of Mexico and other nearby regions. The cooking *cazuelas* or "basins" for the Mazapan and Tollan spheres in the Basin of Mexico (Second Intermediate Phase Two: Sanders, Parsons, and Santley 1979:462, fig. C.21) have a conical form and are quite different from Toza. These conical basins occur in small percentages in settlements of the southern Tula region near the Basin of Mexico and only occasionally in Tula's urban dwellings (Cobean 1990). Thus, like Rebato bowls, Toza is a very useful Tollan sphere diagnostic within the Tula region, but is not a common type in coeval sites elsewhere.

With regard to *ollas*, Soltura Smoothed Red possesses the greatest frequency and most extensive distribution of all the Tollan Complex types in the rural sites and in the city. It occurs in all rural site types in percentages between approximately 30 and 38, except for Type 2 sites where its frequency is 12.21 percent (Fig. 8.2C). The percentages for Soltura in some of the urban excavation type summaries are artificially low because not all projects recorded the body sherds for this type.

Soltura *ollas* are present in 90 percent of the Tollan habitational structures in the Tula area, and show considerable variation in form, surface finish, and paste in rural sites, probably because these vessels are so large that they could not be transported long distances, and thus were produced in numerous workshops in the region (Moncayo 1999). Soltura *ollas* in Tula's ancient city are more uniform than the rural *ollas* in terms of principal attributes, and probably were made by potters living within the urban zone. This type does not appear to be present in significant quantities in Mazapan sphere and Tollan sphere occupations in Central Mexico outside the Tula region, and even the Tollan sites in nearby sectors of the northern Basin of Mexico generally possess *olla* types that are different from Soltura (Jeffrey Parsons, personal communication; Cobean 1978).

Another important *olla* type is Blanco Levantado (also called Levantado Watermarked: Cobean 1990), which is part of an important ceramic tradition in the Bajío and west Mexico that started in the Late Formative and lasted until the Early Postclassic. Key studies of this tradition include Kelly and Braniff (1966) and Braniff (1972, 1975, 1999). The Blanco Levantado tradition does not appear in the Tula region until the Terminal Corral Phase (in very small quantities), even though nearby in the Bajío to the north, Blanco Levantado types are very common in earlier Classic occupations having red-on-brown ceramics similar to some of the types of the Tula region's La Mesa Phase (Braniff 1999).

Blanco Levantado is most common in Type 16 rural sites (complexes of two isolated habitational structures), constituting 10.45 percent of the ceramics in these settlements, and this ware also is fairly frequent (6.40 percent) in the materials for zones of dispersed occupation: Type 15 (Fig. 8.2C). The presence of Blanco Levantado in these isolated rural contexts probably is associated with zones for the cultivation of maguey, the *aguamiel* and *pulque* of which almost surely were stored in these *ollas*. Fernando Lopez (personal communication) observes that the most common form of Blanco Levantado is very similar to that of the small *ollas* that the Otomi in the Mezquital Valley (Hidalgo) still use to transport *pulque*.

In the rural sites, Blanco Levantado possesses some variations in attributes (in paste and appliqué decorations) that suggest that while probably much of this type was locally made, probably a significant portion of Blanco Levantado was imported from northern areas near the Bajío. Mastache and Crespo's (1976) survey identified a probable Tollan Phase Blanco Levantado workshop in the region near Cerro Xicuco (Fig. 10.7), but no workshops for this type have been found yet in the Tula urban zone.

Blanco Levantado *ollas* are more common in the Tula-region sites than in the city, and within the region they are most common in the extreme north—which supports the proposal that at least part of this type probably was imported from northern areas near the Bajío. The increased quantities of Bajío-style Blanco Levantado in the northern region may mark a kind of ethnic frontier between Central Mexico and the Bajío. The high frequency of this type in the north also may be the result of there being more maguey (and *pulque*) cultivation in this part of the area.

The correspondence analysis of the ceramic assemblages concludes that Blanco Levantado (together with Macana Red on Brown and Sillon Incised) constitutes one of the three most diagnostic types for differentiating the rural Tollan Complex from the urban Tollan materials and is more characteristic of the rural complex. Blanco Levantado *ollas* also occur in Mazapan sphere and Tollan sphere occupations in the Basin of Mexico (Cobean 1990; Tolstoy 1958:35, 54–55; Mayer-Oakes 1959:339; Hicks and Nicholson 1962:502; Koehler 1962:56–58).

A final central diagnostic for the Tollan Complex consists of Abra Coarse Brown *braseros,* which generally appear to be more common in the city than the area (Figs. 8.1, 8.2A, and 8.5). The most common form (Abra Variety: 840) was identified in 18 percent of the rural habitation structures. Abra-like spiked hourglass *braseros* are excellent markers for identifying Early Postclassic occupations coeval with the Tollan Phase in Central Mexico. A prototype spiked *brasero* is present in the Terminal Corral Complex at Tula Chico (Cobean and Suárez 1989), but it is sufficiently different in form and decoration to be distinguishable from the Abra type.

There are at least six varieties of Abra Coarse Brown *braseros* in the Tula region (Cobean 1990). The varieties with hourglass or conical forms and appliqué spikes occur in many regions during the Early Postclassic, and have been used to define elements of a Toltec horizon in Mesoamerica (Diehl 1993; Cobean and Mastache in press). Two varieties are decorated with Tlaloc (rain god) images and have been found associated with temples in the urban zone (Acosta 1956: fig. 42; Stocker 1974). In addition to their ceremonial functions, Abra *braseros* also were employed for cooking food and probably for heating rooms. In the Tepetitlán excavation, remains of Abra *braseros* were found in the house group patio associated with burned areas on the floor and food remains, thus suggesting that these *braseros* may have been used as "portable stoves" to cook food (Mastache and Cobean 1999: fig. 8.4). *Brasero* remains also were recovered in numerous domestic contexts in the El Canal excavation, including at least one example of a *brasero* (Mammiform Footed Variety) embedded in the floor of House VI, which probably functioned as a hearth (Healan 1974; Cobean 1990:429).

LESS COMMON MEMBERS OF THE TOLLAN COMPLEX

The most important tradeware of the Tollan Complex is the famous Tohil Plumbate pottery from the Guatemala-Chiapas border area (Shepard 1948; Neff and Bishop 1988). For a foreign ware, this type is surprisingly common at Tula: over five hundred sherds and several complete vessels were recovered in the Missouri Project El Canal excavations (Cobean 1990). Although Tohil Plumbate is less common in the region's rural sites and elsewhere in Central Mexico, our data suggest that when present it can be used along with Jara Polished Orange as an accurate horizon marker for Tula's Early Postclassic apogee.

In Tula's city, this type often constitutes approximately 1 percent of excavated Tollan Phase ceramic assemblages (Fig. 8.4), and in the area Plumbate represents 0.21–0.30 percent of the Surface Collection ceramics (Figs. 8.2A, B, and C and 8.3). In the excavation of one Tollan Phase House Group in Tepetitlán, fifty-five Plumbate sherds were recovered (Moncayo 1999), whereas in excavations of urban House Groups it is common to recover one or more restorable Plumbate vessels in a single house (Cobean 1990). It is probable that Tohil Plumbate trade in Mesoamerica was at least in part controlled by the Toltec state, and that the ethnic group producing Plumbate probably included Nahuatl-speaking Pipiles, who were related to sectors of Tula's population and whose migrations extended through many areas of Central America during the Early Postclassic (Fowler 1989a; Coe 1962).

The trace-element and typological analyses of Hector Neff (1984; Neff and Bishop 1988) have clarified greatly the origins and development of this tradeware in the Soconusco of Guatemala and Chiapas. In addition, an important distributional study for Plumbate in Mesoamerica was published by Fahmel Beyer (1988). Thanks to Neff's investigations, it is clear that the Soconusco, nearly 1,000 kilometers south of Tula, was the only production zone for Plumbate in Mesoamerica. Only the Tohil version (Shepard 1948) of Plumbate was massively exported to other areas in Central America and Mexico, with the period A.D. 900–1100 marking its principal life span as a tradeware (Neff and Bishop 1988). Tohil Plumbate appears to be much more common in the Tula region than other sectors of northern Mesoamerica (Cobean 1990).

Mazapan figurines constitute an important element of the Toltec horizon in Mesoamerica (Diehl 1993; Cobean and Mastache in press). They have been reported in regions as distant as Sinaloa and El Salvador (Stocker 1983; Scott 1993; Cobean 1978, 1990:505, 510; Fowler 1989a). Judging from the number of Mazapan figurine fragments recovered in the excavation of one Tollan Phase House Group at Tepetitlán (Mastache and Cobean 1999a:289–291) (Fig. 8.4), it is probable that these figurines were more common in the area than our project's Surface Collections indicate.

Both in the city and the area, these figurines were not well fired when manufactured, and they tend to erode into irregular lumps of clay when they are exposed on the surface. Over a thousand Mazapan figurine fragments were recovered from the urban El Canal excavations (Stocker 1974, 1983), although many of these were found in trash middens deposited in upper levels after the structures had been abandoned. Stocker's interpretations were that the common female Mazapan figurines at Tula often were used in curing rites. At least two Tollan Phase workshops for Mazapan figurines have been identified in Tula's city: in the northwest urban zone near the west bank of the Tula River (Stoutamire 1975; Healan and Stoutamire 1989:213, fig. 13.12) and in the pottery workshop excavated in the eastern urban zone (Hernández et al. 1999:77, figs. 19–20).

Alicia Openworked incense burners (*incensarios*) possess a distinct globular tripod form with a tail-like handle. During the Early Postclassic, *incensarios* of this general shape occur in the Basin of Mexico, the Valley of Puebla, the Huasteca, and the Valley of Oaxaca, among other regions (Cobean 1990:448). Jorge Acosta (personal communication) proposed that Oaxaca was the place of origin for this form of censer. The fact that Alicia censers have been found both in nonelite dwellings and in monumental public buildings probably indicates that they were used for both domestic and public rituals (Cobean 1990; Moncayo 1999; Acosta 1945:35–37). Alicia probably is not as rare in the area as the excavation and survey data indicate (Figs. 8.1–8.4), because this type is so fragile that it breaks into tiny sherds that are not identified.

Bordo Red on Brown *ollas* may have been produced in the same workshops as Macana Red on Brown bowls, with which these *ollas* share many attributes of color, paste, and surface decorations

(Cobean 1978, 1990). Bordo is a good chronological marker for the Tollan Phase even though it is usually present only in surface or excavated contexts in small quantities. This type is more frequent in the city than in the hinterland, and is quite uniform in attributes throughout the region, which suggests it was mainly produced in only a few workshops. Its higher frequency in Type 2 sites (concentrated settlement with ceremonial structures) and in the city suggests that Bordo may have possessed some value as a "higher-status" commodity (Fig. 8.2C).

Acta Polished Red is a widespread but not very frequent (in terms of sherd counts) type in the urban zone and the region. Because Acta's painted decoration has a brushed texture, it may be related to the orange-and-cream brushed-ware tradition that includes Jara Polished Orange. The most common form for Acta is a *tecomate* (a neckless spherical vessel that probably was used to store liquids or grains). *Tecomates* are mainly diagnostic for Formative lowland Mesoamerican cultures, and this form is a surprise occurring in Postclassic Tula. The Huasteca Postclassic ceramic complexes occasionally include *tecomates,* and it is possible that the Acta type was originally made in Tula by Huastec, who probably were among the artisans producing ceramics in the city's workshops. This type apparently does not occur in Early Postclassic Central Mexican ceramic complexes outside the Tula region (Cobean 1990).

As noted above, Tollan Complex *comals* (Mendrugo Semismoothed) are rare both in the city and the region. These *comals* were recovered in only 38 of the 1,604 URs in the region. In the Tepetitlán excavation, 23 Mendrugo sherds were identified out of nearly 34,000 Tollan Phase sherds (Moncayo 1999:79–80). These *comals* are more common in the city, but only constitute 1.23 percent of the urban ceramic samples (Figs. 8.1, 8.2A, 8.4). In contrast, *comals* are fairly common in Mazapan and Tollan sphere sites in the Basin of Mexico (Evans 1975:28; Koehler 1962:38–40; Blanton and Parsons 1971:290; William Sanders, personal communication). Thus there was a dietary difference in Tollan Phase times, with the people of the Tula region probably consuming maize principally in forms other than tortillas, and possibly consuming more maguey foods than coeval peoples in the Basin.

Ceramic drain tubes were used in the study area during the Tollan Phase to control rainwater in buildings (Healan 1989a). These tubes have not been identified for other periods and may be diagnostic for the Tollan Phase. Healan excavated a small workshop that produced these tubes in House VIII of the El Canal locality in the urban zone, and presents a thorough analysis of a kiln and other workshop remains. Because these tubes are coarsely textured and monochrome (usually brown or red), they often have not been classified in archaeological investigations. In the House Group excavated at Tepetitlán, eighty-six fragments of drain tubes were identified, some of which were still apparently associated with fallen walls and roofs (Moncayo 1999:80; Cobean and Mastache 1999: fig. 1.20). In the urban El Canal excavation, the drain tubes that originally functioned in the houses (not the workshop-associated tubes) sometimes were found fallen in lines indicating their original positions in walls and roofs more clearly than at Tepetitlán (Healan 1989a).

CONCLUDING OBSERVATIONS

Our ceramic analysis determined that the Tollan Complex in the area is very similar to the Tollan assemblage defined for the ancient city, with the same general tendencies and frequencies, especially with regard to the principal diagnostic types. These similarities in the regional and urban ceramics surely constitute one of the elements that defines the city's direct interaction area, especially taking into account that immediately outside the Tula region there is more variation in Early Postclassic pottery complexes than has been documented for the northwest Basin of Mexico (Parsons 2000), the Teotihuacan Valley (Evans 1975; Koehler 1986), and the Ajacuba, Hidalgo, area (Hortensia de Vega, personal communication), among other regions.

In terms of sampling strategies and contextual differences, it is interesting that the frequencies of major Tollan Complex types often are similar in both intensive surface collections and excavations for the same site, as especially is the case for the ceramics recovered in the House Group investigated at Tepetitlán (Moncayo 1999) (Fig. 1.6). There also are a series of significant correlations between ceramic assemblages and specific contexts or structure types studied in the survey of Tula's hinterland. For example, the analysis of the URs showed that the ceremonial structures are associated with unusually large percentages of Mazapa Red on Brown and Proa Polished Cream (Fig. 8.2B), possibly indicating that these buildings often were initially constructed at the beginning of the Tollan Phase (but finding early materials in ceremonial mounds is probably also due to the fact that these structures are often looted and thus have early ceramics on their surfaces). Ceremonial structures also have the highest percentages of Abra *braseros,* which correlates with their ritual functions.

The URs analysis also found that the units classified as habitational structures in Figure 8.2A contain nearly all the principal and less frequent types. These structures possess the highest percentages for Rebato bowls in the hinterland, which correlates with "domestic" food preparing and consuming activities in these buildings. Rebato, however, is even more common in urban habitation structures (Figs. 8.2A, 8.2B, 8.4).

Collection Units of Concentrated Artifactual Material possess all the types, including minor wares, in the Tollan Complex, which is understandable because a large portion of these units probably correspond to habitational structures that have been destroyed or to the peripheries or zones surrounding habitational units (Fig. 8.2B). Units of Dispersed Artifactual Material include at least small quantities of nearly all Tollan Complex types (except for Gulf Coast [888] and Northwest Mexico [890] tradewares), with the most common vessel functions corresponding to storing and serving foods and liquids—for example, Soltura and Blanco Levantado *ollas,* Jara and Proa dishes, and Toza *cazuelas.* At least some of the Dispersed Artifactual Material contexts surely correspond to debris accumulations from intermittently occupied activity areas such as agricultural fields and zones of artisan activities or hunting and gathering, where Tollan Phase people consumed food but did not live full-time.

The statistical analyses of the distribution by zone for each of the four ranks[1] of rural sites (Table 7.2) used by Healan showed significant distributional correlations between some site ranks and specific zones, and also locational correlations between early Tollan Phase sites and previous Classic Teotihuacan tradition occupations. A means of examining possible diachronic trends in rural settlement is to distinguish sites with evidence of an Early Tollan Phase ceramic component from those lacking such evidence, in essence differentiating sites that span the entire Tollan Phase (called here "Full Tollan" sites) from those that were not established until the late phase. Comparison of Full Tollan and Late Tollan Phase rural settlements reveals a number of differences, including somewhat dissimilar preferences for settlement by zone (Table 8.1), in which Full Tollan sites strongly favored Zone 3 over all others, while Late Tollan sites show smaller differences among zones. Full Tollan Phase occupations include disproportionately fewer Rank 5 sites than do those settled in the Late Tollan Phase (Table 8.2A), but this may be a sampling error given the small number of such "sites." Considering only the three largest ranks (Table 8.2B), Full Tollan and Late Tollan sites show a similar "bottom heavy" pattern, although Full Tollan sites show a disproportionately greater number of Rank 3 sites.

Particularly notable is the disproportionately large number of Full Tollan Phase sites exhibiting evidence of prior Classic period occupation (Table 8.3; Fig. 7.7A). It must be noted, however, that the vast majority (sixty) of these eighty sites have no evidence of intervening Epiclassic Coyotlatelco period occupation, hence this association is not indicative of settlement continuity. Perhaps, instead, this overlap represents similar strategies for site location during both Classic and Early Tollan Phase times.

There are statistical tendencies that indicate preferential patterns of consumption between the city and the rural area for the seven or eight most common Tollan Complex types. Soltura *ollas,* constituting the most frequent type in the entire complex, show a tendency to be more common in rural sites than in the city (Figs. 8.1, 8.2A). This is interesting with regard to proposing production models for the city

Table 8.1—Comparative Distribution by Zone of Full Tollan versus Late Tollan Rural Sites

Full Tollan (n=155)		Late Tollan (n=146)	
zone	percent	zone	percent
1	3.23	1	6.16
2	5.16	2	11.64
3	34.84	3	23.97
4	18.06	4	21.23
5	7.74	5	11.64
6	18.71	6	13.70
7	12.26	7	11.64
			$p < .01$

Table 8.2—Comparative Distribution by Rank Size of Full Tollan versus Late Tollan Rural Sites

Full Tollan (n=155)		Late Tollan (n=146)	
A. all sites			
rank	percent	rank	percent
2	8.39	2	8.22
3	16.77	3	3.42
4	52.90	4	39.04
5	21.94	5	49.32
B. five sites removed			
rank	percent	rank	percent
2	10.74	2	16.22
3	21.49	3	6.76
4	67.77	4	77.03
			$p < .01$

Table 8.3—Relative Occurrence of Classic Period Occupation at Full Tollan versus Late Tollan Rural Sites

	Full Tollan	Late Tollan
Classic absent	75* (91)†	101 (85)
Classic present	80 (64)	45 (61)
		$p < .001$

*f_o
†f_e

and the area. Soltura's great uniformity in the urban zone suggests that it was produced in a massive, standardized system, whereas in the rural sites the diverse varieties of this type (Moncayo 1999) indicate the existence of different ceramic workshops from those of the urban zone, along with a more diversified local production.

Jara and Macana, often considered as the central diagnostic types of the Tollan Complex, show a small tendency to be more common in the area (Figs. 8.1, 8.2A), possibly because the inhabitants of the city generally possessed a wider variety of vessels and plates for consuming food, and also because the area's people were mainly of lower social strata, while elite groups among the city dwellers would prefer and have access to other ceramic types such as Sillon, Plumbate, or other imported wares. An important type that definitely is more common in the hinterland than the city is Blanco Levantado (Figs. 8.1, 8.2A), suggesting that the origin area of this tradition could have been a dependent province of the Toltec state.

In contrast, types that tend to be more common in the city than the hinterland (Fig. 8.1, 8.2A) include Bordo *ollas,* Acta *tecomates,* Rebato bowls, Abra *braseros,* Alicia incense burners, Tarea jars, Mendrugo *comals,* Plumbate and most other imported wares, Mazapan figurines, and ceramic drain tubes, all of which, with the exception of Rebato, generally constitute the least-common types of the Tollan Complex. Some are for everyday use, while others of these types could be elite-social-status indicators, such as Plumbate, having a scarce presence in the rural area, along with others that could be mainly for ritual use such as the Alicia incense burners, the figurines, and the Abra *braseros.* Generally, the tendencies for some ceramic types to be more frequent in the city than the rural area indicate differential patterns of consumption between the inhabitants of the city and the rural population that seem to be related to status distinctions.

The presence of workshops for diverse ceramic types in the area and the city (Figs. 6.11, 10.7) indicates that ceramic production was not an exclusively urban or rural activity. Likewise, it is not clear if the rural ceramic workshops only supplied rural populations or specific rural zones. The urban workshops probably distributed their production to a large part of the area, and to more distant regions as is indicated by the homogeneity of some types.

As we mentioned before, the ceramic analyses help us to determine the approximate limits of Tula's core area or rural hinterland, and distinguish it from a second outer ring of regional interaction that was composed of the Basin of Mexico and other surrounding areas that also were integral components of the Toltec state. The hinterland possessed a special distribution and combination of ceramic types that constitute a different complex from the coeval pottery assemblages in the outer ring, including most of the Basin. These differences in the distribution and association of ceramics between the hinterland and the neighboring areas probably are expressions of the different levels of economic and political ties and interaction of these regions with Tula, and the fact that they formed part of different orbits of market systems. Some of these variations in regional ceramic assemblages also can be related to the different ethnic composition of the peoples living in the hinterland and the outlying areas.

Pottery types also frequently reflect the dietary habits of the population. For example, the near absence of *comals* in Tula's hinterland, along with the high frequency of these vessels in coeval occupations of the Basin and other nearby areas, suggest different habits for consuming maize that are perhaps related to ethnic differences and possibly to the fact that this crop would have had a different importance in the diet of the people in these areas.

CORRESPONDENCE ANALYSIS OF TULA REGION URBAN AND RURAL CERAMIC ASSEMBLAGES

Correspondence analysis (Bolviken et al. 1982) was used to determine patterns of interaction among the various ceramic types and assemblages or collections. Like principal components analysis, factor analysis, and other common multivariate analytical methods, correspondence analysis searches for common dimensions of variation, or "factors," among variables and/or cases, but has at least two advantages over the two former methods: first, it can be used in situations like the present one, where there are many more variables (in this case, ceramic types) than cases. Second, the factors defined by correspondence analysis are identical for cases and variables, which can thus can be plotted on the same graphs so that their relationships can be clearly seen. Two factors accounting for over 70 percent of total

Table 8.4—Matrix of Factor Loadings from the Correspondence Analysis

	Factor 1	*Factor 2*
68drain	−0.420	−0.0118
69figs	−0.647	−0.120
794jorob	−0.452	−0.249
796mazap	−0.586	−0.208
800toltc	−0.352	−0.212
806macan	0.154	−0.191
818jara	0.103	0.012
822ira	0.038	−0.108
824proa	−0.088	−0.088
826sill	0.329	−0.288
828rebat	−0.220	0.247
830manl	−0.469	0.003
832toza	0.468	0.185
836blanc	0.455	−0.386
abra	−0.650	−0.180
856alic	−0.762	−0.082
860tarea	−0.941	−0.188
866bordo	−0.249	0.153
868mendr	−0.364	0.469
872acta	0.152	0.935
876borg	−0.175	0.110
878plumb	−0.293	−0.109
886huas	0.869	0.082
888gulf	0.418	0.659
902trade	−0.109	0.141
CIELITO	0.130	0.811
U17	0.171	0.631
TALLER	−0.255	0.012
URBAN	0.083	0.080
RURAL1	0.161	−0.117
TEPET	0.413	−0.195
RURAL2	0.437	−0.111
CANAL EXCV	−0.173	−0.110
CIELITO EXCV	−0.295	−0.135
TALLER ESCV	−0.422	−0.044
TEPET EXCV	0.263	−0.023
% total var	42.59	28.18

variance were extracted (Table 8.4) and depicted graphically in Fig. 8.5.

Perhaps the most striking aspect of Figure 8.5 is that taken together, the two factors clearly differentiate among rural sites, urban-site surface collections, and urban-site excavated assemblages, each of which forms a distinct cluster, along with the ceramic types that principally differentiate the cluster. At the lower right are the four rural collections, including both surface and excavated material from Tepetitlán, along with ceramic types that most notably include Blanco Levantado, Sillon Incised, and Macana Red on Brown, all of which in this case tend to comprise a greater proportion of rural than urban material. At the upper right are two of the three urban surface collections, which contain disproportionately larger amounts of Acta and Gulf Coast tradeware. The third surface collection (Mastache and Crespo 1976, 1982) is only a peripheral member of this cluster, perhaps because of the relatively small size of this collection compared to the other two. Finally, in the lower-left portion of Figure 8.5 the urban excavated materials form their own cluster, along with a large suite of ceramic types that include figurines, drain tubes, Plumbate, Mazapa, and two ritual forms, Alicia and Abra, all of which tend to occur in greater relative frequency in these urban excavated assemblages. Thus, even at a relatively crude level of abstraction, urban and rural sites appear to exhibit distinguishable characteristics in their ceramic assemblages.

NOTE

1. The four rural site ranks are: Rank 2: site Types 1 and 2; Rank 3: site Types 7 and 11; Rank 4: site Types 3, 5, 16, and 19; and Rank 5: site Type 15. See Chapter 7 for zone descriptions.

9
Subsistence Activities

Although the study area is small enough to visit any point from the city of Tula in one day, it has, as we mentioned in previous chapters, diverse ecological niches and different kinds of potential resources that must have been fundamental for the sustenance of the population of the ancient city and its rural environs. This chapter will deal with some aspects regarding the agricultural potential of the area and the possibility of exploiting various natural resources during the Early Postclassic period. We will refer to what seem to have been the principal crops of the area during this period and the role of irrigation agriculture in the sustenance of the populations of the city and its rural hinterland.

In general, regional settlement pattern studies basically consider the area's maize production potential as the principal parameter for calculating a region's agricultural capacity, and the relationship between this factor and the extant population. Thus, we will first refer to maize and the data available for this crop in the Tula area.

Excavations made in domestic Tollan Phase contexts in the city and the area have permitted the recovery of archaeological remains of a wide range of wild and cultivated edible plants, including various races of maize. The excavations include principally a rural habitation complex in the Tepetitlán site at the extreme north of the area (Cobean and Mastache 1999), where numerous samples of carbonized botanical material were recovered, some of them in primary contexts, and in the El Canal and El Corral urban habitation complexes (Diehl 1981; Healan [ed.] 1989), along with the structure we have designated Units 27–28, the latter being close to the monumental center and only partially excavated (Cobean and Mastache 1999; Mastache and Cobean n.d.; Getino n.d.) (see Fig. 1.1).

MAIZE (ZEA MAYS)

The archaeological maize specimens recovered in the aforementioned excavations in Tula were studied by Bruce Benz (1999:157–169). The collection includes fragments of stalks, leaves, roots, grains, cobs, and ears, of which Benz indicates that only a total of twenty samples (cobs) were sufficiently complete to permit the identification and measurement of at least eight morphological characteristics; six of the specimens studied come from the above-mentioned excavations in Tepetitlán, thirteen (from Units 27–28) from the Tollan Phase urban zone, and one from Tula Chico. With the exception of the Tula Chico example, which is the oldest, the rest of the specimens correspond to the Early Postclassic (A.D. 900–1200) and come from habitation contexts (Table 9.1, Fig. 9.1).

It is interesting to mention, albeit briefly, some of the methodological aspects that Benz describes in his study (1999:160). He states that each example was subjected to twelve individual measurements of the rachis—the size and shape of the cob—which refer to the elements that are easiest to measure in archaeological specimens, although only one of them offered significant and relevant information for a racial diagnosis. Using this procedure, the archaeological specimens were compared individually with each one of thirty currently existing races of maize based on statistical measurements of interracial variation and difference multivariables. Each archaeological specimen was given a probability of belonging to a contemporary race in terms of its degree of similarity.

With this kind of identification, it is possible to discuss the evolutionary and biogeographic relationships of the pre-Hispanic and present races. Comparisons were also made between the Tula examples and the collection of archaeological specimens from Teotihuacan, by using a series of statistical tests. Since all the samples in Tula are carbonized, it was necessary to make adjustments for the reduction in size of the examples in order to compare them with the current and the noncarbonized extinct populations (Benz 1999).

Nine different probable races were identified in the sample studied by Benz (1999: table 6.3) (Table 9.1), but this author stresses that the results must be interpreted cautiously, especially because of the small size of the sample and the fact that this is a classification in which some of the examples only have about 50 percent probability of belonging to this race.

The samples studied seem to be associated, based on their general morphology, with the extant races of the Mexican Highlands, for example, with those related to the Mexican Pyramidal Race Complex, although not exclusively. The discriminant analysis classified fifteen of twenty specimens, eleven of which are similar to the Central Highlands races; examples include Cónico, Chalqueño, and Cacahuacintle or Palomero Toluqueño. Four specimens were classified as most similar to the Trans–Sierra Madre Alliance—for example, Elotes Occidentales and Mixteco—and five specimens were classified as being similar to the complex covering races such as Maiz Ancho Olotillo, Pepitilla, and Celaya. Cónico is among the most probable of the races identified. It is important to mention that the classification system used by Benz differs in some ways from the system used by Wellhausen et al. (1987).

Benz states that the Tepetitlán samples are closest to the Mexico Balsas-Occidente and Trans–Sierra Madre groups, while the material of the pre-Hispanic city is visually closer to what he calls the Mexican Pyramidal. The Tula Chico specimen, however, is closer to the Central Highlands group, even though it is different in being more distant from the races corresponding to the other samples and locations and modern populations used in the analysis.

Benz stresses that the maize in the urban zone of Tula seems to be relatively homogenous and shows a higher similarity to the races currently found in the Central Highlands of Mexico, being closer to the races of the Mexican Pyramidal Alliance. The Tepetitlán specimens were divided into two groups that are potentially recognizable as distinct races. One group is more similar to the races that currently exist in the west and northwest at medium to high altitudes, and the other constitutes a race characteristic of high altitude, the Mixteco, that currently exists in the south. The second type is not very different from the maize

Table 9.1—Listing of abbreviations and location of each archaeological maize specimen. Also given are the probability of group membership, racial "identification" and the taxonomic grouping of the racial "identification" for each specimen. Taxonomy follows Benz (1986) (from Benz 1999: fig. 6.4).

Specimen*	DF 1	DF 2	DF 3	Race	Taxonomic Grouping	Probability of Group Membership
56-094-0-03	1.55	−1.24	0.89	Cónico	CHA	0.34
56-107-0-5-03	0.70	1.06	−0.85	Mixteco	TSMA	0.47
56-081-040	−0.22	0.45	0.39	Mixteco	TSMA	0.22
56-077-1-01	0.15	-0.63	−0.23	Maíz Ancho	BWMA	0.24
56-108-0-02	0.03	-0.07	−1.84	Olotillo	BWMA	0.42
56-106-1-04	3.15	1.17	0.66	Cónico	CHA	0.45
28-964-06	1.01	−1.31	-0.66	Pepitilla	BWMA	0.74
27-66-16	2.96	−0.83	1.98	Cónico	CHA	0.67
27-66-13	1.37	2.19	−0.58	Elotes Occidentales	TSMA	0.27
27-66-12	0.44	0.71	−0.59	Mixteco	TSMA	0.41
27-66-12	1.37	0.07	1.18	Cónico	CHA	0.49
27-66-10	2.06	−1.09	2.25	Celaya	U	0.46
27-66-10	2.60	0.30	2.06	Cónico	CHA	0.59
27-66-10	2.69	0.24	−0.06	Pepitilla	BWMA	0.42
27-66-11	1.56	0.28	0.62	Cónico	CHA	0.40
27-449	3.31	1.49	1.28	Cónico	CHA	0.66
27-66-44	2.30	1.03	2.71	Chalqueño	CHA	0.71
28-963-12	0.91	−0.30	0.56	Chalqueño	CHA	0.28
27-66-0-09	3.47	−1.80	0.41	Palomero Toluqueño	CHA	0.56
14-025-180	2.18	3.20	0.47	Cónico	CHA	0.37
mean	1.68	0.25	0.53			
standard deviation	1.14	1.24	1.16			

*56: Tepetitlán; 27, 28: Tula Zona Urbana; 14: Tula Chico

of the Tula urban zone, although according to the statistical analysis it also has some similarities with the modern races of the Trans–Sierra Madre group and the Balsas-Occidente group. He also indicates the possibility that the Tepetitlán groups represent races in the process of evolution or two mixed races. Rafael Ortega observes (personal communication 1996) that this interpretation would not be surprising because currently most of the maize varieties used by campesinos are intermediaries between two or more races, and it is very likely that this was the case in the period in question.

On the other hand, the comparative analysis of the Tula specimens with twenty-two Teotihuacan samples, eighteen of which correspond to the Formative stage, indicates to Benz that there were no significant differences between the average of these samples and the average of the Tula urban zone samples and the Type 2 of Tepetitlán (1999:166). This scholar concludes that among the probable races identified in the Tula and Tepetitlán materials, the most statistically significant similarities are with six races: Palomero Toluqueño, Cónico, Chalqueño, Pepitilla, Mixteco and Olotillo (Table 9.1).

Even with the reservations mentioned by Benz about the exact correspondence of the samples analyzed with current specific races, the study shows that during the Early Postclassic, various races of maize were cultivated in the Tula area, some of which have already been identified in archaeological contexts of other regions, that is, some of them very probably were widely distributed in the pre-Hispanic period. This is the case for the Cónico and Chalqueño maize, which have been found in Tehuacán in Postclassic contexts corresponding to the Venta Salada Phase (Mangelsdorf, MacNeish, and Galinat 1967) and

Palomero Toluqueño and Cónico identified in Teotihuacan (McClung 1977:52, 53).

With reference to the differences between one race and another, a monograph on this plant published by the National Museum of Popular Culture (Museo Nacional de Culturas Populares) mentions that

> the carbohydrate, amino acids, mineral and vitamin contents vary in each race. The ripening periods are also different (early, medium and late) as well as their resistance to plagues, drought, frost, wind, etc. Modern genetics has created new varieties, hybrids, capable of responding favorably to very different conditions . . . in some, the height of the plant is just 80 cm, others are up to 5 m high: There are different degrees of resistance to drought, wind, frost, humidity or excessive heat, different adaptability to soils, altitude, latitude and land slope . . . each variety has its own yields. (Museo Nacional de Culturas Populares 1987:18)

Depending on the maize race in question, the ears have from eight to sixteen rows of kernels and eight to seventeen kernels or seeds; currently there are ears that have up to a thousand or more kernels that may vary greatly in shape and color.

Below, reference is made to those races that, according to Benz's study, probably correspond to the races cultivated in Tula during the Early Postclassic. As noted by Rafael Ortega (personal communication 1994), these archaeological samples exemplify races of maize that are characteristic of different altitudes and suitable for different kinds of cultivation: rainfall, irrigation, or humidity. Early or short-cycle maize varieties such as the Cónico and the Palomero Toluqueño are represented, along with intermediate and late or long-cycle races of maize such as Chalqueño, Pepetilla, and Olotillo; the first is characteristic of irrigation and humidity; the other two are rainfall crops.

Palomero Toluqueño

This race of maize forms part of the group considered by Wellhausen et al. (1987:633–635, 609–732) as Indigenous Ancient Races, which are thought to have originated in Mexico from the primitive maize, and which still maintains many important common characteristics, because it originated from the same progenitor. Four of these races are currently recognized: Palomero Toluqueño, Arrocillo Amarillo, Chapalote, and Nal Tel are all popped-maize varieties with short periods of growth and relatively early ripening.

The first two races have only been found at very high altitudes, above 2,000 meters. Palomero Toluqueño is a variety with very short plants, approximately 1.7 meters tall, and early maturation (ninety days before anthesis or a masculine flowering); it is adapted to altitudes between 2,000 and 2,800 meters. It has currently almost disappeared in its pure form, but it is still found in some high places of the Central Highlands, and is much more frequent in the Valley of Toluca, although even there it has been almost completely replaced by Cónico, which is a more productive race that is derived from this one (Wellhausen et al. 1987).

Cónico

Cónico is the dominant race of the Central Highlands at altitudes that vary between 2,000 and 2,800 meters, with short and intermediate growth periods and early maturation (ninety days to anthesis); it is highly resistant to *chahuixtle* insects that exist in the Central Highlands. Its name is derived from the most outstanding characteristic of the ears, which are conically shaped. It belongs to the designated Prehistoric Mixed Races, and is believed to have originated as a hybrid between the Ancient Indigenous Races and the Exotic Pre-Columbians by the crossing of both varieties with the *teocintle*. Undoubtedly, Cónico resulted from the crossing of the Palomero Toluqueño with the Cacahuacintle, and its distribution center is the Central Highlands, where its supposed ancestors are still cultivated (Wellhausen et al. 1987:654–659).

Pepitilla

This is one of the most distinctive races in Mexico because of its extremely long, narrow, and pointed kernels, which are easily removed from the cob, and because of the high number of rows on the ear; it seems to be derived from a combination of the characteristics of the Palomero Toluqueño and some tropical toothed maize with many rows. The plants are reasonably tall and their average vegetative period (122 days for anthesis), with a medium resistance to the *chahuixtle* insect. It is adapted to altitudes between 1,000 and 1,700 meters. Currently, the center of distribution of the purest forms covers the states of Morelos and the northern part of Guerrero, within the upper basin of the Balsas River (Wellhausen et al. 1987:689–691).

Olotillo

This is a maize race with high plants, approximately 3 meters tall, and a long growing period (148 days to anthesis); its distribution center is in the upper part of the Grijalva River basin at altitudes between 300 to 700 meters. Its predecessors are largely unknown, and it has characteristics that place it near to *teocintle*. It seems to have been the product of a cross between a floury maize with eight rows and a flexible cob with the *teocintle* (Wellhausen et al. 1987:691–694). Is interesting to note that these authors state that Olotillo, or a very similar type, is represented on various Zapotec funeral urns (p. 613).

Chalqueño

This is a race that forms part of what Wellhausen et al. have denominated Modern Incipient Races (pp. 703–706), which as this name indicates are races of fairly recent origin. Chalqueño is adapted to altitudes of between 1,800 and 2,300 meters; the plants are medium to tall, between 2 and 5 meters, with a medium growing period of five to six months (107 days for anthesis). It is almost certainly the product of crossing the Cónico and Tuxpeño; it is similar to Cónico in the high number of rows, kernel length, and resistance to *chahuixtle*. Its geographic distribution is almost identical to that of Cónico in the Central Highlands, but since this is a later maize variety, it differs from Cónico in the adaptation range for altitudes—the upper and lower altitude limits are 1,800 to 2,300 meters, while the altitude for Cónico generally varies between 2,200 to 2,800 meters.

Although both these races are frequently found in the same region and at the same altitude, they do not compete for the same lands. Chalqueño, a productive, vigorous, and late type, is generally planted when the danger of frost has passed (between the end of March and the beginning of April in these zones) on irrigated land or land with subterranean humidity reserves that are sufficient for the germination of deeply planted seeds. However, it may only be planted on rainfall lands at the beginning of the rainy season, that is, at the beginning of June. Since the first frosts occur in the Central Highlands at the beginning of October, a maize race with a shorter period, such as Cónico, which is better-adapted to these conditions, is required; thus Cónico is almost exclusively used.

As mentioned before, the races of maize described represent early or short-cycle maize varieties such as Cónico and Palomero Toluqueño, and intermediate or late or long-cycle varieties such as Chalqueño, Pepitilla, and Olotillo. Cónico maize is a race that is characteristic of rainfall farming, like the Mixteco, although the latter, because it is later, is also suitable for humidity. Chalqueño, however, is common for irrigation and humidity cultivation because it can be planted from the end of March or the beginning of April; it is a race with great potential and high yield capacity because it is the result of a combination of various other races that conserves residual heterosis or hybrid vigor (R. Ortega, personal communication). Although in the study by Wellhausen et al. (originally published in 1952) it was proposed that Chalqueño was a modern race after the Conquest, this proposal is currently not accepted, because we now have archaeological evidence about its existence in pre-Hispanic times. Pepetilla is also a long-cycle maize with a very high potential, and is suitable for irrigation; the kernel is very fine and it is reputed to have very high quality for "nixtamal" (limed maize ground into a moist mash).

Currently Olotillo is not typical of the altitudes of the Tula study area, and in the opinion of R. Ortega, it is probable that the samples identified by Benz (1999) as Olotillo could in fact correspond to the Tabloncillo race, which is very similar and which would be more characteristic of the zone and because it is adapted to higher altitudes (Wellhausen et al. 1987:662–667). Nevertheless, both are eight-row maize varieties typical of the slash-and-burn system, and suitable for poor-quality soils (R. Ortega, personal communication). They are frequent in a large part of the Tula area, especially on hillsides.

Palomero Toluqueño, which is suitable for rainfall cultivation, is currently the least-common maize race and is restricted to high zones, but since it is a primitive maize, it is difficult to determine whether its distribution covered lower altitudes during the Early Postclassic. It should be mentioned that unlike other races present in the Tula area, Palomero Toluqueño is suitable for the "nixtamalization" process because of the characteristics of its kernels, size, and hardness. It is a bursting maize that is suitable for other uses, for example, toasted and popped like popcorn or ground and toasted over hot sand or a *comal*. Given the size of its kernel and hardness of the pericarp, it can be used in the nixtamalization process, although it requires greater cooking time, and obviously more fuel use (Wellhausen et al. 1987).

This is also the case for the Elotes Occidentales races, which apparently are also present in the study zone and are not only planted for the nixtamalization process. This is a wide-kernel maize with soft and flour-rich seeds, which is usually eaten on the cob and may also be employed for symbolic or ritual use due to its kernel colors of red and purple. It is used to make *pinole* and *tesguino,* perhaps because of its flourlike texture and its color (R. Ortega, personal communication).

The Nixtamalization Process and Consumption

Although in both pre-Hispanic times and the present, the consumption of maize is generally associated with the nixtamalization process, it is known that initially this was not the case. Apparently, nixtamalization is very old; MacNeish (1967:284, 302, 303, figs. 185, 187) considers the disappearance of the pericarp of the kernels in samples of human coprolites in Tehuacán during the Abejas Phase (3500–2300 B.C.) as the indicator of the beginning of this process. This author also proposes, based on the abundance of maize remains detected in refuse dumps, that beginning with this phase there was a notable increase in the consumption of the plant.

The purpose of the nixtamalization process, which includes the treatment of maize with lime, is essentially to remove the outer skin or pericarp that covers the kernel, which besides being indigestible interferes with the digestion of other foods, and the phitates it contains are substances that could interfere in the absorption of essential minerals. When maize is treated with lime, it is physically and chemically transformed—the lime and heat not only removes the pericarp, but also produce chemical changes that improve the nutritive value of the kernel. The proteins, for example, have a higher biological value in nixtamal than in the untreated kernel, and many nutrients such as niacin, which is in lower concentrations after the nixtamalization process, are transformed chemically into more digestible forms than in the raw seeds. Additionally, without the nixtamalization process, a diet based on mainly maize would not be possible because this would lead to pellagra, an illness caused by the primary deficiency of niacin (Museo Nacional de Culturas Populares 1982:22–24). As indicated in this study, higher growth rates in animals fed with nixtamalized maize has been reported in repeated laboratory studies, in comparison with those that were fed ground maize without the lime process.

Currently there are many ways of using maize, most of which are undoubtedly of pre-Hispanic origin: tortillas, *totopos, atole, pozole, pozol,* tamales, *esquites,* boiled tender and roasted corn on the cob, *pinole,* honey, and fermented drinks such as *tesguino. Huitlacoche,* the fungus that grows on the maize, is also highly appreciated as food. The tassels of the ear are consumed for their medicinal qualities as an infusion; the roots and stalks are used as fertilizer, the cobs as fuel and food for animals, as well as the stalks, leaves, and grain. The leaves are also used to wrap tamales. A detailed list of the multiple uses, the traditional planting characteristics, rituals, and myths associated with maize cultivation and its consumption in diverse regions of Mexico can be found in the monographs titled *Nuestro Maíz* published by the Museo Nacional de Culturas Populares (1982) and the above-mentioned study of the same institution (1987).

In Tula, there is evidence for diverse forms of consuming maize, although it is difficult to determine whether this grain constituted the fundamental staple of the diet of the region's people, with a relative importance similar to what now exists for a large part of the population of Mexico. For example, the presence of lime sediment in the interior of some of the Soltura-type *ollas,* both in excavations of the urban zone and in Tepetitlán, suggests that these vessels were used in the nixtamal process (Cobean 1990:435). Additionally, metates that would undoubtedly have been used to mainly grind maize are frequent during the Tollan phase, but *comales* (Mendrugo type) are infrequent in the city and in the sites of the area, as mentioned in the chapter on the Tollan Complex, which suggests that tortillas were not the principal way in which the Toltecs consumed maize.

With regard to other forms of consumption, there is an important finding in the habitation structures near the monumental center of some carbonized balls consisting of maize kernel conglomerates, as we could see in the excavations of Carlos Hernández (personal communication). These kernel conglomerates are very similar to the balls of *pozol* that are still consumed in some regions of Mexico. Likewise, in the central patio of the habitation unit excavated in Tepetitlán, two samples of dough with the remains of maize leaves were recorded that seemed to correspond to tamales (Mastache and Cobean 1999a; González Quintero 1999).

Cobean has proposed (1990) that the most common recipient for cooking in Tula is the *cazuela* (Toza Smoothed Brown), which is similar in shape and size to vessels that were used until recently in some regions of Mexico (Morelos, Michoacán) to cook *pozole,* and consequently he considers it likely that this was a common way of consuming maize in Tula. In the University of Missouri excavations of the El Corral unit, part of a Toza *cazuela* was found with some carbonized maize grains stuck to the bottom of the vessel, which seemed to be *pozole* remains.

Production and Yield

In general, regional studies of settlement patterns in Mesoamerica consider an area's maize-production potential as a fundamental indicator in defining its carrying capacity, considering other crops and other biotic resources as secondary to maize. In these studies, various suppositions are implicit, principally:

- That this plant had the same importance in the diet of pre-Hispanic populations of these areas as it currently has for a large part of the country's population
- That the characteristics of cultivation, yield, and uses of the plant are comparable with those of present-day traditional agriculture

Nevertheless, there are many factors and conditions that are either unknown or difficult to determine in relation to the cultivation of maize in the pre-Hispanic period, such as: the races used, their characteristics and size, their genetic potential and yield capacity, forms of use, the predominant systems of cultivation, planting density, soil quality and fertility levels, land fallow cycles, crop association, crop rotation, the use of fertilizers, the limiting conditions under which cultivation was done, climate, temperature, winds, ranges of precipitation, and the frequency of frosts, droughts, and plagues, among others.

Numerous studies on current maize production and cultivation in various regions of the country indicate that changes in any of these variables lead to great differences in terms of production and yields of maize from one year to another in the same region (Montañez and Warman 1985; Ku Naal 1986; Del Amo 1988; Trujillo 1984; LAMP 1991; Finkler 1974; Silva Cifuentes 1992; Del Campo Valle and Luna Flores 1987; Luna Flores and Gutiérrez Sánchez 1990; Museo Nacional de Culturas Populares 1982, 1987).

Nichols (1987) offers information based on various sources about current maize yields in various communities and ecological niches of the Valley of Teotihuacan and Texcoco, for both rainfall and irrigation agriculture. The data she used illustrate the wide range that exists, especially in terms of rainfall maize yields (from 450 to 2,000 kilos per hectare), in terms of various factors: altitude, topography, soil quality, humidity, etc. Thus, determining the maize production and the agricultural capacity of an area in the past is a complex and very speculative task that only leads to very general estimates of the approximate ranges and maximum production limits of the region in relation to a given population.

The Tula region, like a large part of the Central Highlands, is an area with high-risk zones for rainfall cultivation, basically because of the altitude, which is more than 2,000 meters, the existence of frosts, annual precipitation levels (between 420 to 700 millimeters), and the poor quality (see Fig. 2.4) of most of the soils, many of which have a depth of less than 50 centimeters. However, as indicated by R. Ortega (personal communication 1994), this region may also be considered as a typical maize-producing zone, that is, a basically favorable zone for the cultivation of maize. Despite the low precipitation, this is not a zone of excessive evaporation because of its rather low annual temperatures, nor do these conditions favor the development of plagues and diseases. This is also a dry region that is suitable for good conservation and storage of grain.

Because of its altitude and location, the Tula area has the possibility of using or fostering maize types that combine races from the highlands with other tropical maize races, which permits what is known as heterosis or hybrid vigor, the result of crossing races that increases their genetic potential, as in the case of the Chalqueño and Celaya maizes, with a high potential that can be manifested in a suitable and favorable environment (Rafael Ortega, personal communication).

As mentioned in Chapter 2, there are basically two types of climate predominating in this region: zones with a warm climate and zones with a climate that is a semiarid and moderate temperatures, with an average of less than 18°C (microthermic). This means that there are some zones that are favorable for the cultivation of rainfall maize and perhaps maize grown on naturally humid soils and others in which more problematic, marginal sectors predominate, where crops are more frequently lost because of drought in the form of low precipitation, a late start of the rainy season, or droughts during the season at key moments in the development of the plant. According to the data furnished by E. García (1966: table 13), the average precipitation in the area studied ranges between 400 and 700 millimeters annually, and some of the highest rainfall occurs in the southern part of the area.

It is important to clarify that although the amount of precipitation in a region is very important for agriculture, the way in which the precipitation is distributed is more important than the quantity. R. Ortega (personal communication) observes that currently large areas of crops are lost not only because of low precipitation, but also because of erratic rainfall. The date on which the first rains start is fundamental, because a delay could make it impossible to plant maize or the nongermination of the seed, although in this case it is possible to replant with earlier-maturing crops. Droughts are also crucial because if they occur during flowering the crop will be lost, or if there is a drought after flowering, the kernels may not be well formed.

There are also years that, even within the favorable zones having optimum precipitation conditions, the crop may be lost due to frosts, especially the early frosts of September and October, which are a problem at these altitudes and affect all kinds of crops, but especially the rainfall crops that are behind in their vegetative development. Because the irrigated maize crops mature about fifteen days before rainfall crops, they would be less affected. However, the late frosts in the early months of the year affect the humidity or irrigation crops that are usually sown in March, and as Ortega mentions, it is not in the higher elevations but on the valley floors where frosts are the most dangerous.

Sanders (1993b) shows in a recent study that the successful cultivation of maize above 2,000 meters requires a combination of relatively deep soils capable of retaining humidity and an average rainfall of more than 700 millimeters. But at elevations where there is a risk of frost, the rainfall calendar is also crucial; ideally, to minimize the damage caused by frosts it is necessary to plant no later than mid-May, and very often the rainfall is minimal and irregular at this time of the year, which is the moment of germination of the plant; later, rain is necessary in the period of flowering when the plants' water needs increase. Under these conditions, deep soils that store humidity and the closeness of mountains where the rains begin early and the water may be used to irrigate by means of runoffs are very advantageous for maintaining germination of the plants until the rainfall season begins on the plains (Sanders 1993b:23–24).

All of the above makes it possible to understand the number of variables and circumstances that are involved in the yields of this grain in the study area, and the opinion of the campesinos that rainfall agriculture is a very risky and unpredictable endeavor. Chapingo University agronomists (J. Duch, R. Ortega, and Moisés Mendoza, personal communication) observe that a common opinion now is that there are six good years and four bad ones, but it is difficult to establish the real proportion because it depends on so many factors and the zone in question, and because some zones can have several years of consecutive drought. Referring in part to the Tula region, Figueroa (n.d.:20) mentions that "most of the population is in the zone without irrigation . . . maize is planted every year, but there are harvests only every five or six years, because part of the crop is generally lost to frosts or because of the lack of water."

The situation described in a study by Finkler (1974) seems to be very characteristic, and indicates that under rainfall conditions, 350 kilos of maize is the amount taken as the average yield when the maize reaches its bearing stage. "The campesinos say that thirty years ago they harvested such amounts of maize and beans that they were even able to sell the surplus on the market. They rapidly add that rainfall was abundant in those times. In recent years, they indicate 1962 and 1967 as the only two good years for cultivation. One informant said that in 1967 he had harvested approximately 40 bags (approximately 2,800 kilos) of ears on just one hectare. In 1969, the same field only produced two bags and then five bags in 1970 (350 kilos of un-shelled maize)" (p. 174), which, as mentioned before, is the average yield per hectare when the maize reaches the cob stage, because frequently it does not mature and the maize stalk is the only harvest produced on the maize fields, which is, however, an important source of forage.

In this context, it is possible to understand the enormous importance of irrigation in these regions, because irrigation cultivation primarily implies security beyond the risk and chance of rainfall farming, and in some zones the possibility of two or more cultivation cycles on the same land, although this is not the case in the area studied. R. Ortega and M. Mendoza (personal communication 1998) observe that frosts do not permit having two full maize harvests a year, but an extra short growing season is possible between June and October, which could include maize only when it is consumed unripened as *elotes* and not as dry kernels. Currently in the Tula area, there are frequently additional short harvests for beans (*frijol de guía*), *ayocote,* and amaranth. Irrigation agriculture also makes it possible to plant at a higher density and to obtain larger and more developed plants and bigger ears, and also the possibility of mixed crops. According to the probable races identified by Benz, it is very likely in the Tula region that long-cycle maize such as Chalqueño or Celaya would be planted for irrigation or humidity cultivation, because they have a high production capacity under the right conditions (LAMP 1991). Chalqueño is a long-cycle or late-maturing variety (100 days to flowering and 160 days for mature maize) having high yields and good resistance to drought periods (Ortega and Mendoza, personal communication). On the other hand, Cónico maize has a shorter cycle and lower yields.

However, although irrigation is potentially more productive, the yield difference between irrigation and rainfall agriculture sometimes appears to be almost insignificant, as can be seen in the data of Finkler, who mentions that according to the oldest local inhabitants, before the introduction of irrigation with sewage water, 1 hectare produced approximately 535 kilos of maize, which is similar in quantity to the harvest of another informant in the same region whose irrigated land did not include sewage water (1974:97). That is, irrigation offers a degree of security that is not found with rainfall agriculture.

However, in some parts of the study region, under good conditions there are now experimental irrigation crops with very high yields, up to 6 or even 10 metric tons per hectare (LAMP 1991). As mentioned before, it is difficult to determine precisely whether maize was the staple diet of the inhabitants of Tula and the sites of the area, with an importance that is similar to what is seen in a large part of the contemporary rural population of the country, but it is assumed that it was so. In order to obtain a general parameter on the agricultural capacity of the area in study, the following estimates can be made.

Currently it is considered that the average daily consumption of a rural family with a traditional maize-based diet is between 4 and 5 kilos of maize per day, that is, between 1,500 and 1,800 kilos per year (J. Duch and R. Ortega, personal communication). In general terms, the rural people mentioned that they need about 2 metric tons of maize a year for family consumption (Museo Nacional de Culturas Populares 1982), which is a desirable amount to satisfy their needs, although this figure seems to be higher than what is actually available.

Sanders proposes that 600 grams of maize per day provides slightly more than 2,000 kcal per day, which would be a realistic estimate of the per capita consumption in the pre-Hispanic period, while Pollard and Gorenstein, in a study on the Basin of Lake Patzcuaro (1980:275–276), consider that, based on ethnographic data and other sources, the average consumption in this region is 700 grams per day per person, considering that maize accounts for between 80 and 85 percent of the diet and that it produces about 2,400 kcal per day, and they use this figure as a base for their estimates in the production and carrying capacity of the area. In addition, Moisés Mendoza and Rafael Ortega, agronomists at Chapingo University (personal communication), state that 600 grams of maize per day per person is an adequate estimate because surely in pre-Hispanic times *pulque* was consumed along with many plants and other collected wild products, as is still done by the indigenous people in neighboring areas.

In the following tables (Table 9.2) taken from a Museo Nacional de Culturas Populares publication (1987:21), which recorded the nutrients of various food sources, it is indicated that each 100 grams of maize produces 350 kcal. Sanders (1993b), however, based on a study of nutrition in Latin America, recorded the following data on kcal per 100 grams of maize: fresh maize, 129 kcal; dry maize kernels, 354–361; maize dough, 154; tortilla, 202–210; boiled maize, 363; and *pinole,* 370 kcal.

According to Fisher and Bender (1976:185), the FOA's daily recommended intake for adults is 3,200 kcal in the case of men and 2,300 for women. However, a study by Lowenberg et al. (1970:194–195), on two regional groups in the world, records that in one group, which covers the underdeveloped countries, the average daily consumption is: 2,150 total calories, 58 grams total proteins, 9 grams animal proteins, and 38 grams fat. Bourges, in his research on food and nutrition in Mexico (1984:44–46), indicates that the daily intake per capita in this country is about 2,240 kcal and 71 grams of proteins in the urban population, and between 2,131 and 1,911 kcal and 48.4 to 60.8 grams of proteins in rural populations; these figures are very similar to those furnished by Lowenberg.

In Chapter 6, we have indicated that the estimated population for the city of Tula during the Early Postclassic was about 60,000 inhabitants and the population of the hinterland was between 20,000 and 25,000, or a total of between 80,000 and 85,000 people, which means (if this figure is divided by five), that in this period there would be 12,000 families in the urban zone and between 4,000 and 5,000 in the hinterland of the city, or a total of between 16,000 and 17,000 families.

If the estimate that each hectare of irrigated land could produce an average of 1,500 kilos is taken as a base, and the zone with irrigation potential estimated for the Tula area during the Early Postclassic totals about 3,000 hectares, the average annual production of the irrigated land would be 4,500 metric tons. If consumption per person is calculated at 600 grams per day, the total production of the irrigated lands would be sufficient to feed 20,547 people, that is 4,109 families; but if individual consumption were 700 grams per day, the irrigated production would make it possible to feed only 17,612 persons, or about 3,523 families.

In the first case, the production of all the irrigated land would be sufficient to feed only a third of the population of the city, and even less in the second case. This would suggest that the sustenance of the urban and the rural populations of the area would

Table 9.2—Nutrients of Various Food Sources

Nutrients of Diverse Foods in 100 grams of an Edible Portion

Foods	Energy kcal	Proteins g	Fats g	Carbohydrates g
Maize	350	8.9	4.3	72.2
Wheat	330	10.2	2.2	72.1
Rice	362	7.4	1.0	78.8
Nixtamal Flour	377	7.1	4.5	77.4
Wheat Flour	364	10.5	1.0	76.1
Beans	332	19.2	1.8	61.5
Small Squash	18	1.2	0.1	3.7
Fresh Chile	23	1.2	0.1	5.3
Tomato	11	0.6	0.1	2.4
Quelites (Amaranthus hybridus)	39	3.2	1.0	6.4
Squash-Seeds	547	30.3	45.8	14.4
Turkey	268	20.1	20.2	0.0
Rabbit	159	20.4	8.0	0.0

Mineral and Vitamin Content of Some Foods in 100 grams of an Edible Portion: Complex "B"

Foods	Ash g	Calcium g	Phos-phrous g	Vitamin A mg eq	Tiamine mg	Riboflavin mg	Niacine mg	Vitamin C mg
Maize	1.2	22	268	17	0.36	0.12	1.7	0
Wheat	1.7	42	383	0	0.59	0.12	4.4	0
Rice	1.2	24	221	0	0.29	0.05	1.6	0
Nixmatal Flour	—	140	120	1	0.22	0.05	0.2	0
Wheat Flour	0.43	16	87	0	0.06	0.05	0.9	0
Beans	3.9	228	457	—	0.62	0.14	1.7	0
Small Squash	0.6	25	29	27	0.06	0.09	1.0	13
Fresh Chile	1.2	25	49	52	0.22	0.28	3.5	230
Tomato	0.5	13	27	507	0.07	0.05	0.8	17
Quelites (Amaranthus hybridus)	1.4	230	60	400	0.07	0.18	0.8	42
Squash-Seeds	4.9	38	847	15	0.23	0.16	2.9	0
Turkey	1.0	10	212	80	0.09	0.14	8.0	0
Rabbit	1.0	18	352	0	0.18	0.18	10.0	0

(Museo de Culturas Populares 1987: 21)

not be based on irrigation agriculture, but on rainfall farming.

Nevertheless, Moisés Mendoza and Rafael Ortega (personal communication) observe that a current maize production of 3,600 kilos of kernels per hectare of irrigated land is viable for the study area, and thus it would not be an exaggeration to estimate a yield of 2,000 kilos per hectare of irrigated land for the pre-Hispanic period. Based on these figures, 3,000 hectares of irrigated land would produce 6,000 metric tons of maize annually, which would be sufficient for the consumption for 27,397 persons, or about 5,479 families, corresponding to almost half the estimated population for the city.

The calculations for yields under rainfall agriculture per hectare are even more speculative than irrigation because rainfall is more unpredictable and depends on many factors and variables that we do not know, and because there are few studies on rainfall cultivation and yields with traditional instruments. It is also a fact that the pre-Hispanic maize ears were smaller and the planting density was lower, apparently between 30,000 and 35,000 plants per hectare. However, taking into account current yields in regions with a similar habitat, it is feasible to propose a yield of between 500 and 700 kilos per hectare, that is, an average of 600 kilos per hectare.

The above means that in order to produce the 14,115 metric tons necessary for the survival of the 12,891 remaining families (taking 600 grams per day consumption per person as a base), some 23,525 hectares of rainfall land under cultivation would be required, that is, slightly more than 235 square kilometers to produce the 17,209 metric tons required, or 286 square kilometers (28,681 hectares), if per capita consumption is considered at 700 grams per day.

As a point of reference, it should be remembered that as we indicated in Chapter 2, the study area covers approximately 1,000 square kilometers, and its limits include the following present municipalities of Atitalaquia, Atotonilco, Tula, Tepeji de Río, Tepetitlán, Tezontepec de Aldama, Tlaxcoapan, Tula de Allende, and Tlahuelilpan,[1] and that currently, when the area now has more population than in the Early Postclassic, according to Figueroa, only 43 percent of the land can be cultivated, or about 418 square kilometers (Ruiperez Marín 1965; Figueroa n.d.), of which approximately 250 square kilometers (60 percent) is used for rainfall agriculture and only about 165 square kilometers (39 percent) for irrigation agriculture. This author, who used the data of the 1970 census as a basis, indicates that there is also 2.5 square kilometers of moist or humid land (Table 9.3). It should be mentioned that irrigation in the region is currently based principally on the system that is fed by the two large reservoir dams built in the twentieth century, the Requena and the Endó, because their capacity makes it possible to irrigate larger areas of land than would have been possible with the traditional irrigation systems.

On the other hand, according to our study of soil use in the nineteenth century, based on the eighteenth- and nineteenth-century plans of various haciendas and our research on traditional irrigation systems in the region (Mastache 1976) (see Figs. 2.8 and 2.10), the total estimate for agricultural land in the area for that period is approximately 250 square kilometers: 151.44 square kilometers used for rainfall agriculture and 101 square kilometers for irrigation,

Table 9.3—Tula Region*

Municipalities	Total Area (km²)
Atitalaquia	64.2
Atotonilco	30.8
Tepeji del Río	196.6
Tepetitlán	179.9
Tezontepec de Aldama	72.5
Tlaxcoapan	79.2
Tula de Allende	305.8
Tlahuelilpan	31.2
Total	960.2

*Based on Figueroa n.d.: 79.

or 10,191 hectares. This figure is based on the maximum capacity of all the traditional irrigation systems of the villages and haciendas recorded in the area.[2] It should be mentioned that 5,000 hectares of the 15,144 hectares used for rainfall agriculture in this period, was *magueyales*, or land exclusively used for cultivation of maguey. The blank zones in the map are areas for which there is no information, and they could correspond to both grazing areas or rainfall agriculture, which means that the area set aside for rainfall agriculture was probably somewhat larger than the figure mentioned.

The above indicates that it is not feasible to propose that during the Early Postclassic there was such a large area of land under rainfall cultivation (235–286 square kilometers); especially if one takes into consideration the zones that were occupied in this area during this period, the size, their density and population distribution, the topography of the area, and the soil quality. One must also consider the possibility that there were fallow lands, because this would imply having at least double the cultivated land, that is, 470–572 square kilometers, which as we have seen before, exceeds the potential of arable land of the area in any period.

The fallow system of agricultural land varies greatly, as is analyzed in detail by Rojas Rabiela in her study on the agricultural technology of Mesoamerica (1985:131–134). Apparently, in the higher zones of the Central Highlands the so-called short fallow (*barbecho corto*) system is common, in which the fallow periods are similar to the cultivation periods,

Table 9.3a—Classification of Agricultural Lands, Hectares (1970)

	Total 1	Rainfall Agriculture 2	%	Humidity Agriculture 3	%	Irrigation 4
Atitalaquia	4,579.3	3,602.4	79	962.1	21	14.8
Atotonilco	5,136.2	4,843.4	94	279.6	6	13.2
Tepeji del Río	5,167.2	4,264.8	83	894.5	17	5.8
Tepetitlán	6,066.6	2,438.6	80	618.6	20	9.4
Tezontepec de Aldama	4,835.6	835.8	17	3,937.2	81	62.5
Tlaxcoapan	3,829.3	1,009.2	27	2,804.2	73	15.9
Tula de Allende	13,799.6	7,968.4	59	5,703.8	41	127.4
Tlahuelilpan	1,454.2	125.0	9	1,324.6	91	4.6
Totals	41,868.0	25,087.6		16,524.6		255.6

*From Figueroa n.d.: 79, 102.

in general, between one and three years. In the case of the Valley of Teotihuacan, Lorenzo (1968:66–69, quoted by McClung 1984:40–41) estimates in his calculations on the contemporary agricultural potential of this valley that 334.3 square kilometers represent the arable part of an area of 523 square kilometers, and he considers that about 31,630 hectares are used for rainfall cultivation, although only half, 15,815 hectares, could be considered as productive because the rest of the land would be fallow.

On the other hand, Charlton (1970) indicates that the system of fallow land currently has little importance in the Teotihuacan Valley, and Sanders in his study of various communities of the Chalco-Xochimilco lake, conducted at the beginning of the 1950s (1983:127), mentions that in the case of rainfall lands, when fertilizers are not used, the land is left fallow for one year and crop rotation is common when fertilizers are not used. Nevertheless, he also observes (personal communication) that in the Aztec system in the Teotihuacan Valley, about one-third of the land was cropped every year as *calmil*, and these infield gardens were constantly being fertilized so that it was not necessary to fallow that land. The other two-thirds of the land was divided in a fallowing system (Sanders 2000b: chapter 13). On the other hand, Pollard and Gorenstein (1980) propose, for their regional study, a fallow period of one to two years in Class III soils, and rest and crop rotation in the poorer Class IV soils (for the Pátzcuaro, Michoacán, area).

It can be supposed that most of the land in the Tula alluvial valley and zones with Class I and II soils probably would not require a periodic rest, especially if the soils were fertilized in some fashion and if crop mixing was practiced, since it is well known that beans and other plants contribute important nutrients to soils. However, on hill slopes with poorer and shallower soils, it is necessary to rest the land if it is to be used to cultivate maize, although considering the characteristics of these lands, it is probable that they were above all used for the extensive cultivation of maguey.

Nevertheless, the above estimates pose various questions and distinct possibilities of interpretation, of which the following should be mentioned:

1. The agricultural potential of the area studied was not sufficient to sustain its population, and a considerable part of the food came from other neighboring areas that constituted an integral part of the Toltec state or were subjects of it.

In this respect, it must be remembered that our study did not include the small valley that extends to the west of the town of Xochititlán and to the north of San Agustin Buenavista (Fig. 1.4), which obviously formed part of the city's hinterland, and consequently it would be necessary to consider its productive capacity when estimating the agricultural capacity of Tula's sustaining area. Here also, the proposals made by Sanders are of great interest when he mentions that the north of the Basin of Mexico, especially the Zumpango area, should be considered as an integral component of the Tula settlement system, with a regional population that is economically and politically tied to the central nucleus of Tula, as shown by the population distribution and density patterns that existed in the north basin during the Early Postclassic (Sanders, Parsons, and Santley 1979:140–141, 137–149) (see Fig. 9.2).

The above means that this zone would constitute part of Tula's sustaining area, and the same proposals are, in our opinion, valid for part of the Mezquital Valley, especially the zones to the east of Mixquiahuala and the neighboring valley that lies between Ajacuba, Tepepango, and Santiago Tezontlale, to the east of the study zone (see Fig. 1.4), because these zones neighboring the study area undoubtedly must have been crucial for the Toltec state and the sustenance of its population. But since these areas are practically unknown from an archaeological point of view, it is not possible to make more concrete proposals in this respect. The Chapantongo zone to the northwest of the study area, which has been investigated for several years by López Aguilar (López Aguilar et al. 1998), was probably also an integral part of the city's sustaining area.

2. The population estimated for the urban center and the rural sites is too high and the lower ranges considered by some of authors (30,000 inhabitants for the city and 13,000 to 15,000 for the area, or a total of 45,000) are more feasible.

In reality, given the current state of our knowledge, both the upper and lower ranges are highly speculative because of the general characteristics of the surface studies made, especially in the case of the concentrated sites of the area (Types 1 and 2) and the city. In order to obtain more data that would permit more accurate demographic estimates, numerous, extensive, and systematic excavations would be required of habitation units in various zones of the city and the area. As mentioned before, the sample that is now available is very limited (about ten units in the city, some of which are only partially excavated, and only one habitation structure of the Tollan Phase excavated in the area).

3. The maize yields per hectare under irrigation and rainfall farming are higher or lower than the estimates.

In this case, as in other previous possibilities, in order to have a high degree of certainty it is necessary to have detailed ethnographic studies on traditional agriculture in this and in other regions that take into account fundamental aspects—such as work invested (man hours for each stage of the process), tools used, soil quality, planting density, long-term climate charts, etc.—as well as controlled experimental studies with specific races and traditional tools, similar to those done by Drennan and Kirkby in the project directed by Flannery in the Valley of Oaxaca (Flannery 1985:258–263).

4. The potential of the irrigated lands in the area during this period was higher than the somewhat conservative estimate of 3,000 hectares that we have proposed, and closer to what Sanders, Parsons, and Santley (1979) indicated as feasible, taking as a base our estimates on the maximum irrigation capacity in the area during the ninetheenth century, that is, about 10,000 hectares. It also should be taken into account, as Moisés Mendoza and Rafael Ortega (personal communication) emphasize, that even if during the Early Postclassic these 10,000 hectares were not irrigated, they would have included good-quality lands having humidity or deep soils for rainfall that could have given them higher yields than those characteristic of normal rainfall agriculture.

5. Although maize was the principal crop, in the Toltec diet it may not have had the same supposed importance as it does now, and other crops played a relevant role in nutrition as a source of calories and other nutrients. In this respect, we will analyze the possible alternatives or complements offered by plants such as amaranth and maguey, along with beans.

BEANS (*PHASEOLUS VULGARIS*)

Beans are considered the second most important crop in Mesoamerica after maize, and were a fundamental part of the diet of pre-Hispanic peoples and an important source of vegetable protein. Beans are present in almost any archaeological context where vegetable remains are conserved and are mentioned in most of the chronicles of the sixteenth century. As observed by Torres (1985:97), this plant was the second most important tribute good for the Mexica empire.

Like maize, beans are adapted to various latitudes and they are found from sea level to altitudes of 2,800 to 3,000 meters, as mentioned by Rojas Rabiela (1985:168). The plant's adaptability to var-

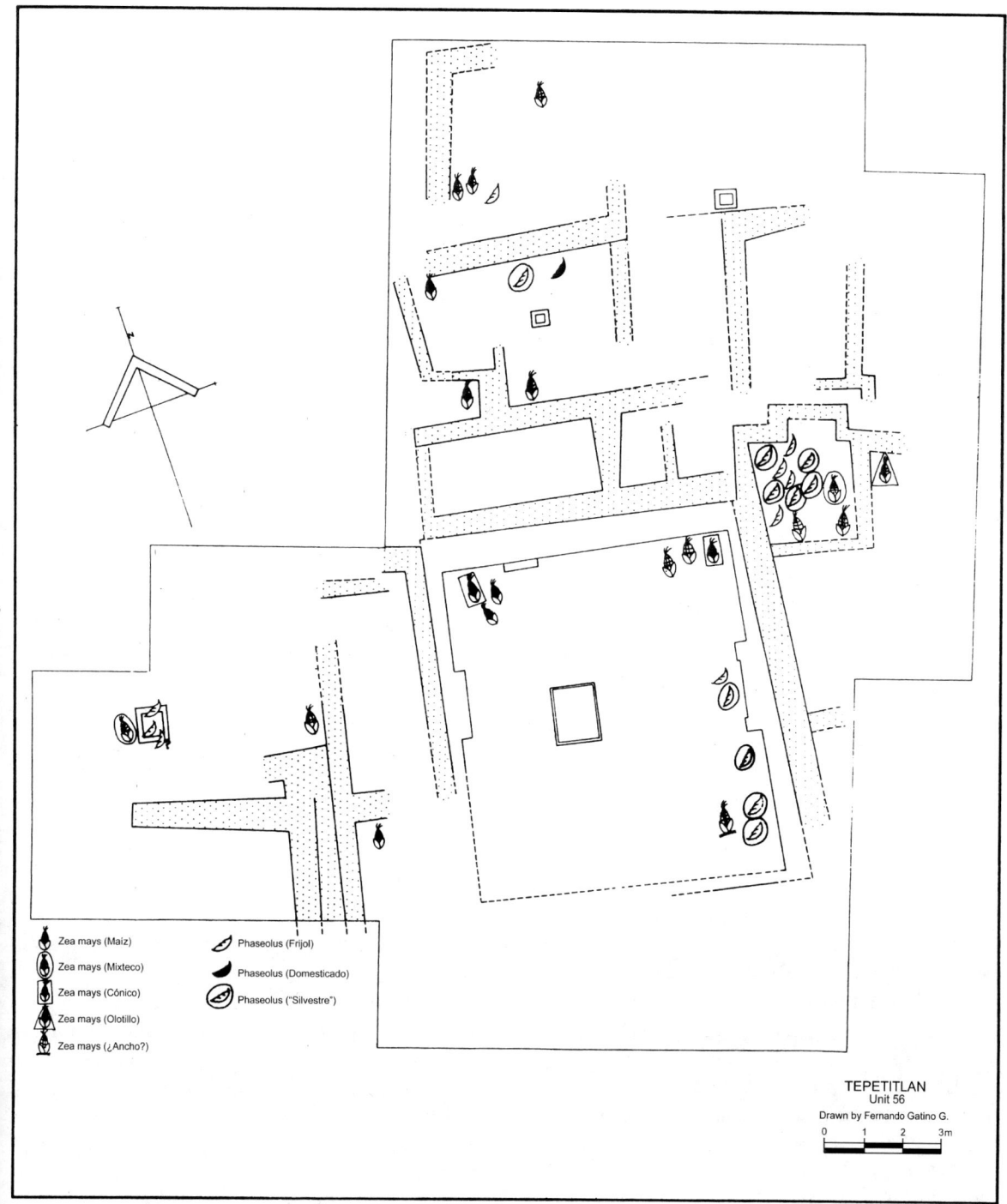

Figure 9.1. Tepetitlán U56: Distribution of *Phaseolus* and *Zea Mays* (Cobean and Mastache 1999).

ious agrosystems has meant that its production is widespread throughout Mexico, thus its geographic diversity is only exceeded by that of maize (Romero Polanco 1993:55).

There is a plethora of varieties of beans, which are characterized by being highly polyform, which according to the agroecological systems where they are found shows distinct vegetative variations in the shape and color of the pods, flower, and seeds. According to Romero Polanco (p. 53), the chemical composition of the green pod contains an average of 85 percent water, 6.1 percent proteins, 0.2 percent fats, 6.3 percent carbohydrates, 1.4 percent fiber, and 0.8 percent ash. The dry seeds contain 11 percent water, 22 percent proteins, 1.6 percent fats, 58.8 percent carbohydrates, 4 percent fiber, and 3.6 percent ash.

Apparently, in pre-Hispanic times beans were above all planted in association with other crops, principally maize, chile, and squash, as is still frequent in traditional systems. It is planted at the same time or after maize, and there is not much competition between these two plants for nutrients and light. As Rojas Rabiela mentions (1985), the climbing variety of beans twine up the maize stalks, thus catching more sun rays. This author quotes numerous sixteenth-century references that refer to the planting of this legume in different regions, in association with other crops.

Although various experiments have shown that beans are more productive as a monocrop than in association with other plants, there are specialists who emphasize the importance of stimulating plant association and crop rotation, because this makes it possible to maintain optimum soil fertility levels by combining high nitrogen consumers such as maize with legumes, which contain bacteria that fix nitrogen in the exhausted soils. Additionally, interspersing crops on the same piece of land has the same effect of alternating legumes and cereals, because it permits better soil exploitation and a more efficient use of labor, due to the better planting, intensive growing, ripening, and harvesting periods (Romero Polanco 1993:59).

Rojas Rabiela indicates (1985:168–169) that it is thus possible to harvest different crops in various states of maturity (green cobs, bean pods, maize, and ripe beans) at various times of the year, thereby constituting "risk distribution" by obtaining a greater variety of products, prorating labor, and involving a better use of vertical space, in addition to the fact that mixed planting determines better overall physical yields than the average of the respective yields if the components were monocrops.

Romero Polanco notes that there is a very wide range of factors that affect the production and yields of beans, such as single or associated cultivation, rainfall or irrigation, regularity of the rainy season, variations in precipitation and temperature during various stages in the development of the plant, as well as different soil types and slopes. Nowadays, the bean harvest largely depends on crops planted in rainfall lands. Rainfall lands produce harvests that cover approximately 75 percent of the total national supply of this product. The most important limiting factor is poor availability of water, which recurrently affects the crops in rainfall zones. In the low- to medium-productivity soils, yields of less than 400 kilos per hectare are obtained. He also mentions that during the spring and summer cycle (when more than 80 percent of the lands used to cultivate beans are planted), the harvest averages 307 kilos per hectare as a monocrop, while in the zones of irrigated beans there are average yields of up to 1,270 kilos per hectare, but these lands only account for 13 percent of the total area cultivated for this legume (1993:55, 56, 57). Moisés Mendoza (personal communication) estimates that in the Tula area 350–450 kilos of beans per hectare can be obtained in rainfall cultivation.

As mentioned before, various archaeological species of *Phaseolus* have been found both in the urban zones and in excavations in Tepetitlán and the results of the study by Kaplan (1999) of the preserved samples are of great interest. All these specimens were carbonized, and Kaplan notes that of the numerous examples recovered, only twenty-three could be measured and only twenty seeds or cotyledons were sufficiently well conserved to be studied.

Eleven of these specimens were found within a small grain bin in a habitation structure (U27–28) of the pre-Hispanic city in Tollan Phase contexts

(Cobean and Mastache n.d., 1999; Getino in press). The bin was a kind of rectangular stone box embedded in a floor with stucco finishes on the interior. The other twelve examples come from the domestic unit excavated in the Tepetitlán site (Cobean and Mastache 1999) (see Fig. 9.1) and they were found principally associated with food-preparation zones.

Kaplan observes (1999:149) that "their identification is based on their overall morphology, the form of the embryo which is discerned from its impression on the cotyledon and the size of the seed." Having identified two groups, he proposes that the largest are *Phaseolus vulgaris,* a climber, and the smallest (originally thought to be tepary beans) are specimens within the size range of wild races of *Phaseolus vulgaris* that grow in Mexico and South America. Kaplan mentions that because of the charring, they are slightly smaller than they would have been when dry and uncharred, primarily as a result of the loss of the seed coat (testa). Even with the seed coat, they would be smaller than any of the well-known land races of *P. vulgaris,* and even smaller than most tepary races.

Kaplan also stresses that the presence of the wild bean in both Tula and in Tepetitlán is interesting in an ecological sense. He mentions that in the Guila Naquitz cave site in Oaxaca, wild beans were present from the earliest preceramic levels to the most recent levels of occupation during the sixteenth century, and as in the case of Tula and Tepetitlán, the wild beans in the site were accompanied by the domesticated bean.

> To the best of my knowledge, wild beans are used at present time only as an occasional supplement by the Tarahumar and probably other groups in those regions where the wild population occurs, especially in west and central Mexico. Does the use of the wild types at Tula suggest hard times? Gathering of wild types as a nonagricultural resource? Or an integrated system of wild-cultivated beans? The latter pattern, an integrated system, may be the most productive hypothesis to consider." (Kaplan 1999:149)

The occurrence of both cultivated and wild types in the same samples suggests that they were harvested together and would be prepared for consumption in the same pot, so to speak. For planting, the seeds of the domesticated type would be separated from the wild types. Each year the wild types would seed themselves and the farmers would plant the domesticates. At the end of the season the harvest would again include both wild and domesticated beans, and the process would continue. Thus, this could be called an integrated system of wild and domesticated races, which does not mean that the domesticated races involved were derived from the wild types in the same system, but rather that there was probably some type of genetic interchange between the wild and the domesticated types (Kaplan 1999).

Although the sample analyzed by Kaplan is relatively small, it seems very significant that most of it, fifteen specimens of a total of twenty (75 percent), was wild. Only five examples corresponded to the cultivated race, four of which originate in the urban zones and one in Tepetitlán, that is, the wild bean predominates both the city and rural samples.

Of the bean fragments from the deposit in the urban habitation unit (U27–28), only nine specimens could be identified by Kaplan, of which six were wild (67 percent) and only three cultivated (33 percent), which means that both types were stored in the same granary, but the wild type dominated. It is very suggestive that the wild beans would predominate in this granary, especially if it is borne in mind that the habitation structure in which it was found could be considered as a habitation of elites, due to its proximity to the ceremonial center.

Although a single sample lacks statistical validity and of course the data cannot be extrapolated to the rest of the city, if it is assumed that the sample of this habitation unit and that of the Tepetitlán structure were representative of the consumption of the city and its sustaining area, it could be proposed at a hypothetical level that the domesticated bean during the Tollan Phase was not the principal source of consumption for this legume and that the population of the area and the city would have basically depended on a type of wild bean. Perhaps this transpired only because of preference and greater ease in obtaining wild beans, but more probably it was due to problems regarding the production capacity of the domesticated

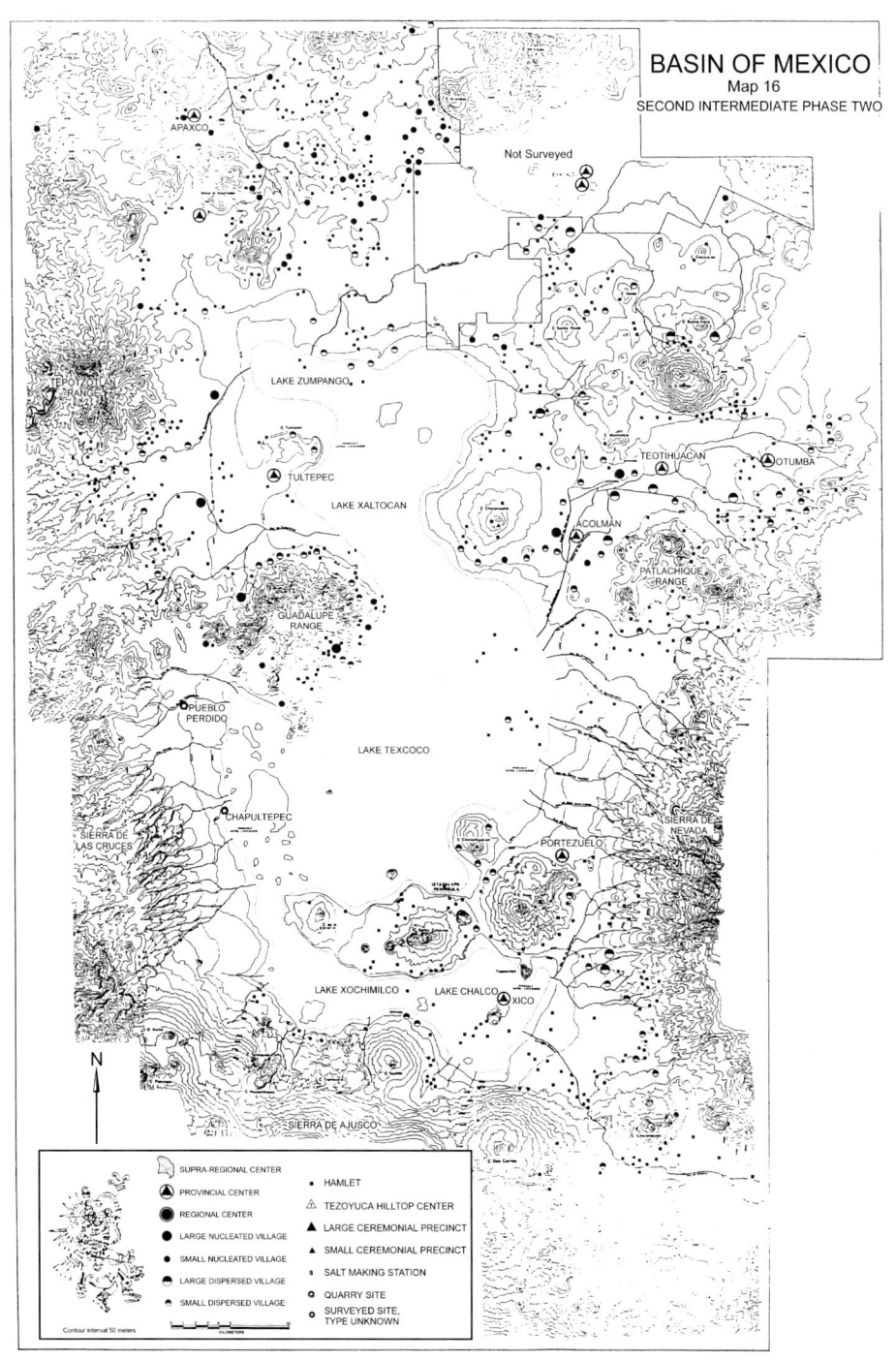

Figure 9.2. The Early Postclassic settlement in the Basin of Mexico (Sanders, Parsons, and Santley 1979). Courtesy, William T. Sanders.

bean in the area, which like maize was also subject to the hazards of rainfall agriculture and its low yields. It must be remembered that the present-day average yields of rainfall bean crops in Mexico are around 300 kilos per hectare.

AMARANTH
(*AMARANTHUS LEUCOCARPUS* OR *A. HYPOCHANDRIAUS*)

It is known that amaranth, which is today also known as *huautli, bledo,* or *alegria,* was in pre-Hispanic times a basic crop in several regions of Mesoamerica. There is archaeological evidence and ethnohistorical data on its cultivation, and together with maize, beans, and chia (sage), it was one of the principal products for the diet of Mesoamerican peoples.

Its diverse uses as food—tamales, *atole,* tortillas, *pinole,* or fresh as a vegetable—and its ritual use in association with important religious ceremonies have been described in detail by various sixteenth-century historians, especially by Sahagún and Hernández. Detailed references to the information contained in these sources and the specific data on ceremonies, along with the diverse products prepared with amaranth and their indigenous names, may be found in Torres (1985:71–72), Rojas Rabiela (1985:185), Ortíz (1997), and especially in the broad study by Sánchez Marroquín about the agro-industrial potential of amaranth (1980:35–40).

Apparently it was precisely amaranth's ritual importance that led to the prohibition of its use after the Conquest, and its cultivation decreased until it almost disappeared in some regions during the colonial period. According to Sánchez Marroquín (1980:102–103, table 3), two species are currently cultivated in Mexico—*Amaranthus leucocarpus* and *Amaranthus cruentus*—although this author indicates that the former, with hard ears, is more important and more extensively used.

This plant is currently sown in some parts of the Federal District, the state of Mexico, Morelos, Tlaxcala, Guerrero, Puebla, Oaxaca, Michoacán, Jalisco, Sinaloa, Sonora, and Chihuahua, although production is on a small scale and in some cases it is only for domestic consumption. In recent decades, research and some economic initiatives have been done in order to promote its rehabilitation as a food based on its high nutritional qualities and industrial potential.

Amaranth is an annual herbacea up to 2 meters tall, with a thick, erect, and reddish stalk; branches start from the base and are marked with longitudinal stripes. The leaves are long, oval-shaped petioles, between 15 and 18 centimeters long and 10 centimeters wide. It has very ramified long stalks with numerous purple or white flowers in a fanlike arrangement. It produces tiny black and white seeds, and the cultivator selects and plants the white seeds, which are preferred (Sauer 1950:614, quoted in Torres 1985:71; Sánchez Marroquín 1980:29–30). The latter author describes the seeds as "smooth and shiny, slightly flat and the size of a mustard grain," and also mentions that three varieties are distinguished in the state of Mexico: Cacahuacentli, "Ojo de Pájaro," and "Cuitlacoche," which is also called "*cimarrona.*" The first of these is more valued because of its larger and better-quality seed, while the third is poorly valued because of its low yield and smaller seed.

Sánchez Marroquín states that amaranth generally grows on fertile, humid, and permeable soils in warm and temperate climates, and even in places that are too hot for other plants. It is drought resistant, although the combination of fertile soil and frequent rain undoubtedly improve crop yields (1980:30–31, 81). "This seed grows on all kinds of lands, provided that they are well fertilized . . . It has been noted that they grow better on loose and porous soils than on solid, clay soils or those which in this area [Cocotitlán, State of Mexico] are known as tesoquites because this kind of land is not suitable for the plant and the yield drops to half of what could be obtained on loose soils" (Granados, Nogueron, and Zarza 1886, quoted by Sánchez Marroquín 1980:30, 77–80).

These authors stress that in another place in the state of Mexico, "land is worked that must be sandy but fertilized with manure"; thus the land preparation is similar to the process for maize, except that the grain is not planted at the bottom of a furrow, but a stick is used to open a narrow furrow and the seeds are sprinkled by hand, while making sure not to have too much grain in just one place. The furrow is then covered with a reed or brush broom so that the layer of earth covering the seed is not too thick to prevent germination or to cause rotting.

In present times, amaranth is also planted by means of the *chinampa* method in the zone of Tulyehualco, which involves germinating plants and transplanting them in the field (Sánchez Marroquín 1980:100). Sanders describes amaranth cultivation in San Gregorio Atlapulco, indicating that it is planted within a system of crop rotation, mixed with tomatoes one year, with maize the next, and with green tomatoes and chilies in the third year. "It is planted in seed beds in the chinampas and transplanted in April. It is more resistant to drought than maize and when the plants are tended and selected in seedbeds, it is possible to plant early in the field" (1983:127–128).

This plant flowers in August and September and early frosts destroy the leaves but have little effect on the grain; it is planted in April and May and harvested at the end of October or in November when the rainy season has finished. The ears become stiff and are easily to shell, but the farmers collect them early in order to avoid seed loss, because later the seeds are eaten by birds or fall to the ground and are very difficult to pick up due to their tiny size. The ears are cut at the base and laid out to dry, and the grain is obtained by beating the ears and with a stick on a piece of cloth; however, this operation does not remove all the seeds, and it is necessary to rub the ears manually, which is difficult because of the sharp spikes; the seeds are then sieved and put in sacks and stored in a dry place (Sánchez Marroquín 1980).

Teresa Rojas indicates that in the *Florentine Codex* there are representations of both the harvesting of the young, tender plant, which was consumed as a vegetable, by pulling it up by the roots, and the harvesting of the mature dry plant to obtain the seed, in this case by breaking the branches without any instrument, and then rubbing them together over a cloth. In reference to storage, she indicates that the representations in the *Mendocino Codex* and the Matricula de Tributos state that, like maize, sage, and beans, it was stored in granaries that are represented as quadrangular wooden structures, while the *Florentine Codex* illustrates the storage of amaranth, sage, and beans in clay *ollas* (Rojas 1985:185).

According to Sánchez Marroquín, the yield in volume of amaranth plants is almost the same as that of the maize plants, but since its cultivation exhausts the soil, consecutive planting on the same ground leads to decreasing yields. Consequently, crop rotation must be practiced by alternating it with beans or another legume (1980:30). In a recent study on some communities in Tlaxcala, Puebla, Morelos, and the Federal District (Del Amo et al. 1988:64), it is clarified that now in all cases chemical fertilization is used along with crop rotation with peanuts, beans, and *habas*.

There is little information on the yields of amaranth per hectare; Sánchez Marroquín indicates that the present-day yields in the states of Mexico and Morelos are between 800 and 1,200 kilos per hectare, depending on the soil conditions (in Tulyehualco, the average is 800 kilos per hectare, while in Huazulco, Morelos, it is between 1,200 to 2,500 kilos per hectare). The author also mentions that controlled crops with the varieties selected in experimental fields have exceeded 1,500 kilos per hectare. But experiments done in 1978 in Tlaxcala and Nayarit with seeds from Tulyehualco, the state of Mexico, and Huazulco, Morelos, in Tlaxcala, produced yields of 600 kilos per hectare (altitude 2,500 meters, precipitation 500 to 600 millimeters per year, very poor soils), and in Nayarit of 480 kilos per hectare (almost sea level, medium-quality soils, high rainfall and greater soil and atmospheric humidity than in Tlaxcala). In the first case, these low yields were attributed to the poor soil quality and, in the second, to the high temperatures of 28° to 35°C during the year (1980:105–108, 150). According to various authors in some parts of Mexico, *huautli* was used as a staple food when maize was in short supply, and amaranth substituted for maize as the principal crop in some places on the Pacific Coast (p. 21).

The oft-cited study by Sánchez Marroquín includes a series of biochemical research data for the nutritional qualities of numerous amaranth species, carried out by various institutions in Mexico and other countries. These studies illustrate the highly nutritional qualities of this plant, both from the seeds, which are more highly valued and have been the most widely used, and the leaves and stalks. According to these studies, some of the nutrients contained in this plant are comparable with what may be found in food sources such as soya, milk, meat, or wheat (pp. 11–173).

The amaranth cultivated in Mexico is a good source of excellent-quality proteins. Such proteins have a high lysine content that distinguishes it from other vegetable proteins; additionally, the seeds contain starch, fats, and other nutritive elements. The leaves of many of the young amaranth species are of extraordinary value as a source of vitamins and essential minerals such as calcium, phosphorus, and iron. The green parts may contain: 1.8–6.9 percent proteins; 400–800 milligrams calcium, and 15–80 milligrams phosphorus; iron is in a ratio of 18:25. On the other hand, the stalks of some black-seed species, which have low fiber and are highly digestible, also have a nutritive value (2.8–5.9 percent proteins, more than 350 milligrams of calcium, about 30 milligrams of phosphorus, and 2 milligrams of iron); the only drawback is the indigestible part of the raw fiber (Sánchez Marroquín 1980:52, 112, 122, 122; Ortiz 1997: table 2).

The most important aspect of the amaranth seed is that it contains an average of 14.7 percent proteins, 3.1 percent fat, and 60.7 percent carbohydrates, and it is rich in minerals: 510 milligrams calcium, 397 milligrams phosphorus, and 11 milligrams iron. The extraordinary aspect of the amaranth protein is its richness in the essential amino acids; the proportion of proteins in amaranth compares favorably with that of other vegetables, as is the case with its amino acids. Its protein quality is comparable to that of soya and yeast, and even to that of meat. It is important to note that the grain of this plant may be stored without suffering notable loss, unlike what happens with other cereals. It has been noted that the lightly toasted seeds, as is currently done to prepare the candy called *alegria,* are more digestible than the raw seeds (Sánchez Marroquín 1980:49, 121, 143).

In the Tula area, in various points of the habitation unit excavated at Tepetitlán, there was a great amount of seeds identified by González Quintero as *Amaranthus leucocarpus* and *Amaranthus hibridus* or quelite. Concentrations of *huautli* or *Amaranthus leucocarpus* were found on the stairs and at the foot of the stairway that connects the central patio with House II (see Fig. 9.3). The grains were dispersed and agglutinated in various points of the zone in a probable ritual context, suggesting that they could have been the remains of a prepared food that is similar to the present candies called *alegria,* or the figures of ritual use described by Sahagún and other historians for different religious ceremonies. Grains were also recorded in other parts of the same habitation unit in contexts that suggest their use as food. In the urban zone, amaranth was recorded in the El Canal habitation unit, although the frequency and specific contexts are not known (Diehl 1981).

The pollen analysis of the drilled stratigraphic core obtained at El Salitre in Tula by González Quintero and Montufar (1980:185–194) contributes very interesting data on amaranth. In the pollen diagram No. 1 and in figure No. 7 (partially reproduced in Figure 9.4), it can be seen that the amaranth chronologically precedes maize in the pollen column, and that later there are two significant concentrations of amaranth that coincide with a hiatus of maize pollen. Later still, there is an absence of amaranth that corresponds to the presence of higher concentrations of maize pollen.

In the opinion of González Quintero (personal communication 1996), this could mean that at the beginning there were two attempts to cultivate amaranth, followed by a preference or substitution of this crop with maize. This author states that the sporadic presence of amaranth seen in this part of the graph cannot be interpreted as meaning that amaranth was wild in this area at an initial moment, because although there are also wild species of amaranth in Mexico, *Amaranthus leucocarpus* is the cultivated species, with pollen possessing a characteristic thinner skin and thicker grain. The final part of the diagram shows the coexistence of both crops, and assuming that the graph directly reflects the higher or lower incidence of each species, amaranth would apparently have been the most abundant crop during this period. It is also very clear in this part of the diagram that the second peak or point of higher concentrations of amaranth pollen once again coincides with a hiatus or moment of reduction of maize pollen. It is important, however, to bear in mind, as González Quintero (personal communication 1996) clarifies, that the amaranth produces more pollen than maize and this should be taken into account in the interpretation of the graphs.

It is also interesting to note that the final part of the diagram where both crops coexist corresponds, according to graphs 2, 3, and 4 of the same study, to the final stage of what González Quintero and Montufar (1980) call the Temperate Humidity Stage and with the beginning of another period called Warm Dry, marked by an increase in the temperature and a decrease riverine water volume. The authors point out that "the record after *Amaranthus* and *Zea* is sporadic during the Warm Humid stage and it is difficult to decide whether man used water" (p. 192) for irrigation. Unfortunately, there are no absolute dates that would make it possible to chronologically place the various parts of the core, although there could be speculation about whether the point on the diagram located at around 140 centimeters corresponds to the period when there was the first significant human occupation of the area in terms of population density.

In summary, the pollen study shows, irrespective of the variations in frequency of amaranth pollen in the pollen column and in the interpretations that this may give rise to, that this plant was an important crop in the Tula region. The above—together with the facts that it has greater resistance than maize to drought and frost, high potential yield in soils of different qualities and characteristics, the ability to be stored for long periods of time without spoiling, and especially that it has high nutritional value—permits us to propose that, in the Tula area, amaranth could have been as important a crop as maize, or perhaps even more important in drought situations, when it could have functioned as an alternative fundamental crop. In this respect there is a very interesting quote by Monjarrez and Zamorano who in 1581 stated: "In the villages where the maize harvest is very low because of the barrenness of the soils, the people eat beans, huautli [alegria] and magueys" (in Hunziker

Metate	Bifacial (Obsidiana)
Mano de metate	Punta de proyectil (Obsidiana)
Machacador (Tejolote)	Punta de proyectil (Sílex)
Molcajete	Núcleo (Obsidiana)
Cepillo (Basalto)	Núcleo (Sílex)
Cepillo (Riolitta)	Núcleo (Riolita)
Raspador (Basalto)	Navaja prismática
Raspador (Riolita)	Excéntrico (Obsidiana)
Raspador (Obsidiana)	Cuenta (Piedra)
Raspador (Sílex)	Cuenta (Turquesa)
Pulidor	Tecalli
Cuchillo tabular o desfibrafor	Cristal de roca
Percutor	Escultura
Hacha (Basalto)	

Concentración de tiestos	
Olla Soltura	
Brasero Abra	
Cajete Jara	
Malacate	Tlecuil
Figurilla	Fogón
Figurilla zoomorfa	Hogar
Molde	Asta de venado
Sello	Hueso humano
Silbata	Restos de fauna
Tiesto recortado	Hueso trabajado
Cascabel de barro	Aguja de hueso
Cuenta de barro	Concha
Pigmento rojo	Concha trabajado

Agave sp. (Maguey)	Heliantus annuus (Girasol)
Agave (Espina de maguey)	P Lemaireocereus (Pitaya)
Amaranthus hybridus (Quelite)	Opuntia (Nopal)
Amaranthus leucocorpus (Amaranto)	Phaseolus (Frijol)
Arachis hypogea (Cacahuate)	Physolus (Tomate de bolsa)
Argemone (Chicalote)	P Pinus (Pino)
Capsicum annum (Chile)	V Portulaca m. (Verdolaga)
Carbón	Prosopis laevigata (Mezquite)
Carbón (Vara)	Prunis capuli (Capulín)
E Chenopodium ambrosoide (Epazote)	S Salvia (Chía)
H Chenopodium nutalis (Huanzontle)	Typha (Tule)
A Ficus (Papel de amate)	Yucca (Palma)
E Chenopodiaceae	Zea mays (Maíz)
G Gramineae	M Zea mays (Masa de maíz)

Figure 9.3. Tepetitlán U56: Locations of diverse archaeological elements.

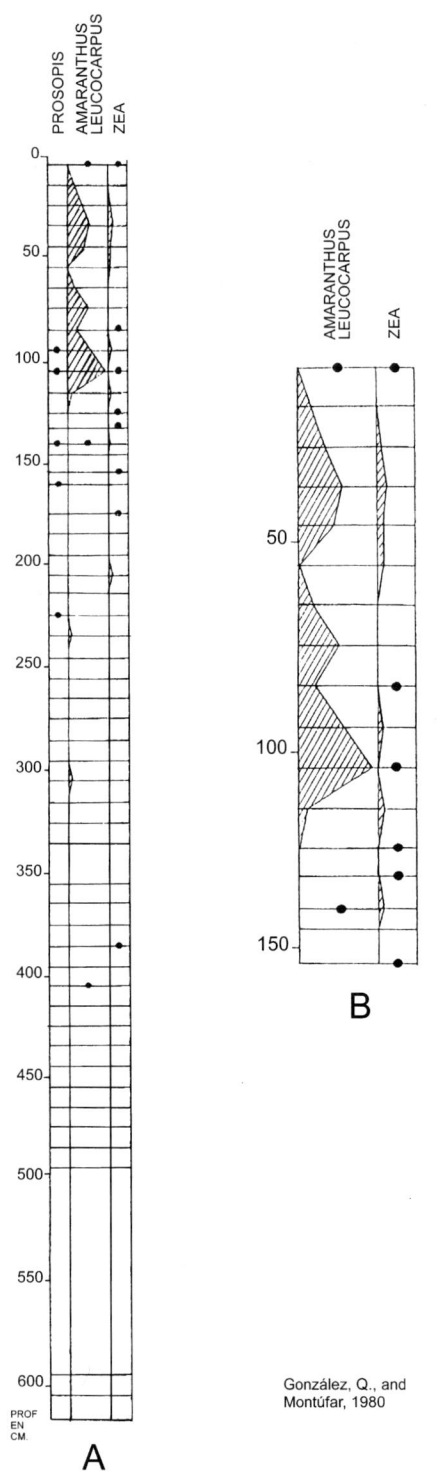

Figure 9.4. Pollen diagram for Tula (González Quintero and Montúfar 1980: fig. 7).

1952, quoted by Del Amo et al. 1988:59). Indeed, if amaranth is a crop that exhausts the soils, as claimed by various authors, its pre-Hispanic cultivation would imply the practice of extensive soil fertilization and planting in association with other crops, perhaps mainly with beans.

Finally, it is interesting to mention that during the Late Postclassic, the provinces of Ajacuba and Jilotepec, which included the Tula region, gave an amaranth tribute to the Triple Alliance in addition to maize and beans, which means that this plant continued to be an important crop in the area during this period (Bedoian 1973: tables 2, 3, and 5). It is interesting to note that in several sixteenth-century sources, such as the *Relaciones geográficas* and other earlier sources, the cultivation of amaranth is not mentioned for this area. This is very probably due to the very early prohibition by the Spanish of the cultivation of amaranth because of its ritual use and its substitution with other crops of greater interest for the conquistadors.

MAGUEY (*AGAVE SP.*)

In recent years, various researchers have stressed the importance of maguey as a source of drink and food in pre-Hispanic times. Parsons and Darling (1993:1) note that the interest of archaeologists in calculating the agricultural capacity of an area is focused on the annual cultivation of grains, principally maize, while ignoring the nutritional potential of maguey and considering this plant supplementary and secondary within the pre-Hispanic diet, when in many regions it is a primary and complementary crop in relation to annual crops. One of these regions is precisely the Tula area, where the cultivation of this plant has undoubtedly been very important during various periods.

According to Sanders (1993b:6), in Mexico there are numerous wild and cultivated species of the *Agave* genus; some authors speak of up to 150 different varieties that grow at different altitudes and are adapted to a wide range of environment conditions. These plants are present in zones with precipitation of less than 200 millimeters per year, extending to zones from 1,200 to 1,500 meters, and in temperatures that range from extremely hot, like the desert of Arizona, to the coldest parts of the Central Highlands of Mexico.

However, there are apparently only about nine or ten species of the plant known as maguey involved in the production of *pulque,* the most outstanding being *Agave salmiana* and *Agave americana,* of which there are several varieties. These species grow on the Central Highlands principally in high, semiarid zones at about 2,000 meters, in areas with minute precipitation and on soils where other crops cannot grow. Although their roots are rather shallow, they can extend to obtain humidity (Parsons and Parsons 1990; Torres 1985:106,109; Guerrero 1981; Finkler 1974).

Although the exploitation of the maguey plant in the production of *pulque* is its most known and most valued function, this plant has other notable uses, and various authors have cited it, not just as a source of drink, but also of food, fiber, fuel, construction material, and animal fodder. *Aguamiel* can be turned into honey and it is possible to store it permanently. The stalk (*quiote*) and possibly part of the leaves are edible when baked and may also be used to cover *barbacoa* and to season food. When planted around fields, the maguey helps prevent erosion.

It is important to note that a given maguey plant can be used for the production of *aguamiel* and *pulque* or for the consumption of its solid parts, but not both. The only major solid edible part of the maguey is the stalk or *quiote,* which never matures if the plant is employed to produce *pulque*. Another limitation of using the solid parts of magueys as food is that while the *quiote* is readily edible, the leaves even when roasted tender are very bitter, burning the mouth, and according to Moisés Mendoza (personal communication) for this reason at present are not commonly consumed. Perhaps in pre-Hispanic times, the solid parts of maguey mainly were consumed principally in difficult times as famine food. Mendoza also observes that perhaps the leaves and other soft parts of some Central Mexican agaves are edible, but these plants do not include the type of maguey that produces *pulque.*

The early physician Francisco Hernández notes that in the sixteenth century "this plant alone could easily provide all that is necessary for a frugal and simple life, because it is not affected by the rigors of the weather, nor does it shrivel in drought. Nothing gives better yields." He enumerates in detail its notable uses:

> The uses of this plant are almost innumerable. The whole plant can be used as fuel and to hedge fields, the stalks are used as wood; the leaves to cover roofs like tiles, as plates or a source to make papyrus, to provide thread with which to make footwear, cloth and all kinds of garments are manufactured, nails and spikes are made from the spines . . . pins, needles, war instruments and brushes to comb the length of cloth. The juice which comes from and is distilled in the central cavity is ordained by cutting the inner parts . . . of which a single plant can sometimes fill 50 amphorae, which are used to make the wines, honey, vinegar and sugar . . . the thicker parts of the leaves and the trunk are baked under the earth . . . they are good to eat and taste like cider laced . . . with sugar . . . wine is made from the same juice by diluting it with water and adding cider and lime skins, gaupatli and other things to make it stronger." (1959: 2, 349, quoted by Parsons and Parsons 1990:275)

The last part of the colonial period and the nineteenth century were a period of apogee for the exploitation of the maguey in the area studied. With the expansion of the *pulque* haciendas, large areas of land were set aside for the cultivation of this agave, basically for the production of *pulque,* which supplied a growing market outside the area, including Mexico City. The map of land use in the nineteenth century (Fig. 2.8) shows the maguey cultivation zones that covered an area of almost 5,000 hectares. Additionally, there were mixed maguey and maize cultivation zones, the size of which is difficult to determine. The traces left by both colonial and nineteenth-century cultivation can still be seen in aerial photographs that, together with current land use, in many cases obscure the remains of the terraces and the pre-Hispanic soil use in these zones.

In present times, the agave is found in family gardens or alternating with maize in the same field. It is also found in extensive plantations, especially in the northwest and southeast of the area, although in the latter zone it is also frequently cultivated as a mixed crop with maize. Terraces are common in the proximity of Tepeji del Río where the natural terracing formed by the erosion of the hills is used and the agave is planted along the edges of these terraces to protect the land and hold water (Crespo 1976:40–41).

In the study zone, there are between five and nine maguey varieties involved in the making of *pulque,* especially the *manso, chacano, samni,* Mexicano, *penca larga,* Santo Domingo, and ordinary maguey types, which according to Finkler grow in the *pulque*-producing regions of the state of Hidalgo. With the exception of the common maguey, a wild type that requires about twenty years to start to produce, these varieties mature at seven, eight, or ten years after having been planted, at which time they yield between 5 and 10 liters of *aguamiel* daily for three to four months. The amount of sap or *aguamiel* produced by the agave depends on the species and the way it is scraped to make the *aguamiel* flow. The juice is collected by suction with a long hollow gourd called an *acocote,* and is then poured into a vessel that contains *pulque* culture; it is left to stand for seventy-two hours to ferment into *pulque* (Finkler 1974:99, 100, 169, 172, 173, 177, 180).

Parsons and Parsons, in an extensive monograph on the maguey, offer a very complete panorama on the traditional uses of this plant and its exploitation, especially as a producer of *pulque* and textile fiber (1990:338). They indicate that between 5 and 10 percent of the maguey plants in a field are in production simultaneously, and that the production period is between three and six months. A single maguey plant produces several hundred liters of *aguamiel,* and one hectare of maguey produces between 5,000 and 9,000 liters per year.

These authors observe that in Meztitlán, the density per hectare is less than 600 plants, and only 5 percent of those plants are in production, and thus the maximum calories that would be obtained per year would be 858,000, which is only the equivalent to a maize yield of 230 kilos per hectare. Even with a density per hectare of 1,000 plants, the production would only be equal to that of 400 kilos of maize (Parsons and Darling 1993). On the other hand, Sanders (1993b) observes that if the production capacity for *pulque,* with an estimated 574 calories per liter, is taken into account, the plants would produce 40,855 liters of *pulque* in one year, that is, 2,786 kcal, which would be the equivalent of the yield per hectare of 800 kilos of maize (pp. 20–21).

This means that if the maguey is cultivated as a single crop for the exploitation of the pulp or as a source of *aguamiel,* one would not obtain the same yields in calories as would be produced by grain crops under rainfall or irrigation regimens, with deep soils, or with a good supply of water. However, in the dry areas of the Basin of Mexico or on hillsides where it is not possible to use rainwater and the soils are shallow, the maguey is the most productive crop, and the one with the least risk, especially when used to produce *aguamiel*. However there is doubt about its consumption in the form of *pulque,* and whether this drink could have functioned as a principal source of calories. This is because of the limitations that *pulque* could have as an alcoholic beverage, due to its physiological effects and the known pre-Hispanic restrictive rules for its consumption (Sanders 1993b).

Crespo, in a study of the Tula area, notes (1976) that according to the 1960 Agriculture, Livestock, and Ejido Census, some 333,100 magueys had been planted, obtaining a yield of 10,835,225 liters of *pulque*. A study by Ruipérez Marín (1965) on the municipality of Tula, also based on the 1960 census data, likewise offers information about the cultivation of the maguey and the production of *pulque* in this area. It indicates that in an area of 112.9 hectares, there is a total of 56,925 plants, of which 19,413 are at the age for extraction and 5,714 are tapped in the year, which means an annual production of 1,323,253 liters (p. 125).

The above means that the density of planting in this zone is an average of 504 plants per hectare, that is, a slightly lower density than what was proposed by Parsons and Darling, which is perhaps due to the poor soil quality in the area. However, the total number of plants that are simultaneously in production is an average of fifty plants per hectare (10 percent of the plants), which is a higher percentage than what was considered by Sanders in his calculations on the yields of kcal per hectare. Thus, in the case of Tula according to Ruipérez's data, the production per hectare would be 11,720 liters, while Parsons and Darling (1993:4) calculated a yield range of between 5,000 and 9,000 liters per hectare per year. The figure of 11,720 liters per hectare, which means an annual yield per plant of 230.7 liters, is a much higher production per plant than what was calculated by Sanders (161.8 liters).

The most productive period of the maguey is especially in the dry season, from the end of March, April, May, and June; in the rainy season, the quality of the *aguamiel* drops because of humidity, the dilution of the sugars, and the proliferation of bacteria and fungi, which spoil it (Granados Sánchez, personal communication). The maguey has a high nutritional value; both the *aguamiel* and the pulp are rich in nutrients and calories; one liter of the maguey sap contains 574 calories, and 100 grams of cooked maguey pulp has 347 calories and 4.5 grams of protein (Parsons and Darling 1993:4). These authors cite a study on an Otomí village in which it is indicated that *pulque* provided 12 percent of the calories and 6 percent of the proteins, 10 percent of the thiamin, 24 percent of the riboflavin, 23 percent of the niacin, 48 percent of the vitamin C, 8 percent of the calcium, and 20 percent of the iron in the daily diets of the Otomí.

Sanders (1993b) draws attention to the fact that the calories and other nutrients of the maguey must be calculated on the basis of the dry plant because of the fact that a large part of the weight of the leaves is water, which could distort calculations. Based on various studies in this field, he proposes the figure of 430 kcal per liter of *aguamiel* instead of the 574 proposed by Parsons and Darling, based on the research of Ruvalcaba. He also indicates, regarding the productive capacity of 1 hectare of maguey in comparison with 1 hectare of maize, that it is important to bear in mind that the maguey needs from six to twenty-five years to mature, and in many cases only 5 percent of the plants in the field are producing simultaneously.

The next section is a summary of some of the principal proposals made by Parsons and Darling (1993), because in our opinion they are of great interest as a general point of reference and working hypothesis. Their main observations are based on the study by Parsons and Parsons (1990).

- There is ethnographic, ethnohistorical, and archaeological evidence for the extensive use of the maguey as food and as a source of textile fiber and especially its use in the Basin of Mexico in various ecological niches, from hillsides to the alluvial plain, in areas with both moderate and light rainfall. However, the maguey does not only grow in marginal lands, it may also be cultivated on any kind of agricultural land, except chinampas, including zones with deep and humid soils.

- This plant's high degree of tolerance to variations in temperature and rainfall makes it a secure source of calories in the marginal areas of the Central Highlands where maize cannot be cultivated or where it is a risky crop; in addition, it can be exploited throughout the year and requires less investment in work than many other crops.

- The calorie production of a field of maguey, taking into account the use of the pulp (heart, leaves) and the liquid produced by the plant in the form of *aguamiel*, is higher than that of maize. That is, the maguey produces more calories per unit of land than grain crops, except on permanently irrigated land and *chinampas* where maize produces higher yields. The fact that the maguey may be planted alone or together with seed crops in almost any environment is very important, and its nutritional value and energy production may be thus increased per unit of land. (This point is debatable because, as mentioned before, maguey cannot be used simultaneously as both a source of *pulque* and for solid food.)

- The maguey is productive all year round, even in months when there are no other kinds of crops, and it can be combined with the grain-storage cycles. Given its resistance to the drought, frost, hail, and low temperatures that destroy other kinds of crops, it is an excellent alternative in situations of crop loss and famine.

- The expansion of the Mesoamerican civilization in the Central Highlands and in north Mexico depended on the total integration of two systems of agricultural production based on seeds and agaves. There was a generalized agricultural pattern based on both types of crops in nuclear zones, especially in the valleys of irrigable rivers, while in the dryer peripheral regions (hillsides and high plains that cannot be irrigated), there would be a more specialized production of the agave, perhaps together with nopal.

- Archaeological records suggest a fundamental change in the technology used in the production of the agave in the center and north of Mexico after the Classic period, related to a more efficient exploitation of the plant, which became a more important resource when the population increased. That is, although the maguey was probably an essential economic element from the earliest phases of occupation of the Basin of Mexico, starting with the Postclassic and the expansion of the population and urban life, its cultivation became more important.

Sanders (1993b:22–23) stated in his comments on the work by Parsons and Darling that it is necessary to ask how many of the maguey's uses could have been complementary and how many were mutually exclusive, and to consider the fact that there is no knowledge of the sequence of exploitation for the different uses of the maguey, especially when it began to be used as a source of *aguamiel* and *pulque*. He also notes, that if the legends about the Toltecs inventing *pulque* reflect a real event, it would indicate that the use of this liquid as a beverage would be relatively late, and that the previous use of this plant would be centered on its use as a source of fiber and in the utilization of the roasted pulp as food.

It is unlikely, however, that the legendary tales about the invention of *pulque* in Tula indeed refer to a real event, because in Teotihuacan there are various representations in mural paintings that, in the opinions of various authors, indicate that *pulque* was already an important beverage in that city. Miller and Taube observe that the *pulque* god appeared for the first time in Teotihuacan, during the Classic Period (1992:138). Taube also states that the masculine anthropomorphic representation conserved on the floor of La Ventilla complex is related to *pulque* (personal communication). Angulo (1996) and Rivas and Lechuga (1987, quoted by Angulo) mention that there are stone instruments in Teotihuacan and in earlier sites in the Basin of Mexico that could have been used to scrape the heart of the maguey to obtain *pulque*. They also note that some representations in the murals of Tepantitla and Tlacuilapaxco show the importance of *pulque* in the urban life of Teotihuacan. Regarding the same period, Angulo cites Müller concerning the mural of the drinkers in Cholula, which is perhaps the oldest pictographic version of a ritual complex dedicated to the god of *pulque* (pp. 126–127).

It is difficult to establish whether the maguey was used extensively in the Tula area during the Teotihuacan occupation; however, the population distribution for this period in the area suggests an economy related to irrigation agriculture and the exploitation of lime. Although the dispersed occupation in the Classic period around Xicuco and on the lower foothills of the sierra that bounds the area to the east, as well as to the south of the Chingú site (see Fig.4.1), is in zones of potential rainfall agriculture, it could have included the cultivation of the agave.

It seems reasonable to the propose (although with indirect evidence) that during the period prior to the development of the urban center (La Mesa Phase: ca. A.D. 550–650), the extensive use and exploitation of the maguey in the area started not only as a textile fiber, but also as a source of beverage and food. If so, its importance as a crop would not be related in this case to the demographic growth and the urban expansion proposed by Parsons and Darling (1993) for these zones, but to situations of adaptation to the ecological niches occupied by these groups and perhaps to a cultural tradition with emphasis on exploitation of the agave. But very likely it was during the apogee of Tula (Tollan Phase) that maguey cultivation extended further and took on greater importance as a beverage and food.

It is very probable that the extensive exploitation of the maguey during the La Mesa Phase is related to the occupation of different ecological niches than those of the previous period, principally on the tops of elevations and hillsides with poorer and shallow soils, without the possibility of irrigation and, in several cases, without direct access to sources of water. From this moment, for the first time great systems of terraces were constructed associated with the principal sites of this period, especially on the Magoni-Bojay sierra and on the extreme east of the sierra that bounds the area to the north, as well as on the foothills of the eastern mountains of the area, including Cerro La Mesa and its foothills to the south (see Fig. 4.6).

In most cases, the boundary walls that bordered the terraces are visible on the surface, along with numerous materials that indicate these they were habitation and cultivation zones. In some cases, the habitation areas are separated from the terrace zones, which seem to have been exclusively agricultural. The surface materials include various kinds of rhyolite and basalt artifacts, especially small "turtle" type scrapers and other larger ones that Jackson (1990) and Rees (1990), who analyzed the lithic industry of these sites in detail, call *cepillos* (high-backed scrapers).

In the analysis of the lithic artifacts of the La Mesa and Atitalaquia sites, Jackson (1990) notes that the obsidian scrapers are scarce, with a predomination of the basalt scrapers and *cepillos* in the first site. He also shows that the absence of wear on the tool edges permits the supposition that they were used to work softer materials, such as leather or vegetable fiber, and that because of their morphology, size, and edge characteristics, the *cepillos* were very well adapted for processing the maguey. There is only one case in which it is obvious that the artifact was used to work hard materials.

Based on the microflaking and microfractures evident in these artifacts, Jackson tries to reconstruct the working angles, concluding that they could be used successfully in the exploitation of maguey. The same observations are valid for the scrapers and *cepillos* of the Atitalaquia site, except that there most of the scrapers are made of chert (1990:209, 210, 275, 276). Jackson's quote that there are obsidian scrapers in the Preclassic of Tulancingo (Hidalgo) that are very similar to the iron ones currently used in the processing of the *pulque* is very interesting (Miller and Ramos 1955, quoted in Jackson 1990:210).

Parsons and Parsons (1990) propose that, based on the experiments carried out by Hester and Heizer with materials from Oaxaca, in the Formative and Classic periods the turtle scrapers had double or triple functions: to soften the maguey leaf, scrape the pulp, and crush the leaf, as is done today by the Tarahumaras. It is interesting to note that the scrapers used by Hester and Heizer are, according to the illustration and the data on their weight (400 grams), very similar to those analyzed by Jackson (1990) in the Tula area (Parsons and Parsons 1990:365).

Parsons and Darling (1993:12–14) likewise indicate that in the Formative and Classic periods the most common agave instruments were chipped scrapers that were used to work fibers and obtain *aguamiel*. During the Postclassic, these artifacts continued to function as scrapers to obtain *aguamiel*, but they were replaced for the fiber work with the basalt slab tools known as *azadas*. Parsons and Parsons stress that these instruments were essentially absent in the Central Highlands before the Postclassic, but Serra (1985) records them in one Formative site. They also propose that the use of this kind of tool and spindle whorls to spin the fiber seem to indicate that the exploitation of the maguey during the Postclassic would have been more efficient, and that they associated this greater efficiency with the development of expansionist urban states.

In the Tula area the slab *azadas*, which were similar to those illustrated by Parsons and Parsons (1990:203, fig. 38), are present in burials in the Coyotlatelco site of La Mesa, but their presence on the surface is not evident in other sites of this period. A characteristic of the Coyotlatelco sites of the area is a high frequency on the surface of sherds corresponding to heavy *ollas* with thick walls that are diagnostic of this period, of the type designated La Luz and variations of this type (Cobean 1990). Cobean indicates that on the sites located on the tops of elevations, such as Magoni and La Mesa, there is a trend toward a gigantic version of these *ollas*. In previous works (Mastache and Cobean 1989, 1990), we have noted that the size and characteristics of these recipients seem to be related to the poor access of these sites to water sources and the need to store liquids: water and perhaps *aguamiel* or *pulque*. In this respect, it is interesting that the necks and profiles of these *ollas* are very similar to those of the vessels for *pulque* illustrated in the Postclassic codices, especially to the types C and D that are reproduced in Figure 36 of the work by Parsons and Parsons (1990:295).

If indeed the Coyotlatelco sites in the Tula region were partially contemporary with the Teotihuacan settlements, two types of agricultural exploitation very probably coexisted in the area at the end of this period, including one with an emphasis on the cultivation and exploitation of agaves on the higher lands with poorer, shallow soils, which were improved by the construction of terraces, some of which were not used again after this period. In addition, there were crops of maize and other plants on alluvial soils and lower, good-quality irrigated and rainfall lands related to the Teotihuacan occupation of the area.

Some of these terrace systems were not occupied again, which is evident in the La Mesa and Atitalaquia sites as well as in some zones of the foothills in the extreme northeast of the area and at the Magoni site. In this latter area, only the top and some of the lower terraces were reoccupied during the Tollan Phase, and new terraces on the lower foothills were constructed and were extensively used during the city's apogee.

Broad systems of terraces were built during the Tollan Phase in zones that were used for the first time; this is the case in the western part of the sierra that limits the area to the north and the foothills of the La Mesa and Los Picachos mountains. There are obsidian scrapers, blades, and other types of instruments associated with these systems of terraces; however, since most of the zones were reoccupied during the Late Postclassic, it is difficult to define accurately whether these instruments correspond to the Tollan Phase. There is the same problem with the spindle whorls of the surface collections and with the tabular fiber scrapers or *azadas* present on the surface in Tollan Phase sites reoccupied during the Late Postclassic (see Fig. 9.5).

There is evidence of the use of the maguey in the plant remains preserved in Tepetitlán, analyzed by González Quintero (1999). These specimens are carbonized, as is the case of other vegetable remains conserved in the site. As can be seen on the corresponding map (see Fig. 9.3), the spines of the plant, found in different points of the habitation compound in diverse contexts, are the predominant remains. There were also fragments of leaf and carbonized fibers associated with a hearth that could be indicators of the preparation and consumption of the pulp as food.

As indicated in Chapter 8, Rosa Moncayo, in her analysis of the Tepetitlán ceramics (1999), concludes that there are several more varieties of the Soltura-type *ollas* in this site than in the Tollan Complex of the city, in addition to other types of *ollas* that have not been recorded in the city of Tula. The *ollas* constitute, as a whole, a greater part of the ceramics of this excavation, and they are more abundant than in urban contexts. Many of the Tepetitlán *ollas* do not seem to have been used for cooking, because there are no signs of soot or having been put on a fire, which suggests that their function was probably for the storage of grains or liquids. Cobean proposes that many of the *ollas* in Tepetitlán could have been used to store *aguamiel* or *pulque,* because the storage of water would be of little importance in this site considering the closeness of permanent water sources.

It should also be stressed that the Blanco Levantado–type *ollas* are more frequent in Tepetitlán than in the city, and that there is a variety of the Soltura *olla* with a narrow neck that is very similar in shape to the Blanco Levantado, which could have had the same function. As indicated in Chapter 8, it is very probable that the function of the Blanco Levantado *ollas* was to transport *aguamiel* or *pulque,* that is, they were used as a sort of individual canteen for drinking and taking it to the field or to market. Regarding this point, it is interesting to mention that these *ollas,* together with the Macana and Jara plates, are the most frequent types in the dispersed-material zones (Type 15), which is a kind of occupation that apparently principally corresponds to cultivation zones.

It is interesting to stress that the lower foothills of the sierra upon which a large part of the Tollan Phase settlement in Tepetitlán extends is a zone with shallow Class IV soils that are suitable for the cultivation of the maguey, and has extensive systems of terraces that are still in use for the cultivation of maguey and maize. We know from the *Suma de visitas,* an early-sixteenth-century source, that the maguey was an important crop in the Tepetitlán area:

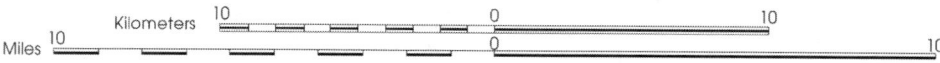

Figure 9.5. Early Postclassic: Distribution of basalt scrapers.

SUBSISTENCE ACTIVITIES

"Viven estos naturales de hacer mantillas de niquen y de hacer cotaras y venden niquen para hacer petates" (*Suma de Visitas* 1905:226). There is also mention of its cultivation in other zones of the area: Tezontepec, Xochitlán, Michimaloya, San Pedro Nextlalpan, Tlamaco, Atotonilco, Tula, and Atitalaquia, although in some cases, for example in Tezontepec, it is stated that it was an unimportant crop (p. 223).

The data on the exploitation of the maguey in the Tula area illustrate that this plant was cultivated in zones with poor soils, because there is no mention of its cultivation or tribute in zones with deep soils with irrigation possibilities. When dealing with towns having different types of lands, it is clarified that the irrigated lands were dedicated principally to the cultivation of maize and wheat. For example in the case of Atotonilco, the same source indicates: "Pasa por un Rio hondo y con el riegan cien hanegas de sembradura de trigo poco mas o menos, todo lo demás es tierra alta que no se puede regar, es fria y seca y llueve poco en ella . . . es tierra que hay muchas heladas. Ay muchos magueyes y tunas y piedra para hacer cal y destas cosas tienen mucha grangería los yndios" (*Suma de Visitas* 1905:2). And the *Descripción del Arzobispado de México* (Ledezma 1905:57) states about the same town of Atotonilco: "Los aprovechamientos de que viven los naturales . . . que es de ser labradores, aunque no siembran mucho por ser la tierra seca; y de quemar cal, y de hacer mantillas de maguey de que se bisten y benden; es toda ella comúnmente gente pobre."

Most other sources of this type only refer to the use of the maguey as a textile fiber; therefore it is interesting to note the data recorded in the *Relaciones Geográficas* of 1580 on Atitalaquia and its dependent towns, where the importance of the maguey as a beverage in this area is clearly mentioned. As we saw in the previous chapter, Atitalaquia, like Atotonilco, is on the Salado River in an area with flat lands and small strips of irrigation, but where heavily eroded soils predominate, in the center of the lime exploitation zone. In this instance it is mentioned that:

> que fuesen estos naturales de sus tierras aprovechados, en tierras asi de temporal como de regadío, donde cogían y de presente cogen mucho mayz y aji y otras semillas de que son aprovechados y entre ellos tienen valor y precio; tenían juntamente con esto por hazienda principal la de los magueyes, de que son muy aprovechados por los particulares y muchos aprovechamientos que de ellos tienen . . . tienen por principales aprovechamientos el ylo mas o menos delgado, según lo benefician: tienen las mantas con que se cubren tan delgadas o bastas como es el beneficio del ylado . . . aprovenchanse de estos magueyes para suelos de calzado.

and then it adds that:

> es este aprovechamiento del maguey como son las cepas en España para el vino del cual se gasta grandisima cantidad de tierra . . . hazeze gran copia de miel de que se aprovechan todos los cinco pueblos de esta jurisdicción, porque se ocupan los naturales de de ellos en el beneficio desta miel . . . no hazen todos estos naturales la miel . . . porque se precian mas de taberneros que de meleros y acese el vino a menos costa y el aprovechamiento del entre ellos es mas común que el de la miel . . . sacan de estos magueyes un aguamiel sustancial y dulce, de tal manera que generalmente se aprovechan mas della para bever que del agua que por estos pueblos pasa por que es salobre y como tengan la dicha miel no echan menos el agua.

Assuming that maize, amaranth, and maguey were the fundamental crops during the period of the apogee of Tula, when the area was populated with tens of thousands of people who lived in the city and in its rural environment, and, therefore, there was a need for a very efficient exploitation of the resources of the area and to maximize the yields of the principal crops, it is very feasible that there would have been a direct correlation between soil classes and specific crop systems. Bearing in mind that Class I and II soils are potentially more productive and more suitable for irrigation and that the most efficient crop in terms of kcal in irrigated lands is maize (Sanders 1993b), it may be supposed that the zones with these soils were almost exclusively used for the cultivation of this grain, especially of the more productive races such as Chalqueño, while the lands with Class III and IV soils would be used for rainfall crops, the main crops being maize of other races, amaranth, and maguey in some cases. The extensive areas of poorer soils (Classes V to VII), located especially on foothills and uneven areas, would essentially be used for the extensive exploitation of the maguey, increasing the possibilities of this crop through extensive terrace systems.

The data that we have discussed on the Tula region make it possible to propose that the traditional concept of the Mesoamerica diet based on the triad of maize, beans, and squash does not seem valid in this case, because it is very likely that the fundamental crops of the Toltec diet constituted a different triad—maize, amaranth, and maguey—crops that may have also been important in other regions with cultural traditions and climatic and geographic characteristics similar to those of the Tula area.

OTHER PLANT RESOURCES, GATHERING, AND HUNTING

It must be remembered that, in addition to the maize, beans, amaranth, and maguey that seem to have been the staple crops in the diet of the inhabitants of the city of Tula and its hinterland, numerous associated and wild species, the consumption of which is still very important in traditional societies, must have been frequently consumed food resources. It should be mentioned that there are between two and five hundred edible plant species recorded in various regions of Mexico, including several varieties of seeds, fruits, roots, and flowers (Cuevas et al. 1991).

As indicated by Granados Sánchez and Hernández (1995:110), in arid areas such as the study region, gathering and hunting occupied a principal role. Gathering and collection included not just all kinds of edible plants (seasonal fruit such as the *garambullo, capulin, tunas,* and mesquites, *garambullo* flowers, palm, and maguey flowers) but also various kinds of animals and insects. Until recently, fishing and the hunting of deer, hares, rabbits, pheasants, and other kinds of birds was also important.

In their research on the Otomí community of Ñahñu, bordering on the study area, Granados Sánchez and Hernández (1995) found that the Otomí practice the collection of spontaneous and perennial products of vegetable and animal origin in their gardens, plots of cultivated land, and in the surrounding zones. Through gathering, they provision themselves with significant amounts of food and other items that are a complement to hunting and the products cultivated in their vegetable gardens and fields. According to these authors, the range of species gathered includes various kinds of mushrooms, diverse varieties of quelites and greens (*Portulaca oleracea, Chenopodium album, Amaranthus hibridus*), leaves, flowers, and fruit of various species of *Opuntia sp.* (nopal), *Opuntia xoconostle, Opuntia streplacantha, Opuntia megacantha, Cururbita pepo* flowers, *Yucca filifera, Dasylirion* and *Agave salmiana* inflorescences, and *Prosopis laevigata* pods, among many other plants, as well as various larvae and insects.

In the archaeological collection of carbonized plants preserved in the Tollan Phase domestic structure excavated in the Tepetitlán site and studied by González Quintero (1999), there are wild plants that are the result of gathering and cultivated species of high nutritional importance. This author states that the species present are characteristic of a xerophytic environment, such as *Mimosa, Prosopis, Koeberlina spinosa, Yucca,* and *viznagas,* along with genuses of vegetable communities that are particular to alluvial lands, as well as species typical of foothills with igneous rock substratum, such as *Dasylirion, Lemaireocerus,* and *Opuntia,* varieties of tule-like *Scirpus* and *Typha* that are characteristic of soils with excessive humidity, *zacatón,* which grows at different altitudes but especially at high altitudes, and *Ficus,* which is alien to the study area. Some of these plants were used as fuel by the occupants of the rural habitation complex excavated. The seeds and fruit of the *Opuntia* genre were also recovered; these and the leaves must have been the nutritional resources of frequent consumption. *Prosopis* and *Lemaireocerus* (*pitaya*) were also undoubtedly important for human consumption, not only as food. The sample also contains species such as *Amaranthus hibridus* or *huanzontle,* quelites, green tomatoes, various kinds of *Chenopodium,* and purslane (*Portulaca*) (Fig. 9.3).

We have included a complete list of the plants identified by González Quintero (1999), Kaplan

(1999), and Benz (1999) in the collection of the Tepetitlán domestic unit, although obviously not all the species are edible:

Agave sp. (maguey), *Amaranthus hybridus* (quelite), *Arachis hypogaea* (peanut), *Amaranthus leucocarpus* (*alegría* or *huautli*), *Argemone* (*chicalote*), *Capsicum annuum* (chile), *Chenopodium ambrosioides* (*epazote*), *Chenopodium nuttalliae* (*huazontle*), *Dasylirion* (*cucharilla*), *Echino-fossulocactus* (*viznaga*), *Eragrostis* (*zacate*), *Ficus* (*amate*), *Helianthus annuus* (sunflower), *Lemaireocereus* (*pitaya*), *Mimosa* (cat's claw), *Muhlenbergia macroura* (*zacatón*), *Opuntia* (nopal), *Physalis* (green tomato), *Portulaca mexicana* (verdolaga), *Portulaca pilos* (verdolaga), *Prosopis laevigata* (mesquite), *Phaseolus* (bean), *Prunus capulli* (*capulín*), *Quercus* (oak), *Salvia* (sage), *Solanum* (*papita de monte*), *Stipa* (*zacate*), *Theobroma cacao* (cacao), *Typha* (tule), *Yucca* (palm), *Zea mays* (maize).

As can be seen, edible weed species such as *Chenopodium, Eragrostis, Helianthus,* and *Portulaca* are present, which have been detected in other archaeological sites of the Central Highlands. The relative abundance of *Zea mays, Amaranthus leucocarpus, Phaseolus,* and *Agave* indicates the importance of these crops in the Tula area during this period. Some of these species had previously been identified in the urban zone in the El Canal excavation: *Zea mays, Chenopodium sp., Opuntia sp., Amaranthus sp., Portulaca sp., Prunus sp., Diospyros sp., Prosopis sp.,* and *Agave sp.* (Diehl 1981: 287).

The presence among the preserved edible species of *Arachis hypogaea* (peanut) and *Theobroma cacao* recorded in the interior of a hearth and in a funerary context respectively is very important, because they are crops that are grown outside the study area and, as stressed by González Quintero (1999), these species are rarely found in archaeological contexts. It is important to note that the peanut was found in a context corresponding to the late Postclassic reoccupation (Mastache and Cobean 1999a:286–290).

A fragment of cacao was associated with a cremation, and it is the only evidence recorded to date for this food item in the Central Highlands. It is very interesting to note that this imported product, which must have been a luxury item with limited consumption in Tula, is present in a rural site of the city's hinterland, albeit only as an offering. As proposed by Diehl (1983) and Cobean (1990), the presence of cacao in the Tula region is very probably associated with the commerce of Plumbate ceramics from the Soconusco regions of the Pacific coast of Chiapas and Guatemala, which was the most important cacao cultivation zone of Mesoamerica, and the only production center of this kind of ceramics.

It is interesting to note the absence of the squash (*Cucurbita sp.*) in both Tepetitlán and the urban zone, since it has been considered as a basic Mesoamerica crop. This fact may not be that important, bearing in mind the limited size of the botanical specimens conserved. However, González Quintero (1999) stresses that he did not find mention of this plant in the *Relacion de Sayula,* a town close to Tepetitlán, and neither did we find reference to its cultivation in the study area in sources published in the sixteenth century, such as the *Suma de visitas* (1905), the *Descripción del Arzobispado de México* (Ledezma 1905), or the *Relaciones geográficas*. It is also interesting that chia (sage) or *Salvia* is only represented by one specimen, although, as mentioned by González Quintero, special effort was made in the search for this plant, bearing in mind that its cultivation covers a large part of the Otomí region, and that Tepetitlán is located almost in the center of the triangle formed by the towns of Huichapan, Chiapa de Mota, and Chiapantongo, all of which are toponyms alluding to chia.

A presence of *Argemone* or *chicalote* is very suggestive; because according to González Quintero (personal communication 1996) it is a wild plant that flourishes in places undisturbed by humans, such as abandoned cultivated fields or fallow lands. This is not an edible species, but the seed has narcotic characteristics, and it is a close relative of the poppy. This author adds that the seeds are found in association with burials, generally not burned, even though in Teotihuacan they have been observed in association with bone ash (González Quintero 1999:146). The presence of the sunflower (*Helianthus*) is also interesting because it has an oleaginous edible seed that could have been used, as this author mentions, toasted and in *atole*.

Nopal (*Opuntia sp.*)

We agree with Granados Sánchez and Hernández (1995) and Rafael Ortega (personal communication) when they stress that the importance of diverse species of *Opuntia* for human consumption in an arid environment such as the study area cannot be underestimated. It is very likely that many of the current uses of this plant by the Otomí people of the area are similar to its utilization in the pre-Hispanic period.

Granados Sánchez and Hernández note (1995) that currently there is very widespread use of both cultivated and wild nopals in the area. This species is divided into races that make up two groups; one of them, whose Otomí name is *hoga xat,a,* is cultivated in crop fields or plots and in vegetable gardens; the other, *mbonga xat,a,* includes the wild races that are exploited due to the plant associations. The Ñahñu Otomí campesinos conceptualize an informal classification according to the morphology of the plant and the botanical characteristics (color) of the fruit. The semideveloped *nopalitos* and *cladolios* (leaves) (*mest,a*) are collected to be consumed as vegetables in various dishes; the fruit (*tunas*) are used for home consumption, gifts, barter, and offerings for the dead; and the mature *cladolios* are used as forage and the dry stalks are used as domestic fuel (p. 113).

In the region, there are various kinds of wild *tuna* species that ripen at different times and have distinct characteristics: "agua mielilla," which is noted for its sweetness; "larga," because of its length; "amarilla" and "rojo" for the color; "shirgu," a very small and seedy *tuna;* and "cuija," which lasts longer after cutting, among others. The *tuna* is not only consumed fresh, but also in a form of *atole,* crushed and without seeds, and maize dough is added to this concentrate. It is interesting to note that *queso de tuna*, which is consumed in various arid regions of the country, is solidified *tuna* juice with a high nutritional value that, once prepared in this manner, may be stored. The nopal is also a source of animal protein; there are colonies of white worms in the old stalks and the bases of the older leaves. These worms are consumed by frying them in lard or toasting with salsa (Granados and Ortega, personal communication 1998).

Other important species in the area include *garambullo* (*Myrtillocactus geometrizans*), *zapote blanco* (*Casimiroa edulis*), and mesquite (*Prosopis sp.*), the last being present in archaeological specimens recorded in Tepetitlán and in the urban zone. Granados Sánchez and Hernández note (1995:115) that the *garambullo* is found in plant associations on foothills and low hills, and that there are various kinds that differ in color, size, and shape of the fruit, which are now collected for home consumption and on some occasions for gifts and barter; the flowers are also collected and used in the preparation of various dishes. The *zapote blanco* is frequently found in inhabited or abandoned households, where it is protected and propagates by means of the seeds of the harvested fruit. There are varieties that are used differentially based on the color of the fruit pulp. This species is valued for its fruit and cool shade, under which the spinning workshops, looms, and *pulque* and water vessels are located, together with the maguey-scraping equipment, tools, and agricultural implements.

Very little work has been done on the potential of the mesquite (*Prosopis sp.*) as a complementary food resource in the pre-Hispanic period, in arid or semiarid regions, although the seedpod has excellent nutritional value. Gómez Lorence (1984:104, 105) indicates that its nutritional value is derived from its chemical composition. This author also notes that in pre-Hispanic times, the seedpods were consumed in the north of Mexico in a kind of *pinole* or prepared in *mezquitamal* or *mezquitole* by combining them with maize or a sunflower flour; this custom still persists in some regions.

The chemical analysis of the seeds has shown a content of between 19.5 and 35.4 percent of good-quality raw protein, integrated by ten essential amino acids. This is an acceptable level when compared with eggs, for instance. The oil content of the seed is about 30 percent. Its nutrient value compares favorably with that of maize, cotton, sunflower, soya, and peanuts (Bernis 1979, quoted by Gómez Lorence 1984:109).

Hernández (1959:III) mentions that the Chichimecas cooked the seeds of the pods to make tortillas, which they used as food, and Sahagún (1975) indicates that the indigenous people sucked and chewed the sweet spongy layer that covers the seed in order to obtain a pleasant juice (quoted by Torres 1985:11–112). In the study area, the *Relaciones Geográficas* (Del Paso y Troncoso 1905–1948: VI, 202) and the *Suma de visitas* (1905:223) mention this plant when referring to Atitalaquia's towns—"hay también unos arboles que hechan unas bainillas ques genero de fruta para ellos"—and in Tlahuelilpan: "tienen algunos tunales y magueyales y mezquiques y caza de liebres y conejos y cordonizes"; both towns are located on the Salado River, and these quotes suggest occasional and low-level consumption.

In the present day, according to Granados Sánchez and Hernández (1995:113–114), mesquite pods found in the study area are used for family consumption, fresh, dry, and toasted, and as forage for animals. This plant is found in the form of dominant groups in the region, and there are types that are differentiated by color, taste, shape, and size of the seedpods. Those that are in the family gardens also provide cool shade for most of the year and lumber that is valued for its characteristics. Granados Sánchez (personal communication 1998) adds that the mesquite seedpods are also consumed boiled and mixed with maize dough in a form of *atole*. Like the nopals, in the foliage of this plant there are insects known as mesquite bugs or *shavis* that are grilled or eaten with salsa.

There is evidence of the mesquite in the carbonized vegetable remains in the Tepetitlán habitation structure. González Quintero (1999) identified a vitroe endosperm, a folio, and a wooden mesquite wedge associated with a burial (Fig. 9.3). This investigator indicates that *Prosopis* is a wild plant that is characteristic of a dry climate and can survive in desert climates or extreme drought conditions because its roots reach underground water for subsistence. Therefore, it can flower in the dry season and give fruit six months later. It takes many years to grow because in its early stages it grows underground to develop and extend its roots; it does, however, flourish with greater humidity (González Quintero, personal communication 1996).

This genus is present in the pollen graph of the area, but the level recorded is low because this plant, like other legumes, achieves pollenization via insects (entomophile), leaving little left for the pollen record. That is, although there is a weak presence in the pollen diagram, this is very properly due to an increase in the frequency of individuals, which may mean higher rainfall. It is clear in the diagram that the period where *Prosopis* is recorded coincides with the hiatus of the amaranth and its substitution by maize; however, at the end mesquite coexists with a sudden increase of amaranth (González Quintero, personal communication 1996).

Nowadays, in addition to the white worms that grow in the nopal and the *shavis* or mesquite bugs mentioned above, the gathering practices in the region include the red maguey worm in September, which is grilled, ant eggs and maize cob worms, which are also used as food, as well as various game birds. *Ajolotes* are also collected in *jagueyes* and then put into buckets and cleaned in the natural dams. They are eaten roasted with chile. *Charales* (small fish) and *acociles* (freshwater shrimp or crayfish) are also consumed (Granados Sánchez and Ortega, personal communication).

In some rivers and dams in the region it is still possible to obtain various kinds of fish. These fish were undoubtedly an important potential source of food for the pre-Hispanic population during the period in question, as a large portion of the sites of the area are close to the main rivers.

There is archaeological evidence in Tepetitlán and in the city for different species of fauna, some of which were undoubtedly important as food for the inhabitants. According to the study by Oscar Polaco (1999), the most commonly recovered faunal remains from Tepetitlán are freshwater mollusks and the bones of dog (*Canis*) and deer (*Odocoileus virginianus*). Less frequently recovered were the following: hare (*Lepus californicus* and *L. callotis*), rabbit (*Sylvilagus auduboniti* and *Sylvilagus sp.*), and turkey (*Meleagris gallopavo* or *guajolote*) (see Fig.

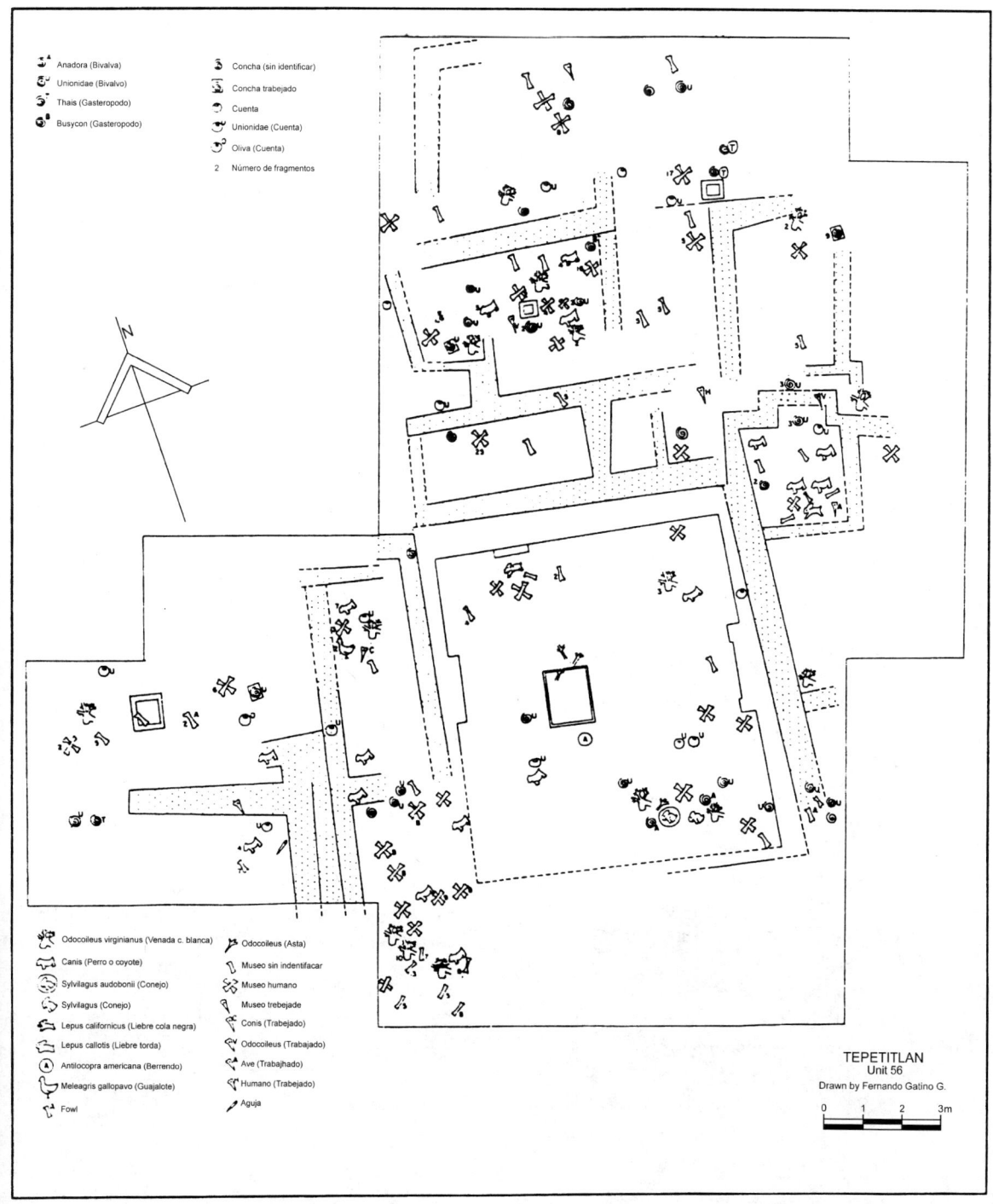

Figure 9.6. Tepetitlán U56: Distribution of faunal remains (Cobean and Mastache 1999).

9.6). The vast majority of these remains were from food waste, though some were used as tools. The faunal remains recovered in the Tepetitlán excavation, including dog and deer, are scarce in comparison to the animal remains recovered from the urban houses at El Canal. For example, Diehl's project (1981, personal communication 1985) identified the remains of twenty-four deer at El Canal, while according to Polaco (1999), only four deer are represented among the remains from Tepetitlán. However, only a single house group was investigated at Tepetitlán, and the majority of the material was recovered from a single house, while the El Canal material came from several different House Groups, and much of it came from dumps or middens formed after abandonment of the houses. In Tepetitlán, the faunal sample only corresponds to the interior of the structure and does not include nearby exterior areas that could have functioned as important waste-disposal zones.

As was the case at El Canal, at Tepetitlán cranium fragments, as well as long bones and small bones, were recovered, indicating that apparently the entire deer was used, not only selected portions. This further suggests that the deer were butchered within the houses. In this respect, the type of use wear patterns identified on stone tools examined by Sánchez (1999) is of interest.

It is notable that there were only two turkey bones in the entire Tepetitlán excavation, even though this bird was domesticated and is considered characteristic of the pre-Hispanic diet. Despite this, in the urban dwellings turkeys also appear to have been very scarce: in the El Corral structure, remains of only one turkey were found, and in the El Canal House Groups no turkey bones were found (Diehl 1981).

Other faunal species that were present in Tula, such as the *Dasypus cf novemcinctus* (armadillo), *Tayassu tajacu* (wild pig), *Terrapene sp.* (turtle), and the sea turtle (Diehl 1981 and personal communication) were not recovered from Tepetitlán.

In summary, there are important differences in the quantities of fauna recorded in the habitation unit at Tepetitlán and those recovered from the urban structures at El Canal. For example, 422 *Odocoileus virginianus* bones representing twnety-four individuals were recovered at El Canal, while only 34 bones, corresponding to only four individuals, were recovered from Tepetitlán. Similarly, there were 111 rabbit and hare bones representing twelve individuals at El Canal, while only 4 bones from these species were recovered from Tepetitlán. Notwithstanding the fact that the El Canal structures consisted of three house groups, if the faunal remains recovered from El Canal and the Tepetitlán were considered representative of the consumption of the species by their inhabitants, we would have a very notable difference of access to these food sources between the two populations and a lower level of meat consumption at Tepetitlán, even though it is logical to suppose that a rural population would have more direct access to these species in its immediate environment than urban inhabitants.

NOTES

1. According to Figueroa (n.d.:79), the area of these municipalities totals some 1,205.1 square kilometers, but since the Tepeji del Río and Tezontepec municipalities are not fully included in the area studied, this figure was adjusted to a total of 960 square kilometers.
2. As mentioned in Chapter 2, it must be borne in mind that our figures are very approximate estimations, due to the schematic characteristics of the old maps used, and because information was not obtained on this period for some zones of the area studied. For further information about the nature of the data and the methodology used, as well as on the characteristics of the irrigation system, the study cited by Mastache may be consulted (1976).

10

Hinterland Settlement

In this chapter we will refer to the characteristics of the Early Postclassic occupation in the area and to the different levels of complexity of the rural sites in relation to the probable territorial units in which the rural environs of the pre-Hispanic city could have been organized.

As we have analyzed in Chapter 6, there is no doubt that the ancient city of Tula was structured into a series of territorial and administrative units; however, given our current level of knowledge, it is not possible to state accurately the exact size and characteristics of these internal subdivisions of the city. Likewise, the hinterland of the city must have been organized in various territorial units of distinct rank and size, but general studies of the settlement patterns pose more questions about the subject, rather than providing answers, especially because there is not the wealth of ethnohistorical information that is available for the Late Postclassic.

It is evident that the differences in the kinds of complexity of the rural sites of the area are related to hierarchical levels and to the function of these entities within the political-administrative structure of the Toltec state and with its internal territorial organization, as well as land tenure, and the particular class structure of the population. But the empirical information available to us is very limited, and it does not permit us to say much about these aspects.

Nevertheless, some ethnohistorical studies based on local sources of different types, such as those of Carrasco (1964, 1972, 1973), Williams (1984, 1991, 1994), Harvey (1984), and Reyes (1973, 1991), among others, constitute, in our opinion, a useful point of reference as an interpretative framework, because they contain valuable information about different forms of land tenure and territorial and political organization in various regions of Central Mexico at the moment of contact and in the early colonial period. Although these early ethnohistorical sources document situations relating to the period immediately before the Conquest, it is not unlikely that, as various studies have proposed, some aspects could date back several centuries.

We make no attempt here to delve into such a complex and specialized subject about which there is wide bibliography, or to make generalizations and to extrapolate to Tula data that refer to other geographic zones and to a much later period, but there is no doubt that some of the situations documented in studies like those mentioned shed light on different possibilities of territorial and political organization in ancient Mexico, and they are a useful point of reference in regional studies of settlement patterns. In the case of our area of study, it is important to bear in mind that in Tula various antecedents to diverse aspects relating to the cosmovision and probably to some religious and political institutions of the Mexica have been found, as indicated by several authors and seen in the analysis of the sacred precinct. Consequently, it would not be surprising that some of the concepts and institutions related to the territorial and political organization of the Mexica and other contemporary peoples of the Central Highlands also developed earlier in Toltec culture.

As we have already seen, the population that inhabited the hinterland of the city of Tula during the Early Postclassic was distributed in numerous settlements of different size and complexity, with diverse forms of dispersed occupation predominating. Many of the sites we have defined consist of isolated habitation structures, or groups of such structures. These are households inhabited by extended families, apparently located in the center of the agricultural space utilized by the family unit. Another part of the settlement consists of concentrated sites, with or without ceremonial architecture, distributed in various zones of the area. It is precisely these zones that were inhabited by most of the rural population of this period, because even though they are less numerous than the dispersed sites, they are more extensive and housed a larger population as a whole.

Nevertheless, the degree of dispersion of a large part of the population of the area and the large number of sites consisting of single isolated households or two or three households is rather surprising. Given this situation at the beginning of our analysis, we even considered the possibility that the archaeological record did not reflect the real characteristics of occupation for this period on the surface, but on analyzing data on the settlement of other regions of the Central Highlands, it is clear that this is not a unique case. Sanders emphasizes that dispersed occupation was very common in Mesoamerica and that the pre-Hispanic settlement pattern in the Basin of Mexico consisted essentially of nucleated villages surrounded by dispersed populations located on more productive land. This dispersed-population pattern is in accordance with the need to have a significant percentage of the land fallow in order to recover soil productivity, and also because the farmers tended to live near their farmland and to reduce the distance between the cultivated fields and their dwellings, with the consequent saving of energy (Sanders 1992:274–275; Sanders and Killion 1992:20–30).

ETHNOHISTORICAL STUDIES

In reference to the pattern of dispersed population combined with nucleated villages to which Sanders refers, which we also find in the sustaining area of the city of Tula, the studies concerning the sixteenth century by Williams (1984, 1991, 1994) on Tepetlaoztoc, Carrasco (1964, 1972, 1976b) on various zones of Morelos, Reyes on Cuautinchan and Tlaxcala (1973, 1991), as well as those by Anguiano and Chapa of this latter region (1976), by Dyckerhoff and Prem (1976) on Huejotzingo, and those by Olivera (1978) on Teccalli, Puebla, are of great interest. We will refer to some of these in detail, because they document different forms of territorial and political organization in various regions of Central Mexico and a population pattern that has elements in common with those of our study area.

Barbara Williams's study treats the *Santa Maria Asunción Codex*. This codex could be dated about 1540, and it contains land records with lists of houses, habitation units, and the locality of a territorial subdivision of the Altepetl or the señorio of Tepetlaoztoc, called the *Tlaxilacalli* de Santa Maria Asunción. During the Late Postclassic, Tepetlaoztoc was a señorio belonging to the district of Acolhuacan; this señorio had (according to research by Parsons 1971, quoted by Williams [1994:78]) a dispersed population pattern covering an area of approximately 450 hectares, with a population estimated at between 6,750 and 13,500 inhabitants for this period. The Tepetlaoztoc territory was under the jurisdiction of a *tlatoani,* and it was subdivided into various units called *tlaxilacalli,* each of which consisted of a set of dispersed rural settlements. Williams notes that the *Vergara Codex,* which is similar to the *Santa Maria Codex* in form and content, contains the records of another adjacent unit similar to the Santa Maria de Asunción *Tlaxilacalli,* corresponding to the present *barrio* of San Jeronimo (Williams 1984:104).

The Santa Maria Asunción *tlaxilacalli,* with an area of approximately 7 square kilometers and a population of 1,324 inhabitants, was in turn subdivided into twelve different localities or political units, which vary greatly in size and population. More than half of the 700 hectares of the *tlaxilacalli* were uncultivated land on the slopes of the Patlachique sierra, and apparently only a relatively small area of 283 hectares was agricultural land (Williams 1991).

Most of these political units at a local level were extremely small. Half of the twelve communities that made up the Santa Maria Asunción *tlaxilacalli* were small settlements of between four and eight households with fewer than fifty inhabitants, that is, settlements that are similar to our Type 7 and Type 11 sites and the "hamlet" category of Sanders, Parsons, and Santley (1979). Three communities had fewer than 100 inhabitants, and only another three of the twelve localities had a population of between 158 and 365 inhabitants. These three entities had the highest rank in the *tlaxilacalli,* and they would be equal to the "small village" of Sanders, Parsons, and Santley and similar to the smaller Type 1 and 2 sites recorded in the Tula area.

Williams (1991) notes that unlike what was recorded in other zones such as Huejotzingo, in the *Santa Maria Asunción Codex* there is no evidence that the *tlaxilacalli* was divided into work groups (*cuadrillas*) of 20 to 100 households and that settlement size was dictated by these tributary units (pp. 196, 205). However, Offner, in his study of the *Vergara Codex,* which dates back to the same period and refers to a similar neighboring unit consisting of fifteen different localities, proposes that the way the codex is organized into groups of five families on each page is compatible with the control and tribute system in which there were some officials in charge of 100 households and others responsible for 20 households (Offner 1984).

The *Vergara Codex* shows that the agricultural land in the *tlaxilacalli* was unevenly distributed at a community, household, and per capita level. Access to agricultural land varied by a factor of two to three. At a community level, the two most important localities were Cuauhtepoztla, which had 82 households and 365 people and almost 73 hectares, and Huiznahuac, which had 64 households and 340 inhabitants on 65 hectares. The eight smallest communities of between 34 and 74 inhabitants had between 6.9 and 27.5 hectares. However, at a household level, the communities with a higher number of inhabitants had less agricultural land per household (0.514, 0.884, and 1.014 hectares per household, respectively) than the smaller localities, where there was from 1 to 2 hectares per household. For the entire sample, the average agricultural land per household is 1.1 hectares. Calculated on a per capita basis, the agricultural land varied greatly within the *tlaxilacalli,* from 0.12 to 0.34 hectares per person (Williams 1991:194–200). This scholar states that not much variation has been detected in terms of the land productivity and that the tribute must have been calculated on the basis of the amount of land and its productivity, as has been documented in other regions.

There are signs of stratification within the *tlaxilacalli* and individuals of higher status lived in the two principal localities. The leading person listed in the codex seems to have been a headman whose household had 5 hectares of land, more than twice the others (Williams 1991:200). Additionally, the Cuautepoztla census for the most important locality of the *tlaxilacalli* begins with ten households whose kinship lines are indicated with red lines, rather than the more common black lines. These were probably high status households within the *tlaxilacalli* (p. 194).

Carrasco (1964, 1972, 1976b), in his studies of censuses that date to about 1540 for various towns of the Marquesado del Valle in Morelos, documents the territorial organization of two distinct entities in Morelos: Yautepec and Tepoztlan. As Sanders, Evans, and Charlton indicate (in press:983–987), in both cases they are *cabeceras* of *señorios* like those that existed in the Valley of Teotihuacan at the beginning of the colonial period. In Tepoztlan, Carrasco analyzes the household and estate of the señorio's Tlatoani, while in Yautepec he studies the household of a *tecuhtli* or ward chief, who is the lord of an entity of a lower rank.

The manuscript on Yautepec written in Nahuatl and analyzed by Carrasco (1972) includes the census of three *calpulli:* Molotla, Tepetenchic, and Panchimalco. In another study, this author (1976b:104–105) mentions that these three *calpulli* had between 120 and 168 households and these were in turn subdivided into units also called *calpulli* or *chinámitl,* which had from 1 to 51 households.

Carrasco (1976b:114) also indicates that Tepetenchic is a *barrio* with 120 households with seven subdivisions. Pedro Tlacochcalcatl ruled in the first of these, with forty-four married dependents in 25 households. Apparently, this subdivision had a total of 41 households. In Tepepan, the second division of Tepetenchic, there are 13 households, all of which are inhabited by subjects of the *tecuhtli,* Domingo Tlacohtecuhtli. Thus, the remaining 66 households of the *calpulli* were distributed among the remaining five subdivisions, from which we can deduce that they would be small localities of a few households and of fewer than a hundred or even fifty inhabitants.

There is no specification of the number of units into which the Panchimalco *calpulli* was divided; we only know that it had 168 households and it is clarified that in the first subdivision, which was also called Panchimalco, there were two *tecuhtli,* whose dependents included 10 of the households of this locality, and that in another subdivision of the Panchimalco, another *tecuhtli* ruled, whose dependents lived in a total of 8 households (Carrasco 1976b).

The information about the Molotla *calpulli* is more detailed because the document analyzed by Carrasco (1972) specifically deals with the family and tenants of Molotecatl *tecuhtli,* the chief of the Molotla *calpulli.* We also know that this *calpulli* had a total of 128 households and 1,057 inhabitants, and that it was subdivided into nine units also called *calpulli,* or in the case of the last three (the smallest), *chinámitl.* In the entire *calpulli* of Molotla, there were two individuals with the title of *tecuhtli.* One is Molotecatl *tecuhtli,* chief of the entire *calpulli* (as in the case of Panchimalco, the same name Molotla is applied to the complex of nine units, as to the first unit), who lived with his family and tenants in the first of the nine subdivisions or localities into which the greater *calpulli* was divided. The other *tecuhtli* is Mateo Tlacatecatl, called *tlacatecuhtli,* who ruled in Atempa, which was the second territorial unit of the greater Molotla territorial unit.

The document analyzed by Carrasco contains precise information about the population, household by household, the land they cultivated, and the tribute they paid. But we do not have, as in the case of Santa Maria Asunción, data on the size, number of houses, and inhabitants of each one of the nine communities that make up the entire territorial entity of Molotla. However, some data may be inferred, because we know that the total population of the *calpulli* was 1,057 inhabitants (this figure is similar to the total population of the Tlaxilacalli de Santa Maria Asunción, and apparently to the Tepetenchic and Tlachimalco *barrios* considering the number of houses mentioned for these *barrios*). We also know that the first subdivision, also called Molotla, where the *cacique* Molotecatl *tecuhtli* lived, had thirty-two households and 333 inhabitants, that is, an entity that is very similar, in terms of population, to the two most important localities of the Tlaxilacalli of Santa Maria Asunción: Cuauhtepoztla and Huiznahuac, which had 365 and 340 inhabitants, respectively. Thus, Molotla, the locality of the highest hierarchy of the *calpulli* of the same name, would also be equivalent to the "small village" of Sanders, Parsons, and Santley (1979) and to the smaller sites of Types 1 and 2 recorded in the Tula area.

We also know that Molotla must have been the highest ranking locality of the *calpulli,* not only because the *tecuhtli* lived there, but also because it housed almost a third of the population of the entire *calpulli* (333 inhabitants of a total of 1,057 inhabitants) and that Atempa, where the other *tecuhtli* lived, would be the community that followed Molotla in importance and in number of inhabitants. In another publication, Carrasco notes that "Atempa had 35 households, without counting the Tlacatecatl tecuhtli" (1976b:109), that is, it would have approximately the same population as Molotla or slightly more, which means that a bit more than 60 percent of the total population of the *calpulli* lived in Molotla and Atempa, and that the remaining 400 inhabitants would be distributed in the other seven hamlets. This means that the latter were small localities with about 50 inhabitants, whose population ranges would be very similar to the hamlets of the *tlaxilacalli* of Santa Maria Asunción, and also equivalent to the sites classified as hamlets by Sanders and the Types 7 and 11 sites in Tula.

In the first instance, the census includes the Molotecatl *tecuhtli* and two additional households occupied by his relatives—the three formed a patio—followed by four other households of Molotecatl's tenants: the total number of inhabitants of these seven households is seventy people; which included seventeen men and twenty-four women available for agricultural work and domestic tasks. This means, as Sanders and Evans (in press) indicate, that there were forty-one economically active people.

As mentioned by Carrasco (1972), the complex of houses described constitutes a unit from the point of view of land use and tributary organization. Molotecatl *tecuhtli* had 400 irrigated land units and 200 *cerro* (hillside) units. The land received by his dependents totals slightly more than a third of the total land and a higher proportion of its productive capacity, because these are mostly irrigated fields. The *tecuhtli* gives 228 *brazas* of land to his dependents and therefore there are 372 for his use. One of the tenants' important obligations is to provide agricultural labor to work the lands of Molotecatl. The six domestic units that provide agricultural labor include seventeen male workers over the age of twenty. The land cultivated for themselves totals 148 *brazas*.

Sanders and Evans calculate that the *braza* or *maitl* "was equivalent to 2 varas, approximately 2 meters. That means that the total land holding of the tecuhtli included irrigated land that measured 800 x 800 m or 64 hectares and 400 x 400m of mountain land or 16 hectares. This amount of land would easily be sufficient to feed 70 people and provide sufficient surpluses" (in press:983).

From the tributary point of view, Molotecatl must pay tribute corresponding to his land and dependents. The tribute (*téquitl*) is of two forms of payment: "contribution" and "food or sustenance given to another." The contribution was paid in cloth (*mantas*) and in decorated clothing, in the case of principals. The "food" was paid in woven fabric of another class ("tribute cloths") and in towels and food as such, which is usually maize, cacao, eggs, chiles, and turkeys. The amount of the tribute is directly related to the amount of land held by the tribute payer. The tenants did not usually pay food, but gave part of the contribution to the señor or provided various personal services, such as cultivating the land reserved for the Molotecatl, who also received other goods such as cotton thread and some finished cloths (Carrasco 1972).

Carrasco (1976b:116) indicates that the dependents of the *tecuhtli* could be slaves or servants maintained by him who provide services of different types, or relatives or individuals without any special kinship priviledges. The relatives could be members of the lord's household or tenants in separate houses. The señor always had lands for his own use, which he cultivated using the members of his own household or the second kind of dependents to whom he gave land in return for tribute or personal services.

Carrasco, in his study of the family structure in Tepoztlan (1964), refers to diverse territorial units of different size and hierarchy into which this señorio was structured a few years after the Spanish had established control. He mentions that Tepoztlan, which had a total of 3,200 married men, was divided into nine *barrios* or major wards, one of which was Tlacatecpan, where the Tlatoani lived. Tlacatecpan (825 married men) was in turn subdivided into five units of different size. One was Tlacatecpan itself; of the other four, the largest had 134 houses and the smallest, called Xoxocotla, had 53. Since the word *calpulli* is also applied here to different hierarchies of territorial units, Carrasco uses "major ward" for the nine subdivisions of Tepoztlan and "ward" for the four subdivisions of Tlacatecpan, each of which was in turn subdivided into units of a smaller size, which he called "subwards." As in the case of Molotla, these localities or subwards had their own names and their size varied from five to thirty-four households.

Tlacatecpan was a territorial unit with a total of 3,100 inhabitants who lived in 549 households: 200 occupied by the *tlatoani* and his subjects (*cacique* subjects), where there was a total of more than 1,262 people, which, according to a clarification made in another article (Carrasco 1976b:113), were distributed in fifteen different localities. This high number of dependents of the *tlatoani* clearly marks the difference in hierarchy that existed between the *tlatoani* of a señorio such as Tepoztlan and the *tecuhtli* or ward chief from a minor territorial unit or ward such as Molotla, because as Sanders and Evans (in press) point out, this offers "a striking contrast to the size of the estate of the tecuhtli of Molotla" (p. 987). As Carrasco indicates, most of the information from the documents analyzed refers to the middle and lower levels of society, that is, to the middle category *tecuhtli* and *macehuales*. There is a dearth of data on important places of specialized artisans and the urban population (Carrasco 1976b:115).

Most of the major ward of Tlacatecpan was occupied by the remaining 348 households with a population of 1,838, who constituted the ward or *barrio* people. Carrasco indicates that there is a marked difference between the subjects of the *cacique* and the ward people, both in family size, amount of land possessed, and the amount of tribute paid. The *cacique*'s household is the largest and the households of his subjects had a higher number of people per unit (6.2) than that of the ward people, where the average was 5.2 inhabitants. The *cacique*'s subjects had less land, but paid less tribute than the ward people, who had to pay three different kinds of tribute—cloth, cacao, beans, eggs, maize, and agricultural and domestic services—while the *cacique*'s subjects only paid cloth, and in lesser amounts. In both groups, the tribute was related to the amount of land possessed; those who had no land did not pay (Carrasco 1964, 1976b).

It is evident that Tlacatecpan was a territorial entity that was almost three times larger than the *tlaxilacalli* of Santa Maria Asunción and the Tepetenchic, Tlachimalco, and Molotla *calpulli*. However, the four units or wards into which Tlacatecpan was subdivided, which had between 134 and 53 households, were equal in rank to the *tlaxilacalli* of Santa Maria Asunción and to the Molotla, Tepetenchi, and Panchimalco *calpulli*, which had between 120 and 168 households. Each ward was also divided into subwards or lesser localities (which had between 5 and 34 households), with a similar rank, in terms of size and number of inhabitants, to the smaller subdivisions of the *tlaxilacalli* and of these *calpulli*. As mentioned before, ten of the twelve subdivisions of Santa Maria Asunción had between 4 and 31 households, and the three *calpulli* of Yautepec studied by Carrasco were subdivided into smaller entities of similar rank.

Among the *señorios* of the Teotihuacan area analyzed by Sanders and Evans on the basis of archaeological and ethnohistorical data (in press:988–1000), it seems that the town or central community (*cabecera*) of Teotihuacan, with an estimated population of between 7,000 and 8,000 or even 12,000 for the Late Postclassic (p. 1013), would be a political territorial unit of similar rank to Tepoztlan. In addition, the *señorios* of Chiconautla, Otumba, Acolman, and Tezoyuca had a *tlatoani*. However, the archaeological data do not make it possible to determine accurately the different level of internal subdivisions of these entities.

Additionally, the ethnohistorical studies by Luis Reyes (1991) and Anguiano and Chapa (1976) on the province of Tlaxcala shed important information concerning the political and territorial organization of this region. In the middle of the sixteenth century, this province was divided into four *señorios* of varying size: Ocotelulco to the south, Tizatlán in the east, Quiahuiztlan in the west, and Tepeticpac in the north (Reyes 1991:6). Each one of these territorial units was governed by a *tlatoani* and was in turn divided into various subunits that covered various towns that were also subdivided into small *barrios* or villages that were also called work squads (*cuadrillas*). In some cases, various squads took the name of the place, that is, they sometimes corresponded to a small locality or *barrio,* but other units were so small that several of them made up one *barrio.*

Anguiano and Chapa (1976) state that each one of the four *señorios* was divided into various *tequitl,* and each *tequitl* consisted of several towns. They note that the *tequitl* seem to be units to provide personal services or tribute payments, since the word *tequitl* means "work." Each *tequitl* covered a variable number of communities; Ocotelulco, with a total of 10,518 inhabitants, consisted of thirty-six towns distributed in six *tequitl,* each one with three to thirteen towns. The *señorio* of Tizatlán, with 14,083 inhabitants distributed in forty-one towns, had six *tequitl*. Quiahuiztlán, a *señorio* with forty-two towns and a population of 7,661, had four *tequitl,* which included from seven to twelve towns.

Thus, the *tequitl* were units of varying size; four of the six of Ocotelulco had between 1,034 and 1,725 inhabitants, and the largest had almost 2,800 people. In Tizatlán, four included between 1,400 and 2,000 inhabitants, and two more had a population of between 3,000 and 3,800. Finally, two of the four *tequitl* of the *cabecera* or *señorio* of Quiahuiztlan had between 1,500 and 1,700 inhabitants, while the other two had around 2,300 (Anguiano and Chapa 1976:127, 134).

However, it is important to clarify, as shown by Luis Reyes (personal communication), that the *tequitl* were not territorial units, but organization units for work and community labor of the *macehual* population who had to provide these services. They worked in squads by shifts or in groups that could cover several towns. There were different levels of group officers or foremen who were given a special name according to the number of workers they controlled: *centecpanpixqui* was in charge of a squad of twenty, and the *macuiltepecpanpixqui* had a higher rank because he was in charge of five squads of twenty. The organization of work squads into twenty men that could include people from several places seems to have been a common form of work organization of pre-Hispanic origin. This work system has also been documented for other places like Cuauhtinchán (Reyes 1972:285), Huejotzingo (Dyckerhoff and Prem 1976:160), Tenochtitlan and Chalco (E. Calnek and Luis Reyes, personal communication).

There were other administrative positions, the rank and obligations of which are not clear in the documents: *tequitato, tepixqui, topilli,* or *coco-scapixqui,* some of which seem to have been a rank above the officer in charge of five squads of twenty (Anguiano and Chapa 1976:123). According to Dyckerhoff and Prem, the *macuiltecpanquixqui* were principals and the men who made up the work squad were tribute payers, that is, married men.

As mentioned before, each one of the four *señorios* with their *cabeceras* of the province of Tlaxcala, or *Tlatocayo*, were subdivided into various territorial units, the best documented being the *centepetl* or *señorio* of Ocotelulco, which was headed by the Maxixcatzin lineage at the end of the fifteenth century, which consisted of various *señorio* households that governed in the five territorial units into which Ocotelulco was subdivided: Cuitlixco, Tlamaoco, Tecpan, Contlazinco, and Chimalpa. Reyes, however, proposes that there are signs that Ocotelulco, with its five divisions, was also divided into two halves (1991). Each one of the five units of Ocotelulco consisted of various towns and various kinds of *señorio* households: *tecalli* (house of the *tecuhtli*), *pilcalli* (houses of the *pilli*), *huehuecalli* (house of the old men), and *yautequihuicalli* (military house). These *señorio* households of differing size and hierarchy had different kinds of lands, and they controlled access to such, with a subject, landless *macehualli* population that worked them. Reyes (1991) states that commerce and the artisans were tied to various kinds of *señorio* houses.

Returning now to the subdivisions in each one of the four divisions of the province of Tlaxcala, we know that the number and size varied greatly (Anguiano and Chapa 1976:36–37). According to the information contained in this study, we can loosely group them into three different ranks: (1) small (less than 100 to 200 inhabitants); (2) medium (200 to less than 600 inhabitants); and (3) large (more than 600 inhabitants). In Quihuiaztlan, more than 60 percent of the communities corresponded to the first rank, that is, towns with less than 200 inhabitants. In Ocotelulco, slightly more than 30 percent belong to this category, while in Tizatlan, the middle groups of between 200 and 600 inhabitants predominate, and only six towns in the three *señorios* have more than 800 inhabitants (one in Quiahuiztlan, two in Ocotelulco, and three in Tizatlan).

Unfortunately, these authors do not provide further information about the work squads or small subdivisions of the towns that would allow us to determine the population dispersion in the different *señorios* of this province. They only indicate, as mentioned before, that these were small *barrios* or villages and in some cases were so small that several *cuadrillas* bore the same place name. Thus, these are small entities with few inhabitants that are very probably similar to the smaller subdivisions of the *calpulli* studied by Carrasco in Morelos or to the *tlaxilacalli* of Santa Maria Asunción analyzed by Williams.

The studies by Dyckerhoff and Prem (1976) on Huejotzingo, based on tributary censuses, also offer very interesting information about the territorial and political organization of another region of Central Mexico in the early colonial period. What these scholars call the key area of Huejotzingo, with an area of about 200 square kilometers, had sixteen towns subdivided into a variable number of *barrios* or localities; from two to fifteen localities. The size of these localities was also variable, although they clarify that in the key area these were very small sites. The two main social strata generally inhabited the towns: the principals as an upper layer, and then the common people or *macehuales*. In the latter group, there is a distinction between *macehuales* who were land-owning members of the *calpulli* and tenant farmers. In some towns there was a high number of tenant farmers. The *macehuales* who were not tenant farmers of the principals were organized in the *calpulli,* and they were known as *calpulleque*. The *calpulli* had their own names, and they constituted subdivisions of the towns. There was also a clear distinction in the work squads into which the population was organized for community work between the *macehuales* who were tenant farmers of the principals and the inhabitants of the barrios or *calpulli* (pp. 158–164).

The above examples of different political territorial units of varying size and hierarchy in various regions of Central Mexico are, as mentioned before, a useful point of reference for interpreting the settlement patterns of the heartland for the ancient city of Tula. This brief survey of ethnohistorical studies covers different hierarchies of territorial and political units, ranging from a kingdom or Tlahtocayo-like Tlaxcala structured in four *señorios* with the respective *cabeceras* and *tlatoanis* to *señorios* such as Tepoztlan, and down to smaller entities such as rural *tlaxilacalli* or *calpulli* under the tutelage of minor *tecuhtli*. It is interesting to note that although there are regional variations in the internal subdivisions and in the hierarchy of the towns and the chain of interrelation and interdependence among them, it could be said that in basically all the cases cited, the settlement patterns of the territorial units that are in the base of the system constitute a combination of two or three towns of several hundred inhabitants and a variable number of small dispersed localities with a few inhabitants who are dependents of these towns.

Apparently, most of the principal towns of the diverse regions mentioned seem to consist of two ranks: one of between 300 and 400 people and another of 600 to 800 inhabitants. The first level includes the *cabecera* communities of the *tlaxilacalli* Santa Maria Asunción and the *calpulli* heads of Yautepec where the *tecuhtli* lived, as well as numerous towns of the four Tlaxcala *señorios*. Some of the larger towns of Tlaxcala and perhaps Tepoztlan are clear examples of the second level. It is interesting to note that both categories of towns would be equivalent to the two main concentrated settlement categories defined by Sanders, Parsons, and Santley (1979:56) in the Basin of Mexico: small nucleated villages (between 100 to 500 people) and large nucleated villages (between 500 and 1,000 people). And they are equivalent to the Type 1 and 2 sites of the Tula area, most of which cover between 10 and 20 hectares and have similar estimated population ranges, although there are some covering 25 hectares.

On this point it is important to stress that the Type 1 and 2 sites of the Tula area include both settlements equivalent to small nucleated villages and large nucleated villages, and only more detailed excavations and surface studies would permit a better definition of these sites. The frequency of Type 1 and 2 settlements in the area studied is not very high. There is a total of twenty-six sites, eleven of which, with ceremonial architecture, constitute Type 2.

TYPE 1 SITES

Eighty percent of the Type 1 sites are found in Zones 2 and 4, that is, the southeast quadrant and the western half of the area, which was lightly populated during this period. Three of these sites have evidence of craft production, and in two of the sites (276 and 277), ground stone tools were produced. These sites are located directly adjacent to outcrops of basalt, which was used as a raw material, and they seem to have been communities dedicated to the production of metates and metate pestles (*manos*). The other site (160) is a semidispersed settlement covering at least 25 hectares where chert bifaces were made, and the remains of the raw material, wasters, and instruments in process are scattered over the entire site (see Figs. 7.6, 7.11, and 7.15).

The location of three of the five sites of this type in Zone 4 (sites 193, 194, and 195) in the heart of the limestone exploitation area suggests a probable relationship between the population of these settlements and this activity. These settlements cover approximately between 15 and 20 hectares and they are close to intermittent streams. The other two Type 1 sites in this zone (216 and 217) are apparently associated with the traditional irrigation system that originates in the El Salto River. Also, sites 246 and 290 and probably sites 302 and 303, all of which are classified as Type 1, seem to be similarly associated with traditional irrigation systems. In summary, it could be said that the Type 1 sites recorded in the area are probably related to specialized economic activities such as craft production (production of grinding instruments and chert bifaces) and perhaps the exploitation of limestone, as well as to small traditional irrigation systems. Most of these sites are not close to the Type 2 sites and it is not clear whether they are surrounded by dispersed occupation (see Figs. 7.6 and 7.7).

TYPE 2 SITES

The Type 2 sites are characterized by the presence of ceremonial architecture, and they are considered as the rural sites of highest rank in the regional hierarchy. They are mostly located on foothills and sides of the sierra, and their distribution in the area gives the impression of surrounding it, as if forming a border (Fig. 10.1). It is very interesting that even though sites of this type seem to surround the alluvial valley, they are not present in this zone (Zone 3), which constitutes what could be called the heart of the rural occupation of this period (see Figs. 7.13 and 7.14).

As stated earlier, the statistical analysis showed that the Rank 2 sites (encompassing Type 1 and Type 2 sites), which have a tendency to occur in peripheral areas, constitute the only site category that possesses correlations with all other ranks of sites, correlations that may reflect the peripheral location of most of the largest rural sites. The peripheral locations of Rank 2 sites may obey an economic strategy in which the largest rural settlements were placed on agriculturally marginal areas to maximize the availability of prime agricultural land.

If, as we believe, ceremonial architecture is an indicator of a site's rank within the political administrative hierarchy of the area, these sites are the highest-ranking in the regional hierarchy and it is feasible to propose that, bearing in mind their characteristics and spatial distribution within the area, as well as their relationship with dispersed occupation zones, that they very probably constitute the *cabeceras* of the territorial and administrative units into which the rural environs of the ancient city could have been divided. That is, they would be an intermediate level between the central power of the state and the rural population.

Although it is highly speculative and difficult to corroborate on the basis of archaeological data, especially just with surface surveys, it is feasible to propose the possibility that these political territorial units could be similar to units like the *tlaxilacalli* of Santa Maria Asunción or the *calpulli* of Yautepec studied by Carrasco. Williams states, "A rural tlaxilacalli was a territorial unit composed of an aggregate of dispersed but discrete rural settlements [with] . . .

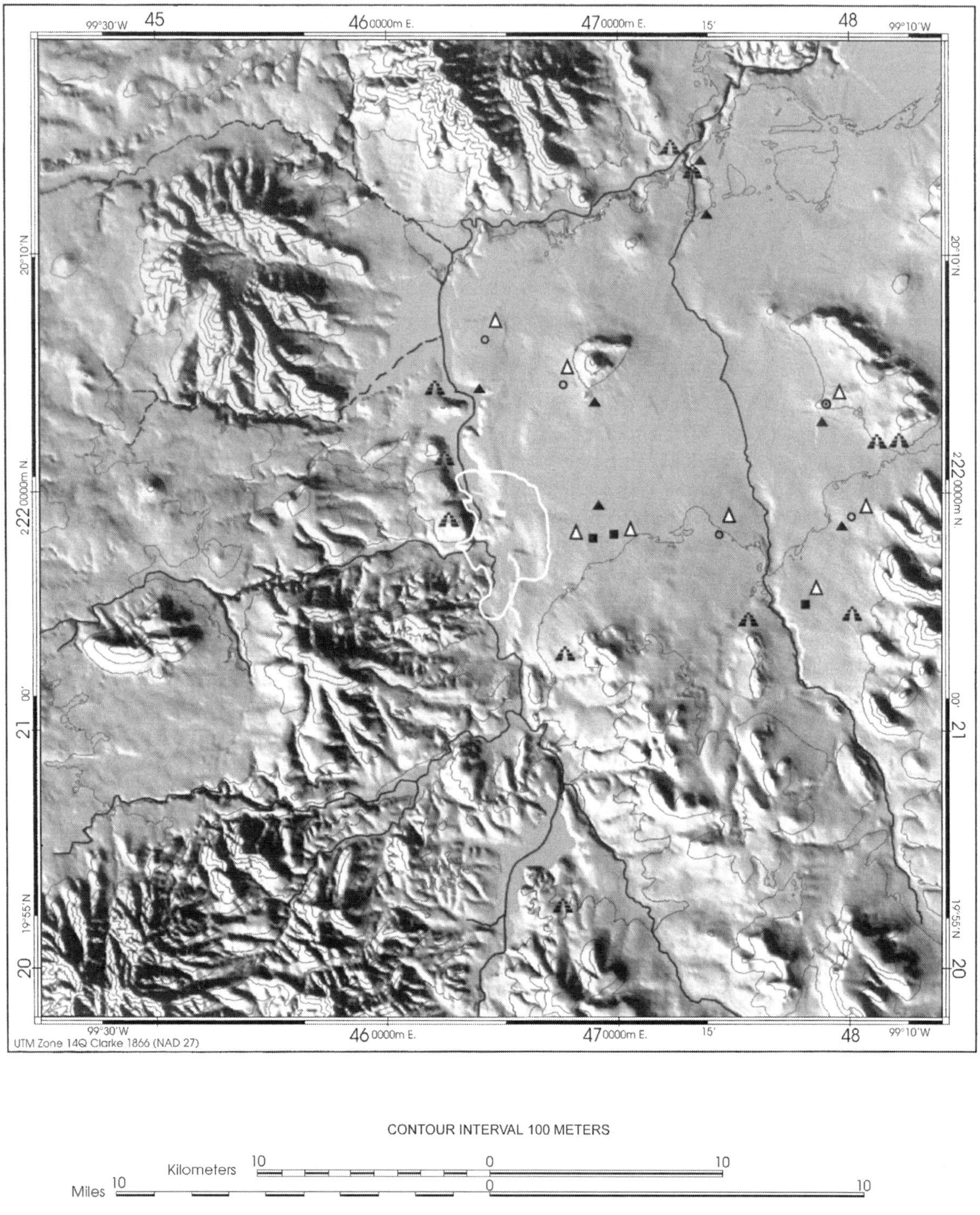

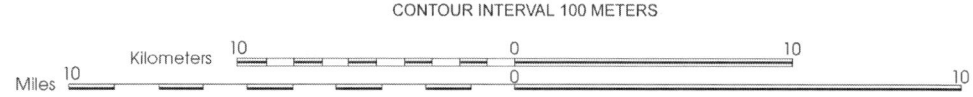

Figure 10.1. Early Postclassic: Sites with ceremonial architecture.

precise spatial boundaries and could encompass a large area of both agricultural and nonagricultural land. Settlement subdivisions within the tlaxilacalli varied greatly in population size, with a tendency towards a hierarchy of small, medium and large communities... Agricultural land within the tlaxilacalli was unequally distributed among communities, among households and on a per capita basis" (Williams 1991:205).

Furthermore, Carrasco's studies show that the *calpulli* he analyzed in Morelos were units related to the use and tenure of the land and tributary organization, with an internal structure that included one or more *tecuhtli* who controlled access to the land, with their relatives and dependents and different ranks of officers, as well as a *macehual* population divided into distinct categories, principally in accordance with their access to land: landless *macehuales* who paid no tribute, *macehuales* with access to communal land, *macehual* tenants farming the land of the *tlatoani* or the principal, and *macehuales* renting from other *macehuales*.

If there really were political territorial entities like the *tlaxilacalli* or *calpulli* mentioned above in the hinterland of Tula during the Tollan Phase, it is very likely that diverse aspects of land tenure, and the organization and stratification of society in these entities, would be expressed in the different hierarchy of the constituent rural sites and in their particular forms of distribution. However, with the information available, it is not possible to establish a correlation between specific social groups and site types; therefore, in the following analysis, there are only very general proposals on this matter.

SETTLEMENT GROUPS

Figure 10.2 shows the groups of sites that could correspond to some of these territorial and administrative units into which the hinterland population of Tula could have been organized. In the definition of these units, we considered those zones where there are Type 2 sites and an occupation that includes sites of different categories. These complexes, called Settlement Groups, are marked with dotted white lines. They basically consist of spatial units where there are one or two sites of higher rank and a variable number of lower-ranking localities, which we suppose were dependents of the higher-ranking settlement or settlements. In some cases, these units coincide with the supraunits, which we call Clusters[1] (Fig. 10.3).

Since the presence of sites with ceremonial architecture (Type 2) was a key indicator in the definition of these units, we would like to clarify why we mark a probable Settlement Group on the west side of Zone 1, even though there is no record of a Type 2 site there. The highest-ranking site in this zone is site 290, classified as Type 1; however, as can be seen in the Appendix, this very extensive site almost uninterruptedly occupies this part of the sierra foothills and it includes a semidispersed occupation zone, as well as an occupation nucleus with ceremonial architecture. But, since there also was heavy Late Postclassic occupation in this sector, it was difficult to place chronologically the ceremonial architecture without excavation and, instead, it was decided to consider it as a Type 1 settlement. However, considering the particular distribution pattern of the Type 2 sites in the area, it is highly probable that the classification of site 290 as Type 1 is erroneous, and that it is in fact a Type 2 site.

It is also interesting to note that the probable Settlement Group located in Zone 7, in an area of low hills between the Tula and the El Salto Rivers (Cluster XXXIII) very probably extends to the lands that were covered by the Requena Dam. On the other hand, as mentioned before, the sites located in the same Zone 7 on the eastern side of the El Salto and Tula Rivers (Clusters XXXII, XXXI, and XXXIV) seem to be associated with two ancient traditional irrigation systems—one on the El Salto River, and the other known as Zanja Romera, which originated to the south of the Requena Dam and terminated in the southern zone of the alluvial valley, as can be seen in Figure 4.2.

Before analyzing some examples of Settlement Groups, we would like to refer to some sites with ceremonial architecture close to the pre-Hispanic city.

It is interesting to note the presence of three Type 2 sites (278, 279, and 280) very close to the city and apparently distributed at regular intervals. The proximity of these sites to the city, and especially of

Figure 10.2. Early Postclassic: Settlement Groups.

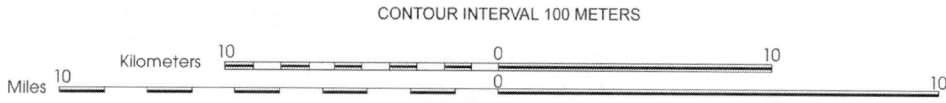

Figure 10.3. Early Postclassic: Clusters and sites with ceremonial architecture.

the two that are closest (278 and 279), is of particular interest regarding the hypothesis that sites of this kind were *cabeceras* of rural territorial entities, since it is not clear in this case that their function would be compatible with their proximity to the city. Both sites seem to mark the commencement of the rural environs of the city, and it is probable that they had a function different to that of other settlements of this kind and a special status within the regional hierarchy of rural settlements. Site 278, with its key placement on the top of the Magoni, would surely have a very special symbolic and strategic importance (see Figs. 10.1 and 7.11).

The third site (280), with ceremonial architecture, borders on the edge of the Endó Dam and currently seems to be isolated and out of context, because an area of various square kilometers that surrounded it was covered by the dam and we do not know the occupation characteristics of this zone. However, it is very likely that there were various kinds of dispersed occupation here, perhaps dependent on this site, and associated with the traditional irrigation systems that originated in the Tula River that we know for certain was below the area covered by the dam (see Fig. 4.2).

Additionally, there is a complex of dispersed sites facing the ancient city at the start of the alluvial valley that were grouped as Cluster XXI and seem to make up a specific unit. This group is of particular interest due to its closeness to the pre-Hispanic city and because it is, like sites 278 and 279, the start of the city's rural environs, except that in this case, in the east, and perhaps because of this, the settlement has some special characteristics, such as the presence of three sites with ceremonial architecture. Two of these sites are isolated ceremonial mounds; the other is a complex formed by a habitational and a ceremonial structure (Type 19). Various kinds of dispersed occupation also form part of this unit, together with complexes of two and three habitational structures and isolated structures (Types 3, 5, 19, and 7).

The location of sites 278 and 279 and those sites with ceremonial architecture of Cluster XXI seems to indicate that the city was flanked to the north, east, and west by sites with a special character, not only because of their ceremonial architecture, but also due to their key placement. It is likely that these sites mark the commencement of the city's rural environs in three different directions, which would give them a special symbolic importance and different status from the rest of the rural settlements.

In order to illustrate the characteristics of the units we have designated as Settlement Groups, we will analyze three of them in some detail as examples, two in Zone 6 and one in the north of Zone 4: the La Mesa Settlement Group, the Atitalaquia Settlement Group, and the Tlamaco Settlement Group.

La Mesa Settlement Group (Zone 6)

The Settlement Group we have called La Mesa covers an irregular area of approximately 6 kilometers long and 2 to 3 kilometers wide. This territory includes at least two zones with distinct topography and different classes of soils, and the modern towns of Tlahuelilpan, Teltipan de Juárez, and Munitepec. The core Tollan Phase occupation nucleus is on the lower foothills of the small mountain range formed by Cerro La Mesa and another hill to the south. The dispersed occupation is mostly located on the strip of lowlands in front of this zone and bounded to the east by the Salado River (Figs. 10.2 and 10.4). As can be seen on Figure 10.3, the principal nucleus of the settlement coincides with the unit defined as Cluster XXIV, while the dispersed occupation on the nearby lowlands corresponds to the zone designated as Cluster XXV.

This is a rural heterogeneous settlement that includes a very varied range of sites. First, in the extreme south there are two sites with ceremonial architecture covering between approximately 10 and 15 hectares (sites 129 and 130). These sites are rather close to each other and somewhat distant from the rest of the settlement (about 2 kilometers). Their placement seems to be very strategic, because both are placed near a natural pass between two mountains that joins the Tula region with the wide neighboring valley of Ajacuba and Tetepango.[2] These sites are followed in size and complexity by a settlement (Type 11) composed of seven structures, two of which are ceremonial (site 124) and three complexes of two habitation units, one consisting of one habitation structure and one ceremonial structure (Type 19). There are also various isolated habitation units and dispersed occupation zones (Fig. 10.4).

The above means that this entity would be made up of two main settlements of between 500 and 750 inhabitants,[3] one locality of about 150 people, three or four smaller localities of approximately 50 persons, and about six smaller dispersed localities, consisting of just one habitational complex housing between 20 and 25 persons each. The dispersed-material symbols (Type 15) that appear on the map very probably represent agricultural land zones.

As mentioned before, Williams (1991) indicates that the *tlaxilacalli* of Santa Maria Asunción, with a total of 1,324 inhabitants,[4] covered an area of approximately 700 hectares, of which only about 280 hectares were agricultural land. The author also mentions that the distance to the cultivated fields does not exceed thirty minutes on foot from the domestic units and she suggests that the settlement pattern seems largely to be the result of the agricultural practice of vegetable gardens or *calmilli* adjacent to the residential units. These vegetable gardens of approximately half a hectare were on the best soils, and therefore they largely determined the location and degree of dispersion of residential sites. Williams concludes that it could be archaeologically expected that most of the residential structures would be located on the best soils, rather than the poorest (1994:80–81).

In reference to this last proposal, in the Tula area, the opposite seems to have occurred, at least in the case of sites Type 1, 2, and 11, that is, the location of these sites on the poorest soils, mainly on slopes with Class IV and worse soils, rather than on better soils. But there seems to be a trend on better lands with dispersed occupation to include isolated habitation structures in the center of the agricultural lands to be exploited. These trends appear clearly in the group we are analyzing.

The settlement distribution in the La Mesa Group also suggests the practice of two different farming strategies. On one hand, the distance between the domestic structures and the three main sites (Types 2 and 11) would permit the existence of vegetable gardens or *calmilli*. Sanders (1992), Evans (1990), and Williams (1994), among other authors, have suggested that the average size of these domestic plots in the Central Highlands was between .25 and .5 hectares. Probably there were nopal, maguey, and some other crops in the fields adjacent to the houses in the zone we are describing. On the other hand, it is probable that the rainfall agricultural fields with fallow and cultivated lands would be located in the dispersed-material zones, especially on the edges of the lower lands and those near the isolated structures. It is also very likely that this entity had irrigated land next to the Salado River, where there are Class 1 soils with a high agricultural potential, in addition to the rainfall land.

It is very interesting to consider the information provided in the *Suma de Visitas* (1905:223–224) about the ecology of this zone; when referring to Tlahuelilpan, it mentions that: "no tienen montes ni pastos ni tiene baldíos; atraviessa un arroyo por el mismo pueblo, algo salobre, y en la madre del salen fuentes más dulces; es tierra llana y buena para trigo y maíz, darse en frutas de castilla, tienen algunos tunales y magueyales y mezquiques y caza de liebres y conejos y codornices; tiene de largo una legua [5 kilometers?] y de ancho tres cuartas."

The presence of three sites with ceremonial architecture stands out in this group. Two of them are Type 2 sites that are rather close to each other and considered as the principal settlements of the entity. The other is a smaller and less complex Type 11 site. Additionally, there is a complex of two structures, one of which is ceremonial (Type 19).

It is pertinent to recall here that in each of the *calpulli* studied by Carrasco in Yautepec, especially those of Tepetenchic and Molotla, there were two *tecuhtli* who lived with their relatives and dependents in the principal localities of the *calpulli*. The one of greater importance, who was the chief of the entire *calpulli*, lived in the principal locality and the *tecuhtli* of lower rank lived in the second community (Tepepan in the case of the *calpulli* of Tepetenchi and Atempa in the case of Molotla). Thus, most of the inhabitants of the entire *calpulli* lived in these two localities, which had a very similar number of inhabitants, while the rest of the population was distributed in various minor localities. Williams documents a similar situation for the *tlaxilacalli* of Santa Maria Asunción. In the *calpulli* of Panchimalco there is a variation because Carrasco notes that in the first subdivision, also called Panchimalco, there were two *tecuhtli,* not one, and that another *tecuhtli* ruled in another locality (1976b:114); thus, in this *calpulli* there were three individuals with the title of *tecuhtli,* and not two.

It seems probable that in the La Mesa Group the situation was similar and that the two principal sites were equal in rank and functions to the two most important localities of the *calpulli,* that is, similar to the places where the principals or señores of highest rank lived with their relatives and dependents and where most of the entity's population was also concentrated. It is also probable that a third personage equal to a lesser *tecuhtli* or officers of lower hierarchy lived in the other two places of lower status with ceremonial architecture.

It must be remembered that Carrasco also states that censuses indicate that there were various persons in positions of authority in these *calpulli,* which is evidenced by their titles as officers or because they were reputedly in charge of collecting tributes or because they distributed the land. There are individuals with the title of *tequitlato,* some of whom were lower level bosses of subdivisions and others who were not. Although there are insufficient data to determine their precise functions, their title seems to have been higher than the minor *barrio* bosses (*mandones*). Carrasco also states that for Molotla there is mention of a *calpixqui* and subordinates or guides whose function is to enforce payment of the tribute (1976b:105–106).

Finally, the La Mesa Group sites that consist of one or two dispersed habitational structures were obviously the least complex of the settlement system, and they would be equivalent to the localities with few inhabitants of the *calpulli* and *tlaxilacalli,* some of which were so small that several were grouped under the same name.

Atitalaquia Settlement Group (Zone 6)

This Settlement Group could be a single entity divided into three distinct units or it could be three different units: one large and two smaller ones, which coincide with the three zones defined as Cluster XXVI (see Fig. 10.3). Within this group, there was also the inclusion of two dispersed-occupation zones next to the Salado River (Cluster XXV), one to the north on the outskirts of the present town of Atitalaquia and the other to the south facing the modern town of Atotonilco. If this were just one entity, it would cover more land than the La Mesa Group, approximately 7 kilometers long and 3 to 4 kilometers wide. It includes two zones with different soil classes and topography; the foothills of the sierra that bound the study area to the southeast and a wide strip of lowlands extending forward up to the Salado River. But in this case, unlike the La Mesa Group, most of the occupation is located in the lower lands.

This group is also an entity with heterogeneous settlement and a very varied range of sites (Fig. 10.4). There are two Type 1 sites and one Type 2 site, and all the variations of dispersed occupation. The Type 1 site (150) in the northern sector of this group covers about 10 hectares and it is located on the slopes of a hill known as Mesa Lechuguilla. There are two sites, Types 7 and 19, with ceremonial architecture and dispersed occupation near here.

The central zone of the group is apparently the most important occupation nucleus. It is almost 4 kilometers long and includes two sites (160 and 161) that cover 20 and 25 hectares each. These are the highest-ranking settlements of the entity, which undoubtedly housed most of the population of this group. The sites are relatively close to each other, and one (160) has ceremonial architecture. The other is very interesting because it is one of the few sites recorded in the area with evidence of craft production. It is a semidispersed settlement of at least 25 hectares where chert bifaces were made. Apparently, this is a community specialized in the production of points and knives made with this material and, as mentioned before, there are remains of the raw materials, wasters, and instruments in progress scattered throughout the site. The finished instruments have been found in various contexts of Tula.

It seems that the main product of these workshops was projectile points with two side notches, probably to be used with an *atlatl*. The point lengths varied from 4.1 to 4.8 centimeters (Mandeville

1974a: figs. 27g, h, i). It is interesting to note that the color of this stone is very characteristic; it ranges from translucent ivory white to pinkish white. Some of the chert points recorded among the materials extracted for the Cenote of Sacrifice in Chichén Itzá, which are illustrated in the catalogue published by Coggins and Shane (1984:47, 100), appear to be virtually identical in shape, size, and color to the bifaces manufactured in the Tula area. A detailed study and petrographic and trace element analyses would make it possible to determine if the bifaces found in Chichén Itzá did indeed come from these workshops.

Surrounding this site and No. 160, there are numerous isolated habitational structures and dispersed-material zones. There are two occupation zones next to the Salado River that seem to form specific complexes that were perhaps some kind of sub-*barrio* or territorial subdivision of the greater unit. There is one complex to the north (sites 143–148, 165, and 166) near the present town of Atitlalaquia, and another to the south (sites 170–173 and 155), facing the present town of Atotonilco Tula. Most of the sites that make up this unit are isolated habitational structures and complexes of two structures.

If the Settlement Group designated Atitalaquia was indeed a single territorial entity, it is evident that it would be larger than the La Mesa Group and perhaps it was subdivided into four distinct territorial units or segments tha may have been equivalent to the neighborhoods or *barrios* it had during the sixteenth century referred to in the *Descripción del Arzobispado de México*.

As mentioned before, in the northern sector there is a settlement (Type 1) that could have housed a population of about five hundred inhabitants, and two smaller sites with ceremonial architecture of less than a hundred inhabitants, as well as isolated habitational units. However, in the central sector the main sites are two settlements that may have had about a thousand inhabitants each (the "large villages" of Sanders, Parsons and Santley [1979]). One of these sites (160) was very probably the principal locality of the entity; the *cabecera,* where the lord or highest-ranking authorities would live. The other site, as mentioned before, was a locality whose population seems to have been specialized in the production of chert instruments. The rest of the population was spread in various smaller, dispersed localities consisting of a single habitation complex that could have housed between twenty and twenty-five persons. It is very probable that the population living next to the Salado River in various dispersed localities of twenty to fifty persons was engaged in irrigation agriculture.

In summary, the Atitalaquia Settlement Group shares with the above-mentioned La Mesa Group the presence of more than one site with ceremonial architecture and the fact that this kind of architecture was present in sites of different ranks: in Type 2 settlements and in two smaller and less complex sites close to each other. There is also a Type 19 site in both groups, that is, a complex formed by two structures: one habitational and one ceremonial. Unlike La Mesa, there are Type 1 sites in this group, one in the northern sector and one in the central sector. Probably this group, which is larger than the La Mesa Group, may have had more-diversified economic activities: rainfall and irrigation agriculture, specialized craft production, and probably the production of lime.

The data recorded in various sixteenth-century sources give us a vivid idea about various aspects of this zone, including its agricultural potential and the exploitation of other products. The *Descripción del Arzobispado de México* (1905:54–55) indicates that in the first half of the sixteenth century Atitalaquia had four neighborhoods or *barrios* that were half a league from the *cabecera*. Additionally, the *Suma de Visitas* records that: "es del mismo temple de México, tiene muchas tierras para trigo y maíz de seca. Alcanzan algún riego . . . tienen pocos pastos, atraviesa el pueblo un arroyo de agua salobre y en la madre del salen algunas fuentes de agua dulce . . . tiene piedra para cal" (1905:21).

On the other hand, the *Relaciones Geográficas* used the following terms to refer to Atitalaquia and its dependent towns, which included the neighboring towns of Tlamaco, Atotonilco, Apazco, and Tlapanaloya.

> Todos estos cinco pueblos están poblados en llano . . . los mantenimientos de que usavan antiguamente

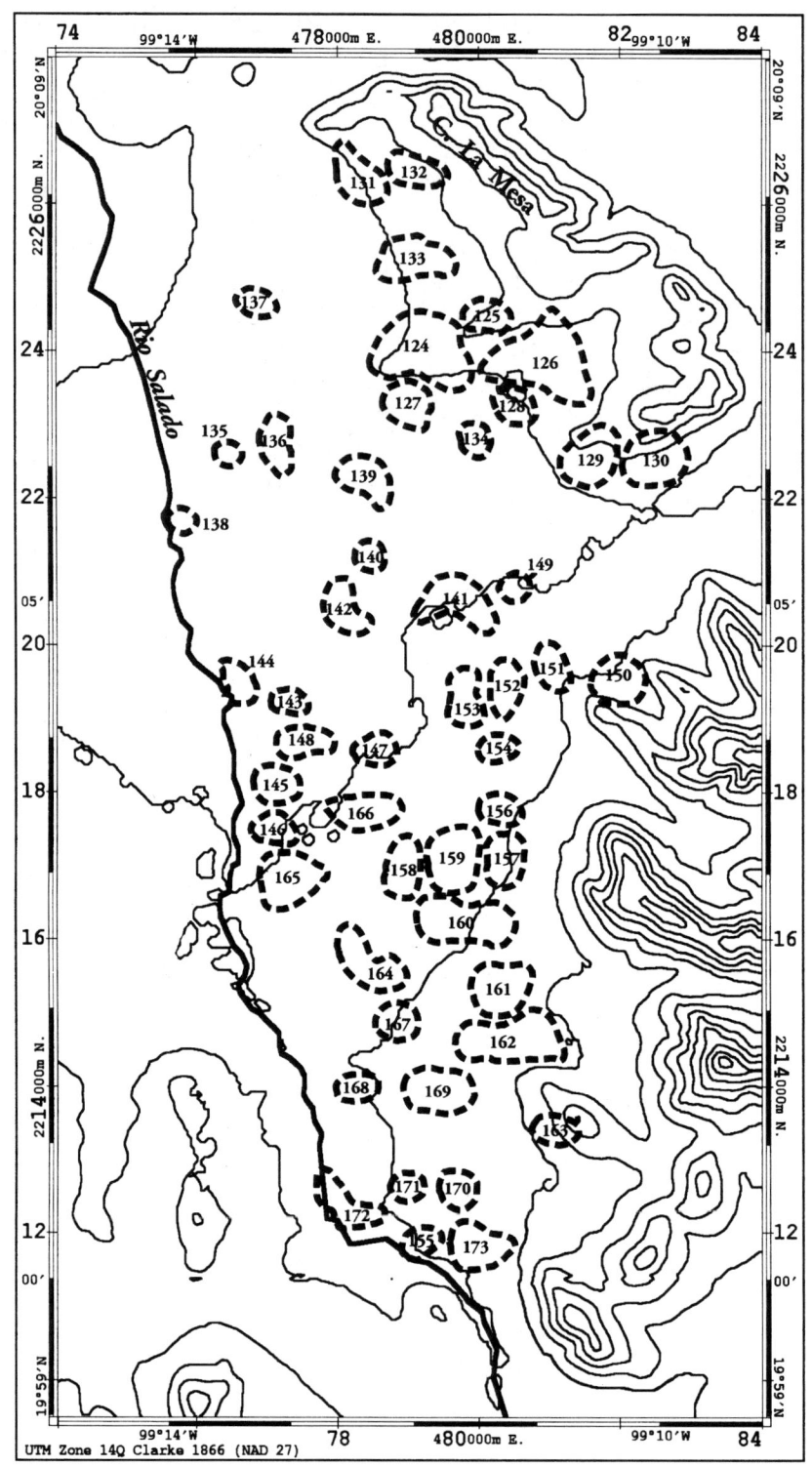

Figure 10.4A. Early Postclassic: Zone 6.

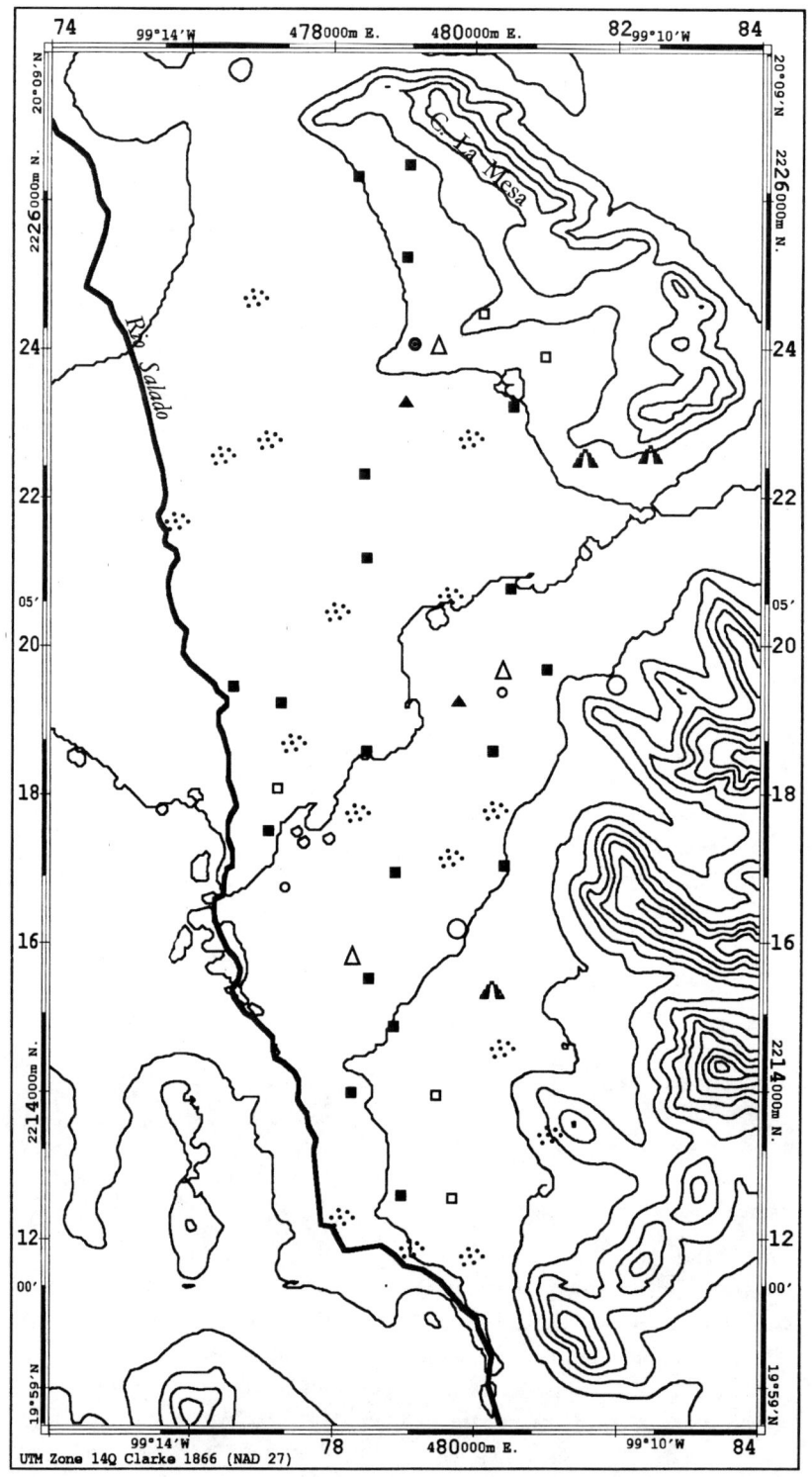

Figure 10.4B. Early Postclassic: Zone 6, site types.

y de presente usan eran y son el mayz, frijoles, calabazas, axi, pepitas, semillas de que tenían en gran cantidad de que hazian diversidad de generos de pan; comían gallos de la tierra . . . todo genero de caza, sin hazer excepción de . . . sapos y culebras, langostas, lagartijas, cigarrones y gusanos . . . hay en estos pueblos caza de venados y liebres y conejos; no hay caza de volatería ni ay otro animal bravo . . . era mucha parte para que fuesen estos naturales de sus tierras aprovechados en tierras así de temporal como de regadío, donde cogían y de presente cogen mucho maíz y aji y otras semillas.

In reference to the importance of maguey cultivation and the production of *pulque* and *aguamiel* in the zone, the text states:

tenían juntamente con esto por hazienda principal la de los magueyes de que son muy apro-vechamiento el hilo mas o menos delgado . . . aprovechanse de estos magueyes para suela de su calzado . . . es este aprovechamiento del maguey como son las cepas de España para el vino, del cual se gasta grandísima cantidad en toda la tierra . . . sacan destos magueyes un aguamiel sustancial, medicinal y dulce, de tal manera que generalmente se aprovechan mas della para bever que del agua que por estos pueblos pasa, porque es salobre y como tengan la dicha miel no echan de menos el agua . . . es tierra llana . . . tienen pocos ríos aunque de algunas fuentes tienen algunos arroyatos que corren y son de provecho a estos naturales porque son faciles de atajar . . . los frutales de este distrito son pocos los de los naturales, porque no tienen otros que los tunales de que a su tiempo se aprovechan . . . hay también unos arboles que hechan unas bainillas que es genero de frutas para ellos . . . y un arbol que da la fruta a manera de las cerezas que llaman calpulies. (Del Paso y Troncoso, vol. IV:204, 205, 206)

Tlamaco Settlement Group (Zone 4)

This group corresponds to Clusters XXIII and XXVII (Figs. 10.2 and 10.3). It is located in the northwestern part of Zone 4 and includes the present towns of Tlamaco and Cardonal and the lands occupied by the former Chingú hacienda (see Fig. 10.4). To the south it borders on the modern towns of Progreso and Atotonilco. It covers an irregular-shaped area of approximately 5 kilometers long by 2–3 kilometers wide. It is a heterogeneous entity that includes a wide array of sites distributed over an area with very even topography: rolling hills and lowlands (Figs. 7.15 and 10.5).

The principal Type 2 site (183) seems to have covered between 5 and 10 hectares, but it is difficult to determine its exact size because a large part of the settlement is in the present town of Tlamaco. There are also three Type 11 sites, which are complexes with six to seven habitation structures. Sites of this kind correspond to a second level of settlement nucleation in the area, and follow Types 1 and 2 in hierarchy. These sites are equivalent to the category of "small nucleated villages" defined by Sanders, Parsons, and Santley (1979). In this group, there are also smaller sites formed by complexes of three to five habitation units (Type 7), which is an intermediate type between dispersed occupation in the area and the nucleated sites. The rest of the occupation consists of complexes of two habitation structures or isolated structures and dispersed-occupation zones (Type 15).

The above means that this Settlement Group had a *cabecera* or principal locality of about 500 inhabitants, three towns of about 160 people, and five smaller localities of slightly more than 100 people, one of which was apparently higher in rank since it had ceremonial architecture. The rest of the population lived dispersed in a dozen small localities of less than 50 inhabitants.

As in the case of the other Settlement Groups mentioned before, in this unit there are also two types of sites with ceremonial architecture: one principal site and one small site. The relatively high frequency of Type 11 and 7 sites is also interesting, because the former is a very scarce type in the area and the Type 7 complexes are more characteristic of the alluvial valley (Zone 3), which is a zone that borders this group to the north.

It is probable that there was rainfall agriculture in addition to irrigation farming on the high-potential agricultural lands adjacent to the Salado River, and that the production of lime was another important economic activity. These specific characteristics of the settlement in this zone are very probably related to this particular combination of economic activities. The *Descripción del Arzobispado de México* men-

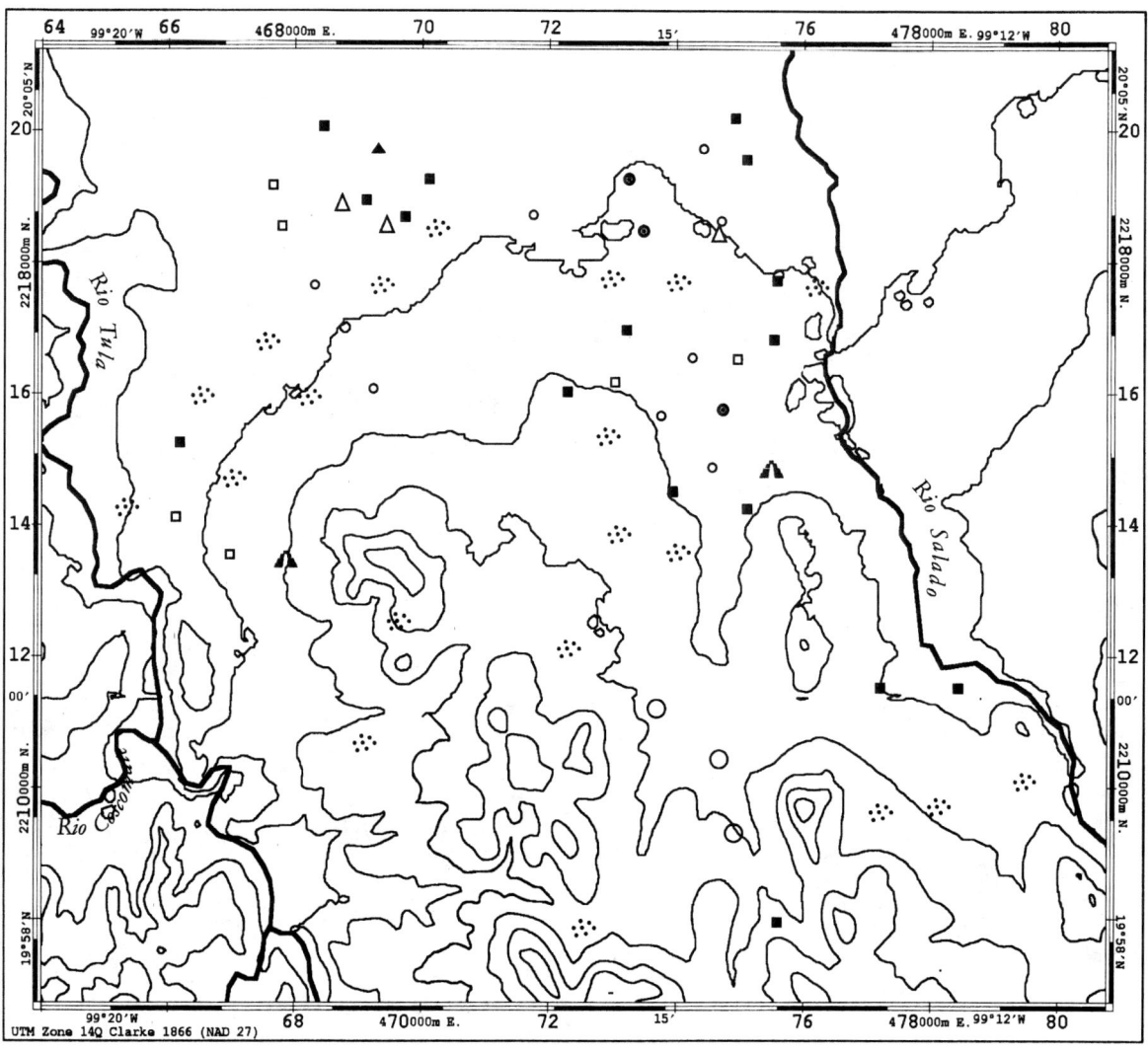

Figure 10.5. Early Postclassic: Zone 4, site types.

tions that Tlamaco, where the Mexican (Nahuatl) tongue and Otomí were spoken, was a "cabecera in itself," divided into two *barrios* separated by the arroyo (1905:55). The *Suma de Visitas*, however, mentions that: "Esta diez leguas de México y es del mesmo temple ... passa por el un arroyo de agua salobre, nacen en el algunas fuentes dulce de que veben, es tierra llana y buena para trigo y maíz, darse an en el frutas de castilla, ay tunales y capulies y canteras de buena piedra y mucha piedra para cal, ay caza de liebres y codornices, alcanzan algun riego aunque poco" (1905:224).

Regarding the Settlement Groups analyzed, in the group of the northwestern sector of Zone 5 there are also sites of different ranks with ceremonial architecture; in this case, it is a Type 2 site and two small Type 19 settlements. The presence of ceremonial architecture in the same unit of sites with different

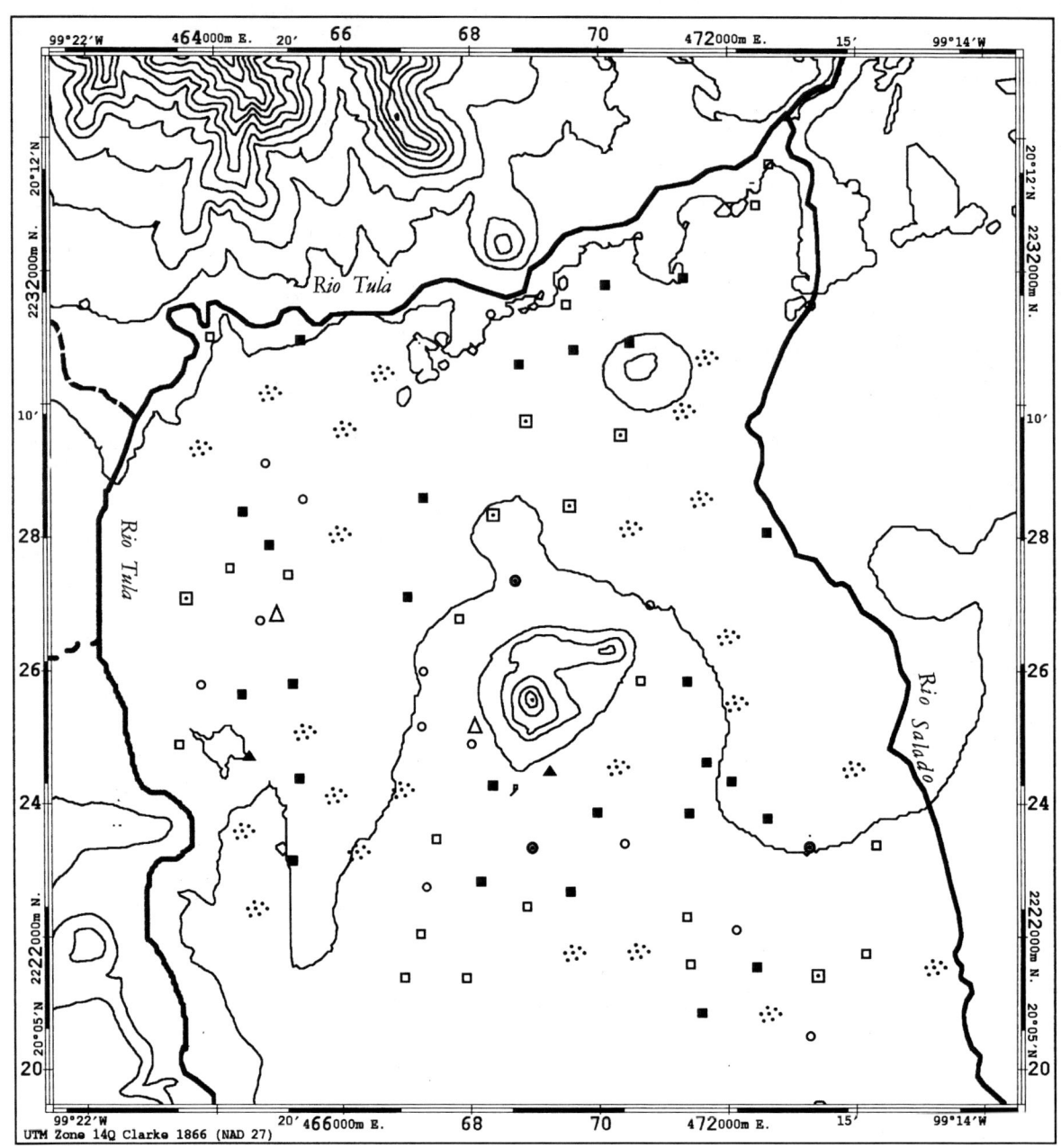

Figure 10.6. Early Postclassic: Zone 3 (alluvial valley), site types.

rank is a fact that seems to be constant in the groups analyzed and could be related to social stratification within these units and to the existence of different levels of administrative and political control that were common to these entities.

THE ALLUVIAL VALLEY (ZONE 3)

It can be said that the alluvial valley is the heart of the rural occupation of the area during this period, not only because it was extensively populated, but also because dispersed occupation predominated in this zone. Isolated extended families (Types 3, 5, and 16) or small groups of extended families (Types 7 and 11) settled directly on the agricultural space exploited by the domestic unit where cultivated and fallow land surely alternated, as was common in Mesoamerican agriculture, to allow soils to recover before being cultivated again. Sites with a higher rank in the regional hierarchy (Types 1 and 2) were not detected in the alluvial valley; however, Type 2 settlements are distributed in such a way that they give the impression of surrounding the alluvial valley, as if delimiting it (Figs. 10.1 and 10.6).

The highest-ranking sites in the alluvial valley are three Type 11 sites, localities probably with 100 to 150 inhabitants that could be considered within the category of "small nucleated villages" of Sanders, Parsons, and Santley (1979). Two of these localities are located to the north and south of Xicuco, and the inhabitants of the village located to the south (site 072) apparently were potters specialized in the production of Toza-type *cazuelas*. The occupants of a nearby habitational structure and those in another site consisting of three habitational units (sites 073 and 074) also probably manufactured the same kind of bowls. There is evidence that the Blanco Levantado–type *ollas* were made in another nearby site (069) (Figs. 10.6 and 10.7).

It should be noted that there are few sites with ceremonial architecture in the alluvial valley. Two of them are to the north and south of Xicuco (sites 061 and 067) and two are on the west side of the valley (sites 261 and 268). In both cases, they are small, dispersed Type 7 and 19 sites, which combine one habitation and one ceremonial structure and small complexes of three to five structures (Type 7). There are three sites with ceremonial structures facing the pre-Hispanic city at the southern end of the valley.

Although various Clusters were defined in the alluvial valley (see Fig. 10.3), the boundaries between these units are not clear because occupation was almost uninterrupted, and the sites have a very similar hierarchy. Thus there are no elements to propose, even hypothetically, whether this was a territorial unit in itself or whether it was divided into various political territorial units. It is clear, however, that the occupation here did have its own characteristics and is different from that of other zones of the area. As mentioned before, the settlement is somewhat homogenous, with only three concentrated localities of perhaps between 100 and 150 inhabitants (Type 11) standing out, in addition to four dispersed sites with ceremonial architecture.

Perhaps these sites functioned as some sort of sub-*cabeceras* that existed in other zones of the area or they were a territory that, from a political and administrative point of view, depended more directly on the city of Tula than other zones of the area. It is also probable that this area had a special kind of land tenure and that some of the dispersed-occupation zones without evidence of permanent settlement (Type 15) detected in the alluvial valley correspond to land cultivated by the urban population, that is, by farmers who usually lived in the city. Here is it important to bear in mind that our estimates for the Tollan Phase rural population, especially that of the alluvial valley, suggest that the economically active population living in the city's hinterland was insufficient to feed the inhabitants of the city and its rural environs.

We know that in Central Mexico during the Late Postclassic, the lands of the *pilli* were of various kinds and they did not necessarily constitute a continuous geographic unit, and that the population subject to the *tecuhtli* or chiefs of entities like the *tlaxilacalli* or *calpulli* did not always live next to the principal localities, but were distributed in various dependent towns housing the people who worked the communal or other lands. We also know that land tenure was very complex and that there were different categories of land: the sovereign's land, the land of the *tlatoanis*,

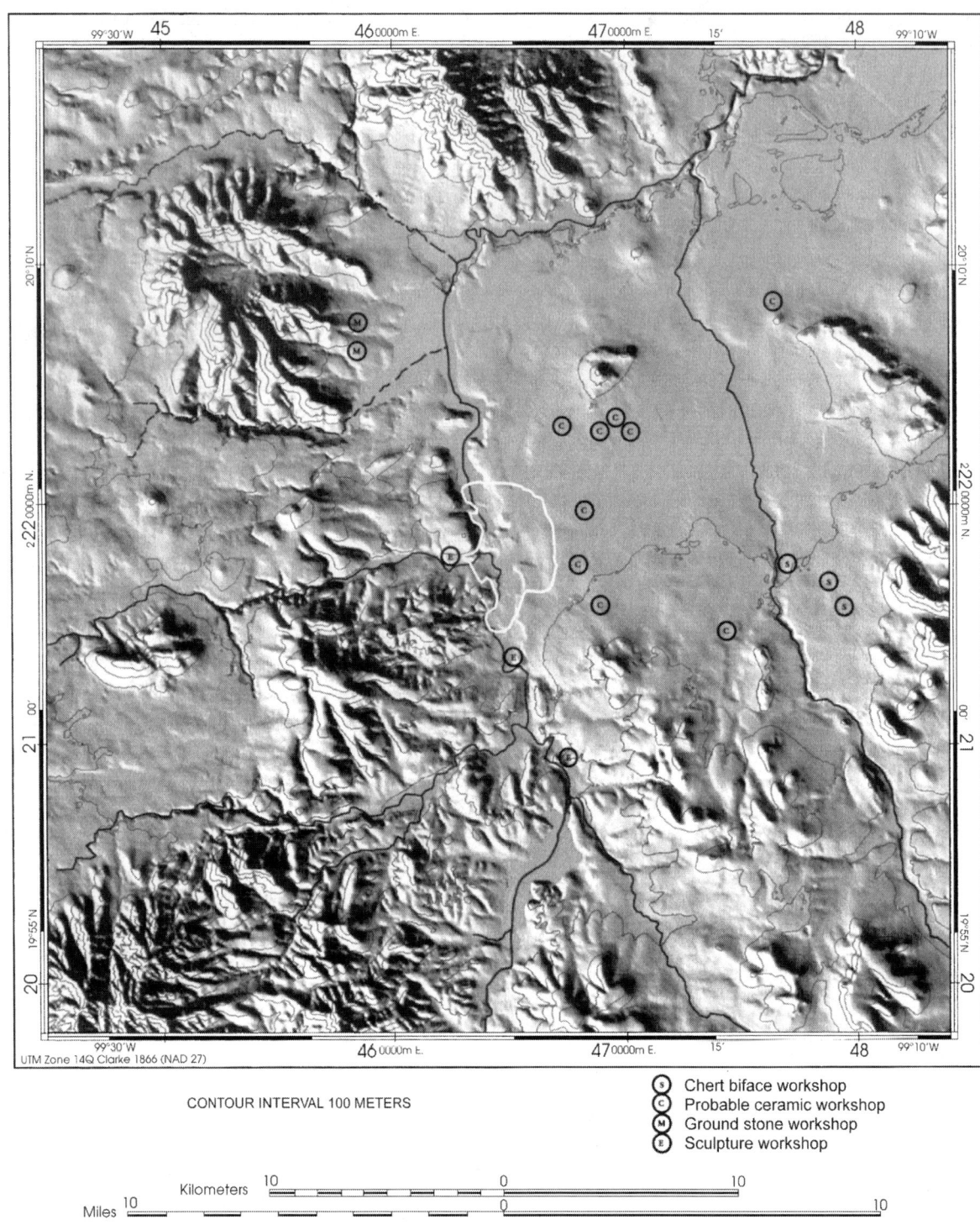

Figure 10.7. Early Postclassic: Lithic and ceramic workshops.

the land of the nobles living in the city, the land of the rural *tecuhtli* and *pilli* of different ranks, patrimonial land, temple land, war lands, and communal lands. It is also known that some of the sites outside Tenochtitlan were estates with people from different *barrios* in the city, and that the children of nobles went to live in various rural communities. Calnek mentions that some lands northwest of Tenochtitlan belonged to warriors or *tepehuani* of the city's four *barrios,* and there are records of *pochtecas* owning land outside the urban zone (personal communication 2000). Calnek also indicates that the nobles had lands in various places, including Azcapotzalco, Coyoacán, and Xochimilco, and that there is information suggesting that the dowries of nobles' wives consisted of lands located outside the city.

Thus it would not be surprising to find that similar political, administrative, and normative institutions regarding land tenure also may have existed in Tula since the Early Postclassic, and that they are related to the specific population-distribution patterns of that period and to the differences observed between the occupation of the alluvial valley and other zones of the city's hinterland. However, given our current level of knowledge, we can only speculate on the matter; more questions arise than are solved, some of which could perhaps be answered with intensive studies of the ancient city's rural environs.

NOTES

1. The units called Clusters that appear in Fig. 10.3 are a tentative category that encompasses various site types, including dispersed-occupation zones (Type 15). One of the criteria for the definition of these units mainly takes into account the spatial distribution of the sites and their topography, by grouping settlements and dispersed-occupation zones together that appear to form complexes, some of which may correspond to units with the same land use.

2. This zone bordering on the Tula region was not part of the study area; consequently, we do not have information about the nature of occupation during this period. However, we do know from a preliminary survey (Hortensia de Vega, personal communication) that there was what seems to have been a significant Tollan Phase occupation around Ajacuba.

3. The criteria of Sanders and Healan were used as a basis in this and subsequent population estimates. Such criteria were used for the general population estimates for the area referred to in Chapter 7.

4. This town was divided into twelve different localities: Cuauhtepoztla (365 inhabitants), Huiznahuac (340), Tlancomolco (158), Antecotla (92), Tlan-chuihca (74), Tlantozcoc (78), Chiauhtenco (45), Chiauhtlan (45), Cuitlahuac (34), Conzotlan (31), Tlaltecahuacan (28), and Zapotla (34) (Williams 1991:194). This author observes that the physical organization of the codex suggests that the first four communities were sufficiently large to be regarded as separate political subdivisions of the *tlaxilacalli,* while the other eight were considered together to form a fifth entity (p. 196).

11
Conclusions

The study of the ancient city of Tula and the settlements in the core of its heartland make it possible to have a regional perspective of the Toltec state and its formation processes. The different forms of populating and the distributions of settlement patterns in the area during three distinct periods are without doubt related to the particular historical conditions for each of these times and show how the continuity of occupation of an area does not necessarily imply the continuity of the social and political structures and of the specific forms of relations with the environment and the potential resources.

During the Classic period, the Tula region constituted part of the sustaining area of a state, the center of which was located in another region. However, the ethnic structure and the economic and political system of the Teotihuacan state are manifest in the particular forms of settlement distribution in the Tula region during that period. For that time in the study area, there is a paramount regional center that reproduces many aspects (such as planning, architecture, and artifact assemblages) of the metropolis. The process of colonizing the area very probably involved people who came directly from Teotihuacan. Regarding this process, the probable presence in sites of this period in our area of ethnic minorities such as the Oaxaca Barrio group, who formed part of the population living in Teotihuacan, is significant.

Archaeological evidence indicates that during this period the area was integrated into the long-distance trade network of the Teotihuacan state. In addition, it is very probable that extensive irrigation systems were constructed, and that the economic importance of the Tula region for the Teotihuacan state was centered on the obtainment of agricultural products and especially the exploitation of the large limestone zone in the south, considering the importance of lime for this city over the centuries.

CONCLUSIONS

In the Late Classic and Epiclassic, there is a different situation, with foreign groups apparently settling in some zones of the area. These people, bearers of a new cultural tradition, probably originated in the northern periphery of Mesoamerica from regions such as the sierra between Jalisco and Zacatecas and some sectors of Guanajuato.

The presence of these groups in the area is very probably tied to general population movements and migrations linked to the decline of the Teotihuacan state as a great center of political, religious, and economic power.

In the study area there are demographic changes and a different population distribution. The sites of this period have characteristics distinct from the Teotihuacan settlements, and in a sense surround the area instead of occupying it. Some of these sites probably are coeval with the final Teotihuacan occupation. The different origin of these populations and their distinct cultural tradition is evident in the planning and internal structure of the sites, their architectural style and construction techniques, as well as the lithic industries and the ceramic tradition, which is generically called Coyotlatelco although this is still an ambiguous term.

At this time there is no evidence in the area for the existence of a center with greater hierarchy upon which the other sites depended politically. Most of these sites are similar in size but they are not homogeneous. Although most of them seem to share a common cultural tradition, there are differences in terms of particular aspects that could be due to their populations having the same origin in general terms but with some specific differences, perhaps from belonging to a regional cultural tradition having significant local variations, or ethnic diversity, or because they may have been the result of different episodes of migration. Another important factor of this diversity could relate to the political fragmentation that is characteristic of this period and the absence of the state, the institutions of which have the tendency to homogenize and make more uniform many aspects of culture.

A crucial transformation took place in the area during the eighth century A.D., the period corresponding to the beginning of Tula's city. The early city apparently integrated ethnically and culturally the preceding Teotihuacan tradition and the people of northern origin, but this is a period full of questions concerning the formation processes of this urban center and the nature of its internal structure and characteristics. There is no certainty concerning whether this early settlement of 5 or 6 square kilometers already constituted a truly developed urban center in terms of the socioeconomic complexity that characterizes a city.

Different kinds of data suggest that the early city had two ceremonial precincts: one in the plaza known as Tula Chico and the second on the nearby hill where the Tollan Phase monumental center eventually was built. The monumental precinct of Tula Chico was abandoned and very probably burned and looted between A.D. 800 and 850. There was then a radical urban transformation that included the construction of a new monumental center of much larger proportions, along with the change in the orientation of the city's urban grid (to approximately 17° to the east), including the new sacred precinct.

It is only possible to speculate about the causes behind this great urban reorganization, but it is evident that the abandonment of Tula Chico and the creation of a new monumental precinct is related to important political and religious events that could have been tied to some of the central incidents referred to in diverse chronicles and historical sources concerning Topiltzin Quetzalcoatl and the followers of Tezcatlipoca. What is certain is that Tula Chico's principal plaza and its buildings were abandoned without having new structures erected there, continuing to be uninhabited for over two centuries even though this zone was surrounded by the Tollan Phase city. This was the first and the most drastic and enigmatic of the two great urban transformations that Tula experienced during its long life of over four centuries.

But it is evident that we have more questions than answers concerning this early city, its ethnic composition, its institutions, and its ideology. In order to understand Tula's formation processes and its urban development, new research that should be centered on the ideological, religious, and political continuity and discontinuity between this initial urban nucleus and the Tollan Phase city is crucial.

CONCLUSIONS

During the following century (Early Tollan Phase), the initial urban nucleus became a more complex city that covered almost 13 square kilometers. Around A.D. 1000 the city lived its period of maximum apogee and expansion as capital of a militarist state having an extensive sphere of influence that included diverse and distant regions of Mesoamerica. The core of this state was formed by the city and its direct hinterland, which constituted an organic political and economic unit. The complexity of this state and its institutions was manifested in the size and internal structure of the city and in the specific forms of settlement of the rural population in its heartland.

The plan and internal structure of Tula differ from the urban conceptions of Teotihuacan and Tenochtitlan in terms of setting, layout, internal thoroughfares, and the organization of urban territory. These differences undoubtedly express cultural and ideological specificities, characteristic institutions, and particular forms of life of these cities. However, there also are some similarities that indicate important continuities in cosmovision and in fundamental ideological concepts shared by these three urban centers.

In the planning of Tula's sacred precinct, and in its iconography and some architectonic elements, cultural and ideological ties with Teotihuacan are evident. Some of the most important of these involve the shared orientation of the sacred precincts and their buildings (approximately 17° to the east of astronomical north) along with fundamental similarities between the Pyramids of the Sun and Moon and Pyramids B and C at Tula that not only include the existence in both cases of two pyramids (with one larger than the other), and that at both centers the largest pyramid faces west and the smallest south, but also, and above all, because these paired monumental structures possess the same spatial setting with regard to each other. There also is a clear architectural similarity between Pyramid C and the two Teotihuacan pyramids in general conception, regarding especially the existence of lateral stairway platforms (*cuerpos adosados*) in the center of the pyramids' principal facades. In this sense Pyramid C represents a continuity with Teotihuacan. This is a clear Teotihuacan presence in the principal structure of Tula's sacred precinct.

In contrast, Pyramid B is conceptually different, integrating in a single architectonic complex a pyramid-temple, a vestibule, and halls with benches and altars; representing essentially innovative aspects characteristic of Toltec culture. Just as Pyramid C links Tula with Teotihuacan, Pyramid B manifests Tula's northern origins with its ties to northern architectural traditions. Thus Pyramid C represents the ancient and ancestral, and Pyramid B the new.

Previously we mentioned that Pyramid B, the Vestibule, and the Palace to the East clearly conformed one basic architectonic unit. Pyramid C, as the principal building on the precinct, was massive and uncovered, dominating the sacred space for public cults, while Pyramid B, with its frontal vestibule and adjacent palace, would have been a more private and restricted space constituting in our opinion a kind of royal sanctuary. This north complex would be a monument linked to royalty, government, and power, with its iconography exalting the royal dynasties and the institution of war, which was a key part of leadership and government at Tula. Apparently, the Palacio Quemado next to Pyramid B was a complementary space of this north complex dedicated also to rituals of kingship and war that very probably were related to Tlaloc.

Some of the sculptural groups in this complex depict personages who clearly are kings and in some cases may represent specific rulers such as Topiltzin Quetzalcoatl. The iconographic corpus of Pyramid B also contains a representation in the same column of a Tlaloc warrior and the only figure of Tezcatlipoca known for Tula, that is, the earliest image of this deity identified in the Central Highlands. It is very significant that the Tezcatlipoca figure appears precisely on the same pillar where there is a probable portrait of Topiltzin Quetzalcoatl. Likewise, the fact that the images of Tlaloc and Tezcatlipoca appear together on the upper section of this column suggests that these could have been the two principal deities or cults at Tula, probably related to royalty. Here also, as with the two main pyramids, Tlaloc would represent Tula's ties with Teotihuacan, and Tezcatlipoca the new god

CONCLUSIONS

and cult, the Toltec god. The same meaning and relationship apparently exists in the two superimposed offerings found in the center of the Palacio Quemado that likewise allude to Tlaloc and Tezcatlipoca. In addition, some sculptures and offerings suggest that in Tula the reigning monarch possessed among his titles and functions being a priest of Tlaloc or, even more, that the king could be the incarnation of Tlaloc.

As in Teotihuacan, important elements of the Toltec iconography in the north complex of the sacred precinct are feathered serpents, which mark the limits of the characteristic procession friezes on the benches of Tula, and occur on the summit of Pyramid B and in the background of some personages in reliefs. It appears that at Tula the plumed serpents, especially those forming an S, are symbols of royalty, possibly signifying the title of ruler. The two probable thrones found at Tula consist of double-headed serpents in stone.

Besides mention in some chronicles, there are elements in the iconographic program of the sacred precinct that point to the existence of a dual government at Tula, such as pairs of personages in the pillars of Pyramid B, the double converging processions of figures in the bench friezes, and the groups of paired reclining personages in the Palacio Quemado roof panels. This probable duality of rulers may have been linked to the binary conception of the universe and to the existence of two major deity cults, along with the basic dual ethnic origins of Tula's ancient city. We must remember that duality also is very evidently present in the architectonic conception of the sacred precinct formed by two opposing L's, among many other elements.

It also is important to point out that the two great ballcourts have clear spatial relationships with Tula's main pyramids: Ballcourt 2, the principal court in the sacred precinct, with Pyramid C; and Ballcourt 1 with Pyramid B. Ballcourt 1 probably was related to the Tlaloc warrior cult, and Ballcourt 2 may have been associated with the same cult as Pyramid C, possibly involving a solar deity.

There are well-defined similarities between Tula's sacred precinct and the great plaza of Tenochtitlan, it being obvious that these are not casual nor merely refer to formal aspects of urban planning and architectural traditions, or to revival manifestations, but instead indicate continuities in cosmovision and fundamental ideological concepts. Shared architectonic and iconographic elements that are cited frequently include warrior-file bench friezes, Chacmools, Atlantes, standard bearers, I-shaped ballcourts, *tzompantli,* along with correlations in the planning and internal structure of both precincts, such as the spatial setting and relations of the main pyramid, the ballcourt, the adoratorio (main altar), and the *tzompantli* in each plaza. But one of the most significant continuities involves the pyramids and goes back to Teotihuacán, because the Sun Pyramid, Pyramid C, and the Templo Mayor have the same orientation, with their main facades facing west, and also due to the importance of the concept of duality in these monuments.

We believe that the existence of two large pyramids at Teotihuacan and Tula, with the aforementioned correlations in placement and orientation, is related to the concept of duality and complementary entities that was fundamental in the cosmovision of Central Highland peoples. It is also very probable that the two pyramids in both centers express this duality and the existence of two principal cults. We think that in the same way that in the Templo Mayor of Tenochtitlan and some other cities of the Late Postclassic, this binary conception is expressed in a single pyramid having two temples on the summit: the north one dedicated to Tlaloc and the south one dedicated to Huitzilopochtli. Very probably the north chapel is smaller as a remembrance that, as at Teotihuacan and Tula, the north temple should be the smallest. We do not know if the deities and cults of both pyramids at Teotihuacan and Tula were similar to those of the two gods of the Templo Mayor at Tenochtitlan, but there is some evidence indicating a probable continuity in this sense involving the three cities.

The notable similarity already mentioned between the so-called Casa de las Aguilas of Tenochtitlan and the Palacio al Este complex, which includes the Vestibule in front of Pyramid B at Tula, is another example of the undoubted cultural ties that existed between both centers. As we have analyzed, correlations involved not only the planning and structuring of both buildings and the existence of specific shared elements such as benches with friezes of warriors and feathered serpents, but also the locations and spatial setting with the pyramids. The placement of this structure in a very prominent place in both cities, on the north side of the Templo Mayor in Tenochtitlan and north of Pyramid C at Tula, points to its important functions and significance. It is very probable that in both cities, this architectural space was linked to key state institutions and ceremonies dedicated to the king and the office of kingship (rituals of enthronement, death, mourning, and war). This strongly suggests that instead of a mere formal revival of a style and of architectural and iconographic elements, we are seeing an important example of ideological continuity between both centers, and that at Tula the direct antecedent for these institutions in Tenochtitlan can be found. In this process, it is probable that some early Aztec centers in the Basin of Mexico such as Culhuacan, where aspects of Toltec culture were preserved after the fall of Tula, played important roles.

Around A.D. 1000 (late Tollan Phase), Tula lived its apogee as the capital of an imperialist state, covering approximately 16 square kilometers. It is very probable that at this time Tula was the largest urban center in Mesoamerica. As we mentioned, this city experienced two great urban transformations. The second of these appears to coincide with its maximum expansion, involving a major change in the orientation of the urban grid, which this time is deviated west of magnetic north. The magnitude of this change is impressive if one considers that it apparently entailed a massive program of construction activities, with streets, avenues, and buildings being constructed or reconstructed according to the new grid orientation. This urban reorganization appears to correspond with changes in the architectonic conception of the domestic structures, along with innovations in the ceramic complexes, such as a drastic increase of types from a new orange-and-creamware tradition.

Undoubtedly, the irregular topography of Tula, which includes hills, slopes, lowlands, and the presence of two rivers along with the small Salitre swamp zone, must have played decisive roles in its planning and layout, because the many natural barriers and uneven topography would have made it difficult to construct straight streets crossing the city from one end to the other. Tula was not articulated along straight axes like Teotihuacan, and we do not know the specific nature of the internal streets and thoroughfares. Some alignments suggest that the streets were interrupted at intervals to form L-shaped turns in 90°. These 90° angles are present in the planning of the sacred precinct and in the structuring of some of its buildings. The accesses of many habitational complexes also are in the form of L's.

Several scholars have calculated that during the late Tollan Phase, Tula had about two thousand multifamily housing complexes including at least three types of habitational units: palaces, House Groups, and Apartment Compounds. The first type (palatial structures) corresponds principally to a series of large structures and platforms located on extensive terraces, especially to the south and east of the monumental center. On the other hand, there are chronological differences between the Apartment Compounds and the House Groups. The Apartment Compounds have planning and internal structure reminiscent of Teotihuacan residential complexes and seem to correspond fundamentally to the early Tollan Phase, while the House Groups were the most common habitational unit during the city's apogee. This means that the last urban transformation not only includes the change of orientation in the plan of the city, but also involves major innovations in domestic architecture and a different concept of dwelling and use of space, changes that surely correspond to important modifications in the socioeconomic structure of the city. The residential compounds called House Groups usually consist of three to five houses placed around a courtyard. The number of House Groups that formed a larger unit varied in ways that seem to be related to the growth of family units; probably because of this, the architectural concept and flexibility of the House Group was more suited to the apparent population boom that took place at Tula during the tenth century A.D.

We know little concerning the internal organization of the city and its territorial divisions. Intensive studies are required to identify its internal struc-

CONCLUSIONS

turing and territorial organization and the distinct levels of spatial units into which the urban territory was divided, along with their religious, economic, social, and political significance. However, at least three different types of spatial units appear to have existed. The smallest ones measure approximately 90 to 100 meters in width, having variable lengths, and may correspond to basic groups of habitation complexes bounded by streets. The two other major kinds of territorial entities that could have political, economic, and social significance cover areas varying between 40,000 and 60,000 square meters and contain numerous habitation compounds The city may have included about two hundred of these larger divisions that could correspond to neighborhoods.

The relationship between two distinct types of ceremonial mounds and the domestic compounds suggests that each probable neighborhood possessed two kinds of temples having different hierarchies: a large temple and a smaller one. We have no information indicating that Tula was divided in four great territorial units like Tenochtitlan, but in Calnek's opinion, Tula seems to have had a territorial organization more similar to that of early sixteenth-century Tlatelolco, structured in *barrios grandes* and *barrios menores* with very variable sizes and populations. Probable temples for *barrios grandes* in Tula were placed on small plazas that very probably, like in Tenochtitlan, included a marketplace and spaces for several kinds of communal activities.

Perhaps, as in Teotihuacan and Tenochtitlan, the economic activity of the inhabitants was an important criteria in the structuring and definition of Tula's neighborhoods. Evidence for many kinds of craft production exists. There are two zones that without doubt were inhabited by specialized craftsmen, and very probably formed *barrios:* an area of obsidian workshops and a large ceramic production neighborhood, both located in peripheral sectors of the city. It is likely that some of the inhabitants in the ceramics *barrio* were related to ethnic groups originating in the Gulf Coast or the Huasteca.

The investigations of Tollan Phase settlement in the core of the city's hinterland show a fundamental difference with other periods. Tula's urban zone was surrounded by an unoccupied strip of between 1 and 3 kilometers wide that clearly marked the limits between the city and its rural environs. There was a much larger population in the area not only due the existence of a great urban center with scores of thousands of inhabitants, but also to the rural population extending to zones that had been only partially occupied before, along with new zones and ecological niches that were then occupied for the first time. Apparently, the occupation and colonization of the area correspond to the two major stages and transformations that the city was known to have experienced during this period.

Numerous settlements of distinct hierarchies, size, and complexity constituted the rural population of the area, with various forms of dispersed occupation predominating. Most of the defined site types are composed of isolated residential compounds or groups of such structures. Regarding their planning and architectural characteristics, these are similar to the House Group compounds of the city, but less complex. That is, apparently just as in the city, in the rural zones the minimum spatial unit was constituted by structures inhabited by an extended family who occupied three or four houses surrounding a central patio.

These isolated structures, which extended throughout distinct zones of the area, constituted the most rural form of settlement having the least hierarchy in the population system, of which there are some variants: two, three, or four habitation structures, that is, isolated extended families and groups of them, apparently located in the center of the agricultural space exploited by the family unit. This settlement pattern is characteristic of extensive cultivation zones, and in some cases areas of new colonization. The fact that some forms of dispersed settlement have ceremonial architecture indicates there were hierarchical levels within this eminently rural occupation of the area.

Another part of the rural occupation consists of concentrated sites with or without ceremonial architecture, distributed in various zones of the area. These sites, even though they are less numerous than the dispersed occupation, collectively housed a larger population. Apparently 75 to 80 percent of the rural population lived in this kind of site, which represented the occupations with highest rank within the rural settlement hierarchy.

The Type 1 sites without ceremonial architecture were probably related to specialized economic activities such as craft production and perhaps the exploitation of limestone as well as to small irrigation systems. The Type 2 sites characterized by the presence of ceremonial architecture were the rural sites of highest rank in the regional hierarchy, and they were very probably administrative centers, a kind of *cabecera* of the territorial and administrative entities into which the rural environs of the city could have been organized.

There are no extensive sites with monumental architecture in the study area during this period, similar to the paramount center of the Teotihuacan era, although equivalent centers must have existed outside the immediate sphere of the city, similar to the site of Temascalapa in the north of the Basin of Mexico that surely functioned as a provincial center for this period. Although the estimates made for the population that inhabited the core of the city's sustaining area are approximate and tentative, they indicate that perhaps up to 70 percent of the global population of the Tula area during this period lived in the city and that the rural dispersed and concentrated sites housed only about 30 percent of the inhabitants of the area.

The presence of workshops for various kinds of goods in the area and in the city indicates that specialized craft production was not exclusively a rural or an urban activity. Even though it is evident that the rural population also was integrated into various systems of markets and commerce and surely in tribute networks of distinct types, there are different frequencies of several products and materials for everyday and ritual use, along with sumptuary goods, in rural and urban domestic contexts. These variations indicate differences in access and consumption patterns among rural and urban populations, and point to the lower status of the rural people in the hierarchy of classes of Toltec society

The fact that Tula subsisted as an urban center with high and rising population density for at least two centuries indicates an adequate use of the distinct ecological niches of the area from the point of view of agricultural exploitation and utilization of other biotic resources. Various kinds of intensive agriculture played a key role in the sustenance of urban populations of this magnitude in the Central Highlands. In the case of Tula, the studies on the irrigation potential of the area provide two distinct estimates for the maximum irrigation capacity of the area with preindustrial technology.

If the lowest figure corresponds to the irrigation capacity of the area during the apogee of the city, the base of sustenance of most of the population would then be rainfall agriculture. This would imply an unstable situation, because this is a region with high-risk zones for the cultivation of rainfall maize, and the surpluses that may be obtained under that system are lower than in the case of irrigation. If, on the other hand, Tula indeed did have as much as 10,000 hectares of irrigable land, the crops would be sufficient to sustain approximately 80 percent of the area's population, including the inhabitants of the urban zone and the rural sites, which means that basically it would be a self-sufficient area. However, it is worth emphasizing that the study area constitutes only the central part of Tula's heartland, and its sustaining area without doubt was a larger geographic unit that included some of the surrounding valleys and part of the Basin of Mexico. Because some of these areas are almost unknown archaeologically, it is not viable to make estimates concerning this aspect.

The estimates for the agricultural potential of the area fundamentally take into account its capacity to produce grains, both under irrigation and rainfall systems. It is very probable that both systems, especially in the case of rainfall cultivation, were more complex and not just based on grains, but included the cultivation of plants with a high nutritional value that are resistant to drought and frost and tolerate shallow soils, such as amaranth and maguey. Perhaps in this region the exploitation of maguey as a source of drink and food could have started with the Coyotlatelco occupation before the existence of Tula's dense city, and that in the later periods this plant undoubtedly became more important. The importance of amaranth in the area is documented, besides in the ethnohistorical data, by the two principal sets of data on plant remains in rural and urban excavations, as

CONCLUSIONS

well as by pollen studies. Various kinds of wild plants very probably were significant sources of food, as they continue to be in this region. The consumption of species such as deer, hare, rabbits, turkeys, and dogs, among others, is shown archaeologically in the domestic contexts of the city and area. Fishing was also undoubtedly an important resource for most of the urban and rural population because of the several rivers in the region.

It is difficult to know whether or not the rural population was sufficiently large to support itself and the populations of the city who were not food producers. In this respect it is important to bear in mind that the capacity of a given productive land unit to obtain a surplus depends largely on the type of crop in question, and, as shown by Sanders, crops grown on *chinampas* make it possible to obtain a surplus of 100 percent, while this figure may be 50 percent for irrigated lands and just 10 to 20 percent for rainfall agriculture, depending on the quality of the soils and other factors. Several kinds of data indicate that it is probable that in addition to the rural population, at least one-third of the inhabitants of the city were also involved in the production of food. A similar situation has been proposed for other centers such as Teotihuacan, Tenochtitlan, and Tzintzuntzan, where an important part of the population was engaged in agriculture.

Surely the problem of self-sufficiency of the nuclear region of a state is a key factor in its eventual decline, and the fact that Tula had a shorter life than Teotihuacan as a city could be related to the limitations of the potential food resources in the Tula region in comparison with those of the Basin of Mexico.

The hinterland of the city must have been organized in various political and territorial units of distinct rank and size. As mentioned earlier, the rural settlement basically combined a pattern of dispersed occupation with nucleated villages where most of the population lived. Considering the characteristics of these sites and their particular forms of distribution, we tentatively propose that these political and territorial units of variable size could be similar to the rural entities (*calpulli* and *tlaxillacalli*) analyzed in Central Mexico by Carrasco, Williams, and Reyes for zones in Morelos, the Basin of Mexico, and Tlaxcala. According to these scholars, these units basically consisted of two or three nucleated villages having a few hundred inhabitants, which were the localities with highest hierarchy, along with variable dispersed populations living in several localities, usually having between fifty and a hundred inhabitants each. These units were related to the use and tenure of land and to the tributary organization, with an internal structure and stratification principally based on access to land. These included one or more *tecuhtli* (señores) of different rank who lived with their relatives and direct dependents in the principal localities, and the extended dependent populations who lived in the small sites. If there really were political territorial entities such as the *tlaxillacalli* and *calpulli* in the Tula area, it is very likely that the diverse aspects of land tenure and tributary organization characteristic of these entities also may have existed in Tula since the Early Postclassic.

Probably there were complex systems of ownership such as those documented by the above mentioned scholars and in several sources for Tenochtitlan and other zones of Central Mexico. The wide variety of soil quality and classes in relatively small zones in the Tula region would permit a system by which the same families of farmers would cultivate various types of land, corresponding to different regimes of ownership—communal, of the local señor, of the temple, of the central power, etc.—and with different functions related to the tributary system and to the organization of labor.

APPENDIX

Site Descriptions and Clusters

Cluster	Site No.	Photo and Square	Unit	Description and Association with Other Periods	Observations
I	1	Photo 064 16 17 10 15 16	1 1, 7 24 5, 10, 17 9	SITE: Type 3 Structure D. Material: concentrated and disperse. TRANSITIONAL CLASSIC COYOTLATELCO: very light. LATE POSTCLASSIC: very light.	UTM: 469500, 2234500 NEAREST TOWN: N of Santiago Acayutlan. LOCATION: Lower slopes; altitude: 2,040 m; barranca; 50 m from the barranca and 1,500 m from the arroyo; moderate to extreme erosion. PROBABLE LAND USE: rainfall agriculture, terraces. PRESENT LAND USE: rainfall agriculture, abandoned terraces. Others: hunting, gathering plants and firewood.
I	2	Photo 064 9	4 2	SITE: Type 3. LOOTED. Structure D (15 m long). Material: concentrated. Probable local ceramic production types 806, 826. COYOTLATELCO: Structures/dense. LATE POSTCLASSIC: light.	UTM: 468400, 2233500 NEAREST TOWN: W of Santiago Acayutlan. LOCATION: Cerro, lower slopes; altitude: 1,980–2,000 m; 50 m from the Rio Tula and from the arroyo; light erosion. PROBABLE LAND USE: rainfall agriculture in terraces. Others: hunting, gathering plants. PRESENT LAND USE: abandoned terraces, herding. Others: hunting, gathering plants and firewood.

APPENDIX

Cluster	Site No.	Photo and Square	Unit	Description and Association with Other Periods	Observations
I	3	Photo 064 11 10 11	2, 8 10, 15, 25 2 10, 11, 14	SITE: Type 7 Complex of 3 Structures, B and C. Material: concentrated and disperse. FORMATIVE: very light. TRANSITIONAL CLASSIC-COYOTLATELCO: very light/light. LATE POSTCLASSIC: very light/light. COLONIAL: light.	UTM: 469800, 2233500 NEAREST TOWN: E of Santiago Acayutlan. LOCATION: Hill; altitude: 1,980–2,000 m; 250–1,300 m from the Rio Tula, arroyo, and barranca; extreme erosion. PROBABLE LAND USE: rainfall agriculture. Others: hunting and gathering plants. PRESENT LAND USE: herding. Others: hunting, gathering plants and firewood. Quarry: Rhyolite.
I	4	Photo 064 5	13	SITE: Type 3 Structure D.	UTM: 469750, 2232900 NEAREST TOWN: Santiago Acayutlan. LOCATION: 150 m to left side of barranca; altitude: 1,980–2,000 m; 750 m from the Rio Tula; extreme erosion. PROBABLE LAND USE: rainfall agriculture/irrigation agriculture. Others: hunting and gathering plants. PRESENT LAND USE: herding.
I	5	Photo 064 6	1	SITE: Type 5 2 Structures C.	UTM: 470100, 2232700 NEAREST TOWN: SE of Santiago Acayutlan. LOCATION: 450 m to north bank of the Rio Tula; no erosion. PROBABLE LAND USE: irrigation agriculture. PRESENT LAND USE: traditional irrigation agriculture, herding.
I	6	Photo 064 6 12 Photo 065 1 7	16 3, 5, 9 19 5	SITE: Type 15 Material: disperse. COYOTLATELCO: very light/light. TRANSITIONAL CLASSIC-COYOTLATELCO: very light. LATE POSTCLASSIC: Structures/very light/light.	UTM: 470900, 2233300 NEAREST TOWN: NW of Tezontepec. Activity area of mencionated sites. LOCATION: Lowlands; altitude: 1,980–2,000m; 300–550 m from the Rio Tula and 50 m from the arroyo; erosion: light to moderate. PROBABLE LAND USE: irrigation agricul- ture/rainfall agriculture. Others: hunting, gathering plants, and fishing. PRESENT LAND USE: traditional irrigation agriculture. Quarry: Rhyolite.
II	7	Photo 065 16	6	SITE: Type 3 Structure D.	UTM: 473300, 2234800 NEAREST TOWN: S of La Palma. LOCATION: Lowlands, 250 m to north bank of the Rio Tula; moderate erosion; moderate vegetation. PROBABLE LAND USE: rainfall agriculture. Others: hunting, gathering plants, fishing. PRESENT LAND USE: rainfall agriculture; herding. Others: hunting, gathering plants and firewood.

APPENDIX

Cluster	Site No.	Photo and Square	Unit	Description and Association with Other Periods	Observations
II	8	Photo 065 9 9 8 9 14 15	5, 12 5 23 2, 21 5 3, 14	SITE: Type 2 Undetermined number of Habitational/Ceremonial Structures, A and B. Extension: approx. 18 ha. Material: disperse. TRANSITIONAL CLASSIC-COYOTLATELCO: dense/very light. COYOTLATELCO: Structures/very light/dense. LATE POSTCLASSIC: Structures/very light/dense.	UTM: 472400, 2234500 NEAREST TOWN: NW of Tezontepec. LOCATION: Lowlands, north bank of the Rio Tula; altitude: 1,980–2,000 m; lower slopes; 200–800 m from the Rio Tula; 300 m from the Rio Salado; moderate erosion. PROBABLE LAND USE: rainfall agriculture. Others: hunting, gathering plants, fishing. PRESENT LAND USE: rainfall agriculture. Others: hunting, gathering plants and firewood.
IV	9	Photo 065 9 9	3, 7 13	SITE: Type 5 2 Structures B. Material: concentrated. COYOTLATELCO: Structures/dense. LATE POSTCLASSIC: very light. Selective Sampling.	UTM: 472650, 2233500 NEAREST TOWN: Panoaya. LOCATION: Plateau between the Rios Tula and Salado; altitude: approx. 2,100 m; 150–250 m from the Rio Tula and 150–250 m from the Rio Salado; moderate erosion. PROBABLE LAND USE: rainfall agriculture/irrigation agriculture. Others: hunting, gathering plants, fishing. PRESENT LAND USE: rainfall agriculture, herding. Others: hunting, gathering plants and firewood.
IV	10	Photo 065 2 3	15 7	SITE: Type 5. DESTROYED. 2 Structures C.	UTM: 472300, 2232850 NEAREST TOWN: Panoaya. LOCATION: Lowlands; altitude: 2,100 m; 500–750 m from the Rio Tula and 850–1,000 m from the Rio Salado; light erosion. PROBABLE LAND USE: rainfall agriculture. PRESENT LAND USE: town; irrigation agriculture from dams.
III	11	Photo 065 4 10	21 6	SITE: Type 2 Undetermined number of Habitational Structures/ Ceremonial Structures, A, B. Ceremonial mounds (30 m diameter and 2 m high) (6 m diameter and 1 m high). TRANSITIONAL CLASSIC-COYOTLATELCO: very light. COYOTLATELCO: very light. LATE POSTCLASSIC: Structures/very light/dense. Selective Sampling.	UTM: 473200, 2233500 NEAREST TOWN: N of Tezontepec. LOCATION: Lowlands; altitude: 2,100 m; 100–150 m from east bank of the Rio Salado; light erosion. POTENTIAL LAND USE: rainfall agriculture/irrigation agriculture. Others: fishing. PRESENT LAND USE: town; irrigation agriculture from dams.

APPENDIX

Cluster	Site No.	Photo and Square	Unit	Description and Association with Other Periods	Observations
III	12	Photo 065 10 10 10 16	 13, 18 25 19 9	SITE: Type 19. DESTROYED. Complex of 2 Structures: Habitational and Ceremonial, B and D. Material: concentrated and disperse. TRANSITIONAL CLASSIC-COYOTLATELCO: Structures/very light/dense. COYOTLATELCO: Structures/dense. LATE POSTCLASSIC: Structures/very light/dense. Selective Sampling.	UTM: 473600, 2233900 NEAREST TOWN: SW of Mixquiahuala. LOCATION: Lowlands, SE of the Rio Tula: altitude: 2,100 m; 300–1,000 m from the Rio Salado; light to moderate erosion. POTENTIAL LAND USE: rainfall agricul-ture/irrigation agriculture. Others: hunting and gathering plants. PRESENT LAND USE: irrigation agriculture from dams.
III	13	Photo 065 18 17	 11 3	SITE: Type 3 DESTROYED. Structure D. Material: disperse. COYOTLATELCO: light. LATE POSTCLASSIC: light. Selective Sampling.	UTM: 475000, 2234600 NEAREST TOWN: SW of Mixquiahuala. LOCATION: Lowlands, SE from the Rio Tula; altitude: 2,100 m; 1,000–1,600 m from the Rio Salado and from the arroyo; moderate erosion. POTENTIAL LAND USE: rainfall agricul-ture/irrigation agriculture. Others: hunting and gathering plants. PRESENT LAND USE: irrigation agriculture from dams.
V	14	Photo 066 8	 25	SITE: Type 3. DESTROYED. Structure D. CLASSIC: very light. LATE POSTCLASSIC: very light.	UTM: 477750, 2234200 NEAREST TOWN: S of Mixquiahuala. LOCATION: Lowlands, near the Rio Tula and the arroyo; light erosion. POTENTIAL LAND USE: irrigation agriculture. PRESENT LAND USE: irrigation agriculture from dams.
V	15	Photo 066 10 10 10 15 16	 11 6 1 20 21	SITE: Type 3 Structure D. Material: concentrated and disperse. FORMATIVE: very light. CLASSIC: very light. TRANSITIONAL CLASSIC-COYOTLATELCO: Structures/very light. LATE POSTCLASSIC: Structures/very light/light.	UTM: 478750, 2233700 NEAREST TOWN: S of Palmillas. LOCATION: Lowlands near the Endó canal; altitude: 2,100 m; light erosion. POTENTIAL LAND USE: irrigation agriculture. PRESENT LAND USE: irrigation agriculture/irrigation agriculture from dams.
V	16	Photo 066 15 15 14	 22 16, 21 15	SITE: Type 3 Structure D. Material: concentrated and disperse. TRANSITIONAL CLASSIC-COYOTLATELCO: very light. LATE POSTCLASSIC: very light.	UTM: 478100, 2233200 NEAREST TOWN: SW of Palmillas. LOCATION: Lowlands near the Endó canal; light erosion, scarce vegetation. POTENTIAL LAND USE: irrigation agriculture. PRESENT LAND USE: irrigation agriculture/irrigation agriculture from dams.

APPENDIX

Cluster	Site No.	Photo and Square	Unit	Description and Association with Other Periods	Observations
VI	17	Photo 076 13 Photo 066 13 31 Photo 076 13 31	23 2, 13, 17 21, 23 18, 23 40	SITE: Type 15 Material: concentrated and disperse.	UTM: 476200, 2232550 NEAREST TOWN: NW of Motovatha. LOCATION: Alluvial valley, between the Requena canal and Rio Salado; light erosion. POTENTIAL LAND USE: rainfall agriculture. PRESENT LAND USE: irrigation agriculture/ irrigation agriculture from dams.
V	18	Photo 076 15	16, 21	SITE: Type 15 Material: concentrated. TRANSITIONAL CLASSIC-COYOTLATELCO: very light. LATE POSTCLASSIC: very light.	UTM: 477900, 2232000 NEAREST TOWN: N of Motovatha. Perhaps concentrated material was permanent occupation. LOCATION: Alluvial valley and lowlands; 4,000–5,300 m from the Rio Salado; light erosion. POTENTIAL LAND USE: rainfall agriculture. PRESENT LAND USE: irrigation agriculture/ irrigation agriculture from dams.
V	19	Photo 066 14 Photo 076 14	4 23	SITE: Type 15 Material: disperse. LATE POSTCLASSIC: very light.	UTM: 477400, 2232400 NEAREST TOWN: N of Motovatha. LOCATION: Alluvial valley; 4,500 m from the Rio Salado; light erosion. POTENTIAL LAND USE: rainfall agricul-ture. PRESENT LAND USE: irrigation agriculture/ irrigation agriculture from dams.
VI	20	Photo 076 7 13 7	3, 14, 24 14 11, 16, 20	SITE: Type 15 Material: concentrated and disperse. TRANSITIONAL CLASSIC-COYOTLATELCO: very light/ light. LATE POSTCLASSIC: very light.	UTM: 476500, 2231000 NEAREST TOWN: E of La Cruz. Four "points" of probable permanent occupation. LOCATION: Near the modern canals; 3,000–3,300 m from the Rio Salado; light erosion. POTENTIAL LAND USE: rainfall agricul-ture. PRESENT LAND USE: irrigation agriculture/ irrigation agriculture from dams.
VI	21	Photo 076 2	11, 16 15, 19 20	SITE: Type 5. DESTROYED. 2 Structures B. Material: disperse. TRANSITIONAL CLASSIC-COYOTLATELCO: Structures/ very light. LATE POSTCLASSIC: Structures/ very light/dense. COLONIAL: very light.	UTM: 476900, 2230300 NEAREST TOWN: SE of La Cruz. LOCATION: Alluvial valley; light erosion; 3,000–4,000 m from the Rio Salado. POTENTIAL LAND USE: rainfall agricul-ture. PRESENT LAND USE: irrigation agriculture/ irrigation agriculture from dams.

APPENDIX

Cluster	Site No.	Photo and Square	Unit	Description and Association with Other Periods	Observations
V	22	Photo 066 5 16 Photo 076 10 16	17 19 20 16, 18	SITE: Type 15 Material: disperse. TRANSITIONAL CLASSIC-COYOTLATELCO: very light. LATE POSTCLASSIC: Structures/ very light/dense.	UTM: 479300, 2232300 NEAREST TOWN: W of Teñhé and Cañada. LOCATION: Alluvial valley between the Requena canal and the Rio Salado; altitude: 2,100 m; light erosion. POTENTIAL LAND USE: rainfall agriculture. PRESENT LAND USE: irrigation agriculture/ irrigation agriculture from dams.
XIA	23	Photo 075 8	22	SITE: Type 3 Structure D. LATE POSTCLASSIC: very light. Selective Sampling.	UTM: 471700, 2231600 NEAREST TOWN: Tezontepec. LOCATION: Alluvial valley between the Rio Tula and the Rio Salado; light erosion. POTENTIAL LAND USE: rainfall agricul- ture/ irrigation agriculture. PRESENT LAND USE: town; traditional irriga- tion agriculture/irrigation agriculture from dams.
VII	24	Photo 075 16	5	SITE: Type 19 Complex of 2 Structures: Habita- tional and Ceremonial, A. TRANSITIONAL CLASSIC-COYOTLATELCO: very light. Selective Sampling.	UTM: 474000, 2231700 NEAREST TOWN: Mangas and Presas. LOCATION: Alluvial valley and lowlands; N of the Requena canal, between Mangas and Presas towns; 1,000 m from the Rio Salado; moderate erosion. POTENTIAL LAND USE: irrigation agriculture. PRESENT LAND USE: traditional irrigation agriculture/irrigation agriculture from dams. Quarry: Sand.
VII	25	Photo 075 4	16, 21	SITE: Type 5. DESTROYED. 2 Structures B. LATE POSTCLASSIC: Structures/ light. COLONIAL: very light/light. Selective sampling.	UTM: 473200, 2230450 NEAREST TOWN: S of Mangas. LOCATION: Alluvial valley; 600–800 m from the Rio Salado; light erosion. POTENTIAL LAND USE: rainfall agricul- ture/ irrigation agriculture. PRESENT LAND USE: town; traditional irri- gation agriculture/irrigation agriculture from dams.
VII	26	Photo 075 4	5, 15	SITE: Type 5. DESTROYED. 2 Structures C. LATE POSTCLASSIC: very light/ light. COLONIAL: very light. Selective sampling.	UTM: 473900, 2230100 NEAREST TOWN: SW of La Cruz. LOCATION: Alluvial valley; 1,500–1,600 m from the Rio Salado; light erosion. POTENTIAL LAND USE: rainfall agricul- ture/ irrigation agriculture. PRESENT LAND USE: town; traditional irriga- tion agriculture/irrigation agriculture from dams.

APPENDIX

Cluster	Site No.	Photo and Square	Unit	Description and Association with Other Periods	Observations
VII	27	Photo 082 17 18 24	22 10, 20, 25 2	SITE: Type 15 Material: disperse. COYOTLATELCO: very light. LATE POSTCLASSIC: Structures/very light/dense. COLONIAL: very light.	UTM: 475600, 2229500 NEAREST TOWN: NW of El Tinaco. LOCATION: Material in altitude 2,000 m; alluvial valley; 2,000–3,800 m from the Rio Salado; light erosion. POTENTIAL LAND USE: rainfall agriculture in lowlands. Others: hunting and gathering plants. PRESENT LAND USE: town; irrigation agriculture/irrigation agriculture from dams.
XIVA	28	Photo 152 16	3	SITE: Type 3 Structure D. LATE POSTCLASSIC: dense.	UTM: 482300, 2232600 NEAREST TOWN: Teñhé—the cerro Loma Larga. LOCATION: Lower slopes of the hill, near the Rio Salado and the arroyo; light erosion, moderate vegetation. POTENTIAL LAND USE: rainfall agriculture in terraces. Others: hunting and gathering plants. PRESENT LAND USE: rainfall agriculture.
VIII	29	Photo 074 17 11	4 24 18, 22 23	SITE: Type 3 Structure D. Material: concentrated and disperse. CLASSIC: light. LATE POSTCLASSIC: Structures/very light/dense. COLONIAL: very light/light.	UTM: 470000, 2231800 NEAREST TOWN: E of San Juan Achichilco. LOCATION: Alluvial valley; 950 m S from the Rio Tula and 550–650 m from the barranca; light erosion. POTENTIAL LAND USE: rainfall agriculture in lowlands/irrigation agriculture. Others: hunting and gathering plants. PRESENT LAND USE: irrigation agriculture/irrigation agriculture from dams.
VIII	30	Photo 074 10 11 10 11 16 17	13, 19 16 20 21 5 1	SITE: Type 5. DESTROYED. 2 Structures B. Material: concentrated and disperse. CLASSIC: light. LATE POSTCLASSIC: Structures/dense. COLONIAL: very light.	UTM: 469300, 2231400 NEAREST TOWN: E of San Juan Achichilco. LOCATION: Lowlands in altitude 2,100 m; S from the Rio Tula; both structures are separated 150 m from the Rio Tula by a cliff; light erosion. POTENTIAL LAND USE: rainfall agriculture/irrigation agriculture. Others: fishing. PRESENT LAND USE: town; traditional irrigation agriculture/irrigation agriculture from dams.
VIII	31	Photo 074 9 8 9	18, 19 20 3, 17, 22	SITE: Type 7. 3 Structures B. Material: disperse. TRANSITIONAL CLASSIC-COYOTLATELCO: very light. COYOTLATELCO: very light. LATE POSTCLASSIC: Structures/light/dense. COLONIAL: very light/light.	UTM: 468300, 2231300 NEAREST TOWN: San Juan Achichilco. LOCATION: Structures are in lowlands, 200 m from bank of the Rio Tula; altitude: 2,100 m; light and moderate erosion. POTENTIAL LAND USE: irrigation agriculture. Others: fishing. PRESENT LAND USE: town; traditional irrigation agriculture/irrigation agriculture from dams, herding.

APPENDIX

Cluster	Site No.	Photo and Square	Unit	Description and Association with Other Periods	Observations
IX	32	Photo 073 11 12	12 4, 5, 6, 8, 12, 13, 14, 17 11	SITE: Type 3 Structure D. Material: disperse. COYOTLATELCO: very light. LATE POSTCLASSIC: Structures/ very light/light/dense. COLONIAL: very light/light.	UTM: 465200, 2230850 NEAREST TOWN: Achichilco-Atengo. LOCATION: Lowlands; 30 m from S bank of the Rio Tula; light erosion. POTENTIAL LAND USE: irrigation agriculture. Others: hunting and gathering plants, fishing. PRESENT LAND USE: town; rainfall agriculture/traditional irrigation agriculture/ irrigation agriculture from dams, herding. Others: hunting and gathering plants, fishing.
IX	33	Photo 073 9	10, 15 13 10, 14, 18	SITE: Type 5. LOOTED. 2 Structures B (1 of them 1,058 m² approx.). Material: concentrated and disperse. COYOTLATELCO: Structures/ very light/dense. LATE POSTCLASSIC: very light/ light. COLONIAL: very light.	UTM: 463900, 2230900 NEAREST TOWN: N of San Gabriel. LOCATION: Lowlands; 20–150 m from S bank of the Rio Tula; light erosion. POTENTIAL LAND USE: irrigation agriculture. Others: hunting and gathering plants, fishing. PRESENT LAND USE: town; traditional irrigation agriculture/irrigation agriculture from dams. Others: hunting and gathering plants, firewood.
XL	34	Photo 12B 20	4	SITE: Type 5. DESTROYED. 2 Structures B. Material: concentrated. LATE POSTCLASSIC: very light. COLONIAL: very light. Selective Sampling.	UTM: 462750, 2230900 NEAREST TOWN: Between Tepetitlán and Atengo. LOCATION: Lower slopes; 150–400 m from the Rio Tula, associated to traditional system of the Tepetitlán canal; light erosion, scarce vegetation. POTENTIAL LAND USE: rainfall agriculture. Others: hunting and gathering plants, fishing. PRESENT LAND USE: rainfall agriculture, herding. Others: hunting and gathering plants, firewood.
X	35	Photo 083 7	16, 17	SITE: Type 5 2 Structures B. Probable local ceramic production type 818. CLASSIC: very light. LATE POSTCLASSIC: very light/ light. COLONIAL: very light.	UTM: 476450, 2228300 NEAREST TOWN: E of El Tinaco. LOCATION: Alluvial valley near the Requena canal, 4,000–4,100 m from the Rio Salado; light erosion. POTENTIAL LAND USE: rainfall agriculture. Others: hunting and gathering plants. PRESENT LAND USE: irrigation agriculture/ irrigation agriculture from dams.
XIV	36	Photo 083 9	24, 25	SITE: Type 5 2 Structures B. CLASSIC: light. COYOTLATELCO: very light. LATE POSTCLASSIC: very light.	UTM: 478700, 2228700 NEAREST TOWN: S of Carrillo Puerto. LOCATION: Alluvial valley, 6,400–6,500 m from the Rio Salado; light erosion. POTENTIAL LAND USE: rainfall agriculture on lowlands. Others: hunting and gathering plants. PRESENT LAND USE: irrigation agriculture/ irrigation agriculture from dams; associated with Requena canal.

APPENDIX

Cluster	Site No.	Photo and Square	Unit	Description and Association with Other Periods	Observations
XIV	37	Photo 083 4 10 Photo 091 18	21 5 16	SITE: Type 15 Material: disperse. CLASSIC: very light. COYOTLATELCO: very light. LATE POSTCLASSIC: very light/light. COLONIAL: very light.	UTM: 479150, 2228000 NEAREST TOWN: Between La Cañada and Hidroeléctrica Juandó. LOCATION: Alluvial valley; 6,000–7,000 m from the Rio Salado; light erosion. POTENTIAL LAND USE: rainfall agriculture. Others: hunting and gathering plants. PRESENT LAND USE: irrigation agriculture/irrigation agriculture from dams.
XIV	38	Photo 083 17	25 15, 18	SITE: Type 3 Structure D. Material: disperse. LATE POSTCLASSIC: very light/light.	UTM: 480400, 2229600 NEAREST TOWN: Between La Cañada and Hidroeléctrica Juandó. LOCATION: Alluvial valley, 8,000–9,000 m from the Rio Salado; light erosion. POTENTIAL LAND USE: rainfall agriculture. Others: hunting and gathering plants. PRESENT LAND USE: irrigation agriculture/irrigation agriculture from dams; terraces.
XIV	39	Photo 083 11 12 17	 5 25 6 2	SITE: Type 3 Structure D. Material: disperse. CLASSIC: very light. TRANSITIONAL CLASSIC-COYOTLATELCO: very light. LATE POSTCLASSIC: Structures/very light/light/dense. COLONIAL: very light.	UTM: 480650, 2228200 NEAREST TOWN: Between La Cañada and Hidroeléctrica Juandó. LOCATION: Lower slopes and alluvial valley Alto Requena, 8,000–9,500 m from the Rio Salado; light and moderate erosion; moderate vegetation. POTENTIAL LAND USE: rainfall agriculture. Others: hunting and gathering plants. PRESENT LAND USE: town; rainfall agriculture on terraces and irrigation agriculture from dams.
XIV	40	Photo 083 16	20	SITE: Type 3 Structure D. LATE POSTCLASSIC: very light. COLONIAL: light.	UTM: 479600, 2229650 NEAREST TOWN: Between La Cañada and Hidroeléctrica Juandó. LOCATION: Alluvial valley, 7,800 m from the Rio Salado; light erosion. POTENTIAL LAND USE: rainfall agriculture. Others: hunting and gathering plants. PRESENT LAND USE: irrigation agriculture/irrigation agriculture from dams.
VI	41	Photo 083 14	11 14	SITE: Type 3 Structure D. Material: concentrated. LATE POSTCLASSIC: very light/light. COLONIAL: light.	UTM: 477250, 2229250 NEAREST TOWN: W of Carrillo Puerto and NE of El Tinaco. LOCATION: Alluvial valley, 4,800–5,800 m from the Rio Salado; light erosion. POTENTIAL LAND USE: rainfall agriculture. Others: hunting and gathering plants. PRESENT LAND USE: irrigation agriculture/irrigation agriculture from dams.

APPENDIX

Cluster	Site No.	Photo and Square	Unit	Description and Association with Other Periods	Observations
X	42	Photo 090 18 Photo 091 8 13	8 17 4, 5, 9	SITE: Type 3 Structure D. Material: concentrated and disperse. LATE POSTCLASSIC: Structures/ very light/light/dense. COLONIAL: very light.	UTM: 476550, 2226600 NEAREST TOWN: SW of Cerro de La Cruz, S of Presas and El Tinaco. LOCATION: Alluvial valley near the Requena canal, 1,000–2,300 m from the Rio Salado; light erosion; moderate vegetation. POTENTIAL LAND USE: rainfall agriculture. Others: hunting and gathering plants. PRESENT LAND USE: irrigation agriculture/ irrigation agriculture from dams; herding. Others: hunting and gathering plants, firewood.
X	43	Photo 082 12 6 5 11 12	12 20, 22 24, 25 9 9	SITE: Type 3. DESTROYED. Structure D. Material: concentrated and disperse. CLASSIC: very light. LATE POSTCLASSIC: Structures/ very light/light/ dense. COLONIAL: very light.	UTM: 475150, 2228200 NEAREST TOWN: W of Cerro de La Cruz, S of Presas and El Tinaco. LOCATION: Alluvial valley near the Requena canal, 1,800–3,000 m from the Rio Salado; light erosion; moderate vegetation. POTENTIAL LAND USE: rainfall agriculture on lowlands. Others: hunting and gathering plants. PRESENT LAND USE: town; irrigation agriculture/irrigation agriculture from dams.
X	44	Photo 082 11 5	1 16, 22	SITE: Type 3 Structure D. Material: disperse. LATE POSTCLASSIC: Structures/ very light/dense.	UTM: 474150, 2228100 NEAREST TOWN: W of Cerro de La Cruz, S of Presas and El Tinaco. LOCATION: Alluvial valley near the Requena canal, 1,300–1,500 m from the Rio Salado; light and moderate erosion, scarce vegetation. POTENTIAL LAND USE: rainfall agriculture. Others: hunting and gathering plants. PRESENT LAND USE: irrigation agriculture/ irrigation agriculture from dams, rainfall agriculture, herding. Others: hunting and gathering plants, firewood.
X	45	Photo 090 17	3 7, 18	SITE: Type 3 Structure D. Material: disperse. LATE POSTCLASSIC: very light/ light.	UTM: 474800, 2226900 NEAREST TOWN: Cuauhtémoc, W of Cerro de La Cruz, S of Presas and El Tinaco. LOCATION: Hill, 700–1,200 m from the Rio Salado; moderate erosion, scarce vegetation. POTENTIAL LAND USE: rainfall agriculture. Others: hunting and gathering plants. PRESENT LAND USE: town; rainfall agriculture.

APPENDIX

Cluster	Site No.	Photo and Square	Unit	Description and Association with Other Periods	Observations
XIA	46	Photo 082 9	8	SITE: Type 3 Structure D. Material: disperse. LATE POSTCLASSIC: very light.	UTM: 472500, 2228000 NEAREST TOWN: Presas and 5 de Febrero. LOCATION: Alluvial valley, 250 m from west bank of the Rio Salado; light erosion. POTENTIAL LAND USE: rainfall agriculture and irrigation agriculture. Others: fishing. PRESENT LAND USE: irrigation agriculture/ irrigation agriculture from dams.
XII	47	Photo 074 4 5	25 22 17	SITE: Type 3. DESTROYED. Structure D. Material: concentrated and disperse. LATE POSTCLASSIC: light. COLONIAL: very light/dense.	UTM: 469350, 2230650 NEAREST TOWN: NW of Huitel and E of Atengo. LOCATION: Lower slopes of the Cerro Huitel and alluvial valley; 1,300–1,700 m from the Rio Tula; light and moderate erosion; scarce and moderate vegetation. POTENTIAL LAND USE: rainfall agriculture, agriculture on terraces. Others: hunting and gathering plants. PRESENT LAND USE: irrigation agriculture/ irrigation agriculture from dams; herding. Others: hunting and gathering plants, firewood.
XII	48	Photo 074 4 3 4	6 14, 15, 18 11, 12, 17, 18, 21, 22, 23	SITE: Type 3. DESTROYED. Structure D. Material: disperse. CLASSIC: light. TRANSITIONAL CLASSIC-COYOTLATELCO: very light. COYOTLATELCO: very light/light. LATE POSTCLASSIC: very light/light. COLONIAL: very light/light.	UTM: 468550, 2230200 NEAREST TOWN: NW of Huitel and E of Atengo. LOCATION: Alluvial valley and lowlands, 700–1,250 m from the Rio Tula and 150–1,000 m from the barranca; light erosion. POTENTIAL LAND USE: rainfall agriculture. Others: hunting and gathering plants. PRESENT LAND USE: irrigation agriculture/ irrigation agriculture from dams.
XI	49	Photo 074 11 6 11 12	4 11, 21 3, 5, 7, 8, 15 3, 6, 11	SITE: Type 3. DESTROYED. Structure D. Material: disperse. TRANSITIONAL CLASSIC-COYOTLATELCO: very light. LATE POSTCLASSIC: Structures/ very light/light/dense. COLONIAL: very light.	UTM: 470200, 2230850 NEAREST TOWN: NW of Huitel and S of Tezontepec. LOCATION: Lower slopes of the Cerro Huitel; alluvial valley, lowlands; 1,000–2,100 m from the Rio Tula and 750 m from the barranca; light and moderate erosion, moderate and dense vegetation. POTENTIAL LAND USE: rainfall agriculture on terraces and irrigation agriculture. Others: hunting and gathering plants. PRESENT LAND USE: town; irrigation agriculture from dams, herding. Others: hunting and gathering plants, firewood. Quarry: limestone.

APPENDIX

Cluster	Site No.	Photo and Square	Unit	Description and Association with Other Periods	Observations
XII	50	Photo 081 21 12 16 Photo 074 4 4 Photo 081 15 16 21 22	 5 3 8 8 9 5, 9, 14, 15, 20, 25 6, 7, 13, 17, 18, 19, 23, 25 3, 4 1	SITE: Type 16 2 Structures D. Material: concentrated and disperse. CLASSIC: very light. TRANSITIONAL CLASSIC-COYOTLATELCO: very light. COYOTLATELCO: very light. LATE POSTCLASSIC: Structures/ very light/light/dense. COLONIAL: very light.	UTM: 468750, 2229800 NEAREST TOWN: NW of Huitel. LOCATION: Lowlands and alluvial valley; 1,400 m from the Rio Tula, N of the old Requena canal; 3,400–3,500 m from the Rio Salado; light erosion. POTENTIAL LAND USE: irrigation agriculture and rainfall agriculture. Others: hunting and gathering plants. PRESENT LAND USE: irrigation agriculture from dams.
XI	51	Photo 081 17 18 11 23 24 Photo 074 5	 5, 8 10, 13, 18, 19, 23, 24 25 11, 12, 13, 16, 21 23 3, 4 1 7, 8, 14, 18	SITE: Type 16 2 Structures D (500 m distance between both structures). Material: disperse. TRANSITIONAL CLASSIC-COYOTLATELCO: very light/ light. COYOTLATELCO: very light. LATE POSTCLASSIC: Structures/ very light/light/dense. COLONIAL: very light.	UTM: 470200, 2229000 NEAREST TOWN: Huitel. LOCATION: Alluvial valley, S of the Cerro Huitel and N of the old Requena canal, 1,400–2,800 m from the Rio Salado; light and moderate erosion; moderate and dense vegetation. POTENTIAL LAND USE: rainfall agriculture. Others: hunting and gathering plants. PRESENT LAND USE: town; rainfall agriculture on terraces and irrigation agriculture from dams, herding. Others: hunting and gathering plants, firewood.
XI	52	Photo 082 13 19	 15 5	SITE: Type 15 Material: disperse. LATE POSTCLASSIC: Structures/ very light/dense. COLONIAL: very light/light.	UTM: 471250, 2229500 NEAREST TOWN: Huitel. LOCATION: Lowlands, lower slopes of the Cerro Huitel, 1,100 m from the Rio Salado; light and moderate erosion, moderate vegetation. POTENTIAL LAND USE: hunting and gathering plants. PRESENT LAND USE: town; irrigation agriculture from dams, herding.
XII	53	Photo 081 10 11 10 9 16 17	 24 7 1 19 18 5 7, 11	SITE: Type 16. DESTROYED. 2 Structures D. Material: concentrated and disperse. CLASSIC: very light. TRANSITIONAL CLASSIC-COYOTLATELCO: Structures/ very light/dense. LATE POSTCLASSIC: very light/ light.	UTM: 469600, 2228400 NEAREST TOWN: S of Huitel, SW of Hacienda de Barrera. LOCATION: Alluvial valley; altitude: 2,040 m; near the old Requena canal, 2,500–4,800 m from the Rio Salado; light erosion, moderate vegetation. POTENTIAL LAND USE: rainfall agriculture. Others: hunting and gathering plants. PRESENT LAND USE: irrigation agriculture from dams, herding. Others: hunting and gathering plants, firewood.

APPENDIX

Cluster	Site No.	Photo and Square	Unit	Description and Association with Other Periods	Observations
XII	54	Photo 081 7 8 15 1 2 7 8 9 14 15	10 1, 4, 7 7 20, 24 25 4, 5, 24 3, 13, 14, 15, 16, 17 21 1, 4, 10, 23 6, 12, 17, 21	SITE: Type 3 Structure D. Material: concentrated and disperse. TRANSITIONAL CLASSIC-COYOTLATELCO: very light. COYOTLATELCO: Structures/ very light/light/dense. LATE POSTCLASSIC: Structures/ very light/light/dense. COLONIAL: very light/light.	UTM: 466550, 2228100 NEAREST TOWN: San Gabriel. LOCATION: Alluvial valley, near the Endó canal; 3,600–6,400 m from the Rio Salado; light erosion. POTENTIAL LAND USE: rainfall agriculture. Others: hunting and gathering plants. PRESENT LAND USE: irrigation agriculture from dams.
XVI	55	Photo 089 15 16 15 16 17	4, 5, 9, 10, 14 1 15, 20 2, 3, 6, 7, 8, 17 7	SITE: Type 11. DESTROYED. Complex of 6 Structures B. Material: disperse. CLASSIC: Structures/light/dense. TRANSITIONAL CLASSIC-COYOTLATELCO: very light/ dense. LATE POSTCLASSIC: Structures/ very light/light/dense. COLONIAL: very light.	UTM: 468300, 2226900 LOCATION: N of Cerro Xicuco. Alluvial valley and lower slopes of Cerro Xicuco, both sides of G-5 canal; 6,000–7,600 m from the Rio Tula; light erosion, moderate vegetation. POTENTIAL LAND USE: rainfall agriculture. Others: hunting and gathering plants. PRESENT LAND USE: irrigation agriculture from dams, herding. Others: hunting and gathering plants, firewood.
XVI	56	Photo 089 9	17, 20 18, 19, 21, 22	SITE: Type 5 Structures C. Material: concentrated and disperse. COYOTLATELCO: very light. LATE POSTCLASSIC: Structures/ very light/dense. COLONIAL: very light.	UTM: 468100, 2226400 LOCATION: NW of Cerro Xicuco. Lower slopes of Cerro Xicuco; altitude: 2,060–2,080 m; above the G-S canal, 5,400–6,600 m from the Rio Tula; light and moderate erosion, moderate and dense vegetation. POTENTIAL LAND USE: rainfall agriculture. Others: hunting and gathering plants. PRESENT LAND USE: rainfall agriculture, herding. Others: hunting and gathering plants, firewood.
XIII	57	Photo 081 10 9 3	4, 6 2, 3, 14 22, 23, 25	SITE: Type 16. DESTROYED. 2 Structures D. Material: disperse. CLASSIC: very light. TRANSITIONAL CLASSIC-COYOTLATELCO: very light/ light. COYOTLATELCO: very light. LATE POSTCLASSIC: Structures/ very light/light/dense.	UTM: 468450, 2228200 NEAREST TOWN: SW of Huitel. LOCATION: Alluvial valley, Hacienda de Barrera's hill; altitude: 2,100–2,120 m; 3,400–4,800 m from the Rio Salado; light and moderate erosion, moderate and dense vegetation. POTENTIAL LAND USE: rainfall agriculture. Others: hunting and gathering plants. PRESENT LAND USE: rainfall agriculture and irrigation agriculture from dams, herding. Others: hunting and gathering plants, firewood.

APPENDIX

Cluster	Site No.	Photo and Square	Unit	Description and Association with Other Periods	Observations
XII	58	Photo 089 8 Photo 088 6 11 12 18 Photo 089 8 13 14 15	17 1 20 16, 21, 22 6 16, 21, 22, 23 3, 4, 8, 10, 20 1, 3, 4, 6, 7, 11, 14, 19, 20 7, 11, 16, 17, 18	SITE: Type 3 Structure D. Material: disperse. CLASSIC: Structures/very light/light. TRANSITIONAL CLASSIC-COYOTLATELCO: very light. COYOTLATELCO: very light. LATE POSTCLASSIC: Structures/very light/light/dense. COLONIAL: very light.	UTM: 466900, 2226500 NEAREST TOWN: SE of Juan Gabriel. LOCATION: Alluvial valley on lower altitude than old Requena canal, 2,500–5,800 m from the Rio Tula; light erosion. POTENTIAL LAND USE: irrigation agriculture and rainfall agriculture. PRESENT LAND USE: irrigation agriculture from dams.
XVI	59	Photo 089 8 3 2 1 2 3 7 8	1, 3 16 16, 19 14, 19, 20, 23, 25 6, 7, 8, 10, 11, 21 6 4, 10 4, 8, 12	SITE: Type 7. DESTROYED. Complex of 5 Structures C. Material: disperse. CLASSIC: Structures/light/dense. TRANSITIONAL CLASSIC-COYOTLATELCO: very light. LATE POSTCLASSIC: Structures/very light/light/ dense. COLONIAL: very light/light. Selective Sampling.	UTM: 467000, 2225700 LOCATION: W of Cerro Xicuco. Alluvial valley, between the G-5 canal and the old Requena canal, 3,800–5,400 m from the Rio Tula; light erosion, moderate and dense vegetation. POTENTIAL LAND USE: rainfall agriculture and irrigation agriculture. Others: hunting and gathering plants. PRESENT LAND USE: irrigation agriculture from dams and rainfall agriculture, herding. Others: hunting and gathering plants, firewood.
XVI	60	Photo 097 14 19 20	17, 18, 25 21, 22, 24 5 5	SITE: Type 7 Complex of 3 Structures B. Material: disperse. CLASSIC: light/dense. TRANSITIONAL CLASSIC-COYOTLATELCO: light. COYOTLATELCO: very light. LATE POSTCLASSIC: Structures/very light/dense. COLONIAL: very light.	UTM: 467050, 2224650 LOCATION: W of Cerro Xicuco. Lowlands, between the G-5 canal and the old Requena canal; between Rio Tula and Rio Salado; light erosion, moderate vegetation. POTENTIAL LAND USE: rainfall agriculture. Others: hunting and gathering plants. PRESENT LAND USE: irrigation agriculture from dams, rainfall agriculture, herding. Others: hunting and gathering plants, firewood.
XV	61	Photo 097 15	13 12, 18 2, 18	SITE: Type 7 Complex of 2 Habitational Structures and 1 Ceremonial Structure B. Material: disperse. CLASSIC: very light. TRANSITIONAL CLASSIC-COYOTLATELCO: very light. LATE POSTCLASSIC: very light. COLONIAL: very light.	UTM: 467750, 2224600 LOCATION: On SW slopes of Cerro Xicuco. Lower slopes of the Cerro Xicuco, on upper altitudes of G-5 canal; between the Rio Tula and the Rio Salado; light and moderate erosion, moderate vegetation. POTENTIAL LAND USE: rainfall agriculture. Others: hunting and gathering plants. PRESENT LAND USE: irrigation agriculture from dams, herding. Others: hunting and gathering plants, firewood.

APPENDIX

Cluster	Site No.	Photo and Square	Unit	Description and Association with Other Periods	Observations
XVII	62	Photo 089 12 18 12 Photo 090 13 Photo 089 12 18	17, 21 1 17 20 11 2, 3	SITE: Type 7 Complex of 3 Structures B. Material: concentrated and disperse. CLASSIC: Structures/very light/light. LATE POSTCLASSIC: very light/light. Selective Sampling.	UTM: 470500, 2226600 LOCATION: NE of Cerro Xicuco. On lower slopes of Cerro Xicuco and alluvial valley, between the G-5 canal and the old Requena canal; 2,500–4,400 m from the Rio Salado and 8,600–8,800 m from the Rio Tula; light erosion, scarce and dense vegetation. POTENTIAL LAND USE: rainfall agriculture. Others: hunting and gathering plants. PRESENT LAND USE: rainfall agriculture and irrigation agriculture from dams, herding. Others: hunting and gathering plants, firewood.
XVII	63	Photo 089 6 12 6 12	 22 1 13 6 2	SITE: Type 5. DESTROYED. 2 Structures D. Material: concentrated and disperse. CLASSIC: Structures/very light/light. LATE POSTCLASSIC: very light/light. Selective Sampling.	UTM: 470500, 2225700 LOCATION: E of Cerro Xicuco. On lower slopes of the Cerro Xicuco; altitude: 2,100 m; above G-5 canal, 4,000–4,500 m from the Rio Salado; light erosion, moderate vegetation. POTENTIAL LAND USE: rainfall agriculture. Others: hunting and gathering plants. PRESENT LAND USE: rainfall agriculture, herding. Others: hunting and gathering plants, firewood.
XVIII	64	Photo 090 1 2	 14 11	SITE: Type 3 Structure D. Material: concentrated. LATE POSTCLASSIC: very light. COLONIAL: very light.	UTM: 471250, 2225500 LOCATION: E of Cerro Xicuco. On lower slopes of the Cerro Xicuco; alluvial valley near G-5 canal, 3,000–3,600 m from the Rio Salado; light erosion, moderate vegetation. POTENTIAL LAND USE: rainfall agriculture. Others: hunting and gathering plants. PRESENT LAND USE: irrigation agriculture from dams, herding.
XVIII	65	Photo 098 20 Photo 090 2 3	 3 8 11	SITE: Type 15 Material: concentrated and disperse. COYOTLATELCO: very light. LATE POSTCLASSIC: very light/light.	UTM: 472100, 2225100 LOCATION: E of Cerro Xicuco. Alluvial valley between the G-5 canal and the old Requena canal, 1,800–2,800 m from the Rio Salado; light erosion. POTENTIAL LAND USE: rainfall agriculture. PRESENT LAND USE: irrigation agriculture from dams.
XVIII	66	Photo 090 8 9	 11, 14 2	SITE: Type 15 Material: disperse. LATE POSTCLASSIC: very light/light.	UTM: 472000, 2226150 LOCATION: E of Cerro Xicuco. Alluvial valley, 1,900–3,100 m from the Rio Salado; light erosion. POTENTIAL LAND USE: rainfall agriculture. PRESENT LAND USE: irrigation agriculture from dams.

APPENDIX

Cluster	Site No.	Photo and Square	Unit	Description and Association with Other Periods	Observations
XV	67	Photo 097 16 10 17	9, 15 2, 4 22 1, 3, 8, 11, 13, 16, 17, 19, 22	SITE: Type 19 Complex of 2 Structures: Habitational and Ceremonial, B and C. Material: disperse. CLASSIC: very light. COYOTLATELCO: very light. LATE POSTCLASSIC: very light/light. COLONIAL: very light.	UTM: 472600, 2226100 LOCATION: E of Cerro Xicuco. On upper slopes of the Cerro Xicuco; altitude: 2,100–2,120 m; between the Rio Tula and the Rio Salado; light and moderate erosion, moderate vegetation. POTENTIAL LAND USE: rainfall agriculture. Others: hunting and gathering plants. PRESENT LAND USE: rainfall agriculture, herding. Others: hunting and gathering plants, firewood.
XV	68	Photo 097 9 9 10	24 17, 18, 19, 22 16	SITE: Type 3 Structure D. Material: disperse. CLASSIC: very light. TRANSITIONAL CLASSIC-COYOTLATELCO: very light. LATE POSTCLASSIC: very light/light. COLONIAL: very light.	UTM: 468250, 2223900 LOCATION: Cerro Xicuco. On lower slopes of Cerro Xicuco; altitude: 2,120 m; between the Rio Tula and the Rio Salado; light erosion, moderate vegetation. POTENTIAL LAND USE: rainfall agriculture. Others: hunting and gathering plants. PRESENT LAND USE: rainfall agriculture, herding. Others: hunting and gathering plants, firewood. Semidisperse site with ceremonial structures. Extension: approx. 2 km^2. The site possibly extends over all the slopes of the sierra, extending from the slopes of Cerro El Culantrillo to the towns of Atengo and Santiago Acayutlán. The most concentrated settlement is on the lower slopes of Cerro Xicuco. Presence of habitational structures on terraces.
XVI	69	Photo 097 8 2 3 9 2 3 8 9 2	3, 9 23 21 2 17, 20, 21, 22, 24, 25 17, 22 4, 5, 8, 10, 14, 15, 20 1, 11, 16 23	SITE: Type 5 2 Structures C. Material: concentrated and disperse. Probable local ceramic production type 836. CLASSIC: very light. TRANSITIONAL CLASSIC-COYOTLATELCO: Structures/very light/dense. COYOTLATELCO: very light. LATE POSTCLASSIC: very light. COLONIAL: very light.	UTM: 467200, 2223300 LOCATION: SW of Cerro Xicuco, between Rios Tula and Salado. Between the G-5 canal and the old Requena canal; altitude: 2,120–2,140 m; light erosion, moderate vegetation. POTENTIAL LAND USE: irrigation agriculture and rainfall agriculture. Others: hunting and gathering plants. PRESENT LAND USE: irrigation agriculture from dams, herding. Others: hunting and gathering plants, firewood.

APPENDIX

Cluster	Site No.	Photo and Square	Unit	Description and Association with Other Periods	Observations
XVI	70	Photo 104 20 20 21 Photo 097 2	5, 10 8 9 3, 6 11, 13	SITE: Type 7. DESTROYED. Complex of 3 Structures B and C (Extension: one structure of 1,024 m² and two structures of 3,600 m² approx.). Material: disperse. CLASSIC: Structures/dense. TRANSITIONAL CLASSIC-COYOTLATELCO: very light. COYOTLATELCO: very light. LATE POSTCLASSIC: Structures/very light/dense. COLONIAL: very light. Selective Sampling.	UTM: 467000, 2222300 NEAREST TOWN: NE of Iturbe. LOCATION: Alluvial valley, between the G-5 canal and the old Requena canal, 3,600–4,000 m from the Rio Tula; light erosion. POTENTIAL LAND USE: rainfall agriculture and irrigation agriculture from dams. PRESENT LAND USE: irrigation agriculture from dams.
XVI	71	Photo 097 3	14 13	SITE: Type 3 Structure D (Extension: 1,496 m² approx.). Material: disperse. TRANSITIONAL CLASSIC-COYOTLATELCO: very light. LATE POSTCLASSIC: very light.	UTM: 468200, 2222800 NEAREST TOWN: NW of Teocalco. LOCATION: Alluvial valley near G-5 canal, between Rios Tula and Salado; light erosion. POTENTIAL LAND USE: rainfall agriculture. PRESENT LAND USE: irrigation agriculture from dams.
XVI	72	Photo 097 4 10 11 4 9 3 4 5 9 10 11	20, 22, 23, 24 3, 4 1 13, 18 10 19, 24, 25 14, 16, 19, 21 16, 17, 21, 22 4, 5 1, 2, 5, 8, 9, 10, 13, 14, 15, 19 2	SITE: Type 11. LOOTED. Complex of 6 Structures B (Extension: 1,215 m², 1,060 m², 1,020 m², 1,600 m², and 1,470 m² approx.). Material: concentrated and disperse. Probable local ceramic production type 832. CLASSIC: Structures/light/dense. TRANSITIONAL CLASSIC-COYOTLATELCO: Structures/very light/light/dense. COYOTLATELCO: Structures/very light/dense. LATE POSTCLASSIC: Structures/very light/light/dense. COLONIAL: very light.	UTM: 468850, 2223100 LOCATION: S of Cerro Xicuco. Alluvial valley, on lower slopes of Cerro Xicuco; altitude: 2,120–2,140 m; north of the G-5 canal, between the Rio Tula and the Rio Salado; light and moderate erosion, scarce vegetation. POTENTIAL LAND USE: irrigation agriculture and rainfall agriculture. Others: hunting and gathering plants. PRESENT LAND USE: rainfall agriculture and irrigation agriculture from dams, herding. Others: hunting and gathering plants, firewood.
XVI	73	Photo 097 11 12 5 12 5 6 11 12	5 1, 6 24 12, 18 19, 20, 23 11, 12, 21 3, 4 7, 8, 13	SITE: Type 7. DESTROYED. Complex of 3 Structures B (Extension of 1 of them: 540 m² approx.). Material: concentrated and disperse. Probable local ceramic production type 832. CLASSIC: very light/light. TRANSITIONAL CLASSIC-COYOTLATELCO: very light. COYOTLATELCO: very light. LATE POSTCLASSIC: very light/light. COLONIAL: very light.	UTM: 470300, 2223200 NEAREST TOWN: N of Teocalco. LOCATION: Alluvial valley, S of Cerro Xicuco and G-5 canal, between the Rio Tula and the Rio Salado; light erosion. POTENTIAL LAND USE: rainfall agriculture. Others: hunting and gathering plants. PRESENT LAND USE: irrigation agriculture from dams.

APPENDIX

Cluster	Site No.	Photo and Square	Unit	Description and Association with Other Periods	Observations
XV	74	Photo 097 11 11	14 8, 12, 13, 19	SITE: Type 3 Structure D. Material: disperse. Probable local ceramic production type 832. TRANSITIONAL CLASSIC-COYOTLATELCO: very light. LATE POSTCLASSIC: very light.	UTM: 470000, 2223700 LOCATION: S of Cerro Xicuco. Lower slopes of the Cerro Xicuco; altitude: 2,120–2,140 m; light erosion. POTENTIAL LAND USE: rainfall agriculture. Others: hunting and gathering plants. PRESENT LAND USE: rainfall agriculture. Others: hunting and gathering plants, firewood.
XV	75	Photo 097 11 12 17 18	24, 25 21 9, 10, 15 1, 2, 6, 8, 11	SITE: Type 15 Material: disperse. COYOTLATELCO: very light. LATE POSTCLASSIC: very light.	UTM: 470300, 2224200 LOCATION: S of Cerro Xicuco. Lower slopes of Cerro Xicuco; altitude: 2,120–2,140 m; between Rios Tula and Salado and G-5 canal; light and moderate erosion, moderate and dense vegetation. POTENTIAL LAND USE: rainfall agriculture. Others: hunting and gathering plants. PRESENT LAND USE: rainfall agriculture, herding. Others: hunting and gathering plants, firewood.
XIA	76	Photo 075 2	24	SITE: Type 15 Material: disperse. TRANSITIONAL CLASSIC-COYOTLATELCO: very light. LATE POSTCLASSIC: very light.	UTM: 472100, 2230600 NEAREST TOWN: Tezontepec. LOCATION: Alluvial valley near Endó canal, 750 m from the Rio Salado; light erosion. POTENTIAL LAND USE: rainfall agriculture. PRESENT LAND USE: town; traditional irrigation agriculture and irrigation agriculture from dams.
XII	77	Photo 082 8	6	SITE: Type 15 Material: disperse. LATE POSTCLASSIC: light. COLONIAL: very light.	UTM: 471500, 2228250 NEAREST TOWN: S of Huitel. LOCATION: Alluvial valley, N of Requena canal, 1,100 m from the Rio Salado; light erosion. POTENTIAL LAND USE: rainfall agriculture in lowlands. PRESENT LAND USE: irrigation agriculture from dams.
XII	78	Photo 081 11 5 6 11	5 20 23 4	SITE: Type 15 Material: concentrated and disperse. LATE POSTCLASSIC: very light/light. COLONIAL: very light.	UTM: 470400, 2227850 NEAREST TOWN: S of Huitel. LOCATION: Alluvial valley, N of Requena canal, 1,200–2,500 m from the Rio Salado; light erosion. POTENTIAL LAND USE: rainfall agriculture. Others: hunting and gathering plants. PRESENT LAND USE: irrigation agriculture from dams.

APPENDIX

Cluster	Site No.	Photo and Square	Unit	Description and Association with Other Periods	Observations
XIA	79	Photo 082 15 21	 6 2	SITE: Type 15 Material: disperse. LATE POSTCLASSIC: Structures/very light/dense. COLONIAL: very light.	UTM: 472550, 2229650 NEAREST TOWN: E of Huitel. LOCATION: Alluvial valley on both banks of the Rio Salado; light erosion. POTENTIAL LAND USE: irrigation agriculture. Others: fishing. PRESENT LAND USE: traditional irrigation agriculture and irrigation agriculture from dams.
XVIII	80	Photo 098 3 9 9 15	 21 7, 17 18, 22 4	SITE: Type 3 Structure D. Material: concentrated and disperse. CLASSIC: very light. TRANSITIONAL CLASSIC-COYOTLATELCO: very light. LATE POSTCLASSIC: very light/light. COLONIAL: very light.	UTM: 472350, 2223150 NEAREST TOWN: S of Manantiales. LOCATION: Alluvial valley, E of G-5 canal, 1,700–3,300 m from the Rio Salado; light erosion. POTENTIAL LAND USE: rainfall agriculture. PRESENT LAND USE: irrigation agriculture from dams.
XVIII	81	Photo 098 14 13 14	 11 9, 24, 25 16	SITE: Type 3 Structure D. Material: disperse. LATE POSTCLASSIC: very light/light. COLONIAL: very light.	UTM: 471500, 2224400 NEAREST TOWN: Near Manantiales. LOCATION: Alluvial valley, E of G-5 canal, 2,400–3,800 m from the Rio Salado; light erosion. POTENTIAL LAND USE: rainfall agriculture. PRESENT LAND USE: irrigation agriculture from dams.
XVIII	82	Photo 098 14 8	 5 21, 23	SITE: Type 3 Structure D. Material: disperse. TRANSITIONAL CLASSIC-COYOTLATELCO: very light. LATE POSTCLASSIC: very light.	UTM: 472200, 2224100 NEAREST TOWN: S of Manantiales. LOCATION: Alluvial valley, E of G-5 canal, 2,000–3,000 m from the Rio Salado; light erosion. POTENTIAL LAND USE: rainfall agriculture. PRESENT LAND USE: irrigation agriculture from dams.
XVI	83	Photo 098 7 8	 14 16	SITE: Type 3 Structure D. Material: disperse. LATE POSTCLASSIC: very light.	UTM: 471150, 2223450 NEAREST TOWN: SW of Manantiales. LOCATION: Alluvial valley, E of G-5 canal, 3,000–4,000 m from the Rio Salado; light erosion. POTENTIAL LAND USE: rainfall agriculture. PRESENT LAND USE: irrigation agriculture from dams.
XIX	84	Photo 098 3 3 10 Photo 105 22 Photo 098 3 4 9	 24, 25 15 6, 16 10 19 21 3, 4	SITE: Type 11 Complex of 6 Structures B and C. Material: disperse. CLASSIC: very light. TRANSITIONAL CLASSIC-COYOTLATELCO: very light. LATE POSTCLASSIC: Structures/very light/light/dense. COLONIAL: very light.	UTM: 473400, 2223000 NEAREST TOWN: NW of Doxey. LOCATION: Alluvial valley, 1,200–2,700 m from the Rio Salado; light erosion. POTENTIAL LAND USE: rainfall agriculture. PRESENT LAND USE: irrigation agriculture from dams.

APPENDIX

Cluster	Site No.	Photo and Square	Unit	Description and Association with Other Periods	Observations
XIX	85	Photo 098 4 5 4 10 4 5 10 11	 19 21 13 3, 9 15, 20, 23 16, 17, 23 5 2, 6	SITE: Type 5 2 Structures C. Material: concentrated and disperse. COYOTLATELCO: very light. TRANSITIONAL CLASSIC-COYOTLATELCO: Structures/very light/dense. LATE POSTCLASSIC: Structures/very light/light/dense. COLONIAL: very light.	UTM: 474250, 2222900 NEAREST TOWN: N and NW of Doxey. LOCATION: Alluvial valley, near Requena canal, 500–1,800 m from the Rio Salado; light erosion. POTENTIAL LAND USE: rainfall agriculture. PRESENT LAND USE: irrigation agriculture from dams.
XIX	86	Photo 098 10 16 4 10 15 16	 18, 23 21 25 13, 14, 24 20 8, 9, 11, 12	SITE: Type 15 Material: concentrated and disperse. LATE POSTCLASSIC: Structures/very light/light/dense. COLONIAL: very light.	UTM: 473900, 2224000 NEAREST TOWN: N and NW of Doxey. LOCATION: Alluvial valley, W of Rio Salado, 600–1,500 m from the Rio Salado; light erosion. POTENTIAL LAND USE: rainfall agriculture. PRESENT LAND USE: irrigation agriculture from dams.
XIX	87	Photo 105 14 14 14 15	 20, 25 18 12, 19, 24 18	SITE: Type 7. LOOTED. Complex of 4 Structures B and C (1 of them: 53 m long approx.). Material: disperse. Probable local ceramic production type 806. TRANSITIONAL CLASSIC-COYOTLATELCO: very light. LATE POSTCLASSIC: very light/light. COLONIAL: very light.	UTM: 472000, 2221850 NEAREST TOWN: NE of Estación Teocalco. LOCATION: Alluvial valley, 2,600–3,900 m from the Rio Salado; light erosion. POTENTIAL LAND USE: rainfall agriculture. PRESENT LAND USE: irrigation agriculture from dams.
XIX	88	Photo 105 13 19 13	 20, 25 5 19	SITE: Type 5. DESTROYED. 2 Structures B. Material: concentrated and disperse. Probable local ceramic production type 818. LATE POSTCLASSIC: very light/light.	UTM: 471400, 2222000 NEAREST TOWN: NE of Estación Teocalco. LOCATION: Alluvial valley, 4,200–4,400 m from the Rio Salado; light erosion. POTENTIAL LAND USE: rainfall agriculture. PRESENT LAND USE: irrigation agriculture from dams.
XIX	89	Photo 105 13 14 8 13 14	 5 1 21 4, 9 6, 7	SITE: Type 5 2 Structures B. Material: concentrated and disperse. LATE POSTCLASSIC: very light. COLONIAL: very light.	UTM: 471400, 2221300 NEAREST TOWN: NE de Estación Teocalco. LOCATION: Alluvial valley, 3,800–4,400 m from the Rio Salado; light erosion. POTENTIAL LAND USE: rainfall agriculture. PRESENT LAND USE: irrigation agriculture from dams.
XIX	90	Photo 105 15 9	 1 21	SITE: Type 3 Structure D. Material: concentrated. LATE POSTCLASSIC: very light/light. COLONIAL: very light.	UTM: 472350, 2221350 NEAREST TOWN: NE de Estación Teocalco and W of Doxey. LOCATION: Alluvial valley, 3,100 m from the Rio Salado; light erosion. POTENTIAL LAND USE: rainfall agriculture. PRESENT LAND USE: irrigation agriculture from dams.

APPENDIX

Cluster	Site No.	Photo and Square	Unit	Description and Association with Other Periods	Observations
XIX	91	Photo 104 12 18	 23 7, 11	SITE: Type 15 Material: disperse. CLASSIC: very light. LATE POSTCLASSIC: very light.	UTM: 470400, 2221400 NEAREST TOWN: NE of Estación Teocalco. LOCATION: Alluvial valley; Rio Salado; light erosion. POTENTIAL LAND USE: rainfall agriculture. PRESENT LAND USE: irrigation agriculture from dams.
XIX	92	Photo 105 2 8 7 8	 22 11 8, 10 6	SITE: Type 3 Structure D. Material: concentrated and disperse. Probable local ceramic production types 806 and 864. COYOTLATELCO: very light. LATE POSTCLASSIC: Structures/very light/dense.	UTM: 471400, 2220250 NEAREST TOWN: NE of Estación Teocalco. LOCATION: Alluvial valley, 3,500–4,700 m from the Rio Salado; light erosion. POTENTIAL LAND USE: rainfall agriculture. PRESENT LAND USE: town; irrigation agriculture from dams.
XIX	93	Photo 105 16 17 10 16	 4 11 19, 25 5, 10	SITE: Type 5 2 Structures C. Material: disperse. TRANSITIONAL CLASSIC-COYOTLATELCO: very light. LATE POSTCLASSIC: Structures/very light/dense. COLONIAL: very light.	UTM: 474150, 2221500 NEAREST TOWN: Doxey. LOCATION: Alluvial valley, E of Requena canal, 1,000–1,500 m from the Rio Salado; light erosion. POTENTIAL LAND USE: rainfall agriculture. PRESENT LAND USE: town; irrigation agriculture from dams.
XIX	94	Photo 105 9 15 10 10 16	 20 10 21 17, 22 7, 17	SITE: Type 16. DESTROYED. 2 Structures D. Material: concentrated and disperse. Probable local ceramic production type 864. LATE POSTCLASSIC: Structures/very light/light. COLONIAL: very light.	UTM: 473300, 2221200 NEAREST TOWN: W of Doxey. LOCATION: Alluvial valley, W of Requena canal, 1,100–2,400 m from the Rio Salado; light erosion. POTENTIAL LAND USE: rainfall agriculture. PRESENT LAND USE: town; irrigation agriculture from dams.
XIX	95	Photo 105 3 10 10 3 4 9 10	 25 1 2 25 22 5 3, 7	SITE: Type 7 Complex of 3 Structures B and C. Material: concentrated and disperse. CLASSIC: very light. LATE POSTCLASSIC: Structures/very light/light/dense. COLONIAL: very light.	UTM: 473200, 2220100 NEAREST TOWN: SW of Doxey. LOCATION: Alluvial valley, N of Endó canal and Requena canal, 1,800–2,500 m from the Rio Salado; light erosion. POTENTIAL LAND USE: rainfall agriculture. PRESENT LAND USE: irrigation agriculture from dams.
XIX	96	Photo 105 9	 6, 8	SITE: Type 15 Material: disperse.	UTM: 472600, 2220400 NEAREST TOWN: Between Teocalco and Doxey. LOCATION: Alluvial valley, N of the Endó canal, 2,600–2,700 m from the Rio Salado; light erosion. POTENTIAL LAND USE: rainfall agriculture. PRESENT LAND USE: irrigation agriculture from dams.

APPENDIX

Cluster	Site No.	Photo and Square	Unit	Description and Association with Other Periods	Observations
XIX	97	Photo 110 17 Photo 105 11	19 14 3, 4, 5	SITE: Type 3. DESTROYED. Structure D. Material: disperse. CLASSIC: Structures/light/dense. COYOTLATELCO: very light. LATE POSTCLASSIC: Structures/very light/light/dense. COLONIAL: light.	UTM: 474900, 2219900 NEAREST TOWN: SE of Doxey. LOCATION: Alluvial valley, 300–800 m from west bank of the Rio Salado; light erosion. POTENTIAL LAND USE: rainfall agriculture. PRESENT LAND USE: town; irrigation agriculture from dams.
XIX	98	Photo 105 11 18	24 1, 7, 12	SITE: Type 15 Material: disperse. LATE POSTCLASSIC: very light/light. COLONIAL: very light.	UTM: 475200, 2221300 NEAREST TOWN: Doxey. LOCATION: Alluvial valley, 50–600 m from the Rio Salado; light erosion. POTENTIAL LAND USE: rainfall agriculture. Others: fishing. PRESENT LAND USE: town; irrigation agriculture from dams.
XVI	99	Photo 104 22 16	2 23	SITE: Type 5. DESTROYED. 2 Structures B (Extension of each structure: 1,640 m² approx.). Material: disperse. COYOTLATELCO: very light. LATE POSTCLASSIC: very light. COLONIAL: very light.	UTM: 468650, 2222300 NEAREST TOWN: NW of Teocalco. LOCATION: Alluvial valley, S of G-5 canal, 5,200 m from the Rio Tula; light erosion. POTENTIAL LAND USE: rainfall agriculture. PRESENT LAND USE: irrigation agriculture from dams.
XVI	100	Photo 104 22 23 Photo 097 5 Photo 104 22 23	10 6 11, 12, 13 5 1	SITE: Type 3. DESTROYED. Structure D. Material: concentrated and disperse. CLASSIC: light. TRANSITIONAL CLASSIC-COYOTLATELCO: very light. COYOTLATELCO: very light. LATE POSTCLASSIC: very light.	UTM: 469300, 2222450 NEAREST TOWN: N of Teocalco. LOCATION: Alluvial valley, between the Rio Tula and the Rio Salado; light erosion. POTENTIAL LAND USE: rainfall agriculture. PRESENT LAND USE: irrigation agriculture from dams.
XX	101	Photo 104 10 11 16 17	19, 25 21 15, 19 7, 12	SITE: Type 15 Material: disperse. COYOTLATELCO: very light. LATE POSTCLASSIC: very light.	UTM: 469400, 2221350 NEAREST TOWN: NW of Teocalco. LOCATION: Alluvial valley, 5,300 m from the Rio Tula; light erosion. POTENTIAL LAND USE: rainfall agriculture. PRESENT LAND USE: irrigation agriculture from dams.
XX	102	Photo 104 14 13 14	13, 18 15, 20 12	SITE: Type 5. DESTROYED. 2 Structures B. Material: disperse. COYOTLATELCO: very light. LATE POSTCLASSIC: very light. COLONIAL: very light.	UTM: 466850, 2221650 NEAREST TOWN: N of Iturbe. LOCATION: Alluvial valley, 3,600–4,400 m from the Rio Tula; light erosion. Structures are to the south of G-5 canal, and disperse material is to the west of G-5 canal. POTENTIAL LAND USE: irrigation agriculture. PRESENT LAND USE: irrigation agriculture from dams.

APPENDIX

Cluster	Site No.	Photo and Square	Unit	Description and Association with Other Periods	Observations
XX	103	Photo 104 8 14 7 8	18 2 4, 5, 15 6, 16, 21, 22	SITE: Type 5. DESTROYED. 2 Structures C (Extension: 1,600 m² and 2,500 m² approx.). Material: disperse. CLASSIC: very light/dense. LATE POSTCLASSIC: Structures/ very light/light/dense. COLONIAL: very light.	UTM: 466800, 2221000 NEAREST TOWN: N of Iturbe. LOCATION: Alluvial valley, on the east side of G-5 canal, 3,000–3,600 m from the Rio Tula; light erosion. POTENTIAL LAND USE: irrigation agriculture and rainfall agriculture. PRESENT LAND USE: irrigation agriculture from dams.
XX	104	Photo 104 9 8 9 15 16	17, 18 15 6, 21, 23 1, 3, 9, 15 11	SITE: Type 5 2 Structures B. Material: disperse. TRANSITIONAL CLASSIC-COYOTLATELCO: very light. COYOTLATELCO: very light. LATE POSTCLASSIC: very light.	UTM: 467700, 2220900 NEAREST TOWN: NE of Iturbe. LOCATION: Alluvial valley, S of G-5 canal, 4,100–4,600 m from the Rio Tula; light erosion. POTENTIAL LAND USE: irrigation agriculture and rainfall agriculture. PRESENT LAND USE: irrigation agriculture from dams.
XVI	105	Photo 097 7 8 7 8 13 14	20, 24, 25 22 13, 15 11, 16, 17, 18, 21, 23, 24, 25 5, 8, 10 3, 4, 5, 6, 14, 15	SITE: Type 15 Material: concentrated and disperse. Probable local ceramic production type 836. FORMATIVE: very light. CLASSIC: very light. TRANSITIONAL CLASSIC-COYOTLATELCO: Structures/ very light/light. COYOTLATELCO: very light. LATE POSTCLASSIC: very light. COLONIAL: very light.	UTM: 466800, 2223900 LOCATION: SW of Cerro Xicuco. Alluvial valley, between the G-5 canal and the old Requena canal; between Rios Tula and Salado; light erosion, moderate vegetation. POTENTIAL LAND USE: irrigation agriculture and rainfall agriculture. Others: hunting and gathering plants. PRESENT LAND USE: irrigation agriculture from dams and rainfall agriculture, herding. Others: hunting and gathering plants, firewood.
XXI	106	Photo 109 16 16 17 11 Photo 104 5	10 4 8, 15 7 22 23	SITE: Type 19 Complex of 2 Structures: Habitational and Ceremonial, B. Material: concentrated and disperse. COYOTLATELCO: very light. LATE POSTCLASSIC: very light.	UTM: 469250, 2219500 NEAREST TOWN: SW of Teocalco. LOCATION: Alluvial valley, N of Endó canal, between the Rio Tula and the Rio Salado; light erosion. POTENTIAL LAND USE: rainfall agriculture. PRESENT LAND USE: irrigation agriculture from dams.
XXI	107	Photo 109 11	19 24	SITE: Type 3 Structure D. Material: disperse. LATE POSTCLASSIC: very light. COLONIAL: very light.	UTM: 470100, 2219100 NEAREST TOWN: SW of Teocalco. LOCATION: Alluvial valley; altitude: 2,080 m; S of Endó canal, between the Rio Tula and the Rio Salado; light erosion. POTENTIAL LAND USE: rainfall agriculture. PRESENT LAND USE: irrigation agriculture from dams.

APPENDIX

Cluster	Site No.	Photo and Square	Unit	Description and Association with Other Periods	Observations
XXI	108	Photo 109 15	10	SITE: Type 3. DESTROYED. Structure D. Probable local ceramic production type 864. CLASSIC: Structures/light/dense. LATE POSTCLASSIC: light.	UTM: 468400, 2219650 NEAREST TOWN: SW of Teocalco. LOCATION: Alluvial valley, 4,000 m from the Rio Tula; light erosion. POTENTIAL LAND USE: rainfall agriculture. PRESENT LAND USE: irrigation agriculture from dams.
XXI	109	Photo 109 9 3	2, 8 16	SITE: Type 5. DESTROYED. 2 Structures C. Material: disperse. LATE POSTCLASSIC: very light/light. COLONIAL: very light.	UTM: 467900, 2218500 NEAREST TOWN: E of Iturbe. LOCATION: Alluvial valley, 3,500–5,000 m from the Rio Tula; light erosion. POTENTIAL LAND USE: irrigation agriculture and rainfall agriculture. PRESENT LAND USE: irrigation agriculture from dams.
XXI	110	Photo 109 9	16	SITE: Type 5 Structures B. LATE POSTCLASSIC: very light.	UTM: 467600, 2219150 NEAREST TOWN: E of Iturbe. LOCATION: Alluvial valley, 3,300 m from the Rio Tula; light erosion. POTENTIAL LAND USE: rainfall agriculture. PRESENT LAND USE: irrigation agriculture from dams.
XXI	111	Photo 109 3 Photo 114 15 16 15 Photo 109 3 4	3 23 16 22, 24, 25 5 2	SITE: Type 7. DESTROYED. Complex of 3 Structures, A and B. Material: concentrated and disperse. Probable local ceramic production types 806, 826, 828, and 832. CLASSIC: Structures/very light/dense. COYOTLATELCO: very light. LATE POSTCLASSIC: very light. COLONIAL: very light.	UTM: 468000, 2217450 NEAREST TOWN: El Llano, Second Section. LOCATION: Lowlands and alluvial valley, E of old pre-Hispanic city, near the modern canal Number 3; 3,500 m from the Rio Tula; light and moderate erosion. POTENTIAL LAND USE: irrigation agriculture and rainfall agriculture. PRESENT LAND USE: town; irrigation agriculture from dams and rainfall agriculture.
XXI	113	Photo 114 16	20	SITE: Type 15 Material: disperse. LATE POSTCLASSIC: very light.	UTM: 469200, 2217200 NEAREST TOWN: Near the El Llano, Second Section. LOCATION: Alluvial valley near the Rio Tula; moderate erosion. POTENTIAL LAND USE: rainfall agriculture. PRESENT LAND USE: rainfall agriculture.

APPENDIX

Cluster	Site No.	Photo and Square	Unit	Description and Association with Other Periods	Observations
XXX	114	Photo 114 4 11 10 10 11	24 1 9 4 4, 5, 9, 14, 18, 19 16	SITE: Type 7. LOOTED. Complex of 4 Structures, B and C (2 with approx. 1,296 m^2 extension and 2 with approx. 650 m^2 extension). Material: concentrated and disperse. Probable local ceramic production types 806, 818, 826, 828, and 864. CLASSIC: Structures/ light/dense. TRANSITIONAL CLASSIC-COYOTLATELCO: very light. COYOTLATELCO: very light. LATE POSTCLASSIC: Structures/ very light/light. COLONIAL: very light. Selective Sampling.	UTM: 469100, 2215800 NEAREST TOWN: S of El Llano, Second Section (Refineria). LOCATION: Alluvial valley and lower slopes of Cerro de Bominzha; 2,000–2,400 m from the manantial and 5,000–6,000 m from the Rio Tula; moderate and strong erosion, scarce and moderate vegetation. POTENTIAL LAND USE: irrigation agriculture and rainfall agriculture on terraces. PRESENT LAND USE: town; rainfall agriculture.
XXI	115	Photo 109 5	23	SITE: Type 3 Ceremonial mound, D.	UTM: 469900, 2218300 NEAREST TOWN: NE of El Llano, Second Section. LOCATION: Alluvial valley, E of old pre-Hispanic city, between the Rio Tula and the Rio Salado; light erosion. POTENTIAL LAND USE: rainfall agriculture. PRESENT LAND USE: irrigation agriculture from dams.
XXI	116	Photo 109 4	23	SITE: Type 3 Ceremonial mound, D.	UTM: 469000, 2218200 NEAREST TOWN: N of El Llano, Second Section. LOCATION: Alluvial valley, E of old pre-Hispanic city, near the Rio Tula; light erosion. POTENTIAL LAND USE: rainfall agriculture. PRESENT LAND USE: irrigation agriculture from dams.
XXI	117	Photo109 11 5 6 11	5 20 12 10	SITE: Type 15 Material: cencentrated and disperse. CLASSIC: very light. LATE POSTCLASSIC: very light.	UTM: 470500, 2218000 NEAREST TOWN: NE of El Llano, Second Section. LOCATION: Alluvial valley, E of old pre-Hispanic city, between the Rio Tula and the Rio Salado; light and moderate erosion. POTENTIAL LAND USE: irrigation agriculture and rainfall agriculture. PRESENT LAND USE: irrigation agriculture from dams.

APPENDIX

Cluster	Site No.	Photo and Square	Unit	Description and Association with Other Periods	Observations
XXIII	118	Photo 110 2 8 8 2 8	25 3 11 21, 23, 24 14, 19	SITE: Type 7 Complex of 3 Structures D (Extension: 480 m², 600 m², and 400 m² approx.). Material: disperse. CLASSIC: Structures/very light/dense. LATE POSTCLASSIC: very light. COLONIAL: very light.	UTM: 471600, 2218500 NEAREST TOWN: W of Hacienda de Chingu. LOCATION: Alluvial valley, between the old La Romera canal and the modern Endó canal. Associated with pre-Hispanic irrigation via the Requena canal; altitude: 2,100 m approx.; 4,500 m from the Rio Salado and 150–1,200 m from the Jagüey; light and moderate erosion. POTENTIAL LAND USE: irrigation agriculture via the La Romera canal and rainfall agriculture. PRESENT LAND USE: irrigation agriculture from dams and rainfall agriculture.
XXIII	119	Photo 110 10 9 10 9 15	23 18, 23 17 14, 15 5	SITE: Type 11 Complex of 7 Structures A, B, C and D. CLASSIC: very light/dense.	UTM: 473000, 2219000 NEAREST TOWN: Hacienda de Chingu. TOLLAN PHASE SITE OF CHINGU. LOCATION: Between altitude 2,100 m and old La Romera canal, on the Hacienda Chingu's hill, 1,500–2,500 m from the Rio Salado; moderate erosion, moderate vegetation. POTENTIAL LAND USE: irrigation agriculture. PRESENT LAND USE: herding. Others: hunting and gathering plants, firewood.
XXIII	120	Photo 110 3 10 3 4	19, 20 3 24 16, 22	SITE: Type 11 Complex of 6 Structures A, B and C. Material: disperse. CLASSIC: dense.	UTM: 473150, 2218250 NEAREST TOWN: W of Dendho. LOCATION: TOLLAN PHASE SITE IN HACIENDA DE CHINGU. Lowlands and hill of Hacienda Chingu; altitude: 2,100 m; S of the old La Romera canal, 2,000–3,500 m from the Rio Salado; moderate erosion, moderate vegetation. PRESENT LAND USE: herding. Others: hunting and gathering plants, firewood.
XXIII	121	Photo 110 17 17 11 17	11 1 17, 18, 21, 22 2, 6, 7, 12	SITE: Type 7. DESTROYED. Complex of 3 Structures, A and B (Extensions: 360 m², 400 m², and 450 m² approx.). Material: disperse. CLASSIC: very light/light. TRANSITIONAL CLASSIC-COYOTLATELCO: very light. LATE POSTCLASSIC: Structures/very light/light/dense. COLONIAL: very light.	UTM: 474250, 2219400 NEAREST TOWN: N of Dendho. 700 m distant from site 139. LOCATION: Below 2,100 m altitude (below the hill); in the alluvial valley between the old La Romera canal and the modern Endó canal, between 1,200–2,300 m from the Rio Salado; moderate erosion, scarce and moderate vegetation. POTENTIAL LAND USE: irrigation agriculture and rainfall agriculture. PRESENT LAND USE: town; rainfall agriculture and irrigation agriculture from dams, herding. Others: hunting and gathering plants, firewood.

APPENDIX

Cluster	Site No.	Photo and Square	Unit	Description and Association with Other Periods	Observations
XXIII	122	Photo 110 5 11 5 11	17 3 18 1, 2, 7, 11	SITE: Type 7 Complex of 3 Structures, A and C (1 is a Ceremonial mound). Material: disperse. CLASSIC: very light. LATE POSTCLASSIC: Structures/ very light/light/dense. COLONIAL: very light.	UTM: 474500, 2218300 NEAREST TOWN: W of Dendho. LOCATION: Southern prolongation (of site 121), E of La Loma, Hacienda de Chingu; altitude: 2,100 m; 1,200–2,000 m from the Rio Salado; moderate erosion, scarce and moderate vegetation. POTENTIAL LAND USE: rainfall agriculture. PRESENT LAND USE: town; rainfall agriculture, herding. Others: hunting and gathering plants, firewood.
XIX	123	Photo 110 17 11 12	4 20 2, 12	SITE: Type 3. DESTROYED. Structure D (Extension: 400 m² approx.). Material: disperse. CLASSIC: very light. LATE POSTCLASSIC: Structures/ very light/light/dense.	UTM: 475000, 2219200 NEAREST TOWN: N of Dendho. LOCATION: Alluvial valley, between the Rio Salado and the Endó canal, 700–1,400 m from the Rio Salado; light and moderate erosion, scarce vegetation. POTENTIAL LAND USE: irrigation agriculture and rainfall agriculture. PRESENT LAND USE: town; rainfall agriculture and irrigation agriculture from dams, herding. Others: hunting and gathering plants, firewood.
XXIV	124	Photo 099 11 11 11 10 11 10 11 12 17	 14, 19 19 12, 13 23 15 6 9, 14 5, 7, 9, 10, 14, 19, 20 6 1, 3	SITE: Type 11. LOOTED. Complex of 8 Structures, A and B (2 Ceremonial mounds and 2 with extensions of approx. 625 m² and 900 m²). Material: concentrated and disperse. CLASSIC: very light. TRANSITIONAL CLASSIC-COYOTLATELCO: very light/ light. COYOTLATELCO: very light. LATE POSTCLASSIC: Structures/very light/light/dense. COLONIAL: very light. Selective Sampling.	UTM: 479100, 2223800 NEAREST TOWN: Teltipan de Juarez. LOCATION: On lower slopes of Cerro El Aguila; altitude: 2,100–2,160 m; E of the Tlamaco-Juando canal, near the Rio Salado; 800 m from site 116; light and moderate erosion, moderate and dense vegetation. POTENTIAL LAND USE: rainfall agriculture and rainfall agriculture on terraces. Others: hunting and gathering plants. PRESENT LAND USE: town; rainfall agriculture, herding. Others: hunting and gathering plants, firewood.
XXIV	125	Photo 099 12 18	 23 17, 19 2, 8	SITE: Type 5. DESTROYED. 2 Structures A. Material: disperse. CLASSIC: very light. LATE POSTCLASSIC: very light. COLONIAL: very light/light.	UTM: 480000, 2223950 NEAREST TOWN: E of Teltipan de Juarez. LOCATION: On lower slopes of Cerro El Aguila; altitude: 2,140–2,160 m; next to an intermittent stream near the Rio Salado; moderate and high erosion, moderate vegetation. POTENTIAL LAND USE: agriculture on terraces. PRESENT LAND USE: rainfall agriculture, herding. Others: hunting and gathering plants, firewood.

APPENDIX

Cluster	Site No.	Photo and Square	Unit	Description and Association with Other Periods	Observations
XXIV	126	Photo 099 12	10, 15 8, 10 13, 20	SITE: Type 5. DESTROYED. 2 Structures B. Material: disperse. LATE POSTCLASSIC: very light. COLONIAL: very light.	UTM: 480350, 2223450 NEAREST TOWN: E of Teltipan de Juarez. LOCATION: On lower slopes of Cerro Los Picachos; altitude: 2,100–2,120 m; near the Rio Salado, 700 m from site 125; moderate and high erosion. POTENTIAL LAND USE: rainfall agriculture on terraces. Others: hunting and gathering plants. PRESENT LAND USE: rainfall agriculture.
XXV	127	Photo 099 5 4 5 10 11	18 21 20 23, 24 2 1	SITE: Type 19. DESTROYED. 2 Habitational and Ceremonial Structures, D. Material: disperse. COYOTLATELCO: very light. LATE POSTCLASSIC: very light. COLONIAL: very light.	UTM: 478950, 2223050 NEAREST TOWN: S of Teltipan. LOCATION: Alluvial valley, W of the Tlamaco-Juando canal, near the Rio Salado; light erosion. POTENTIAL LAND USE: rainfall agriculture. PRESENT LAND USE: irrigation agriculture from dams.
XXIV	128	Photo 099 6 6 Photo 106 24	15 20, 24, 25 10	SITE: Type 3. DESTROYED. Structure D. Material: disperse. TRANSITIONAL CLASSIC-COYOTLATELCO: very light. LATE POSTCLASSIC: Structures/very light/dense.	UTM: 480450, 2222700 NEAREST TOWN: SE of Teltipan de Juarez. LOCATION: On lower slopes of Cerro Buenavista at 2,100 m altitude; above the Tlamaco-Juando canal, near the Rio Salado; moderate and high erosion, scarce vegetation. POTENTIAL LAND USE: rainfall agriculture on terraces. PRESENT LAND USE: rainfall agriculture on terraces.
XXIV	129	Photo 106 18 Photo 152 9	25 2	SITE: Type 2. LOOTED AND DESTROYED. Undetermined number of Habitational Structures/Ceremonial Structures. Ceremonial mound (20 m diam. and 3 m high). Extension: 5 ha approx. Selective Sampling.	UTM: 481350, 2222250 NEAREST TOWN: W of Tetepango. LOCATION: Southern slopes of Cerro Buenavista or "Jaguey de La Palma"; altitude: 2,100–2,140 m; near the Rio Salado and 300 m from the arroyo; light erosion, scarce vegetation. POTENTIAL LAND USE: rainfall agriculture. PRESENT LAND USE: irrigation agriculture from dams and rainfall agriculture.
XXIV	130	Photo 152 10	3	SITE: Type 2 Undetermined number of Habitational Structures/Ceremonial Structures. COYOTLATELCO: Structures/very light/light. LATE POSTCLASSIC: Structures/dense. Selective Sampling.	UTM: 482250, 2222300 NEAREST TOWN: W of Tetepango. LOCATION: Southern slopes of Cerro Buenavista or "Jaguey de La Palma," near the Rio Salado and 500 m from the arroyo; light erosion, scarce vegetation. PRESENT LAND USE: rainfall agriculture, abandoned terraces.

APPENDIX

Cluster	Site No.	Photo and Square	Unit	Description and Association with Other Periods	Observations
XXIV	131	Photo 091 9	4 8, 9, 18	SITE: Type 3. LOOTED. Structure D (50 m large and 5 m high). Material: disperse. CLASSIC: very light. LATE POSTCLASSIC: Structures/ light/dense.	UTM: 478200, 2225850 NEAREST TOWN: NW of Munitepec. LOCATION: On lower slopes of Cerro La Mesa, above altitude 2,100 m, above and to the E of Tlamaco-Juando canal, 2,800–4,000 m from the Rio Salado; high erosion, scarce vegetation. POTENTIAL LAND USE: rainfall agriculture. Others: hunting and gathering plants. PRESENT LAND USE: town; abandoned terraces. Others: hunting and gathering plants, firewood.
XXIV	132	Photo 091 10 10	11 9, 11	SITE: Type 3 Structure D. Material: disperse. FORMATIVE: very light. LATE POSTCLASSIC: Structures/ very light/dense.	UTM: 478800, 2226150 NEAREST TOWN: N of Munitepec. LOCATION: On lower slopes, W of Cerro La Mesa; altitude: 2,160–2,180 m; 3,600–4,700 m from the Rio Salado, 582 m from site 131; light erosion, moderate and dense vegetation. POTENTIAL LAND USE: rainfall agriculture on terraces. Others: hunting and gathering plants. PRESENT LAND USE: abandoned terraces, herding. Others: hunting and gathering plants, firewood.
XXIV	133	Photo 099 23 Photo 091 3 4 5 Photo 099 15 16 17 22	2 10 9, 10 6, 16, 23 25 10, 20, 24, 25 7, 12, 14, 15, 17, 18, 19, 21, 22, 23, 24 2, 3	SITE: Type 3. LOOTED. Structure D (Extension: 1,600 m² approx.). TRANSITIONAL CLASSIC-COYOTLATELCO: light. COYOTLATELCO: very light. LATE POSTCLASSIC: Structures/ very light/light/dense. COLONIAL: very light.	UTM: 479050, 2224900 NEAREST TOWN: S of Munitepec. LOCATION: On lower slopes of Cerro La Mesa, above altitude 2,100–2,200 m, E of Tlamaco-Juando canal, 3,600–5,800 m from the Rio Salado; light and moderate erosion. POTENTIAL LAND USE: rainfall agriculture on terraces. Others: hunting and gathering plants. PRESENT LAND USE: town; rainfall agriculture on terraces, herding. Others: hunting and gathering plants, firewood. Quarry: basalt.
XXV	134	Photo 106 24	1, 6	SITE: Type 15 Material: disperse. COYOTLATELCO: very light. COLONIAL: very light.	UTM: 479900, 2222350 NEAREST TOWN: S of Teltipan. LOCATION: Alluvial valley, W of Tlamaco-Juando canal; altitude: 2,080 m; near the Rio Salado; light erosion. POTENTIAL LAND USE: rainfall agriculture. PRESENT LAND USE: irrigation agriculture from dams.

APPENDIX

Cluster	Site No.	Photo and Square	Unit	Description and Association with Other Periods	Observations
XXV	135	Photo 106 20	2	SITE: Type 15 Material: concentrated. LATE POSTCLASSIC: very light.	UTM: 476300, 2222250 NEAREST TOWN: E of Doxey. LOCATION: Alluvial valley, 800 m from the Rio Salado; light erosion. POTENTIAL LAND USE: rainfall agriculture. PRESENT LAND USE: town; irrigation agriculture from dams.
XXV	136	Photo 099 3 Photo 106 15 20	11 21 10	SITE: Type 15 Material: disperse. LATE POSTCLASSIC: very light. COLONIAL: very light.	UTM: 477075, 2222300 NEAREST TOWN: Between Tlahuelilpan and Tlaxcoapan. LOCATION: Alluvial valley, 1,800 m from the Rio Salado; light erosion. POTENTIAL LAND USE: rainfall agriculture. PRESENT LAND USE: town; irrigation agriculture from dams.
XXV	137	Photo 099 14 15	11 6	SITE: Type 15 Material: disperse. LATE POSTCLASSIC: very light. COLONIAL: very light.	UTM: 476600, 2224200 NEAREST TOWN: Between Tlahuelilpan and Tlaxcoapan, SW of Munitepec. LOCATION: Alluvial valley near the Rio Salado; light erosion. POTENTIAL LAND USE: rainfall agriculture. PRESENT LAND USE: irrigation agriculture from dams.
XXV	138	Photo 105 18	9	SITE: Type 15 Material: disperse. TRANSITIONAL CLASSIC-COYOTLATELCO: very light. LATE POSTCLASSIC: very light.	UTM: 475750, 2221500 NEAREST TOWN: E of Doxey. LOCATION: Alluvial valley, 300 m from east bank of the Rio Salado; light erosion. POTENTIAL LAND USE: irrigation agriculture. Others: fishing. PRESENT LAND USE: irrigation agriculture from dams.
XXV	139	Photo 106 16	17 16 13	SITE: Type 3 Structure D. Material: concentrated and disperse. CLASSIC: light. COYOTLATELCO: very light. LATE POSTCLASSIC: very light.	UTM: 478300, 2222000 NEAREST TOWN: NE of Tlaxcoapan. LOCATION: Alluvial valley, 2,700–3,200 m from the Rio Salado; light erosion. POTENTIAL LAND USE: rainfall agriculture. PRESENT LAND USE: irrigation agriculture from dams.
XXV	140	Photo 106 10	22	SITE: Type 3 Structure D. TRANSITIONAL CLASSIC-COYOTLATELCO: very light.	UTM: 478350, 2221200 NEAREST TOWN: E of Tlaxcoapan. LOCATION: Alluvial valley, 2,700 m from the Rio Salado; light erosion. POTENTIAL LAND USE: rainfall agriculture. PRESENT LAND USE: irrigation agriculture from dams.

APPENDIX

Cluster	Site No.	Photo and Square	Unit	Description and Association with Other Periods	Observations
XXV	141	Photo 106 5 6 11	22 16 1, 4, 5, 9, 10	SITE: Type 15 Material: concentrated and disperse. CLASSIC: very light. LATE POSTCLASSIC: very light/dense. COLONIAL: very light.	UTM: 479650, 2220200 NEAREST TOWN: NE of Tlalminulpa. LOCATION: Lower slopes and alluvial valley, S of Tlamaco-Juando canal, 2,800 m from the Rio Salado; light and moderate erosion. POTENTIAL LAND USE: rainfall agriculture. PRESENT LAND USE: rainfall agriculture and irrigation agriculture from dams.
XXV	142	Photo 106 3 4 9	25 16 10	SITE: Type 15 Material: disperse. LATE POSTCLASSIC: very light.	UTM: 478000, 2220000 NEAREST TOWN: NE of Tlalminulpa. LOCATION: Alluvial valley, 2,800 m from the Rio Salado; light erosion. POTENTIAL LAND USE: rainfall agriculture. PRESENT LAND USE: irrigation agriculture from dams.
XXV	143	Photo 111 7 8	15 7, 14, 23	SITE: Type 3 Structure D. Material: disperse. COYOTLATELCO: very light. LATE POSTCLASSIC: very light. COLONIAL: very light.	UTM: 477000, 2218800 NEAREST TOWN: Tlalminulpa. LOCATION: Alluvial valley, 1,000–1,200 m from the Rio Salado; light erosion. POTENTIAL LAND USE: irrigation agricul-ture and rainfall agriculture. Others: fishing. PRESENT LAND USE: irrigation agriculture from dams and rainfall agriculture on terraces.
XXV	144	Photo 111 7 13	18 18 2, 10	SITE: Type 3. DESTROYED. Structure D. Material: disperse. LATE POSTCLASSIC: very light/light. COLONIAL: very light.	UTM: 476550, 2219000 NEAREST TOWN: Tlalminulpa. LOCATION: Alluvial valley, 30–1,200 m from the Rio Salado; light erosion. POTENTIAL LAND USE: irrigation agricul-ture and rainfall agriculture. Others: fishing. PRESENT LAND USE: irrigation agriculture from dams and agriculture on terraces.
XXV	145	Photo 111 2 1 2	1 10 6, 7	SITE: Type 5 2 Structures B. Material: disperse. Probable chert artifact production. LATE POSTCLASSIC: Structures/light/dense. COLONIAL: very light.	UTM: 477150, 2217600 NEAREST TOWN: E of Atitalaquia. LOCATION: Alluvial valley near and to the north of Tlamaco-Juando canal, 400–500 m from the Rio Salado; light erosion. POTENTIAL LAND USE: rainfall agriculture. Others: fishing. PRESENT LAND USE: town; irrigation agricul-ture from dams.
XXV	146	Photo 111 14 13 14	18 15 6, 11, 16	SITE: Type 3. DESTROYED. Structure D (Extension: 1,600 m² approx.). Material: disperse. COYOTLATELCO: very light. LATE POSTCLASSIC: very light. Selective Sampling.	UTM: 477400, 2217250 NEAREST TOWN: Between Atitalaquia and El Tablón. LOCATION: Lowlands; altitude: 2,100 m; 600–1,000 m from the Rio Salado; light and moderate erosion. POTENTIAL LAND USE: irrigation agriculture and rainfall agriculture. Others: fishing, hunting and gathering plants. PRESENT LAND USE: town; irrigation agricul-ture and rainfall agriculture.

APPENDIX

Cluster	Site No.	Photo and Square	Unit	Description and Association with Other Periods	Observations
XXV	147	Photo 111 3	24 2, 19 7, 11, 12, 17, 18	SITE: Type 3 Structure D. Material: concentrated and disperse. CLASSIC: very light. TRANSITIONAL CLASSIC-COYOTLATELCO: very light. COYOTLATELCO: very light. LATE POSTCLASSIC: Structures/very light/dense.	UTM: 478550, 2218250 NEAREST TOWN: S of Bojayito. LOCATION: Alluvial valley, above Tlamaco-Juando canal; altitude: 2,100 m; light and moderate erosion. POTENTIAL LAND USE: rainfall agriculture. PRESENT LAND USE: town; irrigation agriculture from dams.
XXV	148	Photo 111 2 3 2	17 21 22, 25	SITE: Type 15 Material: concentrated and disperse. FORMATIVE: very light. CLASSIC: Structures/very light/dense. TRANSITIONAL CLASSIC-COYOTLATELCO: very light. LATE POSTCLASSIC: very light/light. COLONIAL: very light.	UTM: 477600, 2218200 NEAREST TOWN: N of Atitalaquia. LOCATION: Alluvial valley, 800–1,600 m from the Rio Salado; light erosion. POTENTIAL LAND USE: irrigation agriculture and rainfall agriculture. PRESENT LAND USE: irrigation agriculture from dams.
XXVI	149	Photo 106 12	3	SITE: Type 3 Structure D. CLASSIC: light. LATE POSTCLASSIC: light. Selective Sampling.	UTM: 480250, 2220300 NEAREST TOWN: E of Bojayito. LOCATION: On lower slopes, N of Cerro Mesa Lechuguilla; altitude: 2,100–2,120 m; near the Rio Salado and 300 m from an intermittent stream; moderate erosion. POTENTIAL LAND USE: rainfall agriculture. PRESENT LAND USE: rainfall agriculture.
XXVI	150	Photo 152 22	3	SITE: Type 1 Undetermined number of Habitational Structures, B. LATE POSTCLASSIC: Structures/dense.	UTM: 481750, 2219250 NEAREST TOWN: E of Bojayito. LOCATION: On lower slopes, 200 m from the arroyo, near the Rio Salado; moderate erosion. POTENTIAL LAND USE: rainfall agriculture on terraces. Others: hunting and gathering plants. PRESENT LAND USE: agriculture on terraces and abandoned terraces.
XXVI	151	Photo 111 18 12 18	2 16 2, 7, 11	SITE: Type 3. DESTROYED. Structure D. Material: disperse. COYOTLATELCO: Structures/dense. LATE POSTCLASSIC: very light. COLONIAL: very light.	UTM: 480800, 2219300 NEAREST TOWN: E of Bojayito. LOCATION: On lower slopes, NW slopes of Mesa Lechuguilla; altitude: 2,140 m; near the Rio Salado and 50–500 m from an intermittent stream and from a Jagüey; light and moderate erosion. POTENTIAL LAND USE: rainfall agriculture. PRESENT LAND USE: irrigation agriculture from dams and rainfall agriculture, herding. Others: hunting and gathering plants, firewood.

APPENDIX

Cluster	Site No.	Photo and Square	Unit	Description and Association with Other Periods	Observations
XXVI	152	Photo 111 11 17	23 18, 23 13 24 3	SITE: Type 5 Complex of 3 Structures (1 Ceremonial mound). Material: concentrated and disperse. TRANSITIONAL CLASSIC-COYOTLATELCO: very light. COYOTLATELCO: light/dense. LATE POSTCLASSIC: Structures/ very light/light. COLONIAL: very light/light.	UTM: 480200, 2219100 NEAREST TOWN: E of Bojayito. LOCATION: Lower slopes, NW of Cerro Mesa Lechuguilla; altitude: 2,120–2,140 m; 20–300 m from the Rio Salado and from an intermittent stream and a Jagüey; light, moderate, and severe erosion. POTENTIAL LAND USE: rainfall agriculture. PRESENT LAND USE: irrigation agriculture from dams, rainfall agriculture, herding. Others: hunting and gathering plants, firewood.
XXVI	153	Photo 111 10 11 10 11 17	25 11 3, 4, 5, 15 1, 6, 12 1	SITE: Type 19. LOOTED. 2 Structures: Habitational and Ceremonial, C. Material: disperse. FORMATIVE: very light. COYOTLATELCO: very light. LATE POSTCLASSIC: Structures/ very light/light/dense. COLONIAL: very light.	UTM: 479800, 2218700 NEAREST TOWN: E of Bojayito. LOCATION: Lower slopes, NW of Cerro Mesa Lechuguilla; altitude: 2,120–2,140 m; 50–3,700 m from the Rio Salado and from the Barranca; light, moderate, and severe erosion. POTENTIAL LAND USE: irrigation agriculture and rainfall agriculture. Others: fishing, hunting, and gathering plants. PRESENT LAND USE: irrigation agriculture from dams and rainfall agriculture, abandoned terraces, herding. Others: hunting and gathering plants, firewood.
XXVI	154	Photo 111 5 11 5	18 23 5 17	SITE: Type 3. DESTROYED. Structure D. Material: concentrated and disperse. CLASSIC: very light. LATE POSTCLASSIC: very light. COLONIAL: very light.	UTM: 480100, 2218100 NEAREST TOWN: E of Bojayito. LOCATION: Lower slopes, NW of Cerro Mesa Lechuguilla; altitude: 2,120–2,140 m; 50–4,000 m from the Rio Salado and from an intermittent stream; light and moderate erosion. POTENTIAL LAND USE: rainfall agriculture. PRESENT LAND USE: rainfall agriculture, herding. Others: hunting and gathering plants, firewood.
XXVI	155	Photo 844 42	6, 7	SITE: Type 15 Material: disperse. Selective Sampling.	UTM: 479100, 2211500 NEAREST TOWN: W of El Refugio. LOCATION: Lower slopes, N of Cerro El Refugio; altitude: 2,160 m; 50 m from the Rio Salado; light erosion. POTENTIAL LAND USE: irrigation agriculture and rainfall agriculture. Others: fishing. PRESENT LAND USE: traditional irrigation agriculture, irrigation agriculture from dams and rainfall agriculture, herding. Others: hunting and gathering plants, firewood.

APPENDIX

Cluster	Site No.	Photo and Square	Unit	Description and Association with Other Periods	Observations
XXVI	156	Photo 842 34	2	SITE: Type 15 Material: disperse. COYOTLATELCO: very light. LATE POSTCLASSIC: very light. Selective Sampling.	UTM: 480200, 2217300 NEAREST TOWN: E of Tezoquipa. LOCATION: On lower slopes, NW of Cerro La Cantera; altitude: 2,160 m; 500 m from the Rio Salado and from the Jagüey; moderate erosion POTENTIAL LAND USE: rainfall agriculture. Others: hunting and gathering plants. PRESENT LAND USE: rainfall agriculture, abandoned terraces, herding. Others: hunting and gathering plants, firewood.
XXVI	157	Photo 842 28	4 2	SITE: Type 3 Structure C. Material: disperse. COYOTLATELCO: Structures/ light/dense. LATE POSTCLASSIC: very light. Selective Sampling.	UTM: 480300, 2216700 NEAREST TOWN: E of Tezoquipa. LOCATION: On slopes, W of Cerro Mesa La Cantera; altitude: 2,160 m; near the Rio Salado, 1,000 m from an intermittent stream; moderate erosion. POTENTIAL LAND USE: rainfall agriculture on terraces. Others: hunting and gathering plants. PRESENT LAND USE: rainfall agriculture, abandoned terraces, herding. Others: hunting and gathering plants, firewood.
XXVI	158	Photo 842 27	3 1 1	SITE: Type 3 Structure D. Material: concentrated and disperse. Probable chert artifact production. COYOTLATELCO: Structures/ dense. LATE POSTCLASSIC: very light/ light/dense. COLONIAL: very light. Selective Sampling.	UTM: 478800, 2216800 NEAREST TOWN: S of Tezoquipa. LOCATION: On lowlands and lower slopes of Cerro La Cantera; altitude: 2,120–2,140 m; near the Rio Salado, 50–300 m from an intermittent stream; moderate erosion. POTENTIAL LAND USE: rainfall agriculture. Others: hunting and gathering plants. PRESENT LAND USE: rainfall agriculture.
XXVI	159	Photo 842 27 28	2 2, 4 1, 3	SITE: Type 15 Material: concentrated and disperse. COYOTLATELCO: Structures/ very light/dense. LATE POSTCLASSIC: very light/ light/dense. COLONIAL: very light. Selective Sampling.	UTM: 479600, 2216600 NEAREST TOWN: Tezoquipa. LOCATION: Lowlands and alluvial valley of the Rio Salado, 50–350 m from an intermittent stream; moderate erosion. POTENTIAL LAND USE: rainfall agriculture on terraces. Others: hunting and gathering plants. PRESENT LAND USE: rainfall agriculture, abandoned terraces.

APPENDIX

Cluster	Site No.	Photo and Square	Unit	Description and Association with Other Periods	Observations
XXVI	160	Photo 842 21 22	4 4 3 2, 4	SITE: Type 1 Undetermined number of Habitational Structures, B and C. Material: concentrated and disperse. Probable chert bifacial artifact production. FORMATIVE: dense. CLASSIC: light. TRANSITIONAL CLASSIC-COYOTLATELCO: very light. COYOTLATELCO: light/dense. LATE POSTCLASSIC: Very light/light/dense. COLONIAL: very light. Selective Sampling.	UTM: 479400, 2215900 NEAREST TOWN: SE of Tezoquipa and N of Texas. LOCATION: At the base of Cerro La Cantera; altitude: 2,140–2,180 m; near the Rio Salado, 30–300 m from an intermittent stream and from the Jagüey; moderate erosion. POTENTIAL LAND USE: rainfall agriculture. Others: hunting and gathering plants. PRESENT LAND USE: rainfall agriculture, herding. Others: hunting and gathering plants, firewood.
XXVI	161	Photo 842 16	4 4	SITE: Type 2 Undetermined number of Habitational Structures/Ceremonial Structures, A. Ceremonial mound: 2 m high and 11 m diam. TRANSITIONAL CLASSIC-COYOTLATELCO: very light. COYOTLATELCO: Structures/very light/light. LATE POSTCLASSIC: very light/light. COLONIAL: very light. Selective Sampling.	UTM: 480200, 2214950 NEAREST TOWN: NE of Texas. LOCATION: Ladera baja, N of Cerro Las Palmas; altitude: 2,180 m; 50–200 m from an intermittent stream and from the Jagüey, near the Rio Salado and the colonial canal; moderate erosion. POTENTIAL LAND USE: rainfall agriculture. Others: hunting and gathering plants. PRESENT LAND USE: rainfall agriculture, terraces and abandoned terraces, herding. Others: hunting and gathering plants, firewood. Site is concentrated on the hill and disperse in surrounding zones.
XXVI	162	Photo 842 17 10 11 16 17	1 13, 15 13, 14, 16 1, 2, 3 2, 5	SITE: Type 15 Material: concentrated and disperse. CLASSIC: light. TRANSITIONAL CLASSIC-COYOTLATELCO: light. COYOTLATELCO: light/dense. LATE POSTCLASSIC: very light/light/dense. COLONIAL: very light. Selective Sampling.	UTM: 480350, 2214300 NEAREST TOWN: E of Texas. LOCATION: On lower slopes and lowlands of the Cerro; altitude: 2,160–2,180 m; 50–500 m from the Jagüey, near the Rio Salado; moderate and high erosion. POTENTIAL LAND USE: rainfall agriculture. Others: hunting and gathering plants. PRESENT LAND USE: rainfall agriculture, herding. Others: hunting and gathering plants, firewood.
XXVI	163	Photo 842 14 20 15 21	4, 6 2, 3 12 1, 2, 3	SITE: Type 15 Material: concentrated and disperse.	UTM: 480150, 2215900 NEAREST TOWN: S of El Tablón. LOCATION: Lowlands; altitude: 2,140–2,160 m; 500–1,000 m from the Rio Salado and from the Jagüey; moderate and high erosion. POTENTIAL LAND USE: rainfall agriculture. Others: hunting and gathering plants. PRESENT LAND USE: rainfall agriculture, abandoned terraces.

APPENDIX

Cluster	Site No.	Photo and Square	Unit	Description and Association with Other Periods	Observations
XXVI	164	Photo 842 20 14 20 21	2 4 2 1	SITE: Type 3 Ceremonial mound D (30 m diam. and 2 m high). Material: concentrated and disperse. CLASSIC: very light. COYOTLATELCO: very light. LATE POSTCLASSIC: very light/ dense. COLONIAL: very light. Selective Sampling.	UTM: 478200, 2215400 NEAREST TOWN: SE of El Tablón. LOCATION: Lowlands; altitude: 2,140–2,160 m; 500–1,000 m from the Rio Salado and from the Jagüey; moderate and high erosion. POTENTIAL LAND USE: rainfall agriculture. Others: hunting and gathering plants. PRESENT LAND USE: rainfall agriculture, abandoned terraces.
XXVI	165	Photo 116 8 14 8 9	 21, 24 2 1 2, 6, 15, 19 6	SITE: Type 7. DESTROYED. Complex of 3 Structures, C (2 with approx. 1,600 m² extension and 1 with approx. 900 m² extension). Material: concentrated and disperse. CLASSIC: very light. COYOTLATELCO: very light. LATE POSTCLASSIC: very light/ light. COLONIAL: very light.	UTM: 477350, 2216450 NEAREST TOWN: El Tablón. LOCATION: Lowlands; altitude: 2,100 m; 700–2,000 m from the Rio Salado; light and moderate erosion. POTENTIAL LAND USE: rainfall agriculture. Others: hunting and gathering plants, fishing. PRESENT LAND USE: town; rainfall agriculture. Possibly formed part of site 146; both sites are the same distance from the Rio Salado.
XXVI	166	Photo 116 15	 17, 18	SITE: Type 15 Material: disperse. FORMATIVE: very light. CLASSIC: very light. LATE POSTCLASSIC: very light/ light. COLONIAL: very light. Selective Sampling.	UTM: 478350, 2217250 NEAREST TOWN: S of Tezoquipa. LOCATION: Lowlands; altitude: 2,100–2,120 m; 2,000 m from the Rio Salado and 200 m from the arroyo; moderate erosion; S of site 146. POTENTIAL LAND USE: rainfall agriculture. Others: hunting and gathering plants. PRESENT LAND USE: town; rainfall agriculture.
XXVI	167	Photo 842 15	 5	SITE: Type 3 Structure D. Material: disperse. CLASSIC: light. TRANSITIONAL CLASSIC-COYOTLATELCO: very light. LATE POSTCLASSIC: Structures/ light. COLONIAL: very light. Selective Sampling.	UTM: 478750, 2214500 NEAREST TOWN: NW of Texas. LOCATION: Lowlands; altitude: 2,140–2,160 m; near the Rio Salado and near a modern canal; high erosion. POTENTIAL LAND USE: rainfall agriculture. Others: hunting and gathering plants. PRESENT LAND USE: rainfall agriculture.
XXVI	168	Photo 842 8	 7	SITE: Type 3 Structure D. Material: concentrated. CLASSIC: Structures/ Light/dense. LATE POSTCLASSIC: very light. Selective Sampling.	UTM: 478250, 2213600 NEAREST TOWN: E of Atotonilco-Tula. LOCATION: Lowlands, near the Rio Tula; altitude: 2,140 m; moderate erosion. POTENTIAL LAND USE: rainfall agriculture. Others: hunting and gathering plants. PRESENT LAND USE: rainfall agriculture.

APPENDIX

Cluster	Site No.	Photo and Square	Unit	Description and Association with Other Periods	Observations
XXVI	169	Photo 842 9 2 9 10 2 3 10 Photo 844 52	4, 6 16 7 9 14 15 3, 5, 6 3	SITE: Type 5 2 Structures C. Material: concentrated and disperse. CLASSIC: light. COYOTLATELCO: very light/light. LATE POSTCLASSIC: very light/light/dense. COLONIAL: very light. Selective Sampling.	UTM: 479200, 2213550 NEAREST TOWN: S of Texas. LOCATION: Lowlands, W of Cerro Las Palmas; altitude: 2,140–2,160 m; near the Rio Salado and 600 m to an intermittent stream; moderate erosion. POTENTIAL LAND USE: rainfall agriculture. Others: hunting and gathering plants. PRESENT LAND USE: rainfall agriculture.
XXVI	170	Photo 844 51 50 51 50	1, 5 4 2 8	SITE: Type 5 2 Structures B. Material: concentrated and disperse. Probable local ceramic production types 806, 826, and 864. CLASSIC: Structures/light. COYOTLATELCO: very light. LATE POSTCLASSIC: very light. COLONIAL: very light. Selective Sampling.	UTM: 479650, 2212250 NEAREST TOWN: NW of El Refugio. LOCATION: Lowlands; altitude: 2,160–2,180 m; 1,000–1,500 m from the Rio Salado; moderate erosion. POTENTIAL LAND USE: rainfall agriculture. Others: hunting and gathering plants. PRESENT LAND USE: rainfall agriculture.
XXVI	171	Photo 844 50	1 3 2, 7	SITE: Type 3. DESTROYED. Structure D. Material: concentrated and disperse. CLASSIC: very light. TRANSITIONAL CLASSIC-COYOTLATELCO: very light. LATE POSTCLASSIC: Structures/very light/dense. COLONIAL: very light. Selective Sampling.	UTM: 478750, 2212250 NEAREST TOWN: N of Vithó. LOCATION: Lowlands; altitude: 2,160 m; 600–1,500 m from the Rio Salado; moderate erosion. POTENTIAL LAND USE: rainfall agriculture. Others: hunting and gathering plants. PRESENT LAND USE: rainfall agriculture. Probably part of site 170.
XXVI	172	Photo 844 41 49	13, 14, 15, 16, 1, 5	SITE: Type 15 Material: disperse. CLASSIC: Structures/light/dense. LATE POSTCLASSIC: Structures/very light/light. COLONIAL: very light. Selective Sampling.	UTM: 478050, 2212000 NEAREST TOWN: NW of Vitho. LOCATION: Lowlands; 50–350 m from east bank of the Rio Salado; altitude: 2,140–2,160 m; moderate erosion, scarce vegetation. POTENTIAL LAND USE: rainfall agriculture. Others: fishing. PRESENT LAND USE: rainfall agriculture, herding. Others: hunting and gathering plants, firewood.

APPENDIX

Cluster	Site No.	Photo and Square	Unit	Description and Association with Other Periods	Observations
XXVI	173	Photo 844 43	1, 8 5, 6	SITE: Type 15 Material: concentrated and disperse. CLASSIC: very light. COYOTLATELCO: Structures/light. LATE POSTCLASSIC: Structures/very light/dense. COLONIAL: very light. Selective Sampling.	UTM: 479950, 2211450 NEAREST TOWN: W of El Refugio. LOCATION: Lower slopes, N of Cerro El Refugio, above altitude 2,160 m, 50–1,000 m from the Rio Salado; moderate and severe erosion, scarce vegetation. POTENTIAL LAND USE: rainfall agriculture on terraces. Others: hunting and gathering plants, fishing. PRESENT LAND USE: town; rainfall agriculture. Quarry: limestone.
XXVII	174	Photo 115 16 10 16 17	8, 9, 10 22 1, 3 11	SITE: Type 7. DESTROYED. Complex of 4 Structures, A and B. Material: disperse. CLASSIC: very light/light. COYOTLATELCO: very light. LATE POSTCLASSIC: very light/light/dense.	UTM: 473700, 2215500 NEAREST TOWN: NW of Tlamaco. LOCATION: Lower slopes of limestone hills of Atotonilco and Bomintza; altitude: 2,140–2,160 m; 2,400–3,800 m from the Rio Salado; moderate and severe erosion. POTENTIAL LAND USE: rainfall agriculture. Others: hunting and gathering plants. PRESENT LAND USE: rainfall agriculture.
XXVII	175	Photo 115 5 10 11 10 11	23 15 12 8 4, 10, 13, 14 1, 2, 3, 6, 11, 16	SITE: Type 7. DESTROYED. Complex of 3 Structures C. Material: concentrated and disperse. CLASSIC: Structures/light/dense. LATE POSTCLASSIC: Structures/very light/light.	UTM: 474250, 2216400 NEAREST TOWN: Estación Bojay, N of Tlamaco. LOCATION: Lowlands of Cerro El Progreso; altitude: 2,140–2,160 m; 1,800–4,100 m from the Rio Salado; moderate and severe erosion. POTENTIAL LAND USE: rainfall agriculture. Others: hunting and gathering plants. PRESENT LAND USE: rainfall agriculture.
XXVII	176	Photo 115 11	5 10, 14	SITE: Type 5 2 Structures B. Material: disperse. CLASSIC: Structures/light/dense. LATE POSTCLASSIC: Structures/very light/light/dense.	UTM: 475000, 2216450 NEAREST TOWN: SW of Cardonal. LOCATION: Lowlands; altitude: 2,100–2,120 m; 1,400–1,700 m from the Rio Salado; moderate and severe erosion. POTENTIAL LAND USE: rainfall agriculture. Others: hunting and gathering plants. PRESENT LAND USE: town; rainfall agriculture.
XXVII	177	Photo 115 6 12	23 2	SITE: Type 3 Structure D. Material: disperse. CLASSIC: very light. LATE POSTCLASSIC: very light/light.	UTM: 475500, 2216600 NEAREST TOWN: S of Cardonal. LOCATION: Lowlands; altitude: 2,100–2,120 m; 1,100 m from the Rio Salado; moderate erosion, moderate vegetation. POTENTIAL LAND USE: rainfall agriculture. Others: hunting and gathering plants. PRESENT LAND USE: town; rainfall agriculture.

APPENDIX

Cluster	Site No.	Photo and Square	Unit	Description and Association with Other Periods	Observations
XXVII	178	Photo 115 6 In photo 115, squares 1, 2, 3, 7, 8, 13, and 14 correspond to the Pemex Refinery and were not systematically sampled.	8	SITE: Type 3 Structure D. CLASSIC: very light. LATE POSTCLASSIC: light.	UTM: 475500, 2217250 NEAREST TOWN: S of Cardonal. LOCATION: Lowlands; altitude: 2,100–2,120 m; 1,000 m from the Rio Salado; moderate erosion, moderate vegetation. POTENTIAL LAND USE: rainfall agriculture. PRESENT LAND USE: town; rainfall agriculture.
XIX	179	Photo 116 13	16, 21	SITE: Type 15 Material: disperse. LATE POSTCLASSIC: very light. Selective Sampling.	UTM: 476200, 2217200 NEAREST TOWN: S of Cardonal. LOCATION: Lowlands; altitude: 2,100 m; 300 m from the Rio Salado, near the Dendho canal; moderate erosion. POTENTIAL LAND USE: irrigation agriculture and rainfall agriculture. Others: fishing. PRESENT LAND USE: rainfall agriculture and irrigation agriculture from dams.
XXVII	180	Photo 115 17 17 11 17 11 17	10 5, 9, 14 18, 23 13 25 4, 12	SITE: Type 11. DESTROYED. Complex of 6 Structures A, B, and C. Material: concentrated and disperse. CLASSIC: very light/light. LATE POSTCLASSIC: Structures/ very light/light/dense.	UTM: 474650, 2215500 NEAREST TOWN: NW of Tlamaco. LOCATION: Lowlands; altitude: 2,100–2,120 m; 1,500–2,400 m from the Rio Salado; light and severe erosion. POTENTIAL LAND USE: rainfall agriculture. Others: hunting and gathering plants. PRESENT LAND USE: town; rainfall agriculture.
XXVII	181	Photo 841 21	2, 4 3 4	SITE: Type 7 Complex of 4 Structures, B and C. Material: disperse. Probable local ceramic production types 818 and 826. CLASSIC: very light. COYOTLATELCO: Structures/ very light/dense. LATE POSTCLASSIC: Structures/very light/light/dense. Selective Sampling.	UTM: 474450, 2214700 NEAREST TOWN: W of Tlamaco. LOCATION: Lower slopes of limestone hill El Progreso; altitude: 2,120 m; near to an intermittent stream, 2,000–2,800 m from the Rio Salado; severe erosion. POTENTIAL LAND USE: rainfall agriculture. Others: hunting and gathering plants. PRESENT LAND USE: rainfall agriculture. Probably part of site 180.
XXVII	182	Photo 841 22	3	SITE: Type 3 Structure D. CLASSIC: very light. LATE POSTCLASSIC: light. Selective Sampling.	UTM: 475150, 2214350 NEAREST TOWN: Tlamaco. LOCATION: Lower slopes, N of limestone hill El Progreso; altitude: 2,120–2,140 m; 1,400 m from the Rio Salado; moderate erosion, scarce vegetation. POTENTIAL LAND USE: irrigation agriculture and rainfall agriculture. PRESENT LAND USE: town; traditional irrigation agriculture, herding.

APPENDIX

Cluster	Site No.	Photo and Square	Unit	Description and Association with Other Periods	Observations
XXVII	183	Photo 841 22	4	SITE: Type 2 Undetermined number of Habitational and Ceremonial Structures.	UTM: 475450, 2214750 NEAREST TOWN: Tlamaco, below the 16th century church. LOCATION: Lowlands; altitude: 2,120–2,140 m; 700 m from the Rio Salado; moderate erosion, scarce vegetation. POTENTIAL LAND USE: rainfall agriculture. Others: hunting and gathering plants. PRESENT LAND USE: town. Probably is part of a single site, with sites 181 and 182.
XXVII	184	Photo 115 9 10	19, 20 10, 14, 24, 25 16, 17 21	SITE: Type 5. DESTROYED. 2 Structures B. Material: disperse. CLASSIC: very light. LATE POSTCLASSIC: very light/ light/dense.	UTM: 472750, 2215900 NEAREST TOWN: NW of Tlamaco. LOCATION: Lowlands; altitude: 2,140–2,160 m; 3,200–4,000 m from the Rio Salado; severe erosion. POTENTIAL LAND USE: rainfall agriculture. Others: hunting and gathering plants. PRESENT LAND USE: rainfall agriculture.
XXVII	185	Photo 115 9 3 4	5 24 19, 20, 24 16, 17, 22, 23	SITE: Type 3 Structure D. Material: concentrated and disperse. FORMATIVE: very light. CLASSIC: Structures/light/dense. LATE POSTCLASSIC: Structures/very light/light/dense. COLONIAL: very light.	UTM: 472900, 2216600 NEAREST TOWN: NW of Tlamaco. LOCATION: Lowlands; altitude: 2,120–2,140 m; 3,500–4,400 m from the Rio Salado; moderate and high erosion. POTENTIAL LAND USE: rainfall agriculture. Others: hunting and gathering plants. PRESENT LAND USE: rainfall agriculture.
XXVII	186	Photo 115 15 9	1 11, 16, 22	SITE: Type 3 Structure D. Material: disperse. CLASSIC: Structures/very light/ light. LATE POSTCLASSIC: Structures/very light/light/dense.	UTM: 472100, 2215700 NEAREST TOWN: W of Tlamaco and N of Bomintza. LOCATION: Lowlands; altitude: 2,160 m; 4,200–4,900 m from the Rio Salado; moderate and severe erosion, scarce vegetation. POTENTIAL LAND USE: rainfall agriculture on terraces. Others: hunting and gathering plants. PRESENT LAND USE: rainfall agriculture, abandoned terraces, herding.
XXVII	187	Photo 115 15 16	13 11	SITE: Type 15 Material: disperse. CLASSIC: Structures/light. LATE POSTCLASSIC: Structures/very light/dense. Selective Sampling.	UTM: 472900, 2215050 NEAREST TOWN: NW of Progreso and N of Bomintza. LOCATION: Lowlands; altitude: 2,160 m; 3,200–4,000 m from the Rio Salado; light and severe erosion. POTENTIAL LAND USE: rainfall agriculture. Others: hunting and gathering plants. PRESENT LAND USE: rainfall agriculture on terraces.

APPENDIX

Cluster	Site No.	Photo and Square	Unit	Description and Association with Other Periods	Observations
XXVII	188	Photo 841 12 20	 2, 3, 4 4	SITE: Type 3 Structure D. Material: disperse. CLASSIC: very light. LATE POSTCLASSIC: very light/ dense. COLONIAL: very light. Selective Sampling.	UTM: 473750, 2213950 NEAREST TOWN: W of Progreso. LOCATION: Lowlands; altitude: 2,160 m; 2,700 m from the Rio Salado; moderate and high erosion. POTENTIAL LAND USE: rainfall agriculture. Others: hunting and gathering plants. PRESENT LAND USE: rainfall agriculture, herding.
XXVII	189	Photo 841 4 5	 2 1 3	SITE: Type 15 Material: concentrated and disperse. CLASSIC: Structures/light/dense. LATE POSTCLASSIC: very light/ light. COLONIAL: very light. Selective Sampling.	UTM: 474150, 2213450 NEAREST TOWN: W of Progreso. LOCATION: Lowlands; altitude: 2,160 m; 3,500–3,700 m from the Rio Salado; severe erosion, scarce vegetation. POTENTIAL LAND USE: rainfall agriculture. Others: hunting and gathering plants. PRESENT LAND USE: town; herding.
XXVII	190	Photo 841 3 12	 4 2, 4	SITE: Type 15 Material: disperse. CLASSIC: light. COYOTLATELCO: very light. LATE POSTCLASSIC: very light/ dense. COLONIAL: very light. Selective Sampling.	UTM: 473100, 2213700 NEAREST TOWN: W of Progreso. LOCATION: Lowlands; altitude: 2,160 m; 3,800–4,900 m from the Rio Salado; moderate and severe erosion, scarce vegetation. POTENTIAL LAND USE: rainfall agriculture. Others: hunting and gathering plants. PRESENT LAND USE: rainfall agriculture, herding.
XXIII	191	Photo 110 2 3 Photo 115 3 4	 9 6 4, 5 1	SITE: Type 15 Material: disperse. CLASSIC: Structures/light/dense. LATE POSTCLASSIC: very light/ light. COLONIAL: very light.	UTM: 472550, 2217600 NEAREST TOWN: W of Cardonal. LOCATION: Power station. Site on Chingu's periphery; alluvial valley; altitude: 2,100–2,120 m; 3,800–4,400 m from the Rio Salado and 300 m from the Jagüey; moderate erosion, scarce vegetation. POTENTIAL LAND USE: irrigation agriculture and rainfall agriculture. Others: hunting and gathering plants. PRESENT LAND USE: rainfall agriculture, herding, abandoned terraces. Others: hunting and gathering plants, firewood.
XXVII	192	Photo 115 4 5	 10 9	SITE: Type 15 Material: disperse. LATE POSTCLASSIC: Structures/ light/dense.	UTM: 473900, 2217300 NEAREST TOWN: SW of Cardonal. LOCATION: Lowlands; altitude: 2,100–2,120 m; 2,200–3,000 m from the Rio Salado; moderate erosion. POTENTIAL LAND USE: rainfall agriculture. Others: hunting and gathering plants. PRESENT LAND USE: rainfall agriculture.

APPENDIX

Cluster	Site No.	Photo and Square	Unit	Description and Association with Other Periods	Observations
XXVIII	193	Photo 843 36 44 36 44	14 6 12, 14 3, 4, 7	SITE: Type 1 Undetermined number of Habitational Structures, B. Material: concentrated and disperse. CLASSIC: Structures/light/dense. LATE POSTCLASSIC: very light. COLONIAL: very light. Selective Sampling.	UTM: 473500, 2211150 NEAREST TOWN: S of Zacamilpa. LOCATION: Slopes of limestone hill; altitude: 2,160–2,200 m; 30–900 m from the arroyo and near the Rio Salado; light to severe erosion. POTENTIAL LAND USE: irrigation agriculture and rainfall agriculture. Others: hunting and gathering plants. PRESENT LAND USE: rainfall agriculture on terraces, irrigation agriculture, herding. Quarry: limestone.
XXVIII	194	Photo 843 37 38	4 6	SITE: Type 1 Undetermined number of Habitational Structures, B. Material: disperse. LATE POSTCLASSIC: very light. COLONIAL: very light. Selective Sampling.	UTM: 474700, 2210300 NEAREST TOWN: La Cañada. LOCATION: Slopes; altitude: 2,060–2,080 m; 500 m from the arroyo, near the Rio Salado; light and moderate erosion. POTENTIAL LAND USE: rainfall agriculture on terraces. Others: hunting and gathering plants. PRESENT LAND USE: traditional irrigation agriculture and rainfall agriculture. Quarry: limestone.
XXVIII	195	Photo 843 29 21 22	3, 8 15 13	SITE: Type 1 Undetermined number of Habitational Structures, A. Material: disperse. TRANSITIONAL CLASSIC-COYOTLATELCO: very light. LATE POSTCLASSIC: very light. COLONIAL: very light. Selective Sampling.	UTM: 474750, 2209400 NEAREST TOWN: N of Conejos. LOCATION: Slopes of limestone hill; altitude: 2,200–2,250 m; near the Rio Salado and 50–400 m from the arroyo; light to severe erosion, scarce vegetation. POTENTIAL LAND USE: rainfall agriculture on terraces. Others: hunting and gathering plants. PRESENT LAND USE: town; rainfall agriculture on terraces, abandoned terraces. Quarry: limestone.
XXVIII	196	Photo 843 14 15 14 22	16 9 14 6	SITE: Type 3 Structure D. Material: concentrated and disperse. CLASSIC: very light. COYOTLATELCO: very light. LATE POSTCLASSIC: very light. Selective Sampling.	UTM: 475650, 2208200 NEAREST TOWN: S of Las Trancas, SE of Conejos. LOCATION: Slopes of limestone hill; altitude: 2,200 m; near the Rio Salado and 300–800 m from the Barranca; light to severe erosion, scarce vegetation. POTENTIAL LAND USE: rainfall agriculture. Others: hunting and gathering plants. PRESENT LAND USE: rainfall agriculture, herding. Quarry: limestone.

APPENDIX

Cluster	Site No.	Photo and Square	Unit	Description and Association with Other Periods	Observations
XXVIII	197	Photo 843 32	2, 10	SITE: Type 15 Material: disperse. TRANSITIONAL CLASSIC-COYOTLATELCO: light. LATE POSTCLASSIC: very light/light. Selective Sampling.	UTM: 477100, 2209600 NEAREST TOWN: S of Atotonilco. LOCATION: Lowlands; altitude: 2,260–2,280 m; near the Rio Salado; moderate erosion. POTENTIAL LAND USE: rainfall agriculture. Others: hunting and gathering plants. PRESENT LAND USE: rainfall agriculture. Quarry: limestone.
XXVIII	198	Photo 844 25 25	7 2, 6, 9, 10, 13	SITE: Type 15 Material: concentrated and disperse. CLASSIC: Structures/very light/dense. LATE POSTCLASSIC: very light/light. Selective Sampling.	UTM: 478100, 2209700 NEAREST TOWN: S of Atotonilco. LOCATION: Lowlands; altitude: 2,160–2,200 m; 800–1,750 m from the Rio Salado; moderate erosion. POTENTIAL LAND USE: rainfall agriculture. Others: hunting and gathering plants. PRESENT LAND USE: rainfall agriculture. Quarry: limestone.
XXVIII	199	Photo 844 26	15	SITE: Type 15 Material: disperse. TRANSITIONAL CLASSIC-COYOTLATELCO: very light. LATE POSTCLASSIC: very light. Selective Sampling.	UTM: 479300, 2210150 NEAREST TOWN: Vitho. LOCATION: Lower slopes of limestone hill; altitude: 2,160–2,200 m; 50 m from the Rio Salado; light erosion. POTENTIAL LAND USE: irrigation agriculture. Others: fishing. PRESENT LAND USE: traditional irrigation agriculture and irrigation agriculture from dams.
XXIX	200	Photo 843 35 43 49 51	14 13 8 2	SITE: Type 15 Material: disperse. CLASSIC: very light/light. LATE POSTCLASSIC: Structures/very light/dense. Selective Sampling.	UTM: 472200, 2212000 NEAREST TOWN: Bomintza. LOCATION: Slopes of limestone hill; altitude: 2,200–2,250 m; 100 m from the Rio Salado; moderate erosion. POTENTIAL LAND USE: rainfall agriculture. Others: hunting and gathering plants. PRESENT LAND USE: town; rainfall agriculture. Quarry: limestone.
XXVIII	201	Photo 844 41 Photo 843 48	11 7, 10, 13 12	SITE: Type 3 Structure D. Material: disperse. CLASSIC: Structures/very light/dense. LATE POSTCLASSIC: Structures/very light/light/dense. COLONIAL: very light. Selective Sampling.	UTM: 478200, 2211600 NEAREST TOWN: NW of Vitho. LOCATION: Lowlands, near the west bank of the Rio Salado and 100 m from the Jagüey; light and moderate erosion, scarce vegetation. POTENTIAL LAND USE: irrigation agriculture and rainfall agriculture. Others: fishing, hunting, and gathering plants. PRESENT LAND USE: traditional irrigation agriculture and irrigation agriculture from dams, rainfall agriculture, herding. Others: hunting and gathering plants, firewood.

APPENDIX

Cluster	Site No.	Photo and Square	Unit	Description and Association with Other Periods	Observations
XXVIII	202	Photo 843 48	2	SITE: Type 3 Structure D. LATE POSTCLASSIC: light. COLONIAL: very light. Selective Sampling.	UTM: 477100, 2211300 NEAREST TOWN: S of Atotonilco. LOCATION: Lowlands and lower slopes of hill; altitude: 2,120 m; 500 m from the Rio Salado; moderate erosion. POTENTIAL LAND USE: rainfall agriculture. Others: hunting and gathering plants. PRESENT LAND USE: rainfall agriculture. Quarry: limestone.
XXXI	203	Photo 121 9 15	 18 20 2	SITE: Type 3 Structure D. Material: disperse. LATE POSTCLASSIC: Structures/light/dense. COLONIAL: very light/dense. Selective Sampling.	UTM: 467100, 2209100 NEAREST TOWN: S of Ciudad Cruz Azul. LOCATION: Slopes and lowlands; altitude: 2,040–2,100 m; near east bank of the Rio Tula; light to moderate erosion, dense vegetation. POTENTIAL LAND USE: irrigation agriculture and rainfall agriculture. Others: hunting and gathering plants, fishing. PRESENT LAND USE: traditional irrigation agriculture, irrigation agriculture from dams, rainfall agriculture, herding. Others: hunting and gathering plants, firewood. Quarry: limestone.
XXXIV	204	Photo 120 10 11 12 10 11 12	 2 12, 23 14 4 1, 23 15	SITE: Type 15 Material: concentrated and disperse. LATE POSTCLASSIC: Structures/very light/light/dense. COLONIAL: very light.	UTM: 468850, 2210650 NEAREST TOWN: NE of Ciudad Cruz Azul, E of San Miguel Vindho. LOCATION: Lowlands and lower slopes of hill and limestone hill; altitude: 2,200 m; 2,000 m from the Rio Tula and 50–700 m from the arroyo; moderate and severe erosion, scarce and moderate vegetation. POTENTIAL LAND USE: rainfall agriculture. Others: hunting and gathering plants. PRESENT LAND USE: rainfall agriculture, herding. Others: hunting and gathering plants, firewood. Quarry: limestone.
XXXII	205	Photo 121 6	 17	SITE: Type 3 Structure D. LATE POSTCLASSIC: very light.	UTM: 469500, 2208150 NEAREST TOWN: E of San Jose Acoculco. LOCATION: Slopes of limestone hill; altitude: 2,120 m; near the arroyo and near the Rio Tula; moderate erosion. POTENTIAL LAND USE: rainfall agriculture. Others: hunting and gathering plants. PRESENT LAND USE: rainfall agriculture. Quarry: limestone.
XXXI	206	Photo 121 4	 13	SITE: Type 3 Structure D. LATE POSTCLASSIC: very light. Selective Sampling.	UTM: 467900, 2208100 NEAREST TOWN: NW of San Jose Acoculco. LOCATION: Lowlands; altitude: 2,080 m; near the old Requena canal, 500 m from the Rio Tula; moderate erosion. POTENTIAL LAND USE: rainfall agriculture. Others: hunting and gathering plants. PRESENT LAND USE: rainfall agriculture.

APPENDIX

Cluster	Site No.	Photo and Square	Unit	Description and Association with Other Periods	Observations
XXXIV	207	Photo 121 5 4	16 20	SITE: Type 15 Material: concentrated and disperse. LATE POSTCLASSIC: very light. Selective Sampling.	UTM: 468800, 2208200 NEAREST TOWN: N of San Jose Acoculco. LOCATION: Lowlands; altitude: 2,100–2,150 m; near the Rio Tula and 30–50 m from the arroyo; light erosion. POTENTIAL LAND USE: irrigation agriculture and rainfall agriculture. Others: hunting and gathering plants. PRESENT LAND USE: traditional irrigation agriculture and rainfall agriculture. Quarry: limestone.
XXXI	208	Photo 121 9 10	9 1	SITE: Type 5 2 Structures B. Material: disperse. Probable local ceramic production type 806. CLASSIC: very light. TRANSITIONAL CLASSIC-COYOTLATELCO: very light. LATE POSTCLASSIC: very light. COLONIAL: very light. Selective Sampling.	UTM: 467100, 2208700 NEAREST TOWN: NE of Caltengo. LOCATION: Lowlands; altitude: 2,060–2,080 m; near west bank of the Rio Tula and Schmeltz canal; no erosion. POTENTIAL LAND USE: irrigation agriculture. Others: fishing. PRESENT LAND USE: traditional irrigation agriculture and irrigation agriculture from dams.
XXXI	209	Photo 121 10	2, 3	SITE: Type 15 Material: disperse.	UTM: 467800, 2208500 NEAREST TOWN: W of Acoculco. LOCATION: Lowlands, on right side of the Rio Tula; no erosion. POTENTIAL LAND USE: irrigation agriculture. Others: fishing. PRESENT LAND USE: traditional irrigation agriculture and irrigation agriculture from dams.
XXXIV	210	Photo 121 10 11	18 11	SITE: Type 15 Material: disperse. CLASSIC: very light. LATE POSTCLASSIC: light/dense. COLONIAL: very light. Selective Sampling.	UTM: 468300, 2209200 NEAREST TOWN: N of Acoculco. LOCATION: Slopes; altitude: 2,100–2,140 m; 100–500 m from the Rio Tula and 30 m from the arroyo; light erosion. POTENTIAL LAND USE: irrigation agriculture. Others: hunting and gathering plants, fishing. PRESENT LAND USE: traditional irrigation agriculture and irrigation agriculture from dams; herding.
XXXII	211	Photo 122 17	16, 17 10, 17 3, 17	SITE: Type 5 2 Structures B. Material: concentrated and disperse. FORMATIVE: very light. CLASSIC: Structures/very light/light/dense. LATE POSTCLASSIC: Structures/very light/dense.	UTM: 468500, 2207400 NEAREST TOWN: S of San Jose Acoculco. LOCATION: On the top and slopes of San Jose Acoculco's hill; altitude: 2,180–2,200 m; 300–800 m from the Rio El Salto; severe erosion, scarce vegetation. POTENTIAL LAND USE: rainfall agriculture and rainfall agriculture on terraces. Others: hunting and gathering plants. PRESENT LAND USE: rainfall agriculture, abandoned terraces, herding. Quarry: limestone. UTM: 469650, 2206550

APPENDIX

Cluster	Site No.	Photo and Square	Unit	Description and Association with Other Periods	Observations
XXXII	212	Photo 122 18 12	3 11	SITE: Type 15 Material: concentrated and disperse. FORMATIVE: very light. CLASSIC: Structures/very light/dense. LATE POSTCLASSIC: very light.	NEAREST TOWN: NW of El Salto (Melchor Ocampo). LOCATION: Slopes of El Salto's mountains; altitude: 2,150–2,200 m; 30 m from the Rio El Salto; light and moderate erosion. POTENTIAL LAND USE: rainfall agriculture. Others: hunting and gathering plants. PRESENT LAND USE: traditional irrigation agriculture and rainfall agriculture. Quarry: limestone.
XXXII	213	Photo 122 5	20	SITE: Type 15 Material: disperse. LATE POSTCLASSIC: light. Selective Sampling.	UTM: 469200, 2205600 NEAREST TOWN: NW of El Salto (Melchor Ocampo). LOCATION: Slopes of El Salto's mountains; altitude: 2,150–2,200 m; 50 m from the Rio El Salto; light erosion. POTENTIAL LAND USE: irrigation agriculture. PRESENT LAND USE: traditional irrigation agriculture. Quarry: limestone.
XXXII	214	Photo 122 10	4	SITE: Type 15 Material: disperse. CLASSIC: very light. LATE POSTCLASSIC: very light. Selective Sampling.	UTM: 468200, 2205900 LOCATION: Eastern slopes of Cerro El Venado; altitude: 2,150 m; 1,000 m from the Rio Tula; moderate erosion, scarce vegetation. POTENTIAL LAND USE: rainfall agriculture. Others: hunting and gathering plants. PRESENT LAND USE: rainfall agriculture, herding.
XXXII	215	Photo 122 6	23	SITE: Type 3 Structure D. CLASSIC: light. COYOTLATELCO: Structures/very light. LATE POSTCLASSIC: very light. COLONIAL: very light.	UTM: 469950, 2205700 NEAREST TOWN: N of El Salto (Melchor Ocampo). LOCATION: Lowlands and slopes; altitude: 2,180 m; near an intermittent stream and 30 m from the Rio El Salto; no erosion. POTENTIAL LAND USE: irrigation agriculture. Others: fishing. PRESENT LAND USE: traditional irrigation agriculture and irrigation agriculture from dams.
XXXII	216	Photo 20B 27	3	SITE: Type 1 Undetermined number of Habitational Structures, A.	UTM: 471300, 2204750 NEAREST TOWN: E of El Salto (Melchor Ocampo). LOCATION: Altitude: 2,200 m approx.; next to an intermittent stream, associated with colonial irrigation systems of the Hacienda El Salto; moderate erosion, scarce vegetation. POTENTIAL LAND USE: rainfall agriculture. Others: hunting and gathering plants. PRESENT LAND USE: rainfall agriculture, herding. Others: hunting and gathering plants, firewood.

APPENDIX

Cluster	Site No.	Photo and Square	Unit	Description and Association with Other Periods	Observations
XXXII	217	Photo 20B 15	1	SITE: Type 1 Undetermined number of Habitational Structures, A. LATE POSTCLASSIC: very light. Selective Sampling.	UTM: 471200, 2203800 NEAREST TOWN: S of El Salto (Melchor Ocampo). LOCATION: Next to the El Salto dam, associated with colonial irrigation systems of the Hacienda El Salto; altitude: 2,180–2,220 m; moderate erosion, moderate vegetation. POTENTIAL LAND USE: irrigation agriculture and rainfall agriculture. PRESENT LAND USE: traditional irrigation agriculture.
XXXIII	218	Photo 124 17 11 17	5, 9 24 8, 20	SITE: Type 5 2 Structures B. Material: concentrated and disperse. CLASSIC: very light/light. LATE POSTCLASSIC: very light/light. COLONIAL: very light.	UTM: 469100, 2203900 NEAREST TOWN: SW of El Salto (Melchor Ocampo). LOCATION: On present crop fields; altitude: 2,180–2,200 m; 500 m from the Rio El Salto; moderate and severe erosion, scarce vegetation. POTENTIAL LAND USE: rainfall agriculture. Others: hunting and gathering plants. PRESENT LAND USE: rainfall agriculture, herding. Quarry: limestone.
XXXIII	219	Photo 124 12	16 6, 11	SITE: Type 3. DESTROYED. Structure D. Material: disperse. CLASSIC: very light. LATE POSTCLASSIC: very light/light. Selective Sampling.	UTM: 469600, 2203550 NEAREST TOWN: SW of El Salto (Melchor Ocampo). LOCATION: Lowlands, on present crop fields; altitude: 2,180 m; near the Rio El Salto; moderate erosion. POTENTIAL LAND USE: rainfall agriculture. Others: hunting and gathering plants. PRESENT LAND USE: rainfall agriculture. Quarry: limestone.
XXXIII	220	Photo 124 4	22	SITE: Type 2 Undetermined number of Habitational and Ceremonial Structures, A (Ceremonial precinct: plaza with mounds and surrounding habitational area). CLASSIC: very light. COYOTLATELCO: very light. LATE POSTCLASSIC: light. Selective Sampling.	UTM: 467800, 2202700 LOCATION: On the top of Cerro El Borrego; altitude: 2,220 m; near the Rio El Salto; moderate erosion. POTENTIAL LAND USE: rainfall agriculture. Others: hunting and gathering plants. PRESENT LAND USE: rainfall agriculture. Quarry: limestone.

APPENDIX

Cluster	Site No.	Photo and Square	Unit	Description and Association with Other Periods	Observations
XXXIII	221	Photo 124 5 10 11 17	17 23 10 6, 17, 22 3	SITE: Type 3 Structure D. Material: disperse. CLASSIC: very light. LATE POSTCLASSIC: very light/ light.	UTM: 468650, 2202800 NEAREST TOWN: Ciénega de Flores. LOCATION: On the top of hill near site 220 and present crop fields; altitude: 2,220–2,250 m; 3,200–3,600 m from the Rio Tula; moderate erosion. POTENTIAL LAND USE: rainfall agriculture. Others: hunting and gathering plants. PRESENT LAND USE: rainfall agriculture and rainfall agriculture on terraces. Quarry: limestone.
XXXIII	222	Photo 124 9 8 9 14 15 16	8 5, 13, 19 3 9 8, 14 11	SITE: Type 15 Material: concentrated and disperse. FORMATIVE: very light/dense. CLASSIC: Structures/very light/ light/dense. COYOTLATELCO: very light. LATE POSTCLASSIC: very light/ light. Selective Sampling.	UTM: 466500, 2203200 LOCATION: E of Requena dam. Top of the hill; altitude: 2,200 m; Cerro El Tesoro and nearest hills, 400–2,000 m from the Rio Tula and near the Rio El Salto; moderate erosion, scarce and moderate vegetation. POTENTIAL LAND USE: rainfall agriculture on terraces. Others: hunting and gathering plants. PRESENT LAND USE: rainfall agriculture on terraces, abandoned terraces, herding. Others: hunting and gathering plants, firewood. Quarry: limestone.
XXXIII	223	Photo 124 9 10	7, 9 11	SITE: Type 15 Material: disperse. CLASSIC: light/dense. LATE POSTCLASSIC: very light.	UTM: 467400, 2204300 LOCATION: E of Requena dam. Hill slopes; altitude: 2,200 m; Cerro El Tesoro and nearest hills, 1,500–2,400 m from the Rio Tula, near the Rio El Salto; moderate erosion, scarce vegetation. POTENTIAL LAND USE: rainfall agriculture on terraces. Others: hunting and gathering plants. PRESENT LAND USE: rainfall agriculture and rainfall agriculture on terraces, herding. Others: hunting and gathering plants, firewood. Quarry: limestone.
XXXIII	224	Photo 124 16	23	SITE: Type 15 Material: disperse. CLASSIC: very light. LATE POSTCLASSIC: very light. COLONIAL: very light.	UTM: 468100, 2204800 LOCATION: E of Requena dam. Slopes and lowlands; altitude: 2,050 m; 500 m from the Rio Tula and from the Barranca; light erosion. POTENTIAL LAND USE: irrigation agriculture. Others: fishing. PRESENT LAND USE: traditional irrigation agriculture and irrigation agriculture from dams.

APPENDIX

Cluster	Site No.	Photo and Square	Unit	Description and Association with Other Periods	Observations
XXXV	225	Photo 122 1 2 7 8	24 12 22 4 2, 6, 7, 9, 13, 14	SITE: Type 15 Material: concentrated and disperse. CLASSIC: very light. TRANSITIONAL CLASSIC-COYOTLATELCO: very light. COYOTLATELCO: very light/light. LATE POSTCLASSIC: Structures/very light/light/dense. COLONIAL: very light.	UTM: 465700, 2205900 NEAREST TOWN: S of Caltengo. LOCATION: Slopes and small hills, NW of Requena dam; altitude: 2,040–2,080 m; 800–1,500 m from the Rio Tula and 30 m from the arroyo; moderate and severe erosion. POTENTIAL LAND USE: rainfall agriculture. Others: hunting and gathering plants. PRESENT LAND USE: rainfall agriculture. Quarry: limestone.
XXXV	226	Photo 821 25 Photo 822 33 39	1 4 4	SITE: Type 15 Material: concentrated and disperse. COYOTLATELCO: very light. LATE POSTCLASSIC: light/dense. COLONIAL: light. Selective Sampling.	UTM: 463550, 2206050 LOCATION: Mesa Redonda hill. On the top and upper slopes of Mesa Redonda hill, W of Requena dam; altitude: 2,150–2,200 m; near the Rio Tlautla, 150–300 m from the arroyo; moderate erosion. POTENTIAL LAND USE: rainfall agriculture. Others: hunting and gathering plants. PRESENT LAND USE: town; rainfall agriculture and rainfall agriculture on terraces. Quarry: limestone.
XXXV	227	Photo 821 24	1	SITE: Type 15 Material: concentrated. LATE POSTCLASSIC: Structures/dense. COLONIAL: very light. Selective Sampling.	UTM: 462500, 2205750 LOCATION: W of Requena dam. Top of hills, W of Requena dam, Cerro El Tejocote, and Mesa Redonda; altitude: 2,150–2,200 m; near the Rio Tlautla and 300 m from the Barranca; moderate erosion. POTENTIAL LAND USE: rainfall agriculture on terraces. Others: hunting and gathering plants. PRESENT LAND USE: rainfall agriculture on terraces.
XXXV	228	Photo 821 13	3	SITE: Type 15 Material: concentrated. LATE POSTCLASSIC: dense. Selective Sampling.	UTM: 462450, 2204600 LOCATION: W of Requena dam. Top of hills, W of Requena dam and Cerro El Tejocote; altitude: 2,150–2,200 m; near the Rio Tlautla and 300 m from the Barranca; moderate erosion. POTENTIAL LAND USE: rainfall agriculture on terraces. Others: hunting and gathering plants. PRESENT LAND USE: rainfall agriculture on terraces.

APPENDIX

Cluster	Site No.	Photo and Square	Unit	Description and Association with Other Periods	Observations
XXXV	229	Photo 121 1 2	 15 11	SITE: Type 15 Material: disperse. TRANSITIONAL CLASSIC-COYOTLATELCO: very light. LATE POSTCLASSIC: very light/dense. Selective Sampling.	UTM: 465400, 2208150 NEAREST TOWN: S of Pueblo Nuevo. LOCATION: Slopes of small hills, N of Requena dam; altitude: 2,100 m; near the Rio Tlautla; moderate and severe erosion, scarce and moderate vegetation. POTENTIAL LAND USE: rainfall agriculture. Others: hunting and gathering plants. PRESENT LAND USE: abandoned terraces, herding. Others: hunting and gathering plants, firewood. Quarry: limestone.
XXXV	230	Photo 121 8 14 9 15	 8, 18 1 11 6	SITE: Type 15 Material: concentrated and disperse. CLASSIC: very light. LATE POSTCLASSIC: Structures/very light/light/dense. COLONIAL: very light.	UTM: 466100, 2209250 NEAREST TOWN: Pueblo Nuevo. LOCATION: Slopes, hills to the N of Requena dam, near the Schmeltz canal; altitude: 2,100 m; 30–300 m from the Rio Tula; light to severe erosion. POTENTIAL LAND USE: irrigation agriculture and rainfall agriculture on terraces. Others: fishing. PRESENT LAND USE: traditional irrigation agriculture, irrigation agriculture from dams, and rainfall agriculture.
XXX	231	Photo 120 7 8 9 14	 23 18 11 8	SITE: Type 15 Material: disperse. CLASSIC: Structures/dense. LATE POSTCLASSIC: very light/dense. Selective Sampling.	UTM: 466350, 2210850 NEAREST TOWN: San Miguel Vindho. LOCATION: Lowlands and slopes of San Miguel Vindho's hills; altitude: 2,100 m; 250–800 m from the Rio Tula; light and moderate erosion, moderate vegetation. POTENTIAL LAND USE: irrigation agriculture and rainfall agriculture. Others: hunting and gathering plants, fishing. PRESENT LAND USE: town; traditional irrigation agriculture and irrigation agriculture from dams, herding. Others: hunting and gathering plants, firewood. Quarry: limestone.
XXX	232	Photo 118 8	 11	SITE: Type 2. LOOTED. Undetermined number of Habitational and Ceremonial Structures, B.	UTM: 467800, 2213300 NEAREST TOWN: E of Zaragoza. LOCATION: Cerro Mogote's slopes; altitude: 2,140–2,160 m; near the Rio Tula and the Barranca; severe erosion. POTENTIAL LAND USE: rainfall agriculture. PRESENT LAND USE: rainfall agriculture. Quarry: limestone.

APPENDIX

Cluster	Site No.	Photo and Square	Unit	Description and Association with Other Periods	Observations
XXX	233	Photo 118 7 2 7	18 18 20 9	SITE: Type 5 2 Structures B. Material: concentrated and disperse. CLASSIC: very light. COYOTLATELCO: very light. LATE POSTCLASSIC: very light. Selective Sampling.	UTM: 466900, 2213300 NEAREST TOWN: N of Zaragoza. LOCATION: Lowlands and lower slopes of Cerro Bomintza; altitude: 2,140–2,160 m; 2,500–2,900 m from the Rio Tula; light and severe erosion, scarce vegetation. POTENTIAL LAND USE: rainfall agriculture. Others: hunting and gathering plants. PRESENT LAND USE: rainfall agriculture, herding. Quarry: limestone.
XXIX	234	Photo 120 24	18	SITE: Type 15 Material: disperse. CLASSIC: very light. LATE POSTCLASSIC: very light. Selective Sampling.	UTM: 469500, 2212400 NEAREST TOWN: Bomintza. LOCATION: On lower slopes of Cerro Bomintza; altitude: 2,260 m; near the Rio Tula; light erosion. POTENTIAL LAND USE: rainfall agriculture. Others: hunting and gathering plants. PRESENT LAND USE: rainfall agriculture on terraces. Quarry: limestone.
XXX	235	Photo 118 15	3	SITE: Type 15 Material: disperse. COYOTLATELCO: very light. LATE POSTCLASSIC: very light. COLONIAL: very light. Selective Sampling.	UTM: 467000, 2214450 NEAREST TOWN: SE of San Pedro Alpuyeca. LOCATION: Lowlands; altitude: 2,120–2,140 m; 2,500 m from the Rio Tula; moderate erosion. POTENTIAL LAND USE: irrigation agriculture and rainfall agriculture. PRESENT LAND USE: rainfall agriculture.
XXII	236	Photo 118 10	7, 13 5, 8	SITE: Type 5 2 Structures B. Material: disperse. CLASSIC: very light. TRANSITIONAL CLASSIC-COYOTLATELCO: very light. LATE POSTCLASSIC: very light.	UTM: 466200, 2213950 NEAREST TOWN: San Marcos. LOCATION: Lowlands, near the Number 3 canal; altitude: 2,080 m; 2,000–2,600 m from the Rio Tula; light and moderate erosion. POTENTIAL LAND USE: irrigation agriculture and rainfall agriculture. PRESENT LAND USE: traditional irrigation agriculture and irrigation agriculture from dams.
XXII	237	Photo 117 1 3 6 7	19 8 6 7	SITE: Type 15 Material: disperse. CLASSIC: very light. COYOTLATELCO: very light. LATE POSTCLASSIC: Structures/ very light/dense. COLONIAL: very light.	UTM: 465200, 2214000 NEAREST TOWN: W of San Marcos. LOCATION: Lowlands, 200–1,500 m E of Rio Tula; light and moderate erosion, moderate vegetation. POTENTIAL LAND USE: irrigation agriculture and rainfall agriculture. Others: hunting and gathering plants, fishing. PRESENT LAND USE: town; traditional irrigation agriculture and irrigation agriculture from dams, herding. Others: hunting and gathering plants, firewood.

APPENDIX

Cluster	Site No.	Photo and Square	Unit	Description and Association with Other Periods	Observations
XXII	238	Photo 117 7 Photo 114 1 2	10 3 16	SITE: Type 3 Structure D. Material: disperse. COYOTLATELCO: very light. LATE POSTCLASSIC: very light. COLONIAL: very light.	UTM: 465800, 2215000 NEAREST TOWN: S of San Pedro Alpuyeca. LOCATION: Alluvial valley; altitude: 2,060–2,080 m; 1,800–2,500 m from the Rio Tula and 1,500 m from the Manantial; light erosion, scarce vegetation. POTENTIAL LAND USE: irrigation agriculture and rainfall agriculture. Others: hunting and gathering plants. PRESENT LAND USE: town; traditional irrigation agriculture, irrigation agriculture from dams, rainfall agriculture. *This is the closest rural structure to the south edge of Tula's pre-Hispanic city.
XXIA	239	Photo 114 7 8	3, 4, 9 1, 6, 21	SITE: Type 15 Material: disperse. COYOTLATELCO: very light. LATE POSTCLASSIC: very light/light. COLONIAL: very light.	UTM: 466500, 2215850 NEAREST TOWN: San Lorenzo. LOCATION: Alluvial valley; altitude: 2,060–2,080 m; 2,000–2,500 m from the Rio Tula and 800–1,200 m from the Manantial; light erosion. POTENTIAL LAND USE: irrigation agriculture and rainfall agriculture. PRESENT LAND USE: town; traditional irrigation agriculture and irrigation agriculture from dams.
XXI	240	Photo 114 8 9 15	25 18, 21 1	SITE: Type 15 Material: disperse. TRANSITIONAL CLASSIC- COYOTLATELCO: very light. COYOTLATELCO: very light. LATE POSTCLASSIC: very light. COLONIAL: very light.	UTM: 467700, 2216400 NEAREST TOWN: El Llano, Second Section. LOCATION: Alluvial valley; altitude: 2,080–2,100 m; 1,000 m from the Rio Tula, near the Manantial; light erosion, moderate vegetation. POTENTIAL LAND USE: irrigation agriculture and rainfall agriculture. PRESENT LAND USE: town; irrigation agriculture from dams and rainfall agriculture.
XXX	241	Photo 114 3 9	22, 24 10	SITE: Type 15 Material: disperse. COYOTLATELCO: very light. LATE POSTCLASSIC: very light. COLONIAL: very light.	UTM: 468100, 2215600 NEAREST TOWN: El Llano, Second Section. LOCATION: Lowlands; altitude: 2,100–2,120 m; 1,000 m from the Rio Tula; light and severe erosion, scarce and moderate vegetation. POTENTIAL LAND USE: irrigation agriculture and rainfall agriculture. PRESENT LAND USE: town; traditional irrigation agriculture, rainfall agriculture, herding.

APPENDIX

Cluster	Site No.	Photo and Square	Unit	Description and Association with Other Periods	Observations
XL	242	Photo 843 11 12	6, 11, 13 7	SITE: Type 15 Material: disperse. CLASSIC: very light. TRANSITIONAL CLASSIC-COYOTLATELCO: very light. LATE POSTCLASSIC: Structures/very light/light/dense. COLONIAL: very light. Selective Sampling.	UTM: 472550, 2207900 NEAREST TOWN: SW of Conejos. LOCATION: Northern slopes of Cerro El Salto; altitude: 2,200–2,250 m; near the Rio El Salto; moderate erosion, moderate vegetation. POTENTIAL LAND USE: rainfall agriculture. Others: hunting and gathering plants. PRESENT LAND USE: rainfall agriculture on terraces, herding. Others: hunting and gathering plants, firewood. Quarry: limestone.
XXXIA	243	Photo 120 7 7	23 22	SITE: Type 3. LOOTED. Structure D. Material: concentrated. LATE POSTCLASSIC: Structures/very light. COLONIAL: very light. Selective Sampling.	UTM: 465200, 2211000 NEAREST TOWN: NE of Santa Maria Ilucan. LOCATION: Lowlands; altitude: 2,000 m; 50–100 m from west bank of the Rio Tula; light erosion. POTENTIAL LAND USE: irrigation agriculture and rainfall agriculture. Others: hunting and gathering plants, fishing. PRESENT LAND USE: traditional irrigation agriculture, irrigation agriculture from dams, herding.
XXXIA	244	Photo 120 7	8	SITE: Type 15 Material: disperse. LATE POSTCLASSIC: very light. Selective Sampling.	UTM: 465250, 2210500 NEAREST TOWN: Cruz Azul. LOCATION: Lowlands, east bank of the Rio Tula; light erosion. POTENTIAL LAND USE: irrigation agriculture. Others: fishing. PRESENT LAND USE: town; traditional irrigation agriculture and irrigation agriculture from dams.
XXXV	245	Photo 125 5	1	SITE: Type 1 Undetermined number of Habitational Structures, B. CLASSIC: very light. COLONIAL: light. Selective Sampling.	UTM: 463950, 2201000 NEAREST TOWN: Around Tepeji del Rio and atrium of town's church. LOCATION: Top of the hill and terraces on slopes of Cerro El Tepeyac, 800 m from the Rio Tula; moderate erosion. POTENTIAL LAND USE: rainfall agriculture on terraces. Others: hunting and gathering plants. PRESENT LAND USE: town; rainfall agriculture on terraces.
XXXVI	246	Photo 833 21	2 1	SITE: Type 1 Undetermined number of Habitational Structures, A. Material: disperse. LATE POSTCLASSIC: Structures/very light/dense. COLONIAL: very light. Selective Sampling.	UTM: 460400, 2208800 NEAREST TOWN: Santa Maria Magdalena. LOCATION: Upper and lower slopes; altitude: 2,100–2,150 m; 30–100 m from the Rio Tlautla and near the arroyo; light erosion, moderate vegetation. POTENTIAL LAND USE: rainfall agriculture on terraces. Others: hunting and gathering plants, fishing. PRESENT LAND USE: rainfall agriculture, herding. Others: hunting and gathering plants, firewood.

APPENDIX

Cluster	Site No.	Photo and Square	Unit	Description and Association with Other Periods	Observations
XXXVI	247	Photo 833 22	2	SITE: Type 15 Material: concentrated. Selective Sampling.	UTM: 461800, 2208750 NEAREST TOWN: S of San Lucas Teacalco. LOCATION: On lower slopes, S of Mesa El Lindero, 100 m from north bank of the Rio Tlautla and near the Barranca; light erosion, moderate vegetation. POTENTIAL LAND USE: rainfall agriculture on terraces. Others: hunting and gathering plants, fishing. PRESENT LAND USE: rainfall agriculture, herding. Others: hunting and gathering plants, firewood.
XXXV	248	Photo 833 22	2	SITE: Type 15 Material: disperse.	UTM: 462000, 2208350 NEAREST TOWN: N of Santiago Tlautla. LOCATION: Slopes and lowlands; altitude: 2,100–2,150 m; 50 m from south bank of the Rio Tlautla.
XXXV	249	Photo 833 14	1, 2	SITE: Type 15 Material: disperse. CLASSIC: Structures/light. LATE POSTCLASSIC: Structures/dense. Selective Sampling.	UTM: 462050, 2207650 NEAREST TOWN: N of Santiago Tlautla. LOCATION: Lowlands; altitude: 2,100–2,150 m; 50–150 m from the Rio Tlautla, near the arroyo; light erosion. POTENTIAL LAND USE: rainfall agriculture on terraces and irrigation agriculture. Others: hunting and gathering plants, fishing. PRESENT LAND USE: traditional irrigation agriculture, rainfall agriculture, and rainfall agriculture on terraces.
XXXV	250	Photo 833 5	4	SITE: Type 15 Material: disperse. CLASSIC: light. LATE POSTCLASSIC: Structures/dense. COLONIAL: very light. Selective Sampling.	UTM: 461250, 2207200 NEAREST TOWN: Santiago Tlautla. LOCATION: Lowlands; altitude: 2,100–2,150 m; 150 m from the Rio Tlautla, near the arroyo; light erosion. POTENTIAL LAND USE: irrigation agriculture and rainfall agriculture. Others: fishing. PRESENT LAND USE: traditional irrigation agriculture and rainfall agriculture.
XXXVII	251	Photo 833 11 5 10 11 17 22 23	2, 11, 21 22 15, 20 7, 11 3 5, 8 2	SITE: Type 7. DESTROYED. Complex of 3 Structures C. Material: disperse. CLASSIC: Structures/very light/light/dense. TRANSITIONAL CLASSIC-COYOTLATELCO: very light. COYOTLATELCO: very light. LATE POSTCLASSIC: very light/light. COLONIAL: very light/light/dense.	UTM: 464950, 2228200 NEAREST TOWN: E of Estacion Carrasco. LOCATION: Alluvial valley; altitude: 2,020 m; 1,500–3,000 m from the Rio Tula; light erosion. POTENTIAL LAND USE: irrigation agriculture and rainfall agriculture. PRESENT LAND USE: town; irrigation agriculture from dams.

APPENDIX

Cluster	Site No.	Photo and Square	Unit	Description and Association with Other Periods	Observations
XXXVII	252	Photo 080 10 16 16 10 15 16	23 3 11 4 18, 22, 25 5, 20 2, 6, 8, 9, 10, 12, 13, 21, 22, 24	SITE: Type 7. DESTROYED. Complex of 3 Structures, B and C. Material: concentrated and disperse. CLASSIC: Structures/very light/light/dense. TRANSITIONAL CLASSIC-COYOTLATELCO: Structures/very light/dense. COYOTLATELCO: very light. LATE POSTCLASSIC: Structures/very light. COLONIAL: very light.	UTM: 464300, 2228800 NEAREST TOWN: General Anaya. LOCATION: 500 m from site 251; alluvial valley; altitude: 2,020 m; 1,200–2,500 m from the Rio Tula; light erosion. POTENTIAL LAND USE: irrigation agriculture and rainfall agriculture. PRESENT LAND USE: irrigation agriculture from dams.
XXXVII	253	Photo 080 9 3 8 9 10	4 5 23 10 15 6, 7, 11, 12	SITE: Type 3 Structure D. Material: concentrated and disperse. CLASSIC: Structures/very light/dense. TRANSITIONAL CLASSIC-COYOTLATELCO: very light. LATE POSTCLASSIC: very light. COLONIAL: very light.	UTM: 463700, 2227900 NEAREST TOWN: W of Estacion Carrasco. LOCATION: Alluvial valley; altitude: 2,020 m; 600–1,800 m from the Rio Tula; light erosion. POTENTIAL LAND USE: irrigation agriculture and rainfall agriculture. PRESENT LAND USE: irrigation agriculture from dams.
XXXVII	254	Photo 073 6	6	SITE: Type 15 Material: disperse. COYOTLATELCO: Structures/dense.	UTM: 465750, 2230300 NEAREST TOWN: Atengo. LOCATION: Alluvial valley; altitude: 2,020 m; 900 m from the Rio Tula. POTENTIAL LAND USE: irrigation agriculture. PRESENT LAND USE: town; traditional irrigation agriculture.
XXXVII	255	Photo 080 17 17 18	14, 25 15 1, 21	SITE: Type 15 Material: concentrated and disperse. CLASSIC: very light/light. TRANSITIONAL CLASSIC-COYOTLATELCO: very light/light. COYOTLATELCO: very light/light. LATE POSTCLASSIC: very light. COLONIAL: very light.	UTM: 465600, 2229350 NEAREST TOWN: W of San Gabriel. LOCATION: Alluvial valley; altitude: 2,020 m; 2,400–3,500 m from the Rio Tula; light erosion. POTENTIAL LAND USE: irrigation agriculture and rainfall agriculture. PRESENT LAND USE: irrigation agriculture from dams.
XXXVII	256	Photo 080 5 12	20, 25 1	SITE: Type 15 Material: disperse. LATE POSTCLASSIC: very light.	UTM: 465650, 2227500 NEAREST TOWN: E of Estacion Carrasco. LOCATION: Alluvial valley; altitude: 2,020 m; 3,000–3,500 m from the Rio Tula; light erosion. POTENTIAL LAND USE: irrigation agriculture and rainfall agriculture on lowlands. PRESENT LAND USE: irrigation agriculture from dams.

APPENDIX

Cluster	Site No.	Photo and Square	Unit	Description and Association with Other Periods	Observations
XXXVII	257	Photo 080 9 15	22 7, 8, 17, 18	SITE: Type 15 Material: disperse. CLASSIC: Structures/very light/light/dense. LATE POSTCLASSIC: very light/light. COLONIAL: very light/dense.	UTM: 463300, 2229000 NEAREST TOWN: NW of General Anaya. LOCATION: Alluvial valley, 500–850 m from the Rio Tula; light erosion. POTENTIAL LAND USE: irrigation agriculture and rainfall agriculture. PRESENT LAND USE: town; irrigation agriculture from dams.
XXXVII	258	Photo 080 10	3	SITE: Type 3 Structure D. CLASSIC: light. LATE POSTCLASSIC: very light. COLONIAL: very light.	UTM: 464400, 2227700 NEAREST TOWN: SE of General Anaya. LOCATION: Alluvial valley; altitude: 2,020 m; 2,000 m from the Rio Tula; light erosion. POTENTIAL LAND USE: irrigation agriculture and rainfall agriculture. PRESENT LAND USE: irrigation agriculture from dams.
IX	259	Photo 073 4 Photo 080 21	21 7, 8	SITE: Type 15 Material: disperse. COYOTLATELCO: very light. TRANSITIONAL CLASSIC-COYOTLATELCO: Structures/very light/dense. LATE POSTCLASSIC: Structures/very light/dense. COLONIAL: light.	UTM: 463450, 2229850 NEAREST TOWN: W of San Gabriel. LOCATION: Alluvial valley, near San Gabriel canal, 100–400 m from the Rio Tula; light and moderate erosion. POTENTIAL LAND USE: irrigation agriculture and rainfall agriculture. Others: fishing. PRESENT LAND USE: town; traditional irrigation agriculture and irrigation agriculture from dams.
XXXVII	260	Photo 088 4 5	15, 19 15, 19 11, 16	SITE: Type 5 2 Structures B. Material: disperse. TRANSITIONAL CLASSIC-COYOTLATELCO: very light. COYOTLATELCO: very light. LATE POSTCLASSIC: very light. COLONIAL: very light. Selective Sampling.	UTM: 464700, 2227250 NEAREST TOWN: S of Estacion Carrasco. LOCATION: Alluvial valley; altitude: 2,020 m; 2,100–2,400 m from the Rio Tula; light erosion. POTENTIAL LAND USE: irrigation agriculture and rainfall agriculture on lowlands. PRESENT LAND USE: irrigation agriculture from dams.
XXXVII	261	Photo 088 4 4 10 4 10 11 4 5 10 11	4 3 12, 17, 29, 25 2 8, 10, 11, 24 11 1, 7, 10 1, 7 4, 5, 9, 13, 14, 15, 20, 21, 22 6, 16	SITE: Type 7 Complex of 6 Structures, B (1 is a Ceremonial mound). Material: concentrated and disperse. CLASSIC: Structures/very light/light/dense. TRANSITIONAL CLASSIC-COYOTLATELCO: very light. COYOTLATELCO: very light. LATE POSTCLASSIC: Structures/very light/light/dense. COLONIAL: very light. Selective Sampling.	UTM: 464350, 2226500 NEAREST TOWN: Between Santa Ana Ahuehuepan and General Anaya. LOCATION: Alluvial valley, near the Dendho canal; altitude: 2,020 m; 1,400–2,600 m from the Rio Tula; light erosion. POTENTIAL LAND USE: irrigation agriculture and rainfall agriculture on lowlands. PRESENT LAND USE: irrigation agriculture from dams.

APPENDIX

Cluster	Site No.	Photo and Square	Unit	Description and Association with Other Periods	Observations
XXXVII	262	Photo 088 3 4	15, 20 19 11, 12	SITE: Type 5 2 Structures B. Material: disperse. CLASSIC: light. TRANSITIONAL CLASSIC-COYOTLATELCO: Structures/dense. LATE POSTCLASSIC: Structures/very light/light/dense. COLONIAL: very light.	UTM: 463800, 2227250 NEAREST TOWN: S of General Anaya. LOCATION: Alluvial valley; altitude: 2,020 m; between Santa Ana Ahuehuepan aqueduct and Dendho canal, 1,100–1,700 m from the Rio Tula; light erosion. POTENTIAL LAND USE: irrigation agriculture and rainfall agriculture on lowlands. PRESENT LAND USE: irrigation agriculture from dams.
XXXVII	263	Photo 088 3 9 3 9 2 3 8 9	 8 24 6 25 4, 5, 9, 10, 18, 19 2, 7 19 12, 18, 21, 23	SITE: Type 16. DESTROYED. 2 Structures D (1 m high). Material: concentrated and disperse. CLASSIC: Structures/very light/light/dense. TRANSITIONAL CLASSIC-COYOTLATELCO: light. LATE POSTCLASSIC: Structures/very light/light/dense. COLONIAL: very light/dense.	UTM: 463600, 2226800 NEAREST TOWN: Between General Anaya and Santa Ana Ahuehuepan. LOCATION: Alluvial valley; altitude: 2,020 m; between Santa Ana Ahuehuepan aqueduct and Dendho canal, 150–2,300 m from the Rio Tula; light and moderate erosion, moderate vegetation. POTENTIAL LAND USE: irrigation agriculture and rainfall agriculture on lowlands. Others: hunting and gathering plants, fishing. PRESENT LAND USE: irrigation agriculture from dams and rainfall agriculture, abandoned terraces, herding. Others: hunting and gathering plants, firewood.
XXXVII A	264	Photo 088 15 14 15	 8 15, 20 3, 12, 18	SITE: Type 7 3 Structures A. Material: disperse. CLASSIC: Structures/light/dense. TRANSITIONAL CLASSIC-COYOTLATELCO: very light. COYOTLATELCO: very light. LATE POSTCLASSIC: Structures/very light/light/dense. COLONIAL: very light.	UTM: 463250, 2225350 NEAREST TOWN: NW of Santa Ana Ahuehuepan. LOCATION: Near west side of Santa Ana Ahuehuepan aqueduct; altitude: 2,040 m; 250–900 m from the Rio Tula; light erosion. POTENTIAL LAND USE: irrigation agriculture and rainfall agriculture on lowlands. PRESENT LAND USE: town; irrigation agriculture from dams.
XXXVII	265	Photo 088 15 Photo 096 21	 24 2	SITE: Type 3. DESTROYED. Structure D. Material: disperse. CLASSIC: light. LATE POSTCLASSIC: very light. COLONIAL: very light/light.	UTM: 463800, 2225700 NEAREST TOWN: Between General Anaya and Santa Ana Ahuehuepan. LOCATION: Alluvial valley, between Santa Ana Ahuehuepan aqueduct and Dendho canal; altitude: 2,020–2,040 m; 500–1,200 m from the Rio Tula; light erosion. POTENTIAL LAND USE: rainfall agriculture and irrigation agriculture. Others: hunting and gathering plants, fishing. PRESENT LAND USE: town; irrigation agriculture from dams and rainfall agriculture.

APPENDIX

Cluster	Site No.	Photo and Square	Unit	Description and Association with Other Periods	Observations
XXXVII	266	Photo 088 16 11 16	14 3, 4, 10 4	SITE: Type 3 Structure D. Material: disperse. CLASSIC: very light. LATE POSTCLASSIC: very light. COLONIAL: very light.	UTM: 464650, 2225400 NEAREST TOWN: NE of Santa Ana Ahuehuepan. LOCATION: Alluvial valley, between Dendho canal and old Requena canal; altitude: 2,020–2,040 m; 1,900–3,400 m from the Rio Tula; light and moderate erosion. POTENTIAL LAND USE: irrigation agriculture and rainfall agriculture on lowlands. PRESENT LAND USE: town; irrigation agriculture from dams and rainfall agriculture.
XXXVII A	267	Photo 088 16 17 Photo 096 17	25 1, 2, 3, 6, 16, 21, 22 16	SITE: Type 15 Material: disperse. CLASSIC: very light. TRANSITIONAL CLASSIC- COYOTLATELCO: very light. COYOTLATELCO: very light. LATE POSTCLASSIC: Structures/ very light/dense. COLONIAL: very light/light.	UTM: 465150, 2224750 NEAREST TOWN: Santa Ana Ahuehuepan. LOCATION: Near west side of aqueduct; altitude: 2,020–2,040 m; 1,100–2,800 m from the Rio Tula; light and moderate erosion. POTENTIAL LAND USE: irrigation agriculture and rainfall agriculture on lowlands. PRESENT LAND USE: town; irrigation agriculture from dams and rainfall agriculture.
XXXVII A	268	Photo 096 16 16	3 7	SITE: Type 19. LOOTED. 2 Structures: Habitational and Ceremonial, B (Ceremonial mound: 15 m diam. and 2 m high). COYOTLATELCO: very light. LATE POSTCLASSIC: Structures/ light/dense. COLONIAL: very light. Selective Sampling.	UTM: 464150, 2224400 NEAREST TOWN: Santa Ana Ahuehuepan. LOCATION: Lowlands, near Endó dam; altitude: 2,020–2,040 m; 50–500 m from the Rio Tula; light to severe erosion, scarce vegetation. POTENTIAL LAND USE: rainfall agriculture. Others: fishing. PRESENT LAND USE: town; rainfall agriculture, abandoned terraces.
XXXVII A	269	Photo 096 15	10, 11 17	SITE: Type 5 2 Structures, B. Material: disperse. COYOTLATELCO: very light. LATE POSTCLASSIC: very light/light. COLONIAL: very light. Selective Sampling.	UTM: 463200, 2224500 NEAREST TOWN: W of Santa Ana Ahuehuepan. LOCATION: Lowlands, near Endó dam; altitude: 2,020–2,030 m; 100–150 m from the Rio Tula; light and moderate erosion, scarce vegetation. POTENTIAL LAND USE: irrigation agriculture and rainfall agriculture. Others: fishing. PRESENT LAND USE: town; rainfall agriculture.
XXXVII A	270	Photo 096 17	2	SITE: Type 3 Structure D. LATE POSTCLASSIC: very light. Selective Sampling.	UTM: 465100, 2224000 NEAREST TOWN: E of Santa Ana Ahuehuepan. LOCATION: Lowlands; altitude: 2,040 m; between aqueduct and Endó canal, 1,100 m from the Rio Tula; moderate erosion, scarce vegetation. POTENTIAL LAND USE: rainfall agriculture. PRESENT LAND USE: town; rainfall agriculture, herding.

APPENDIX

Cluster	Site No.	Photo and Square	Unit	Description and Association with Other Periods	Observations
XXXVII	271	Photo 096 5 5	11 12, 13, 16, 17, 21, 22	SITE: Type 3 Structure D. Material: disperse. COYOTLATELCO: very light. LATE POSTCLASSIC: Structures/ very light/light. COLONIAL: very light.	UTM: 464900, 2222600 NEAREST TOWN: SE of Santa Ana Ahuehuepan. LOCATION: Lowlands; altitude: 2,040–2,050 m; between aqueduct and Endó canal, 1,000–1,300 m from the Rio Tula; light and moderate erosion, scarce vegetation. POTENTIAL LAND USE: irrigation agriculture and rainfall agriculture. PRESENT LAND USE: rainfall agriculture and irrigation agriculture from dams, herding. Others: hunting and gathering plants, firewood.
XXXVII A	272	Photo 096 10	2, 7	SITE: Type 15 Material: disperse. COYOTLATELCO: light. LATE POSTCLASSIC: Structures/ very light/dense.	UTM: 464250, 2223150 NEAREST TOWN: Between Santa Ana Ahuehuepan and Julian Villagran. LOCATION: Lowlands, W of aqueduct; altitude: 2,060 m; 1,200 m from the Rio Tula; high erosion, scarce vegetation. POTENTIAL LAND USE: rainfall agriculture. Others: fishing. PRESENT LAND USE: town; abandoned terraces, herding.
XXXVII A	273	Photo 096 5 11 12 17	25 14, 20 11, 16, 21 3	SITE: Type 15 Material: disperse. COYOTLATELCO: very light. LATE POSTCLASSIC: very light. COLONIAL: very light.	UTM: 465550, 2223400 NEAREST TOWN: E of Julian Villagran and Santa Ana Ahuehuepan. LOCATION: Between old Requena canal and Endó canal; altitude: 2,040 m; 1,400–2,100 m from the Rio Tula; light erosion. POTENTIAL LAND USE: irrigation agriculture and rainfall agriculture. PRESENT LAND USE: irrigation agriculture from dams.
XXXVII A	274	Photo 103 24 17 Photo 096 6 12 Photo 097 1	6 10, 15 16, 22 2 23	SITE: Type 15 Material: concentrated and disperse. FORMATIVE: very light. TRANSITIONAL CLASSIC-COYOTLATELCO: very light. COYOTLATELCO: light. LATE POSTCLASSIC: very light/light. COLONIAL: very light.	UTM: 465700, 2222150 NEAREST TOWN: NW of Iturbe. LOCATION: Alluvial valley, between old Requena canal and G-5 canal; altitude: 2,040 m; 1,800–2,300 m from the Rio Tula; light erosion. POTENTIAL LAND USE: irrigation agriculture and rainfall agriculture. PRESENT LAND USE: town; irrigation agriculture from dams and rainfall agriculture.
XXXVII A	275	Photo 103 10	24 17	SITE: Type 15 Material: concentrated and disperse. CLASSIC: Structures/dense.	UTM: 464450, 2221850 NEAREST TOWN: S of Julian Villagran. LOCATION: Lowlands; altitude: 2,060 m; 2,000 m from the Rio Tula; moderate erosion. POTENTIAL LAND USE: irrigation agriculture and rainfall agriculture. PRESENT LAND USE: town; rainfall agriculture.

APPENDIX

Cluster	Site No.	Photo and Square	Unit	Description and Association with Other Periods	Observations
XXXIX	276	Photo 12B 4 5 4 5 6	 4 3 3 4 3	SITE: Type 1. DESTROYED. Habitational Structures, A. Material: disperse. Ground stone workshop. LATE POSTCLASSIC: Structures/ very light/light. COLONIAL: very light. Selective Sampling.	UTM: 458600, 2226500 NEAREST TOWN: W of Santa Maria Daxtho. LOCATION: NW lowlands area, Barranca Honda; altitude: 2,060–2,100 m; near the Rio Tula, 50–600 m from the Arroyo Las Adjuntas, 100–600 m from the Barranca and Manantial; moderate and severe erosion, scarce vegetation. POTENTIAL LAND USE: rainfall agriculture. Others: hunting and gathering plants. PRESENT LAND USE: town; rainfall agriculture, herding. Others: hunting and gathering plants, firewood. Quarry: basalt.
XXXIX	277	Photo 12B 16 24 16 20 24	 1 2 1, 3 1 1	SITE: Type 1. DESTROYED. Habitational Structures, A. Material: disperse. Ground stone workshop. LATE POSTCLASSIC: Structures/ very light/light/dense. COLONIAL: very light. Selective Sampling.	UTM: 458750, 2227700 NEAREST TOWN: W of San Pedro Nextlalpan. LOCATION: Lower slopes, NW mountains of area, Barranca Honda; altitude: 2,100–2,140 m; 3,000 m from the Rio Tula, 100–300 m from the Arroyo El Dagul, and 150–200 m from the Barranca; moderate and severe erosion, moderate and dense vegetation. POTENTIAL LAND USE: rainfall agriculture on terraces. Others: hunting and gathering plants. PRESENT LAND USE: town; rainfall agriculture on terraces, abandoned terraces, herding. Others: hunting and gathering plants, firewood. Quarry: basalt.
XXXVIII	278	Photo 12B 21 20 3 15 20 21	 3 2 1 3 2, 4 3	SITE: Type 2. LOOTED. Habitational and Ceremonial Structures, A. Material: concentrated and disperse. COYOTLATELCO: Structures/ very light/light/dense. LATE POSTCLASSIC: Structures/ very light/light. COLONIAL: very light. Selective Sampling.	UTM: 462750, 2218800 LOCATION: Top of hill and west slopes of Cerro Magoni; altitude: 2,100–2,150 m; 300–2,200 m from the Rio Tula and 200–500 m from the Rio Rosas; moderate erosion, scarce and moderate vegetation. POTENTIAL LAND USE: rainfall agriculture on terraces. Others: hunting and gathering plants. PRESENT LAND USE: rainfall agriculture, herding. Others: hunting and gathering plants, firewood. The concentrated zone is on top of the hill. Concentrated and disperse material is on west slope terraces.

APPENDIX

Cluster	Site No.	Photo and Square	Unit	Description and Association with Other Periods	Observations
XXXVIII	279	Photo 12B 14 8 10 14	 4 23 3 3, 4	SITE: Type 2 Habitational and Ceremonial Structures, A. Additional sampling by George Bey. Material: concentrated. COYOTLATELCO: very light/light. LATE POSTCLASSIC: very light. COLONIAL: very light. Selective Sampling.	UTM: 462550, 2221400 Site Hacienda Bojay. NEAREST TOWN: On lands of former Hacienda Bojay. LOCATION: Adjacent to the W of Endó dam, lower slopes; altitude: 2,020–2,030 m; 200–1,000 m from the Rio Tula; moderate erosion, scarce and moderate vegetation. POTENTIAL LAND USE: irrigation agriculture and rainfall agriculture on terraces. Others: fishing. PRESENT LAND USE: rainfall agriculture, abandoned terraces, herding. Others: hunting and gathering plants, firewood.
XXXVIII	280	Photo 096 14 20	 1 1	SITE: Type 2. LOOTED. Undetermined number of Habitational Structures with Ceremonial mound on the hill and semidisperse Structures in periphery, A and C. Additional sampling by George Bey. Material: disperse. COYOTLATELCO: very light/light. LATE POSTCLASSIC: Structures/very light/dense.	UTM: 462350, 2224400 NEAREST TOWN: Barrio El Retiro. LOCATION: Hill, S of El Retiro; altitude: 2,020–2,040 m; 30–200 m from the Rio Tula; moderate erosion, moderate vegetation. POTENTIAL LAND USE: irrigation agriculture and rainfall agriculture on terraces. Others: fishing. PRESENT LAND USE: rainfall agriculture, abandoned terraces, herding. Others: hunting and gathering plants, firewood.
XXXVIII	281	Photo 103 8		SITE: Type 15 Material: disperse.	UTM: 462950, 2220750 NEAREST TOWN: S of Hacienda Bojay. LOCATION: Slopes of Cerro Magoni; altitude: 2,030–2,040 m. Material between the Hacienda Bojay and NW of pre-Hispanic city.
XL	282	Photo 12B 17	 4	SITE: Type 5 2 Structures A. LATE POSTCLASSIC: very light. COLONIAL: very light. Selective Sampling.	UTM: 459000, 2233500 NEAREST TOWN: NE of Sayula. Lowlands; altitude: 2,040 m; near the Rio Tula and 500 m from an intermittent stream; moderate erosion. POTENTIAL LAND USE: rainfall agriculture on terraces. Others: hunting and gathering plants. PRESENT LAND USE: town; rainfall agriculture on terraces.

APPENDIX

Cluster	Site No.	Photo and Square	Unit	Description and Association with Other Periods	Observations
XL	283	Photo 12B 16 26 31	 2 2, 3, 4 2	SITE: Type 15 Material: disperse. CLASSIC: very light. COYOTLATELCO: very light. LATE POSTCLASSIC: very light. COLONIAL: very light. Selective Sampling.	UTM: 459700, 2232500 NEAREST TOWN: S of Sayula. LOCATION: Lowlands, between El Calvario's hill and S of Sayula; altitude: 2,030 m; 50–600 m from the Arroyo Tepetitlan and Arroyo Grande, near the Rio Tula; light and moderate erosion, moderate vegetation. POTENTIAL LAND USE: irrigation agriculture and rainfall agriculture on terraces. Others: hunting and gathering plants. PRESENT LAND USE: town; rainfall agriculture, herding. Others: hunting and gathering plants, firewood.
XXXIX	284	Photo 12B 21 22 20 22 23	 3 1 4 3 2	SITE: Type 15 Material: concentrated and disperse. COYOTLATELCO: very light. LATE POSTCLASSIC: very light. COLONIAL: very light. Selective Sampling.	UTM: 457650, 2228450 NEAREST TOWN: NW of San Pedro Nextlalpan. LOCATION: On both sides of the Arroyo La Joya, slopes of Cerros El Garambuyo and Dagui; altitude: 2,060–2,100 m; near the Rio Tula, 50–300 m from the Arroyo La Joya; moderate and severe erosion, moderate vegetation. POTENTIAL LAND USE: rainfall agriculture and rainfall agriculture on terraces. Others: hunting and gathering plants. PRESENT LAND USE: town; rainfall agriculture and rainfall agriculture on terraces, herding. Others: hunting and gathering plants, firewood.
XXXIX	285	Photo 12B 14 19 13 19	 4 3 2, 4 2	SITE: Type 15 Material: concentrated and disperse. FORMATIVE: very light. LATE POSTCLASSIC: very light. Selective Sampling.	UTM: 459100, 2230000 NEAREST TOWN: S of Tepetitlan. LOCATION: Slopes, N and E of Cerro El Garambuyo; altitude: 2,040–2,070 m; near the Rio Tula and the arroyo; light and moderate erosion. POTENTIAL LAND USE: rainfall agriculture on terraces. Others: hunting and gathering plants. PRESENT LAND USE: town; rainfall agriculture, herding. Others: hunting and gathering plants, firewood.
XXXIX	286	Photo 12B 19	 4	SITE: Type 15 Material: disperse. LATE POSTCLASSIC: light. Selective Sampling.	UTM: 458800, 2231450 NEAREST TOWN: W of Tepetitlan. LOCATION: Lowlands and slopes, S of Cerro Santa Cruz; altitude: 2,070 m; near the Rio Tula and 250 m from the arroyo; moderate erosion. POTENTIAL LAND USE: rainfall agriculture. Others: hunting and gathering plants. PRESENT LAND USE: rainfall agriculture.

APPENDIX

Cluster	Site No.	Photo and Square	Unit	Description and Association with Other Periods	Observations
XL	287	Photo 80 14 13 14	 17 1, 23 7, 12	SITE: Type 15 Material: concentrated and disperse. CLASSIC: light. COYOTLATELCO: very light/ light. LATE POSTCLASSIC: very light. COLONIAL: very light.	UTM: 462100, 2229200 NEAREST TOWN: S of Tepetitlan. LOCATION: Alluvial valley, between Rio Tula and Tepetitlán canal; altitude: 2,000 m; 300–1,600 m from the Rio Tula; light and moderate erosion, moderate and dense vegetation. POTENTIAL LAND USE: irrigation agriculture and rainfall agriculture. Others: hunting and gathering plants. PRESENT LAND USE: town; traditional irrigation agriculture and irrigation agriculture from dams, herding. Others: hunting and gathering plants, firewood. Probable irrigation zone.
XLI	288	Photo 12B 27 29 27	 4 3 1	SITE: Type 5 2 Structures A. Material: concentrated and disperse. LATE POSTCLASSIC: Structures/ light/dense. Selective Sampling.	UTM: 459900, 2235500 NEAREST TOWN: S of Xithi. LOCATION: Slopes of Cerro Xithi, E of El Culantrillo dam; altitude: 2,100–2,150 m; 100–600 m from both sides of Arroyo El Culantrillo; moderate erosion, scarce and moderate vegetation. POTENTIAL LAND USE: rainfall agriculture on terraces. Others: hunting and gathering plants. PRESENT LAND USE: rainfall agriculture on terraces, abandoned terraces, herding. Others: hunting and gathering plants, firewood.
XLI	289	Photo 12B 28 29 27 28	 1 1 1 1, 2	SITE: Type 16 2 Structures D. Material: disperse. COYOTLATELCO: very light. LATE POSTCLASSIC: Structures/ very light/dense. COLONIAL: very light. Selective Sampling.	UTM: 460700, 2235100 NEAREST TOWN: SE of Xithi. LOCATION: Slopes and lower slopes of northern mountains; altitude: 2,130–2,150 m; between two arroyos and near the Rio Tula; light and moderate erosion, scarce and moderate vegetation. POTENTIAL LAND USE: rainfall agriculture and rainfall agriculture on terraces. Others: hunting and gathering plants. PRESENT LAND USE: rainfall agriculture on terraces, herding. Others: hunting and gathering plants, firewood.

APPENDIX

Cluster	Site No.	Photo and Square	Unit	Description and Association with Other Periods	Observations
XLI	290*	Photo 12B 22 22 31 23 31 23 31	 2 2 3 1, 3 3 1 3	SITE: Type 1 Undetermined number of Habitational Structures, A. Material: concentrated and disperse. TRANSITIONAL CLASSIC-COYOTLATELCO: very light. COYOTLATELCO: Structures/very light/dense. LATE POSTCLASSIC: very light/light. COLONIAL: very light. Selective Sampling.	UTM: 461100, 2233600 NEAREST TOWN: NE of Sayula and Tepetitlan. LOCATION: Lower slopes of northern mountains; altitude: 2,000–2,100 m; near the Rio Tula and 50–300 m from the Arroyo El Sabino; moderate erosion, moderate vegetation. POTENTIAL LAND USE: rainfall agriculture on terraces. Others: hunting and gathering plants. PRESENT LAND USE: rainfall agriculture and rainfall agriculture on terraces, abandoned terraces, herding. Others: hunting and gathering plants, firewood.
XXXVIII	292	Photo 12B 15	 1	SITE: Type 15 Material: disperse. COYOTLATELCO: dense. LATE POSTCLASSIC: light. COLONIAL: very light. Selective Sampling.	UTM: 461700, 2221400 LOCATION: On the top and upper slopes, SE of Cerro Bojay; altitude: 2,050–2,100 m; 1,000 m from the Rio Tula; moderate erosion, scarce and moderate vegetation. POTENTIAL LAND USE: hunting and gathering plants. PRESENT LAND USE: herding. Others: hunting and gathering plants, firewood.
XXXVIII	293	Photo 096 7	 9, 10	SITE: Type 15 Material: disperse. COYOTLATELCO: light. LATE POSTCLASSIC: Structures/very light/dense. COLONIAL: very light/light.	UTM: 461750, 2223100 NEAREST TOWN: Barrio El Retiro. LOCATION: Hill; altitude: 2,050 m; 1,100 m from the Rio Tula; light and moderate erosion, moderate vegetation. POTENTIAL LAND USE: rainfall agriculture. Others: hunting and gathering plants. PRESENT LAND USE: abandoned terraces, herding. Others: hunting and gathering plants, firewood.

*SITE 290:

Flanks and lower slopes of northern mountains; altitude: 2,000–2,100 m, NE of Sayula and Tepetitlan towns.

Probably, this settlement extents to the slopes of the mountains, from the dam and the Arroyo Culantrillo to the Arroyo Las Ánimas, to the east.

The main nucleus of settlement is associated with the Manantial and Arroyo El Sabino, on man-made terraces, principally at altitudes 2,050–2,100 m, and extending over the southern slopes of Cerro Tasguada, which have Ceremonial mounds of uncertain chronology because of the high density of Late Postclassic occupations.

There are semidisperse Habitational Structures between the Arroyo El Sabino and the Arroyo Peña Honda. Possibly the settlement extends to the east on slopes of mountains to the town of Atengo. Sampling and delimitation of the site are only preliminary.

There are remains around the Manantial El Sabino, a colonial irrigation system belonging to the Hacienda de Tepetitlán.

One Habitational Structure was excavated in 1984. See Cobean and Mastache (1999) for the site excavation report.

APPENDIX

Cluster	Site No.	Photo and Square	Unit	Description and Association with Other Periods	Observations
XXXVIII	294	Photo 096 2	1	SITE: Type 15 Material: disperse. COYOTLATELCO: very light. LATE POSTCLASSIC: very light. COLONIAL: very light. Selective Sampling.	UTM: 462000, 2222650 NEAREST TOWN: Barrio El Retiro. LOCATION: Lower slopes of Cerro; altitude: 2,050 m; 400 m from the Rio Tula; moderate and high erosion, scarce vegetation. POTENTIAL LAND USE: rainfall agriculture. Others: fishing. PRESENT LAND USE: rainfall agriculture, herding. Others: hunting and gathering plants, firewood.
XXXVIII	295	Photo 096 9	12	SITE: Type 15 Material: disperse. LATE POSTCLASSIC: very light. COLONIAL: very light.	UTM: 463100, 2223500 LOCATION: Hill, E of the Cerro El Venado; altitude: 2,050 m; 350 m from the Rio Tula; high erosion, scarce vegetation. POTENTIAL LAND USE: rainfall agriculture on terraces. Others: fishing. PRESENT LAND USE: abandoned terraces, herding.
XXXVIII A	296	Photo 102 7 10 Photo 12B 20 21	2 6 3 3	SITE: Type 15 Material: disperse. COYOTLATELCO: very light. LATE POSTCLASSIC: very light/dense. Selective Sampling.	UTM: 459050, 2221500 LOCATION: Loma Larga; lowlands; altitude: 2,050–2,100 m; near the Rio Tula, 500 m from the Arroyo San Antonio and 600 m from the Barranca; light to high erosion. POTENTIAL LAND USE: irrigation agriculture and rainfall agriculture. Others: hunting and gathering plants. PRESENT LAND USE: traditional irrigation agriculture and rainfall agriculture, herding. Others: hunting and gathering plants, firewood.
XXXVIII A	297	Photo 12B 15 Photo 152 21 Photo 102 8	3 2 11	SITE: Type 15 Material: disperse. COYOTLATELCO: Structures/very light/light. LATE POSTCLASSIC: Structures/very light/light. COLONIAL: very light. Selective Sampling.	UTM: 458650, 2222450 LOCATION: Loma Larga; lower slopes, between Arroyo El Venado and Arroyo Troneras; altitude: 2,050–2,100 m; near the Rio Tula and 200–600 m from the Arroyo San Antonio; moderate erosion, scarce to dense vegetation. POTENTIAL LAND USE: rainfall agriculture on terraces. Others: hunting and gathering plants. PRESENT LAND USE: rainfall agriculture, abandoned terraces, herding. Others: hunting and gathering plants, firewood.
XXXVIII A	298	Photo 102 5	18, 20	SITE: Type 15 Material: disperse. COYOTLATELCO: Structures/dense. LATE POSTCLASSIC: very light.	UTM: 459750, 2220750 LOCATION: S of Loma Larga; lower slopes, between the Arroyo El Venado and Arroyo Troneras, near the Rio Tula, 700–1,000 m from the arroyo; moderate erosion. POTENTIAL LAND USE: rainfall agriculture. Others: hunting and gathering plants. PRESENT LAND USE: rainfall agriculture.

APPENDIX

Cluster	Site No.	Photo and Square	Unit	Description and Association with Other Periods	Observations
XXXVIII A	299	Photo 12B 4	6	SITE: Type 15 Material: disperse. COYOTLATELCO: very light. LATE POSTCLASSIC: very light. COLONIAL: very light. Selective Sampling.	UTM: 460200, 2219250 NEAREST TOWN: N of San Andres. LOCATION: On lower slopes, near the Rio Tula, 1,000 m from the arroyo; moderate erosion, scarce vegetation. POTENTIAL LAND USE: rainfall agriculture. Others: hunting and gathering plants. PRESENT LAND USE: rainfall agriculture, herding. Others: hunting and gathering plants, firewood.
XXXVIII A	300	Photo 12B 1 2 3	4 3 16	SITE: Type 15 Material: disperse. COYOTLATELCO: Structures/ light. LATE POSTCLASSIC: very light. Selective Sampling.	UTM: 459100, 2219800 LOCATION: S of Loma Larga; lowlands, 2,500 m from the Rio Tula and 300–500 m from an intermittent stream; moderate erosion, scarce and moderate vegetation. POTENTIAL LAND USE: rainfall agriculture on terraces. Others: hunting and gathering plants. PRESENT LAND USE: rainfall agriculture on terraces, abandoned terraces, herding. Others: hunting and gathering plants, firewood.
XLII	301	Photo 12B 16	10, 12	SITE: Type 3 Structure D. Material: disperse. LATE POSTCLASSIC: dense. COLONIAL: very light. Selective Sampling.	UTM: 456050, 2217000 NEAREST TOWN: Xochitlan. LOCATION: Lowlands; altitude: 2,220–2,240 m; 1,000 m from the Rio Rosas; light erosion. POTENTIAL LAND USE: irrigation agriculture and rainfall agriculture. PRESENT LAND USE: town; traditional irrigation agriculture. Material found in downtown Xochitlan.
XLII	302	Photo 12B 7 8 15	8 2 2, 6	SITE: Type 1 Undetermined number of Habitational Structures, A. Material: disperse. COYOTLATELCO: very light. LATE POSTCLASSIC: very light. Selective Sampling.	UTM: 452450, 2220650 NEAREST TOWN: W of San Antonio Tula. LOCATION: Lowlands, near the El Huizache dam; altitude: 2,200–2,240 m; 50–500 m from the Arroyo El Tecolote; light and moderate erosion. POTENTIAL LAND USE: rainfall agriculture. Others: hunting and gathering plants. PRESENT LAND USE: traditional irrigation agriculture and rainfall agriculture.
XLII	303	Photo 12B 15 21	11 2	SITE: Type 1 Undetermined number of Habitational Structures, A. LATE POSTCLASSIC: Structures/ dense. COLONIAL: dense. Selective Sampling.	UTM: 449050, 2221200 NEAREST TOWN: SW of Carranza. LOCATION: Lowlands, SE of Julian Villagran dam; altitude: 2,260–2,280 m; 50 m from the arroyo, light erosion. POTENTIAL LAND USE: irrigation agriculture and rainfall agriculture. PRESENT LAND USE: town; traditional irrigation agriculture.

Cluster	Site No.	Photo and Square	Unit	Description and Association with Other Periods	Observations
XLII	304	Photo 12B 31	2	SITE: Type 1. LOOTED. Undetermined number of Habitational Structures, A. LATE POSTCLASSIC: light.	UTM: 446700, 2223400 NEAREST TOWN: Between Xiteje and San Juan Daxthi. LOCATION: Hill, near the Macua dam; altitude: 2,340 m; on basaltic outcrop, 100 m from the arroyo; moderate erosion, scarce vegetation. POTENTIAL LAND USE: rainfall agriculture. Others: fishing. PRESENT LAND USE: traditional irrigation agriculture and rainfall agriculture, herding.
XLII	305	Photo 12B 14	10	SITE: Type 15 Material: disperse. COYOTLATELCO: very light. LATE POSTCLASSIC: very light. Selective Sampling.	UTM: 453100, 2222000 NEAREST TOWN: NW of San Antonio Tula. LOCATION: Lowlands, N of El Temporal dam; altitude: 2,220–2,250 m; 1,500 m from the Barranca; moderate and severe erosion. POTENTIAL LAND USE: rainfall agriculture. PRESENT LAND USE: rainfall agriculture.
XLIII	306*	Photo 12B 26 27 35	4 3 4	SITE: Type 15 Material: disperse. COYOTLATELCO: very light/ dense. LATE POSTCLASSIC: very light. Selective Sampling.	UTM: 463800, 2216250 NEAREST TOWN: N of San Marcos. LOCATION: Lowlands, upper slopes and on the top of Cerro, 300–2,000 m from the Rio Tula; light and severe erosion, scarce vegetation. POTENTIAL LAND USE: irrigation agriculture, rainfall agriculture, and rainfall agriculture on terraces. Others: hunting and gathering plants, fishing. PRESENT LAND USE: town; irrigation agriculture from dams, abandoned terraces, herding.

*The total number of sites is 304, because there are no sites having the numbers 112 and 291.

List of Clusters

I   Lower foothills and slopes southeast of the sierra that limits the area to the north; northern side of the Tula River; approximate altitude of 1,980 to 2,080 m. It is divided into two sub-zones: the foothills and slopes as such, and the lowlands adjacent to the Tula River on the northern edge.

II   Northern side of the Tula River; highlands with an altitude of approximately 1,980 m.

III   Southeast of the Tula River and east of the Salado River at an altitude between 2,060 and 2,100 m.

IV   Meseta between the Tula and Salado Rivers, approximately 2,100 m.

V   The beginning of the Valle del Mezquital. A small valley to the south of the present town of Mixquiahuala. An altitude of approximately 2,100 m. Next to the modern Endó canal.

VI   South Mixquiahuala Valley to the east of the town of Tezontepec; on lower lands than Zone V, at an altitude of 2,020 to 2,100 m.

VII   South Mixquiahuala Valley, extreme southwest. At an altitude of 2,080 m, to the north of the modern Requena canal, between the present towns of Mangas and Presas.

VIII   South bank of the Tula River, at an altitude of approximately 2,100 m.

IX   Prolongation of Zone VIII; lowlands; south bank of the Tula River.

X   Zone between the Salado River and the foothills of the sierra that limits the area to the east. The sites to the west of Cerro de la Cruz next to the modern Requena canal and on higher lands nearby.

XI   Cerro Huitel, north, east, and south foothills.

XII   Alluvial valley to the north of Cerro Xicuco at an altitude of 2,020 to 2,040 m; that is, between the old Requena canal and the modern Endó canal. It extends to the south of Cerro Huitel on a narrow strip with scarce and very dispersed material.

XIII   Hill to the north of Cerro Xicuco, at an altitude of approximately 2,040 m; including lands above the old Requena canal.

XIV   Foothills of the sierra limiting the area to the east. Northwest of Cerro La Mesa and Cerro Tumba of Mixquia-huala, at an altitude of 2,020 to 2,040 m; the zone between the modern Requena and Alto Requena canals.

XV   South Xicuco. South foothill of Cerro Xicuco at an altitude of 2,060 and 2,100 m; in lands higher than the modern G-5 canal, which constitutes the arbitrary limit used to separate this cluster from cluster XVI on lower lands.

XVI	Alluvial valley and foothills of Cerro Xicuco, to the south and west of the modern G-5 canal, on lower lands at an altitude of 2,040 to 2,060 m. This and the previous cluster should probably not be separated given the continuity and characteristics of the occupation; the criterion for the separation into two clusters is their different altitudes.
XVII	Eastern foothills of Cerro Colorado, which constitute the NE prolongation of Cerro Xicuco at an altitude of 2,040 to 2,100 m.
XVIII	East Xicuco, foothills, at an altitude of 2,040 to 2,060 m; east of the G-5 canal.
XIX	Alluvial valley to the west of the Salado River divided into three sub-zones: center and west; the latter has very dispersed occupation near the Salado River.
XX	Alluvial valley to the south of Xicuco divided into three sub-zones. The latter borders on the extreme northeast of the pre-Hispanic city. Sub-cluster XIX could form part of this zone and not part of XIX.
XXa	Eastern periphery of the pre-Hispanic city.
XXI	East of the pre-Hispanic city on lowlands at an altitude of 2,080 to 2,100 m; with irrigation potential. The zone between the modern Endó and No. 3 canals.
XXII	Lowlands below an altitude of 2,100 m to the southeast of the pre-Hispanic city; scarce occupation. A cluster with irrigation potential divided into two sub-zones: north and south.
XXIII	Loma Hacienda de Chingú and surrounding area; associated with the colonial irrigation system. La Romera and the irrigable strip surrounding it at an altitude of 2,080 to 2,100 m. It is divided into three sub-zones: west, center, and east. The center sub-zone corresponds to the area sampled by Clara Díaz as part of the project and published in her monograph on the Classic settlement of Chingú (1980).
XXIV	Sierra to the east of the area; western foothills of Cerro La Mesa, El Aguila, Picachos, and Buenavista; principally between an altitude of 2,100 and 2,140 m. Settlement to the east (above) the modern Tlamaco Juando canal.
XXV	Lowlands between the Salado River and the sierra to the east of the area (Cerro La Mesa, El Aguila, Picachos, Buenavista, and Mesa Lechuguilla) at an altitude of 2,060 to 2,100 m, that is, below the modern Tlamaco Juando canal. It is divided into four sub-zones: north, center, east, and south.
XXVI	Foothills and lowlands of the sierra to the southeast of the area, between the Salado River and Mesa Lechguilla, Cerros La Cantera and Las Palmas, at an altitude of 2,100 to 2,180 m; divided into three sub-zones: north, center, and south.
XXVII	Hills to the west of the Salado River at an altitude of 2,120 to 2,160 m. It covers an area between the modern towns of Bominza, Progreso, and Tlamaco; that is, the zone of extensive pre-Hispanic limestone exploitation, which is probably associated with sites with this activity and rainfall agriculture. The CFE Thermoelectric Station and the Pemex Refinery were built to the west and northwest of this area. These facilities cover squares 1, 2, 3, 7, 8, 13, and 14 of Photo 115; squares 5, 6, 11, 12, 17, and 18 of Photo 114; square 6 of Photo 109; and square 1 south of Photo 110. Thus, the area could not be systematically surveyed and the periphery was partially sampled. Consequently, the void that appears on the map is due to this and the settlement could have continued without interruption between this cluster and No. XXX sierra to the south of the area.
XXVIII	Hills and foothills at an altitude of 2,150 to 2,200 m. It is divided into three sub-zones: east, west, and southwest. Intensive limestone exploitation. The sub-zone with highest occupation density is between the modern towns of Ocampo, Conejos, and Cañada. The second with dispersed occupation is south of the town of Atotonilco. The third is southwest of the town of Conejos. Dispersed materials.
XXIX	Sierra on the southeast of the area; south Bominza at an altitude of 2,100 to 2,200 m. Very dispersed occupation.
XXX	Hills north and east of Cerro Bominza at an altitude of 2,100 to 2,200 m. Rainfall agriculture.
XXXI	Lowlands on both banks of the Tula River. A sector with pre-Hispanic irrigation potential.

XXXIa	Lowlands on both banks of the Tlautla River.
XXXII	Sierra to the east and west of the El Salto River. Foothills and hills principally between altitudes of 2,150 and 2,200 m. It is divided into two sub-zones: north and south, the former with more dispersed occupation. These sites are apparently associated with colonial irrigation systems. This cluster was not fully surveyed.
XXXIII	Hills between the El Salto and Tula Rivers at an altitude of 2,180 to 2,200 m. Southeast of the Requena Dam. Dispersed occupation.
XXXIV	Sierra east of the Tula River, hills and foothills at an altitude of 2,100 and 2,200 m between the modern towns of San Miguel Vindho and San Jose Acocula. This sector is currently subject to intensive limestone exploitation.
XXXV	Sierra to the west of the Tula River, between the Tlautla River and the Requena Dam. Hills and foothills at an altitude of 2,080 to 2,200 m. It is divided into four sub-zones with dispersed occupation, separated by areas without occupation. This cluster does not have a full systematic survey.
XXXVI	Sierra to the north of the Tlautla River. Hills and foothills. There was no systematic survey in this cluster.
XXXVII	Alluvial valley to the east of the Tula River. Lowlands with irrigation potential at an approximate altitude of 2,020 to 2,040 m. The modern Dendho canal and Santa Ana pipeline to the west cross this area. The traditional San Gabriel Canal runs to the north. The south sub-zone is a narrow strip of dispersed material to the east and west of the old Requena Canal.
XXXVIIa	To the west of the above cluster, it is divided into two sub-zones: north and south, the latter with very dispersed occupation borders on the north of the pre-Hispanic city.
XXXVIII	Sierra Magoni–Bojay–El Venado borders in the east with the Tula River and the pre-Hispanic city. It is at an altitude of 2,000 to 2,100 m and is divided into four sub-zones: Magoni, Bojay, Venado, and Retiro.
XXXVIIIa	Foothills and hills to the west of zone XXXVIII, between the Rosas River and Arroyo Los Organos. Very dispersed occupation zone.
XXXIX	Sierra to the west of the area, foothills at an altitude of 2,040 to 2,140 m from Cerro de la Santa Cruz on the north and Santa Ma. Daxtho on the south.
XL	Zone next to the Arroyo Grande Sayula Tepetitlan and the traditional Tepetitlán canal. At an altitude of 2,000 to 2,040 m the sub-zone to the southwest is between the northern channel of the Tepetitlán canal and the Tula River. A zone with potential pre-Hispanic irrigation.
XLI	Foothills of the Sierra Norte of the area between the El Culantrillo Arroyo and the Las Animas Arroyo. It is divided into two sub-zones: northwest and northeast, both of which are associated with springs. The first is associated with the El Culantrillo Spring and the second with El Sabino. The area between this cluster and cluster I was not studied and it is probably that the occupation continued almost without interruption along the foothills up to Cerro de la Cruz and the present town of Santiago Acuyutlán.
XLII	Diverse sites on the northwest sierra of the area associated with various traditional irrigation systems and probably related to their care and maintenance during the Toltec period. There is no full systematic survey for the area.

Bibliography

Abascal Macías, R. (editor)
  1982. *Proyecto arqueológico Tula.* 9 vols. Archivo Técnico de la Coordinación Nacional de Arqueología, INAH. México.

Acosta, Jorge R.
  1940. "Exploraciones en Tula, Hidalgo, 1940." *Revista Mexicana de Estudios Antropológicos* 4: 172–194. México.
  1941. "Los últimos descubrimientos arqueológicos en Tula, Hidalgo, 1941." *Revista Mexicana de Estudios Antropológicos* 5: 239–243.
  1942. "La ciudad de Quetzalcoatl." *Cuadernos Americanos* 1, no. 2: 121–131.
  1943. "Los colosos de Tula." *Cuadernos Americanos* 1, no. 2: 133–146.
  1944. "La tercera temporada de exploraciones arqueológicas en Tula, Hgo., 1942." *Revista Mexicana de Estudios Antropológicos* 6: 125–164.
  1945. "La cuarta y quinta temporada de exploraciones arqueológicas en Tula, Hgo." *Revista Mexicana de Estudios Antropológicos* 7: 23–64.
  1956a. "Resumen de los informes de las exploraciones arqueológicas en Tula, Hidalgo, durante las VI, VII y VIII temporadas 1946–1950." *Anales del INAH* 8: 37–115.
  1956b. "El enigma de los Chac Mooles de Tula." *Homenaje al Dr. Manuel Gamio:* 159–170. INAH.
  1956–1957. "Interpretación de algunos de los datos obtenidos en Tula relativos a la época tolteca." *Revista Mexicana de Estudios Antropológicos* 14: 75–110.
  1957. "Resumen de los informes de las exploraciones arqueológicas en Tula, Hidalgo, durante las IX y X temporadas, 1953–54." *Anales del INAH* 9: 119–169.
  1959. "Técnicas de reconstrucción." *Esplendor de México Antiguo* 11: 501–518. Centro de Investigaciones Antropológicas de México.
  1960. "Las exploraciones en Tula, Hidalgo, durante la XI temporada, 1955." *Anales del INAH* 11: 39–72.

1961a. "La doceava temporada de exploraciones en Tula, Hidalgo." *Anales del INAH* 13: 29–58.

1961b. "La indumentaria de los cariátides de Tula." *Homenaje a Pablo Martínez del Río:* 221–228. INAH.

1964. "La décimo tercera temporada de exploraciones en Tula, Hgo." *Anales del INAH* 16: 45–76.

1967. *Tula* (Guía). INAH. México

1968. *Tula: Official Guide.* INAH. México.

1974. "La Pirámide del Corral de Tula, Hgo," in *Proyecto Tula,* 1a. parte. Colección Científia No. 15: pp. 27–56, INAH. México.

1983. "Datos arqueológicos de la zona de Tula," in *Antología de Teotihuacan a los Aztecas. Fuentes de interpretación históricas:* pp. 86–107. Lecturas Universitarias 11, UNAM. México.

Acosta, Jorge R., and Pablo Martínez del Río
1957. *Tula* (Guía). INAH. México.

Acosta, Jorge R., and Hugo Moedano
n.d. Unpublished field notes, 1942. Archivo Técnico, Coordinación Nacional de Arqueología, INAH. México.

Adams, Robert McC.
1981. *Heartland of Cities.* University of Chicago Press. Chicago.

Alden, John R.
1979. "A Reconstruction of Toltec Period Political Units in the Valley of Mexico," in C. Renfrew and K. Cooke (editors), *Transformations: Mathematical Approaches to Culture Change:* pp. 169–200. Academic Press. New York.

Altschul, Jeffrey H.
1981. "Spatial and Statistical Evidence for Social Groupings at Teotihuacan, México." Ph.D. dissertation. Brandeis University. Waltham, MA.

Anales de Cuauhtitlan
1945. *Códice Chimalpopoca: Anales de Cuauhtitlan y leyenda de los soles,* P. F. Velázquez (editor). UNAM. México.

Anguiano, Marina, and Matilde Chapa
1976. "Estratificación social en Tlaxcala durante el siglo XVI," in Pedro Carrasco, Johanna Broda et al. (editors), *Estratificación social en la Mesoamérica prehispánica:* pp. 118–156. SEP-INAH. México.

Angulo, Jorge
1996. "Teotihuacan: Aspectos de la cultura a través de su expresión pictórica," in Beatriz de la Fuente (coordinator), *La pintura mural prehispánica en México: Teotihuacan:* vol. II, pp. 65–186. UNAM. México.

Armillas, Pedro
1947. "La serpiente emplumada, Quetzalcoatl y Tlaloc." *Cuadernos Americanos* 1: 161–178.

1950. "Teotihuacan, Tula y los toltecas: Las culturas post-arcaicas y pre-aztecas del centro de México: Excavaciones y estudios, 1922–1950." *RUNA* 3: 37–70.

Avilez, María Rosa
1997. "Noticias de Soyaniquilpan, Estado de México." *Expresión Antropológica* 4–5: 49–59. Toluca.

Bedoian, William H.
1973. "Oro y Maíz: The Economic Structure of the Mexica Empire and Its Effects on Social Stratification and Political Power." Master's thesis. Pennsylvania State University. University Park.

Benfer, Alice N.
1974. "A Preliminary Analysis of Obsidian Artifacts from Tula, Hidalgo," in Richard A. Diehl (editor), *Studies of Ancient Tollan:* pp. 88–94. University of Missouri. Columbia.

Benz, Bruce F.
1986. "Taxonomy and Evolution of Mexican Maize." Ph.D. dissertation. University of Wisconsin. Madison.

1987. "Racial Systematics and the Evolution of Mexican Maize," in L. Manzanilla (editor), *Studies in the Neolithic and Urban revolutions:* pp. 12–136. BAR International Series No. 349. Oxford.

1999. "Morphological Studies of Maize from Tula, Tepetitlán and Tula Chico," in R. H. Cobean and A. G. Mastache (coordinators), *Tepetitlán: Un espacio doméstico rural en el area de Tula:* pp. 157–170. INAH–University of Pittsburgh. México.

Bernal, Ignacio
1963. *Teotihuacan: Descubrimientos, reconstrucciones.* INAH. México.

Bey, George
1986. "A Regional Analysis of Toltec Ceramics, Tula Hidalgo, Mexico." Ph.D. dissertation. Tulane University. New Orleans.

Beyer, Hermann
1955. "La procesión de los señores." *El México Antiguo* 8: 8–42.

Binford, L. R., S. R. Binford, R. Whallon, and M. A. Hardin
1970. "Archaeology at Hatchery West." *Society for American Archaeology Memoirs* 24.

Blanton, R. E., and J. R. Parsons
1971. "Ceramic Markers," in J. R. Parsons (editor), *Prehistoric Settlement Patterns in the Texcoco Region, Mexico:* pp. 255–314. Memoirs of the Museum of Anthropology, No. 3. University of Michigan. Ann Arbor.

Bolviken, E., E. Helskog, K. Helskog, I. Olsen, L. Solheim, and R. Bertelsen
1982. "Correspondence Analysis: An Alternative to Principal Components." *World Archaeology* 14: 41–60.

Bonfil Olivera, Alicia
1998. "Areas de actividad en La Mesa, Hidalgo: Ejemplo de una sociedad del Epiclásico en la región de Tula, Hidalgo." Tesis de licenciatura. Escuela Nacional de Antropología e Historia. México.

Boone, Elizabeth H. (editor)
1987. *The Aztec Templo Mayor*. Dumbarton Oaks. Washington, DC.

Borah, W., and S. F. Cook
1963. "The Aboriginal Population of Central México on the Eve of the Spanish Conquest." *Ibero-Americana* 54. University of California Press. Berkeley.

Bourges, Héctor
1984. "Panorama de la alimentación y la nutrición en México," in T. R. Trujillo (editor), *Seminario sobre la alimentación en México:* pp. 27–49. Instituto de Geografía. UNAM. México.

Braniff, Beatriz
1961. "Artefactos líticos de San Luis Potosí: Ensayo de sistematización." Tesis de maestría. ENAH. México.
1972. "Secuencias arqueológicas en Guanajuato y la Cuenca de México: Intento de correlación," in *Teotihuacan: Onceava Mesa Redonda*. SMA. México.
1974. "Oscilación de la frontera septentrional mesoamericana," in B. Bell (editor), *The Archaeology of West Mexico*. Ajijic. México.
1975. "La estratigrafía de Villa de Reyes, S.L.P.: Un sitio en la frontera de Mesoamérica." *Cuadernos de los Centros* No. 17, INAH. México.
1998. *Morales, Guanajuato y la tradición Chupicuaro*. Colección Científica, INAH. México.
1999. *Morales, Guanajuato y la tradición Tolteca*. Colección Científica, INAH. México.

Broda, Johanna
1976. "Los estamentos en el ceremonial Méxica," in Pedro Carrasco, Johanna Broda et al. (editors), *Estratificación social en la Mesoamérica prehispánica:* pp. 37–66. SEP-INAH. México.
1982. "El culto mexica de los cerros y el agua." *Revista Multidisciplinaria*, año 3, no. 7: 45–56. Escuela Nacional de Estudios Profesionales Acatlán. UNAM. México.

Brown, Roy B.
1992. *Arqueología y paleoecología del norcentro de México*. Colección Científica 262. INAH. México.

Brumfiel, Elizabeth M., and John W. Fox (editors)
1994. *Factional Competition and Political Development in the New World*. Cambridge University Press. Cambridge.

Cabezas, L. G., and R. H. Cobean (coordinators)
2009 *Proyecto de Investigación, Conservacion y Mantenimiento para la Zona Arqueologica de Tula, Hidalgo*. (4 vols.). Archivo Tecnico, Coordinacion Nacional de Arqueologia, INAH, México.

Calnek, Edward E.
1974. "Conjunto urbano y modelo residencial en Tenochtitlan," in A. Moreno Toscano (editor), *Ensayos sobre el desarrollo urbano de México*. SEP-Setentas. México.
1976. "The Internal Structure of Tenochtitlan," in E. Wolf (editor), *The Valley of México: Studies in Prehispanic Ecology and Society:* pp. 287–302. University of New Mexico Press. Albuquerque.
n.d. *The Urban Structure of Tenochtitlan*. Manuscript.

Camargo Valverde, Lourdes
n.d. "La población prehispánica de La Mesa, Hgo." *Informe, Proyecto Tula y su Area directa de Interacción*. INAH. México.

Carrasco, Pedro
1964. "Family Structure in Sixteenth-Century Tepoztlan," in R. A. Manners (editor), *Process and Pattern in Culture:* pp. 185–210. Aldine. Chicago.
1967. "Relaciones sobre la organización social indígena en el siglo XVI," *Estudios de Cultura Nahuátl* 7: 119–154. UNAM. México.
1971. "The Peoples of Central Mexico and Their Historical Traditions," in R. Wauchope (editor), *The Handbook of Middle American Indians*, vol. 11: 459–473. University of Texas Press. Austin.
1972. "La casa y la hacienda de un señor tlahuica." *Estudios de Cultura Nahuátl* 10: 225–244. UNAM. México.
1973. "Los documentos sobre las tierras de los indios nobles de Tepeaca en el siglo XVI." *Comunicaciones, Proyecto Puebla-Tlaxcala* 7: 89–91. Fundación Alemana para la Investigación Científica. Puebla.
1976a. "La sociedad mexicana antes de la conquista." *Historia General de México* 1: 165–288. El Colegio de México. México.
1976b. "Estratificación social indígena en Morelos durante el siglo XVI," in Pedro Carrasco, Johanna Broda et al. (editors), *Estratificación social en la Mesoamérica prehispánica:* pp. 102–117. SEP-INAH, México.
1996. *Estructura político-territorial del imperio Tenochca.* El Colegio de México. México.

Carrasco, David (editor)
1991. *Aztec Ceremonial Landscapes.* University Press of Colorado. Niwot.

Caso, Alfonso
1941. "El complejo arqueológico de Tula y las grandes culturas indígenas." *Revista Mexicana de Estudios Antropológicos* 5: 85–95.
1956. "Los barrios antiguos de Tenochtitlan y Tlatelolco." *Memorias de la Academia Mexicana de la Historia* 15: 7–63.

Caso Alfonso, I. Bernal, and J. R. Acosta
1967. *La cerámica de Monte Albán.* Memorias del INAH, vol. 13. México.

Castañeda, Carlos
1989. "Los talleres de obsidiana en San Bartolo Agua Caliente, Gto.," in M. Gaxiola G. and John E. Clark (editors), *La obsidiana en Mesoamérica:* pp. 277–295. INAH. México.

Castells, Manuel
1982. *La cuestión urbana.* Siglo XXI. México.

Castillo, Noemí, and Alfredo Dumaine
1988. "Escultura en piedra procedente de la zona arqueológica de Tula, Hidalgo, México." *Beitrage zur Allgemeinen und Vergleichenden Archaologie* 8: 213–282. Verlag Philipp Von Zabern. Mainz.

Charlton, Thomas
1970. "Contemporary Agriculture of the Valley," in W. T. Sanders (editor), *The Natural Environment, Contemporary Occupation and Sixteenth-Century Population of the Valley.* The Teotihuacan Valley Project Final Report, vol. 1. Pennsylvania State University. University Park.
1972. "Population Trends in the Teotihuacan Valley, A.D. 1400–1969." *World Archaeology* 4 (11): 106–123.

Charlton, Thomas H., and Deborah H. Nichols
1997. "Diachronic Studies of City-States: Permutations on a Theme: Central Mexico from 1700 B.C. to A.D. 1600," in D. L. Nichols and T. H. Charlton (editors), *The Archaeology of City-States:* pp. 169–207. Smithsonian Institution. Washington, DC.

Charnay, Desire
1885. *Les anciennes villes du nouveau monde.* Hachette. Paris.
1887. *The Ancient Cities of the New World.* Chapman and Hall. London.

Claessen, Henry, and Peter Skalnik (editors)
1978. *The Early State.* Mouton Publishers. The Hague.

Cobean, Robert H.
1974. "Archaeological Survey of the Tula Region," in R. A. Diehl (editor), *Studies of Ancient Tollan: A Report of the University of Missouri Tula Archaeological Project.* University of Missouri. Columbia.
1978. "The Pre-Aztec Ceramics of Tula, Hidalgo, Mexico." Ph.D. dissertation. Harvard University. Cambridge, MA.
1982. "Investigaciones recientes en Tula Chico, Hidalgo," in A. G. Mastache, A. M. Crespo, R. H. Cobean, and D. M. Healan (editors), *Etudios sobre la antigua ciudad de Tula:* pp. 37–122. Colección Científica No. 121. INAH. México.

1990. *La cerámica de Tula, Hidalgo*. Estudios sobre Tula 2, INAH. México.
1991. "Un definición de los principales yacimientos de obsidiana en el Centro de México." *Arqueología* 5. INAH. México.
1994. "El mundo tolteca." *Arqueología Mexicana*, vol. 2, no. 7: 14–19. INAH–Editorial Raíces. México.
2000. "A Chronological Framework for the Beginnings of Tula." Paper presented at the 65th Annual Meeting of the Society for American Archaeology, Philadelphia.
In press. *A World of Obsidian: The Mining and Trade of Volcanic Glass in Ancient México*. INAH–University of Pittsburgh. México.
n.d. "La ocupación clásica en la región de Tula." INAH. México.

Cobean, Robert H. (coordinator)
1994. *Proyecto: Mantenimiento, conservación y estudio de la Zona Arqueológica de Tula, Hidalgo*, 6 vols. Informe al INAH. México.

Cobean, R. H., and A. G. Mastache
1985. "La cerámica importada de Tula, Hgo." *Arqueología* 1: 89–132. INAH.
1988. "La excavación monumental en Tula," in C. García Mora and M. L. del Valle Berrocal (editors), *La antropología en México: Panorama histórico*, vol. 6. Colección Biblioteca, INAH. México.
1989. "The Late Classic and Early Postclassic Chronology of the Tula Region," in D. M. Healan (editor), *Tula of the Toltecs:* pp. 34–46. University of Iowa Press. Iowa City.
1995. "Tula," in Leonardo López Luján, Robert H. Cobean, and Alba Guadalupe Mastache, *Xochicalco y Tula:* pp. 143–237. Jaca Book. Milan.
1999. "Jorge R. Acosta," in Tim Murray (editor), *The History of Archaeology: An Encyclopedia: The Great Archaeologists*. Garland Press. New York.
In press. "Toltec," in David Carrasco (editor), *The Oxford Encyclopedia of Mesoamerican Cultures*. Oxford University Press. New York.

Cobean, R. H., and A. G. Mastache (coordinators)
1999. *Tepetitlán: Un espacio domestico rural en el area de Tula*. INAH–University of Pittsburgh. México.

n.d. *Ofrendas en un palacio tolteca: Turquesa y concha en el Palacio Quemado de Tula, Hidalgo*. INAH. México.

Cobean, R. H., E. J. Garcia, and A. G. Mastache
2012 *Tula*. Fondo de Cultura Economica. México.

Cobean R. H., A. G. Mastache, A. M. Crespo, and C. L. Díaz
1981. "La cronología de la región de Tula," in E. Rattray, J. Litvak K., and C. L. Díaz (coordinators), *Interacción cultural en México central:* pp. 187–214. UNAM. México.

Cobean, R. H., and M. E. Suárez
1989. *Informe de las excavaciones en Tula Chico, temporada 1989*. Archivo de la Coordinación Nacional de Arqueología, INAH. México.

Codex Aubin
1963. *Códice Aubin, historia de la nación mexicana*. Charles E. Dibble, translator and editor. Edición José Porrúa Turanzas. Madrid.

Codex Ixtlilxóchitl
1976. *Codex Ixtlilxóchitl, Bibliothéque Nationale, Paris (Ms. Mexicain 65–71)*. Jacqueline de Durand-Forest, commentator. Akademische Druck-u. Verlagsanstalt. Graz.

Codice Borgia
1963. With commentaries by Eduard Seler. 3 vols. Fondo de Cultura Económica. México.

Coe, Michael D.
1962. *Mexico*. Frederick A. Prager. New York.
1994. *Mexico: From the Olmecs to the Aztecs*. 4th ed. Thames and Hudson. London.

Coggins, Clemency Chase
1987. "New Fire at Chichen Itza," in *Memorias del Primer Coloquio Internacional de Mayistas:* pp. 427–484. UNAM. México.

Coggins, Clemency Chase, and Orín C. Shane III
1984. *Cenote of Sacrifice: Maya Treasures from the Sacred Well at Chichen Itzá*. University of Texas Press. Austin.

Cohen, Ronald, and Elman R. Service
1978. *Origins of the State*. Institute for the Study of Human Issues. Philadelphia.

Cook de Leonard, Carmen
1956– "Algunos antecedentes de la cerámica tolteca."
1957. *Revista Mexicana de Estudios Antropológicos* 14: 37–43.

Cowgill, George L.
1979. "Teotihuacan, Internal Militaristic Competition and the Fall of the Classic Maya," in N. Hammond and G. R. Willey (editors), *Maya Archaeology and Ethnohistory:* pp. 51–62. University of Texas Press. Austin.
1997. "State and Society at Teotihuacan, México." *Annual Review of Anthropology* 26: 129–161.

Cowgill, George, Jeffrey H. Altschul, and Rebeca S. Sload
1984. "Spatial Analysis of Teotihuacan: A Mesoamerican Metropolis," in Harold J. Hietala (editor), *Intrasite Spatial Analysis in Archaeology:* pp. 154–195. Cambridge University Press. Cambridge.

Crespo, Ana María
1970. "Artefactos líticos de un sitio rural en la frontera norte de Mesoamérica," in *35 Reunión de la Society for American Archaeology.* México.
1976. "Uso del suelo y patrón de poblamiento en el área de Tula, Hgo." *Proyecto Tula,* 2a. parte. Colección Científica No. 33, INAH. México.

Crespo, Ana María, and Alba Guadalupe Mastache
1973. "Reconocimiento de superficie en el area de Tula, Hgo." *Balance y Perspectiva de la Antropología:* 365–371. Sociedad Mexicana de Antropología, XIII Mesa Redonda. Jalapa.
1981. "La presencia en el area de Tula, Hgo. de grupos relacionados con el Barrio de Oaxaca en Teotihuacan," in E. C. Rattray, J. Litvak K., and Clara Díaz O. (editors), *Interacción cultural en México central:* pp. 99–106. UNAM. México.

Crumley, Carole
1976. "Toward a Locational Definition of State Systems of Settlement." *American Anthropologist* 78: 59–73.

Cuellar, Alfredo
1981. *Tezcatzoncatl Escultórico o el Chac-Mool.* Avangráfica, S.A. México.

Cuevas, J. A., E. Hernández X., T. Rojas R., and J. García
1991. "Estudio de recursos fitogenéticos en el Totonacapan," in R. Ortega et al. (editors), *Avances en el estudio de los recursos fitogenéticos de México:* pp. 137–160. Sociedad Mexicana de Fitogenética, A.C. México.

Davies, Nigel
1977. *The Toltecs: Until the Fall of Tula.* University of Oklahoma Press. Norman.
1980. *The Toltec Heritage: From the Fall of Tula to the Rise of Tenochtitlan.* University of Oklahoma Press. Norman.

De la Fuente, Beatriz
1990. "Retorno al pasado tolteca." *Artes de México.* Nueva Epoca 7: 36–53. México.

De la Fuente, Beatriz (coordinator)
1995. *La pintura mural prehispánica en México,* vol. 1: *Teotihuacan.* 2 vols. UNAM-INAH. México.

Del Amo, Silvia
1988. *Cuatro estudios sobre sistemas tradicionales.* INI. México.

Del Amo, S., A. L. Anaya, J. Jiménez, and E. Fernández
1988 "Algunos aspectos ecológicos y económicos de amaranto (alegría): Un cultivo tradicional en México," in Silvia Del Amo (editor), *Cuatro estudios sobre sistemas tradicionales.* INI. México.

Del Campo Valle, Salvador, and M. Luna Flores
1987. "Respuesta de grupos de maíz de diferente precocidad a etapas de sequía controlada." *Fitotecnia* 9: 13–26. México.

Del Paso y Troncoso, Francisco (editor)
1905– *Papeles de Nueva España.* 9 vols. Sucesores
1948. de Rivadeneyra. Madrid and México.

Díaz, Clara
1980. *Chingú: Un sitio clásico del área de Tula, Hidalgo.* Colección Científica No. 90, INAH. México.

Diehl, Richard A.
1971. *Preliminary Report of the University of Missouri Archaeological Project at Tula, Hidalgo, Mexico: 1970–1971 Field Seasons.* Mimeograph.
1976. "Prehispanic Relationships between the Basin of Mexico and North and West Mexico," in E. Wolf (editor), *The Valley of Mexico: Studies in Prehispanic Ecology and Society:* pp. 249–286. A School of American Research Book. University of New Mexico Press. Alburquerque.
1981. "Tula," in J. Sabloff (editor), *Supplement to the Handbook of Middle American Indians,* vol. 1: pp. 277–295. University of Texas Press. Austin.

1983. *Tula: The Toltec Capital of Ancient Mexico.* Thames and Hudson. London.
1989. "Previous Investigations at Tula," in Dan M. Healan (editor), *Tula of the Toltecs: Excavations and Survey:* pp. 13–29. University of Iowa Press. Iowa City.
1993. "The Toltec Horizon in Mesoamerica," in Don S. Rice (editor), *Latin American Horizons:* pp. 263–294. Dumbarton Oaks. Washington, DC.

Diehl, Richard A. (editor)
1974. *Studies of Ancient Tollan: A Report of the University of Missouri Tula Archaeological Project.* University of Missouri. Columbia.

Diehl, Richard, and Robert Benfer
1975. "Tollan: The Toltec Capital." *Archaeology* 28, no. 2: 112–124.

Diehl, Richard A., and Lawrence H. Feldman
1974. "Relaciones entre la Huasteca y Tollan." *Proyecto Tula,* part 1: pp. 105–108. Colección Científica No. 15, INAH. México.

Diehl, Richard, Roger Lomas, and Jack Wynn
1974. "Toltec Trade with Central America: New Light and Evidence." *Archaeology* 27, no. 2: 182–187.

Diehl, R. A., and E. G. Stroh
1978. "Tecali Vessel Manufacturing Debris at Tollan, Hidalgo." *American Antiquity* 43: 73–79.

Diehl, Richard A., and Janet Catherine Berlo (editors)
1989. *Mesoamerica after the Decline of Teotihuacan: A.D. 700–900.* Dumbarton Oaks. Washington, DC.

Dumond, D. E., and F. Muller
1972. "Classic to Postclassic in Highland Central Mexico." *Science* 175: 1208–1215.

Dunnell, Robert C., and W. S. Dacey
1983. "The Siteless Survey: A Regional Scale Data Collection Strategy," in M. Schiffer (editor), *Advances in Archaeological Method and Theory,* vol. 6: pp. 267–288. Academic Press. New York.

Dutton, Bertha
1955. "Tula of the Toltecs." *El Palacio* 62: 195–250. Santa Fe.

Dyckerhoff, Ursula, and Hanns S. Prem
1976. "La estratificación social en Huexotzinco," in Pedro Carrasco, Johanna Broda et al. (editors), *Estratificación social en la Mesoamérica prehispánica:* pp. 157–183. SEP-INAH. México.

Ekholm, G. F.
1944. "Excavations at Tampico and Panuco in the Huasteca, Mexico." *Anthropological Papers* 38: 319–512. American Museum of Natural History. New York.

Elson, Christina M.
1999. "An Aztec Palace at Chiconautla, Mexico." *Latin American Antiquity* 10, no. 2: 151–167.

Evans, Susan Toby
1975. "Toltec Ceramics from the Teotihuacan Valley." Master's thesis. Pennsylvania State University. University Park.
1986. "Analysis of the Surface Sample Ceramics," in W. T. Sanders (editor), *The Toltec Period Occupation of the Valley, Part 1.* The Teotihuacan Valley Project Final Report, vol. 4. Pennsylvania State University. University Park.
1990. "The Productivity of Maguey Terrace Agriculture in Central Mexico during the Aztec Period." *Latin American Antiquity* 1–2: 117–132.
1991. "Architecture and Authority in an Aztec Village: Form and Function of the Tecpan," in H. R. Harvey (editor), *Land and Politics in the Valley of Mexico:* pp. 63–92. University of New Mexico Press. Albuquerque.
1992. "The Productivity of Maguey Terrace Agriculture in Central Mexico during the Aztec Period," in Thomas W. Killion (editor), *Gardens of Prehistory: The Archaeology of Settlement Agriculture in Greater Mesoamerica:* pp. 92–116. University of Alabama Press. Tuscaloosa.
1993. "Aztec Household Organization and Village Administration," in R. S. Santley and K. G. Hirth (editors), *Prehispanic Domestic Units in Western Mesoamerica:* pp. 173–190. CRC Press. Boca Raton, FL.
1998. "Sexual Politics in the Aztec Palace." *RES: Anthropology and Aesthetics* 33: 166–183.
2000. "The Cerro Gordo South Slope: An Aztec Period Rural Settlement in the Teotihuacan Valley," in William T. Sanders and Susan T. Evans (editors), *The Aztec Period Occupation of the Valley:* pp. 687–709. The Teotihuacan Valley Project Final Report, vol. 5, part 2. Pennsylvania State University Press. University Park.
2001. "Aztec Noble Courts," in T. Inomata and S. Houston (editors), *Royal Courts of the Ancient Maya.* Westview Press. Boulder.

Evans, Susan Toby (editor)
1988. *Excavations at Cihuatecpan: An Aztec Village in the Teotihuacan Valley.* Vanderbilt University Publications in Anthropology 36. Nashville.

Evans, Susan Toby, and Ann Corinne Freter
1996. "Teotihuacan Valley, Mexico, Postclassic Chronology." *Ancient Mesoamerica* 7: 267–280.

Fahmel Beyer, Bernd
1988. *Mesoamérica tolteca: Sus cerámicas de comercio principales.* UNAM. México.

Fash, William L.
1991. *Scribes, Warriors and Kings: The City of Copan and the Ancient Maya.* Thames and Hudson. London.

Fash, William L., and Barbara W. Fash
2000. "Teotihuacan and the Maya: A Classic Heritage," in D. Carrasco, L. Jones, and S. Sessions (editors), *Mesoamerica's Classic Heritage:* pp. 433–464. University Press of Colorado. Boulder.

Feldman, Lawrence
1974a. "Tollan in Central Mexico: The Geography of Economic Specialization," in R. A. Diehl (editor), *Studies of Ancient Tollan:* pp. 150–189. University of Missouri Monographs. Columbia.
1974b. "Tollan in Hidalgo: Native Accounts of the Central Mexican Tolteca," in R. A. Diehl (editor), *Studies of Ancient Tollan:* pp. 130–149. University of Missouri Monographs. Columbia.

Feldman, Lawrence, and Alba Guadalupe Mastache
1990. *Indice de documentos sobre el Centro de México y cartografía antigua del área de Tula, Hidalgo.* Colección Fuentes, INAH. México.

Fernández, Enrique
1986. "Nivel de producción y especialización artesanal en un taller de producción de materiales líticos en Tula, Hgo." Tesis de licenciatura. ENAH. México.

Fernández, Enrique (coordinator)
1994. *Simposium sobre arqueología en el estado de Hidalgo: Trabajos recientes, 1989.* Colección Científica No. 282, INAH. México.

Figueroa N., Ramón
n.d. *Aspectos generales sobre la tenencia de la tierra en el Distrito de Riego del Valle del Mezquital.* Instituto de Investigaciones Económicas. UNAM. México.

Figueroa Silva, Javier
1994. "Conservación en 'El Corral,'" in Robert H. Cobean (editor), *Proyecto: Mantenimiento, conservación y estudio de la zona arqueológica de Tula, Hidalgo,* vol. 6. INAH. México.

Finkler, Kaja
1974. *Estudio comparativo de la economía de dos comunidades de México: El papel de la irrigación.* Colección SEP-INI No. 23. INI. México.

Fish, Suzanne K., and Stephen A. Kowalewski (editors)
1990. *The Archaeology of Regions: A Case for Full-Coverage Survey.* Smithsonian Institution Press. Washington, DC.

Fisher, Patty, and Arnold E. Bender
1976. *Valor nutritivo de los alimentos.* Editorial Limusa. México.

Flannery, Kent V.
1985. "Los orígenes de la agricultura en México: Las teorías y las evidencias," in T. Rojas and W. T. Sanders (editors), *Historia de la agricultura. Época prehispánica—siglo XVI,* vol. 1: pp. 237–266. INAH. México.
1986. *Guilá Naquitz: Archaic Foraging and Early Agriculture in Oaxaca.* Academic Press. New York.

Fowler, William R.
1989a. *The Cultural Evolution of Ancient Nahua Civilizations: The Pipil-Nicarao of Central America.* University of Oklahoma Press. Norman.
1989b. "Nuevas perspectivas sobre las migraciones de los pipiles y los nicaraos." *Arqueología* 1: 81–88. INAH.
2000. "Toltec Related Cultures of Prehispanic Central America." Paper presented at the 65th Annual Meeting of the Society for American Archaeology, Philadelphia.

Franco, José Luis
1945. "Comentarios sobre tipología y filogenia de la decoración negra sobre el color natural del barro en la cerámica Azteca II." *Revista Mexicana de Estudios Antropológicos* 7: 163–186.

García, Enriqueta
1966. *Los climas del Valle de México*. Colegio de Postgraduados, Escuela Nacional de Agricultura. Chapingo, México.

García Cook, Ángel
1981. "The Historical Importance of Tlaxcala in the Cultural Development of the Central Highlands," in V. R. Bricker and J. A. Sabloff (editors), *Supplement to the Handbook of Middle American Indians*, vol. 1: pp. 244–276. University of Texas Press. Austin.

García Cook, Ángel, and Beatriz Leonor Merino Carrión
1996. "Investigaciones arqueológicas en Cantona, Puebla." *Arqueología* 15: 55–78. INAH.
1998. "Cantona: Urbe prehispánica en el altiplano central de México." *Latin American Antiquity* 9, no. 3: 191–216.

García Cubas, Antonio
1873. "Ruinas de la antigua Tollan." *Boletín de la SMGE* 3, no. 1: 173–187.

George, Pierre
1974a. *Población y poblamiento*. Ediciones Península. Barcelona.
1974b. *Geografía rural*. Colección El Cano, Editorial Ariel. Barcelona.
1974c. *Geografía urbana*. Editorial Ariel. Barcelona.
1976. *Geografía económica*. Colección El Cano, Editorial Ariel. Barcelona.

Getino, Fernando
1994. "Informe de excavación de la Estructura K," in Robert H. Cobean (editor), *Proyecto: Mantenimiento, conservación y estudio de la zona arqueológica de Tula, Hidalgo*, vol. 1: pp. 7–46. INAH. México.
2000. "El Edificio K de Tula, Hidalgo." Tesis de licenciatura. ENAH. México.
n.d. *Análisis de las estructuras de las unidades 27 y 28, Tula, Hidalgo*.

Getino Granados, Fernando, and José Rodolfo Cid Beziez
2000. "Astros y montañas: Elementos rectores para el trazo urbano en Teotihuacan y Tula." *Arqueología* 24:87–106. INAH.

Getino, Fernando, and Javier Figueroa
n.d. "Las ofrendas del Palacio Quemado: Una interpretación," in Robert H. Cobean and Alba Guadalupe Mastache (editors), *Ofrendas en un Palacio Tolteca: Turquesa y concha en el Palacio Quemado de Tula, Hidalgo*. INAH. México.

Getino Granados, F., and J. Fuentes Martínez
1986. "Informe sobre las excavaciones en Tula: 1986." Archivo de la Coordinación Nacional de Arqueología. INAH. México.

Gómez Lorence, Federico
1984. "Recursos alimentarios potenciales de las zonas áridas," in T. R. Trujillo (editor), *Seminario sobre la alimentación en México*: pp. 103–113. Instituto de Geografía, UNAM. México.

Gómez, Susana, Javier Sansores Francisco, and Enrique Fernández
1994. *Enterramientos humanos de la época prehispánica en Tula, Hidalgo*. Colección Científica No. 276, INAH. México.

González de Cossío, F.
1952. *El libro de las tasaciones de pueblos de la Nueva España*. Archivo General de la Nación–UNAM. México.

González de Cossío, F. (editor)
1946. *Nuevos documentos relativos a los bienes de Hernán Cortés*. Archivo General de la Nación–UNAM. México.

González Quintero, Lauro
1967. *Tipos de vegetación del Valle del Mezquital*. Paleoecología No. 2. Departamento de Prehistoria, INAH. México.
1988. *Análisis de los restos orgánicos de Tepetitlán*. Informe del Departamento de Salvamento, INAH. México.
1999. "Implicaciones sociales del material vegetal de Tepetitlán, Hidalgo," in R. H. Cobean and A. G. Mastache (coordinators), *Tepetitlán: Un espacio doméstico rural en el area de Tula*: pp. 139–147. INAH–University of Pittsburgh. México.

González Quintero, L., and A. Montúfar López
1980. "Interpretación paleoecológica del contenido polínico de un núcleo cercano a Tula, Hgo.," in F. Sánchez (editor), *III coloquio sobre paleobotánica y palinología: Memorias*. Colección Científica No. 86, INAH. México.

Granados Sánchez, D., and J. Hernández H.
1995. "Sistema de recolección en una comunidad Nahñu en el Valle del Mezquital, Hidalgo." *Revista Chapingo*. Ciencias Forestales 1: 109–115.

Graulich, Michel
1984. "Quelques observations sur les scupltures mesoamericanes dites 'Chac Mool.'" *Jaarboek:* 51–72. Vlaamse Institut Voor Amerikaanse Kulturen. Belgium.
1998. "El rey solar en Mesoamérica." *Arqueología Mexicana* 6 (32): 14–21.

Griffin, J., and A. Espejo
1947. "La alfarería correspondiente al último periodo de ocupación nahua del Valle de México, I." *Memorias de la Academia Mexicana de Historia* 6: 131–147.
1950. "La alfarería del último periodo de ocupación nahua del Valle de México, II: Culhuacan, Tenayuca y Tlatelolco." *Memorias de la Academia Mexicana de Historia* 9: 118–167.

Guerrero G., Raul
1981. *El Pulque*. INAH. México.

Harrison, Peter D.
1970. *The Central Acropolis, Tikal, Guatemala: A Preliminary Study of the Functions of Its Structural Components during the Late Classic Period*. Ph.D. dissertation. University of Pennsylvania. Philadelphia.

Harvey, H. R.
1984. "Aspects of Land Tenure in Ancient Mexico," in H. R. Harvey (editor), *Land and Politics in the Valley of Mexico: A Two-Thousand-Year Perspective:* pp. 83–101. University of New Mexico Press. Albuquerque.

Hassig, Ross
1992. *War and Society in Ancient Mesoamerica*. University of California Press. Berkeley.

Haviland, William A.
1970. "Tikal, Guatemala and Mesoamerican Urbanism." *World Archaeology* 2, no. 2: 186–197.

Healan, Dan M.
1973. "Residential Architecture and Household Patterning in Ancient Tula." Ph.D. dissertation. University of Missouri. Columbia.
1974. "Residential Architecture at Tula," in R. A. Diehl (editor), *Studies of Ancient Tollan:* pp. 16–24. University of Missouri. Columbia.
1977. "Architectural Implications of Daily Life in Ancient Tollan." *World Archaeology* 9, no. 2: 140–156.
1982. "Patrones residenciales de la antigua ciudad de Tula." *Estudios de la Antigua Ciudad de Tula:* 123–147. Colección Científica No. 121, INAH. México.
1986. "Technological and Nontechnological Aspects of an Obsidian Workshop Excavated at Tula, Hidalgo." *Research in Economic Anthropology* 2: 133–152.
1989a. "The Central Group and West Group," in D. M. Healan (editor), *Tula of the Toltecs: Excavations and Survey:* pp. 97–148. University of Iowa Press. Iowa City.
1989b. "House, Household and Neighbourhood in a Postclassic City," in S. Mac Eachern, D. Archer, and R. Gavin (editors), *Households and Communities*. University of Calgary. Calgary.
1989c. "Synopsis of Structural Remains in the Canal Locality," in D. M. Healan (editor), *Tula of the Toltecs: Excavations and Survey*. University of Iowa Press. Iowa City.
1992. "Local Versus Non-Local Obsidian Exchange at Tula and Its Implications for Post-Formative Mesoamerica." *World Archaeology* 24: 449–466.
1993. "Urbanism at Tula from the Perspective of Residential Archaeology," in R. S. Santley and K. G. Hirth (editors), *Prehispanic Domestic Units in Western Mesoamerica:* pp. 105–120. CRC Press. Boca Raton, FL.
1997. "Prehispanic Quarrying in the Ucareo-Zinapecuaro Obsidian Source Area." *Ancient Mesoamerica* 8: 77–100.
1998. "La cerámica coyotlatelco y la explotación del yacimiento de obsidiana de Ucareo-Zinapécuaro," in Véronique Darras (editor), *Génisis, culturas y espacios en Michoacán:* pp. 101–113. CEMCA. México.

Healan, Dan M. (editor)
1989. *Tula of the Toltecs: Excavations and Survey*. University of Iowa Press. Iowa City.

Healan, D. M., R. H. Cobean, and R. A. Diehl
1989. "Synthesis and Conclusions," in D. M. Healan (editor), *Tula of the Toltecs: Excavations and Survey:* pp. 239–252. University of Iowa Press. Iowa City.

Healan, Dan M., and Christine Hernández
1997. "Neither Tarascan nor Aztec: Interpolity Regions as Dynamic Interfaces in Prehispanic Eastern Michoacán." Paper presented at the 62nd Annual Meeting, Society for American Archaeology, Nashville.

Healan, D. M., Janet Kerley, and George Bey III
1983. "Excavation and Preliminary Analysis of an Obsidian Workshop in Tula, Hgo., Mexico." *Journal of Field Archaeology* 10: 127–145.

Healan, D. M., and J. W. Stoutamire
1989. "Surface Survey of the Tula Urban Zone," in D. M. Healan (editor), *Tula of the Toltecs: Excavations and Survey:* pp. 203–236. University of Iowa Press, Iowa City.

Hernández, Christine
2000. "A History of Prehispanic Ceramics, Interaction, and Frontier Development in the Ucareo-Zinapecuaro Obsidian Source Area, Michoacán, México." Ph.D. dissertation. Tulane University. New Orleans.

Hernández, José
1959. *Obras Completas* (1570). 5 vols. UNAM. México.

Hernández Reyes, Carlos
1994 "Rescate de una tumba zapoteca en Tepeji del Río," in E. Fernández (coordinator), *Simposium sobre arqueología en el estado de Hidalgo:* pp. 125–142. Colección Científica No. 282, INAH. México.
1995. "Talleres toltecas para el labrado en basalto." Paper presented at the Jornada de Difusión de la Investigación Antropológica e Histórica en el Estado de Hidalgo, Actopan. Centro INAH, Hidalgo, México.

Hernández, Carlos, Robert H. Cobean, Alba Guadalupe Mastache, and María Elena Suárez
1999. "Un taller de alfareros en la antigua ciudad de Tula." *Arqueología* 22: 69–88. INAH.

Hers, Marie-Areti
1976. "Primeras temporadas de la Misión Arqueológica Belga en la Sierra de Nayar." *Boletín del INAH* 2, no. 16: 41–44.
1989. *Los Toltecas en tierras chichimecas.* UNAM. México.

Hers, Marie-Areti, and Beatriz Braniff
1998. "Herencias chichimecas." *Arqueología* 19: 55–80.

Heyden, Doris
1973. "¿Un Chicomóztoc en Teotihuacan? La cueva bajo la Pirámide del Sol." *Boletín del INAH* 2, no. 6: 3–18.

Hicks, F., and H. B. Nicholson
1962. "The Transition from Classic to Postclassic at Cerro Portezuelo, Valley of Mexico." *Actas del XXXV Congreso Internacional de Ameri-canistas* 1: 493–505.

Hirth, Kenneth
2000. *Ancient Urbanism at Xochicalco.* University of Utah Press. Salt Lake City.

Hirth, Kenneth, and Jorge Angulo
1981. "Early State Expansion in Central Mexico: Teotihuacan in Morelos." *Journal of Field Archaeology* 8: 135–150.

Hirth, Kenneth G., and Ann Cyphers Guillén
1988. *Tiempo y asentamiento en Xochicalco.* Instituto de Investigaciones Antropológicas, UNAM. México.

Historia de los mexicanos por sus pinturas
1941. *Historia de los mexicanos por sus pinturas,* J. García Icazbalceta (editor). México.

Hodge, Mary G., and Leah D. Minc
1990. "The Spatial Patterning of Aztec Ceramics: Implications for Prehispanic Exchange Systems in the Valley of Mexico." *Journal of Field Archaeology* 17: 415–436.
1991. *Aztec-Period Ceramics Distribution and Exchange Systems.* University of Michigan. Ann Arbor.

Hopkins, Joseph W.
1983. "The Tomellín Cañada and the Postclassic Cuicatec," in K. V. Flannery and J. Marcus (editors), *The Cloud People.* Academic Press. New York.

INEGI
1984. *Hidalgo demográfico.* Breviario 1983. INEGI. México.

Ixtlilxochitl, F.
1952. *Obras históricas.* Editorial Nacional. México.

Jackson, Donald
1990. "Análisis sobre la producción y el uso de lítica en el sitio de La Mesa," in A. G. Mastache, R.

H. Cobean, C. Rees, and D. Jackson (editors), *Las industrias líticas coyotlatelco en el área de Tula.* Colección Científica No. 221, INAH. México.

Jaso, Valentín
1905. "Relación de Atitalaquia y su partido," in F. Paso y Troncoso (editor), *Papeles de la Nueva España 1905,* vol. 6: 199–208. Sucesores de Rivadeneyra. Madrid and México.

Jiménez García, Elizabeth
1998. *Iconografía de Tula: El caso de la escultura.* INAH. México.

Jiménez Moreno, Wigberto
1941. "Tula y los toltecas según la fuentes históricas." *Revista Mexicana de Estudios Antropológicos* 5: 79–83.
1954– "Síntesis de la historia precolonial del Valle de
1955. México." *Revista Mexicana de Estudios Antropológicos* 14: 219–236.
1959. "Síntesis de la historia pretolteca de Mesoamérica." *Esplendor del México Antiguo,* no. 2: 1019–1108.
1966. "Los imperios prehispánicos de Mesoamérica." *Revista Mexicana de Estudios Antropológicos* 20: 179–195.

Jiménez, Peter
1989. "Perspectivas sobre la arqueología de Zacatecas." *Arqueología* 5: 7–50.

Jones, Emrys
1971. *Geografía humana.* Editorial Labor, S.A. Barcelona.

Jones, Lindsay
1995. *Twin City Tales: A Hermeneutical Reassessment of Tula and Chichen Itza.* University Press of Colorado. Niwot.

Kaplan, Lawrence
1986. "Informe sobre los frijoles arqueológicos de la región de Tula," in *Informe, Proyecto Tula y su área directa de interacción.* INAH. México.
1999. "Estudio de phaseolus arqueológico de Tepetitlán y Tula," in R. H. Cobean and A. G. Mastache (coordinators), *Tepetitlán: Un espacio doméstico rural en el area de Tula:* pp. 148–155. INAH–University of Pittsburgh. México.

Kelley, J. Charles
1971. "Archaeology of the Northern Frontier: Zacatecas and Durango," in R. Wauchope (editor), *Handbook of Middle American Indians,* vol. 11: pp. 768–804. University of Texas Press. Austin.

Kelley, J. C., and E. A. Kelley
1971. "An Introduction to the Ceramics of the Chalchihuites Culture of Zacatecas and Durango, México, Part I: The Decorated Wares." *Mesoamerican Studies* No. 5. Southern Illinois University. Carbondale.

Kelly, Isabel, and Beatriz Braniff
1966. "Una relación cerámica entre Occidente y la Mesa Central." *Boletín del INAH* 23: 206–207.

Killion, Thomas W.
1992. "The Archaeology of Settlement Agriculture," in Thomas W. Killion (editor), *Gardens of Prehistory: The Archaeology of Settlement Agriculture in Greater Mesoamerica:* pp. 1–13. University of Alabama Press. Tuscaloosa.

Kirchhoff, Paul
1947. "Prologo," in *Historia tolteca-chichimeca: Anales de Quauhtichan.* Fuentes para la Historia de México, vol. 1. México.
1955. "Quetzalcoatl, Huemac y el fin de Tula." *Cuadernos Americanos* 84, no. 6: 163–196.
1976. *Historia tolteca-chichimeca.* INAH. México.
1985. "El imperio tolteca y su caída," in J. Monjarás, R. Brambila, and E. Pérez-Rocha (editors), *Mesoamérica y el Centro de México:* pp. 249–272. Colección Biblioteca del INAH. México.

Klein, Cecilia F.
1987. "The Ideology of Autosacrifice at the Templo Mayor," in Elizabeth H. Boone (editor), *The Aztec Templo Mayor:* pp. 293–370. Dumbarton Oaks. Washington, DC.

Koehler, T. H.
1962. "Late Toltec Ceramics in the Valley of Teotihuacan." Master's thesis. Columbia University. New York.
1986. "Excavations at Maquixco Bajo," in W. T. Sanders (editor), *The Toltec Period Occupation of the Valley,* part 1. The Teotihuacan Valley Project Final Report, vol. 4. Pennsylvania State University. University Park.

Kolb, Michael J., and James E. Snead
1997. "It's a Small World After All: Comparative Analyses of Community Organization in Archaeology." *American Antiquity* 62, no. 4: 609–620.

Koontz, Rex
2000. "A Ballcourt Dance at Tula." Paper presented at the 65th Annual Meeting of the Society for American Archaeology, Philadelphia.

Kovar, Anton
1970. "The Physical and Biological Environment of the Basin of Mexico," in W.T. Sanders (editor), *The Natural Environment, Contemporary Occupation and Sixteenth-Century Population of the Valley*. The Teotihuacan Valley Project Final Report, vol. 1. Pennsylvania State University. University Park.

Kristan-Graham, Cynthia
1989. "Art, Rulership and the Mesoamerican Body Politic at Tula and Chichen Itza." Ph.D. dissertation. University of California at Los Angeles.
1993. "The Business of Narrative at Tula: An Analysis of the Vestibule Frieze, Trade, and Ritual." *Latin American Antiquity* 4, no. 1: 3–21.

Kubler, George
1961. "Chichen Itza y Tula." *Estudios de Cultura Maya* 1: 47–80.

Ku Naal, Roberto
1986. *Cambios en la tecnología de cultivo de la milpa: Rosa-tumba-quema en Yaxcabá, Yucatán, México*. Tesis profesional. Universidad Autónoma de Chapingo. México.

LAMP
1991. *Catálogo del germoplasma de maiz*, vol. 2. Proyecto Latino-Americano de Maiz (LAMP). México.

Ledezma, Bartolomé (compiler)
1905. *Descripción del Arzobispado de México*, F. Del Paso y Troncoso (editor). Papeles de la Nueva España, vol. 3. Madrid and México.

Lefebvre, Henri
1976. *De lo rural a lo urbano*. Editorial Paulinas. México.
1983. *La revolución urbana*. Alianza Editorial. Madrid.

Linné, S.
1934. *Archaeological Research at Teotihuacan, Mexico*. Ethnographic Museum of Sweden, n.s., Publication 1. Stockholm.

Lombardo de Ruiz, S.
1973. *Desarrollo urbano de México-Tenochtitlan según las fuentes históricas*. SEP-INAH. México.

López Aguilar, F., R. Nieto, and R. Cobean
1989. "La producción de obsidiana en la Sierra de las Navajas, Hgo.," in M. Gaxiola and J. Clark (editors), *La obsidiana en Mesoamérica*: pp. 193–198. Colección Científica No. 176, INAH. México.

López Aguilar, Fernando, Laura Solar Valverde, and Rodrigo Vilanova de Allende
1998. "El Valle del Mezquital: Encrucijadas en la historia de los asentamientos humanos en un espacio discontinuo." *Arqueología* 20: 21–40. INAH.

López Austin, Alfredo
1973. *Hombre-Dios: Religión y política en el mundo nahuátl*. UNAM. México.
1980. *Cuerpo humano e ideología: Las concepciones de los antiguos Nahuas*. 2 vols. UNAM. México.

López Austin, Alfredo, and Leonardo López Luján
1999. *Mito y realidad de Zuyuá: La serpiente emplumada y las transformaciones mesoamericanas del clásico al posclásico*. El Colegio de México. México.

López Luján, Leonardo
1993. *Las ofrendas del Templo Mayor de Tenochtitlan*. INAH. México.

Lorenzo, José Luis (editor)
1968. *Materiales para la arqueología de Teotihuacan*. Serie Investigaciones No. 17, INAH. México.

Lothrop, Samuel K.
1952. *Metals from the Cenote of Sacrifice, Chichen Itza, Yucatan*. Memoirs of the Peabody Museum of Archaeology and Ethnology, Harvard University. Vol. 4, No. 2. Cambridge, MA.

Lowenberg, Miriam E., E. Neige, E. D. Wilson, M. C. Feeney, and J. R. Savage
1970. *Los alimentos y el hambre*. Limuse-Wiley. México.

Luna Flores, Máximo, and J. R. Gutiérrez Sánchez
1990. "Relación entre el clima y el rendimiento de maiz de temporal en Zacatecas." *Revista Fitotécnica Mexicana* 13: 104–116.

MacNeish, Richard
1967. "A Summary of the Subsistence," in D. S. Byers (editor), *The Prehistory of the Tehuacan Valley,* vol. 1: *Environment and Subsistence:* pp. 290–310. University of Texas Press. Austin.

Mandeville, M.
1974a. "Chipped Stone Points from Tula," in R. A. Diehl (editor), *Studies of Ancient Tollan: A Report of the University of Missouri Tula Archaeological Project:* pp. 95–104. University of Missouri. Columbia.
1974b. "A Study of Contemporary Ceramic Techniques at Tula and a Possible Archaeological Application," in R. A. Diehl (editor), *Studies of Ancient Tollan: A Report of the University of Missouri Tula Archaeological Project:* pp. 122–129. University of Missouri. Columbia.

Mandeville, Margaret, and Dan M. Healan
1989. "Architectural Remains in the El Corral Locality," in Dan M. Healan (editor), *Tula of the Toltecs: Excavations and Survey:* pp. 171–199. University of Iowa Press. Iowa City.

Mangelsdorf, P. C., R. MacNeish, and W. C. Galinat
1967. "Prehistoric Wild and Cultivated Maize," in D. S. Byers (editor), *The Prehistory of the Tehuacan Valley,* vol. 1: *Environment and Subsistence.* University of Texas Press. Austin.

Marcus, Joyce
1983. "On the Nature of the Mesoamerican City," in E. Vogt and R. Leventhal (editors), *Prehistoric Settlement Patterns:* pp. 195–242. University of New Mexico Press. Albuquerque.

Márquez Calderón, Rafael
1986. "Aspectos geológico y geomorfológico de la región de Tula, Hgo." Unpublished manuscript.

Marquina, Ignacio
1964. *Arquitectura prehispánica.* Memorias del INAH No. 1, 2nd ed. México.

Martín, Paul S.
1963. *Last 10,000 Years.* University of Arizona Press. Tucson.

Martínez Magaña, Ricardo
1994. "Un rescate en el Cerro el Elefante, Tunititlán," in E. Fernández (coordinator), *Simposium sobre arqueología en el Estado de Hidalgo:* pp. 143–150. Colección Científica No. 282, INAH. México.

Martínez Valenzuela, Balbina, and Luis Felipe Nieto
1987. "Distribución de asentamientos prehispánicos en la cuenca central del Río Laja (Guanajuato)." Tesis de licenciatura. ENAH. México.

Mastache, Alba Guadalupe
1976. "Sistemas de riego en el área de Tula, Hgo." *Proyecto Tula,* Part 2. Colección Científica No. 33, INAH. México.
1996a. "El estado tolteca: Una investigación sobre su proceso de desarrollo y estructura social, económica y política." Ph.D. dissertation. UNAM. México.
1996b. "El amaranto y el maguey en la dieta tolteca," in A. G. Mastache et al. (coordinators), *Arqueología mesoamericana: Homenaje a William T. Sanders:* vol. 1, pp. 365–374. INAH–Arqueología Mexicana. Mexico.

Mastache, A. G., and R. H. Cobean
1985. "Tula," in Jesus Monjarás-Ruiz, Rosa Brambila, and Emma Pérez-Rocha (recompilers), *Mesoamérica y el Centro de México:* pp. 273–307. Colección Biblioteca del INAH. México.
1988. "La arqueología," in C. García Mora and M. Del Valle Berrocal (coordinators), *La antropología en México: Panorama histórico,* vol. 5: pp. 39–82. INAH. México.
1989. "The Coyotlatelco Culture and the Origins of Toltec State," in R. A. Diehl and J. C. Berlo (editors), *Mesoamerica after the Decline of Teotihuacan:* pp. 49–68. Dumbarton Oaks. Washington, DC.
1990. "La cultura coyotlatelco en el area de Tula," in A. G. Mastache, R. H. Cobean, C. Rees, and D. Jackson (editors), *Las industrias líticas coyotlatelco en el area de Tula.* Colección Científica No. 221, INAH. México.
1999a. "Activity Areas," in R. H. Cobean and A. G. Mastache (coordinators), *Tepetitlán: Un espacio doméstico rural en el area de Tula:* pp. 239–294. INAH–University of Pittsburgh. México.
1999b. "Conclusions," in R. H. Cobean and A. G. Mastache (coordinators), *Tepetitlán: Un espacio doméstico rural en el area de Tula:* pp. 295–312. INAH–University of Pittsburgh. México.

2000. "Ancient Tollan: The Sacred Precinct." *RES: Anthropology and Aesthetics* 38: 100–133.
n.d. *Proyecto Tula y su area directa de interacción: Temporada 1984–1985.* Informe. Archivo Técnico, Coordinación Nacional de Arqueología. INAH. México.
n.d.2. "An Analysis of the Pillar Reliefs of Pyramid B at Tula, Hidalgo." Unpublished manuscript.

Mastache, A. G., R. H. Cobean, C. Rees, and D. Jackson
1990. *Las industrias líticas coyotlatelco en el área de Tula.* Estudio Sobre Tula 3, Serie Arqueología. Colección Científica No. 221, INAH. México.

Mastache, A. G., and A. M. Crespo
1974. "La ocupación prehispánica de Tula, Hgo." *Proyecto Tula,* part 1: pp. 71–103. Colección Científica No. 15, INAH. México.
1976. "El area de Tula." Ponencia presentada en el XLII Congreso Internacional de Americanistas, París.
1982. "Análisis sobre la traza general de Tula, Hgo." *Estudios sobre la antigua ciudad de Tula:* pp. 11–38. Colección Científica No. 121, INAH. México.

Mastache, A. G., A. M. Crespo, R. H. Cobean, and D. M. Healan
1982. *Estudios sobre la antigua ciudad de Tula.* Colección Científica No. 121, INAH. México.

Matos Moctezuma, Eduardo
1974. "Excavaciones en la microarea: Tula Chico y la Plaza Charnay," in Eduardo Matos Moctezuma (editor), *Proyecto Tula,* part 1: pp. 61–69. INAH, México.
1976. *Tula* (Guía). Editorial Orto. México.
1988. *The Great Temple of the Aztecs.* Thames and Hudson. London.
1999. "Los edificios aledaños al Templo Mayor," in Eduardo Matos Moctezuma (editor), *Estudios Mexicas,* vol. 1: pp. 77–192. El Colegio Nacional. México.

Matos Moctezuma, Eduardo (coordinator)
1974. *Proyecto Tula,* part 1. Colección Científica No. 15, INAH. México.
1976. *Proyecto Tula,* part 2. Colección Científica No. 33, INAH. México.

Mayer-Oakes, W. J.
1959. "A Stratigraphic Excavation at El Risco, Mexico." *Proceedings of the American Philosophical Society* 103: 332–373.

McClung de Tapia, Emily
1977. "Recientes estudios paleoetnobotánicos en Teotihuacán, México." *Anales de Antropología* 14: 49–61. UNAM.
1984. *Ecología y cultura en Mesoamérica.* UNAM. México.

McCullough, John
1966. "Toltec Ceramics of the Lower Teotihuacan Valley." Paper presented at the 64th Annual Meeting of the American Anthropological Association, Denver.

Medellin Zenil, Alfonso
1960. *Cerámicas del Totonacapan: Exploraciones en el centro de Veracruz.* Universidad Veracruzana. Jalapa.

Melville, Elinor
1994. *A Plague of Sheep: Environmental Consequences of the Conquest of Mexico.* Cambridge University Press. Cambridge.

Merino, L., and A. García Cook
1987. "Proyecto Arqueológico Huaxteca." *Arqueología* no. 1: 31–72. Dirección de Monumentos Prehispánicos, INAH. México.

Miller, Mary
1985. "A Re-examination of the Mesoamerican Chacmool." *Art Bulletin* 67, no. 1: 7–17.

Miller, Mary, and Marco Samayoa
1998. "Where Maize May Grow: Jade, Chacmools, and the Maize God." *RES: Anthropology and Aesthetics* 33: 54–72.

Miller, Mary Ellen, and Karl Taube
1992. *The Gods and Symbols of Ancient Mexico and the Maya.* Thames and Hudson. London.

Millon, Rene
1976. "Social Relations in Ancient Teotihuacan," in E. R. Wolf (editor), *The Valley of Mexico: Studies in Prehispanic Ecology and Society.* University of New Mexico Press. Albuquerque.
1981. "Teotihuacan: City, State and Civilization," in Victoria Bricker and Jeremy A. Sabloff (editors), *Handbook of Middle American Indians,* Supplement 1: *Archaeology:* pp. 198–243. University of Texas Press. Austin.
1988. "The Last Years of Teotihuacan," in N. Yoffee and G. L. Cowgill (editors), *The Collapse of*

Ancient States and Civilizations: pp. 102–164. University of Arizona Press. Tucson.

Millon, Rene (editor)
1973. *Urbanization at Teotihuacan, Mexico,* vol. 1: *The Teotihuacan Map.* University of Texas Press. Austin.

Moedano, Hugo
1944. "La diosa raptada." *Nosotros* 1, no. 19: 24–26.
1946a. "Tollan." Master's thesis. Escuela Nacional de Antropología e Historia. México.
1946b. "La cerámica de Zinapécuaro, Michoacán." *Anales del Museo Michoacano* 4: 39–49.
1947. "El friso de los caciques." *Anales del INAH* 11: 113–136.

Moguel Cos, Antonieta, Fernando Getino Granados, and Javier Martínez González
1999. *Rescate 10 km., Carretera: Pachuca-Tula-Jilotepec.* Informe. Dirección de Salvamento Arqueológico. INAH. México.

Molina Montes, Augusto
1987. "Templo Mayor Architecture: So What's New?" in Elizabeth H. Boone (editor), *The Aztec Templo Mayor:* pp. 97–107. Dumbarton Oaks. Washington, DC.

Moncayo, Rosa E.
1988. "Análisis cerámico del sitio de Tepetitlán en Tula, Hgo." Tesis de licenciatura. ENAH. México.
1999. "Análisis de la cerámica," in R. H. Cobean and A. G. Mastache (coordinators), *Tepetitlán: Un espacio doméstico rural en el area de Tula:* pp. 75–109. INAH–University of Pittsburgh. México.

Moncayo, Rosa Elena, and José López-Rivera Cuessy
1985. "Tula Zona Urbana 17." *Proyecto Tula y su área directa de interacción: Temporada 1984–1985.* Informe. Archivo de la Coordinación Nacional de Arqueología. INAH. México.

Monjaras-Ruiz, Jesús, Rosa Brambila, and Ema Pérez-Rocha (recompilers)
1989. *Mesoamérica y el Centro de México.* Colección Biblioteca del INAH. México.

Montañez, Carlos, and Arturo Warman
1985. *Los productores de maíz en México: Restricciones y alternativas.* Centro de Ecodesarrollo. México.

Mountjoy, Joseph.
1982. *Proyecto Tomatlán de salvamento arqueológico.* Colección Científica No. 122, INAH. México.

Müller, Florencia
1970. "La cerámica de Cholula." Proyecto Cholula, INAH Serie Investigaciones 19: 129–142.

Museo Nacional de Culturas Populares
1982. *Nuestro maíz: Treinta monografías populares.* 2 vols. Secretaría de Educación Pública. México.
1987. *El maíz.* SEP. México.

Nabhan, Gary, Wendy Hodgson, and James Hickey
n.d. "Domestication, Cultural Diffusion and In Situ Conservation of *Agave murpheyi Gibson:* An Ethnoecological Perspective." Unpublished manuscript.

Nalda, Enrique
1975. "U A San Juan del Río: Trabajos arqueológicos preliminares." Tesis. ENAH. México.
1991. "Secuencia cerámica del sur de Queretaro," in A.M. Crespo and Rosa Brambila (editors), *Queretaro Prehispánico.* Colección Científica No. 238: pp. 31–57. INAH. México.

Navarrete, Carlos
1986. "The Sculptural Complex at Cerro Bernal on the Coast of Chiapas." *Notes of the New World Archaeological Foundation* 1: 1–28.

Neff, Hector
1984. "Developmental History of the Plumbate Pottery Industry in the Eastern Soconusco Region, A.D. 600 through A.D. 1250." Ph.D. dissertation. University of California at Santa Barbara.

Neff, Hector, and Ronald L. Bishop
1988. "Plumbate Origins and Development." *American Antiquity* 53: 505–522.

Nelson, Ben A.
1997. "Chronology and Stratigraphy at La Quemada, Zacatecas, México." *Journal of Field Archaeology* 24, no. 1: 85–109.

Nichols, Deborah L.
1987. "Risk and Agricultural Intensification during the Formative Period in the Northern Basin of Mexico." *American Anthropologist* 89: 596–616.

1996. "An Overview of Regional Settlement Pattern Survey in Mesoamerica: 1960–1995," in A. G. Mastache et al. (coordinators), *Arqueología mesoamericana: Homenaje a William T. Sanders* 1: pp. 59–96. INAH–Arqueología Mexicana. México.

Nichols, Deborah L., and C. D. Frederick
1993. "Irrigation Canals and Chinampas: Recent Research in the Northern Basin of Mexico." *Research in Economic Anthropology,* supplement 7: 123–150. JAI Press. Greenwich, CT.

Nichols, Deborah L., and J. McCullough
1986. "Excavations at Xometla," in W. T. Sanders (editor), *The Toltec Period Occupation of the Valley,* part 1: pp. 53–194. The Teotihuacan Valley Project Final Report, vol. 4. Pennsylvania State University. University Park.

Nicholson, H. B.
1957. *Topiltzin Quetzalcoatl of Tollan: A Problem in Mesoamerican Ethnohistory.* Ph.D. dissertation. Harvard University. Cambridge, MA.
1961. "The Chapultepec Cliff Sculpture of Motecuhzoma Xocoyotzin." *El México Antiguo* 9: 379–444.
1971. "Major Sculpture in Prehispanic Central Mexico," in R. Wauchope (editor), *Handbook of Middle American Indians,* vol. 10: pp. 92–134. University of Texas Press. Austin.
1978. "Western Mesoamerica: A.D. 900–1520," in R. E. Taylor and C. W. Meighan (editors), *Chronologies in New World Archaeology.* Academic Press. New York.

Offner, Jerome A.
1984. "Household Organization in the Texcocan Heartland," in H. R. Harvey and H. Prem (editors), *Explorations in Ethnohistory:* pp. 127–147. University of New Mexico Press. Albuquerque.

Olivera, Mercedes
1978. *Pillis y macehuales: Las formaciones sociales y los modos de producción de Tecali del siglo XII al XVI.* CIESAS. México.

Ortíz, Ricardo
1997. *Amaranto: Historia y perspectivas.* Editora y Distribuidora Yug, S.A. México.

Ortíz Villanueva, Bonifacio, and Carlos Alberto Ortíz S.
1990. *Edafología.* Universidad Autónoma Chapingo. México.

Palerm, Angel
1955. "The Agricultural Basis of Urban Civilization in Mesoamerica," in J. H. Steward (editor), *Irrigation Civilizations: A Comparative Study:* pp. 28–42. Pan American Union. Washington, DC.

Paredes Gudiño, Blanca
1990. *Unidades habitacionales en Tula, Hidalgo.* Colección Científica No. 210, Serie Arqueología, INAH. México.

Parsons, Jeffrey R.
1966. "The Aztec Ceramic Sequence in the Teotihuacan Valley, México." Ph.D. dissertation. University of Michigan. Ann Arbor.
1971. *Prehistoric Settlement Patterns in the Texcoco Region, Mexico.* Memoirs of the Museum of Anthropology 3, University of Michigan. Ann Arbor.
1974. Unpublished field notes for Cerro La Mesa Ahumada. Manuscript.
1976. "Settlement and Population History of the Basin of México," in E. R. Wolf (editor) *The Valley of Mexico: Studies in Pre-Hispanic Ecology and Society.* University of New Mexico Press. Albuquerque.
1990. "Critical Reflections on a Decade of Full-Coverage Regional Survey in the Valley of Mexico," in S. K. Fish and S. A. Kowalewski (editors), *The Archaeology of Regions: A Case for Full-Coverage Survey:* pp. 7–32. Smithsonian Institution. Washington, DC.
2000. "The Toltec World as Reflected by Changing Settlement Systems in the Basin of Mexico." Paper presented at the 65th Annual Meeting of the Society for American Archaeology, Philadelphia.

Parsons, Jeffrey R., Elizabeth Brumfiel, and Mary Hodge
1996. "Developmental Implications of Earlier Dates for Early Aztec in the Basin of Mexico." *Ancient Mesoamerica* 7, no. 2: 217–230.

Parsons, Jeffrey R., and J. Andrew Darling
1993. "A Reconsideration of Maguey in Mesoamerican Civilization." Paper presented at the 13th

International Congress of Anthropological and Ethnological Sciences. México.

Parsons, Jeffrey R., Elizabeth Brumfiel, Mary H. Parsons, and D. J. Wilson
1982. *Prehispanic Settlement Patterns in the Southern Valley of Mexico: The Chalco-Xochimilco Region.* Memoirs of the Museum of Anthropology 12, University of Michigan. Ann Arbor.

Parsons, J. R., and M. H. Parsons
1990. "Maguey Utilization in Highland Central Mexico." Anthropological Papers No. 82, Museum of Anthropology, University of Michigan. Ann Arbor.

Pastrana, Alejandro
1990. "Producción de instrumentos de obsidiana. División del trabajo (Proyecto Tula)," in M. D. Soto de Arechavaleta (editor), *Nuevos enfoques en el estudio de la lítica:* pp. 243–296. Instituto de Investigaciones Antropológicas, UNAM. México.

Pasztory, Esther
1997. *Teotihuacan: An Experiment in Living.* University of Oklahoma Press. Norman.

Patiño, Héctor
1994a. *Arquitectura coyotlatelco: Un análisis en la región de Tula.* Tesis de licenciatura. ENAH. México.
1994b. "La conservación del Juego de Pelota 2," in Robert H. Cobean (editor), *Proyecto: Mantenimiento, conservación y estudio de la zona arqueológica de Tula, Hidalgo,* vol. 4. INAH. México.

Peña, Agustín, and C. Rodríguez
1976. "Excavaciones en Dainí, Tula, Hgo.," in E. Matos (coordinator), *Proyecto Tula,* part 2. Colección Científica No. 33, INAH. México.

Pérez Castro, Guillermo, Pedro Sánchez Nava, María Estefan, Judith Padilla y Yedra, and Antonio Gudiño Garfias
1989. "El Cuauhxicalli de Moctezuma I." *Arqueología* 5: 131–151.

Polaco, Oscar
1988. "Análisis de los restos de fauna de Tepetitlán, Hgo." *Informe del Laboratorio de Paleozoología.* INAH. México.
1999. "Analysis of the Faunal Remains," in R. H. Cobean and A. G. Mastache (coordinators), *Tepetitlán: Un espacio doméstico rural en el area de Tula:* pp. 125–138. INAH–University of Pittsburgh. México.

Pollard, Helen Perlstein
1993. *Tariacuri's Legacy: The Prehispanic Tarascan State.* University of Oklahoma Press. Norman.

Pollard, H. P., and S. Gorenstein
1980. "Agrarian Potential, Population and the Tarascan State." *Science* 209: 274–277.

Pool, Christopher A.
1990. "Ceramic Production, Resource Procurement, and Exchange at Matacapan, Veracruz, México." Ph.D. dissertation. Tulane University. New Orleans.
1997. "Prehispanic Kilns at Matacapan, Veracruz, México," in W. D. Kingery and P. R. Rice (editors), *The Prehistory and History of Ceramic Kilns:* pp. 149–171. The American Ceramic Society. Westerville, OH.

Porter, M. N.
1956. "Excavations at Chupicuaro, Guanajuato, México," *Transactions of the American Philosophical Society* 46 (5). Philadelphia.

Raisz, Irving
1959. *Land Forms of Mexico.* Map prepared for the Geography Branch of the Office of Naval Research. Cambridge, MA.

Rattray, Evelyn C.
1966. "An Archaeological and Stylistic Study of Coyotlatelco Pottery." *Mesoamerican Notes* 7–8: 87–211.
1973. "The Teotihuacan Ceramic Chronology: Early Tzacualli to Early Tlamimilolpa Phases." Ph.D. dissertation. University of Missouri. Columbia.
1990. "New Findings on the Origins of Thin Orange Ceramics." *Ancient Mesoamerica* 1–2: 181–195.
1991. "Fechamientos por radiocarbono en Teotihuacan." *Arqueología* 6: 3–18. INAH.
1993. "The Oaxaca Barrio at Teotihuacan." *Monografías Mesoamericana* 1, Universidad de las Américas. Cholula, México.
2001. *Teotihuacan Ceramics: Chronology and Cultural Trends.* INAH–University of Pittsburgh. México.

In press. *Excavaciones en el Barrio de los Comerciantes, Teotihuacan.* Instituto de Investigaciones Antropológicas, UNAM. México.

Rees, Charles
1990. "Estudios sobre la cantera taller del sitio de Magoni, Hgo.," in A. G. Mastache, R. H. Cobean, C. Rees, and D. Jackson (editors), *Las industrias líticas Coyotlatelco en el área de Tula:* pp. 23–145. Colección Científica No. 221, INAH. Mexico.

Reyes García, Luis
1972. "Ordenanzas para el Gobierno de Cuauhtinchan, año 1559." *Estudios de Cultura Nahuatl,* vol. 10.
1973. "Cuauhtinchan del siglo XII al XVI," in *Comunicaciones, Proyecto Puebla-Tlaxcala* 7: pp. 87–88. Fundación Alemana para la Investigación Científica. Puebla.
1991. "Materiales etnohistóricos de la cabecera de Ocotelulco, Tlaxcala." Manuscrito, CIESAS. México.
n.d. "Notas sobre organización social y política de los toltecas según fuentes históricas." Paper presented at the 65th Annual Meeting of the Society for American Archaeology, Philadelphia (2000).

Rice, Prudence R.
1976. "Rethinking the Ware Concept." *American Antiquity* 41: 538–543.
1987. *Pottery Analysis: A Sourcebook.* University of Chicago Press. Chicago.

Ridings, R.
1996. "Where in the World Does Obsidian Hydration Work?" *American Antiquity* 61, no. 1: 136–148.

Rojas, José Luis de
1986. *México Tenochtitlan: Economía y sociedad en el siglo XVI.* Fondo de Cultura Económica. México.

Rojas Rabiela, Teresa
1983. *La agricultura chinampera.* Universidad Autónoma Chapingo. México.
1985. "La tecnología agrícola mesoamericana en el siglo XVI," in T. Rojas and W. T. Sanders (editors), *Historia de la agricultura: Epoca prehispánica–siglo XVI,* vol. 1: pp. 129–232. INAH. México.

Rojas, Teresa (coordinator)
1991. *La agricultura en tierras mexicanas desde sus orígenes hasta nuestros días.* Editor Grijalbo. México.

Romero Polanco, Emilio
1993. "El frijol y la alimentación," in C. González and F. Torres (coordinators), *Los retos de la soberanía alimentaria de México,* vol. 1. UNAM. México.

Roper, Donna
1976. "Lateral Displacement of Artifacts Due to Plowing." *American Antiquity* 41: 372–375.

Ruipérez Marín, Rosario
1965. "Estudio geográfico del Municipio de Tula de Allende, Hidalgo." Tesis de licenciatura en geografía. UNAM. México.

Sahagún, Fray Bernardino de
1956. *Historia general de las cosas de Nueva España.* Angel María Garibay (editor), 4 vols. Editorial Porrua. México.

Salazar Avendaño, José Clemente
1991. *Análisis tecnológico de artefactos en obsidiana de un conjunto residencial en Tula, Hidalgo.* Tesis de licenciatura. ENAH. México.

Sánchez Marroquín, Alfredo
1980. *Potencialidad agroindustrial del amaranto.* Centro de Estudios Económicos y Sociales del Tercer Mundo. México.

Sanders, William.T.
1965. *The Cultural Ecology of the Teotihuacan Valley.* Pennsylvania State University. University Park.
1983. "El lago y el volcán: La chinampa," in Teresa Rojas (editor), *La agricultura chinampera:* pp. 115–158. Universidad Autónoma Chapingo. México.
1986. *The Toltec Period Occupation of the Valley,* part 1: *Excavations and Ceramics.* The Teotihuacan Valley Project Final Report, vol. 4. Pennsylvania State University. University Park.
1989. "Household, Linage and State in Eighth-Century Copan," in D. Webster (editor), *The House of the Bacabs, Copan: A Study of the Iconography and Social Context of a Maya Elite Structure:* pp. 89–105. Dumbarton Oaks. Washington, DC.

1992. "Summary and Critique," in Thomas W. Killion (editor), *Gardens of Prehistory: The Archaeology of Settlement Agriculture in Greater Mesoamerica:* pp. 273–284. University of Alabama Press. Tuscaloosa.

1993a. "Mesoamerican Household Archaeology Comes of Age," in R. S. Santley and K. G. Hirth (editors), *Prehispanic Domestic Units in Western Mesoamerica:* pp. 275–284. CRC Press. Boca Raton, FL.

1993b. "Commentary," in *Simposio: Agave in Prehistoric Mesoamerica and the Southwestern United States,* 13th International Congress of Anthropological and Ethnological Sciences. México.

1997. "El final de la Gran Aventura: El Ocaso de un Recurso Natural." *Arqueología* 17: 3–20. INAH.

2000a. "The Natural Environment and Twentieth-Century Occupation," in S. T. Evans and W. T. Sanders (editors), *The Aztec Period Occupation of the Valley.* The Teotihuacan Valley Project Final Report, vol. 5, part 1: pp. 5–58. Pennsylvania State University. University Park.

2000b. "Methodology: The Surface Survey," in S. T. Evans and W. T. Sanders (editors), *The Aztec Period Occupation of the Valley.* The Teotihuacan Valley Project Final Report, vol. 5, part 1: pp. 59–73. Pennsylvania State University. University Park.

Sanders, William T., and Susan T. Evans
In press. "The Teotihuacan Valley and the Temascalapa Region during the Aztec Period," in W. T. Sanders and S. T. Evans (editors), *The Aztec Period Occupation of the Valley.* The Teotihuacan Valley Project Final Report, vol. 5, part 3. Pennsylvania State University, University Park.

Sanders, William T., Susan Toby Evans, and Thomas Charlton
In press. "Colonial Period Cultural Geography of the Teotihuacan Valley," in W. T. Sanders and S. T. Evans (editors), *The Aztec Period Occupation of the Valley.* The Teotihuacan Valley Project Final Report, vol. 5, part 3. Pennsylvania State University. University Park.

Sanders, William T., and Thomas W. Killion
1992. "Factors Affecting Settlement Agriculture in the Ethnographic and Historic Record of Mesoamerica," in Thomas W. Killion (editor), *Gardens of Prehistory: The Archaeology of Settlement Agriculture in Greater Mesoamerica:* pp. 14–32. University of Alabama Press. Tuscaloosa.

Sanders, W. T., J. R. Parsons, and R. S. Santley
1979. *The Basin of Mexico.* Academic Press. New York.

Sanders, William T., and Robert S. Santley
1983. "A Tale of Three Cities," in Evon Vogt and Richard Leventhal (editors), *Prehistoric Settlement Patterns:* pp. 243–291. University of New Mexico Press. Albuquerque.

Sanders, William, and David Webster
1988. "The Mesoamerican Urban Tradition." *American Anthropologist* 90: 521–546.

Schele, Linda, and Peter Mathews
1998. *The Code of Kings: The Language of Seven Sacred Maya Temples and Tombs.* Scribner's. New York.

Schondube Baumbach, O.
1974. "Deidades prehispánicas en el área de Tamazula-Tuxpan-Zapotlán en el Estado de Jalisco," in B. Bell (editor), *The Archaeology of West Mexico:* pp. 168–181. Ajijic. Jalisco.

Scott, Sue
1993. *Teotihuacan Mazapán Figurines and the Xipe Totec Statue: A Link between the Basin of México and the Valley of Oaxaca.* Vanderbilt University Publications in Anthropology No. 44. Nashville.

Seler, Eduard
1915. "Die Teotihuacan-Kultur des Hochlands von Mexiko." *Gesammelte Abhandlungen zur Amerikanischen Sprach-und-Alterthumskunde* 5: 405–585. Ascher. Berlin.

Serra Puche, Mari Carmen
1985. "Terremote Tlaltenco: Los Recursos Lacustres de la Cuenca de México durante el Formativo." Ph.D. dissertation. Universidad Nacional Autónoma de México. México.

Serra Puche, Mari Carmen, and J. Carlos Lazcano Arce
1997. "Xochitecatl-Cacaxtla en el Periodo Epiclásico." *Arqueología* 18: 85–102.

Shepard, Anna O.
1948. *Plumbate: A Mesoamerican Trade Ware.* Carnegie Institution of Washington. Publication 573. Washington, DC.

Silva Cifuentes, Edison
1992. *Estudio agronómico y taxonómico de colecciones de la raza de maíz "cónico," su colección central y perspectivas de uso en mejoramiento genético.* Tesis de maestría. Colegio de Posgrados, Centro de Genética. Montecillo, México.

Smith, Michael E.
1992. *Archaeological Research at Aztec-Period Rural Sites in Morelos, México,* vol. 1: *Excavation and Architecture.* University of Pittsburgh Memoirs in Latin American Archaeology No. 4. Pittsburgh.

Smith, Virginia
2000. "The Art and Iconography of the Xochicalco Stelae," in Kenneth Hirth (editor), *The Xochicalco Mapping Project,* vol. 2. University of Utah Press. Salt Lake City.

Spence, Michael W.
1971. "Some Lithic Assemblages of Western Zacatecas and Durango." *Mesoamerican Studies* 8. University Museum, Southern Illinois University. Carbondale.
1974. "Residential Practices and the Distribution of Skeletal Traits in Teotihuacan, Mexico." *Man* 9: 262–273.
1981. "Obsidian Production and the State in Teotihuacan." *American Antiquity* 48: 769–788.
1989. "Excavaciones recientes en Tlailotlaca, El Barrio Oaxaqueño de Teotihuacan." *Arqueología* 5: 81–104. INAH.

Spencer, Charles S.
1982. *The Cuicatlan Cañada and Monte Alban: A Study of Primary State Formation.* Academic Press. New York.

Stocker, Terrance L.
1974. "Mazapan Figurines from Tula," in R. A. Diehl (editor), *Studies of Ancient Tollan: A Report of the University of Missouri Tula Archaeological Project:* pp. 42–55. Columbia.
1983. "Figurines from Tula, Hidalgo, Mexico." Ph.D. dissertation. University of Illinois. Urbana.

Stone, Andrea
1989. "Disconnection, Foreign Insignia, and Political Expansion: Teotihuacan and the Warrior Stelae of Piedras Negras," in R. A. Diehl and J. C. Berlo (editors), *Mesoamerica after the Decline of Teotihuacan A.D. 700–900.* Dumbarton Oaks. Washington, DC.

Stoutamire, James
1974. "Archaeological Survey of the Tula Urban Zone," in R. A. Diehl (editor), *Studies of Ancient Tollan: A Report of the University of Missouri Tula Archaeological Project.* University of Missouri. Columbia.
1975. "Trend Surface Analysis of Survey Data from Tula, Hidalgo, Mexico." Ph.D. dissertation. University of Missouri. Columbia.

Stresser Pean, Guy
1971. "Ancient Sources on the Huasteca," in R. Wauchope (editor), *Handbook of Middle American Indians,* vol. 11: pp. 582–602. University of Texas Press. Austin.

Stuart, David
1998. "Testimonios sobre la guerra durante el Clásico Maya," *Arqueología Mexicana* 6 (32): 6–13.
2000. "The Arrival of Strangers: Teotihuacan and Tollan in Classic Maya History," in David Carrasco, Lindsay Jones, and Scott Sessions (editors), *Mesoamerica's Classic Heritage: From Teotihuacan to the Aztecs:* pp. 465–514. University Press of Colorado. Boulder.

Sugiura Y., Yoko
1993. "El ocaso de las ciudades y los movimientos poblacionales en el Altiplano Central," in M. C. Serra Puche (coordinator), *El poblamiento de México: Una visión histórico-demográfica,* vol. 1: pp. 190–215. Consejo Nacional de Población. México.

Sugiyama, Saburo, and Rubén Cabrera
1999. "Se descubren dos ofrendas de notable importancia en la Pirámide de la Luna en Teotihuacan." *Arqueología Mexicana* 7, no. 40: 71–73.
2000. "El Proyecto Pirámide de la Luna: Algunos resultados de la Segunda Temporada 1999." *Arqueología* 23: 161–172.

Suma de visitas
- 1905. "Manuscrito 2800 de la Biblioteca Nacional de Madrid, de la mitad del siglo XVI," in F. Del Paso y Troncoso (editor), *Papeles de Nueva España*, vol. 1. Sucesores de Rivadeneyra. Madrid and México.

Taube, Karl A.
- 1992. "The Iconography of Mirrors at Teotihuacan," in Janet C. Berlo (editor), *Art, Ideology, and the City of Teotihuacan:* pp. 169–204. Dumbarton Oaks. Washington, DC.
- 1993. *Aztec and Maya Myths.* British Museum. London.
- 1994. "The Iconography of Toltec Period Chichen Itza," in H. J. Prem (editor), *Hidden among the Hills: Maya Archaeology of the Northwest Yucatan Peninsula.* Verlag von Flemming. Mockmuhl.
- 2000. *The Writing System of Ancient Teotihuacan.* Center For Ancient American Studies. Washington, DC.
- In press. "Tetitla and the Maya Presence at Teotihuacan," in Geoffrey Braswell (editor), *Teotihuacan and the Maya: Reinterpreting Early Classic Maya Interaction.* University of Texas Press. Austin.
- n.d. "The Mirrors of Offerings 1 and 2 of Sala 2 in the Palacio Quemado at Tula: An Iconographic Interpretation," in R. H. Cobean and A. G. Mastache (editors), *Ofrendas en un Palacio Tolteca: Turquesa y concha en el Palacio Quemado de Tula, Hidalgo.* INAH. México.

Thompson, J.E.S.
- 1942. "Representations of Tezcatlipoca at Chichen Itza." *Carnegie Institution of Washington Notes 12.* Washington, DC.

Torres W., Bárbara
- 1985. "Las plantas útiles en el México Antiguo según las fuentes del siglo XVI," in T. Rojas and W. T. Sanders (editors), *Historia de la agricultura: Epoca prehispánica–siglo XVI,* vol. 1: pp. 53–128. INAH. México.

Tolstoy, Paul
- 1958. "Surface Survey of the Northern Valley of Mexico." *Transactions of the American Philosophical Society* 48, no. 5.
- 1978. "Western Mesoamerica before A.D. 900," in R. E. Taylor and C. W. Meighan (editors), *Chronologies in New World Archaeology.* Academic Press. New York.

Tovalin Ahumada, Alejandro
- 1990. "Tlalpizahuac: Un sitio del Postclásico Temprano de la Cuenca de México," in Federica Sodi Miranda (editor), *Mesoamerica y el Norte de México: Siglos IX–XII:* pp. 321–336. INAH. México.

Townsend, Richard
- 1992. *The Aztecs.* Thames and Hudson. New York.

Tozzer, Alfred M.
- 1921. *Excavations of a Site at Santiago Ahuitzotla, D.F., México.* Bureau of American Ethnology, Bulletin 74. Washington, DC.
- 1930. "Maya and Toltec Figures at Chichen Itza." *Proceedings of the 23rd International Congress of Americanists.* New York.
- 1957. *Chichen Itza and Its Cenote of Sacrifice.* Memoirs of the Peabody Museum of Archaeology and Ethnology 12, Harvard University. Cambridge, MA.

Trombold, Charles D.
- 1985. "A Summary of the Archaeology in the La Quemada Region," in M. Foster and P. C. Weigand (editors), *The Archaeology of West and Northwest Mesoamerica.* Westview Press. Boulder, CO.

Trujillo, Teresa Reyna (editor)
- 1984. *Seminario sobre alimentación en México.* Instituto de Geografía, UNAM. México.

Umberger, Emily
- 1987. "Antiques, Revivals, and References to the Past in Aztec Art." *RES: Anthropology and Aesthetics* 13: 62–105.

Universidad Autónoma Chapingo
- 1985. *Xolocotzia: Obras de Efraín Hernández Xolocotzi.* 2 vols. Revista de Geografía Agrícola. Universidad Autónoma de Chapingo. México.

Urcid, Javier
- 1993. "The Pacific Coast of Oaxaca and Guerrero: The Westernmost Extension of Zapotec Script." *Ancient Mesoamerica* 4 (1): 141–165.

Vaillant, G. C.
1931. *Excavations at Ticoman.* American Museum of Natural History, Anthropological Papers, 32-2. New York.
1938. "A Correlation of Archaeological and Historical Sequences in the Valley of Mexico." *American Anthropologist* 40: 535–573.
1941. *Aztecs of Mexico.* Doubleday and Co. New York.

Vega Sosa, Constanza
1975. *Forma y decoración en las vasijas de tradición azteca.* Colección Científica No. 23, INAH. México.

Vega Zaragoza, Gabriel
1973. "Estudio de la infiltración genética de los maíces mejorados sobre los criollos de temporal de los estados de México, Puebla y Tlaxcala." Tesis de maestría. Escuela Nacional de Agricultura, Chapingo. México.

Velasco Mireles, Margarita
1989. "La arqueología en Querétaro," in M. Mejía Sánchez and C. García Mora (editors), *La antropología en México: Panorama histórico,* vol. 13: pp. 231–253. INAH. México.

Vogt, Evon, and Richard M. Leventhal (editors)
1983. *Prehistoric Settlement Patterns: Essays in Honor of Gordon R. Willey.* University of New Mexico Press and Peabody Museum of Archaeology and Ethnology, Harvard University. Cambridge, MA.

Weigand, P. C.
1979. "The Formative-Classic and Postclassic Transitions in the Teuchitlan-Etzatlan Zone of Jalisco." *XV Mesa Redonda: Los procesos de cambio en Mesoamérica y áreas circunvecinas,* vol. 1: pp. 413–423. Sociedad Mexicana de Antropología. México.
1985. "Evidence for Complex Societies during the Western Mesoamerican Classic Period," in M. Foster and P. C. Weigand (editors), *The Archaeology of West and Northwest Mesoamerica.* Westview. Boulder, CO.

Wellhausen, E. J., L. M. Roberts, E. Hernández Xolocotzi, and P. C. Mangelsdorf
1987. "Razas de maíz en México." *Xolocotzia* vol. 2: pp. 609–732. Universidad Autónoma de Chapingo. México.

Whalen M. E., and J. R. Parsons
1982. "Ceramic Markers Used for Period Designations," in J. R. Parsons et al. (editors), *Prehispanic Settlement Patterns in the Southern Valley of Mexico: The Chalco-Xochimilco Region:* pp. 385–460. Memoirs of the Museum of Anthropology 12. University of Michigan. Ann Arbor.

Wicke, Charles R.
1976. "Once More Around the Tizoc Stone: A Reconsideration." *Actas del XLI Congreso Internacional de Americanistas* 2: 209–222. México.

Willey, Gordon R., and Jeremy A. Sabloff
1993. *A History of American Archaeology.* 3rd ed. W. H. Freeman and Company. San Francisco.

Williams, Barbara J.
1984. "Mexican Pictorial Cadastral Registers," in H. R. Harvey and H. J. Prem (editors), *Explorations in Ethnohistory:* pp. 103–125. University of New Mexico Press. Albuquerque.
1991. "The Lands and Political Organization of a Rural Tlaxilacalli in Tepetlaoztoc, c. A.D. 1540," in H. R. Harvey (editor), *Land and Politics in the Valley of Mexico: A Two-Thousand-Year Perspective:* pp. 187–208. University of New Mexico Press. Albuquerque.
1994. "The Archeological Signature of Local Level Polities in Tepetlaoztoc," in M. H. Hodges and M. E. Smith (editors), *Economies and Polities in the Aztec Realm:* pp. 73–87. Institute for Mesoamerican Studies, SUNY. Albany.

Wolf, Eric R.
1959. *Sons of the Shaking Earth.* University of Chicago Press. Chicago.

Wolf, Eric R. (editor)
1976. *The Valley of Mexico.* University of New Mexico Press. Albuquerque.

Wolfman, Daniel
1990. "Mesoamerican Chronology and Archaeomagnetic Dating A.D. 1–1200," in J. L. Eighmy and R. S. Sternberg (editors), *Archaeomagnetic Dating:* pp. 261–391. University of Texas Press. Austin.

Yadeun, Juan
1975. *El estado y la ciudad: El caso de Tula, Hgo. Colección Científica No. 25, INAH. México.*

Index

Page numbers in *italics* indicate illustrations or tables.

Abandonment, 59, 74, 75
Abra Coarse Brown, *47,* 48, 49, 224, 229, 232, 235
Acoculco, 57, 59
Acolhuacan, 276
Acolman, 280
Acosta, Jorge R., 2
Acta Polished Red, 46, *47,* 48, 231, 233, 235
Adoratorio, 129, 131
Agave salmiana, 269. *See also* Maguey
Agriculture, 191–92, 209, 277, 289, 291; amaranth and, 255–58; beans and, 250–53; fallow system in, 248–49; maize, 243–50; maguey, 260–69, 294; rainfall, 33, 35, 195, 197, 247–48; Tula area, 249–50, 307–8. *See also* Irrigation systems
Aguamiel, 229; production of, 261, 262, 263, 265, 266, 294
Ajacuba Valley, 227, 231, 260, 288, 299(n2)
Ajolotes, 272

Alegria. See Amaranth
Alicia Openworked incense burners, *47,* 48, 230, 233, 235
Alpuyeca spring, 82–83
Altar Q (Copán), 142
Altars, 176; friezes on, 111–12
Alta Vista, 69, 107
Amanalco, 170
Amaranth (*Amaranthus* spp.), 269, 270; cultivation and use of, 245, 255–58, 268, 307–8
Amate (*Ficus*), 270
Animals, 141; use of, 272–74, 308. *See also* by type
Apartment Compounds, 152, 155, 159; El Corral as, 156–58; at Tula, 161, 167, 305
Aquila chrysaetos, 141, 148–49(nn2, 5)
Arachis hypogaea, 270
Archaeoastronomy, 148(n1), 152
Architecture, 43, 70; Coyotlatelco occupation and, 62, *64, 65–66,* 68, 69. *See also* by structure type

Argemone, 270
Armadillo (*Dasypus* cf *novemcinctus*), 274
Arrocillo Amarillo race (maize), 240
Artifactual material, 185
Artisans, 144. *See also* Craft production
Atempa, 289
Atenantitech, 170
Atengo, 35, 212
Atetelco, 141
Atezcapan, 170
Atitalaquia, 9, 17, 45, 203, 265, 266, 272; Coyotlatelco occupation in, 60, 68; irrigation systems in, 38, 212
Atitalaquia Settlement Group, 288, 290–94
Atlante sculptures, 95, 96, 304
Atlatongo Complex, 225
Altars, friezes on, 111–12
Atotonilco, 32, 57, 212, 268, 290, 294
Atotonilco Tula, 9, 17, 291
Atzacualpa, 169, 170

INDEX

Atzompa, 133
Autosacrifice, 111, 126, 149(n8)
Axayacatl, 104
Axis mundi, pyramids as, 135, 148(n1)
Ayocote, 245
Azadas, 265
Azcapotzalco, 299
Aztec occupation, 42, 43, 46, 131, 132, 134, 137; palaces and, 144–45, 147

Bajío zone, 48, 70, 71, 229
Ballcourt 1 (Tula), 89, 132, 133, 134, *135,* 141
Ballcourt 2 (Tula), 91, 129, 132, 133, 135
Ballcourts, 64; at Tula, 89, 91, 132–*35,* 141; at Tula Chico, 74, 75
Ball players, depictions of, 133
Balsas River, 241
Barrios, 163, 291, 306; craft production and, 167–69; organization in, 280–82; social status and, 169–70; temples and, 171, 173–76
Barrios Grandes (Tlatelolco), 170, 171, 173
Barrios Menores (Tlatelolco), 170
Basalt, 169, 265, *267*
Batha, 45
Beans (*Phaseolus* sp.), 245, 250–53, 255, 270
Benfer, Robert, 3
Blanco Levantado, *47,* 49, 49, 71, 224, 228–29, 232, 233, 235, 266, 297
Bledo. See Amaranth
Bone production areas, 4
Bordo Red on Brown, 46, *47,* 48, 230–31, 233
Braseros, 47, 48, 125–26, 229, 232
Building 1. *See* Palace of Quetzalcoatl
Building 4. *See* Palace to the East of the Vestibule
Building J. *See* Building to the South of Pyramid C
Building K (Tula), 42, 72, 89, 91, 128–29, *131,* 135, 148
Building 6 (Cihuatecpan), 145, *147*
Building to the South of Pyramid C, 127–28, *130,* 135
Burials, at La Mesa, 66, *67*
Burning, 74, 89

Cabaceras, 227, 281, 282, 291, 294; Type 2 sites as, 283, 288
Cacahuacentli race (amaranth), 255
Cacahuacintle race (maize), 238, 240
Cacao (*Theobroma cacao*), 270
Cacaxtla, 105
Cacaxtla-Xochitecatl, 89
Cadenas irrigation system, 35
Calmecatlaca, 177
Calmilli, 289
Calpolleque, 177
Calpulli, 170, 278–79, 280, 282, 283, 297, 308; distribution of, 289–90
Canals, Classic period, 52, 59
Canines, 141, 272
Canis lupus, 141, 148(n2)
Cantona, 2, 87, 89, 132, 167
Canutillo Phase, 70
Capsicum annuum, 252, 270
Capulín (*Prunus capulli*), 270
Cardonal, 294
Caryatids. *See* Atlantes
Casa de las Aguilas (Tenochtitlan), 111, *115,* 127, 136, 149(n8), 304–5; and Palace to the East of the Vestibule, 113–14
Casa Tolteca, 4
Casimiroa edulis, 271
Cathartidae, 141, 148(n2)
Cat's claw (*Mimosa*), 270
Cazuelas, 228, 232, 243, 297
Ce Acatl Topiltzin, 112
Celaya race (maize), 238, 245
Cenote of Sacrifice (Chichén Itzá), 291
Cenozoic era, 19–20, 22
Centeotl, 65
Central Group (El Canal), 152, *154,* 210
Central Highlands, 89, 270, 276; agave cultivation in, 261, 263; cosmovision of, 137–38; fallow system in, 248–49; maize races from, 238, 240; political and economic reorganization in, 59–60; *tzompantli* in, 132–33
Central Plateau, 17
Ceramic drain tubes, 231
Ceramic production, 217, 219, 225
Ceramics, 12, 57, 71, 127; and chronology, 41, 42; Classic period, 55, 57, 59; Coyotlatelco occupation, 51, 60, 67, 68, 69, 70, 71; cultural sequences and, 43, 44, 45–46; distributions of, *14, 15,* 231–34; Early Tollan Phase, 218–20; production areas, 4, 297, *298;* Tollan Complex, 46–50, *222–23;* Tollan Phase, 199–200, 217–18, 224–29, 234–35; tradeware, 229–30
Ceramics production barrios, *157,* 167–69, 219, 227
Ceramic tubes, 4
Ceremonial mounds, 185; in residential sectors, 166–67, 171–76
Ceremonial precincts, 302; Coyotlatelco occupation and, 62, *64,* 68, 69; entrances to, 134–35; at Tula, 82, 88, 89; at Tula Chico, 72, 74–75. *See also various structures by name or type*
Ceremonial structures, 185, 191, 384; and ceramics, 224, 232; distribution of, *187,* 289, 290, 291, 295, 297, 307; sites with, 283–85, *287*
Chac Mool sculptures, 95, 131, 149(n10), 304; in Palacio Quemado, 124–25
Chahuixtle, 241
Chalchihuites culture, 89; influence of, 69–70, 71
Chalco, 281
Chalqueño race (maize), 238, 239, 241–42, 245
Chapalote race (maize), 240
Chapantongo region, 19, 250
Charnay Palace, 145–47, 152
Chenopodium spp., 269, 270
Chert, 265, 290–91
Chia, 270
Chiapa de Mota, 270
Chiapantongo, 270
Chiapas, ceramics from, 229–30
Chicalote (*Argemone*), 270
Chichén Itzá, 108, 125, 131, 132, 291; deity depictions at, 100, 103–4; iconography at, 105, 149(nn10, 12); personages depicted in, 106, 112
Chiconautla, 147, 280
Chiles (*Capsicum annuum*), 252, 270
Chimalpa, 281
Chinampa agriculture, 256, 308
Chingú, 13, 35, *56,* 57, 80, 294; Classic occupation of, 52, 55
Chingú hacienda, 212

404

INDEX

Chingú Phase, 45
Cholula, 2, 177, 264
Chronology, 41, *42*, 51, 71, 74; Tula region, 43–46
Cihuacóatl, 104
Cihuatecpan, 144, 145, *147*
Cipactli symbols, 98
Circular structures, 70
Cities: location of, 78–79; organization of, 77–78; shape and plan of, 81–85
Ciudadela, 55
Classic period, 12, 43, 51, 65, 70, 71, 88, 264, 265, 301; settlement pattern during, 52–60, 193–94
Climate, 9, 40(n1), 258; bean cultivation and, 252, 255; and erosion cycles, 22–23; maguey distribution and, 260–61; maize cultivation and, 244–45
Cloth production, 147
Clusters, site, 211–12, *213*, 299(n1)
Coatepantli, 133–34
Cold-Dry Stage, 28
Collection Units (URs), 183, *184, 185–86*, 193, 194–95, 232
Colonia Pemex, 4
Colonization, of rural areas, 220–21
Comales, 228, 231, 233, 234, 243
Communities, 183; organization of, 277–79, 280–81, 282–83, 299(n4), 308; population distribution in, 279–80; sizes of, 281–82
Complexes, site type, 190–91
Concentrated Artifactual Material, 185, 186–87, 232
Conch shells, representations of, 95, *96*, 117, 133
Conflicts, Topiltzin Quetzalcoatl and Tezcatlipoca, 74, 75, 104
Cónico race (maize), 238, 239, 240, 241, 245
Construction stages; of monumental architecture, 89–148
Contlazinco, 281
Copán, 142, 143, 149(n18)
Corral Phase, 41, 42, 43, 46; at Tula Chico, 71, 72, *73*, 74
Correo Mayor, Zanja del, 35, 212
Coscomate River, 17, 19, 204, 205, 207
Cosmogony, cosmovision, 91, 137–38, 304
Coyoacán, 299

Coyotlatelco, 45
Coyotlatelco Complex ceramics, 68
Coyotlatelco occupation, 51, 72, 89, 194, 218; maguey production and, 265, 266, 307; northen influences on, 69–71; settlement pattern of, 60, 62–69, 194–95, 198
Coyotlatelco Red on Brown, 69
Coyotlatelco Sphere complexes, 41, 42, 45–46
Craft production, 225; and neighborhoods, 167–69; sites and, 283, 290–91
Crayfish, 272
Crop rotation, 249, 256
Cuahxicalli, 104, 111, 124
Cuauhtemoc, 98
Cuauhtepoztla, 277, 278, 299(n4)
Cuauhtinchán, 281
Cucurbita pepo, 269
Cuepopan, 169, 170
Cuicatec, 133
Cuicatlán Cañada, 133
"Cuitlacoche" (amaranth), 255
Cuitlixco, 281
Culhuacan, 305
Cults, 104, 124, 125–26, 133, 135, 138
Cultural sequences: characteristics of, 42–46; ceramics and, 46–50

Daini, 157–58
Dams, 33, 35
Dart House, 126–27
Dasylirion spp., 269, 270
Dasypus cf *novemcinctus*, 274
Deer (*Odocoileus virginianus*), 272, 274
Defensive sites, 60, 62, 68, 79
Deforestation, 28
Denguí, 32
Diehl, Richard, 3
Deities, 138; on Pyramid B pillars, *96, 98*, 99–104. *See also by name*
Descending-bird motifs, 105–6
Descripción del Arzobispado de México, 291, 295
Diet, and pottery types, 234
Diospyros sp., 270
Dispersed Artifactual Material, 185, 186, 197–98, 209, 232
Dispersed Habitat, 209–10
Dogs, 272, 274
Dos Pilas, 149–50(n19)

Duality, 149(n14), 304
Durango, 71
Dynasties, 99

Eagles (*Aquila chrysaetos*), 141, 148–49(nn2, 5)
Early Classic period, 45, 132–33, 193
Early Postclassic, 12, 30, 46, 77, *189, 267, 275*, 276; agriculture, 248, 250; ceramics of, 218, 229, 231; irrigation systems of, 212, *214*–15; maize races of, 238, 239, 240–42; settlement pattern of, 179–82, 194, *200, 202, 203, 204, 205, 206, 207, 254*, 283–99
Early Tollan Phase, 161, 303; ceramics of, 218–20
East Group (El Canal), 152, 154
Echinofossulocactus, 270
Economy, 10; barrios and, 167–68, 306
Effigies, Tlaloc, 125–26
El Aguila, 45, 68
El Canal, 4, 14, 166, 257, 274; ceramics from, 57, 229, 230; excavations at, 43, 57, 79; House Groups at, *152–55, 156*, 159, 162, 165, 210; plant production and use, 237, 270; temples in, 173, *174–75*
El Cielito, 14, 57, 72, 83, 169
El Corral, 4, 173, *176*, 237, 243; as Apartment Compound, 156–58, 159; excavations at, 43, 79; panel reliefs at, 128, 149(n17)
El Elefante, Cerro, 68
Elites, 104, 227; land tenure, 297, 299
El Llano, 83
Elotes Occidentales race (maize), 238
El Sabino spring, 35, 195
El Salitre, 4, 57, 82, 257
El Salitre swamp, 28
El Salto, Zanja de, 207
El Salto del Agua, 32
El Salto River, 17, 200, 204, 207, 283
El Tajín, 128
El Tesoro, 57, 59
El Venado, 13
El Vivero, 4, 157
Endó Canal, 199
Endó Dam, 33, 38, 288
Environment, 9
Epiclassic period, 12, 51, 89, 302

405

INDEX

Eragrostis sp., 270
Erosion cycles, 22–23
Ethnic groups: craft production and, 169, 225; at Tula, 159, 167, 177; at Tula Chico, 74, 75–76
Ethnohistories, 275–83
Etzalqualiztli, 123
Excavated areas, 4, *5*
Exotic Pre-Columbian races (maize), 240

Fallow system, 248–49, 270
Families, 246; 278; extended, 162–63; and habitational structures, 190–91; territory and, 279–80
Farming. *See* Agriculture
Fauna. *See* Animals
Feathered-serpent motifs, 108, 113, 304
Felines, 141, 148(n2)
Fertilizer, 249
Ficus sp., 270
Figurines, Mazapan, 230, 233, 235
Firewood, as tribute, 144
Fishing, fish, 269, 272, 308
Foods, 253, 263, 279; amaranth as, 256–57; gathering and hunting of, 269–70; maize as, 242–43, 246
Formative period, 265
Friezes, 134; in Palace East of the Vestibule, 111–12; in Palacio Quemado, 117–18, 119–22, *124*, *125*; in South Vestibule, 107–11
Friso de los Caciques, 107, *110*, 111; personages on, 108–9
Fruit trees, 33
Fuego Phase, 41, 42, 43, 46
Funeral rites, 149(n8); Palacio Quemado and, 126–27

Garambullo (*Myrtillocactus geometrizans*), 271
Gardens, vegetable, 289
Gathering, 269, 308
Geology, 19, *21*
Geomorphology, 19–20, 22–23
Glyphs, on Pyramid B pillars, 98, 105–6
Government: palaces and, 143–44; Tula's dual, 105, 142
Greens, 269
Grijalva River basin, 241
Group of the Thousand Columns (Chichén Itzá), 125

Guanajuato, 70
Guatemala, ceramics from, 229–30
Guerrero, 241

Habitation units/complexes, 4, 85, 183; characteristics of, 165–67; types of, 152–63. *See also* Apartment Compounds; House Groups
Habitation structures, 185, *187,* 210; complexes of, 190–91; distribution of, 187–88
Hacienda Bojay, 13
Haciendas, 32, 33, 35
Hare (*Lepus* sp.), 272
Helianthus annuus, 270–71
Heroes de Carranza, 9
Hidalgo, 72
Historia tolteca-chichimeca, 176–77
House Groups, 176, 230; at El Canal, 152–55, *156*, 210; rural, 158–59, *160*; at Tula, *157*, 161–62, 166, 167, 305
Households: and community organization, 278–79, 280, 305; settlement distribution and, 289–90
Huasteca, 70; ceramics and, 72, 225, 231; cultural influences from, 46, 48, 79
Huautli. *See* Amaranth
Huejotzingo, 277, 281, 282
Huichapan, 270
Huistle, Cerro de, 69; *tzompantli* at, 132–33
Huitel, 199
Huitzilopochtli, 304; temples to, 137, *139*, 140, 149(n14)
Huiznahuac, 277, 278
Human figures. *See* Personages
Hunting, 269, 308

Iconography, 138; of La Mesa sculpture, 65–66; on Pyramid B pillars, 98–106; of Pyramid B sculptures, 95–96; Toltec, 303–4. *See also* Symbolism
Icxicouatl, 177
INAH. *See* Instituto Nacional de Antropologia e Historia
Incense burners (*incensarios*), 230, 233
Indigenous Ancient Races (maize), 240
Inferred habitation structures, 185
Insects, consumption of, 271, 272

Institution Nacional de Antropologia e Historia (INAH), 3, 11
Ira Stamped Orange, *47,* 49, 219, 225, 227
Irrigation District of the Ministry of Water Resources, 33
Irrigation systems, 10, 11, 32–33, 35–40, 201; Classic period, 52, 59; collection points of, 198–99; Early Postclassic, 212, *214*–15, 283, 289; maize cultivation and, 245–47; Xochitlán, 38–40; zones of occupation and, 195, 198–99, 201–2
Isolated Habitational Structures, 188
Ixmiquilpan, 33
Izcoatl, 98

Jade, 4
Jalisco, 70, 71
Jara Polished Orange, *47,* 48, 49, 218, 219, 224–25, 227, 231, 232
Jasso, 32
Jilotepec, 9, 39, 260
Joroba Orange on Cream, *47,* 48, 49, 195, 218–19
Juandó hydroelectric station, 33
Julián Villagrán, 55

K'inich Yax K'uk' Mo', 142
Kings: depictions of, 98, 104–5, 106, *107*, 118, 136, 142; rituals of, 111, 149(n8)

La Cañada, 32
La Goleta, 32, 35, 40
La Loma, 44–45
La Malinche, 83, 169
La Malinche, Cerro, 4, 72, 157
La Mesa, 45, 69, 107, 265, 266; Coyotlatelco occupation of, 60, 62, 64–67
La Mesa, Cerro, 203, 265, 288
La Mesa Ahumada, Cerro, 68–69
La Mesa Phase, 45, 67, 264
La Mesa Settlement Group, 288–90
La Mesa sierra, 201, 266
La Quemada, 65, 69, 89, 107
La Romera, 35, 199, 201, 212
Land use and tenure, *31,* 181; farming and, 85, 277, 289; nineteenth-century, 30, 32–33, *34*; pre-Hispanic, 198, *199*, 279, 297, 299; surveys of, 10–11
Las Cadenas Dam, *39*

406

Las Flores, 225
Las Ranas, 65
Las Ventanas, 69
Late Classic period, 89, 302
Late Formative period, 44–45, 133
Late Postclassic period, 70, 133, 144, 147, 260, 280, 304; reoccupation during, 89, 129
Late Tlamimilolpa phase, 45, 57
Late Tollan Phase: ceramics of, 224, 225; spatial units of, 163–65; urban layout of, 161–62
Lemaireocereus sp., 269, 270
La Ventilla complex, 264
Lepus sp., 272
Lime, production and use of, 59, 268, 294–95
Limestone, 283, 301
Lineages, iconography of, 105
Lithic industries, 265, *298*; Atitalaquia Settlement Group, 290–91; Coyotlatelco, 68, 69, 70; at Tula Chico, 71–72
Loma Alta, 70
Los Picachos mountains, 266

Macana Red on Brown, 46, *47,* 48, 49, 224, 227, 229, 230, 235
Macehuales, 282
Macua Dam, 199
Magoni, 45, 288; Coyotlatelco occupation at, 60, 62, 67–68, 69
Magoni, Cerro, 3, 68, 79, 169, 198, 288
Magoni-Bojay mountain range, 79, 82, 198; terraces and, 264–65
Maguey (*Agave* sp.), 229, 294; Coyotlatelco occupation and, 66–67, 68; cultivation and use of, 33, 249, 260–69, 307
Maiz Ancho Olotillo, 238
Maize (*Zea mays*), *251,* 270; cultivation of, 33, 252, 268; and maguey cultivation, 261–62; preparation and consumption of, 228, 231, 242–43; production and yield of, 237, 243–50; races of, 238–42
Man-bird-reptile motifs, 128, *130,* 140
Manuelito Plain Brown, 46, *47,* 48, 195, 218, 219
Marketplaces, neighborhood, 173
Marquesado of Morelos, 153
Maya, 142, 143

Maya Chac, 128
Mazapan Complex, 218; figurines, 230, 233
Mazapa Red on Brown (Wavy-Line Mazapan Red on Brown), 46, 48, 49, 195, 218, 232, 235
Meleagris sp., 272, 274
Mendrugo *comals, 47,* 48, 233
Mercado (Chichén Itzá), 112, 113
Merchant's Barrio (Teotihuacan), 70, 167
Mesa Lechuguilla range, 202, 290
Mesozoic era, 19
Mesquite (*Prosopis* sp.), 270, 271–72
Metepec Phase, 45, 51, 55, 57, 60
Mexican Pyramidal Race Complex (maize), 238
Mexica rulers, 98, 104
Mexico, Basin of, *254,* 308. *See also various sites; regions*
Mexico Balsas-Occidente maize group, 238, 239
Mezquital Valley, 33, 201, 229, 250
Meztitlán, 262
Miccaotli Phase, 52, 57
Michimaloya, 39, 40, 268
Michoacán, 43, 66, 71, 79
Middle Formative occupation, 44, 70
Migrants, Toltec, 177, 301
Mimosa, 270
Mines, obsidian, 72, 79
Mirrors: as offerings, 123–24; as pectorals, 101, 103; symbolism of, 104, 138, 140, 149(nn10, 15)
Mixquiahuala, 9, 13, 33
Mixteco race (maize), 238–39
Moctezuma I, 104
Moctezuma II, 144
Modern Incipient Races (maize), 241
Mollusks, 272
Molotecatl, 279
Molotla, 278–79, 280, 289, 290
Monte Albán, 57, 59, 133
Monte Albán I phase, 57
Monte Albán II phase, 57
Monumental precincts, 87, 303–4, 307; at Teotihuacan, 92–93, *94;* at Tula, 82, *87–91,* 89–92, 142–48; at Tula Chico, 93–94. *See also various structures; structure types*
Morelos, 60, 153, 241, 278, 308
Moyotlan, 169, 170
Muhlenbergia macruoura, 269, 270
Multifamily complexes, 153, 162

Munitepec, 288
Mushrooms, 269
Myrtillocactus geometrizans, 271

Nal Tel race (maize), 240
Navajas, Sierra de las, obsidian from, 72, 79
Nayar, Sierra del, 70
Nearest neighbor coefficients, and site distribution, 208–9
Neighborhoods. *See* Barrios
Neo-Volcanic Axis, 19
Netzahualcoyotl, 144
New Fire, 149(n10)
Nextlalpan, 40
NIDE. *See* Sites with Indeterminate Number of Structures
NIDE Sites with Ceremonial Architecture, 188
9-Hand, 128
Nixtamalization, 242–43
Nonoalcas, 159
Nopal (*Opuntia* spp.), 270; production and use of, 264, 269, 271
Nueva, Zanja, *54,* 59, 201

Oak (*Quercus* sp.), 270
Oaxaca, 55, 57, 59, 230, 265
Oaxaca barrio (Teotihuacan), 57–58, 59, 167, 301
Obsidian, 43, 66, 78; maguey production and, 265, 266; at Tula Chico, 71–72
Obsidian workshops, 4, 14, *15,* 218; at Tula, 154–55, *168,* 227
Ocampo, 57
Ocotelulco, 280, 281, 282
Odocoileus virginianus, 272, 274
Offerings, 131, 141; mirrors in, 138, 140; found in Palacio Quemado, 123–24, *126*
"Ojo de Pájaro" (amaranth), 255
Ollas, 228–29, 230–31, 243; Coyotlatelco occupation and, 67, 68, 71; maguey processing and, 265, 266; Soltura, 232–33
Olmeca-Xicalanca, 105
Olotillo race (maize), 239, 241
Opuntia sp., 264, 269, 270
Organos, Arroyo de los, 198
Otomí, 229, 262, 263, 269, 270, 271
Otumba, 280
Oxtotipac Complex, 60
Pachuca, Sierra de, 43, 79

INDEX

Palace of Axayacatl, 144
Palace of Moctezuma II, 144
Palace of Quetzalcoatl (Tula), 96, 113, 114, 137, 145; form of, 115–16
Palace to the East of the Vestibule (Tula), *109,* 116, 136, 137, 145, 303, 304–5; altar frieze in, 111–12; and Casa de las Aguilas (Tenochtitlan), 113–14
Palaces: functions of, 143–44; Tecpan, 144–45; at Tula, 142, *146,* 147–48
Palacio Charnay. *See* Charnay Palace
Palacio Phase, 41, 42, 46
Palacio Quemado (Tula), 42, 64, 72, 96, 104, 113, 114, 115, 133, 135, 136–37, 145, 148, 227, 303; artwork in, 117–23; iconography of, 126–27, 149(n10), 304; offerings found in, 123–24; ritual and, 124–25; structure of, 116–17, *118, 119*; Tlaloc cult and, 141, 142
Palacio Tolteca, 4
Paleoenvironment, 28–30
Palomero Toluqueño race (maize), 238, 239, 240, 242
Panchimalco, 278, 290
Panoaya, 60
Pánuco River, 17, 79
Papita de monte (*Solanum* sp.), 270
Patios, in residential architecture, 162, 167
Patlachique sierra, 277
Patron gods, 173
Patzcuaro Basin, Lake, 246
Peanuts (*Arachis hypogaea*), 270
Peccary (*Tayassu tajacu*), 274
Pectorals, 100, 101, 103, 149(n12)
Pepitilla race (maize), 238, 239, 240–41
Periodification, 41–42
Personages, 134, *135,* 138; on Palace East of the Vestibule friezes, 111–12, *113*; in Palacio Quemado artwork, 117–19, *120, 122–23, 124;* on Pyramid B pillars, 96, *98,* 99–*106*; on South Vestibule friezes, 107–11. *See also various deities by name*
Phaseolus sp., 245, 250–53, 255, 270
Physalis (green tomato), 269, 270
Pillar 3, sculpture on, 99–106
Pillars, on Pyramid B, 96–106

Pilli, 297, 298
Pintura Roja, 227
Pipiles, 230
Pitahaya (*Lemaireocereus* sp.), 269, 270
Plants: production and use of, 237, 269–71; wild, 253, 257, 308. *See also* Agriculture; *various plants by type*
Plataforma de Venus (Chichén Itzá), 131
Platforms, 152, 185; *talud,* 115–16; at Tula, 88, 91; at Tula Chico, 93–94
Plaza Charnay, 57, 134
Plazas, 93, 132, 166, 171, 185; accesses to, 134–35; Coyotlatelco, 62, 64, 69; at Tula, 90–*91*. *See also* Ceremonial precincts
Plazoleta Norte, 116, 132, 134, 135
Plazoleta Sur, 134
Plumbate ceramics, 270
Pochteca, depictions of, 108–9
Political-religious organization, at Tula Chico, 74–75
Political systems, 10, 69
Pollen, and paleoenvironment reproduction, 28–30
Population distribution, 210–11, 250, 277–78, 297; communities and, 279–80, 281–82, 289–90
Population movements, 59–60
Porticos, 107
Portulaca spp., 269, 270
Postclassic period, 43; maize in, 239–40
Pottery. *See* Ceramics
Pozole, 243
Prado Complex, 45, 71
Prado Phase, 41, 42, 43, 45, 60, 71
Prehistoric Mixed Races (maize), 240
Presa Requena, 169
Presa Vieja irrigation system, 35
Priests, 100, 105, 177
Proa Polished Cream, *47,* 48, 49, 219, 224, 225, 232
Processions, depictions of, 108–12, 119, 122–23, *125,* 141
Production areas, 4, 198; at Tula, 167–69
Progreso, 57, 294
Projectile point workshops, 290–91
Prosopis laevigata, 269
Prunus capulli, 270
Puebla, 87

Pueblo, Cerro del, 69
Puebla-Tlaxcala, 60
Puente Colgante, 212
Pulque, 33, 229, 261; production of, 262, 263, 264, 265, 266, 294
Puma concolor, 141, 148(n2)
Purslane (*Portulaca* spp.), 269, 270
Pyramid B (Tula), 64, 90, 91, *92, 93, 108,* 114, 115, 116, 134, 135, 140, 148(n1), 303, 304; architectonic complex of, 136–*37*; and Ballcourt 1, 132; pillars on, 96–106; sculptures on, 65, *107,* 127, 128, 149(n12); structure of, 95–96; and Tlaloc cult, 141, 142. *See also* South Vestibule
Pyramid C (Tula), 65, 90, 91, *92,* 93, 114, 129, 132, 134, 140, 148(n1), 303, 304, 305; structure of, 94–95, 135
Pyramid of the Moon (Teotihuacan), 92, *94,* 115, 136, 138, 141, 148(n1), 149(n16), 303
Pyramid of the Sun (Teotihuacan), 92, 136, 138, 148(n1), 149(nn15, 16), 303, 304
Pyramids, 132, 173, *176,* 303; cosmovision and, 137–38; at Tula, 88, 90–92, *93,* 94–96, 135–36. *See also* Pyramid B; Pyramid C; Ceremonial mounds; Temples; Templo Mayor

Quelites, 269
Querétaro, 70
Quetzalcoatl, 95, 100, 104; and pyramids, 140–41; representations of, 96, 105, 112, 128
Quetzalteueyac, 177
Quiahuiztlan, 280, 281–82

Rabbit (*Sylvilagus* sp.), 272
Radiocarbon dates, 74
Rainfall. *See* Climate
Rainfall farming, 33, 35, 289
Ranas, 70
Real habitation structures, 185
Rebato Polished Red, *47,* 48, 224, 227–28, 232
Red, use in houses, 144, 48
Red House, 144, 148. *See also* Tecpan
Relaciones Geográficas, 291, 294
Religious organization, of Tula Chico, 74–75
Requena Canal, 171, 199

Requena Dam, 33, 35, 38, 57, 205, 207
Residential architecture: Coyotlatelco occupation, *65–66*, 68, 69; Tollan Phase, 151–77; at Teotihuacan, 162–63; at Tula, 151–62, 163–77
Rhyolite instruments, 68, 265
Rituals, 111, 123, 265: amaranth use in, 255, 257, 260; funeral, 126–27; sacrificial, 124–25
Romera, Zanja la, 35, 52, *54*, 59
Rosas River, 17, 19, 82, 169, 181, 197, 198
Rulers, royalty: depictions of, 98, 104, 118, 136, 142; and descending-bird motifs, 105–6; funeral rites of, 126–27; palaces and, 144, 145, 152
Rural areas, 13, 14, 275, 308; ceramics on, 218–20, 224, 225, 227, 228–29, 232–33; residential architecture of, 158–59; settlement groups in, 288–99; site distribution in, 207–15, 285–88, 289, 306–7; site ranking in, 283–85; site types in, 188, 190–92; zones of occupation in, 193–207

Sacred precincts, Tula, 135–42, 303. *See also* Ceremonial precincts; Monumental precincts; *various structures by name or type*
Sacred space, defining, 133–34
Sacrifice, rituals of, 124–25, 127
Sage (*Salvia* sp.), 270
Salado River, 17, 33, 68; agriculture on, 268, 289; irrigation systems on, 35, 38; settlement pattern and, 199, 200, 201, 202, 288, 290, 291, 294–95
Salvia sp., 270
San Agustin (La Goleta), 40
San Andrés Nantza, 39, 212
San Antonio, 40
San Antonio Tula, 32
San Bartolo, 65
San Francisco Bojay, 13, 32, 38, 212
San Francisco Soyaniquilpan, 39
San Francisco spring, 39
San Gregorio Atlapulco, 256
San Isidro Bojay, 32, 35
San Jeronimo, 277
San José Bojay, 32
San José del Tinto, 70

San Juan del Río, 70
San Juan Rojo/bayo ceramics, 70
San Lorenzo, 38, 83, 212
San Lorenzo Endó, 32
San Lorenzo Xipacoya, 38, 212
San Luis Potosi, 70
San Marcos, 38, 83
Santa Maria Asunción, *Tlaxicalli* de, 276–77, 278, 279, 280, 282, 289, 290
Santa Maria Asunción Codex, 276–77
Santa María Illucan, 212
Santa María Macua, 197
Santa María Magdalena, 33
San Miguel, Zanja, 198
San Miguel Chingú, 32, 59
San Miguel de Allende, 70
San Miguel Vindhó, 38, 212
San Pedro Nextlalpan, 32, 212, 268
San Pedro Tlaxcoapan, 33
Scirpus spp., 269
Scrapers, basalt and rhyolite, 265, *267*
Sculptures, 131, 133, 134; on Building to the South of Pyramid C, 127–28; at La Mesa, 65–66; mirrors in, 138, 140; on Pyramid C, 94–95; on Pyramid B, 95–96; on Pyramid B pillars, 96–106. *See also* Friezes
Señorios, 276–77, 280–81, 282
Serpentine production areas, 4
Serpents, 112; depictions of, 134, 149(n6). *See also* Feathered-serpent motif
Settlement Groups, 285–87; alluvial valley and, 297, 299; Atitalaquia, 290–94; La Mesa, 288–90; Tlamaco, 294–97
Settlement patterns, *61,* 237; Classic era, 52–59; Classic Teotihuacan, 193–94; Coyotlatelco occupation and, 62–71; dispersed and nucleated occupation and, 209–11; Early Postclassic, 276, 283–99; habitation structures, 187–88; regional, 9–15; Teotihuacan's decline and, 59–60; Tollan Phase, 179–82, 195–209; use of elevations in, 88–89
Shell production areas, 4
Shrimp, freshwater, 272
Sierra Madre Occidental, 19
Sillón Incised, 46, *47,* 224, 225, 226, 229, 235

Site location, 78–79
Sites: defining, 182–83; hierarchical ranking of, 191–92, 293–94; identifying, 186–88; and settlement groups, 285–88, 289–90, 295, 297, 306–7; types of, 188–92; and zones of occupation, 207–15
Sites with Indeterminate Number of Structures (NIDE), 188
Skulls, representations of, 138, 140, 149(n17)
Slab construction, 65
"Sloppy" Red on Brown, 218
Social status, 177, 226; and neighborhoods, 169–70, 282; and settlement patterns, 289–90
Socioeconomic units: extended family as, 162–63; habitation complexes and, 165–66
Soconusco, 230
Soils, 266, 289; and agriculture, 249, 268–69, 308; classes of, 24, 26, 27; and maize cultivation, 244–45; regional, 23–24, *25*
Solanum sp., 270
Solar deities, 138, 149(n15)
Soltura Smoothed Red, *47,* 48, 224, 228, 232–33, 243, 266
South Vestibule (Tula), 96, 136, 303; characteristics of, 106–7, 114; friezes in, 107–11
Soyaniquilpan springs, 198
Space, 152; organization of, 77–78; sacred, 133–34; urban, 142–43, 161–62
Spatial units, 163–65
Spindle whorls, 147
Springs, 39, 195, 198
Squash, 252
Stipa sp., 270
Stone disk sculpture, 138
Storage areas, 127
Street of the Dead (Teotihuacan), 92–93
Suma de Visitas, 295
Sunflower (*Helianthus annuus*), 270–71
Surface collections, *220, 221, 219, 222*
Survey, regional, 7–12
Swamps, 82–83
Symbolism, 94; on Pyramid B sculptures, *97,* 98–99; Quetzalcoatl, 140–41. *See also* Iconography

INDEX

Tabloncillo race (maize), 241–42
Talud platforms, 94, 115–16, 129
Tamuín, 70
Tanleón, 70
Tarea jars, 48, 233
Tasguada, 19, 195, *198*
Tayassu tajacu, 274
Tecalli objects, 4
Tecomates, 231, 233
Tecpan, 281
Tecpan, 144–45, *147,*
Tecpancalli, 144
Tecuhtli, 278, 290, 297, 299
Tehuacán valley, 239–40
Teltipan, 13
Teltipan de Juárez, 288
Temascalapa, 307
Temperate-Humid Stage, 28–29
Temperate Humidity Stage, 258
Temple of Quetzalcoatl (Teotihuacan), 93
Temple of the Jaguars (Chichén Itzá), 105, 106, 112, 132
Temple of the Warriors (Chichén Itzá), 132, 149(n12)
Temples: and *barrios,* 169–71, 173–74
Templo Mayor (Tenochtitlan), 93, 114, 137, *140,* 149(n14), 304, 305; cults of, 137, 138; rituals and, 126–27
Templo Mayor (Tezcoco), *139,* 140
Tenochtitlan, 2, 88, 111, 125, 138, 144, 167, 281, 299; Casa de las Aguilas, 113–114, *115,* 136; layout of, 169–70; residential complexes at, 162, 163, 306; rituals in, 126–27; Templo Mayor at, 93, 137, *140;* and Tula, 304–5
Tenzompa, 69
Teocintle, 240, 241
Teopan, 169, 170
Teotenango, 89
Teotihuacan, 2, 45, 52, 55, 70, 108, 115, 138, 149(n16), 155, 159, 167, 249, 264, 280, 301, 307; decline and collapse as, 59–60; layout of, 85, 87; maize from, 238, 239, 240; monumental zone at, 88, 92–93, *94;* neighborhoods in, 167, 171; Oaxacan barrio at, 57, 59; people from, 75–76; pyramids at, 136, 137; residential architecture at, 65, 162–63; Tlaloc cult, 141–42; and Tula, 303–4

Teotihuacan occupation, 51, 193–94, 195
Teotihuacan Valley, 210, 225, 249
Tepantitla, 264
Tepeji del Río, 9, 17, 33, 59, 212, 262
Tepeji Phase, 45
Tepeji River, 59
Tepeji River Dam, 33, 35
Tepepan, 289
Tepetenchic, 278, 280, 289
Tepeticpac, 280
Tepetitlán, 9, 13, 14–*15,* 17, 32, 43, 195, 212, 218, 257, *259, 291*; animal use at, 272–74; beans in, 252–53; ceramics of, 225, 227, 229, 230, 232, 235; domestic units at, 152, 158–59, *160, 161,* 210; maguey use at, 266, 268; maize from, 237, 238, 239, 243; wild plant use at, 269–70, 271
Tepetitlán, Arroyo, 13, 195
Tepetlaoztoc, 276–77
Tepoztlan, 278, 279–80, 282
Tequitl, 281
Terminal Corral Complex, 220, 229
Terminal Corral Phase, 41, 42, 43, 74, 218, 228
Terminal Formative period, 45, 59
Terraces, 88; maguey cultivation and, 261–62, 264–65, 266
Terrapene sp., 274
Territorial units, 279–80, 308
Tesoro Phase, 41, 42, 46
Tetepango, 288
Teuchitlán culture, 70
Texcoco, 144
Textiles, maguey fiber and, 263, 268
Tezcacuitlapilli, 138, 140
Tezcatlipoca, 74, 75, 125, 127, 302, 303, 304; depictions of, *101,* 103–4
Tezcoco, Templo Mayor at, *139,* 140
Tezontepec, 35, 212, 268
Tezontepec de Aldama, 17
Tezoyuca, 280
Theobroma cacao, 270
Thin Orange, 55
Tikal, 143
Tizatlán, 280, 281, 282
Tizoc Stone, 104
Tlacatecpan, 279–80
Tlachimalco, 280
Tlacochcalcatl, Pedro, 278
Tlacochcalco, 126–27, 149(n8)
Tlacohtecuhtli, Domingo, 278

Tlacuilapaxco, 264
Tlahtocayo, 282
Tlahuelilpan, 9, 13, 17, 32, 62, 203, 227, 288, 289; irrigation system, 35, 38, *39*
Tlahuizcalpantecuhtli, 65, 140; representations of, 96, *97,* 128, 134
Tlaloc, 303; cult of, 104, 124, 125–26, 133, 135, 141–42, 149(n10), 304; depictions of, 101, *102,* 119, 123, 128, *130,* 149–50(nn18, 19); pyramids and, 137, 138, *139*
Tlaloc Temple (Tenochtitlan), 125
Tlamaco, 212, 268, 294
Tlamaco Settlement Group, 288, 294–97
Tlamaco feeder dam, 33
Tlamaoco, 281
Tlamimilolpa Phase, 55, 59
Tlatelolco, 149(n14), 170, 306
Tlatoani, 280
Tlaxcala, 280–81, 282, 308
Tlaxcoapan, 17, 38, 203
Tlaxilacallis, 170, 276–77, 278, 279, 280, 297, 308; rural, 283, 285, 290, 299(n4)
Tohil Plumbate pottery, *47,* 48, 49, 229–30, 235
Tollan Complex, 13–*14; braseros* of, 125–26; ceramics of, 46–50, 217, 220–32
Tollan Phase, 13, 41, 42, 43, 51, 76, 82, 89, 129, 132, 237, 266, 302; ceramics and, 167, 218–34; residential architecture, 65, 148, 151–77; settlement pattern of, 179–82, 193–215, 299(n2); Tula's layout in, 85, 161–62
Tollan Sphere, 49
Toltec A orientation, 159, 161, 220
Toltec B orientation, 159, 161, 163, 220
Tolteca A (Tula), *84*
Tolteca B (Tula), *86*
Tolteca-Chichimeca, 159
Toltec culture, 303–4; agriculture, 249–50; ceramics of, 46, 48
Toltec House, 156
Toltec Palace, 145–47
Toltec Red on Brown ("Sloppy" Red on Brown; Toltec Red on Buff), 218
Toltecs, 96, 105–6, 177
Toltec state, 51, 301

Toluca, Valley of, 60
Toluquilla, 65
Tomatlán, 70
Topiltzin Quetzalcoatl, 74, 75, 302, 303; depictions of, 100, *102, 103*, 104
Topography: Tula River Basin, 17, 19; and urban layout, 169–70
Toza Smoothed Brown, 224, 227; *cazuelas* of, *47,* 48, 228, 232, 297
Trade, 72; ceramic, 229–30; obsidian, 43, 66, 71
Transitional occupation, 60, *61,* 194
Trans–Sierra Madre Alliance, 238, 239
Tres Pueblos, Zanja de los, 38, 212
Tribute, 144, 260, 279
Triple Alliance, tribute to, 260
Tula, 1, 17, 78, 138, 140, 159, 253, 264, 274; agriculture and, 249–50, 268–69, 307–8; amaranth in, 257, 258, 260; archaeological studies of, 2–3; ceramics of, 218, 219; ceremonial mounds in, 171–76; Classic period, 55, *58,* 301; core area–hinterland relationships in, 233–34; craft production in, 167–69, 227; Early Postclassic, 77, 276; expansion of, 220–21, 302–3; internal organization of, 305–6; irrigation system, 39, 212; layouts of, *84, 85, 86,* 87, *164;* location of, 79–*80, 81*; maguey cultivation and processing in, 262–63, 265, 268; maize processing and consumption at, 242–43; maize races of, 240–42; modern destruction of, 3–4; monumental precinct in, 87–*91*, 142–48; neighborhoods in, 163, 165, 167–68, 170–71; palaces at, 145, *146,* 147–48; pillar sculptures at, 96–106; pyramids at, 91–*92, 93*, 94–96; residential structure of, 65, 151–77; sacred precinct in, 89–148, 135–42, 303–5; settlement pattern of, 282–83; shape and general plan of, 82–83, 85; Tlaloc cult in, 125–26, 141–42; Toltec state and, 301–2; tradewares at, 229–30. *See also various buildings by name*
Tula and Its Direct Interaction Area Project, 12
Tula Chico, 41, 42, 45, 57, 67, 82, *83,* 169, 220, 238, 302; Coyotlatelco occupation and, 60, 195; early structure of, 71–76; monumental architecture at, 93–94
Tula de Allende, 17, 44, 55, 82
Tulancingo, 265
Tula Project of the INAH, 11
Tula Region Project, goals and methods of, 7–15
Tula River, 33, *38,*68, 79, 83, 169, 181; irrigation systems on, *38,* 212; sites on, 195, 196, 199, *201*
Tula River Basin, 8, 17–19
Tultengo, 83
Tuna, 271. *See also* Nopal (*Opuntia* sp.)
Turkey (*Meleagris* sp.), 272, 274
Turtle (*Terrapene* sp.), 274
Tutul Xiu, 105
Type 1 sites, 282, 283, 289, 290, 291, 307
Type 2 sites, 282, 283–85, 308; and settlement groups, 288, 289, 290, 291, 294
Typha spp., 269, 270
Tzacualli Complex, 59
Tzacualli Phase, 52, 59
Tzompantli, 132–33

Ucareo, 43, 71, 79
Ulapa, 35
Unit U27, 4
Unit U 28, 4
Unit U98, 4
University of Missouri Project, 3, 11, 42
Urban zone, 13, 14, 275; ceramics of, 218, 219, 224, 227–28; habitation units in, 165–66; maize from, 238–39; Tula's, 85, 165–66, 302–3
Urban centers, 1, 72; government and, 142–43; habitation units and, 165–66; location of, 78–80; organization of, 77–78, 305–6; and rural site distribution, 285, 288; shape and general plan of, 81–85; socioeconomic units of, 162–63; study of, 1–2
Urban layouts, 87; topography and, 169–70; of Tula, 78, 82–85, 161; of Tula Chico, 72, *73*
Urban zone, 3, *83*
URs. *See* Collection Units
Valleys, alluvial, 297, 299
Vegetation, 26–28

Venta Salada Phase, 239–40
Venus, 148(n1); symbolism of, 95, 96, 140
Veracruz, 72
Verdolaga (*Portulaca* spp.), 270
Vergara Codex, 277
Vesuvio Phase, 70
Villa de Reyes, 70
Villages. *See* Barrios
Visnaga (*Echinofossulocactus*), 270
Volcanoes, 19–20
Vultures, 141, 148(n2)

Warm-Dry Stage, 28–30, 258
Warriors: depictions of, 122–*23,* 126, 131, 133, *135,* 138, 148–49(n5); Tlaloc cult and, 104, 124, 125, *141*–42, 304; Toltec, 96, 117–18
Water distribution, at Xochitlán, 39–40. *See also* Irrigation systems
Weeds, edible, 270
West Group (El Canal), 152, 154, 210
Wheat, 33
World view, and spatial organization, 77–78

Xicuco, 13, 55, 62, 181–82, 199, 227, 264, 297
Xicuco, Cerro, 19, 228
Xitejé, 39, 40
Xitejé, Zanja, 198
Xiuhtecuhtli, 105
Xiuhtotol, 105
Xochicalco, 89, 133, 149–50(n19)
Xochimilco, 299
Xochitlán, 33, 268; irrigation system, 38–40, 198, 212
Xolalpan, 170
Xolalpan Phase, 55, 57, 60
Xoxocotla, 279–80

Yautepec, 278, 280, 282
Yocua Dam irrigations ystem, 35
Yopico, 170
Yucatán, 105, 128, 148(n2)
Yucca filifera, 269, 270
Yucuñunahui, 133

Zacatapayolli, 111
Zacate (*Eragrostis* sp.; *Stipa* sp.), 270
Zacatecas, 70, 71
Zacatón (*Muhlenbergia macruoura*), 269, 270

411

Zacualtipan, 72, 79
Zapote blanco (*Casimiroa edulis*), 271
Zinapécuaro-Ucareo region, 66
Zone 1, 195, *197, 198*
Zone 2, 197–99, *200*, 207
Zone 3, 199–200, *201, 202, 203*, 207
Zone 4, 200–201, *204*
Zone 5, 201–2, *205,* 207
Zone 6, 202–4, *206*
Zone 7, 204–5, *207*
Zones of Dispersed Occupation, 191–92, 203–4, 207, 209–11
Zones of occupation, 72; descriptions of, 195–209; site distribution and, 207–15
Zones with an Undetermined Number of Structures, 185–86, 187
Zoomorphs, *97. See also* Animals
Zumpango area, 249